**John
Hohenberg**
Columbia University, Emeritus
Syracuse University

Fifth Edition

The
Professional
Journalist

Holt, Rinehart and Winston
New York   Chicago   San Francisco   Philadelphia   Montreal   Toronto
London   Sydney   Tokyo   Mexico City   Rio de Janeiro   Madrid

For Monty Curtis

John Hohenberg, a working journalist for 25 years in New York, Washington and abroad, has served as Administrator of the Pulitzer Prizes and Professor of Journalism at Columbia University, Meeman Distinguished Professor of Journalism at the University of Tennessee, Gannett-Professional-in-Residence at the William Allen White School of Journalism, University of Kansas, Gannett Distinguished Professor of Journalism at the University of Florida, and Newhouse Distinguished Professor at Syracuse University. In 1974, he was named the nation's outstanding teacher of journalism by the Society of Professional Journalists/Sigma Delta Chi, and he has won SDX-SPJ Prizes for three of his eleven books as well as a Pulitzer Prize Special Award for his services to American Journalism.

Other Books by John Hohenberg

The Pulitzer Prize Story: An Anthology
Foreign Correspondence: The Great Reporters and Their Times*
The New Front Page: An Anthology
Between Two Worlds: Policy, Press and Public Opinion in Asian-American Relations*
The News Media: A Journalist Looks at His Profession
Free Press/Free People: The Best Cause
New Era in the Pacific: An Adventure in Public Diplomacy
The Pulitzer Prizes: A History
A Crisis for the American Press*
The Pulitzer Prize Story II, 1959–1980: An Anthology

*Winner, Society of Professional Journalists/Sigma Delta Chi Prize for distinguished research in journalism

Library of Congress Cataloging in Publication Data
Hohenberg, John
 The professional journalist.

 Includes bibliographical references and index.
 1. Journalism. I. Title.
PN4775.H44 1983 070.4 82-23256

ISBN 0-03-062582-3

Published by CBS College Publishing
Printed in the United States of America
Published simultaneously in Canada
 4 5 6 090 9 8 7 6 5 4 3

CBS COLLEGE PUBLISHING
Holt, Rinehart and Winston
The Dryden Press
Saunders College Publishing

Preface

There have been so many dramatic and far-reaching changes in both print and broadcast journalism in this decade that I have made major revisions in *The Professional Journalist* for this fifth edition. Much of the new material applies equally to all forms of journalism, with primary emphasis on the following:

1. Better training for writers, provided in the Writers' Guide and elaborated upon in numerous examples of how to improve written work for the print and broadcast media. One of the principal changes is a basic 1-2-3 summation on how to write news, assembled in the second chapter and intended for the beginner.
2. Broader patterns of general local and investigative reporting, based upon personal experiences of young investigative and local reporters for the print and broadcast media with their own explanations of their work.
3. A detailed consideration of the ethical, legal and moral responsibilities of today's journalists, not only in the special chapters devoted to these subjects, but also throughout the book.
4. A description, with pertinent definitions, of the latest technological advances in both print and broadcast journalism, including the broad electronic spectrum of cable TV news, teletext and other new methods of mass communications.

There are many other additions. The treatment of reporting on local government and the budget-making process, police reporting and court reporting has been expanded, with new examples of the best work at the professional level. In chapters on Washington and foreign correspondence, there is more information on how major developments in these areas can be followed and expanded at the local level. After each chapter, there is a brief summary, Short Takes, which provides a review of the principal points that should be remembered by the student and young professional. Throughout, new examples of professional excellence, a number of them by young writers, have been excerpted from the latest Pulitzer Prize-winning materials.

The plan of organization follows a useful teaching and study pattern. After the introductory chapter, which illustrates in a striking manner how young broadcast and print journalists work, the book is organized in four parts:

The Writers' Guide
The Writer as Journalist
Principles of Reporting
Interpretive Journalism

Many journalists, public officials and teachers of journalism have helped me assemble the material for this fifth edition and I am most grateful to all of them. In particular, my warmest thanks go to the following for having contributed either information and written commentaries, or outstanding examples of journalism, and, in some cases, both:

David Andelman, foreign correspondent, *CBS Evening News*
Lyn Bailey, reporter, *Watsonville* (CA) *Register-Pajaronian*
Susan Biskeborn, and Paul Vitello, reporters, *Newsday*, Melville, NY
Edna Buchanan, reporter, *Miami Herald*
Thomas F. Chester, reporter, *Knoxville* (TN) *Journal*
J. Montgomery Curtis, former director, American Press Institute, and former vice president, Knight-Ridder Newspapers Inc.
Sharon Fitzgerald, reporter, *The Oak Ridger*, TN
Steve Fry, reporter, *Topeka* (KS) *Capital-Journal*
Lewis A. Gorham Jr., director, Office of Management and Budget, Knoxville, TN, and Thomas Sherran, of the Department of Public Administration, University of Tennessee
Henry Beetle Hough, editor, *Vineyard Gazette*, Edgartown, MA
Leah Keith, reporter, KXAS-TV, Fort Worth, TX
Peter Kihss, reporter, *The New York Times*
Andy Knott, reporter, *Chicago Tribune*
Bob Matthews, sports columnist, *Rochester* (NY) *Times-Union*
Ned McCormack and Nancy Quirk Keefe, reporter and rewrite, respectively, *Nyack* (NY) *Journal-News*
Ken McLaughlin, *Watsonville* (CA) *Register-Pajaronian*
Robert B. McFadden, rewriteman, *The New York Times*
Anita Miller, reporter, *Topeka (KS) Capital-Journal*
Sylvia Moreno, reporter, *Newsday*, Melville, NY
David Perlman, science editor, *San Francisco Chronicle*
Doug Tunnell, foreign correspondent, *CBS Evening News*
Brenda Webber, court reporter, *Gainesville* (FL) *Sun*
Jennie Williams, columnist, *Rochester* (NY) *Times-Union*
William J. Woestendiek, executive editor, *Arizona Star*, Tucson

To this list, I also add numerous others whose bylines appear over their articles in this and previous editions and who have thereby continued to contribute to this book's usefulness.

My gratitude also goes to the following for material assistance in the form of advice and the use of texts, partial texts, background information and much-appreciated cooperation in general: Buddy Baker, executive editor, *Today*, Cocoa, FL; Joseph P. Bellon, CBS News; Barry Bingham Jr., publisher, *Louisville (KY) Times* and *Courier-Journal*; Louis D. Boccardi, executive editor, the Associated Press; Wallace Carroll, former editor, *Winston-Salem* (NC) *Journal & Sentinel*; Rick Dalton, managing editor, *Topeka* (KS) *Capital-Journal*; Robert P. Early, managing editor, *Indianapolis Star*; William H. Fields, executive editor, Atlanta *Constitution*; John R. Finnegan, executive editor, *St. Paul Pioneer Press*; Reuven Frank, president, NBC News; Earl Foell, editor, *Christian Science Monitor*; William German, managing editor, *San Francisco Chronicle*; Gene Giancarlo, managing editor, *The Bulletin of the American Society of Newspaper Editors*; Robert H. Giles, editor, Gannett Rochester Newspapers; William E. Giles, editor, *Detroit News*; John R. Harrison, president, New York Times Group Newspapers, Lakeland, FL; Randall C. Hatch, managing editor, *Ogden* (Utah) *Standard-Examiner*; James F. Hoge Jr., publisher, *Chicago Sun-Times*; Dana Hornig, editor, *The Register*, Barnstable, MA; William Jones, managing editor, *Chicago Tribune*; Peter Kamm, associate publisher, *Wall Street Journal*; Dick Leonard, editor, *Milwaukee Journal*; Lawrence K. Miller, editor, *Berkshire Eagle*, Pittsfield, MA; John McMullan, executive editor, *Miami Herald*; Ted M. Natt, editor, *Longview* (WN) *Daily News*; Rob Oglesby, managing editor, *Gainesville* (FL) *Sun*; Richard A. Oppel, editor, *Charlotte* (NC) *Observer*; Frank F. Orr, editor, *Watsonville* (CA) *Register-Pajaronian*; Ralph Otwell, editor, *Chicago Sun-Times*; Cruise Palmer, former managing editor, *Kansas City Star*; Eugene C. Patterson, president and editor, *St. Petersburg* (FL) *Times*; Donald A. Pels, president, Lin Broadcasting Co.; Robert H. Phelps, executive editor, *Boston Globe*; Terry C. Plumb, editor, *Island Packet*, Hilton Head, SC; Gene Roberts, executive editor, *Philadelphia Inquirer*; A. M. Rosenthal, executive editor, *The New York Times*; Lou Schwartz, managing editor, *Newsday*, Melville, NY; John Seigenthaler, publisher, *Nashville Tennessean*; Howard Simons, managing editor, *Washington Post*; Dick Smyser, editor, *Oak Ridger*, Oak Ridge, TN; H. L. Stevenson, vice president and editor, United Press International; Tom Sweeten, managing editor, *Knoxville* (TN) *Journal*; W. F. Thomas, editor, *Los Angeles Times*; Ron Thornburg, executive editor, *Fort Myers* (FL) *News-Press*; Paul H. Tracy, editor-in-chief, *New Hampshire Sunday News*, Manchester; Joseph M. Ungaro, executive editor, Gannett Westchester-Rockland Newspapers; Steve Vaughn, managing editor, *Orlando* (FL) *Sentinel-Star*.

All are hereby absolved of responsibility for what is written here. I also acknowledge, in general, the copyright ownership of the material herein reproduced with the permission of the news organizations involved. A listing of story-by-story permissions and copyrights is included.

Finally, my heartfelt gratitude goes once again to my wife, JoAnn F. Hohenberg, and my children, Pamela and Eric, for making life so pleasant for me during the preparation of this fifth edition.

John Hohenberg
Gainesville, Florida

Contents

Introduction

Part 1   The Writers' Guide

Part 2   The Writer as Journalist

7   Problems of News Writing   105

8   Writing Obituaries   119

9   Writing Human Interest Stories   127

10   Writing About Disasters   139

Part 3 Principles of Reporting

Introduction

CHAPTER 1

Journalists at Work

We have an insatiable demand for news. The surprise, the shock, even the turmoil of the unexpected have a continual fascination for us.

We want to know, at all costs, what's going on and why. At any minute, at any hour of the day or night, we expect information at the twist of a television dial, over automobile radios in heavy traffic, in the newspapers that are picked up at newsstands or delivered to our homes, in the newsweeklies that come through the mail.

Nor is that all. From our burgeoning cable information systems, we demand instant retrieval of information. And we are supporting research for even more complex systems. In one way or another, we insist on knowing the latest, even if it is only a sports score or the weather.

Reporters in Action

The patterns of the news are endless in their variety and appeal. To develop them, to give them shape and meaning, our corps of journalists — professionals all — serve us around the clock. Here is how they go about their work:

Getting out a Verdict The courtroom doors were locked. A frowning bailiff was guarding them. And Brenda Webber, anxious to telephone a guilty verdict in the drug smuggling case she had been covering, was minutes away from her deadline at the *Gainesville* (Florida) *Sun*. She said to the bailiff, "You'll either have to open those doors or arrest me." He turned and glared at the small but determined young black reporter, but she did not waver. "What'll I do about her?" the bailiff asked a nearby policeman. "Open up," was the response. And with that, Brenda Webber ran to a telephone and made her edition.

An Exclusive for CBS-TV   In the Italian hilltop village of Castel Gandolfo on a sunny summer's day, Doug Tunnell was gambling that he could zing his American television competition. The young reporter for the Columbia Broadcasting System had come here with a cameraman, hoping for an exclusive report on the arrival of Pope John Paul II at his summer palace following his escape from an assassin. CBS's rivals evidently thought it wouldn't be much of a story and hadn't assigned anyone. Tunnell himself wasn't sure. But once the smiling pope emerged from his white helicopter to the cheers of the villagers and tourists, all doubts vanished. "We zunged 'em," Tunnell said.

Covering a Tragedy   At Pomona Lake, near Topeka, Kansas, a steamboat had capsized with a large toll of dead. Anita Miller of the *Topeka Daily Capital* was putting together a list of the identifiable dead, talking with bereaved relatives, phoning others, getting names of still others from the authorities at the scene. After a time, she phoned a clergyman who told her, as best he could, that he had lost his wife, his daughter and his granddaughter when the boat sank. With professional calm, the young reporter made notes, finished her work and wrote her story. Then, unable to forget the clergyman and his broken life, she went home and cried.

Reporting a Life-Saving Effort   Inside a water tower that loomed over eastern Long Island's flat farmlands, three painters had crashed to the bottom of a huge tank they were whitewashing. Two reporters for the Long Island, New York, daily *Newsday*, Susan Biskeborn and Paul Vitello, mingled with a hundred or more rescuers and wondered how they could convey the enormity of this life-saving effort to their readers. One painter already was known to be dead. Another was pulled from the tank but died later. However, the third victim was saved, and that was the story. "The scene," Vitello wrote, "became a little bubble of hell."

For $25, a Mail Order Ministry   Back in the beautiful East Tennessee hill country, in the village of Pigeon Forge, Thomas F. Chester of the *Knoxville Journal* found a 76-year-old man who dispensed mail-order chaplains' credentials for $10 a year or $25 for a lifetime. Mindful of all the faithful clergy who had worked and studied for years for their ordination, Chester investigated the latest type of diploma mill. He bought a chaplain's certificate for $25, then did a lot of interviewing and eventually produced eight articles for his newspaper. The series gave fair warning to the credulous — and to the Internal Revenue Service.

The Challenge of Journalism

These instances of journalists at work illustrate the attraction of the profession for young people, women as well as men. The challenge, the colorful variety of the work, the opportunity to be of service and the rising prestige of the profession itself are magnets that are attracting newcomers in increasing numbers.

To dedicated journalists, nothing can match the thrill of pursuing the news, pinning it down and spreading it quickly before a mass public. That is what journalism is all about. And that, too, is why it beckons to the idealistic, the adventurous and the young in our multifaceted society. For in the three centuries since the first newspaper was founded on this continent, journalists have never enjoyed greater opportunities than are available to them today.

The Testing of Journalists   There is no doubt that journalists of ability tend to question established values to a greater extent than members of any other profession. And this is as it should be.

Skepticism has always been the hallmark of journalism. No news organization can exist for very long if it has a cheerleader complex, if it continually registers contentment with things as they are, if it does not delve beneath the surface of events, if it fails to sound the alarm over the shortcomings of society.

For journalism, in its broadest sense, incites change. And change, therefore, remains the first law of journalism.

The element of credibility, too, enters into everything the journalist says, does and writes. In its simplest form, this calls for the accurate reporting of factual material, from the exact time of an earthquake to the closing words of a presidential address, from the precise shade of the bridal gown to the correct spelling of the name of a murder suspect.

But of what use is it to report the middle initial of a speaker and his title with unfailing accuracy, yet ignore the inconsistency of his remarks? Or to make certain that the city's budget totals are correct to the penny, yet fail to point out that projected outlays are inadequate to meet the requirements of the city's schools, its needy and its aged?

Is Factual Accuracy Enough?   It is in these larger areas of journalism that its practitioners are tested far more than in the achievement of minimal accuracy, necessary though it is. For in all things, journalists must prove themselves worthy of public belief and public trust. They are, in a broad sense, the surrogates of the public, the public's eyes and ears.

Now, in the closing years of the century, it is commonly accepted that journalists are something more than news stenographers; for, in all that they say and do, they must try to determine the truth. Unhappily, since news and truth are not always synonymous, this is seldom easy to accomplish. Moreover, it can scarcely be assumed that what is true today will necessarily remain true tomorrow. Presidents, governors and mayors can and do change their minds. Laws can be repealed. Court verdicts can be overturned on appeal. And even warring couples, who seem to be on the verge of divorce, have been known to kiss and make up.

Thus, time has an uncomfortable way of changing the perspective from which events are viewed. Unlike historians, who are preoccupied with the past, journalists must deal with the present and, very often, with the future as well. They must cope with the reluctance of their sources, both official and unofficial, to spell out the facts under certain circumstances. They must face up to the perils of writing quickly while the course of events is still imprecise. And always, of course, they work under the tyranny of the deadline.

How they are able to do these things often becomes a small miracle of professionalism. For a better understanding of their work, it is worth examining in some detail the case histories outlined at the beginning of this chapter.

Anatomy of Court Reporting

When Brenda Webber was assigned to cover the drug smuggling trial in Gainesville's federal court, the first thing she tried to do was to gather background information on the 15 Floridians who were the defendants. It seemed a simple job. But it turned out to be unexpectedly difficult.

"The difficulty," she said, "was in getting background information that was in a court file that I had no opportunity to see. Because the federal court functions out of Tallahassee for this district, getting file information is difficult, particularly in a case involving multiple defendants, prosecutors and defense attorneys."

Problem-Solving on the Job Webber had then been on the *Gainesville Sun*'s staff for five years and was still well under 30. She had been a copy writer for two Savannah radio stations for a year after graduation from the University of Georgia's journalism school. After that, she worked on the *Sun*'s public school beat for four years and was just rounding out her first year as a court reporter when the drug smuggling trial opened.

"As to that story," she went on, "the first difficulty was in trying to beat the clock and get something into our first edition, which goes to the specific areas involved in the drug investigation.

"The second problem was having to write a piecemeal story as things happened and then try to put that information into sequence for a publishable story."

It was 10:45 on a Saturday night when the jury handed up guilty verdicts against 11 of the 15 defendants. For security reasons, the judge had ordered the courtroom doors locked. But even after Webber forced the unwilling bailiff to open the doors, she still had a problem. It was too late for her to write the story. Instead, she had to dictate to a typist at the office.

A Dictated Story This was her story, run across the top of Page 1:

By Brenda Webber

After 18½ hours of deliberation over two days, Federal jurors last night convicted 11 of 15 Floridians charged with smuggling marijuana along the Suwannee River in Dixie and Taylor Counties.

"We feel like this is the first signal to the people down there that we are going to do something and we're not going

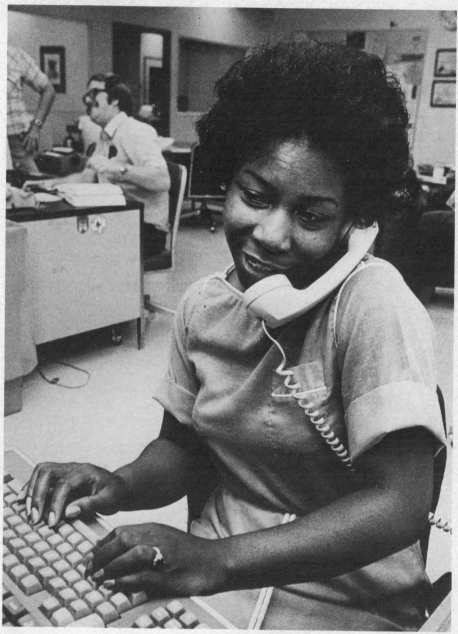

Brenda Webber, court reporter for the *Gainesville* (Florida) *Sun* at work in the newsroom. (Photo by Kevin Kolczynski, staff photographer. Copyright, the *Gainesville Sun.* Used by permission.)

to stop," Federal prosecutor Lynda Kent said after the verdict. "We think it is time the law-abiding citizens of Dixie and Taylor Counties realize people are interested in the problem and we've got to do something about it. There will be more trials happening in the future."

Jurors had begun deliberations at 5:20 p.m. Friday but U.S. District Court Judge Lynn Higby released them after three hours and allowed them to return to their motel for the night.

Court reconvened at 8 a.m. Saturday and deliberations went on until 10:45 p.m. Jurors did not leave the Federal courthouse throughout Saturday.

Defendants Felix Miranda and his two sons, Jorge and Rudy, were found guilty of conspiracy to possess more than 1,000 pounds of marijuana and a second count of possession of marijuana.

Also found guilty on the same charges were brothers Ira and Howard Reed. Former Taylor County Sheriff's Deputy Broward Reed was found guilty of possession of less than 1,000 pounds of marijuana and of three counts of perjury. Broward Reed had been charged with lying before a Federal grand jury.

Brothers Wesley and Herbert Corbin, Dennis Neilson, Oscar Hall and Elvin (Bud) Colson were found guilty of conspiracy with intent to possess and possession of more than 1,000 pounds of marijuana.

Cecelia Reed, the wife of Ira Reed, was found not guilty of the same charges, along with Luis Leon and Dudley Reed. Joseph (Butch) Stewart was found not guilty on possession and conspiracy charges.

The defendants had been indicted by a Federal grand jury as part of the Federal government's crackdown on drug smuggling in North Florida. Those convicted face a maximum of 15 years in prison and $125,000 in fines on the conspiracy and possession charges.

While sentencing and appeals procedures remained in the offing, Webber said after it was all over: "I haven't had that much fun doing a story in a long time."

Best of all, the *Gainesville Sun* gave it a good ride.

Zinging 'em on Network TV

Doug Tunnell's problem in covering Pope John Paul II's arrival at his summer retreat in Castel Gandolfo was entirely different. In the first place, it wasn't a bang-bang news story. Moreover, the chances were slim that it would make the other networks. But the young CBS correspondent decided there was a chance for a lovely pictorial feature.

It really hadn't been Tunnell's line. Immediately upon graduating from

Columbia's journalism school, he had taken his chances as a stringer (temporary correspondent) during the Lebanese civil war and had caught on with CBS. Since then, he had been under fire many times as a war correspondent in Beirut, at the Israeli border, in Iran and in Northern Ireland.

Young and daring as he was, he had remained unscathed. And he had prizes and awards, one of them from the Overseas Press Club, to show for his relatively brief career. So the mission to Castel Gandolfo in the peaceful summer sunshine was a novelty for him.

Planning "What If" Coverage   This is how Tunnell laid out his problem:

> With the Pope just out of the hospital, we planned "what if" coverage of his annual trip to his summer residence. We knew both the other networks were planning the same, just in case another would-be assassin should try again. But beyond that there was no clear-cut "news" in the event. Chances that the day's trip would make the air on the other networks were slim.
>
> CBS in Rome, however, enjoys the talents of some of the finest cameramen in the world, in my judgment. It was a lovely day in August for the shooting, and in this I suspected that if we could come up with an editorial line of some sort, we might zing the guys from NBC and ABC with a story they didn't have.
>
> The angle was the tourist industry built around the Holy Father . . . and we "zung" 'em.

From the *CBS Sunday Night News*   This is how the script began that Sunday evening over CBS, with Phil Jones as anchorman:

JONES   Pope John Paul II will spend the rest of the summer in the
        country. He left Rome today after another public appearance at
        the Vatican. Doug Tunnell reports.
            [Singing]

TUNNELL   There was certainly no lack of devotion at St. Peter's,
        nor any shortage of exuberance among the pilgrims who gathered
        there today. But it just wasn't the throng of thousands one
        might expect to join Pope John Paul II in prayer. The reason?
        It is vacation time in Italy. Fully half of this nation's
        population is away on holiday. After this service, the Holy
        Father was to join them.

        [Tunnell commented:

> From opening prayer service in St. Peter's in Rome, the story developed chronologically. Since we had put Saturday's massive service there on the air the day before, I wanted to use contrast in this Sunday report to carry the pictures. My first paragraph was therefore delivered at a slow pace, with plenty of space to bring up the sounds of choir groups and the prayer between each sentence.

Then, an abrupt change of scene to the all but deserted streets of Castel Gandolfo at high noon on Sunday. Again, contrast was the objective, this time more visual than editorial.]

High season in the village of Castel Gandolfo should have started long ago. But the merchants and restaurant owners of this hilltop resort say their profits are only half of what they were last summer. For the three months the Pope spent recovering in Rome, Castel Gandolfo's tourist industry was left to languish in the summer sun. But when the only resident of the village who has his own helicopter finally arrived, so did the tourists--right on cue. . . .
[Singing]

[Here, Tunnell explained the visuals in his running commentary after the fact:

A lovely shot of the papal helicopter brought the Pope to town for us, and then contrast again played an important part in the story.

The previously empty streets and squares were seen in a series of quick cuts to be bustling with activity. Both the cameraman and the editor exercised their ability to the fullest here. It is worth a note of caution. Television can make empty villages seem full, and crowded squares seem empty, if the scene is shot and edited with that intent.

But in this case, the image was correct. As I witnessed them, the tourists did indeed arrive 'right on cue.']

[The script continued while the visuals unfolded:]
TUNNELL   There were choirs from Warsaw and tour groups from Dublin. Even the odd Italian or two. All clamored inside the courtyard of what has been the summer home for Popes for centuries to hear a heartfelt apology from the Holy Father. He confessed to having stayed away too long, and told the mayor of Castel Gandolfo how sorry he was that he was late in coming. The Pope is to stay here and rest, his doctors say, at least until October. It may be too late for the village to recoup; too many package tours have already passed this stop by. But there is at least some consolation in knowing the village population increased today, if only just by one.

Doug Tunnell, CBS News, Castel Gandolfo.

The Way It Turned Out   For the young CBS correspondent and his cameraman, the results were eminently satisfactory. The story was handsomely displayed on the *CBS Sunday Night News.* Afterward, Tunnell commented:

The Pope spoke only in Italian; a message clearly directed at the townspeople. He, too, was aware of the story, which made it all the more valid for us. I was left to paraphrase the remarks that seemed to highlight our storyline. Nothing else of editorial import was said. Then I went out on a high note.

For me, it was the end of the saga of an attempt on the life of the Pontiff and a very happy one at that.

At no time did I put myself on camera. The Pope was the man I assumed America wanted to see, not Doug Tunnell. Our pictures were strong; a lovely village, a gleaming helicopter, St. Peter's Square in Rome. My smiling face just cannot compare to visuals like those.

This was one of the most enjoyable stories I did that summer and a good part of the concept of the piece was to communicate that enjoyment to our viewers.

It isn't often that an editorial plan can be carried out with such finesse in journalism, particularly on network television. But this is one time everything clicked. As Tunnell said, he "zunged" 'em.

The Story Behind a Casualty List

One of the most difficult and dreary assignments in journalism is the compilation of a casualty list after a disaster, natural or manmade. When Anita Miller was assigned to that task for the *Topeka Daily Capital* after a showboat capsized on Pomona Lake, she had just been graduated from the William Allen White School of Journalism at the University of Kansas. But despite her youth, she was a skilled and well-trained professional and had been working on the *Capital* nights and summers while completing her education.

And so Miller set out on her task with care and determination because she knew it was important.

A Reporter's Thoughts   To many reporters, the almost daily presence of turmoil, hardship and death, when they go on general assignment, causes them to build a shield of detachment, even indifference. It enables them to keep their emotions in check. Anita Miller knew this instinctively; certainly, she hadn't yet learned it from experience. In consequence, when she began assembling her casualty list, she adopted the detached attitude so common to journalists in the face of disaster. As she explained her thoughts:

The capsizing of the Whippoorwill steamboat at Pomona Lake was big news in Topeka, since many folks from our town were involved or had visited the novelty steamboat on occasion.

My assignment was to find who was on board that tragic night and why. I also compiled a list of the dead.

For this story, I spoke mainly with families, because I was trying to get factual information in a short amount of time about a number of people. The hardest call I've ever made was on this story.

I had to call a minister who lost his wife, daughter and granddaughter in the capsizing of the steamboat.

That really got to me. I think I related it to my own family. I dropped that barrier reporters put up to keep a detached front, almost insensitive to what's really happening. I think we need to drop that barrier sometimes just to stay human. . . .

Tragedy Rides a Showboat   But there was no hint of emotion in Miller's story for the *Capital*. It was a completely factual, professional accounting, written in the measured cadence of a straight news story—no comment, no editorialization, no sob stuff. And it went right to the point that had touched the young reporter. This is how she began:

By Anita Miller

Many of those aboard the double-decked steamboat Whippoorwill Saturday night were celebrating family occasions or just wanted a relaxed cruise around Pomona Lake when the scene turned into a nightmare.

A tornado, so small it wasn't detected on weather radar, capsized the 100-foot showboat, tossing 47 passengers and 13 crew members into the water.

Fourteen bodies, some badly bruised, were recovered by Sunday night by divers and a drag team. One person remained missing as of midnight Sunday.

Fourteen persons were injured and four remained hospitalized Sunday. Two of those four were in serious condition.

The Rev. Milton Vogel, former executive secretary of the Kansas Council of Churches and a United Methodist minister in Topeka for many years, was aboard the showboat with his wife, Grace, 66, for their 40th wedding anniversary. He was accompanied by five family members.

Only three survived.

The Rev. Vogel, 5707 W. 16th, lost his wife, daughter and granddaughter in the lake waters.

Mrs. Vogel was found Saturday and the Vogels' daughter, Sandy Vogel Wright, 34, who taught music at Potwin and Stout elementary schools in Topeka, was found Sunday afternoon after a drag team pulled lines through the lake.

Melisa Leigh Wright, nine, who lived with her mother and brother at 1223 Glendale Drive, was still reported missing Sunday night.

The Rev. Vogel and his son, Lynn Vogel, Chicago, and grandson, Alan Wright, five, survived the ordeal. Lynn Vogel had come to Topeka for the celebration of his parents' anniversary. . . .

The End of the Assignment   The story ran on for another column and a half, taking up the stories of the victims and their families, one by one, with the same meticulous care for factual detail and the firm suppression of reportorial comment. But reporters *are* affected by such assignments, whether they are young or old; they can't help themselves. It is the human condition.

When it was over, Anita Miller told of her own reactions:

> After I wrote this story, I went home and cried. When I write something really sensitive, especially where there's been human suffering or death, I can keep my cool when interviewing and writing the piece, but when I leave the office for home it suddenly hits me and often I can't get it out of my mind. Sometimes it takes crying to get it out of my system.

It has made Miller a better reporter. Three years after the Whippoorwill tragedy, she was covering courts, police, City Hall and some of the proceedings of the Kansas Legislature for her paper.

Inside a Water Tower

It is simple enough to take viewers to the scene of a news story on television. You show them exactly what is going on with relatively few words of explanation and you've grabbed their attention for the 60 or 90 seconds of a routine news event.

But what if the story is not routine? What if the problem is to bring *readers* to the scene with the quality and skill of your writing and reporting? This was the challenge faced by the *Newsday* reporters Susan Biskeborn and Paul Vitello when they covered the struggle of police and volunteers to save two of the three painters who had tumbled to the bottom of a whitewashed Long Island water tower.

Finding a Story Pattern   Paul Vitello summed it up this way:

> Water tanks are common sights on the suburban landscape. There is nothing exotic or other-worldly about them. From the outside, what few people know—and what we had to get across—was that the interior of a whitewashed, empty water tower is like a zero-gravity simulator. Venturing inside induces instant vertigo.
>
> Add to that the slippery surface [from wet paint], the paint fumes, the deafening noise from a gigantic fan that was supposed to be clearing the fumes, two men dying inside . . . and the scene of our story became a little bubble of hell.
>
> We tried to get that across to readers by entering the story—and the tank—through the eyes of the mountain-climbing rescuer, who described in good detail the sensation of lowering himself inside the tank and the steps he took to get two men out. [A third was already dead.] In a sense, it was the story of how an experienced rescuer, using a combination of craft and rote method, took on the bad old Abyss. . . .

Death in a Water Tower   This was the essential part of the two reporters' story in *Newsday*:

By Susan Biskeborn and Paul Vitello

CENTEREACH—As he lowered himself into the freshly whitewashed interior of a 500,000-gallon water tank to try to rescue two men who lay dying Thursday night, John Flynn said he felt like a mountaineer in an avalanche: blinding whiteness and mind-bending noise everywhere.

Reporters and rescuers watching efforts to save a worker from the Long Island water tower where two others perished. (Copyright, *Newsday*. Used by permission.)

The noise roared from giant fans that pushed fresh air into the fume-filled tank. The great expanse of curved, white-washed walls made him feel nauseous.

The white, epoxy-based paint covered everything, including the semi-conscious bodies of painters Peter Koustas, 32, and Leslie Salomon, 31, who had been overcome by fumes in the late afternoon. A third painter, John Bakalopoulos, 34, had slipped down a 110-foot pipe to the ground earlier and was dead.

"Their eyes were wide open and they were mumbling something I couldn't hear with all the noise," said Flynn, a 37-year-old Suffolk County police emergency specialist, a former Green Beret and an avid mountain climber. "I had to read lips."

Both of the injured men, one of whom died yesterday, muttered the same thing, Flynn said: "Please help us . . . please help us. . . ."

[In graphic detail, the reporters then described the many desperate but vain efforts that had been made by firefighters, police and volunteers for many hours to get the two men out before Flynn took over. Then the story continued.]

Flynn, called on his day off, arrived at 8 p.m. With mountaineering equipment he uses on hiking trips, he lowered himself in a Swiss mountain seat with nylon ropes. "It was white as a snowstorm in the Alps," he said. "Completely disorienting. It made me nauseous."

He hit the floor in a few minutes, slid on the wet paint—toward the hole leading to the pipe that had swallowed Bakalopoulos—then recovered his balance and got to work. He told the men, "You're going to be all right. We're going to get you out of here."

Then began a five-hour exercise in attention to detail: setting up block-and-talley pulleys, tying bowline knots, adjusting straps on stretchers, attaching safety lines and double safety lines—double-checking and triple-checking each step.

Salomon, at 200-plus pounds, was hoisted up through the top of the tank despite a near-accident when he suddenly awoke from his stupor and grabbed at the ropes. Koustas, who died yesterday, was lowered through the feeder pipe. When it was over, Flynn came down the same way. "I love my work," Flynn said later, "but I hope I never have to do anything like this again."

The Reporters' Work   During the many hours they waited outside the water tower, the reporters interviewed rescuers and would-be rescuers. But they weren't able to get to Flynn for his key story until 10 hours afterward. And that gave them what they needed. As Vitello concluded: "It was a simple, linear story that acquired whatever depth it had by recording the details of the failed rescue attempts as well as the last, successful one." But it was the saving of a life that counted most.

Investigating a Diploma Mill

The term "investigative reporter" has a special appeal for this generation of young journalists. It conjures up the image of two youngsters on the *Washington Post*, Bob Woodward and Carl Bernstein, uncovering the seamy truth behind the bungled break-in at Democratic headquarters in the Watergate complex in Washington, the exploit that eventually forced the resignation of President Nixon. The phrase epitomizes the work of Neil Sheehan, a reporter for the *New York Times*, who single-handedly produced the top-secret Pentagon Papers, the inside story of how the United States was maneuvered into the Vietnam War—and spread them before a wondering nation. And it celebrates many another feat of derring-do that has been crowned with Pulitzer Prizes and other journalistic awards.

But not all investigations are so dramatic and not all either put people in jail or get them out of jail. There are literally hundreds of reporters, working quietly on newspapers or at a few of the nation's radio and TV stations, who produce results that benefit their communities and strike a blow at sham and fraud.

Beginning an Investigation   The sale of "mail-order ministries" that Thomas F. Chester investigated was an example of this kind of reporting. Like so many others who attend universities in these times of inflated costs, Chester had worked his way through the University of Tennessee's College of Communications. He had attended classes days and worked nights on the *Knoxville Journal* as a reporter and deskman.

As a result, once he received his degree and was able to devote his full interests to newspaper work, he already had experience and was prepared for the tough story. This, as he explained it, was how the tip for his investigation came his way:

> The first thing that happened was a call from a friend who works in social services in Knoxville. He told me about this guy who sold ministers'/chaplains' credentials by mail. He also put me in touch with two social service workers who had checked out this man's own credentials after he had applied to adopt a child.
>
> From then on, I spent three months in interviewing—along with my regular work for the *Journal*. I also became a minister myself to obtain a lot of material from the man involved. It cost me $25. And I also interviewed people as far away as West Virginia, Florida and Ohio to find out what the man's past had been like.

Always, Chester had in mind the many dedicated, hard-working clergy in the South and elsewhere who had struggled for an education, obtained their degrees by dint of hard work and self-sacrifice and served their congregations with selfless devotion. If he could expose the operations of a mail-order diploma mill, he reasoned that it would at least serve as a warning to the public. And that is how he proceeded.

"Ministries by Mail"   This was the opening of the *Knoxville Journal*'s six-part series:

By Thomas F. Chester

For $10 a year or $25 a lifetime, Alvin O. Langdon will sell you a chaplain's credentials. He'll also give you literature that tells you how to avoid paying income tax and how to avoid the draft.

Claims similar to these and the proliferation of mail-order ministries such as Langdon's prompted the Internal Revenue Service earlier this year to begin a national investigation of their promoters.

Langdon, who works out of his home at 717 Hitching Post Drive at Pigeon Forge, Tenn., has sold hundreds and perhaps thousands of ordination certificates to buyers who may now be caught in the web of an IRS tax-avoidance inquiry.

Langdon says his home is the headquarters for the National Chaplains' Association (NCA), an international religious organization, the Calvary Grace Christian Church and a boys' lodge. He is 76 years old and says he has not been interviewed by the IRS in its current investigation.

"In the first place," he said, "the IRS cannot investigate or look at the books of any religious organization except only for one reason. If they think you own a filling station or parking lot somewhere or something else that's not connected or affiliated with the church, they might have a right to do that."

Literature from Langdon says that by buying an ordination certificate from the National Chaplains' Association, benefits include:

• Elimination or savings on taxes—"even on your home."
• Substantial discounts on "almost everything you buy, including your auto."
• Your own license plates and decals for your auto.
• Recommendation for a college degree.
• The rearing of your children in case you should die.
• Draft-exempt status.

If an NCA member and two other persons wish to form a church, Langdon will "grant the group the use of a legal charter complete with the NCA tax-exemption number"—for $10. He's the national commander of the NCA, he says, and the fee covers printing, postage and the filing of legal documents. . . .

Results of an Investigation   There was a lot more of this in the first article and in the rest of the series, plus reactions from various parts of the country that put a crimp in Langdon's operations in Tennessee.

"After our story ran," Chester said, "several others like it popped up across the country. I received calls from the Dallas Better Business Bureau, the Cherokee

Indian Boys' Home, preachers from all over Tennessee and a district attorney who was interested in the way money was being raised."

For such investigative work and other reportorial assignments, Chester accumulated an impressive list of local and state journalistic awards early in his career. Those were a tribute to his skill and his tenacity as a reporter, as well as a source of encouragement to others to follow his example.

State of the Profession

These examples of journalistic activity reflect the range of interest and the influence of the news media in the United States. Here, we have today the most powerful engine of information that the world has ever seen and a stronger, better-educated and better-trained corps of journalists than we have ever had before.

Everybody recognizes that the three television networks, the newsmagazines and the great metropolitan dailies, such as the *Washington Post*, the *Wall Street Journal*, the *New York Times*, the *Chicago Tribune*, the *Los Angeles Times* and their competitors, have a major impact on public attitudes. What is not generally realized is the extent to which smaller news organizations in cities throughout the country influence public affairs.

"The Backbone of the Press" Sir Denis Brogan, the distinguished British historian who specialized in American history at Cambridge University, often said he learned more about America from reading small-city newspapers than he did from the giants of American journalism. He called them "the backbone of the press." The record of accomplishment in this area bears him out.

Not long ago the *Lufkin News* in Texas investigated the death of a local Marine recruit, exposed the brutality of Marine drillmasters and forced widespread reforms in the recruiting and training operations of the United States Marine Corps.

In California, a tiny weekly, the *Point Reyes Light*, took on a large and powerful organization that it believed to be a menace to citizenry in its own county and forced an investigation of its activities.

In Nebraska, the weekly *Sun* Newspapers of Omaha became troubled by the fund solicitations from the charitable organization behind Boystown, conducted a thorough inquiry into its practices and brought about some major reforms.

In Kansas, the *Hutchinson News* saw that there were widespread injustices in the political divisions of the state and, through painstaking inquiry and editorial persuasion, brought about legislative reapportionment on a more equitable basis.

In North Carolina, the *Winston-Salem Journal and Sentinel* stopped a strip mining company from destroying one of the most scenic parts of the state and brought the firm's proposed operations to a halt.

In North Carolina, also, the *Tabor City Tribune* and the *Whiteville Reporter*, two small weeklies, took on the Ku Klux Klan in their own backyards and broke its influence in their communities.

In Alabama, the *Tuscaloosa News* steadfastly advocated adherence to law and peaceful integration of the University of Alabama at a time when angry mobs were threatening to use violence against the few brave black students who stood up for their rights.

In Florida, the *St. Petersburg Times* exposed chicanery in the construction of the state's highway system and, some years later, attacked a strange religious cult that was attempting to intimidate the citizens of Clearwater.

In Nevada, the *Reno Evening News* and the *Nevada State Journal* combined forces to expose a local brothel keeper who had gained influence over some of the state's politicians.

All these feats won Pulitzer Prizes. And for every award that came to one newspaper or to some reporters and editors on its staff, there were many other journalists who worked in obscurity but recorded accomplishments of benefit to their communities.

Of course, the primary mission of newspapers is to present the news, to examine important events in depth, to explain and interpret them. Good newspapers invariably devote their best efforts to that endeavor. But the press's watchdog function in society cannot be minimized. Moreover, because so much of the broadcast media is given over to entertainment, it falls to newspapers to provide their communities with an open forum for ideas, popular or not, and for the presentation of conflicting points of view.

The Responsibility of TV   Fortunately for the public interest, broadcast journalism has come into its own in the 1980s. After a long battle by dedicated television journalists, even the most conservative station owners have realized that it is in their own interest, as well as the public's, to present well-rounded news reports. And so the tendency in recent years has been to expand the time given over to news and special events not only on network TV but on local stations as well. TV journalism, too, has developed an interest in public service and investigative reporting with the commercial and professional success of the *60 Minutes* program on CBS. Both the rival networks have come up with their own versions of probing journalism, as have some of the larger local stations.

The Media—Print and Broadcast

All in all, American journalism is undergoing tremendous changes in the concluding years of the 20th century. All forms of news media are breaking out of established patterns through advances in science. As our journalistic horizons have brightened, new technologies have developed with dramatic impact on the future of both newspapers and their electronic competitors.

Through the computer and the Video Display Terminal (VDT), the photocomposition machine and the offset printing press, newspapers today are being produced by vastly more efficient processes. In effect, production has become an editorial function that has all but eliminated the old-time hot-type composing room. And the end is not yet in sight, for a beginning has been made on electronic home delivery of great volumes of news.

Nor is television immune from change. On the contrary, we have witnessed the development of cable television and such special data processing services as CEE-FAX, Prestel and Teletext. Thus, the severe limits of network television news have been shattered and a multichannel era in home viewing already has begun. This cuts both ways, for newspapers are bound to be even more affected by electronic news than the broadcast media by the time the next century begins.

The Press Newspapers in the 1980s remain the largest single compilers and distributors of news in the United States and, despite the gains of their competitors, they remain the largest advertising medium as well.

As an overview, there are about 1,745 daily newspapers in the United States, with a daily average circulation of 62.2 million and an average cost of somewhere between 20 and 25 cents a copy. Because of the inroads of television and the growth of suburban newspapers, the big-city afternoon newspapers are shrinking in number, with some turning to "all-day" circulation and others shifting to the morning field. There have been distinguished casualties in recent years, among them the *Washington Star*, the *Philadelphia Bulletin*, *The Minneapolis Star* and the *Chicago Daily News*, but the tremendous growth of suburban publications like *Newsday* and others shows the shape of the future. The ratio of afternoons to mornings still is about 3-to-1, because the pressure of TV competition in smaller cities is less dramatic than it is in the big cities. In fact, more than half the dailies have circulations of under 15,000 and mainly they are doing well.

It is the Sunday newspapers that have shown the greatest gains over all. The number of Sundays published by dailies runs around 740, and Sunday circulation is up to around 55 million, a healthy increase. There are more all-day papers, too.

Group ownership is the dominant feature of American dailies. The giants — the Gannett Company, with more than 80 newspapers, and the Knight-Ridder Newspapers, with about 35 dailies — each have a total daily circulation of about 3.5 million. The other leaders are the Newhouse Newspapers, Chicago Tribune Company, *Los Angeles Times* (Times-Mirror Company), Scripps-Howard, the *Wall Street Journal* (Dow Jones-Ottaway papers), Hearst, Cox and the New York Times–Ochs Estate Newspapers. The *Washington Post*, which is developing a group ownership of its own, predicts that by the next century "virtually all daily newspapers in America will be owned by perhaps fewer than a dozen communications conglomerates."

That kind of consolidation is still far off, however. In the 1980s there were about 170 newspaper groups in the country with around 50 percent of the nation's daily newspaper circulation. The tendency toward still greater contraction depends to a very large extent on how federal tax laws develop in the next decade. The prime reason for the current consolidation is the heavy penalties that inheritance taxes levy on the heirs to a family newspaper, a major inducement for sales to the chains. These laws, however, are being liberalized.

In any event, the nation's larger newspapers and the groups are so profitable, even in periods of recession, that they are acquiring television stations; some are going heavily into cable television and the various new data processing and distribution systems. Among the leaders in the new technology, the *Wall Street Journal* maintains the largest circulation, with around two million copies a day printed at some 13 different centers in the United States through electronic means.

While the weeklies also are affected by the trend toward group ownership, their numbers are not being reduced to any significant extent. About 7,000 of them are still being published, from one to three times a week, including a number of the so-called "shoppers" or free newspapers. In self-defense, legitimate dailies and weeklies that feel themselves threatened by upstart "shoppers" tend to start rival "shoppers" to drive the competition out of business.

Broadcast Media   The statistics for broadcast journalism are stunning. There are almost 10,000 broadcasting stations in the nation, about 9,000 radio and 1,000 TV stations. The growth of electronic news-gathering devices (ENG) enables TV to flash news pictures directly from the scene. There also are hundreds of low-power TV stations, citizens' band radios in the millions — mainly in automobiles — and rapid developments in cable and other forms of pay television.

The broadcast media blanket 99 percent of American homes that have nearly 100 million sets, some 80 percent of them in color. And radio transmitters service 425 million receivers.

Whereas newspaper advertising schedules can be expanded, there is a limit to precious TV network prime time and more than 600 wealthy advertisers do battle for it. Thus, a 30-second commercial in prime time now goes for as high as $175,000 except in the sluggish summer period, but it can exceed $350,000 for a spectacular like the annual pro football Super Bowl. TV is in 80 million U.S. homes.

Out of total annual advertising expenditures of about $50 billion, TV accounts for about $10 billion and radio $3.4 billion, for a combined total of $13.4 billion, which is not far from the $14.5 billion spent on advertising in newspapers.

As is the case with the press, group ownership is dominant in TV. Aside from the owned and operated stations of the three networks, the largest TV groups, based on net weekly audiences, include Metromedia, RKO-General, Westinghouse, WGN (Chicago), Continental, Kaiser and Storer. Such newspaper groups as *Post-Newsweek*, Scripps-Howard, Hearst, Newhouse and Cox also are important in the broadcast industry. Groups outside the networks may own up to seven TV stations each under current law, but only five of these can be VHF stations.

Low-Power TV   "Poor Man's TV" is now possible, thanks to a new ruling by the Federal Communications Commission. Some estimates are that a low-power station, which has a range of about 10 to 20 miles, can be put on the air for as little as $50,000. Accordingly, the FCC has been besieged by thousands of people who want licenses and have made applications, whether qualified or not.

The first interim license awarded by the FCC went to John Boler, a 73-year-old retired broadcasting executive, who put the country's first low-power TV station on the air at Bemidji, Minnesota, a farming community. He had a 16-hour-a-day routine of high school sports, country-western music and local news for his neighbors.

"I'm really going to make something of this," he said. "Low-power TV is going to be a very important development."

A lot of other backyard impresarios agree with him.

Cable and Data Services The growth of cable has been phenomenal. In relatively few years, it has achieved about 30 percent penetration of the nation's 80 million TV households, which means that more than 20 million homes are wired for cable. Most cable companies operate in conjunction with the American Telephone and Telegraph Company, using AT&T poles on which to mount their wires and their lead-in cables to subscribers.

Cable has spawned numerous pay-TV services, like Home Box Office; a rise in video games; the first all-news national program in Ted Turner's Cable News Network (CNN), and a formidable array of teletext services. For the future, such news and information delivery systems as Prestel, CEEFAX and others in the viewdata field will be racing to gain acceptance as push-button home news and advertising services. As for predictions that they will substantially reduce the cost of newspaper delivery or provide a printout electronic newspaper of their own, that is very far off indeed.

Because of the high cost of such systems today, they cannot yet challenge newspapers in either cost or effectiveness in presenting a complete news report. The teletext services, too, have yet to become cost-effective, but that isn't stopping the giant information conglomerates from investing in them.

Magazines With TV prime time advertising at a premium, national advertisers have turned to large, nationally circulated magazines for greater exposure for their products. And with the rise in magazine advertising to $3 billion annually, the magazine business has become a magnet for risk-takers. Between 200 and 350 new magazines are begun each year, but only the best-financed and best-staffed of them catch on.

In the news field, the leaders continue to be *Time*, with a circulation of 4.5 million; *Newsweek*, with almost 3 million; *U.S. News & World Report*, with 2 million, and *Sports Illustrated*, with 2.3 million. The most successful newcomer, *People*, the feature and gossip magazine begun by Time Inc., has achieved 2.3 million. The checkout counter tabloids, led by the *National Enquirer*, match and sometimes exceed these figures, but have very little appeal to national advertisers.

Among general magazines, the leaders are *TV Guide*, with 18.8 million; *Reader's Digest*, with 18.2 million; *National Geographic*, with 10 million; *Better Homes and Gardens*, with 8 million, and *Woman's Day* and *Family Circle*, with more than 7 million each. While thousands of magazines are published in the United States, the number of nationally circulated publications is generally estimated at 950 to 1,000.

The Integrity of the Journalist

The professional aspect of journalism long ago prevailed over the commercial side. Those who regarded it in the past as merely a money-making enterprise or a bald technique that could be practiced by semiliterate tradespeople under loose editorial direction were proved wrong. Still, journalism is also a business in somewhat the same sense that law and medicine are. It is, in fact, a most necessary business, because it sustains the independence of the news media by keeping them solvent and profitable.

However, it is also true that where there is no profession of journalism, there can be no business of journalism. Neither one can exist in a closed society, where the state owns all the means of communication. In American journalism, it is an article of professional faith that the editorial side must be separated from the commercial side and that at all costs advertising influence must be kept out of the news columns. Whenever there is a violation of this credo, the incident rightfully becomes a matter of general public concern, and that is all to the good.

● Short Takes

Here is what journalism is all about:

- News, first of all. It may be defined as current information that interests and affects the public.
- In the United States, the First Amendment guarantees free speech and a free press. That places the news media under special obligation to report the news quickly and honestly without being subject to distortion or special influence of any kind.
- Journalists are surrogates of the public. They must be more than news stenographers. It is their mission, no matter how difficult it may be, to search for the truth.
- As public surrogates, journalists are bound to act as the public's watchdogs. This is the reason for the spread of investigative reporting.
- The state of the profession, even in times of recession, shows continuing prosperity. That is as it should be. For a prosperous press and prospering broadcast media can be depended on to maintain their independence from outside pressures.
- Because of their economic strength, the news media have developed the most powerful and dependable engine of public information in this country that the world has ever seen.
- It is traditional in the American press that news must be set apart from editorial comment and that the news and editorial function must be rigidly separated from the business side of journalism.
- Journalism in the 20th century has become one of the most vital forces in our society, an essential link between the people and the government.
- Its challenge, excitement and opportunity for service have attracted young men and women in increasing numbers. More than one commentator has called it "the profession of youth."

1

The Writers' Guide

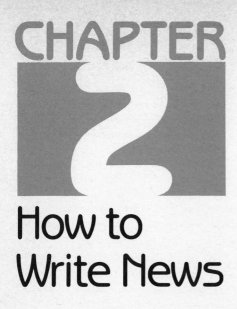

CHAPTER 2

How to Write News

The basis for all good news writing is good reporting. Accuracy, clarity, timeliness and interest are also necessary. So are the broader ingredients such as fairness (which some call objectivity), good taste and good judgment.

But good reporting is the one indispensable quality that makes all others possible. Without it, the writer is lost.

Basis for a News Story

Because writers know the importance of careful and thorough reporting, most of them prefer to gather their own facts. But under the pressures of today's journalism, print and broadcast alike, that isn't always possible. A beginner on a small daily may have to depend on notes like these, telephoned from a nearby village by a part-time reporter:

The Facts for a Story   "This is Paul Lukens in Clearview. Here's an obit of a woman 100 years old."

Name: Mary Adelaide Ward. [Carefully spelled out.]
Address: 153 Main Street. [Repeated.] It's a one-story white clapboard cottage.
She was born there.

Don't know cause of death. She was found at 7:30 a.m., dead in bed, by a neighbor who came in to light her kitchen stove.

Neighbor's name: Wall Weaver [spelled out], 82, retired postman, 155 Main Street.

Here's a quote from Weaver: "She was a good woman."

Funeral services Thursday, 2:30 p.m., Old Steeple Congregational Church, Clearview.

By the way, Mrs. Ward observed her 100th birthday two days ago. Baked a cherry pie, Weaver said, and gave him the first slice. Said she smiled and said, "Guess this is the last cherry pie I'll ever make."

Husband, Samuel J. Ward, stone mason. Died 40 years ago and she's lived alone ever since. Survivors: two sons, four daughters, 18 grandchildren. How many names d'ya want? . . .

The Writer's Problem The writer is told to do a short piece for the first page with the edition deadline only 20 minutes away. By tradition, a newspaper obit would be told "straight" in inverted pyramid style, the most important fact first and others following in diminishing importance. The writer begins:

A 100-year-old woman was found dead today in her home in Clearview. She was Mrs. Mary Adelaide Ward, of 153 Main Street. . . .

It's not very good. Even a beginning news writer understands that a story must be interesting to be published on the first page. This one is dull-dull-dull. The question must be asked, and every writer does it from time to time: "Is that all there is to the story? Isn't there something that makes this obit *different*?"

The clock is running. The writer tries again:

Two days after celebrating her 100th birthday, Mrs. Mary Adelaide Ward was found dead today in the white clapboard cottage at 153 Main Street, Clearview, in which she was born. . . .

It's a lot better. But few newspapers use 30-word lead sentences nowadays if they can avoid it. The most important news stories can be told in less. While the writer hesitates, an assistant city editor asks, "How's that obit coming along?" It isn't. And the clock is still running. There's time for just one more try.

A Different Type of Story The writer attempts something different:

Mary Adelaide Ward celebrated her 100th birthday two days ago at her home, 153 Main Street, Clearview, by baking a cherry pie.

"Guess this is the last cherry pie I'll ever make," she said as she gave the first slice to a neighbor, Wall Weaver, an 82-year-old retired postman, of 155 Main Street.

Today, Weaver found her dead in bed. He recalled the cherry pie incident after reporting her death. He had come to her white clapboard cottage, in which she had been born, to light a fire in her stove.

She had lived there alone since the death of her husband, Samuel J. Ward, a stone mason, 40 years ago. Funeral services will be held Thursday at 2:30 p.m. in the Old Steeple Congregational Church, Clearview. Survivors include two sons, four daughters and 18 grandchildren.

The Basic Principle   With the coming of the electronic revolution, better reporting and writing are essential to newspapers. The immediacy of television has caused many an editor to shake off the shackles of tradition, which decreed that all except feature material had to be told deadpan. Writers who wanted to play it safe, therefore, clung to the inverted pyramid form of story organization, which is better adapted to breaking news and deadline writing.

Leads for such stories, following an older pattern of journalism, often tried to sum up the who, what, where, when, why and how of the event — the 5W's and H, as they were known. Rudyard Kipling, as a young newspaperman in India in the 1890s, called them his "six faithful serving men." The trouble was that they stretched leads to unnecessary length. Gradually, it became the practice to emphasize the who or the why or another of the 5W's and H, by not in the same lead sentence.

The press has progressed. The general rule now is: *Do it differently if you can.* But you do need an idea for a story line first.

The News Feature Approach   The final Ward story shows how some of the devices of the news feature are applied to "hard news" or "spot news," both terms for events that should be reported at once.

- The writer tells a *story* instead of throwing a collection of undigested facts at the reader.
- The story deals in specifics, not generalities. The quote about the cherry pie makes the story interesting because it is unusual. The banal quote "She was a good woman" is not used. Not everything people say is worth writing about.
- The writing style is simple, unaffected. It shuns personal opinion. Paragraphs and sentences are short. The words are familiar, most of them being limited to one or two syllables.
- The story is clear and coherent. There are no unconnected paragraphs (called block paragraphs, usually found in deadline material).
- The writer remains in the background. As a rule, the first person singular appears in the news columns only in eyewitness stories.

"When in Doubt ..."   If a fact cannot be verified, it must be omitted until it can be checked. Thus, in the Ward story, the cause of death is not reported even though it is probably the ills of old age. But the writer, ever vigilant to avoid leaving holes in a story, cannot guess or make up something. One of the most important rules in journalism is: *When in doubt, leave out.*

This is not a defense of timidity. It is good sense. The *Washington Post* used it to advantage in the Watergate inquiry but didn't let it slow the drive for results.

The Deadline Rule   Making the deadline is journalism's most inflexible rule. The writer of the Ward story had 20 minutes, no more. Despite two false starts, the story was in on deadline for Page 1 use. There was no special praise for this. Journalists are expected to make deadlines, regardless of the medium they work in.

The finest reporting, the best writing, the most impressive segment of a TV news program are worthless if they are not ready in time. And so, inevitably, there comes a moment when fact-gathering must end and writing must start. At that instant, journalists know there is no escape from the deadline rule: *Go with what you've got!*

Procedure and Substance

Copy Preparation Most copy for newspapers is prepared today on Video Display Terminals. While the amount of information varies for the top of the first take of copy (the first page), depending on editorial requirements, the material generally includes fuller information than typewritten copy.

The basics are the same for both, however. In typewritten copy, the name of the writer and the source are placed at the top left, followed by a one-word slug (the name of the story) two inches below the writer's name. Copy begins one-third of the way down the first take with one-inch margins around the side and bottom. The first line of a paragraph is indented two inches.

Sentences and paragraphs end on a page. There are no runovers. If the copy ends on a page, an end mark is used: (xxx) or merely the word (end). If there is more to the story, the word "more" appears at the lower right. For the second and subsequent pages, the slug appears at the upper left with the page number after it. For VDTs, this material is rearranged and amplified. For details, see Chapter 3.

Matters of Style In newspapers, most news accounts are told in the past tense. In the broadcast media, except in the roundup evening news programs, the present tense is more often favored to denote the immediacy of events. In both, the time element — today, last night, yesterday — is emphasized, either in the first sentence or close to it.

The Ward story thus conforms to general newspaper practice. The opening anecdote is past-tensed. The fact that her death was discovered *today* (many newspapers now use the day of the week instead) appears at an appropriate point high in the story.

The obit also conforms to the principles of syntax in well-written news accounts. The emphasis is on nouns and verbs in the active voice. The unnecessary adjective and the adverb, that weasel among the parts of speech, are shunned.

That does not excuse the omission of a brief description of the centenarian. Somewhere, it should have been possible for the writer to let the reader see this woman as her neighbors knew her: "In fine weather, she often sat in an ancient maple rocker on her front porch — a frail, white-haired figure in black — and waved at passersby."

But the reporter didn't know Mrs. Ward and never thought of asking the neighbors what she was like.

Sourcing the News Following general newspaper style, the Ward story is organized in two parts: (1) the lead, which may be a sentence, a paragraph or a section of several paragraphs, and (2) the body, which documents the lead. In this instance, the documentation — or proof — for both the death and the cherry pie incident is supplied by the neighbor, Weaver. He is the source for the story.

This kind of proof is all-important in the telling of the news.

If two persons die in a fire, that is the lead; to document it, the source of the news and the identities of the victims, if available, are noted. If there is a marriage, unless the reporter witnesses it, the source of the announcement and the pertinent details are given. Should a snowstorm tie up a city, there must be documentation from the Weather Bureau, City Hall and the police on the extent of the storm and the damage.

The rules are:

Never take anything for granted in journalism.
Support all conclusions with facts.
Document everything with trustworthy sources and, except in the rarest of instances, name them.

The unsourced story is not for beginners.

The Break from Routine

Writers with marginal experience in journalism often complain that it is impossible to be interesting about all subjects. Very true, for the public can scarcely be expected to read about something in which the writer is profoundly uninterested. It takes a specialist, very often, to carry the public through a story about such arcane subjects as price fixing, the gross national product or the mathematics behind a poll of public attitudes.

In the general run of the news, however, any editor has a right to assume that a writer will carry out minimal basic research on most items destined for publication. Unhappily, such an assumption is not always well based.

The journalist is usually pressed for time; too often, that becomes an excuse for giving routine treatment to something that looks like a routine item. And in some cases, it isn't at all routine.

Reporting a Marriage   In a Midwestern city, a relative of Mrs. Marjorie Robinson, 73, of 226 Volunteer Road, telephones the city desk of the local newspaper to report that she will be married tomorrow to Cyrus Hadley, 76, a retired lawyer, who lives in New York City. It will be her third marriage, Mr. Hadley's second, the relative says, and the details of time, place and the officiating clergyman are all given with care.

The reporter who takes the notes contents himself with a routine callback to make sure the caller really is a relative of the bride. (Some newspapers insist on written confirmation.) Then he writes a routine item:

> Mrs. Marjorie Robinson, 73, will be married tomorrow to Cyrus Hadley, 76, a retired New York City lawyer, at the First Presbyterian Church of Central City. . . .

But in the newspaper's library, there is a clipping file on Mrs. Robinson that shows she was born in New York City, was married at 18 and obtained a divorce two years later, then was married to Herbert F. Robinson, a local architect who died three years ago. Who was the first husband?

For the journalist, no detail is too small. It's worth checking. A telephone call to Mrs. Robinson quickly yields the first husband's identity. He was Cyrus Hadley, then a poor law student, and she says she can't recall why she divorced him. Now the story is anything but routine and begins:

> Fifty-three years after their divorce, Marjorie Robinson, 73, and Cyrus Hadley, 76, will be remarried tomorrow.
>
> Mrs. Robinson said today she didn't remember why she gave up on him the first time. "It was so long ago," she explained, "and it doesn't matter very much now...."

Handling a Hostage Story   There was a much bigger story in Kansas City and it was a lot more difficult to handle. There had been a bank robbery, but the police had cornered the bandits in a house some distance away. In desperation, the bandits had seized hostages in the house. And at that point, a reporter saw Detective Sylvester Young, Sr. getting out of a patrol car. Why Young? And why the belated arrival?

The reporter waited, listened and soon discovered the reason. Next morning when the story appeared in the *Kansas City Times,* there was no "Bang-Bang-You're-Dead" lead on the piece about Detective Young. This is how it began:

> It was raining when Sylvester Young Sr. got there yesterday morning, the kind of good, soaking rain the city needed a month ago.
>
> Young, a member of the Kansas City Police Department for nearly 23 years, paused for a minute at the intersection of 44th and Highland. Just down the street police had surrounded a house that contained, they thought, some bank robbers and some hostages.
>
> A patrolman came up to Young and asked him gently, "That your boy in there?"
>
> "Yeah," Young said, "I've talked to him."
>
> So there it was. Dozens of police cars, barricaded streets, guns galore. And one of the men wanted on suspicion of robbing the Central Bank of Kansas City yesterday morning was Sylvester Young Jr., the son of the long-time Kansas City detective....

The Importance of Quotes   In these instances, and in many others that could be cited, the colorful direct quote helps bring the story to life. Writers, in their anxiety to use the cadences of people talking to each other, sometimes clutter their copy with slush. Such as:

> "Well, it's a nice day," she said.
>
> The secretary said, "Just sit down and wait a minute and I'll tell him you're here for the interview."
>
> "My, isn't New York a big city?" he asked.

These come in the category of dumb quotes. Like quotes used in dialect, they seldom contribute much to any story. The reporter and writer need keen ears to note the difference between something a person says that is worth repeating and the usual flow of trite remarks that sinks many an interview.

In a story about New Orleans just before a recent Super Bowl, Mike Tierney of the *St. Petersburg Times* included the following:

> Hookers left the street corners and back alleys to work the brightly lit hotel lobbies and special parties. They were everywhere, making their pitches even to unsuspecting bystanders.
>
> "How much?" one man asked, strictly out of curiosity.
>
> "A hundred bucks," she answered.
>
> The man shook his head. "No, thanks."
>
> "Creep," she replied.
>
> Another man was approached by, of all people, the maid in his hotel room.
>
> "I can show you a good time for $100," she said to him.
>
> "How about $20?" he counter-offered.
>
> "No way."

That put a little life in the story. When editors emphasize the need for good quotes and want them high in a story, writers would do well to listen. And that goes for reporters, too.

Crisis in a Small City

There is a popular fallacy, which is current chiefly among those dazzled by big-city life, that writing for a small city paper has to be dull. Few young journalists would be bored by Oak Ridge, a middle-class community of 30,000 that grew with the atomic age in the lush green hills of eastern Tennessee, or its daily newspaper, the *Oak Ridger*, with its 12,000 circulation.

The latest scientific developments in the atomic era are not the regular news that makes the *Oak Ridger* go. The community, despite the comfortable lives led by most of its people, is subject to the same hazards of life as any other.

One cold November night, a motorist who had been stopped for questioning in Oak Ridge kidnapped Police Officer Jon Shipley, shot him in the head three times and left him for dead. That same night, Tommie Okoh Warner, who had escaped several weeks earlier from an Oak Ridge jail, was arrested and charged with the crimes.

Dick Smyser, editor of the *Oak Ridger*, directed his small staff in a thorough coverage of the story and missed no detail. But all the while, he knew he had an even more difficult problem ahead of him. As he explained: "The whole incident became a major community concern as the police officer made a miraculous recovery and became a local hero. The atmosphere surrounding the case led to claims by the defense [for Warner] that a fair trial could not be given the defendant."

Writing for a Small City   When Warner was brought to trial eight miles away in the Anderson County seat, Clinton, the atmosphere was tense. The worst thing that could have happened would have been the publication of inflammatory stories under sensational headlines. But neither Smyser nor the publisher, Tom Hill, would have permitted the *Oak Ridger* to go that route, either on this story or any other.

An editor and his newsroom motto. Dick Smyser, editor of the Oak Ridge (Tennessee) *Oak Ridger*, beside his ever-present newsroom admonition: "Accuracy, accuracy, accuracy." At the time this photograph was taken, he was treasurer of the American Society of Newspaper Editors and scheduled to become the organization's president. (Copyright, the *Oak Ridger*. Used by permission.)

For the trial assignment, Smyser chose a relatively inexperienced 25-year-old reporter, Sharon Fitzgerald, who had recently graduated from the University of Tennessee and had served for a year as the news editor of a nearby weekly newspaper. Her stories were complete, impartial, objective in the best sense and packed with sharply observed detail and key quotes from important testimony.

For her final story, she chose not to go with a straight news lead. Rather, she gave a news feature twist to what might otherwise been a colorless, straight news account. This was what she wrote:

By Sharon Fitzgerald

News feature lead

Today is Tommie Okoh Warner's 27th birthday.

And today Warner was sentenced to more than 50 years in a state penitentiary for the Nov. 30 shooting, abduction and robbery of Oak Ridge Police Officer Jon Shipley, and for a Sept. 14 escape from the Anderson County jail.

Color

The courtroom had been nearly deserted in Clinton this morning as the jury continued deliberating—asking for lunch to be brought in—after the trial.

The lead is documented

The eight men, four women jury returned with guilty verdicts on all four counts against Warner at 1:06 p.m. after more than 12 hours of deliberation that began shortly after the jury retired Thursday afternoon.

Warner was found:

Exact sentence on each count

- Guilty of attempted murder in the first degree and sentenced to 20 years in the state penitentiary;
- Guilty of armed robbery and sentenced to 10 years;
- Guilty of aggravated kidnaping with injury and sentenced to 20 years
- Guilty of jail escape and sentenced to the term in the

state penitentiary of not less than one year nor more than two years.

The latest move   At press time today Judge James B. (Buddy) Scott was preparing a charge for the jury on an habitual criminal indictment against Warner from the Anderson County Grand Jury.

Explanation   Under state law, only certain felonies can trigger an habitual criminal action. After three or more such felony convictions, a person can be declared an habitual criminal and sentenced to prison for life.

Warner pleaded not guilty to the habitual criminal charge. Jan Hicks, assistant attorney general, told the Oak Ridger that defense attorneys have asked to argue the charge. These proceedings were to continue this afternoon.

Ms. Hicks said that although the law is clear, "some juries don't follow the law."

The lead is further documented   Warner sat quietly, head bowed, when Jury Foreman Warren Hensley reported the verdicts to the court. Shipley sat motionless, staring straight ahead.

Following the judgment from the court, Warner made an emotional statement calling the trial "a masquerade." He spoke for about three minutes, stopping frequently and sighing loudly.

Warner quote   "Justice never reigned here, only dictatorship and force," he said. "The anti-social source of crime should be destroyed." He added that it is the system that should be punished, not the individual.

Color   There were about 30 persons in the courtroom to hear the jury's verdict, and one could have heard a pin drop as Warner made his statement.

Detail on record and trial   Warner was indicted by Anderson County's Grand Jury for a Sept. 14 escape from the Anderson County jail, and for assault with intent to commit murder in the first degree, armed robbery and the aggravated kidnaping of Officer Shipley.

Warner had been convicted Feb. 1, 1972 of assault with intent to commit voluntary manslaughter. On March 23, 1977 he was convicted of grand larceny. And on June 3, 1977 he was convicted of armed robbery.

Summary   Ms. Hicks elected this afternoon to go with the armed robbery conviction in pressing the habitual criminal prosecution.

Warner's trial began Monday with jury selection being completed by noon Tuesday. Shipley took the stand Tuesday afternoon and Warner admitted to the shooting on Wednesday afternoon.

There was no need for Dick Smyser of the *Oak Ridger* to worry about prejudicial trial coverage. The story was handled professionally throughout by a young journalist with scanty experience. Not long after, she went on to the staff of the *Philadelphia Inquirer,* and Smyser began breaking in another newcomer. Over 30 years, he has had a lot of them.

A Pulitzer Prize Story

The *Longview* (Washington) *Daily News*, with a circulation of 27,000, had a staff of 11 cityside reporters, three photographers and four news editors early in 1980. Its editor and publisher, Ted M. Natt, had been trying to improve the writing in the paper for some time. He held "writers' lunches" to discuss better ways of handling the news. He sent some of his editors and reporters to attend regional writing seminars. And he delegated some of his editors to be "writing coaches."

When Mount St. Helens Erupted   Natt's efforts yielded results in an unexpected way. Less than 35 air miles away, a formidable volcano, Mount St. Helens, began rumbling ominously in March of that year. Bob Gaston, the *News*'s managing editor, was quick to cover the story, not really knowing what would happen but sensing an impending catastrophe.

Among the earliest stories the *News* published was one in which the earth-

Andre Stepankiwski (left) and Tom Paulu of the *Longview* (Washington) *Daily News*. Reporters and photographers of the *News* were watching Mount St. Helens months before the volcano erupted. The newspaper's coverage was so comprehensive when the volcano erupted that the paper won a Pulitzer Prize. (This photograph and photographs of Mount St. Helens erupting on pages 37–38: copyright by the *Longview Daily News*. Used by permission.)

quakes that were shaking the mountain, according to scientists, pointed to renewed volcanic activity. Up to that time, there hadn't been an eruption in years.

On May 17, 1980, *News* reporters were at the mountain interviewing three people who lived on the slopes. Next day, with a roar that echoed through the countryside, a blast tore the top off the volcano. The three people who had been interviewed were among the first to die. Other victims were discovered later.

For miles around, the area was devastated. A whole lake vanished. Silt threatened the valley and flood waters raged through hamlets and farms. Through it all, *News* reporters moved by every possible means, including helicopters, to find out what had happened. One even climbed across housetops to interview a family fleeing from its mud-choked home.

When the *News* came out the next morning, there was a complete summary of casualties and property damage on Page 1, plus pictures showing the volcano shooting a fiery plume 10 miles high. Every story in the paper was stamped with the special training in writing that had been given to the small staff. In particular, there was an unsigned eyewitness account of the devastation as seen from a helicopter. It was headed, simply, "RAMPAGE".

"A Spectacle from Hell"   This was what the reporters saw from their helicopter:

Concrete bridges crumbled.

Steel railroad trestles rammed by logjams became screaming, twisted toys.

Mud enveloped riverfront homes.

Uprooted trees bounced into the air, tossed from rampaging waters like surfboards caught in crashing waves.

Cars and pickup trucks careened end over end in the muddy wall of water.

It was a spectacle from hell.

Crisscrossing the Toutle River Valley Sunday afternoon in a helicopter, we saw what few persons believed would happen. The scientists' warnings over the past few weeks had predicted the growing destruction below us.

Both forks of the Toutle River had gone berserk since the morning lava eruption on Mount St. Helens. Walls of mud resembling wet cement filled the North Fork, topping its banks, oozing and spreading, crushing everything in its path.

At 3 p.m., we landed on a ridge above the North Fork west of Hoffstadt Creek near Weyerhaeuser Co.'s Camp Baker—some 15 miles from the volcano.

The logging yard below us was filled with rushing muddy water that picked up stacks of logs, shooting them down the growing rapids. Giant ice chunks floated by.

The deluge knocked aside logging trucks like so much trash.

The torrent pushed over an empty logging train, burying it within minutes.

Whole trees rammed up against a green steel bridge on Spirit Lake Highway. It bowed in half like a Tinker Toy and sounded like metal railroad cars banging together. The

bridge ripped loose and joined thousands of trees and logs in the rushing river.

Trees snapped loudly under the force of pounding water. A stand of more than 40 trees disappeared within minutes. It sounded like combat.

Flying north toward Green River, we came upon an eerie scene that could have come from a science fiction movie. Acres of tall trees miles from the volcano, powdered with ash, had been uprooted and flattened, apparently in the initial explosion. Their tops pointed west like giant tombstones in a prehistoric graveyard.

Back on the North Fork, one mile above Kid Valley, we watched in shock as the swollen river overran every home on the shore. Within six minutes nothing was left but mud as the houses joined the mass of debris cascading down the river toward Interstate Highway 5.

When the wall of mud and logs reached the concrete bridge just east of Toutle Lake School, nature smashed man's creations. While reporters, sightseers and police stood on Spirit Lake Highway, the bridge broke away in one piece, cracking at both ends in billowing clouds of yellow dust.

The river swept the bridge into the mighty fray. It, too, began moving at a speed of more than 50 mph before breaking into large chunks and sinking under the deep churning water.

Large arms of gray, ugly mud soon covered farmlands. Fences, power lines, telephone poles and tractors were sucked into the muck. Only a few pieces of the highway east of Toutle were visible. The North and South Forks met, engulfing the entire valley.

The Toutle River Fish Hatchery was wiped out. . . . We could see people loading their belongings into a pickup truck and a station wagon and racing out on a logging road.

The scene was the same everywhere in the valley. River banks, except for the very steepest, no longer existed. Thick expanses of trees suddenly became small isolated islands. . . .

It was, as Lew Pumphey observed in his Page 1 lead, a catastrophe that "has left scars on the terrain of Southwest Washington that will remain for years." For many days thereafter, the *Daily News*'s small staff covered what was, for them, the biggest story of the year. All told, between March 24 and December 31, 1980, the newspaper published 2,200 of their stories and 500 of their photos of the volcano.

For the work of its staff, the *Longview Daily News* won the Pulitzer Prize for Local Reporting in 1981. A distinguished jury of journalists called their coverage "superb" and commented: "When the eruption occurred, the coverage blended the tragedy, drama, scientific and human interest elements into well-written, thoughtful main stories and sidebars. Presentation of the material was highly dramatic and effective. The relatively small staff made maximum use of limited resources and continued its fine coverage into the weeks of aftermath."

Nothing ever happens in a small town? Don't believe it! There are many more reporters in small- and medium-size cities in the United States today than there are in the big cities. That's where many of the newspapers are and most of them are prospering. Ted Natt, for one, is not likely to complain from now on that he is in a "soft-news" town.

The Assignment Sheet

City desks on smaller papers and metropolitan desks on larger ones draw up assignment sheets to show at a glance what the staff is expected to do. Assignments are given to reporters on the basis either of assigned beats or general assignments taken from a "Day Book" (a record of scheduled events). The daily news breaks, which cannot be anticipated, are assigned on the basis of the availability of some reporters, the special knowledge of others.

Assignments for a Smaller Newspaper At the *Knoxville Journal*, a morning newspaper in a city of nearly 200,000 people, the staff is mainly assigned to beats except for a few general assignment reporters. This is what the weekly assignment sheet there looks like:

Staff	Assignment
Moxley	City Hall
Hetherington	General assignment
Day	Energy
Beazley	General assignment
Greene	Courts
Jones	Business
Womack	Knox County
Glenn	On vacation
McWilliams	Higher education
Chester	Desk & general assignment
Griffith	Day police
Frary	Night police
King	State news
Ray	State news
Klebenow	Westward section
Roberts	Handling copy
Ethridge	Handling copy

Assignments for a Larger Newspaper The newsroom of the *New York Times* is so large, and there are so many reporters in all sections of the newspaper, that a public address system is used to call reporters to the metropolitan desk. Standing in any one corner, you can't see the entire newsroom—only a major part. In consequence, there is little sense in reproducing the entire *Times* assignment sheet. The following shows how a section of the staff was assigned for a day picked at random:

Staff	Assignment
Dionne	Albany. State's bridges, roads, sewers in bad shape.
Reif	Guns. Color story on gun auction.
Haberman	Exhibit. Make-it-in-New York exhibit was made in N.J.
Sulzberger	Shop. Mayor announces Brooklyn "shopsteading" project.
Hanley	Rich. How the rich live in the suburbs.
R. Sullivan	Hosp. Dispute over Federal support for city hospitals.
Shipp	Abbott. Suspect arraigned.
Perlez	Jerpols. Jersey political campaign financing.
Maitland	Export. Exclusive. Details later.
Feron	Scarsdale. DA's response in Jean Harris case appeal.
Wires	Buffalo. Opening of Christopher trial.

Source Books for Journalists

Every journalist should own—*and use*— a certain number of important source books. They are the tools of the profession. My own basic list follows:

Writing and Usage

Bernstein, Theodore M. *The Careful Writer*. New York: Atheneum, 1965.

Bremner, John B. *Words on Words: A Dictionary for Writers and Others Who Care About Words*. New York: Columbia University Press, 1980.

Fowler, H. W. *A Dictionary of Modern English Usage*. 2nd ed. New York: Oxford University Press, 1965.

Strunk, William, Jr., and White, E. B. *The Elements of Style*. 3rd ed. New York: Macmillan, 1979.

Dictionaries

Payton, Geoffrey, ed. *The Merriam-Webster Pocket Dictionary of Proper Names*. New York: Pocket Books, 1972.

Webster's New International Dictionary. 2nd ed. Springfield, Mass.: G. & C. Merriam, 1959.

Webster's New World Dictionary of the American Language. 2nd coll. ed. Cleveland and New York: William Collins & World Publishing, 1974, 1976.

Texts and Guides

Associated Press Stylebook. New York: Associated Press, 1980.

Congressional Directory. Washington: Government Printing Office; issued annually.

Editor & Publisher International Year Book. New York: Editor & Publisher; published annually.

Opdycke, John B. *Harper's English Grammar*. New York: Harper & Row, 1966.

The World Almanac. New York: Newspaper Enterprise Assn.; published annually.

Anthologies

Hohenberg, John, ed., *The Pulitzer Prize Story*. New York: Columbia University Press, 1959, and *The Pulitzer Prize Story II*. New York: Columbia University Press, 1980.

Pickett, Calder M. *Voices of the Past.* Columbus, Ohio: Grid, 1977.

Snyder, Louis M., and Morris, Richard B., eds. *A Treasury of Great Reporting.* Rev. ed. New York: Simon & Schuster, 1962.

● Short Takes

Here is a summary of the basic rules for news writing:

- The purpose of all news writing is to communicate information, opinions and ideas in an interesting and timely manner. Stories must be accurate, terse, clear and easily understood.
- Writers should use relatively short, simple sentences and paragraph liberally. Two or three sentences to a paragraph are sufficient. Occasionally, a one-sentence paragraph may be used for emphasis. Unity and coherence should be maintained throughout.
- Wherever possible, use one idea to a sentence. To do so, separate sentences should be made out of qualifying or descriptive clauses if it is necessary.
- Short, familiar words are preferred over long, strange words. Don't make readers run to a dictionary. Unfamiliar words should be defined. Geographical points should be located.
- Use vigorous verbs. Wherever possible, use the active voice. Use adjectives and adverbs sparingly.
- Be positive, not negative. This means to emphasize what *is* happening and to avoid leads that report no change in events or a mere continuation of developments that are already known.
- Be specific. Instead of reporting that a woman is tall, she should be described as being six feet two. Instead of writing that a speaker was upset, it would be better to report that he shouted and banged on the table with his fist.
- A news event outside the news organization's own area should be related to the local community if possible. Five dead in an Atlanta fire means little in Chicago unless some of the dead are from Chicago.
- Statistics should be related to something a mass public can understand. Instead of calling India a needy nation, write that the average Indian earns less than $100 a year. Instead of calling Lebanon a tiny country, it should be pointed put that Lebanon's coastline is only 120 miles long, about the size of Long Island's Atlantic coastline.
- The simplest form of a news story is divided into two parts—the lead and body. The lead tells what happened, but it should not be crowded with all the 5Ws and H. The body documents the lead.
- In a hard news story, everything must be attributed to an identifiable source. If it cannot be done, there should be an explanation. ("The source asked not to be identified.")
- In reporting a speech, interview or public statement, all statements made by speakers must be attributed directly to them. In reporting an arrest, it must be specified that the police version of the alleged crime is being given.
- Use meaningful quotations high up and throughout a story. Use partial quotations sparingly. When a quotation is used, it should begin a new paragraph.

- When in doubt, leave it out.
- Make deadlines. Go with what you've got.
- Don'ts:
  Don't write tortured, unnatural or excitable prose.
  Don't write topsy-turvy sentences.
  Don't overwrite in length or meaning. Be moderate.
  Don't editorialize. Personal views must be kept out of the news columns except for an important eyewitness story.
  Don't switch tenses except for good reason. Most news for newspapers is told in the past tense. Breaking news of immediate interest is told in the present tense for broadcast journalism.
  Don't forget the time element in newswriting. In hard news, it generally goes in the lead. But it must be high up always.

CHAPTER 3

Working with the News

Most journalists have their own pet definitions of news.

Keith Fuller, president of the Associated Press, suggests that when somebody says, "Gee whiz, I didn't know that," it's news. Turner Catledge used to tell the staff of the *New York Times* when he was its executive editor, "News is anything you didn't know yesterday." A cynic's definition is: "News is what editors say it is." And finally, here is a statement of fact: "News is what is printed in newspapers or broadcast."

The pattern of the news operation varies from print to broadcast organizations, from daily to weekly newspapers, from wire services to news magazines. The operation of the daily newspaper, from which the others developed, is described here. The broadcast operation is detailed in Chapter 15.

The Electronic Newsroom

Nearly all American dailies and many weeklies are produced be electronic means. Production is carried out by a combination of Video Display Terminals, computers, photocomposition machines and offset printing presses. Reporters and writers, who turn in their copy on VDTs instead of a typewriter, are the main cogs in this reproduction process.

The newcomer, far from fearing the electronic newsroom, should welcome it. Most editors agree that it requires only about 48 hours of work on a VDT to convince the beginner that the machine is a blessing for the working journalist. It is, in fact, as big an advance over the typewriter as the typewriter was over the quill pen a little more than a century ago.

Handling the VDT   Chuck Johnson, assistant news editor of the *Milwaukee Journal*, has this to say about writing on the VDT:

> No question about it: Writing on the VDT is much easier than writing on a typewriter.
>
> The advantages are obvious, even to veteran reporters who swore they would never part with their typewriters in favor of computerized electronic devices.
>
> For one thing, a letter, a word, a sentence, a paragraph — even a whole book — can be inserted anywhere the writer chooses. For another, parts of a story can be moved about without scissors and paste and the attendant messiness.
>
> For still another, a writer can start over any time he or she wants. It isn't necessary to rip the paper (with carbons) out of the typewriter and replace them. Rather, the whole story or just the lead, or any part of both, can be killed in a couple of key strokes and a replacement started.

A quiet moment in the electronic newsroom of the *Rochester* (New York) *Times-Union* with a reporter, foreground, working on his story on the VDT. Note the absence of typewriters and spikes for copy and other equipment of the age before computers supplanted copy paper. (Copyright, the Gannett Rochester Newspapers. Used by permission.)

Or a false start can be filed, then brought back, to work parts of it into a new version if the writer wants.

If the electronic editing system works better for the reporter and writer, it slows things down for the copy editor. With paper and pencil, an editor could glance through the copy, say, to check the spelling of a name. With the VDT, the story must be scrolled up on the screen and back down for such a simple check.

That is one reason the *Milwaukee Journal* kept the paper copy to go with the electronic version. The paper can be marked as a road map in a difficult job and then the electronic version can be put together accordingly. Trying to mark the screen of a VDT would be like trying to put an X on a location in a lake so you could come back next day to the exact place where the fish were biting.

How the VDT Works This marvelously adaptable machine has a typewriterlike keyboard attached to a small TV screen, on which the news appears when it is written, edited or called up from computer storage. In addition to the usual arrangement of keys on a typewriter, there are extra keys for the broad range of VDT operations. The basic steps are these:

Signing on Generally writers use the first four letters of their names, or their initials plus a code word, and push the SIGN ON button that produces a SIGN ON response. If editing is to be done, the editor's initials plus the call letter of the queue or story placed on the screen will produce the SIGN ON response.

Execute mode A light on the right side of the keyboard will show under the label EXEC. This means the VDT is in the EXECUTE mode. When the SLUG key is touched, a one- or two-line form, depending on the type of machine, will appear at the top of the screen. Next, a small block of light, one character in size, will appear behind the word SLUG. This block of light is called a *cursor*. The writer then fills in the blanks in the SLUG form (name of the writer, whether it is city desk or sports or other copy, the date, the slug, or one-word name of the story and so on). Now the VDT is ready for copy.

Cursor There is no guesswork about where to start the story. The cursor positions itself where the writing should begin when the HOME key is pressed. As the writer types the story, the copy comes up silently on the screen. With the use of the cursor, copy can be changed, shifted, corrected or inserted at the touch of a key. When a take (page) is completed, it can be stored in the computer at the touch of another key. Or it can be sent instead to an editor's VDT or to the photocomposition machine to be set in type. Editors, too, can operate the machine in the same manner by calling up this or any other story they wish. (See Chapter 12.)

Continuation If the story is to be continued beyond the first take, the word "more" should be inserted after the last sentence and paragraph on the first take and the story routed to the editing desk by touching the proper button. The SLUG key will now produce another form to be filled in for the top of the second take and the writing proceeds until the story ends.

End/send When the story ends, whether it is after the first or second take or the tenth, the END/SEND button is pressed and the terminal returns to the EXECUTE mode.

It should be emphasized that VDTs vary and so do the operating instructions. Depending on the type of machine used, some of the specific details outlined here may change slightly.

VDT Copy Preparation Here is an example of how copy is prepared on the VDT by filling in the SLUG form as it comes up on the top of the VDT screen:

Barbara Abel is ready to write a story about a parade for the city desk of the *Milwaukee Journal*. She signs on at her Hendrix 3400 VDT, presses the SLUG key, and this form, known as a "header," pops up at the top of the screen:

SLUG:	ABEL SLUGIT 01Z	STATUS:	R1	TIME:	09:23 MON	REF:	
EDN:	DAY:	PAGE:	SET:	012			OK:

CY is entered for city desk, PARADE is the slug, 01 is the page number (the z is dropped because that signifies the last take), R1 means the piece is routine (urgent, or U, means faster handling) and 1 means it is the first version. One L is the name of the edition and 012 is the code for body type. Abel writes a take and the city desk gets it:

SLUG:	CY ABEL PARADE 01	STATUS:	R2	TIME:	09:23 MON	REF:	ABEL PARADE
EDN:	ONE L	DAY:	MON	PAGE:	SET:	012	OK:

Automatically, when the story comes up for editing on a city desk VDT, it becomes version R2. There happens to be another PARADE slug, so the desk changes Abel's story to FROLIC and decides to set it in wide measure and put it on a page designated as H. Note that the initial time, 09:23, has not yet changed. The codes appear in these spaces and the take goes to the copy desk:

SLUG:	LD ABEL FROLIC 01	STATUS:	R2	TIME:	09:23 MON	REF:	ABEL PARADE
EDN:	ONE L	DAY:	MON	PAGE:	HHH	SET:	042	OK:

When the copy editor finishes with the take on another VDT, Abel's second and last takes are ready and these, too, are handled and sent to the composing room. This is the second take slug when it reaches the composing room at 10:10 a.m.:

SLUG:	NA ABEL FROLIC 02Z	STATUS:	R3	TIME:	10:10 MON	REF:	ABEL PARADE
EDN:	ONE L	DAY:	MON	PAGE:	HHH	SET:	042	OK: SR

The Computer Newcomers to journalism need not know any more about computers than the average driver knows about the engine of an automobile.

But a few words of explanation may be helpful because of the machine's importance in the news operation.

A computer is an electronic machine that works at very high speeds for sorting, storing and processing the news. It has a fabulous memory, is far more accurate than any other tool that has been used to process the news and can perform tasks within seconds that formerly would have required a long time to accomplish.

Within a single day, a computer can make several billion calculations without mistakes as it stores information, changes it, organizes it and puts it out as tape, cards, microfilm, or impulses to operate a photocomposition machine or a laser beam. The machine can be programmed to perform quickly and efficiently a great many tasks that formerly tied up a composing room for hours. It also can handle banks of VDTs, accept instructions from a variety of sources and even "talk" with other computers such as those that transmit wire service news at very high speeds.

Other Machines and Processes Here is a brief summary of the other machines and processes that are used in the electronic newsroom, but seldom involve the writer:

Photocomposition This is a photographic printing process that is done on paper. The machine receives electronic signals that make up the letters of a news account or other material and transfers them to paper by photographic means. The paper, in column lengths, is pasted by experts on page-size sheets called "flats." With headlines, illustrations and advertisements, these "flats" then become the basis for the printing of the newspaper.

Material for use in photocomposition machines may be transmitted by an operator at a keyboard, from a tape or directly from a computer. As for headlines, they can be attached to stories for which they are written in whatever type sizes an editor may designate.

Phototypesetters, used in conjunction with computers, are usually accurate. But when an error does occur in a line, a new tape must be produced and a pasteup expert must impose the single corrected line over the original film printout. To avoid such complications, many newspapers do proofreading on VDTs so that corrections are made on the screen and error-free tapes result.

Pagination machine This is a machine designed to shorten the time for the imposition of type on a page. It was developed for making up and placing advertisements and illustrations on a page but now is being used by some newspapers, notably the Gannett Westchester-Rockland Group, for laying out editorial matter in the process, including headlines. Joseph Ungaro, executive editor of the Westchester-Rockland Group, believes that the Pagination machine eventually will do away with the pasteup process and make up an entire page electronically. This already is being done in Japan by the newspaper *Asahi Shimbun*.

Offset This is an indirect printing process. The positive image of a page — either from the pasteup of type, headlines, pictures and ads or the Pagination machine — is sent to the camera room, where a film negative of the page is produced.

The negative in turn is transferred to a thin metal plate by an automatic platemaking machine. An oil-based ink adheres to the parts of the plate that retain the image of the page; the rest of the plate is washed clean by water.

Next, the inked image is imposed on a rubber roller as a negative which, when

The shape of the future. One of the earliest pagination machines, which enables editors to make up pages electronically in the newsroom. The nearly made-up page is on the oblong screen in the middle, and the editor is working keyboards on both machines. (Copyright, Westchester-Rockland New York Newspapers, Inc. Used by permisson.)

transferred to a roll of newsprint in an offset printing press, again becomes positive and presents a sharp, clean appearance. Most American newspapers now use offset exclusively.

The News Organization

The publisher, the top executive of a newspaper, oversees five departments — editorial, advertising, mechanical, circulation and business. On a large newspaper, each department has its own executive and table of organization. On a small weekly, necessarily, the departments are combined and the actual printing usually is done on contract elsewhere.

Delegation of Authority Most newspaper publishers delegate authority over the news operation to the editor, who is responsible for the paper's editorial policy and the editorial page. Many editors then delegate responsibility for the news operation to their managing editor.

Sometimes, that job is given the loftier title of executive editor. But whatever the title, the individual becomes principally responsible for covering the news and getting out the paper.

Editorial departments on larger newspapers are divided roughly into three parts that are generally known as the news side, the city side, and the various departments such as sports, financial, life-style and amusements. Each operates under the general directives given to the individual editors and department heads by the managing editor.

The News Side   The news side VDTs receive all copy from the city, sub-urban, telegraph and cable desks for processing. The departmental copy is handled directly by the people in charge, also on VDTs.

One individual (who may be called news editor or assistant managing editor) evaluates this flow of copy for the paper, edition after edition, day after day. It has to be scanned for news value and length and given a particular headline designation and place in the paper unless it is a short.

Once the news editor's directions are recorded on the VDT copy, it is processed on VDTs at the copy desk where it is read for errors of fact, style, grammar and spelling, given the designated headline, trimmed to appropriate length and dis-patched to the phototypesetter.

The makeup editor then takes over with a dummy of Page 1, made up by the managing editor or news editor after a brief editorial conference. There also may be dummies for other pages, depending on the size of the paper and the importance of the edition. It is the makeup editor's job to put the paper together so that the mechanical department can complete the process of production.*

To sum up the news side process: Whether it is handled entirely by one person on a small daily or weekly, or whether there is an elaborate staff and electronic processing that is typical of a large metropolitan daily, it is the heart of the news production operation. The news side ties in with the mechanical department, which gets out the paper; the circulation department, which distributes it; the advertising department, which brings in the ads that actually determine the size of the news hole before any news goes into the paper, and the business department, which must meet all expenses and attempt to show a profit.

The City Side   Whether the city side is run by a metropolitan editor, a city editor or a combination of city and suburban editors, it is responsible for local coverage. The top editor on a large newspaper has a number of assistants who handle the staff on an around-the-clock basis; generally, too, the city desk also is responsible for photo coverage. On a small daily or weekly, one person handles the whole assignment.

Departmental Desks   Everything on a large newspaper proceeds in channels. If a copy editor wants to consult a reporter or writer, it must be done through the city desk and vice versa. The same is true of the work of departmental desks. The sports side, for example, has its own space assignment and fills its pages with its own copy. The same is true of financial, amusements, life-style and others.

The Individual   In a profession that is seemingly so casual, this chan-neling of the individual is always something of a surprise to the newcomers to jour-

---

*Note: Pagination, an electronic makeup process, is used for much advertising and is in limited use for editorial matter. But for the most part editorial makeup is still done from hand-written dummies.

nalism. Even if the lines of authority are few and not clearly visible, they are scrupulously observed.

A local reporter, for example, must call back the same assistant city editor who
issued the assignment or the individual who replaced that person on a later shift.
Except in an emergency, the reporter stays within this chain of command. Reporters
do not write headlines or picture captions, except on smaller papers, and have no
authority over the play of the story. Nor does the reporter have anything to say to
the copy editor who handles the story. These operations are entirely separate. So is
the electronic process of putting the story in type and placing it in the newspaper.

How Many to a Staff?   News staffs vary widely in size. A survey of
small-city dailies has shown that a daily of 5,000 circulation has four full-time staffers and one part-timer, while another of 8,400 circulation has six full-time staffers.
Weeklies are even smaller, except when they are combined into a group publishing
operation. Most large dailies, however, have staffs in the hundreds and the giants of
daily journalism employ more than 1,000 persons on the news side alone.

News Style

Style in journalism is a two-faced word. To the reader, it means an individualistic
manner of writing. But to journalists, it refers to uniform rules for spelling, syntax,
abbreviations and the like.

Many news organizations of substance, such as the larger newspapers, have
their own stylebooks. But the most influential stylebook in the nation by far is the
one issued by the Associated Press and updated annually. It is the accepted standard
for American journalism and may be found in the reference rooms of all news organizations worthy of the name.

The use of the *AP Stylebook* is widespread because of the need for standard
stylistic practices in the operations of computers, VDTs and photocomposition
machines. Says the AP of its stylebook: "Presentation of the printed word should be
accurate, consistent, pleasing to the eye and should conform to grammatical rules.
The English language is fluid and changes incessantly. . . ."

What Stylebooks Cannot Do   Despite the importance of a stylebook,
it cannot substitute for the hard work, acquired skills and natural artistry that are
the mark of the professional writers of news.

It cannot be used to decide what points are most important in a story. Nor can
it develop hints on how news should be presented or organized either in print or in
the broadcast media. No rules have yet been devised to substitute for thinking.

The Pad and Pencil Journalist

Despite the dominance of the electronic newsroom, it would be premature to say
goodbye to pad and pencil journalists. Even though portable VDTs are used by many
reporters on numerous assignments ranging from sports events to political conven-

tions, there are still many times when journalists on assignments out of town and out of the country must use typewriters. We cannot completely dispense, therefore, with the rules for nonelectronic copy preparation and editing. That is why they are given here, both for professional and classroom use or wherever else they are applicable.

Copy Preparation on Paper   Writers using typewriters for news stories generally work on 8½-x-11-inch sheets of copy paper, on one side only.

The first take (page) of a story should begin one-third of the way from the top, with margins of an inch or more at either side and a bit more at the bottom. All sentences and paragraphs should end on a take. It is also standard practice not to split words at the end of a line.

The first thing that goes on a story is the name of the writer, top left, with a few words to indicate the source (name of source, wire service, clip from another newspaper and so on). Reporters doing their own stories write "assigned" after their name. Those using the telephone use "by phone," with the name of the persons interviewed; others, who rewrite publicity, use "handout" plus the source's name.

Essentially, the information is the same as that for a VDT "header" block except for the placement of the slug, the one-word designation for the story. The slug in typewritten copy goes about two inches under the name of the writer and is repeated, top left, on succeeding pages with the page number.

If a story ends on one page, it should be given an end mark such as xxx, ### or even the word "end," plus the time the piece was finished. Now and then, the figure "30" — the old telegraphers' signal for the end of a message — is still used.

When a story runs to more than one page, the word *(more)* in parentheses is typed in the lower right-hand corner. The process continues, page after page, until the writer concludes with an end mark and time indication. Some newspapers use wire service continuation procedures, which will be found in Chapter 14.

After the first take, all succeeding ones begin with copy about an inch and a half under the slug and page number in the top left-hand corner.

Slugging   The preparation of copy on terminals has emphasized the importance of choosing a proper and characteristic slug for a story. For example, if an auto accident is slugged "auto," the chances are that at least one other piece with the same slug might be called up from a terminal if the initials of the writers happen to coincide. Such general slugs as "auto," "obit" and "weather" must be avoided on terminals because they are too general. This is even more true for stories written on copy paper.

Because there is more space for slugs on copy paper, a report about a death could carry the name of the dead person as a slug: "Obit-Mays." A City Council speech could also carry a joint slug: "Council-Roe," Roe being the name of the speaker.

On terminals, a brief slug is mandatory.

Handing in Copy   When a story written on copy paper is handed to the city desk, or other units in the editorial department, it should be folded in half with the typed side up and the name of the writer visible. This should also be done with printouts of VDT stories or wire copy, if it is pulled off the printers. It is standard operating procedure and the way editors want copy handled.

Copy Editing Terms and Symbols

Copy editing and headline writing are generally done on VDTs. However, on some newspapers, printouts of the VDT copy may be used on specific events for the convenience of the editors. The standard copy editing terms and symbols, in use for more than a century in the hot type era, still are a part of newsroom lore and are summarized here with examples of how each may used on the copy desk:

Symbol	Meaning	Example
⌞ or ¶	Begin new paragraph (pgh).	⌞This was the result.
No ¶	No pgh. Run in.	No ¶ Rain soon ended.
(MORE)	Continued on next page.	Goes in lower right corner.
XXX ###	End of story. Use one symbol.	Center on page after last pgh.
John Smith (double underscore)	Capitalize letters.	Double underscore means caps.
Really? (single underline)	Use italics.	Single underline means italics.
(BF)	Set in boldface type.	(bf) **Scene of wreck.**
⊙ ⊗	A period, inserted in copy. Use one or the other.	The sun was shining⊙
,/	A comma, inserted in copy.	He said,/ "This is it."
"̂ " ˅/	Quotation marks, inserted.	˄"Let's have dinner,"˅/
ʌ	Caret, used to insert a word, phrase or punctuation.	The ʌ *meaning* was unclear.
=̄ ˄	Insert a hyphen.	Sing=song.
6̇ (Gov.)	Spell out word or figure.	Six. Governor
(One hundred)	Use figures.	100.
(Colonel) Jones	Use abbreviation.	Col. Jones.
would (underscored)	underscore w and u.	Draw lines under letters.

Symbol	Meaning	Example
ñeverm̃ore	overscore n and m.	Draw lines over letters.
STET	Restore text.	(STET) Then he went home.
Thund⌢ous	Transpose letter, word or phrase.	Thunderous.
⌐	Indent from left.	News Names.
⌐	Indent from right.	News Names.
⌐⌐	Center the words. Indent both sides.	News Names.
gentle͡man	Close up, eliminate space.	gentleman
Boy/Scout	Separate.	Boy Scout
Here's the ⌿ook.	Use lower-case letter.	Here's the book.
The ~~pretty~~ girl	Eliminate copy and close up.	The girl
(set 2 col 10 pt)	Circled copy is not to be set in type. These are instructions to the typesetter.	The words are left out.
blue - ~~black~~-covered	Substituting a word or phrase.	blue-covered

• Short Takes

Here are the basic things to remember about putting out the news:

- Keith Fuller's definition: When somebody says, ''Gee whiz, I didn't know that,'' it's news.
- There's more to news than crisis, conflict, disaster and controversy. New times and new issues have broadened the news field beyond shock and sensation. The public is well-nigh shockproof now.
- Journalists customarily pay more attention in these times to public service and general information that is relevant and useful to the needs of a mass public.
- Individual journalists can't do as they please in a newsroom. They fit into a tight line of organization and must submit to a certain rough discipline. Above all, they must learn to keep their cool.
- Working with a VDT is much easier than using paper and typewriter, and it doesn't take long to learn to use a terminal. The adaptable newcomer usually fits into the electronic newsroom with 48 hours of instruction.
- Writers have little trouble learning the few necessary rules of copy preparation on a VDT, and editors sometimes still want them to know the rules for preparing copy on copy paper, especially where VDT printouts are used. These rules are

included here and should be memorized, along with the relatively few copy editing symbols.

- Writers should be familiar with the electronic machines—computers, photocomposition units, Pagination and the like—in the same manner that drivers know about the complicated engines under the hoods of their autos. Expert knowledge, however, is not required.

- The important things for every journalist to check in writing, either on the VDT or copy paper, include sources, slugging and continuation and end marks.

CHAPTER 4

News Writing Is Clear Writing

There is no mystery about good writing. The principles have been put into practice by the masters of literature since the time of Homer. To apply them properly is a challenge for any young journalist.

The Uses of Clarity

E. B. White, whose writing graced the pages of the *New Yorker* magazine for many years, offered this advice to the beginner:

> Young writers often suppose that style is a garnish for the meat of prose, a sauce by which a dull dish is made palatable. Style has no such separate entity; it is nondetachable, unfilterable. The beginner should approach style warily, realizing that it is himself he is approaching, no other; and he should begin by turning resolutely away from all devices that are popularly believed to indicate style—all mannerisms, tricks, adornments. The approach to style is by way of plainness, simplicity, orderliness, sincerity.

Structure and Style   Late in life, Winston Churchill recalled how he had been left back twice in the lowest grade at the Harrow school in England because he was a dilatory pupil:

> By being so long in the lowest form [grade], I gained an immense advantage over the cleverer boys. I got into my bones the essential structure of the ordinary British sentence, which is a noble thing.

British or American, that "noble thing" is the basis for clear and effective writing. It is the essence of good journalism in all its forms.

What Editors Believe   Henry Beetle Hough, editor of the weekly *Vineyard Gazette* on the island of Martha's Vineyard, Massachusetts, expressed the problem in these terms:

> It's hard to get someone to write freely and naturally nowadays unless you take him young. Most of the sophisticated feel they must follow an adaptation of *Timestyle* or else write in a stutter.
>
> But we believe it is still deep in the nature of writing men and women to be articulate, even fluent, and the opposite only seems to be true because of limited opportunities. To sharpen a story into vivid and economical language is not the same thing as discarding most of the values and seeking to represent them through a few clipped sentences. . . .

Evidently, a number of editors throughout the land shared Hough's faith. For in the 1980s, what was called a "writing movement" developed momentum in widely separated newsrooms. Writing seminars, writing conferences, even writing coaches made their appearance on newspapers as different in size, location and philosophy as the *Boston Globe*, the *Providence* (Rhode Island) *Journal-Bulletin*, the *St. Petersburg* (Florida) *Times* and the *Longview* (Washington) *Daily News*.

On some newspapers, the effort was prolonged and produced results. On others, it was tried and abandoned because both editors and staff were too busy with their usual tasks. But the display of interest did make newspaper people think just a little more about better ways to make words flow on paper and VDTs.

James P. Gannon, executive editor of the *Des Moines Register and Tribune*, put it this way: "What does a newspaper have to offer the reader if not good stories well-told? . . . Yes, suddenly we care about writing because it is the heart of our enterprise and our medium of exchange."

"Who's Going to Love Judith Bucknell?"   The story of Judith Bucknell is an example of the modern writing method. Bucknell was Homicide 106 in a recent year in Miami. At first nobody paid much attention to the murder of Judith Bucknell, a 38-year-old Miami businesswoman and divorcee. She was an item in the news, to be flicked over with a casual eye as the reader turned the pages. "Somebody else murdered? Ah, yes, lived alone . . . wasn't careful. Too bad. Let's see what the Dolphins are doing. . . ."

Madeleine Blais was different. She was a reporter for the *Miami Herald*, a skilled writer who cared about the English language and used it with grace and devotion. She examined Judith Bucknell's diaries and talked to police, the neighbors, the few people who knew the murdered woman.

It took Blais a long time to put Judith Bucknell's life together. And when she wrote a two-part series about the case for the *Herald*, she prefaced it as follows:

Madeleine Blais of the *Miami* (Florida) *Herald* with colleagues. (Photograph by Mary Lou Foy. Used by permission of the *Miami Herald*.)

By Madeleine Blais

There are so many calls.

The phones in a newsroom are forever ringing: dishonest mechanic calls, barking-dog calls, calls about the man across the street dealing in drugs. A black Mercedes shows up at his house every evening at the same time; the details of color and make are offered as proof that this must be true.

People call wondering why there is never any good news in the paper, and if you want some good news, just interview their grandchildren. Some call to say they have led interesting lives, and somebody should write them up. Others call to settle bets and grievances. Once, on the full moon, somebody called and asked, simply, "How do you spell psychopath?"

This call was different.

It was from a stranger, a woman, the tenant in 2-B at 3204 Aviation Ave., in Coconut Grove. She said on Wednes-

day of the previous week, July 9, her next-door neighbor—
the girl in 2-A—had been murdered. . . .

Judith Iris Bucknell was Miami Homicide 106, Dade
County Homicide 268 in a year in which the number of violent
deaths exceeded all records, including that for 1979, itself a
record breaker. Judith Bucknell was strangled. She was hung
from the knob of the door of her bedroom. She was stabbed
seven times. The knife was left in her. . . .

All summer long the heat was like an invisible prison and
the fear grew and blistered in the heat. There was a sense
that things were out of control, and the worst could happen
to anyone. The way summer was going, everybody expected
a hurricane.

There were fires in the ghetto and refugees in the waters.
There was no sense of mercy, all justice seemed denied.
People were killed during traffic arguments; honking was
practically a suicide gesture. Life, which had been comfortable, was becoming cheap. Was this the price of constant
sun? . . .

For the tenants at 3204 Aviation Ave., Judith Bucknell
was one more burden in a trying summer. . . . After her death
they finally had something in common beyond her address.
They traded rumors: white man, black man, stranger, friend,
drugs, Mafia. No one knew her well.

At Aviation Ave., they complained. The rent is high. The
pool is dirty. The barbecue doesn't work. The girl in 2-A is
dead. . . .

"You who enter here upon these pages want something
from me—you want to take from me what is mine, and you
give me nothing in return."

This is the opening passage in a diary begun by Judith
Bucknell on June 30, 1976. The police found two diaries and
many unsent letters among her belongings; these writings
proved to be crucial to the investigation. . . .

There is something juicy, prurient, about these diaries,
something indecent about our posthumous access to this
woman's secrets, her recesses. It is a violation, if not of the
body, then of the soul. But in a way she invites the violation
by anticipating it, and the anticipation seems to invite
forgiveness.

"Who's going to love Judy Bucknell? I feel so old.
Unloved. Unwanted. Abandoned. Used up. I want to cry and
sleep forever. . . ."

What Is Style?   The effectiveness of this story depends almost entirely on
the reporter's observations and insights. If the piece is analyzed for style, it would
be called plain, simple, orderly, sincere. The trouble, as E. B. White admits, is that
no single definition can capture the meaning of style in its many guises. Not everything can be reported in terms of the violent death of a friendless woman.

Expository writing requires a different style. Such complicated matters as SALT (Strategic Arms Limitation Talks), the reporting of budgets and taxes and the opening of a new atomic energy plant require more background, a more deliberate approach and much more explanation. Those who write on science or sports, fashions or home economics, life-style or diplomacy will find conventions in each field that will require some adjustment in style.

Above all else, assuming the writer is accurate and orderly in the presentation of the facts, the most important ingredient in all forms of writing is clarity of expression.

Mixing Fact and Fiction

Writers who are opaque in their presentation, whether they deal in science, semantics, news or love letters, are storing up trouble for themselves. It takes more effort to be simple, clear and direct. Sometimes it also takes more courage. Those who weary of the struggle sometimes are tempted to mingle fiction with fact to make their work more interesting.

The New Journalism   *New York* magazine and *Esquire* introduced the public to the "New Journalism" in the 1960s with somewhat dubious results. Writers like Gay Talese, a former *New York Times* reporter, and Tom Wolfe, a Ph.D.-turned-freelance, pioneered in adapting the methods of fiction to fact.

This went far beyond mere form, which has always been useful in newspaper feature copy. The New Journalists re-created events, read minds, neglected to identify sources and went as far as possible toward the techniques of the short story and the novel without actually calling their work fiction.

What made this colorful writing style even more popular was the use novelists made of it. Truman Capote, a popular author, promoted his book *In Cold Blood* by calling it a "nonfiction novel." Norman Mailer, a Pulitzer Prize-winner, wrote what he termed a "true-life novel" in *The Executioner's Song.* Both descriptions defy logic, and are pure hype.

"Blurring the Line ..."   The New Journalism ran into trouble when *New York* magazine published an article by Gail Sheehy about a character named "Redpants," who was identified as a prostitute. Very soon, it turned out that "Redpants" was a myth. The author pleaded that she *had* identified the woman as a "composite character" in the article but that her editor, Clay Felker, had taken the caveat out. Felker admitted it.

There have been many other misadventures since then among the practitioners of the New Journalism, some of which are considered under journalism's ethical problems, in Chapter 22. The format lingers on, mainly in books and magazines. Newspapers are wary of it now. The credibility of the press has been damaged by too many unsourced stories, trick reconstructions of events and reports about "inner thoughts" that have no factual basis.

David Shaw of the *Los Angeles Times* summed up the position when he expressed his gratitude to the New Journalists for breaking the rigid forms of news-paper feature writing. He explained:

> A good newspaper story can read like good fiction. Beginning, middle and end. Strong characters. Conflict. Suspense. Similarly, good narrative profiles can take a reader into the subject's home and heart and mind and soul—just as a good short story or novel does. But some liberties taken in the name of such experimentation blur the line between journalism and fiction, and when that happens, we risk losing our integrity and our credibility.
>
> The rule is: *The line must be carefully and clearly drawn to separate truth from fiction, fact from imagination, dream from reality.*

The Writing Habit

Those who have spent most of their lives as writers know that it is a habit. Good writers cultivate good habits—a sensitive approach to the use of the English language, self-discipline, a continual concern over grammar and spelling, a willingness to rewrite as well as to write and to make a realistic appraisal of the product. Bad writers generally have slovenly habits—wretched composition, lack of coherence, factual inaccuracies, overwriting, inexcusable errors in grammar and spelling and a lamentably short attention span.

Words About Words   John Harrison, a Pulitzer Prize-winner in editorial writing, once wrote: "Words are the crude, blunt instruments by which we in communications earn our way.... We try to fashion these crude, blunt instruments into shining, gleaming tools of power and beauty and precision and effectiveness. But, as Jacques Barzun has told us, 'Simple English is no one's mother tongue. It has to be worked for.'"

It is easy enough to say that a writer can stay out of trouble by using short words and shunning the polysyllables. It's not quite that simple, however.

The word *peace* is on a list of words intelligible to fourth graders. But what is peace? In four years of attendance at a seminar at Columbia University, I heard professors trying to work out a definition of peace acceptable to all. What they had to settle for was: "Peace is the absence of war."

Many other apparently simple words have widely varying meanings for different audiences, as these few examples show:

bananas   To some it is a fruit. To others, "going bananas" means to be driven out of one's mind.

bread   Normally, it is food. But in street talk it can mean money.

creep   Formally, it describes movement. Informally, it may mean an objectionable person.

democracy   This drives diplomats to distraction. In America, it means a system of government that protects individual liberties. In Russia, it means a system of government that subordinates individual liberties to the state.

gay   Once, it was a beautiful word denoting happy, light-hearted conduct. Now, it is also used as a popular term for homosexuals.

split   Usually, this means that an object is divided. In street talk, it means to depart.

square   It is a geometrical form in one sense; in another, it is a hopelessly conventional person.

table   In America, it means that a proposal has been shelved. In most other countries, it means that a proposal has been introduced.

total   This is, normally, the sum of all parts. But in a wretchedly coined word that appears in some newspapers, "totaled" — used as a verb — means an automobile has been demolished.

These illustrations underline a basic principle of clear writing: *It is not enough for writers to be understood. They should be certain that they are not misunderstood.*

Debasing the English Language   Street talk is not the worst danger to the purity of the English language. Nor is slang the threat it once appeared to be. Many useful words have emerged from both to be sanctified in dictionaries and recommended by English teachers.

But in the higher reaches of our society, among people who should know better, there are fashionable words and phrases that are misused and overworked. One example is the word "terribly" as an adverbial synonym for "very." It leads to aberrations like this: "She wasn't a terribly bright child." Or "He wasn't terribly impressed."

Another widely misused word is "real," a perfectly good adjective meaning authentic or genuine, which has been worked into a popular cliché, "It's for real." Some supposedly educated people also exclaim, "Real good!" or "Real fine!" It's a case of an adjective modifying another adjective, a no-no among professional writers except in quotations.

These are a small part of the penalty for permissiveness in the oral and written use of the English language. There are other phrases that are just as debasing. Even well-educated Americans are falling victim to the tendency to drop the words "You know" and "I mean" into ordinary speech so that they become a monotonous refrain, which sounds something like this: "I read a terribly good book last night, yunno, it's real fine, holds your attention and all that. It's like, yunno, something you wish you wrote yourself. Eyemean, you oughta read it." Ow.

When this bit of functional illiteracy becomes a part of written English, it is intolerable.

Teachers are not exempt from this linguistic plague. Some have their own baffling language, which includes such expressions as "a learner-centered merged curriculum," an "empirically validated learning package with cognitive values" and a "life-oriented curriculum." Business people and scientists also have their own jargon, which can be just as baffling.

Rudolph Flesch, in the *Associated Press Writing Handbook*, gave this advice to writers who want to avoid these thought-deadening words and phrases:

> Don't use words that are not generally used in everyday conversation if you can help it. Remember, the AP isn't in the business of increasing people's vocabulary. If you *have* used a word that *may be* unfamiliar to an ordinary reader, explain it.

Follow the example of the reporter who explained that tularemia is rabbit fever. In particular, be sure to explain geographical terms for readers who live at a distance.

Gobbledegook The worst offenses of all are committed in the name of government.

Gobbledegook perverts the meaning of much that is done in Washington, the governments of the 50 states and the thousands of city halls and town halls in the land. This is the kind of nonsense that led the Agriculture Department to announce solemnly that, in school lunchrooms, ketchup was to be considered a vegetable and tofu, a soybean-meal curd, was to be classed as meat. This lamentable attempt to use gobbledegook to disguise an effort to save money at the expense of schoolchildren was abandoned when it was discovered and ridiculed.

What is gobbledegook? it is a coined word to describe semantic confusion. In government circles, for example, a problem is not examined; it is "scoped." If costs are embarrassingly high, they are called "social diseconomies" to disguise them. If a project is well conceived, it is "maximally valuable"; if it is abandoned, however, it is "defunded." A wild guess is dignified as a "ballpark estimate." Even the most stupid procedure is termed a "game plan." Officials seldom say "now"; it is usually "at this point in time." They seldom "resist." Instead, they "stonewall." And they always refer to "the bottom line" rather than to results.

Such expressions defile the clarity of news writing. Nor does it help to drop the word *clearly* into a sentence to show that an effort is being made to avoid obscuring an issue. *Clearly* is one of the most overworked words in the English language.

The Jargon of Journalism Writers should make a special effort to eliminate the jargon of journalism from their work. It can wither the freshest news. It can also make certain types of stories sound alike regardless of when and where they occur.

The examples of journalese are numerous, but a few here will suffice to illustrate the problem:

A ship that has a mishap *limps into port*, which would be quite a performance if it ever happened.

A collision between automobiles, trains, planes or ships is a *crash*. The investigation is, of course, a *probe*.

If more deaths occur, the *death toll mounts*.

When someone is criticized, he is *flayed*.

In police cases, when a witness is questioned, he is *grilled*.

If he says nothing, he *defies the police*.

Should the police issue an alarm for a suspect, they *throw out a dragnet*.

When someone is arrested, he is *seized*.

If the police have no clues or are too lazy to find some, quite naturally, *mystery surrounds the case*.

On election day, voters invariably *troop to the polls* under (check one) *sunny, cloudy, rainy, snowy skies*.

Should the voting be close, the victor wins through *a late surge at the polls*.

If the contest isn't close, the victory is always a *landslide*.

When opposing politicians meet, it is often a *showdown*.

If the issues at the meeting are unresolved, as frequently happens, it is either a *crisis* or a *deadlock*.

In international affairs, it is a safe assumption that when representatives of the United States and the Soviet Union meet, it will be a *clash*.

And when royal visitors pass through an American community, even though it may be for only ten minutes, readers may be sure that they will *reign over the city*.

The worst offenders in journalism are sports writers and sportscasters. Red Smith once illustrated his colleagues' weakness with this mythical interview between a sports editor and an applicant for a baseball writer's job:

Q. What is baseball? A. The national pastime.
Q. Good, very good. Now what is the game played with? A. The horsehide and ash.
Q. Excellent. And what else? A. The sphere, hassocks.
Q. Yes, yes. And what is the game played on? A. A velvety sward.
Q. What does the rookie run like? A. A deer.
Q. What has he for an arm? A. A rifle.
Q. Describe the man who has played baseball for five years. A. An old pro with know-how.

There is a lot more of this in football, which is played with the *old pigskin*; basketball, with a *casaba*, and hockey, with a *rubber spheroid*.

In short, few writers can be original as often as they would like but no writer is justified in trying to convey meaning with clusters of tired words—the hallmark of journalistic jargon. It is easier to tell it in English. It is also more refreshing.

Beware of the Cliché Writers, particularly on deadline, often are tempted to use trite expressions because they have no time to think of better ones. These hackneyed phrases, clauses and sentences, known as clichés, constitute still another objectionable part of journalese. It would be better to omit them.

These are examples of timeworn language that have been rightly condemned:

along these lines	old Jupe Pluvius, for rain
meets the eye	a goodly number
a long-felt want	budding genius
Old Sol, for the sun	at one fell swoop
sadder but wiser	method in his madness
launched into eternity	busy as a bee
last but not least	cool as a cucumber
green with envy	wild and woolly
with bated breath	white as a sheet
fair maidens	dull thud
the blushing bride	a shot rang out
the great beyond	fast as a jackrabbit

There are thousands more.

Dr. Bergen Evans, the lexicographer, put a few of them together to illustrate cliché-stuffed writing in the following, a description of an audience reacting to a political orator:

They know they are in the presence of a man who gets down to brass tacks, hits the nail on the head and doesn't beat around the bush; a man who means business, who is fully aware that although we have entered the atomic age, we have not relinquished the faith of our fathers, and who believes that although we cannot rest upon our laurels, we must not rush in where angels fear to tread. Such a speaker is a man after our own hearts. He has his feet on the ground. He knows the score.

Alas, the 5Ws and H This was the way leads used to be written, as witness the following from the *Washington Post:*

A revolutionary $3 billion foreign military aid bill carrying $1.5 billion in weapons credits for Israel and unprecedented Congressional powers to monitor the $12 billion annual U.S. overseas arms trade won Senate approval yesterday, 60–30.

That is a mouthful of lead. It is based on the theory that the 5Ws and H — who, when, where, what, why and how — must be covered in a news lead. But today, simpler leads are required even on complicated stories. Writers who put everything into the first sentence are bound to come up with 35- to 100-word leads and no editor will pass them. The broadcasters are even more insistent on slimmer, stronger leads.

The *Washington Post* lead could easily have been rewritten:

The Senate yesterday voted 60–30 for a $3 billion foreign aid bill. It permits Congress to monitor the $12 billion annual U.S. arms trade overseas and also provides $1.5 billion in weapons credits for Israel.

Most editors today prefer a single idea in the lead sentence followed by a summary of the rest of the story in a paragraph or two for most hard news accounts. Sometimes, the *who* may be featured, or the *why* but the cluster effect of the 5Ws and H in a single catch-all sentence is gone forever.

It forces writers to make up their minds, which is an advancement in journalism.

Word-Counting It follows that reasonably short sentences are preferred for wire services, newspapers and broadcasters.

Few editors bother to count words, but there is general agreement that the 30- to 35-word sentence creates reading difficulty. Most well-written newspapers average somewhere between 15 and 20 words to a sentence. Saul Bellow, the American Nobel Prize novelist, is said to average 11 or 12 words to a sentence.

But it is not word-counting that matters. Everything depends on the clarity with which the sentences are written. After all, a short sentence can create just as much confusion as a long one if it is poorly written.

The difference between *The Reader's Digest* and Henry Thoreau, for example, is not in the length of their sentences or the number of syllables in their words, but in what they have written. Or consider the "reading ease" of Walt Whitman:

I celebrate myself, and sing myself,
And what I assume you shall assume,
Every atom belonging to me as good belongs to you.

Obviously, "Song of Myself" requires careful reading even though the words and sentences are reasonably short. Or consider the "reading ease" of Lewis Carroll:

'Twas brillig and the slithy toves
Did gyre and gimble in the wabe
All mimsy were the borogroves,
And the mome raths outgrabe.

All things considered, the King of Hearts was a readability expert, too. In *Alice in Wonderland*, he said this was how to tell a story:

Begin at the beginning, and go on until you come to the end, then stop.

Try to improve on that.

• Short Takes

Here are the rules that will help you develop a clear writing style:

- The main characteristics of a clear writing style are plainness, orderliness, simplicity and sincerity.
- The line must be drawn carefully to separate truth from fiction, fact from imagination, dream from reality.
- In using interpretation and analysis, the facts on which such material is based should be cited so that readers and viewers can make up their own minds.
- A separate analytical or interpretive article must be so labeled in the news columns.
- Unless reporters are reasonably sure their interpretation of a story is correct and they have the facts to support it, they should omit all interpretation. Guessing doesn't pay.
- Continual practice and the cultivation of good writing habits are essential to the achievement of clarity.
- It is not enough for writers to be understood. They should be certain they are not misunderstood.
- Avoid clichés, gobbledegook and journalistic jargon.
- Never try to work the 5Ws and H (who, when, where, what, why and how) into a lead sentence. Try to feature a single idea in a lead sentence when it is possible to do so.
- Try to write sentences averaging 15 to 20 words to maintain readability, but don't be a slave to word-counting.
- Do not be afraid to use models or learn from others. Above all, do not sulk when your work is criticized. Try always to take advantage of fair-minded criticism.

CHAPTER 5

Hits and Errors for Writers

The news media cannot be casual about the uses of language. They must transmit news, opinions and ideas to mass audiences as efficiently as possible. Their standards of English usage must be at least as high as those of the best-educated elements of their readers, listeners and viewers if they are to retain the public's respect.

Slovenly or unnecessarily offensive language may not prevent 100,000 people from buying a book, listening to a rock record or seeing a new Broadway play, but either would be well-nigh fatal, if continued for very long, to the reputation of a news organization.

A Grammatical Checklist

There are no exceptions to the rule that correct grammatical usage is essential to good journalism. The precision of language sharpens the meaning of fact. That is why the two go hand in hand.

Here, in condensed and practical form, is a grammatical checklist. It includes some of the principal shortcomings of professional journalists and suggests procedures for remedial writing that are generally acceptable in American newsrooms:

Adjectives It is customary in every professional work on writing to caution against the use of too many adjectives, certainly sound advice. Most writers, even inexperienced ones, quickly learn that adjectives can be treacherous and are cautious about selecting the few they use.

Adverbs   In the use of copulative (linking) verbs (appear, feel, look, seem, smell) writers must choose carefully between the use of a predicate adjective and an adverb modifier. "He feels *bad*," connotes illness. To write, "He feels *badly*," would mean that something was wrong with his sense of touch.

Antecedent   A noun or noun equivalent, whether word, phrase or clause, is referred to by a personal or relative pronoun. The pronoun and antecedent must agree in number. The pronoun *it* is nearly always a danger signal in copy because it may be the source of grammatical error. Always check the antecedent.

> **Wrong**   He was one of four students whom two *teachers* at Greenwood Academy put on probation in *their* freshman year.
> **Right**   He was one of *four students* who were put on probation in *their* freshman year by two teachers at Greenwood Academy.

The students, not the teachers, were in their freshman year when probation was ordered. Usually, the pronoun has an affinity for the nearest noun.

Articles   There is a notion among some editors that an article can be dispensed with in some sentences. This, they believe, has the effect of "speeding up the action." It doesn't. It just encourages a species of telegraphic writing in which *the, a* and *an* are bowled over like tenpins. Some samples:

> Sense of the meeting was against zoning.
> Rash of activity broke out in City Council last night.
> Dedication of bridge was set for Tuesday.

Collective Nouns   *Congress*, the *government* and the *Cabinet* are among the collective nouns that are singular in American usage and plural in Britain and other Commonwealth countries. Plural nouns such as police and fish should not be mistaken for collective nouns.

The principal errors that result from confusion over the use of collective nouns are disagreements in number. For example:

> **Wrong**   The *government* is deciding *their* policy.
> **Right**   The *government* is deciding *its* policy.
> **Wrong**   The *company* wanted *their* product displayed.
> **Right**   The *company* wanted *its* product displayed.

Ellipsis   The omission of words necessary to complete a sentence involves the use of ellipsis. There is a rule, modified by exceptions, that a word may be omitted if its meaning can be supplied or understood from a corresponding part of a compound sentence. The word to be supplied must be in the same grammatical form as the one to which it corresponds.

> **Wrong**   One person was killed and 12 injured in the fire.
> **Right**   One person was killed and 12 *were* injured in the fire.

Euphemisms   The use of euphemisms is seldom necessary in today's realistic atmosphere. Fifty years ago, writers on so-called family newspapers of the era were instructed to use the word *attacked* instead of *raped* and *social ailment* instead of *venereal disease*. Most of these code words, which were intended to soothe the sensibilities of gentlefolk unused to plain speaking, have now been dropped. Some of the last to go were *house of ill fame*, or *bagnio* or *sporting house*—euphemisms that were found in some of our best newspapers.

It's   This is the source of more student and professional errors than any other three letters in the English language. *It's* means *it is* and cannot be used as a possessive pronoun.

Wrong   Every day has it's joys and trials.
Right   Every day has its joys and trials.

Media   This is a plural noun.

Not Only   The rule for correlative conjunctions is that one must parallel the other; that is, it must follow the same part of speech. Thus, the expression *not only* is usually paired with the expression *but also*.

Wrong   The defendant was not only found guilty of grand larceny but also of assault.
Right   The defendant was found guilty not only of grand larceny but also of assault.

To make sense, each of the phrases directly precedes the preposition "of" and is parallel in construction. Other correlative conjunctions that are used in pairs, and that follow the same rule, include such expressions as *either-or*, *neither-nor* and *both-and*.

Number   The number of the *subject* determines the number of the *verb*. Any word, phrase or clause that intervenes between subject and verb does not affect the number of the verb.

Wrong   A *box* of hand grenades and rifles, discovered on the ship, *were seized* by federal agents.
Right   A *box* of hand grenades and rifles, discovered on the ship, *was seized* by federal agents.

The subject, *box*, is singular, and it takes a singular verb because the intervening material must be discounted.

When a compound subject is joined by *or*, *nor*, *either-or* or *neither-nor*, the verb agrees with the subject nearest to it. When both nouns are singular, no problem; the verb must be singular. But when one noun is singular and the second is plural, the verb is plural. For example: "Neither the prisoner nor his associates were harmed."

Preposition at the End of a Sentence   The rule against prepositional endings has been relaxed by most editors. A few still remain who, when confronted with a preposition at the end of a sentence, ask what in the world the writer was thinking of.

Sequence of Tenses   The first thing to remember, in solving this grammatical puzzle, is that the alignment of tenses should follow the rules of parallelism and normal time sequence. Thus, it is normal to write: "The President says he feels fine." Also, transposing to the past tense, it is correct to write: "The President said he felt fine." But it is awkward to write, as so many do, "The President said he feels fine," thus mixing the tenses. However, sometimes it has to be done to make sense.

For example, it is silly to write: "Columbus said the world was round." It still is. (Well, anyway, it's pear-shaped.) Therefore, the correct method of writing current truths expressed in the past is to break parallel construction and write: "Columbus said the world is round."

Split infinitive   Infinitives are split at will in some universities but it's still a no-no in many newsrooms. Reason: It's one of the few grammatical rules that journalists remember. So if the young writer slips an adverb between "to be," "to have" or "to split," there should be no surprise if the copy desk corrects the supposed infraction. It isn't a serious grammatical fault any longer, but the notion persists in newsrooms that it is.

Subjunctive   Too much of a mystery has been made out of the subjunctive mood. This is the way it works:

In the case of a clause that is completely hypothetical or contrary to fact, the use of the subjunctive mood is proper, as follows:

Wrong   It's *as if* the moon *was* made of green cheese.
Right   It's *as if* the moon *were* made of green cheese.

For other conditional clauses, most writers agree that the indicative mood should be used. For example:

Wrong   *If* the mayor *were* involved, he didn't say so.
Right   *If* the mayor *was* involved, he didn't say so.

That and Which   This is an old puzzler but it can easily be solved. *Which* is used when it introduces a clause that could be enclosed in parentheses or even omitted without affecting the noun it modifies. Here is an example:

Wrong   New York City, *that* consists of five boroughs, is best known for the borough of Manhattan.
Right   New York City, *which* consists of five boroughs, is best known for the borough of Manhattan.

Such a clause, generally set off by commas, is called a nondefining clause. It should always be introduced by *which*. With only two exceptions, *that* should be used in the following manner:

Wrong   Manhattan is the best known of the five boroughs *which* are included in New York City.

Right   Manhattan is the best known of the five boroughs *that* are included in
New York City.

The clause introduced by *that* above is called a limiting or defining clause. It
is used far more often than the parenthetical clause. So many a *which* should be
turned into a *that*.

Verbs   Every beginning or inexperienced writer is advised to use verbs in
the active voice. The proposition is insisted upon throughout this book. And yet the
device can be overused.

Sometimes, an intransitive verb can be effective in reporting a great event. For
instance:

> The ship is sinking.
> The president is recovering.
> The pope is dying.

A verb in the passive voice also is not to be despised. Now and then, it can be
used with dramatic results:

> CAPE CANAVERAL—A space shuttle was fired into orbit today.

Not all the smashing, lashing, dashing, crashing pileup of verbals can create
the effect of a simple, dramatic statement of big news. Where verbs in the active
voice contribute to the clarity and mood of a story they are, of course, to be preferred.
But verbs in the passive voice can be used, particularly in reports of storms and other
natural disasters.

Writers also should be careful not to switch from active to passive voice, and
vice versa, in the same sentence. This is guaranteed to turn off the most devoted
reader.

Verbals   We now enter the grammatical chamber of horrors.

Exhibit A is the dangling participle. A participle is a verb used as an adjective.
When it dangles, it is an erratic modifier. For example:

Wrong   *Walking* from the room, *his eyes* blinked.
Right   *Walking* from the room, *he* blinked.

The point is that *he* did the walking, not his eyes. Dangling participles may
be avoided by putting the participle in direct contact with the noun or pronoun it
modifies.

Exhibit B is the misused gerund. A gerund is a verb used as a noun. It may
take a modifier but, if so, the noun or pronoun must be in the possessive case. For
example:

Wrong   He did not approve the *candidate speaking* first.
Right   He did not approve the *candidate's speaking* first.

The candidate was not the object of disapproval. It was the *candidate's speaking* that was disapproved and this is the way the sentence must be written.

The rule is that the intent of the sentence should be the basis for determining whether the gerund takes a possessive. It is useful to use the words *act of* as a test. For example, insert *act of* in the text of the *wrong* sentence above just before the gerund *speaking* and see what happens:

> He did not approve the candidate (act of) speaking first.

It is awkward. It doesn't fit. It doesn't even make sense. Therefore, the use of the possessive, the *candidate's speaking*, is demonstrably correct.

Will and Shall   This one is almost a lost cause. And yet the distinction between will and shall is a good one.

Shall is used with the *first* person and *will* with the *second* and *third* persons when simple future or mere expectation is to be expressed. Thus: "*I shall* try if *you will* help me."

But in expressing determination, command, promise or obligation, the order is reversed. Thus: "*I will be* heard." Or "*You shall obey* me."

The trouble is that such language as "I shall go" or "I should like" sounds too prissy for most American ears.

Who and Whom   *Who* is used as the subject of a clause or sentence. *Whom* is the object. The reason for confusion is entirely the fault of the writer who can't tell a subject from an object. A simple test may be made by substituting the pronouns *he* or *him*, or *she* or *her* for *who* or *whom*. Let's try it for size:

Wrong   The mayor was the only candidate *whom*, in the opinion of the committee, *would be acceptable* to the voters.
Test   . . . in the opinion of the committee, *(he) would be acceptable*. . . .
Right   The mayor was the only candidate *who*, in the opinion of the committee, *would be acceptable* to the voters.

It is obvious, if the prepositional clause is removed, that *who* is the subject of the clause, and the test confirms it. The pronoun cannot be the object of the first verb if it is the subject of the second.

Let's try it again:

Wrong   The mayor was the candidate *who the committee preferred.*
Test   . . . the committee preferred *(him).*
Right   The mayor was the candidate *whom the committee preferred.*

It is apparent that the subject of the verb *preferred* is the *committee*. In addition to the *he and him* test, as shown above, a simple reversal will show that the pronoun must be the object of the clause and not the subject: " . . . the committee preferred *whom*," not "*who*." Thus, *whom* is the correct pronoun.

Usage and Misusage

Here are a number of words and expressions that are frequently misused by writers:

all-America   Often misused as *All-American*, referring to members of all-America teams.

all right   Often incorrectly spelled *alright*. It is two words.

all-round   Misused as *all-around*. The correct expression is *all-round athlete*.

as a result of   Usually misused as "*the* result of . . ." Often something happens as "*a* result of. . . ." In other words, more than one result is possible.

author   This is a noun. Do not use as a verb. Nothing is *authored*. It is *written*.

banquet   Usually it is a dinner. There hasn't been a dinner worth calling a banquet in years. Ask any veteran of the rubber chicken circuit.

boat   A small craft, propelled by oars. It is often misused for a ship, which is a larger, seagoing craft.

bride   A woman about to be married, as well as a newly married woman. Her husband is a *bridegroom*, not just a *groom*, whose primary mission is to take care of horses.

broadcast   Present and past tenses of the verb are identical.

burglary   Often misused. There must be breaking and entering before a larceny can be called a burglary. The act of stealing is more often a theft or a robbery.

by   A preposition expressing relations of place or direction and commonly referring to persons. *Through* may refer either to persons or things.

capital   Washington, D.C., is the capital. The building is called the *Capitol*.

casualties   In war these refer to both dead and injured. The term means losses from any cause.

chair   Misused as a verb. To write that someone chaired a meeting is incorrect. He or she presided.

claim   It is not correct to write, as so many do, that a district attorney claims a defendant is guilty. This is not a claim. It is a charge or an accusation. Frequently, writers also misuse the word to indicate argument: "She claimed that it was a good film." This however, is a contention, while the word *claim* is an assertion, a demand, an assertion of one's rights. When in doubt, instead of using *claim*, use *said*.

compare   Two like objects are compared *to* each other. Two unlike objects are compared *with* each other. The two should not be confused.

comprise   Do not confuse with *compose*. *Comprise* means to consist of.

counsel   Used as a noun, this refers to a person or persons who give advice. They may be part of a *council*, which is a deliberative body.

couple   A collective noun and a puzzler. Many American writers, in defiance of logic, use it as a singular noun. However, the word means more than one person and my preference has always been for plural usage, taking a plural verb. If in doubt, follow the rules of your news organization, print or broadcast.

data   This is plural. The singular, *datum*, is seldom used.

different than   Use *different from*.

don't   It means *do not* and must never be used for *doesn't*, meaning *does not*.

disinterested   It means no selfish interest is involved. Do not confuse with *uninterested*, meaning lack of interest.

due to   Must refer to a noun if used. Often, *because of* is better.

facts   Some write, *true facts*. Don't do it. Facts are facts.

farther   Refers to physical distance. *Further* is used for time and all else.

figuratively   Do not confuse with *literally*, which refers to the actual, unvarnished truth.

finalize   A coined word. It comes out of government gobbledegook. Do not use.

from   People do not die *"from* heart failure." They die *"of* heart disease." The word from is often misused in this manner.

hanged   People are *hanged.* A picture is *hung.*

hopefully   Often misused. Avoid it.

infer   Not to be confused with *imply.* To *infer* is to derive by reasoning. To *imply* is to suggest.

kind of   It is popular to use it in street language: "He's some *kind of* creep." In news writing, except when quoted, forget it.

lawyer   A member of the bar is a lawyer, not an attorney. However, a lawyer may be an attorney (adviser) to an accused person.

less   A reference to quantity: "Less than one-third remains." Fewer refers to numbers: "Fewer than ten persons attended."

lie, lay   *Lay* is the past tense of *lie:* "He lay down." *Lie* is present tense: "It lies there."

like   A preposition that expresses comparison: "He looks like a movie star." The word *like* cannot be substituted for the conjunction *as.* Proper usage is, "The prisoner did as he was told." Not "like he was told."

majority, plurality   The winning margin between two candidates in an election is a majority. If more than two are running, the first candidate has a plurality over the second. In addition, the first candidate might even win a majority of all the votes cast.

media   It's a plural noun. And it takes a plural verb. The singular, *medium*, is seldom used in describing a means of communication.

narcotics   Do not use the expressions *dope* and *drugs* or such variants as *pot, grass, angel dust* and the like when narcotics or habit-forming drugs are meant. In describing illegal narcotics, it is best to say exactly what they are.

none   It's singular, except when the usage is awkward.

numbers   There is an old rule of journalism, going back to the days of the quill pen, that a sentence should not begin with a number or numbers unless they are spelled out. Few pay much attention to it now.

over   Not to be used for the expression *more than. Over* means above. *More than* means in excess of. Don't confuse the two.

percent   It is one word.

person   Refers to individuals. It should not be confused with *people,* which refers to a group, but in today's usage the line is blurred.

plenty   A noun. Cannot be used as an adjective or an adverb.

practically   It is the opposite of *theoretically.* Not to be confused with *virtually*, which means in effect, but not in fact.

principal   Don't confuse this adjective with *principle,* a noun meaning a general truth.

proven   The correct word is *proved.*

providing   *Provided* is better: "The plane was due at JFK Airport in New York at 8 a.m., provided its schedule could be maintained."

raise   Children are reared. Pay is raised.

reason is because   Don't use. *Because* means "for the reason that."

render   Fat is rendered, not music.

St. James's   The United States has an ambassador at the Court of St. James's, the name of the palace in London. It's not the *Court of St. James.*

Scots   The people of Scotland are Scots. Sometimes they drink Scotch and soda.

sustain   Injuries are received or suffered. Not sustained.

toward   Journalists in the United States drop the final *s* in *toward, afterward, forward.*

this point in time   An overstuffed cliché, a heritage of the Watergate hearings. It means *now*, which is easier to use.

transpire   Means to become known gradually. It should not be used in the sense that something has happened or occurred.

try   The old college try has made this verb into a noun.

whether   Do not use *whether or not* unless an alternative must be given the same weight. Generally, the word *whether* is sufficient. The *or not* may be dropped.

Spelling

Editors are not alone in complaining that newcomers to journalism are poor spellers. Young lawyers, doctors and engineers also have been criticized for the same failing. Not even the most familiar spelling rule — *i* before *e* except after *c* — appears to have made much impression, as witness the frequent misspelling of those two ancient teasers: *believe* and *receive*. These are at or near the top of every teacher's list of most misspelled words.

Here are some others. The list includes words that have been chronically misspelled for many years by both older and younger generations of journalists:

abrogate	assassin	colloquy	discernible
accessible	assault	commiserate	dissension
accelerate	atoll	commitment	drunkenness
accessory	ballistic	conceit	ecstasy
accommodate	battalion	consensus	effect
acquit	bettor	contemptible	embarrass
aggravate	buses	council	encomium
aggression	cabal	counsel	endorse
all right [2 words]	canoeist	curlicue	eying
analogous	capital	defense	fascinate
appall	capitol	deity	frivolous
appendicitis	carousal	demurrer	fulfill
apprize*	carrousel	dependent	furor
arraignment	changeable	dietitian	gaiety
ascendant	claque	diphtheria	gauge

*Apprise is also correct. So is adviser-advisor.

glamor	kidnapped	peaceable	timbre
guerrilla	kimono	permissible	tincture
hemorrhage	liaison	Philippines	toboggan
hygiene	likable	phony	torque
hyperbole	mangy	plaque	transcendent
immolate	Manhattan	Portuguese	traumatic
impeccable	marshal	propeller	ukulele
incalculable	mercenary	queue	unctuous
incompatible	mien	recommend	under way [2 words]
incorruptible	mulct	regrettable	vacillate
indispensable	naphtha	renege	vacuum
indomitable	nickel	sacrilegious	vain
inevitable	niece	sanitarium	vein
ingenious	ninety	saxophone	vilify
ingenuous	observer	seized	weird
innocuous	occult	stationary	whisky [or whiskey]
inoculate	occurred	stationery	wield
inseparable	oculist	supersede	withal
insistence	offense	tiara	wrack
judgment	ophthalmologist	tidbit	yield

The pitfalls in this list are not entirely of a writer's own making. Some of these words have several accepted spellings, but only one is used generally in American journalism. (Observer is accepted by most news organizations, but observor is equally correct.) Others, correct by American standards, are incorrect by those of Britain and other Commonwealth countries. (We spell glamor, offense; the British, glamour, offence.) There are also homonyms—words that sound alike but are spelled differently and have different meanings (council, counsel). Of course, there also are many words that are exceptions to what we regard as normal spelling.

Good spelling requires a good memory and a good dictionary. The particular dictionary that will be found in most newsrooms is *Webster's New World Dictionary of the American Language*, second college edition (Cleveland and New York: William Collins & World Publishing, 1974, 1976).

Conciseness

Every newcomer to a newsroom quickly learns that conciseness is a virtue. Clichés are stricken ruthlessly from a beginner's copy. And editors pride themselves on their wisdom in preserving the elementary truth that copy should be tightly written.

In every shop, there are words and expressions that writers are forbidden to use. Most of these lists are handed down from one generation of journalists to another. A few are preserved in journalism textbooks. Here are the ones that I inherited during 25 years of daily newspaper work:

at the present time   Use *at present, now.*
before in the past   *Before* indicates it was in the past.
big in size   Big is size.

biography of his life That's what a biography is.

checked in If it is applied to entering a hotel or motel, use *registered*.

check out This has a supermarket flavor about it now. As used by TV detectives, in the sense of investigating clues, it is redundant. Drop the *out*. It also does heavy duty in the sense of departure from a hotel or motel. Why not say, "He left the hotel"? So much easier.

combined together Drop the *together*.

conspicuous by their absence Cliché. Use: "Their absence was noticed."

consensus of opinion A consensus means opinion. Use *consensus*.

dead body A body is presumed to be dead.

early pioneer How late can a pioneer be?

entire monopoly Either it is or is not a monopoly. Drop the *entire*.

falsely fabricated It is either false or it is fabricated.

if and when Eliminate *and when*.

head up The *up* is superfluous.

high-powered rifle Rifles are. If it is a popgun, say so.

lady In Britain, it is a title. In the United States, all ladies are women but all women are not necessarily ladies. It is equally true that all gentlemen are males, but all males are not necessarily gentlemen.

lit up like a Christmas tree Cliché. Drop it.

matinee performance A matinee is a performance.

most unique It cannot be. Drop *most*. It's like saying somebody is very dead.

present incumbent Drop the *present*.

repeat again That's what repeating is — again.

Sahara desert That's what Sahara means — desert.

Sierra mountains Sierra means mountains.

simple reason Instead of the cliché *for the simple reason*, use because.

strangled to death Strangling is a final act. It causes death.

tonight at 10 p.m. It's just as redundant when it is written, "At 5 a.m. this morning. . . ."

two alternatives An alternative is a choice between two things.

unknown person Correct expression is unidentified person.

well-known Do not use. If a person is well known, people need not be told. The same is true of *prominent citizen*.

whether or not drop the *or not*.

win it This is a fad expression among sportscasters. The *it* is superfluous.

There are other pet hates among journalists. One of the most despised, particularly among people over 50 or thereabouts, is *senior citizens*. The list could grow to unreasonable length. It is intended primarily as a compilation of the most common offenses.

Punctuation

The best advice that can be given to young or inexperienced writers is: "Always keep a pocketful of periods and use them frequently." It avoids a lot of trouble.

Unskilled writers use too much punctuation. There are too many quotation marks around single words and partial quotations. There also are too many dashes and hyphens, too many commas, semicolons and colons. If more periods were used, there would be less clutter in news writing.

In an effective writing style, punctuation is generally distinguished by its sparseness and utility. Naturally, there are exceptions. But as the *AP Stylebook* puts it:

> Punctuation is visual inflection. The marks should clarify meaning and, like shouting, should be employed sparingly. Skillful phrasing avoids ambiguity, insures correct interpretation and lessens the need for punctuation. When punctuation is used, it should be employed solely to bring out what is intended. If punctuation does not clarify, it should be omitted.

Some of the principal rules for punctuation follow.

Periods   They end declarative sentences and imperative sentences that are not exclamations. They are used with abbreviations, as a decimal point and after a series or list of items.

If an entire sentence is enclosed in parentheses, the period goes inside the last parenthesis.

It is omitted after nicknames, after *percent* and after most tabulated matter. It is also omitted after the S in Harry S Truman because the S stands for nothing but the letter itself and that is how he signed his name.

Commas   They clarify meaning by separating words and figures when necessary. *(Whatever will be, will be.)*

They also separate a series of qualifying words except the last in a series. *(It is either red, white or brown.)*

They separate parenthetical matter in a sentence and also are used to set off appositives, and appear between a list including name, title and organization.

Commas are usually omitted between the name and a designation such as *Jr.* or *Sr.*, before a dash or an ampersand, in street addresses, years and serial numbers.

Semicolons   Their principal use is to separate phrases containing commas in order to avoid confusion, to separate statements of contrast and statements too closely related.

They separate names and addresses in series: *John Jones, Riverhead; Doris Smith, Greenport; David Johnson, Southold.* They are also used in sports scores and balloting: *Yankees, 6; Dodgers, 5. Yeas, 22; Nays, 15.*

Colons   They are usually avoided in news writing. Where an essayist would use a colon, a journalist uses a period. Mainly, colons are used in news writing to introduce listings and statements, in reporting time, introducing a resolution and separating chapter and verse in scriptural references.

Quotation Marks   The failure to place commas and periods inside quotation marks is frequently noted in news copy.

Another error is the placement of quotation marks in several paragraphs of quoted matter that follow one another. All that is required is to place a quotation mark at the beginning of each paragraph in the series and to omit it from the end of all paragraphs except the last quoted one.

Often quotation marks are placed around single words and phrases when they are not needed. In general, writers should avoid quoting a word or a phrase unless there is specific justification for it.

To quote a word or a phrase because it is unusual, slangy or cute is an error, unless it can be directly attributed to someone in the story and has a special meaning that requires quotation marks.

As for double attribution, single quotation marks within double quotation marks, it should be used sparingly and with great care to avoid confusion.

Semicolons and colons always follow quotation marks.

Apostrophes   Use the apostrophe for possessives and for some abbreviations. In possessives, the apostrophe generally is used between a singular noun and the added *s* (except when the noun ends in *s*). For plural nouns ending with *s* or *ce* the apostrophe only is added. *(David's wife. James's son. Both her daughters' dresses.)*

When the apostrophe is not a part of a proper name (as in *Governors Island*), it should be omitted. When common possession is indicated, only one apostrophe is used (as in the *Army, Navy and Air Force's joint maneuvers*).

The apostrophe also marks the omission of such word contractions as *it's, I've, I'll, we're* and so on.

Hyphens and Dashes   Hyphens pull language together. Dashes perform the opposite function. A dash should be used in a sentence only when there is an abrupt change of thought. The hyphen forms compound words, and is used in abbreviations and sports scores.

As a general rule, "like" characters take the hyphen but "unlike" characters do not. (*A-bomb* and *U-boat,* but not *B52, IC4A.*) Hyphens should not be used for *commander in chief, vice president, upstate, downstate, homecoming, cheerleader, textbook* and *bookcase,* among others.

Two or more words that form a compound adjective are hyphenated but the combined adjective elements that follow a noun do not take a hyphen.

The best rule of all concerning hyphens is to consult a good dictionary if there is any doubt about correct usage.

Exclamation Point   Use it sparingly. The "astonisher," as old-time copy editors called it, should indicate only the strongest emotions such as surprise, incredulity, appeal or intense excitement. Too many exclamation points, dashes and quotation marks about single words make news copy look like a schoolgirl's letter to her boyfriend.

Question Mark   In addition to its normal use after a direct question, it also marks a gap or an uncertain point in a sentence. Like the exclamation mark, question marks should be used sparingly except after a direct question.

Ampersand   Its formal use is restricted to abbreviations and firm names: *AT&T; Smith, Jones & Co.*

Capitalization

While proper nouns are capitalized, proper names that have acquired a common meaning are lower cased (i.e., the Dutch people, but make it dutch oven; Brussels, Belgium, but make it brussels sprouts). Terms like Arctic Circle and Antarctica are capitalized, but not arctic or antarctic. A title like Joint Chiefs of Staff takes upper case, but not chiefs of staff.

In general, the *AP Stylebook* is followed for specific directions. However, when a newspaper hews to a lower-case, or down, style, it often goes farther in this direction than it may wish. The reason is that copy editors are generally so rushed that they miss capitalizing some proper nouns on the VDT. And the machine, unlike the old-time printers, can't cover up their mistakes.

The result is that, in many a newspaper of excellent reputation, there will be illogical instances of what should be capitalized and what should not be. For example, the Congress will be correctly treated as a proper noun in one story and as a common noun in another. To young journalists, this kind of thing may not seem like a serious fault but it is an annoyance to discriminating readers. While a newspaper is not intended to be a copy book, it should not be turned into a typographical nightmare by carelessness in following accepted style, down or not.

Conclusion

Such are the basic uses of language that must be known to every serious journalist. They must be practiced faithfully. Without them, journalism would become undisciplined, even chaotic. Sensitive and experienced writers are well aware that these techniques and general practices contribute to the expressiveness and versatility of the English language. They determine the manner in which journalists give their written work added depth and meaning.

• Short Takes

All the hits and misses described in this chapter are important to careful writers, but these are the major ones:

- A pronoun and its antecedent must agree in number. Always check the antecedent.
- Don't drop articles *(a, an, the)* in news copy. It leads to writing in telegraphese.
- Many collective nouns such as the *government*, the *Congress* and the various state *Legislatures* are singular. Others like *police* and *media* are plural.
- Avoid euphemisms. There is no need to disguise a rape or venereal disease with a fancy word. This is an age of plain speaking and writing.

- In using such phrases as *not only-but also, either-or, neither-nor* or *both-and,* parallel construction should be observed—that is, each part of the phrase should follow the same part of speech in the sentence.
- Subject and verb must agree in number. The subject always determines the number of the verb. This is the grammatical rule that is most violated.
- The old rules against splitting an infinitive and against ending a sentence with a preposition are still strictly enforced on some newspapers, but not all. At any rate, neither is now considered a serious grammatical infraction.
- The subjunctive mood ("If I were . . .") is used with a clause that is hypothetical or contrary to fact. The indicative mood is used for a conditional clause.
- While good writers insist on using verbs in the active voice, there are times when an intransitive verb can be effective in the report of a great event. (*The President is dead.*)
- Avoid dangling participles and misused gerunds. It pays to review these rules for verbals in some detail.

CHAPTER 6

How to Improve Your Writing

Most newcomers say they are attracted to journalism because they "want to write." However, it takes more than a declaration of intent to make a writer. Training, study, self-discipline and the continual reading of established writers are among the requirements for success in this demanding field.

In this chapter, some of the factors that lead to improvement in writing are alphabetically listed and discussed. The most important ones are examined in greater detail in subsequent chapters.

Accuracy

Most editors and broadcasters agree that accuracy continues to be one of the dominant problems for all journalists, particularly for writers. Some believe it is the outstanding issue.

It is so important that virtually all American newspapers run daily correction boxes. A number have outside sources telephone interviewees and other figures in news stories every week to determine if they have been correctly quoted and if other facts about them are accurately written. Some papers even print house ads inviting public comment on the accuracy of their news reports.

This concern follows a number of polls that indicate a rising public mistrust of journalistic accuracy in general. A Gallup Poll, for example, found that only 33 percent of 760 people interviewed by telephone believed that most news media reports are valid and only 5 percent believed everything they read and heard. However, Gallup said that 61 percent believed "very little" or "only some" of the news.

When specific parts of the nation's engine of information were mentioned, the showing was better. Television news, for example, received a 71 percent vote of confidence in the accuracy of network reportage, with newsmagazines receiving a 66 precent rating and newspapers 57 percent. But that does not allay the justified concern over improving the accuracy of journalists in general.

If reporters and writers can't get their facts straight, mere word-slinging isn't going to help convince the public of their credibility. An old news agency motto was: "Get if first but get it right." There's not much sense in having the wrong information and presenting it exclusively.

The only way to insure accuracy is to check all sources continually and leave nothing to guesswork or chance.

Attitudes

Writers in all forms of journalism are well advised to maintain a cool, detached, even skeptical attitude as they approach their material. Their task calls for a high degree of skill in the use of language, organization and dexterity on both the Video Display Terminal and, in declining importance, the typewriter. The newsroom is no place for histrionics, displays of temperament, excitement or loud talk. These are the tell-tale signs of the amateur.

Everything depends on the ability of the writer to concentrate and work efficiently under pressure. Some despair, at the beginning, of ever being able to achieve that kind of attitude on deadline. It does come — with patience and experience and training.

Attribution

The newcomer to journalism is told at the outset that everything in a news story must be attributed. Such writers seldom understand, at the beginning, that this can be done without affecting the readability of the story. All they can think of is that they must write "he said . . . he said . . . he said . . ." in almost every sentence. Often, it is the only word that fits. (See also "Elegant Variation.")

Breeziness

The part-time country journalist, in notes from Cutchogue, New York, for the weekly paper, used to write:

> Good old Daddy Dockweiler had a terrific blowout at his place on Peconic Boulevard Sunday. He served fried bluefish to all his neighbors until it came out their ears. . . .

That kind of writing went out with the horsecars, even for country journalism. Breeziness sounds amateurish even on the sports page, where it still crops up now and then.

For some peculiar reason, inexperienced writers also feel obliged, at the end of an interview about some earnest and well-meaning person, to add a benediction something like this:

> But with the spirit Mrs. Sudenthaler has always shown, she is bound to overcome her difficulties. In any case, she remains an inspiration to all who know her.

This is a no-no on two counts: (1) It is editorial opinion; (2) it is unnecessary.

Checking Copy

Several safeguards are generally used in copy whether it is produced on terminal or typewriter. The process varies from one news organization to another, but the responsibilities for attention-calling devices are always put on the writer. The desk person or copy editor then must be sure they are eliminated before the story is set, taped or put in a script for a news program.

Names   When a new or a strange name appears for the first time in the news, several methods are used to call attention to it. One is to repeat the name in brackets to indicate that it is properly spelled. Or, CQ or OK may be inserted after the name, the notation being in brackets. In copy edited with a pencil, these symbols may be placed in a circle above the name; also, for that matter, above any unusual fact or figure.

Figures   The use of figures in the news always entails risks and much checking, but that is no reason for not using them. For reasons of newspaper style, figures are never used to begin a sentence but are spelled out instead. This is one way to be sure the figure is correctly used.

Another is to repeat a key figure in brackets, [M] for millions and [B] for billions.

The general rule is to spell out figures below 10, use numerals for 10 and above. In money amounts of more than a million, round numbers take the dollar sign, and million, billion and trillion are spelled. Decimals are carried to two places: $4.75 million. Exact amounts are written: $4,372,356 [M]. In amounts of less than a dollar, the figure is used and "cents" is spelled out.

The same style is used for figures other than money. But cardinal numbers (four, 12, 15, etc.) are used for most purposes such as ages, dates, distances, heights and weights while ordinal numbers (10th, 12th, 21st, etc.) are used for addresses and sequences (32nd Street, the 41st in line).

Claiming Credit

The lower forms of print and broadcast journalism revel in credit claiming. It is not unusual to pick up a sensational paper and find that "the *Daily Intruder* exclusively reveals today the horrendous details of a criminal plot." It is just as common to hear an enthusiastic broadcaster exclaim, in reporting a news conference attended by 30 reporters, "Our Joe Blow has the story!" intimating that good old Joe alone talked with the news source.

The writing of news also suffers from overstatement through the use of such credit-claiming verbs as "disclosed" and "revealed." If there is a real disclosure or revelation, the use of such verbs is, of course, justified. But it arouses merriment even among less sophisticated readers or viewers when a reporter says, or writes, with ponderous solemnity, that the United States Weather Bureau "revealed" that tomorrow's weather would be fair and warm.

This is gas-light journalism and it should remain decently interred in the files of newspaper morgues.

Clutter

Clutter in news writing is the equivalent of spouting a mouthful of meaningless words. It is the foe of clarity. It deadens interest. It makes writing a mindless chore.

In the main, clutter is attributable to a writer's effort to relate too many things at once. The result resembles a frumpy dress — too much material put together in a disorderly way with bulges in all the wrong places. Instead, a good writer tries to use the material smoothly where it fits best.

This is clutter:

> Peter Wyczinski, acting chairman of the City Council's Special Committee on Consumer Affairs, presented a committee report today that charged Greenwich Supermarkets Inc., with headquarters at Fifth Ave. and 10th Street, with "deliberately short-weighting customers in its meat department" in some of its stores.

It would be simpler to write:

> A City Council committee report today charged Greenwich Supermarkets Inc. with "deliberately short-weighting customers in the meat department" in some of its stores.
>
> The report was presented by Peter Wyczinski, acting chairman of the Council's Special Committee on Consumer Affairs.

Coherence

Nearly all American schoolchildren are told to write with "unity, coherence and emphasis," but few are able to do it without effort and training. By the time they reach college, some have even forgotten the importance of maintaining continuity in their writing.

Except for brief news items or breaking news on deadline, writers must make an attempt to link the various parts of a story in readable order. Unimaginative writers use such transitional phrases as "earlier in the evening," "prior to this development," "just before the vote," "in another move during the meeting," and similar connecting material. The most overworked of all transitions is the word "meanwhile."

Here are some others that journalists have put into their copy over the years to indicate that another phase of the story is about to be told:

> The *next* speaker was . . .
> The proposal *also* called for . . .
> *But another* speaker objected that . . .
> It *soon* became clear that . . .
> *Before* the accident . . .
> *After* the performance ended . . .
> *In spite of* opposition . . .
> *With* the help of others . . .
> He *followed* with . . .
> *However*, many others were in favor . . .
> *As for* the wounded man, he suffered . . .
> *With* that statement, the defense rested . . .
> *Without* such formality, the meeting proceeded . . .
> *Nearby*, several eyewitnesses concluded . . .
> *Then came* a flower-filled carriage . . .
> *For example*, this was a reminder of . . .
> *Finally*, the resolution read . . .
> *In conclusion*, the speaker said . . .
> *A newer* development was better (or worse) . . .
> *Farther off*, flood waters were rising . . .

This list could be extended. Such simple connecting words and phrases do make for a certain amount of coherence. So does the conjunction "and" at the beginning of a sentence. But more artful writers, given time, try to work their transitions into a newsworthy sentence or paragraph so that readers are not conscious of being mentally pulled and hauled from one point to another.

Credibility

Basically, journalists are only as credible as their news sources and the willingness of those sources to be identified. They must, in the first instance, be prepared to pass the test of truth.

Where the outcome of a news event has a finite result, there is no excuse for errors. This would include everything from the reporting of elections to box scores and financial markets, the casualty figures in natural or manmade disasters, the outcome of most police investigations, the result of court trials and the minutae of vital statistics of individuals who make news.

For the variables, which would include everything from the weather to predictions affecting the economy, the most that can be done is to use the best possible sources, name them, quote them and hope that the outcome will be somewhere near the truth.

The credibility of the historian rests on the truth as reflected over centuries. The credibility of the journalist sometimes turns on a perception of truth in a matter of minutes. And this, finally, is the burden the journalist must bear.

Current Timing

Unlike news broadcasts, which have a sense of immediacy, the news written for a newspaper may not be read for hours later by its subscribers. Timing, therefore, creates special problems for the press in an era when major news events can be seen unfolding on television by tens of millions of viewers. And this is as true of newsmagazines as it is of newspapers.

When Did It Happen?   In most instances, your favorite newsmagazine reports vaguely that an event took place last week, but the exact time and date are mentioned only if there is some need for it. This is called fuzzing up the timing.

In newspaper work, editors prefer using either the day of the week or a broad stretch of time — today, yesterday, last night — as the time element in leads. Except when it is important, the exact time of an event is seldom used.

The Present Tense   Much broadcast news is written in the present or present perfect tense. Newspapers also resort to this device to try to bridge the gap between events at the hour of publication and the time lapse before the paper is read. For example:

> A congressional committee convenes today to investigate the nation's defense program.
> The New York Yankees and the Boston Red Sox open the baseball season today.
> The UN Security Council meets today on the crisis in the Middle East, with the United States demanding a cease fire.
> The City Council decides today whether to approve the mayor's proposal for a tax increase.

Starting the Action   One of the minor crimes of journalism is to write something that "dates the paper." Thus, all kinds of devices are used to indicate that the paper is on top of a story that actually hadn't begun to unfold when the edition went to press. The trick is to be perfectly accurate and still indicate the shape of the expected news. These are some examples of how it is done:

> A 21-year-old clerk was held for arraignment today as a suspect in the murder of his 23-year-old girlfriend.
> The sidewalks of Knoxville blossomed in green today as marchers lined up for their annual St. Patrick's Day parade.
> The State Convention moved today to nominate Marvin McAllister as the Republican candidate for governor.

The one thing that cannot be done is to past-tense a story without waiting for it to happen. There have been too many instances in which people were severely injured or died before they acted out the roles ordained for them in press releases. The rule is: *You may anticipate the news, but you must wait until it happens before reporting it.*

Datelines

A dateline is the name of the city or town at the beginning of print stories not of local origin. Broadcast people do not have to worry about datelines. Newspapers do. The general practice is not to use a dateline on news of the community in which the paper is published, nor a given area surrounding the community (generally a 20- or 25-mile radius). In addition, when broad leads are written on such general stories as storms, holidays, elections, and so on, datelines are omitted. These are termed "undated leads."

When datelines are used, they should be written as part of the lead, beginning exactly where news accounts normally would start on terminal or page. The text of the lead then follows on the same line without a break.

Very few papers now use the date in the dateline, arguing that the date is on the whole paper. General wire service and newspaper practice is to use only the place name. (See also "Time Element.")

Designing a Story

Any story in the news other than an item, a brief straight news account or a deadline piece develops a pattern all its own. If the writer is not firm and knowledgeable, that pattern will be a crazy quilt. In mature hands, however, the pattern will follow a useful and even pleasing design.

Writers have always known this. In newsrooms, the search for a design is variously known as an "angle," a "handle," a "slant." If these terms were used perjoratively, the public might well believe that journalists try to doctor up everything they write. Indeed, quite the opposite is the case. For the design of a story determines whether it will be worth the readers' trouble to peruse it or, for that matter, whether it will be worth printing or broadcasting in the first instance.

In its simplest form, the story's structure might follow a basically chronological pattern. Or it might begin with the statement of a problem area in the news and proceed with an analysis of the difficulty. It might be told entirely in the form of questions and answers. Or it could conceivably follow the pattern of a short short story, provided the writer had all the necessary facts for such a design.

No matter what, for a story of any substance, there does have to be a plan and a pattern. Otherwise the whole thing collapses into utter confusion.

Dialect

Around the turn of the century, dialect stories were popular. But times and styles have changed. Few news organizations permit writers to use quotations in dialect any longer. Ethnic and racial groups are too easily affronted. If it becomes necessary to quote someone in dialect, the uneasy choice is either to use paraphrase or the exact statement with some indication of why it was important to present the material as it was uttered.

Distortion

The warning to avoid unnatural prose may be illustrated by the following type of nuisance lead:

> Quit.
> That's what Housing Commissioner Ringwood did today.

It is a ridiculous way of writing news or anything else. A simple statement that Commissioner Ringwood resigned is shorter and more pointed. It takes more than a trick approach to startle today's readers and viewers. They're usually shockproof.

James Thurber of *The New Yorker* is credited with having written the ultimate in ridiculous leads when he turned out the following as a young reporter, in a mild protest against unnatural writing:

> Dead.
> That's what Joe Schmaltz was today after he fell down a manhole.

Editorializing

The principle of separating the news from editorial opinion is supported in every responsible area of American journalism. What it means is that writers may not inject their own point of view in the news columns unless they are authorized to do so. Generally, that kind of authorization is limited to special stories, labeled "Analysis." These accounts consist of interpretation and background material assembled in an effort to explain the news.

The Urge to Advise What is editorializing? Basically, it means that writers in one way or another are trying to put their own personal stamp on events, to make every news story a column of opinion, to urge a course of conduct on either the public or some facet of the private or public sector in American life.

It is, in short, a belief that the writer must give advice. Mainly, it arises from the popularity of advocacy journalism as practiced by a few magazine writers and novelists who began calling themselves the "New Journalists" in the 1970s and still are around. Most of these writers were well established, commanded large fees or royalties (sometimes both) and never lacked an outlet for their product.

Clearly, it would be difficult for young journalists to emulate them on well-edited newspapers or broadcast news programs, but that hasn't deterred some of the free spirits from trying. The result is usually mutual embarrassment between journalists and their news organization and a rather abrupt divorce.

Personal Pronouns Personal journalism has enjoyed a revival on TV, particularly in broadcast news programs, which are dominated by highly paid and glamorous anchor people. Except among columnists, there isn't much of that in print journalism. No "I" stuff is wanted, either on wire services or newspapers, unless it is necessary to write an eyewitness story of some major event. Even then, the writer's experiences are stressed, not thoughts or opinions.

Inadvertent Comment   A critical adjective in a newscast or the lead of a news story can be damaging to a person or a proposal. An unnecessary descriptive phrase, mainly to make a story more readable, also can be prejudicial. The *Wall Street Journal*, in carrying a report about Knoxville, Tennessee, affronted a large part of its population by calling it a "scruffy little city."

These things hurt. They cause unnecessary injury to others. But mainly they hurt journalism itself. A little self-restraint has never injured any writer.

Loaded Words   These are commonly used loaded words and phrases:

> A little-known group *claimed credit* for the assassination.
> The *Right-to-Life* movement opposes abortion.
> Social Security supports *socialized medicine*.
> The local union, which is not on strike, *honored the drivers' picket line*.
> The Legislature was asked to endorse a *right-to-work* law.
> The suspects belong to a *terrorist* group.
> The *gay community* is powerful in San Francisco.

Writers ought to realize, whenever they use such terminology, that they are picking up propaganda with it. Whether the cause is just or unjust, right or wrong, the words and phrases still are intended to influence people for or against a particular cause or group. And loaded words make loaded journalism.

How bizarre it is, after all, to write that a band of murderers "claimed credit" for an assassination or attempted assassination of a president, pope or other world leader! It would be more in keeping with the loathesome character of the deed to write that the group opened itself to public condemnation. But that, too, would be loaded. It is best to note the fact that a particular organization said it had been involved in a particular event and let it go at that.

It is just as difficult to characterize certain groups as *terrorists* or *guerrillas*. Who, other than the reporter and editor, would make such a judgment? Reporters who have to cope with stories of this nature have learned to use a certain number of circumlocutions — *extremists, leftists, Moslem fundamentalists, activists* — to describe ill-defined groups that have cropped up as major forces in the news.

Such concepts as Right-to-Life movement, right-to-work laws, socialized medicine and honoring picket lines are phrases with public relations connotations that are intended to influence the public toward one cause or another. There are many others, all of which should be approached with caution and used only with justification.

Making up the News   This is a form of editorialization that entails outright deception. It includes fake quotes, fake interviews, the restaging of a conversation long past that occurred without the presence of witnesses, composite figures in the news that never existed and deplorable efforts to twist the news into phony drama.

It goes under many guises, ranging from New Journalism to Gonzo Journalism. Years ago, this kind of thing used to be termed "piping a story," meaning that the writer was smoking an opium pipe at the time of composition. Today, among the indiscriminate newcomers to journalism, it has acquired a certain amount of cachet because it is supposed to be fun.

There's only one trouble with that point of view. Lies, by whatever name they are called, aren't funny.

Elegant Variation

Nobody would call a banana "an elongated yellow fruit" or describe a black-haired young woman as a "maiden with raven tresses." Nor should a writer use verbal exaggeration when attributing a quote, including such words as *opined* and *averred*. These are all prima facie evidence of the literary crime known as elegant variation — the use of a big or unfamiliar word where a small, common word will do.

There is no reason why a banana should not be called a banana. And we have passed the era when it was permissible to describe women in terms we would not use for a man in a similar situation. A young woman is a young woman, preferably identifiable by age (if it can be obtained), address and occupation, if any. We do not use "willowy brunette" or "sexy blonde" in the news columns any more than we would describe a young man as "curvaceous" or "loaded with sex appeal."

As for the use of *said* in attributing a quote, it's the handiest and most applicable verb for the situation. Some believe it is overused, particularly in wire service copy. Perhaps so. But Ernest Hemingway rarely used any other verb in reporting a conversation and won both the Nobel and Pulitzer Prizes for his writing.

If someone shouts or murmurs, naturally that should be reported. There also are other useful verbs in covering speeches, debates and the like, among them recalled, protested, insisted, admitted, conceded, asserted and declared. But there's nothing wrong, either, with the use of said — said — said.

Every authority on written English from E. B. White to Winston Churchill has stressed the importance of using words of Anglo-Saxon derivation, which are usually short, rather than words derived from Latin, which are generally longer. As one Midwestern editor used to tell his writers: "Don't give me any of these $10 words. I like mine out of the five and dime store."

False Titles

It's easy to write *President Jones, Governor Smith, Mayor Brown* or *Councilman Black*. These are legitimate titles, all of them capitalized when used with the name of the title-holder.

There is no trouble, either, with using longer designations such as these: *John Davis, Democratic candidate for councilman-at-large; James White, former chairman of the Republican County Committee,* or *Eunice Johnson, director of the Nurses' Association of St. Luke's Hospital.*

Where writers stub their toes is in the creation of false titles, most of which precede the name of the false title-holder. For example: sparkling television personality Josie Hawkins, local fashionplate and man-about-town Mac Thompson and champion whiz kid Sammy Simpson. If these observations are accurate, it would be better to work them into the story rather than thrust them before the name of some hapless figure in the news.

It would make for better reading, too.

Foreign Expressions

Don't use them. Most young writers can't spell them correctly, much less define them. Usually, foreign words and expressions—used out of context—are an embarrassment in the news columns. It's a fair assumption, too, that the general public won't understand foreign terminology scattered through a newspaper; in broadcast journalism, the result would be even more confusing.

It's best to stick to English. And simple English at that.

Good Taste

When President Nixon used gamy language in discharging the duties of his high office, most papers published the unexpurgated text. The networks ran enough of it on slides to give the viewing public the general idea. Not all the Nice Nellies in journalism could protest, in this case, that obscenities should *never* appear in a family newspaper. Public policy demanded that the public should know how the presidency was being conducted.

In today's realistic society, the words and deeds of public figures must be made known if they bear on the manner in which they discharge their duties. The same is true of material emanating from police files, courts and public health offices among others. If news organizations have a contrary policy, forbidding the use of obscenities under any circumstances, the writer will quickly be made aware of it. Circumstances, however, generally govern usage today. This problem is discussed at greater length in Chapter 16.

Handouts

This is the general newsroom term for public relations releases. Any first rate news organization, large or small, will check any handout as to origin and veracity before attempting to use it in a news report. If the handout passes these tests, the writer assigned to the story usually works the telephone for a different angle from the one featured in the release. This is done, as a rule, to blunt the factor of self-interest that is the essence of most handouts. There is no reason for a news organization to carry a public relations message, particularly when advertising time or space is easily available. Handouts should be rewritten.

Hard Words

The theory of unique occurrence has been used so often and for so many years that, with few exceptions, it has become a public bore. The theory is based mainly on a few hard words that are painfully familiar to every journalist. These are among the superlatives that have automatically signaled too many stories:

> The *largest* crowd in some place's history.
> The *lowest* or *highest* temperature on record.
> The *smallest* or *largest* person in a school or other institution, not to overlook
the *youngest* and the *oldest*.

The oldest settler, the cutest baby, the closest athletic contest, the prettiest girl, the first person in line at the opening of the World Series or the Super Bowl—all these, too, have been overused. In fact, most of them are so well worn as to be predictable by the unlucky reporter who is assigned, once again, to try to make them come alive.

These are among the words that could be honorably retired.

Honorifics

Most news organizations refuse to *Mr.* anybody. Only a few still do it for the president of the United States. However, they do use titles, academic or military rank and other honorifics. The rule is to use the honorific with the full name of the person when it first appears. Thereafter, most news organizations use only the last name, but a few still use the title as well.

The same general practice applies to women with titles, but there is a wide variation in the use of *Mrs.*, *Miss* and *Ms.* In a valiant effort to defer to the Modern Woman, many newspapers have dropped all honorifics for women without title or rank, applying the same rule by which men are addressed. However, in any proceeding involving a man and a woman of the same name, whether related or not, this does become confusing.

In the interests of clarity, the writer should conform to the rules of the news organization involved.

Hunches

Some journalists have a mysterious faith in playing hunches or trusting their intuition. As a reporting device, there's nothing wrong with this. Sometimes, a hunch can lead to positive results. But hunches and intuition can be very misleading if they are blindly followed in writing a news story. There is no magic way of doing a lead.

Negative News

Editors ask writers to be positive, not negative. This means more than dropping "not" out of a lead. Negative news means that nothing has happened — that a trial continues, that reactions to a speech are awaited, that negotiations are marking time.

However, when a bride refuses to be married, that is the most positive kind of news for her bridegroom. Moreover, if the president of the United States announces he will not run for re-election, it has to be the biggest positive story of the day.

To translate this attitude into action requires a bit of dexterity, as witness the following editing changes:

Negative Police Commissioner Hamilton said today he would not adopt Mayor Riddle's plan to shake up the police force.

Positive Police Commissioner Hamilton today rejected Mayor Riddle's demand for a police shakeup.

Negative There was no chance left today that the Warrington Woolen Mills would remain here instead of moving south.

Positive The Warrington Woolen Mills, once a major source of local income, prepared to move south today.

The point to remember is that news organizations dislike reporting that something didn't happen or that someone didn't do anything, unless there is a positive element to be made known in such cases.

"Now"

The use of a verb in the present tense indicates immediacy. It is not necessary to use "now," "at present" or "presently" when the verb tense so clearly indicates the time element. "Now" may be used, however, in place of such a redundant phrase as "at this point in time."

Omission of Necessary Detail

One of the sources of murky writing is the constant effort to shorten sentences by dropping articles. Thus:

Council voted last night to halt action boosting parking meter rates.
Commission at final fiscal year meeting today approved $4.65 million budget.

What this sounds like is telegraphese. It's bad enough in leads. But when it is continued in the body of news stories, the effect is akin to a person tripping over the multiplication tables. Where the ordinary forms of written English require the use of an article, it should not be omitted.

Another familiar shortcoming is the use of inference to hook up the action between the lead and body of a news story. This situation occurs when persons not generally known to the public must be introduced in some way other than by using their name in the lead. For example:

> A teenage messenger today saved 30 fellow-employees from a fire that razed McMichael's Department Store.
>
> Sammy Jones, 17, gave the alarm. . . .

One Idea to a Sentence

Madeleine Blais wrote of her mother in a piece called "The Last Christmas," published in the *Miami Herald:*

> Blasphemy served her like a trumpet. A decision had to be reached. The best way to face loss was to celebrate it; it was the way of her people; Irish wakes, last hurrahs. Everyone must come home. . . . They must all come home and take part in the ritual of the last Christmas Eve in the big house. . . . The mother of six would wear the diamond necklace she reserved for special occasions. It was not just holiday; it was elegy.

This is what is meant by writing with one idea to a sentence. The style is effective, but it doesn't apply to every story. Nor can it be used in every sentence and every situation. But graceful writers who have a good ear and a sense of the fitness of things know how to use this method. There is no doubt that the process increases comprehension.

Of course it is possible to exaggerate and go back to kindergarten writing: "Oh, see the cat. It is a gray cat. Its eyes are green." Nobody seriously proposes that. The suggestion of one idea to a sentence does have its uses, but it isn't recommended for inept writers.

Overwriting

An explosion of adjectives and adverbs is the most familiar sign of overwritten copy. An intensely dramatic treatment of a mild incident in the day's news also amounts to literary overkill. The most regrettable of all forms of overwriting, however, is the story that runs for a thousand words and could easily be compressed into three short paragraphs.

Writers should always remember not to offer readers more than they wish to know about a given incident in the news, especially one that verges on the routine. The cure for the disease is brutal. Either the overwritten story is sharply edited or, if a writer shows signs of being overwhelmed by the urge to pile words on words, the editor signals a cutoff in the labor of composition with a curt, "Keep it short. That's enough."

Paragraphing

The news paragraph is more of a typographical device than a unit of composition. In much of print journalism, with the exception of magazines like *The New Yorker*, most paragraphs run only a few lines. Sometimes, when emphasis is needed, there may be only one sentence to a paragraph. It is not often, in consequence, that a topical sentence and fully developed paragraph will be found in most newspapers and newsmagazines.

The concern over reader fatigue, caused sometimes by great masses of unrelieved print, has prompted journalists in general to write short paragraphs.

Objections to Short Paragraphs Editors on some of the quality newspapers in the land have made no secret of their dislike for the three- or four-line paragraph. In reaction to the bang-bang-bang style of paragraphing, many of these editors have been encouraging their writers to use paragraphing in a normal manner as a means of achieving greater coherence. The trend, however, is not overwhelming.

There are a few points on which there is general agreement:

- A new paragraph should be used to begin a quote.
- Large blocks of quotes should be broken up by paragraphing.
- A paragraph that is unnecessarily long should also be chopped up and transitions should be added, where necessary, to maintain coherence.

Beginning Paragraphs Differently Editors sometimes get strange ideas. A few here and there advocate beginning every paragraph differently to avoid monotony. What this accomplishes is the almost certain destruction of a writer's peace of mind. It is not a good rule.

Pseudo-events

Politicians and entertainers are adept at drumming up staged events to attract TV coverage and news space. It is apparent to everybody, including the news media, that the so-called news is being manufactured. This kind of hype can be applied to all kinds of situations—gatherings of famous people to publicize a cause, colorful parades sponsored by department stores or other commercial enterprises, dramatic exhibits of everything from rare jewels to new types of military weapons, even speeches by eminent figures delivered in praise of something or someone.

The news media know they are being had, but they cover anyway. Some say it is harmless. Perhaps. But there are quite a few in journalism who believe it is demeaning.

Qualifying a Story

Every writer knows that the use of qualifying words and phrases weakens the effect of a story. But in journalism, there is sometimes no way of avoiding qualification of a report in the interests of both accuracy and clarity.

If a president is shot at or a pope dies, if a bridge collapses or a bank is robbed, if an airplane crashes or a film star vanishes, there is no way of presenting the facts in five seconds. Everything has to be qualified as to source. And the source has to be official as a guarantee against the deadly accusation that the news media are spreading unconfirmed rumors. (See also "Rumors and Reports.")

Quotes

Quotes often make or break a story. A good quote, used high up, can dramatize a difficult situation far more than a lengthy exposition. Where journalists get into trouble is in the use of quotes for the sake of slapping quotation marks around a few words. There is no reason to use a banal quote ("How nice of you to come," he said) or a meaningless quote ("I like animals, don't you?" she asked).

Often, a good quote can be ruined by mistakes in punctuation. The few rules that apply are worth reviewing:

- All direct quotations, complete or partial, are enclosed in quotation marks.
- When there are several paragraphs of continuous quotations, each paragraph should start with a quotation mark, but the quotation mark should be omitted from the end of all paragraphs except the final one.
- The attribution of a quotation should be placed where it fits.

For a long block of quotes, the attribution might be at the beginning (The statement follows:). In a paragraph of quotes, the identity of the speaker could be inserted after the first clause ("It has happened as was to have been foreseen," wrote Alexander Hamilton, "the measures of the Union have not been executed."). But in no case should the speaker's identity be deferred beyond the end of the first sentence of quotes. And it should never be put off until the end of the paragraph. Other rules:

- Commas and periods go inside quotation marks. Other punctuation marks go inside quotation marks only when they are part of the quoted matter.
- Semicolons and colons always follow quotation marks.
- Interior quotes take single quotation marks and follow the same rules as full quotations in every other respect.
- Beware of using partial quotes at the expense of clarity. It would be better to use a paraphrase in a lead and use the full quote as documentation in the following sentence or paragraph. Too many partial quotes can lead to muddy writing and complete confusion.
- Do not put quotes about a perfectly acceptable phrase. (George was "bright" and "liked to play.") Use quotes sparingly for ironical observations, coined words or words of unusual meanings.
- In newspaper usage, titles of books, plays, movies, operas, statuary, paintings, ships and aircraft take quotation marks. If a comma or period is included, it goes inside the end quote.
- In using trial testimony from a court record, do not use quotes. This material runs as Q. and A.

Rumors and Reports

Journalists have a special nomenclature for news that cannot be immediately substantiated. Developments that have at least a degree of authenticity from trustworthy sources, even if they cannot be identified, are termed "reports." Thus, if a respected colleague of Senator Augustus Regas says he has learned the senator won't run for re-election and the senator's office refuses to confirm or deny, it may be used as a report as follows:

> WASHINGTON—Senator Augustus Regas may refuse to run for re-election, it was reported today. The senator's office refused to confirm or deny the report, which originated with a close associate who would not be named.

But if the same story comes to the reporter from an office worker, who heard it from another Senate employee, it must be dismissed as an unauthenticated rumor unless and until it can be checked from firmer and more reputable sources.

There is an enormous difference between the use of rumors, a term that covers most unverified material, and reports, news that is unquestionably correct but cannot be given immediate official confirmation. For example, when President Anwar el-Sadat of Egypt was assassinated in 1981, all major news agencies and networks carried his death as a report (based on authentic sources in the Egyptian government) until the government itself made the formal announcement three hours after he was fatally shot. Even the United States government refused to confirm his death until the official announcement was made from Cairo.*

Specific News Writing

One of the first rules of news writing is: *Be specific. Use language that is concrete. Be definite. Avoid generalities.*

Give Meaning to the News   Generalities often blur the news picture. Instead of writing that a man is tall, describe him as 6 feet 4. Instead of writing that he is heavy, write that he weighs 258 pounds.

Generalities blur written work. The specific brightens and enlivens copy.

If statistics are used, they must be given meaning. To say that New York City's subways have an illumination of only one candlepower means little. It is more informative to write that the average New York subway rider sometimes reads the paper by less light than Abe Lincoln had when he studied by firelight in a log cabin.

Certain other types of news must be related to the specific, too. Five dead in a San Francisco fire is of little interest in Des Moines. But let five in a family from Des Moines die in a San Francisco fire and Iowans are bound to take notice. Anti-American demonstrations in Western Europe or the Middle East usually bore Amer-

---

*To avoid semantic confusion, the beginner should be aware that the journalistic meaning of the term "report"—used as a verb—differs from the conventional use of the word as a noun, which usually is applied to a document of one kind or another.

ican audiences, but let someone from Topeka or Bloomington be involved, and Kansas and Indiana news media are on the alert at once. We cannot ignore hometown interests.

Names Make News   Any hometown personality who says or does something differently or is involved in the news in one way or another is a fit subject for a profile, an interview or a commentary. Every journalist knows that when subjects are too large, complex and indefinite for the public to grasp, the story had best be told in terms of personalities.

It is a truism that people like to know about other people. When a young woman reporter went on a tour of Russia with a YWCA group, she made it her business to interview the wives and children of Russian farmers and did a feature series about their lives on Russian farms for the Associated Press. The series was popular in the Midwest farming belt, where it attracted favorable attention. Whenever reporters visit American military installations abroad, they invariably look up members of the armed forces from their respective areas and write about their lives overseas.

Even buildings, monuments, bridges and other familiar sights in the modern world have names that automatically awaken images and yearnings in the minds of many readers. Who cannot feel just a bit involved with the Statue of Liberty, the 110-story Sears Tower in Chicago, San Francisco's Golden Gate Bridge, California's Death Valley, Arizona's Grand Canyon and such wonderful place names as Ten Sleep, Wyoming, and Paradise Valley, Washington?

Color   Journalists have often been criticized for trying to characterize a person, place or situation with a bright phrase or a vivid sentence. It is difficult to do well but it is an important part of writing for the news media. The television cameras catch these details automatically with a sweep of the lens—the black-haired small boy in a blue stocking cap clutching his mother's hand, the old man in blue overalls nodding over his newspaper on a park bench, the bright, laughing girl in a yellow dress walking in the park on a sunny afternoon, the stern financial authority arising after testimony before a Senate committee in the nation's capital and displaying a hole in the seat of his pants, the great opera singer opening her mouth wide and choking over an insect that darts into her throat.

This, too, is the stuff of life and it is a part of the art form we call journalism.

Time Element

Every story must have a time element. For current material, it is usually established in the first sentence. For feature material, it may be deferred in favor of an anecdotal beginning. In investigative, interpretive and analytical stories, it is likely to include a more detailed report of the period involved. For space or time fillers, set aside for use to fill out a page or program when needed, the time may be very general. But in some way, some place and by some method, the time of the news must be specified.

Defining the Time Element As was pointed out under "Current Timing," the definition of the time element varies. Most morning newspapers now use the day of the week in straight news but a declining number of afternoon papers still cling to the use of the word "today." The former practice of using "yesterday" in morning paper leads, or the word "today" with yesterday's date in the dateline, still appears here and there, the *New York Times* being a notable example. For the broadcast news media, the problem is simplified because the telling of the news is far more immediate.

Usually, in newspaper copy, the time element goes into the story where it naturally belongs. For straight news, that is usually close to the verb in the opening sentence. For example:

> A new military jet plane flew Tuesday from London to Kennedy Airport in New York City in record time.

Confusing the Public The reason for simplifying the time element, either by using the day of the week or eliminating the date from the dateline, is made clear in the following:

> CENTRAL CITY, June 30 — Gov. Amberwell said today that he would announce tomorrow whether he will run for re-election.

When this appears in a morning paper that carries the date Tuesday, July 1, the reader must realize that the tomorrow in the lead of June 30 actually means today, and today means yesterday (Monday). It's guaranteed to confuse the public. That's why such a lead is generally written:

> CENTRAL CITY — Gov. Amberwell will announce Tuesday whether he will run for re-election.

That's clear enough for everybody.

When Yesterday Is Taboo With the decline of afternoon papers in number, the various PM taboos aren't as important as they once were. But some editors are still around who will not tolerate the use of the word "yesterday" in a straight news lead in today's paper. It really doesn't matter much. Broadcast journalism has made the public realize that newspapers can't present the news as quickly as the electronic news gatherers.

• Short Takes

This summarizes major writing problems and suggests ways to improve writing:

- It takes more than a declaration of intent to make a writer. A lot of hard work is involved, including training, study and self-discipline.
- Accuracy is one of the major problems in all news writing. Some authorities believe it is the principal problem today. Checking facts and checking copy help eliminate errors.
- Writers should strive for a cool, detached, skeptical attitude.

- Every story of consequence should have a suitable design and organization. Cluttered writing should be avoided at all costs.
- Avoid dialect, distortion, editorializing, the overstuffed word or phrase, clichés, false titles and foreign expressions.
- It is true that qualifying words or phrases weaken the strength of a writer's work, but not everything in the news can be told in terms of clear black and white, heroes and villains, cops and robbers. There are many gray areas in which qualifiers must be used as a matter of elementary fairness. But do not overqualify.
- Watch for a lack of coherence in writing news. It is a major fault that can easily be avoided with a judicious use of connecting words, phrases, clauses and— sometimes—sentences or paragraphs. There must be a sense of unity in writing for publication or broadcast.
- When stories are overwritten, a writer's credibility suffers. As many facts as possible should be put into a story to make it credible to readers and viewers, but it isn't necessary, in a fire story, to locate each fire plug. There is a limit to what the public can absorb in any given situation.
- The stiff and stylized news stencil, sometimes called formal news writing, is the bane of journalism. It is guaranteed to produce dull copy. Writers should not be afraid to weave the wonderful rhythms of the English language into their copy, to seek new ways of telling old stories, to try for originality.

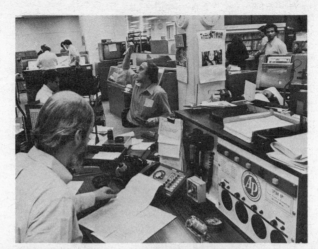

2
The Writer as Journalist

CHAPTER

7

Problems
of News Writing

Many a beginner sits around a newsroom for what seems like hours, waiting for an assignment. Then, without warning, comes the first test. Sometimes it is an obit or a bit of wire copy that has to be rewritten with a local angle. Or it could be a handout in which there is a kernel of news that must be checked. Now and then, the newcomer will be instructed to listen to a reporter on the phone and write a brief account of a two-alarm fire, a small theft or an auto accident.

Fighting Time and Space

Whatever the material, once the writer asks the city desk for a space estimate, the instructions come back to do a "short"—sometimes called a "brief" or a "brite" (which is bright, misspelled for no apparent reason).

All of a sudden, the writer is caught up in the journalist's eternal struggle against the limits of time and space in a highly personal manner. After all, how short is a "short"? It depends on the story and the skill of the writer. The piece could be three or four lines, figuring 10 words to a line on the VDT, or it might be as much as 10 lines if the story is worth it.

And what of time? How quickly will the story have to be written? Once again, that depends on the writer.

Writing a "Short"   Every young man and woman who has survived that first test vividly remembers the circumstances and the inevitable inner question: "How can I tell a story in so short a time and with so little space?" How indeed? But somehow, those initial moments of panic subside and the writer begins turning out the story, trying all the while to show no hint of turmoil.

All newspapers and local broadcast media carry such news items. Here is one example:

> A northeast Gainesville resident lost two shotguns and a revolver to a burglar early Wednesday afternoon, police reported. Two 12-gauge shotguns and a .41-caliber Magnum pistol were taken from the NE 8th Ave. home of James White, 39, Officer Tim Good reported.
>
> —*Gainesville* (Florida) *Sun*

For broadcast, this would be written in the present perfect tense.

This "short" follows the first principles of news writing. There is a brief summary lead, then a sentence that documents it with supporting factual material. No color, no comment, no attempt to do anything more than to describe a brief event in the day's news.

Handling a "Brite"   Sometimes the "short" has the germ of a story in it. Then the wise writer follows the prescribed pattern, but at the same time tries to arrange the facts in such a way that they tell a *story*. It's tricky because the story still has to be brief. A delayed beginning, a clever tag line, chronological construction, a quote — any of these devices may be used to make a "short" come alive.

But if the writing is forced, or if there is an attempt at humor, the piece is likely to die on the editor's VDT. Here are two "brites" that survived on the news wires:

> WASHINGTON — At a cost of $144,012, a National Science Foundation project found that pigeons sometimes follow generally accepted human consumer patterns. The study won Sen. William Proxmire's monthly "Golden Fleece" award for the most ridiculous example of waste of taxpayers' money.
>
> "This is one project that should be pigeonholed," the Wisconsin Democrat said.

> Entertainer Sammy Davis Jr. has been awarded an honorary doctor of literature by Atlanta University. Davis, subdued after receiving the degree and the white-and-crimson hood for his academic robe, noted that he had never had a formal education.

Such pieces relieve the monotony of straight news writing and are a little more lively than the items that exist to fill out columns, often in the back of the paper. It helps young writers if they are able to do them quickly and cleanly without trying to make them seem of more consequence than they actually are.

Writing a Short Feature

Another hurdle for newcomers to the newsroom is the short feature. The first question they ask is, "What is it? What makes it different from the usual run of the news?" Generally, a feature story is based on that mysterious ingredient in journalism called human interest—an event that appeals to us because we can relate to it.

The categories that lend themselves to feature treatment run the gamut of human experience. They include stories about the young and the elderly, happily married couples and those who can't get along, strange names and familiar places, ways to make money and a great many more ways to lose it, encounters with dangerous creatures or with household pets, contests of strength and beauty and skill. The list could go on indefinitely. It is certainly more inclusive than the snappy reply attributed to an old-time New York city editor: "Features? Just give me anything about blood, money and broads."

Starting a Short Feature　You can use almost anything for a lead on a short feature as long as it is interesting, accurate and gets the reader into the story. While it is always possible to start with a straight beginning, such leads tend to be deadpan, and a feature should be told with at least a flash of interest. The *Wall Street Journal* was the first among larger newspapers to toss the rulebook out the window and instruct its writers to stay away from straight leads. Here is a sample of the kind of writing the *Journal* offers its two million readers—a short feature based on an unlikely subject, a fire alarm box:

By William M. Bulkeley

Say you're near the high school in North Providence, R.I., and you want to call in a fire alarm. Nearby is a bright red cylindrical booth marked "Fire Alarm. Enter Only in Emergency." So you step in, close the door, pull the alarm and *voilà!* You're locked in and stay that way for five minutes, or until police or firefighters free you.

The booth is the brainchild of a 48-year-old former truckdriver named Lawrence Hartshorn, who says he came up with the idea while sitting in a phone booth and reading a newspaper article about the cost of false alarms.

Since it was installed in July, there hasn't been a single false alarm from the booth, in contrast to 54 from that spot last year.

"I think it's working out real well," says Mayor Salvatore Mancini. Kids were pulling the alarm when they got out of school, and to get out of tests. We stopped that. . . ."

A TV Feature Story　Often these feature pieces are not all that simple. Here is one that David Andelman did for the *CBS Evening News* (with Leslie Stahl substituting for Dan Rather on anchor) about an incident in Moscow:

STAHL:　The U.S. Embassy in Moscow is closely guarded by Soviet
　　police, their job not so much to protect the Americans inside
　　as to keep out any unauthorized Russians. Well, those guards

were surprised today by some unexpected callers. David
Andelman reports from Moscow.

ANDELMAN: It was a tense three-and-a-half-hour ordeal from the
moment their aging Moskvich sedan sped past the heavily armed
Soviet guards into the compound of the American Embassy in
Moscow. But for 54-year-old Vasily Nazarov and his 74-year-
old mother, Natalia, from a small northwest suburb of Moscow,
their reasons for their desperate dash were compelling: he,
fired repeatedly from his job as engineer for reasons he
failed to clarify; his mother, he said, beaten by thugs after
she went to protest her son's plight; both then followed and
harassed by the authorities. That was the tale they told to
American officials who secluded them in the inner courtyard of
the embassy compound.

   [Vasily Nazarov speaking in Russian on camera]

   And after more than three hours of talks, it was the tale
they told to a swarm of Western correspondents who followed
them from the compound to their car parked three blocks away,
moved by U.S. officials apparently to prevent an incident in
front of the embassy itself. "From the start, they were not
seeking asylum," said an embassy source, "merely a
sympathetic ear." Yes, the two said later, they were aware of
the dangers involved. "But," said Vasily Nazarov today, "You
can't be afraid all your life." As his car pulled off into
heavy traffic, three other cars apparently carrying
plainclothes police pulled off after them.

What the Reporter Did   Seemingly, all David Andelman had to do
was stand there, watch, listen and take notes while a camera crew recorded the
scene. Not so. Here is what actually happened, as Andelman reported after his piece
was broadcast:

   This was a classic "crash" story, as it's known around CBS. The story broke
   about 3 p.m. Moscow time (7 a.m. in New York). We knew immediately there was
   no chance of satelliting the story from the Soviet Union (Soviet officials would never
   have allowed that).

   So our deadline was the departure of the last flight to the West—a 7:15 p.m.
   flight to Frankfurt-am-Main, West Germany. As it developed, the story broke
   perfectly but with a razor-thin margin of time. The crew and I spent most of the time
   at the embassy during the three-and-one-half hours the couple was inside.

   We never had any idea when they might emerge and, frankly, there was little
   reporting to be done until they did come out. But unlike the other networks (we were
   the only ones to have a story on the air that night—the others told the story over still
   pictures), we laid our logistical plans early.

   I taped a stand-up close that was valid whether the couple left the embassy or
   elected to stay inside and request asylum. It was never used, due to a technical snafu
   in Frankfurt. The crew divided their time between arranging to get the tape out (it

was hand-carried by the wife of a CBS cameraman) and shooting whatever was available.

As soon as the couple left and the story was wrapped up, the crew sped to the airport. I returned to the bureau to handle the script. There were two key elements that were absent: first, the couple spoke no English, so that no interview was possible; second, the pictures were "thin," though what we had was most dramatic.

The drama had to be conveyed by a tight script and some nice closeup shots of the tortured faces of the pathetic couple, although we were able to make some use of the "natural sound" of the two speaking in Russian when they walked away from the embassy.

The real drama was the three cars of secret police that could be clearly seen in the closing shot, pulling out after the couple, preparing to pounce on them. A perfect example of pictures and words meshing.

Telling a Story Through Dialogue

Edna Buchanan, police reporter for the *Miami Herald*, looks death in the face almost every day. It's part of her job. Jim Bishop, who knows all about police reporters, has called her "Hildy Johnson in earrings." (For the new generation of journalists who never knew Hildy Johnson, he was the Chicago police reporter who became the hero of the old Hecht-MacArthur play *The Front Page*.)

It isn't often that Edna Buchanan is able to do a feature of any kind, particularly one in which life is spared rather than ruthlessly taken. But one day there was a police signal that an elderly couple had been trapped in an accident on the Intracoastal Waterway's drawbridge at Sunny Isles, and this was the story she wrote for *The Herald*.

By Edna Buchanan

For the first time in 52 years of marriage, 80-year-old Paul Finkelstein screamed at his wife, Elizabeth, "Shuddup!"

The circumstances Friday were extenuating.

They were trapped in their car—Elizabeth, 77, at the wheel, suspended in the air at a 70-degree angle, staring into the Intracoastal Waterway 60 feet below.

The Sunny Isles drawbridge had opened when they were driving eastbound across the span and suddenly, for them, every South Florida motorist's worst nightmare came true.

"I would have had a heart attack," Metro Police Sgt. Robert Johns said. "It's a long drop into the water."

"They were sitting there scared, their eyes kind of wide," said Metro Fire Lt. Victor Manoccio, a member of the team that rescued the couple from their car after an hour-long ordeal.

The Finkelstein car had crossed the center of the bridge when the spans began to open. Their Plymouth slid forward down the rising span and smashed into the crevice between the bridge and the roadway.

"It was like looking down on a roller coaster ride," Police Officer Laurence Noon said.

Bridgetender Minerva Duncan, 40, was "concerned but maintained her cool," Noon said. "If she had tried to let the bridge down, it would have been disastrous."

"They could have gone into the Intracoastal," Manoccio agreed.

Dripping gasoline added to the emergency. "I wanted to jump out," said Finkelstein. But the front doors were wedged shut.

As they sat, fearful, his wife panicked.

"I never talk rough to her," Finkelstein said later. "I just told her that 'we'll wait until they [rescuers] come.' It was a bad experience. You see God. I told her, 'Don't get hysterical, honey.' Then I said, 'Shuddup!'"

Elizabeth Finkelstein was surprised to learn later that they had been trapped for less than an hour. "Oh, my goodness," she said. "It must have been longer."

The firefighters—"nice boys," Finkelstein said—erected platforms and a ladder. Lt. Ralph Torres climbed into the back of the car and helped him out first. He climbed down the ladder himself.

"They had to put a rope around my wife," he said. . . .

Had a less experienced writer handled the story, it might have been overdone. But Edna Buchanan's decision to tell the whole story as it was related by the participants gave it a sense of reality that might otherwise not have come through to her readers. She kept herself and her feelings out of it and let the quotes tell the story. They did more than a lot of fancy language could have, under the circumstances. It was a lesson in reportorial restraint.

Building Blocks of News

Once writers move away from short news stories, more complicated forms of organization take over. The lead and its phrasing are bound to determine in large part the organization of the story. After all, the function of the lead is to focus the attention of the reader. This is true whether the article is long or short, straight news or feature, background or in-depth reporting, analysis or interpretation.

The Importance of the Lead   Here is how the lead influences what the writer must do about the rest of the story:

If the lead is based on a single incident, the body of the story must document that incident first and briefly summarize other pertinent facts. If several incidents make up the lead, each incident must be documented in turn in the body of the story and the various parts must be linked by connectives. Should there be an anecdotal lead or a delayed lead of another type, the lead must first be explained before the writer takes up the documentation of the various points. For analysis and interpretation, the format depends to an even greater extent on the basic idea with which the article begins.

These are, in effect, the building blocks of news. When they are properly handled and neatly laid in place, cemented by connectives to the rest of the story, they form an enduring structure for the telling of the news.

Organizing Single-Incident Leads

Having shown how leads so often determine the pattern of a news story, we now go on to consider the organization of a complete news account.

The simplest story is based on several points in the news that are taken up one at a time and related to a single subject. This could be a story about a speech, a public relations statement, a weather story, an accident or similar news development. In such accounts, the point that seems most important to the writer would be made the lead, with documentation; then, with a connecting phrase or clause or sentence, the second point and its documentation would follow. In the same manner, the third point would be introduced and documented.

Such pieces are described as news stories with single-incident leads, as contrasted with news of a more complex nature that is best handled with a cluster of events at the top, called multiple-incident leads. Both are known as "spreads" in newspaper newsrooms because they take headlines that are spread across one, two or more columns.

The organization of a story with a single-incident lead takes the form of a ladder:

Lead incident
    Documentation
        Connecting element

        Second incident
            Documentation
            Connecting element

            Third incident
            Documentation

                Summary of other facts
                End of story

The length of such a story can be calculated in advance by limiting the number of news ideas that are selected for development and using only the most essential documentation for each (i.e., attributing to known sources, using quotes, getting eyewitness accounts). Anything worth mentioning that is left over goes into the summary at the end.

There isn't anything very rigid about this format. It won't be found in any handy set of tables, like chi square values, and nobody is going to stand over a writer's terminal and proclaim, "For this story, use a single-incident lead." The writer makes such a determination in a few seconds before beginning the story without consulting anybody. What the city desk gives him or her is a space estimate, by which everybody is bound.

Story of a Missing Child   Steve Fry, who reports on law enforcement for the *Topeka Capital-Journal*, used this simple, basic format in a story about a missing child. He had three purposes in mind: to write about the child, the progress of the investigation and the detective who was handling the case.

Fry summarized his own concept of the story:

> Besides being brought up to date on the search for the missing girl, Jackie Hay, the *Capital-Journal*'s readers learned of the frustration detectives felt in their inability to develop concrete leads about the girl's disappearance. Many readers, I think, feel that any crime or disappearance can be solved if investigators work hard enough and use sophisticated gadgetry to find and analyze the evidence. The public needs to be told that not all crimes are resolved.
>
> With this story, too, readers got a glimpse of the man leading the search and learned that missing children are particularly difficult to find.

This was the story:

By Steve Fry

Lead incident: child missing

Telephones in the Topeka police missing-persons unit rang constantly Wednesday as citizens suggested places where investigators should look for Jackie F. Hay, the five-year-old Topeka girl who disappeared five days ago.

Documentation for lead incident

Detectives patiently listened and occasionally jotted down the location of a house or landmark. Most were citizens asking whether police had checked this abandoned house or that creek. Some identified themselves as psychics who envisioned a landmark that might lead police to the child. So far, none has provided any solid information in the case.

Jackie, the daughter of Mr. and Mrs. Olen Hay, 3124 Colfax, was reported missing at 4:40 p.m. last Saturday. She had been playing with friends at Colfax and Golf Park. Police questioned one man in connection with the disappearance, but he was released Saturday.

Second incident: pursuit of a promising tip

Following a tip that appeared to be more promising than others, about 20 off-duty officers searched vainly in several fields behind K-Mart, 240 E. 29th, Wednesday afternoon. Earlier, Fire Department inspectors had returned to search a fire-damaged house at 2710 Cunningham but found nothing.

Documentation of second incident: child's friends quizzed

Police questioning of the girl's playmates, massive searches by volunteers near the Hay home and aid from psychics have turned up nothing. The lack of a recent photograph has been a problem for police.

Third incident: the detective speaks

When last seen, the girl was clad in a white, ruffled, cotton midriff top and light blue cotton pants. She is three feet one inch tall, has blue eyes and blond hair cut in Dutch boy style.

Notes and reports dealing with the search were scattered over the desk of Detective Sgt. Bill Beightel, the investigator leading the search for Jackie. Beightel has handled eight to 10 missing persons cases since being assigned to the unit.

Documentation of third incident: the interview

"There's always a lot more emotion and frustration in a case connected with a child," he said. "It becomes a personal drain on you."

He said the disappearance of the Hay girl still is classified as an investigation, explaining, "You can't call it a crime until you have some evidence. When a child has disappeared, then the only recourse you have is to seek out acquaintances of the child and look for leads that way. But children just don't communicate on the same level that we do. Their attention to detail isn't nearly that of an adult.

"I'm going to do anything that will get Jackie back."

Fry's story yielded one small result. A recent picture of the missing girl was found, but for a long time nothing more was learned about what had happened to her. As the reporter had said, not all such cases are solved.

Multiple-Incident Leads

The story with several angles that must be featured high in the lead, with each being documented in turn, becomes a fairly complicated matter to organize. Once again, the selection of news ideas that are to be featured is the key to the amount of space that will be required. This type of organization is more akin to the inverted pyramid, but it cannot be bitten from the bottom as recklessly as that old sponge for printer's ink.

This is generally the organization scheme for a multiple-incident lead, when writers have the time to figure out exactly how they want to construct it. Assuming three major news ideas must be included near the top of the story, with proper connectives between them and the documentation that follows, the ladder would look like this:

Lead incident
    Second lead incident
        Third lead incident
            Connecting paragraph, usually a high quote
                Documentation for lead incident
                    Connecting clause or sentence
                        Documentation for second lead incident
                            Connecting clause or sentence
                                Documentation for third lead incident
                                Other details, summarized

If each major news idea is easy to explain, the three top incidents may be summarized in one paragraph each. This is often not possible, and two or more paragraphs may be required to give the highlights of each news idea. It is likely that a key quotation, another paragraph of importance, or some other part of the documentation may have to be placed high in the story to call it immediately to the readers' attention.

This is the fundamental reason for difficulties in estimating the length of leads for news stories. Some may be a few sentences, others will take 500 words and sometimes more. It all depends on the complexity of the story and the skill of the writer.

A multiple-incident lead can easily be messed up. A writer who ignores connectives (or bridges, as some call them) can butcher an important news account. Equally dangerous is the writer who omits a necessary fact in the lead, which transforms the whole business into mud. To make certain that nothing of importance is omitted, some writers circle or number important points in their notes and cross them off as they cover each one. Others, who have more time, set down a series of slugs (each a word or two) denoting the way the story is to be organized and check each one off as it is handled.

This is the essential point to be remembered: Some scheme, some plan, some design does have to be kept in mind as the piece develops and the transitional material must be inserted as the story weaves from one phase to another.

The temptation of inexperienced writers, confronted with this kind of a problem, is to write involved sentences in an effort to glue their paragraphs together. It is disastrous to yield to this kind of complication. There is no necessity for it. Whether the facts are complicated or not, simplicity and clarity remain the essential ingredients of good writing.

To go to the other extreme and write block paragraphs can be just as disastrous. What comes up on the VDT then is little more than a series of unconnected bulletins. They can be scrambled and rearranged and they'll still be block paragraphs, having little or no relation to one another.

There is no mystery about the use of transitional phrases, clauses or sentences. Sometimes a single word will do. The artful writer, who has a feel for words, can put together a story with such skill that the transitions will seem entirely natural and an intrinsic part of the process of telling the news.

A Multiple-Incident Story   Here is a simple but well-told account of the historic manner in which Sandra D. O'Connor became the first woman member of the United States Supreme Court, published in the *Washington Post* on September 26, 1981:

By Fred Barbash

Lead incident: first woman joins the high court	Sandra D. O'Connor became an associate justice of the Supreme Court yesterday, the first woman in U.S. history to bear that title.
Second incident: O'Connor takes the oath	Chief Justice Warren E. Burger administered the constitutional oath of office at 2:16 p.m. before about 400 dignitaries and friends of the O'Connor family who packed the mammoth Supreme Court chamber.

Third incident: She is seated in the Court	"Justice O'Connor, welcome," Burger said simply. Then, after being helped into her black judge's robe, O'Connor took the chair assigned to her by seniority, the one on the end of the bench to Burger's extreme left. Sitting next to her was her Stanford law school classmate, Justice William H. Rehnquist.
Transition: O'Connor's reaction	From the raised bench, where no woman has sat in the 191-year history of the Supreme Court, she smiled down on President Reagan just below her.
Lead incident detail: the 102nd justice and the youngest	O'Connor is the 102nd justice and the first appointment to the court by Reagan. At 51, she is the youngest member of the court, which has five justices over 70. Her first public appearance at the court came at noon yesterday. She and Burger, his snow-white hair glistening in the sun, descended the front steps to pose for pictures. Burger clutched her arm and commented to reporters, "You've never seen me with a better-looking justice."
Second incident detail: the formalities and the first oath	O'Connor's husband, three sons and mother and father joined them on the court plaza for the pictures. She shouted to a friend to take pictures of the photographers for her scrapbook. She then went inside to take her first oath of the day, the "judicial oath," which calls upon her to "do equal right to the poor and the rich" in the privacy of Burger's chambers.
Third incident detail: she takes her seat and is sworn in	Shortly after 2 p.m., Supreme Court Chief Clerk Alexander Stevas escorted her into the silent but jammed Supreme Court chamber, where she sat alone in a chair used by Chief Justice John Marshall in the 19th century. Attorney General William French Smith presented her to the eight other justices. Placing her left hand on a Bible and raising her right hand, she took the constitutional oath, swearing that she will "well and faithfully discharge the duties of the office on which I am about to enter, so help me God."

A Different Type of Story

When the principal facts of a story are known and the writer has the time to try something different, the result can be a welcome deviation from routine. Here, for example, is the way a straight news writer would handle what appeared to him to be a clergyman's death from natural causes:

> A clergyman who was falsely accused of kidnapping two children at gunpoint died today of a heart attack at a police station.

This is a story that cries out for a feeling of human sympathy, of originality, of compassion. When Tom Fitzpatrick of the *Chicago Sun-Times* assembled the facts, this is how he wrote it:

Setting the scene   The well-worn Bible was on the living room table, still open to the passage that the Rev. James Jackson had been reading when the knock came at the door.

His glasses were still on the table, too, right where Mr. Jackson had placed them as he got up to greet the policemen and the 7-year-old boys who would cause his death.

Developing the main character   Mr. Jackson was 62 years old and the pastor of St. Luke's Community Church, which holds its services in the Washington Park YMCA at 50th and Indiana.

He had done so much work with the young people in his neighborhood that it wasn't surprising that the boys would know that Mr. Jackson lived on the third floor of the old building at 4550 S. Cottage Grove and that he drove a black car.

"He was such a wonderful man, my grandfather was," the young girl was saying now.

Mrs. Olivia Williams, 27, was sitting in the same chair her grandfather always used when reading. It is near the window and it offered him the opportunity to look at the passing cars on Cottage Grove when his eyes grew tired from reading.

"I keep thinking that this is some awful dream," Mrs. Williams said now. "I keep thinking maybe I'll wake up and it won't be true."

But it is true that Mr. Jackson is dead, and on Wednesday afternoon his widow got on a bus and went downtown to buy some new clothes to wear to his funeral, which will be held Saturday.

The tragedy, normally the lead   Mr. Jackson died Monday after suffering a heart attack while being questioned in the brand-new police building at 51st and Wentworth.

He had been taken into custody after the two youngsters told police that he had kidnapped them at gun point and forced them into his home.

"But I haven't been out of the house all day," Mr. Jackson pleaded when the boys made the charge. "Ask my wife and sister. They've been with me all the time."

The two women pleaded with the police but it was to no avail.

Documentation of the lead   The mothers of the two boys were with the police at the time and they kept shouting terrible things at Mr. Jackson and demanding that the police "get to the bottom of this thing."

"But I've never even seen these two boys before," Mr. Jackson said over and over again. "I don't even know them. I've never held a gun in my hand in my whole life and I certainly don't even have one."

Details of the arrest   "Sorry," said one of the police officers. "You'll have to come down to the station. Get your hat and coat."

Mr. Jackson was distraught. There was nothing he could do but follow orders. He was under arrest.

At the station, the mothers signed complaints charging Mr. Jackson with illegal restraint and he was taken into a small room for more questioning.

"I don't even like to think about it," Sgt. Sam Babich said Wednesday. "It was just an awful thing. Those kids fingered him and there was nothing else we could do.

"They picked out his car and they knew where he lived and they told a pretty convincing story."

It was while Mr. Jackson was attempting to refute this "pretty convincing story" that he suffered the heart attack. The police rushed him to Provident Hospital but there was nothing anyone could do.

The climax   Oh, yes, there was one thing. When the boy who had been making most of the charges heard that Mr. Jackson was dead, he did what he could.

"I think we'd better tell you we weren't really telling the truth," the youngster said. "Rev. Jackson never did anything to us. We just made up the story because we ditched school and we had to have a good excuse."

Mr. Jackson's wife was in the police station when the 7-year-olds and their parents emerged from an interrogation room and headed for the door. There were tears in her eyes but Mrs. Jackson spoke with great control

Conclusion   "Son," she said to the boy who had done most of the talking, "whatever you do, as long as God gives you life, don't ever tell another lie. You told a lie today and it cost a good man his life."

The effectiveness of the piece depends almost entirely on the manner in which it is organized, once the anecdotal approach catches the reader's attention. But even tight and logical organization would not suffice, were it not for the neat manner in which each part of the story is joined to the next without artifice or strain. The writer's reportorial eye for color, detail and nuances of speech thus turned what might have been a routine story into an interesting and dramatic narrative.

This is the kind of thing experienced writers put together without thinking too much about detailed organization or fussing about artistry. Having had to learn how through years of practice, they do what comes naturally.

● Short Takes

These are some of the principal problems of news writing and how to learn to handle them:

- Every journalist must contend with the pressures of time and space. Some never feel comfortable with them. Those who do learn with experience how to make necessary adjustments without sacrificing their skill or style.
- There is an art to writing a good "short" or "brite." However, it doesn't help much to labor over them. The writer either develops an idea quickly for such

stories, or settles for a brief, professional account. The point is never to over-write or overdramatize a piece that is at best worth only a few lines of type.

- Almost anything can be made interesting if writers have the time, skill and idea for the job. That goes for stories about personalities and anniversaries, places and things, investigations and backgrounders and all the other facets of modern journalism.
- Every writing assignment, large or small, is worth all the trouble it takes to do it well. That is the professional's view of journalism. Careless handling of a story is almost always an invitation to disaster for it invites error and, sometimes, a libel suit.
- Originality nearly always pays off. Telling a story through dialogue, through anecdotes, through a central personality, all have their place in journalism. The trick is to know when to use them and that, too, comes with experience.
- The way different types of leads are handled frequently determines how a story is to be organized. There are set ways of doing this, some derived from the inverted pyramid form of organization (main fact first, others thereafter in diminishing order of importance). When the facts and time permit, different ways to tell the story often prove to be effective.
- One of the most familiar forms for important stories, the single-incident lead, may be used when the main facts can be told in sequence. Thus, the lead will be based on the main incident with documentation, followed in turn by others.
- The more complicated news stories generally fall into the pattern set by multiple-incident leads. The principal facts, in this format, are clustered in a lead of several hundred words, with documentation for each following in the body of the story.
- All forms of news organization depend heavily on the use of transitions to bind the separate parts of a story together. They cannot be ignored.
- For some stories with intense human appeal, normal organizational patterns can be discarded. The rule then is: Get out of the way of the story and let it tell itself.

CHAPTER 8

Writing Obituaries

Each life is different. Each obituary, therefore, should be different. But getting at the facts is not always a simple matter. Nor is an obituary always easy to write, particularly when death has occurred through accident or natural calamity rather than behind the drawn curtains of a sorrowful home or in a carefully sanitized hospital room.

Generally, the death that is more-or-less anticipated is written for an obit column or page except when the person is of such prominence as to merit Page 1 and the TV evening news. The accidental death, however, often is run in the news columns outside the space set aside for the formal obits plus obit advertising.

Biography on Deadline

There are so many automobile accidents that the police seldom do more than record the barest and most necessary details for their records. If a reporter wants a story, he or she either has to know the victim or stumble across a vagrant fact that points to a tangle of circumstances worth researching. In any event, when the facts are assembled, the writing nearly always amounts to the first draft of a biography done under deadline pressure.

Death on a Country Highway   Anita Miller, a young reporter for the *Topeka Capital-Journal*, came across a note during her regular routine that Becky Jackson, an 18-year-old girl from a nearby town, had been killed on a Saturday night in a single-car accident on a country highway in Kansas.

That was on a Sunday morning, Anita Miller recalled:

> I remembered that Becky's stepfather had been convicted of the shooting death of her mother and that Becky had been a key witness at the trial.
>
> It triggered interest in me, so I began contacting schoolmates, church friends and others in the small town of Perry who might have known Becky. Finally, I was able to develop information that I thought gave good coverage to an incident that would never have been told had someone not taken the time to look into it.
>
> The story also showed that Becky had been more than a witness at a murder trial, which was the only way our readers knew her. She had been a real person with plans and dreams, but her life ended before she had a chance to fulfill them.

Writing About a Funeral   It was no ordinary funeral Anita Miller covered three days after Becky Jackson's death. For Becky had not been an ordinary person, as the story clearly showed.

By Anita Miller

PERRY—The townspeople of Perry said their goodbyes to Becky Jackson Tuesday afternoon.

Funeral services for the 18-year-old Perry–Lecompton High School senior were held in the Perry United Methodist Church, where services for her mother were held just seven months ago. It was also where Becky had planned to be married on June 5.

Becky was killed in a one-car crash Saturday night on a county road between Lecompton and Perry as she was returning home from a trip to Topeka.

She had been a key witness in October in the murder trial of her father, Arthur Machacek, who was sentenced to life imprisonment Dec. 2 in the shooting death of her mother, Betty Machacek, last May.

The townspeople were overwhelmed by Becky's death. Many grieved and wept, holding onto each other for support. Becky had been one of them. The sadness in the town was as gray as the sky.

"After her mother was killed we all worried about her but she seemed to take it OK," said Jan Crain, a neighbor, friend and mother of one of the pallbearers. Her son, Steven, 18, had gone through school with Becky since fourth grade.

Becky was industrious, happy and insightful, her friends said. Her high school principal, Richard Lauffer, called her a "super kid."

At school she was the editor of the Kaw, the school yearbook, a member of the National Honor Society and Future

Business Leaders of America. She had been a cheerleader. In addition, she was active in her church.

Becky also had worked as a waitress at Walgreen's restaurant in White Lakes for three years until she recently began working at the Topeka Steak House. "She was one of the best," said Jan Valdivia, assistant manager of Walgreen's.

William D. Jackson, her father, said, "She was the greatest there was. I hate to have her remembered because she saw her mother shot eight times."

Friends said Becky was excited about her June 5 marriage to LeRoy Dunn, a Perry boy who is serving in the U.S. Navy in Chicago. He sat beside her father at the funeral.

The accident Saturday night changed everything. According to Kansas Highway Patrol Trooper Dean Riedesel, who investigated the accident, the northbound car Becky was driving was traveling at "excessive speed" when it went off Lecompton Road, the stretch that connects Lecompton and Perry.

When the tragedy occurred, Becky was being followed in another vehicle by a young man, a former classmate, Riedesel said. The youth told the trooper Becky had seemed quite upset and was crying when he spoke to her at an East Topeka convenience store. What had upset her was unknown, Riedesel said.

The classmate asked her if he could drive her home. She declined but asked him to follow her in his vehicle. Just after crossing a bridge over the Kansas River, Becky's car sharply accelerated around a curve and pulled away from the youth, Riedesel said. The youth tried to catch up, saw a cloud of dust from her car leaving the road and discovered the accident. . . .

What distinguishes this story is the careful, detailed reporting and the restrained manner in which it is written. In less professional hands, it could have been a sentimental tale. But Anita Miller is no kin to the sob sisters of another era. The reader's emotions are affected by the facts, not the histrionics of the writer.

Biography for the Millions

Most of the deaths in homes, hospitals, nursing facilities and the like are recorded in paid obituary notices in newspapers. These are often placed by funeral directors on the basis of information on forms filled in by family members. Many smaller newspapers also have longer and more complete forms that are used as the basis for brief obits run in the news columns. The question of which persons' deaths are to be reported as news is always a matter of editorial judgment. It depends largely on the prominence of the person in the community and the public interest in the story of a particular life.

Principal Points in Obits When obits are written for the obit column or obit page, and sometimes for Page 1 in the case of a big news name, they should include the following:

- Name, age, identification by title or position, business, trade, public office or profession.
- Time and place of death, and home address, if it is not the place where death occurred.
- Cause of death, if it can be obtained and verified.
- Principal facts about the subject's life — parents' names, education, highlights of career.
- Survivors. Stylebooks always caution that a man is survived by his wife, not his widow; a woman is survived by her husband, not her widower.
- Funeral arrangements, if available.

For people of great prominence, the circumstances of death are reported in more detail and the persons present at the time of death are noted. Anecdotes, recollections, comments and the like are solicited from friends, business associates and family members. In rare cases, such as the death of Elvis Presley, it may be necessary to interview physicians and others about the cause of death.

Writing a Short Obit The usual obit, which is destined for the obit page, may not cover all the points obtained by a reporter, telephoned in by a family member or friend, or taken from a form sheet. That is because the story must be held to modest length, perhaps 100 to 200 words.

The first thing a writer must always do is to check the source of the information by calling either the funeral director or the home of the subject. There are instances in which false death notices have been deliberately sent to news organizations, either by pranksters or others with more sinister intent. The rule is: Never take a chance on an obit if there is any doubt of its authenticity.

Another rule is never to demean the dead. Crimes or other sensational aspects of their lives that must be recalled should be handled tactfully. Moreover, a woman should not be written about merely as someone's wife, nor should a man be characterized mainly as the husband or ex-husband of a woman of prominence. The children of famous parents, who have spent their lives in the shadow of greatness, are at least entitled in death to be written about as individuals. Of course, mention must be made of all such circumstances but they should not dominate the obit.

Here is a brief obit from the *Register*, a weekly of Yarmouth Port, Massachusetts, which includes most of the essential information:

C. Dwight Perry, 81, of Cummaquid, died August 19 at South Shore Hospital, Weymouth, after a brief illness.

He was a senior master and former teacher at the Fountain Valley School, Colorado Springs, Colo. He was born in Rockland and was graduated from Harvard College in 1921 and taught at several East Coast preparatory schools before he joined the faculty of Fountain Valley in the 1930s. He remained there until his 1976 retirement when he moved to Cape Cod.

Mr. Perry was a member of the Dennis Forum and the Historical Society of Old

Yarmouth. He is survived by his wife, Marcelle; one son, one daughter, one sister and seven grandchildren. Burial was at Spring Lake Cemetery, Rockland.

Doing It Differently A number of newspapers, large and small, have tried to do obits differently. Instead of listing survivors and other details, they emphasize the *stories* of people's lives. The *Los Angeles Times* features nearly a page of such obits. Usually, these obits begin with an observation or an anecdote, a form of delayed lead, and back into the news peg, either the details of the death or the funeral announcement. It takes a bit more thought, a lot more reporting and considerable writing skill to do them.

Death of a Patriarch The deaths of people who live to a great age are often given a good play in the news sections, as witness the following:

NIAGARA FALLS (AP)—Friends say many people never realized how old David P. (Doc) Livingston really was.

Some neighbors recall that back in the 1960s, when he was climbing a ladder one day, he offered to show off his birth certificate. They urged him to stop climbing ladders after reading that he was 104 years old.

And after Livingston died of an apparent heart attack Wednesday at Memorial Medical Center, Coroner James Joyce of Niagara County said he was startled to read records that showed Livingston to be 119 years old.

The records indicate he was born in Charleston, S.C., on June 10, 1862, in the midst of the Civil War.

Friends say he smoked unfiltered cigarettes and chewed tobacco. "And he'd drink anything if it was good," said Inez Caver, his landlady, who said she had known him for 35 years. He prayed and sang a lot and was a member of the New Hope Baptist Church, friends said.

Mrs. Caver said Livingston came to Niagara Falls in 1937 and worked at the Union Carbide plant until the 1940s, when the company learned he was in his 80s and forced him to retire. After that, she said, he became a construction worker and kept working until he was 92. . . .

Some Do's and Don'ts

Many troubling questions arise among young or inexperienced journalists when they are assigned to obit writing. Some of them are easily resolved by following the general policy of the paper. Others are just as vexing to the editor and publisher of the paper.

Criminal Records One of the most frequent puzzlers is what should be done about recalling a criminal record, early in life, of a citizen who otherwise has led a blameless career.

Most papers have a policy on such things, but the policy can change with circumstances and the person who is involved.

In the death of Harry Golden, the best-selling author, most obits recalled that he had been convicted as a young man in connection with a fraud case. Golden himself never tried to conceal it, although it must have been a source of embarrassment to him.

People who were known to be alcoholics, former drug addicts and former mental-hospital patients have achieved prominence despite their failings. In their obits in metropolitan newspapers, these facets of their lives were usually recalled. But sometimes, when nothing derogatory had ever been written about them, the obit writer looked the other way with — and sometimes without — the permission of editors.

Embarrassing Details Then there is the perennial argument over what to do when an important person dies under circumstances that raise questions, to say the least.

For example, when Nelson A. Rockefeller died in New York City, a young woman was with him and explained she had been an office assistant. However, she had called in a girlfriend before notifying the authorities.

Because it had happened to a Rockefeller — and a Rockefeller who had been governor of New York and vice president of the United States — the story was played, in fact overplayed, from coast to coast.

But when President Franklin D. Roosevelt died at Warm Springs, Georgia, the world did not know for many years thereafter that a woman artist and a former secretary of Mrs. Roosevelt's, Lucy Rutherford, had been visiting him at the time.

Once the story was published in *Life* magazine by Jonathan Daniels, who had been the White House press secretary under FDR, some Washington correspondents contended that they had known it all along and hadn't written it. The same protection was given to President John F. Kennedy in some of his private relationships until a few young women, after his assassination, told their stories.

Suppressing Causes of Death Usually, on large newspapers and small ones, causes of death are published when available, but no special effort is made to invade a family's privacy if no announcement is made. The exception, of course, comes when suspicious circumstances are involved in the death.

Neither physicians nor bereaved families like to issue statements that a loved one's death was attributed to a cause that might imply alcoholism or drug abuse. And most newspapers respect their wishes. But when someone of the prominence of Elvis Presley, William Holden or John Belushi dies and the cause of death is blurred, the news media have no choice other than to investigate.

It's different on country weeklies. There, when something tragic happens, everybody knows about it before the paper comes out, and editors know they can be bitterly criticized for giving undue publicity to the cause of death.

For example, a country editor learned of a tragic incident in which a father, backing his car out of his garage, killed his four-year-old daughter, who had run from their home to be with him. In using the story, the editor wrote that the little girl had died in an unspecified accident.

"What good would it do," he asked, "if I used the whole story and in effect pilloried the father? I didn't do it then and I wouldn't do it if it had happened today."

Helping Bereaved Families Sometimes bereaved families will ask newspapers to omit obituaries for one of their number. This often happens in the case of a suicide, particularly when the person involved has never before figured in the news. When such things are published in large cities, some families feel a sense of shame and do not understand why their personal tragedy should be publicized.

It all depends on the editor at the city or metropolitan desk. The request may be granted, or the editor may decide that the affair must be published, if only in a few lines, just to show that the paper plays no favorites. It's not the kind of thing over which an editorial conference is called.

Of much less importance is the more familiar request, if an obit is being written, to omit flowers but send contributions to a specified charity or religious organization. Sometimes, a sentence to that effect is included; sometimes, too, it is cut out on the copy desk.

Advance Obits

Wire services, large newspapers and other news organizations maintain hundreds of obits of prominent people, and update them from time to time, for use as reference material, features or when death occurs. A few even send out reporters to interview such subjects for obituary material, to be held for later use.

The *Nashville Tennessean* is reputed to be the first newspaper to do this. On the national and international level, the *New York Times* has also done "live" reporting for obits. A former chief obit writer for the *Times*, Alden Whitman, once interviewed C. P. Snow, the British novelist, who good-humoredly called the reporter a "ghoul." To which Whitman replied, "The eye of the beholder in this, as in other matters, is where ghoulishness is perceived — and resides."

● Short Takes

These are the main points to remember in writing obituaries:

- No set of facts for an obit should be taken for granted. First of all, the death should be verified carefully. Next, all available records should be checked to make certain that the material in hand is correct. If there is any doubt whatever, the obit should be withheld pending further checking.
- Whether death came by accidental means or illness, the story should be researched by making calls to those who knew the subject well—friends, business associates, family if available. In the case of someone of prominence, no angle should be overlooked.
- While most obits and funerals are written about in a formal style, there is no rule that binds a journalist to tradition if the story warrants more extended treatment.
- Always check names, ages, addresses, identities of survivors, funeral arrangements and other details. Bereaved families and even official records are fallible, and mistakes can easily be made if a reporter is not careful.

- Instead of writing a blueprint second-day angle on an obit, once it is published, it is worth considering whether a human-interest story about the subject might be more fitting.
- The use of a criminal record or other embarrassing details in an obit about a person of prominence in the community depends in part on circumstances and in part on the paper's policy. In any event, the facts should be established, whether or not it is decided to use them.
- No writer should suppress details, such as the cause of death, unless there is a consultation with the editor in charge.

CHAPTER 9

Writing Human Interest Stories

The rainbow of human interest arches over the entire field of journalism today. Almost anything can be turned into an interesting feature involving the human condition if the writer knows how. A well-researched, brightly written story that appeals to people is one of the essential ingredients of the modern newspaper.

"Examples," Vladimir Nabokov once said, "are the stained glass windows of the mind." They are also the basis for any story involving human interest.

Making a Story Come Alive

Basically, what innovative writers try to do is to apply the feature touch to otherwise dull and sometimes difficult news stories that generally are handled in traditional style. The human interest patterns, the elements that have a special appeal to people, are fitted into what was once considered to be straight news, deadpanned from beginning to end.

A Difficult Subject Don Olesen of the *Milwaukee Journal*'s "Insight" section drew a difficult assignment for one of his Sunday stories. As he put it:

> How do you tell a reader about something that can't be seen, smelled or touched? How do you communicate concern for the possible effects of that

something—effects that may not be felt in our natural world for years, a generation or even longer?

That, briefly, was the problem I faced in assembling and writing "Facing the Acid Truth," an article about the effects of acid rain on Wisconsin's lakes, trees, crops and wildlife.

Olesen had a personal problem, too. His background in science was limited; consequently, he had a lot of catch-up reading to do before he could translate highly technical terms into words that meant something to his readers. He also had to relate the acid rain problem to the daily lives of people in Wisconsin without, to use his own terms, "hype or overdramatization." He went on:

I faced still another hurdle. Although the ill effects of acid rain have been demonstrated amply in other regions, the impact has yet to be proved in Wisconsin. Under the circumstances, no honest writer could throw paragraphs of impending doom at his readers by way of grabbing their lapels and their attention.

I have tackled some tough assignments during more than three decades of newspaper writing. This, by far, was the toughest.

Solving a Writing Problem   Here, in essential part, is the way Olesen solved his writing problem at the beginning of his long and important article:*

By Don Olesen

You can't see it, smell it or feel it. Its effects, if any, are slow to appear and unbelievably subtle. Yet, the unnatural phenomenon called "acid rain" has touched and twitched a public nerve like no other environmental concern in recent years.

Even the name sounds ominous. The rain, our friend, no longer is benign. Here is an international concern; a national concern; Wisconsin's concern.

Precipitation sampled in northern Wisconsin is at least 10 times more acid than normal. Still, despite the furor, acid rain has no proven impact—yet—on assets dear to Wisconsin and its dollar-dropping visitors: our lakes, forests, fields or fish.

In fact, preliminary findings of one recent study seem to show that a glitter of selected northern Wisconsin lakes are somewhat *less* acidic than they were a half century ago.

Almost nobody claims the stuff is good for you or for the plant and animal community that shares our world. Still, here and there, you do find acid rain apologists. Nothing about acid rain is predictable. Except for the fact that it's here. . . .

Up there in the sky, in a process still not fully understood

---

*pH, literally hydrogen power, is the symbol for acid or alkaline concentration. pH 7, the value for distilled water, is neutral. pH from 0–7 indicates acidity, from 7–14 alkalinity. Mussels die at pH 6, mayflies and smallmouth bass at 5.5, lake trout and yellow perch at 4.5. The problem is not unique to the United States.

by scientists, gases react with sunlight and other chemicals to form sulfates and nitrates, which then combine with moisture to form mild solutions of sulfuric and nitric acids. Every time it rains—it rains acid. . . .

Lloyd (Duke) Andrews props one foot against the trailer of a small outboard boat, one of the fleet used by the Department of Natural Resources for fish research. It is a glowing day in Oneida County, a day to put you in mind of a lazy fishing trip.

Andrews is talking about acid rain. He's a DNR fishery biologist at the Woodruff area headquarters.

During his 20 years of resource work, he says, he doesn't recall such a public reaction to an environmental issue—except perhaps to DDT during the '60s. Upwards of one-third of the mail he sees here concerns acid rain. Most of it comes from lake property owners, who fear it will ruin their fishing and their property values.

"People are concerned, scared," Andrews says. "There's a lot of emotionalism in it."

These days in the North Woods, it's not unusual for city folks shopping for lakeside property to ask the real estate agent, "Hey, what's the pH of that lake?"

Scary headlines appear. "Acid Rain Could Peril Tourism," reads one in the Milwaukee Journal. "Verify Acid Rain Is Hurting Lakes," the Vilas County News Review declared. . . .

Yet, as Andrews sees it, time and research are needed to pinpoint the problem. Man isn't always the villain. In Wisconsin, acid bog lakes have been with us a long, long time.

"The dinosaurs came and went," he says, "and we weren't here to screw it up." . . .

As the article continued, the writer viewed acid rain through the eyes of Dick Freeman, a state forest-fire-control and acid-rain-testing official; Robert Martini, a state water-quality specialist; John Magnuson, a university scientist, and numerous others.

"Personalizing" a Story   What Olesen did was what experienced writers in journalism nearly always do with abstruse subjects they must explain to a mass audience. They "personalize" them. They tell them through the eyes of the people who are directly involved in the project, the issue, the crisis.

This serves to fit the matter into an understandable context.

Stories About People

In most stories about people, one of the first things a writer has to do is to find a handle, as the old newsroom expression goes. Usually that involves answering the nagging question "Why should I write about this person?" Or, to put it another way, "Why should anybody want to read about this person?"

The News Angle   The easiest answer, of course, is that the person is in the news. For example, a hard-working superintendent of a large office building would be a most unlikely subject for a story. But let him win millions in a lottery and the world will come clamoring to his door. Or consider the case of a dry-as-dust professor of physics engaged in an abstruse laboratory experiment that even his colleagues do not understand. Sorry, no story. However, when the news breaks that he has been awarded $500,000 by a scientific foundation, everybody wants to know how he did it.

The news can make overnight folk heroes out of quite ordinary people. It can, by unhappy chance, create a few villains as well.

There is a very special art to writing about people. Some have it, others do not. A few, by doing a lot of reading and writing and rewriting stories, can develop it. Here is a sketch from life, a vignette that is the very basis for most stories about people.

Portrait of an Indian   John R. Camp of the *St. Paul Pioneer Press* was strongly attracted to Indian people when he moved to the Midwest. For a while, he lived among them. Then he persuaded his paper to let him do an in-depth study of Indian life. This is his classic word portrait of The Man Who Stands in Two Places, his Ojibway name, whose white name was Bill Chatfield:

> The Man Who Stands in Two Places is getting old.
> Seventy-four years are printed in his face. Wrinkle lines have eroded into small canyons cutting across his forehead, down the sides of his nose, around his mouth. His left eyelid flutters over an empty socket: the eye was cut out when it went blind and began giving him pain. It no longer hurts, but now his good eye waters constantly, and he dabs at it with a paper napkin. He has coarse hair twisted into a defiant braid more gray than black, a braid the color of the granite in Confederate war monuments and Yankee tombstones.
> Around his neck he wears a bead totem.
> The Man Who Stands in Two Places is so much an Indian, so much Leech Lake Ojibway, that he might have had his profile hammered on a nickel; so Indian that his speech is a disappointment—instead of the guttural movie-Indian pidgin, he rolls out the long mellifluous vowels of Swedish-settler English. . . .
> The Man Who Stands in Two Places is a serious human being. He speaks for the record: "The Ojibway name for a white man is *Jomokomon Eeshish*, dirty old butcher knife. . . ."

The handle in this case is the difference between the Indian and the white man. The Man Who Stands in Two Places emphasizes the contrast.

A Mother for the Retarded   Vantrease Russell is the founder of the first nonprofit institution in Orange County, Florida, for brain-damaged children. She displayed her Certificate No. 1, issued on November 13, 1951, when a reporter for the *Orlando Sentinel Star* visited the Russell Home more than 30 years later. This is how the reporter, Michelle Naspinski, saw her:

Every night after making the rounds, the white-haired woman shuffles in her slippers to the living room, where she opens a pull-out couch into a bed.

She lies on a thin, sagging mattress and closes her eyes, sleeping lightly, so that she will hear if anyone awakens during the night.

She has been performing this routine since 1951, when she officially turned her rural Orlando home, set on a dirt road off Holden Avenue, into an institution for the mentally retarded. . . .

The Inner Story   Some of the most fascinating stories about people are based on an account of their motivation. As one reporter put it, "I want to know what makes them tick." Accounts of courage and hope and self-sacrifice, of love and devotion, of martial ardor and persistence and eternal friendship invariably create a strong response among readers and viewers.

A Little Boy's Courage   One of the most remarkable stories in recent years began in a small California town where a little boy, born without arms and with stubby, partially formed legs, was selected as a Poster Boy for the March of Dimes. His name was Marco Cordova, but to many who later read about him and saw him on national television, he was Marco the Magnificent. Everybody in Watsonville loves him. Lyn Bailey of the *Watsonville Register-Pajaronian*, who wrote the first of many stories about him, says:

> In the three years I have written for the Watsonville paper, I have never come across a more remarkable young man. He is extremely self-confident and intelligent. He has adapted to his severe physical disability in a way that shows much courage and strength for such a little boy.
>
> Writing about Marco was a challenge. What I tried to do was to bring out his individual characteristics and the manner in which he has learned to cope with his disability on an everyday basis.
>
> In the story that follows, many of the questions were directed toward his mother, Vicki Cordova, who was very helpful in explaining the problems she had encountered in dealing with her son's handicap.
>
> Marco mostly talked about his animals and their family ranch and how he enjoyed riding the horses after school.

Marco's Story   This is Marco's story. It was written originally for the family page, but it attracted attention far beyond that:

By Lyn Bailey

"Marco, come into the living room and show Grandpa your new shirt," Vicki Cordova called to her son.

Marco yelled back that he couldn't find his shoes, then proceeded down the hallway. When the four-year-old boy entered the living room, his smile warmed the room, and attention was focused on his new shirt with the greeting, "Nanu Nanu," of television's spaceman, Mork.

Lyn Bailey, reporter for the *Watsonville* (California) Register-Pajaronian, with Marco the Magnificent. This picture was taken just after Mrs. Bailey had given birth to her own first child. (Copyright, 1982, the *Watsonville Register-Pajaronian*. Used by permission.)

You'd never know from Marco's eyes and smile that he is handicapped.

He was born without arms and with legs that are only partially formed. "He has always been a friendly little boy and loves to meet people, especially men," said Marco's mother, a bus driver for the Pajaro Valley School District. His father is a horseshoer and rancher.

The little, brown-eyed boy has adjusted amazingly to his handicap and lives his life with great determination. His mother believes the deformity was caused by a drug taken during early pregnancy to relieve her rheumatoid arthritis.

Because of Marco's delightful personality and his gift of getting along with others, he has been chosen as the Poster Boy for the March of Dimes in the Monterey Bay District.

In last year's March of Dimes Walkathon, Marco drove his battery-operated four-wheel cart, which he manipulates with his toes. He uses the cart for long distances, but usually he prefers to walk. One aid he isn't particularly fond of is the mechanical arms he is learning to use at Duncan Holbert School for the Handicapped.

"He's so independent. He doesn't want any help if he thinks he can do it himself," said Marco's grandfather, Vic Amato.

When Marco is eating, he gets so frustrated using his artificial arms that he insists on using his toes, his grandfather said. The boy has learned to do just about everything with his toes, including brushing his teeth and combing his hair.

His parents stress, however, that he must learn how to use his artificial arms in public places.

Pride and self-confidence, given from a loving family, allow Marco to be himself. "Other people don't bother me," he says.

His mother explained that when other children ask Marco why he doesn't have any arms, he just stands up and looks them straight in the eye and says something like, "I was born like that," or "I left them home for now."

Marco and his brother, Tony, 11, have shared some great times at their parents' ranch on Mt. Madonna Road. The 20 acres—with horses, chickens, pigs, dogs and cats—keep the boys occupied. There is even time for imaginary games.

A favorite game is to pretend that they're bull-riding. Marco climbs on Tony's back, holds on with his feet and has the time of his life trying to hang on as Tony bucks. Marco also spends hours riding around the ranch on his imaginary motorcycle, with his red, white and blue helmet, his mother says.

Other playtime favorites are riding his skateboard, back flips off the couch, dancing and imitating "The Fonz" and members of the "Kiss" band.

"Little things in life seem to make Marco happy," his

mother says. "He is so appreciative when he can spend happy times with others."

It wasn't really necessary to find a handle for the story about Marco, even though the announcement of his Poster Boy selection was the obvious reason for it. The *inner story*—the demonstration of his courage and determination and his love for people—is so universal that it needs no peg, no excuse, for the telling.

This is the kind of feature that has transformed the old newspaper family page (now called the family living page or the life-style section) into something worth reading. It was once a mere receptacle for press-agentry about flour companies, dress designers and interior decorators. In its reincarnation on better newspapers, it has become more realistic and often deals with such once-taboo issues as divorce, homosexuality and the handicapped. Stories like the one about Marco have played an important part in the change.

The General Feature Story

General stories about people take many forms. One of the most popular is the column of briefs, mostly rewritten from wire services, about people of prominence. The profile, often called man- or woman-in-the-news, is another. Then there are all kinds of human interest features, ranging from snake-charmers to elderly artists, curious sentences by experimental judges to the woes of opera stars. Much of it makes for interesting reading.

Tracking down a Feature   Stories based on human interest crop up in unexpected places. Sylvia Moreno of *Newsday*, the Long Island daily, came across a good one by answering an ad for a surrogate mother, placed in her own paper. She said:

> I wasn't at all sure the advertiser would reply to a request for a story. But he did, thanked me for my interest but refused to consent to an interview. Although I wanted to delve into the details of his personal plight, I told him the article would discuss the surrogate parenthood issue as a whole. A week later, he called back and agreed to an interview on the basis that his and his wife's names would not be used.
>
> I was able, through the story, to discuss a nationwide trend and highlight the issue by portraying the personal trauma of a couple obsessed with the wife's infertility and their desire to have a child. Although not every couple in search of a surrogate mother launches a worldwide search, many couples generally experience the same problems, indecision and emotional torment.

Handling an Unusual Story   The writer had more that the usual problems in handling this story. It was sensitive in the extreme. Improperly done, it could have given offense and aroused criticism over the intrusion of a reporter into

Sylvia Moreno, a reporter for *Newsday*, the Long Island daily, developed a sensitive story about surrogate mothers by following up a classified advertisement. (Copyright, *Newsday*. Used by permission.)

a highly private matter. But Moreno, with the support of her editors, was able to do the story justice. Here is the heart of the matter, as she wrote it:

By Sylvia Moreno

Separated by thousands of miles, they live day to day on the thread of hope that the right woman will come forward and volunteer to bear their child.

He gave up his job as an executive to carry their quest around the world. Ensconced in his brother's neat home on one of the pleasant, tree-lined streets in Hicksville, L.I., the 51-year-old husband patiently awaits replies to his newspaper ad for a surrogate mother and writes his wife almost daily.

"As long as I am here, she has hope," he says.

His wife, a 42-year-old executive secretary for an international organization in a Southeast Asian capital, busies herself with her work and her "chapel." It's just a corner in a room in the couple's home, but it contains clusters of statues of deities and pictures of modern-day prophets who never answered her prayers for a child.

The couple offers $10,000, room and board, career training and a monthly allowance to the surrogate if she chooses to spend the term of her pregnancy with them overseas. If she chooses to stay in the U.S., she will receive a monthly stipend. In either case, all medical and insurance bills up to six weeks after delivery will be paid.

They are seeking a married or single woman from 21 to 30 with Rh-negative blood, who has had at least one child and preferable is of Jewish/Spanish ancestry, like the wife.

They are a dramatic example of the many childless couples who are increasingly turning to surrogate pregnancy— the latest and, to date, the most controversial use of artificial insemination. For the modern phenomenon of professional baby-making has become embroiled in ethical, medical and legal controversies.

Like many social and technological developments, the practice of surrogate motherhood has preceded the law.

"I admire tremendously those couples who embark on this journey because it is so perilous and yet they're willing to go ahead with it," says Jerry Simon Chasen, a Manhattan attorney who researched the issue for two New York couples exploring the possibility of hiring surrogate mothers. "It's legally dangerous. Our clients got advice telling them that we can't tell you the definitive answer."

Most cases follow the same pattern. After a contract is signed and a fee agreed upon, the surrogate is inseminated with the husband's sperm. When the baby is born, the woman turns it over to the couple for adoption.

But there are complications. The most recent challenge to the procedure—the right of a surrogate mother to back out of a baby-by-contract deal—occurred in California. Other challenges are pending elsewhere, including the legality of paying a woman to have a baby. In the meantime, legal and medical circles continue to research the issue. . . .

Is this a matter of buying or selling a child? Does anybody have the right to contract for somebody else's baby before it is born? Suppose something happens and the child turns out to be deformed? Who sues whom? The questions raised by this story are endless and it will be a long time before they are answered. In the interim, many more such features will be researched and written.

The Surprise Feature   Reporters who attend what they believe will be a cut-and-dried court sentencing procedure are sometimes surprised. There was once a judge in Knoxville, Tennessee, who required speeders who also were first offenders to write a long essay on reckless driving and its perils and read it to an organized group—a club or class—of not less than 100 people. To comply, and present adequate proof, was to qualify for a suspended sentence. To refuse meant a jail sentence and a $50 fine. Except for one balky college boy, all the offenders agreed.

There are other surprises in the courts of the land from time to time. One occurred in Cocoa, Florida, when a reporter for *Today*, the local paper, was present. And this is her story:

By Gina Thomas

Timothy Barrett thought his day in court would be followed by 365 days in the slammer. The 19-year-old Titusville man, who pleaded guilty to possession of less than 20 grams of marijuana, found himself on Thursday facing a year in jail, a $1,000 fine and a judge who said he was going to throw the book at him.

Brevard County Judge Larry Johnston meted out the sentence: sixty days' suspended sentence and one year's self-supervised probation.

And there was one more thing.

Barrett must ask 100 people if they know it is illegal to possess marijuana. If they don't know, he must tell them. . . .

Love and Marriage, New Style Almost anything new that bears on love and marriage commands interest among mass audiences. Marriage by computer, for example, is a story that was widely published. This is how it came over the wire:

SUNNYVALE, Calif. (AP)—Bride and bridegroom stand before a computer terminal. Rev. Ron types "RUN WED." And the rites of marriage light the screen of the world's first marrying computer, the latest fad in Silicon Valley.

"HELLO, MY NAME IS REV. APPLE. (Press space bar to continue)," reads the Apple II computer screen. "GROOM, WHAT'S YOUR NAME?"

So far, six couples have exchanged vows via video display terminal. One bride and bridegroom took a printout of the ritual as a souvenir.

"In Silicon Valley, a computer wedding is a very appropriate means of self-expression, since so many people work for computer companies or chip companies," said Reinhard Jaenisch, who likes to be called Rev. Ron.

Silicon Valley is the name given to an area north of San Jose that has become a world center for the production of computers and computer parts.

Jaenisch, 31, is an executive and part-time mail order minister of Universal Life Church Inc., of Modesto. He is also a computer buff.

"I come from a marketing background and when you mix ministry and marketing, this is what you get. Too often, a wedding is a ho-hum affair. But this gets people's attention," he said.

Using an Unnamed Source

Case histories involving real people who are not identified continue to appear regularly in the news media. They are often necessary to illustrate perplexing social problems. Indeed, even on such renowned TV programs as *60 Minutes*, national audiences hear stories of criminals and criminal informants whose identities are at least partially protected because their faces aren't shown.

Writing a Sensitive Story Any story about rape, incest or homosexuality has to be written with a great deal of reserve. This is not so much because of the fear of libel. The equally important matter of good taste is involved, especially if the story appears on Page 1 or, as frequently happens nowadays, in the family living page or life-style pages or section of a newspaper. Sometimes the writer withholds the identity of the source or explains that a pseudonym is being used to protect the person from harm, or another sound reason for allowing confidentiality. It is not only necessary to protect sources in investigative stories. It is equally urgent, sometimes, in human interest pieces.

● Short Takes

Here are the essentials about writing human interest feature stories:

- Difficult stories, such as a piece about acid rain, are best told through the eyes of the people who deal with the phenomenon. This is what is called "personalizing" a story.
- Many human interest stories develop a life of their own. Never begin with a fixed idea, but let the facts point in the direction in which you must go as a writer.
- When a story line changes, follow it to its conclusion before attempting to write. It can take surprising turns.
- Most stories require a handle, a news peg, a reason for writing about a particular person, and it should be worked into the opening paragraphs.
- It always helps to give a word portrait of the subject in vivid terms.
- Writers should show the reader what the person is like through anecdotes, quotes, brief descriptive passages and other familiar devices of journalism. It is always a mistake to say someone is "good" or "bad," "tough" or "easygoing." Actions speak louder than words.
- One of the best methods for hitting off a character is to pile fact on fact, observation on observation, so that the writer sketches a portrait of a personality.
- One of the most fascinating types of human interest, the *inner story* about a person, is based on an examination of his or her motivation. These are stories in the main about people who are driven by strong emotions—love or friendship, hope or self-sacrifice. It takes a lot of good reporting to make these stories come alive, however.
- In doing a *general story* about people, writers must be conscious of special problems that require sensitivity in handling—problems dealing with such aspects as infertility, sexual abuse of children, alcoholism and other ills that afflict humankind in the modern world.
- Any story about a person is useless unless names, ages, addresses and pertinent other facts are checked for accuracy with scrupulous care.

CHAPTER 10

Writing About Disasters

Natural disasters afflict millions of Americans each year. In various sections of the land, people struggle through wintry rain and snowstorms, springtime floods, summer and fall droughts, tornadoes, hurricanes and an occasional earthquake. The plague of accidental and manmade calamities is an unwelcome addition to life in these United States—the automobile and air crashes, the fires, the train and ship collisions and, in more recent years, the threat of a nuclear holocaust.

It falls to the lot of journalists to cover them all, to write about them, talk about them and photograph them, often at considerable risk to themselves.

The Responsibility of Journalists

Nobody profits from a disaster, least of all a newspaper cut off from its advertisers and sometimes from its own plant, or a TV or radio station that gives its time to public service in an emergency.

Reasons for Disaster Coverage It cannot be fairly said that disaster reporting is of particular benefit to the news media. It doesn't sell newspapers. On the contrary, the regular circulation routes of the press are often disrupted in a stricken community. And on TV, the part of the public that lusts for entertainment at all costs often resents looking at scenes of disaster instead.

Why, then, do the news media go to such effort to cover this type of news regardless of risk and cost? Quite simply, it is a part of the tradition of good journalism. TV and radio, the most immediate sources of such news, serve as the faithful watchmen. The news agencies and newspapers follow up, in the most intricate detail, with casualty lists, the extent of damage to the community and the myriad additional facts that cannot be made available to the public by broadcasters in comparable volume.

The News Nobody Likes Covering and writing disaster news isn't exciting or glamorous, as anybody knows who has ever walked wearily through mud, rain and darkness to the scene of a fatal wreck. Like the news of a defeat in war, such material cannot benefit anybody — even the survivors. It is the news nobody likes. But it is also the news the public must have.

Writing Disaster Stories

The leads in any account of a disaster must summarize the event, which can make for dull writing if it isn't carefully done. For in the opening paragraphs, the writer must

- Describe the extent of the storm or other natural calamity.
- Report the casualties high up and make sure they are reasonably accurate. List school closings and transportation tieups.
- Give the United States Weather Bureau forecast.
- Cover the extent of material damage — the homeless, the wreckage of businesses, factories and houses, the power outages in specific areas.
- Report efforts to rescue victims.
- Detail the plans to restore normal living conditions.

It requires a certain amount of skill in organization as well as in writing to do all these things and still make the story readable.

Reporting a New England Blizzard Here is the *Boston Globe*'s story about a recent December blizzard that raged over New England:

By Peter Mancusi

Lead: blizzard hits all New England
A powerful ocean storm that veered unexpectedly inland buried most of New England in snow yesterday, producing accumulations not seen in many areas of the region since the Blizzard of '79.

Results: airport closed, power off, four dead
Driven by gale-force winds upwards of 50 m.p.h., the storm, termed a blizzard by the National Weather Service in Boston, forced the closing of Logan Airport, left thousands throughout the region without electricity and was blamed for the deaths of at least four persons.

Forecast: iced roads
As the snow began tapering off last night, the weather service warned that high winds would continue and that tem-

peratures would drop into the low 20s by morning, causing roads to ice and making driving extremely hazardous.

Additional results: schools closed

The Boston School Department canceled classes for today, as did dozens of other communities. State and city offices, however, are expected to be open. The Massachusetts House of Representatives canceled today's session.

Train delays

Commuter trains and the MBTA will be running today but delays are expected. Delays in excess of two hours were common on the MBTA yesterday. But the transit authority said yesterday it would keep trains running overnight in hopes of keeping tracks clear and that it expected to begin service on schedule today.

Snow depth in and out of Boston

By late yesterday, as much as two feet of snow had fallen in areas south of Boston and in southeastern Rhode Island, among the hardest hit by the blizzard. In Boston, 13 inches of snow had fallen as of 10:30 p.m., topping the 12 inches that fell on Dec. 5–6, 1926. That made the blizzard the worst storm to hit the city so early in the season since that time, according to the weather service.

Forecasters surprised

The weather service had forecast only moderate accumulations when the snow began falling in Boston Saturday afternoon.

A key quote on why it happened

"We knew we had a very large storm out there," said Monte Glovinsky, a weather service meteorologist, "but all indications that we had said that it was going to take a northeast track and not give us too much snow."

But when the storm system stalled, he went on, it gradually began an "explosive intensification. It backed in and made a more westerly track. . . ."

Cleanup hampered

For Boston, the unexpected storm came at a time when its snow-plowing capabilities have never been worse and crews were hard-pressed to do much more than clear major arteries.

At a city hall press conference yesterday, Joseph Casazza, commissioner of the Department of Public Works, said budget reductions forced by Proposition 2½, the tax-limiting proposal, were to blame for the poor showing. . . .

The *Globe's* lead story continued, in extensive detail, following in general the outline of the lead and elaborating on each point. The four deaths, for example, were painstakingly reported with full identification and the reasons each fatality was attributed to the storm. The tone of the story was brisk, unemotional, thoroughly professional. All the gee-whiz stuff was eliminated.

Casualty Lists

In these days of instant reportage, with the public watching on TV as news people go about their work, it is folly to guess at a total of dead and injured. It never was sound practice, but in the earlier years of the century reporters at least had time to do their work and weren't often tempted to gamble. Under current circumstances, the safest thing for any reporter to do on reaching the scene of a disaster is to say quite frankly what people can see for themselves—that no one has any accurate casualty figures and that it may take some time to arrive at an accurate count.

Of course, there is always pressure when a wire service or rival reporter for radio or television jumps out in front with a figure derived, usually, from a wandering official who is even more confused than the press corps. But the reporter has to assume, sometimes against the body of evidence, that editors are reasonable people and will wait a reasonable time for a more soundly based figure.

Precautions for Reporters No reporter should accept a casualty estimate from a hysterical or unqualified person. Nor should those who claim to have been eyewitnesses to an accident be permitted to give their stories without a precautionary warning that the statement will require verification. Often, eyewitnesses turn out to be very inaccurate and biased reporters.

Figures even from authoritative sources should be checked carefully, and the sources identified as far as possible so that first reports from a disaster scene are not ridiculously out of line. If there are conflicting estimates, which may seem to be worth examining, a casualty figure within a certain range—from the lowest to the highest—may serve as a temporary expedient.

As soon as possible, reporters should begin working on their own to gather their figures, documented by the names of the dead and injured. If a count shows that 20 bodies have been recovered (and it is one of the most distasteful parts of a reporter's job to make such a tally), then the reporter eventually must have 20 names in the list of dead. Until the list is complete, partial identifications are acceptable if they are so specified. The list of the injured, and their identities, is compiled from the various hospitals and emergency shelters at which the victims are treated.

Storms Defined

What is a storm? The news media must be precise in announcing that a tornado, hurricane, or blizzard has struck the area. The United States Weather Bureau designations are offered as standard here, but it should be noted that they differ slightly from the standard of the familiar Beaufort's scale. These are the Weather Bureau's definitions:

Designation	Miles per Hour
Calm	less than 1
light air	1–3
light breeze	4–7
gentle breeze	8–12
moderate breeze	13–18
fresh breeze	19–24
strong breeze	25–31
near gale	32–38

gale	39–46
strong gale	47–54
storm	55–63
violent storm	64–73
hurricane	above 74

Beaufort's scale, devised by Sir Francis Beaufort, of the Royal Navy, in 1805, describes a whole gale as one that uproots trees and defines a hurricane as a wind of more than 75 miles an hour velocity. Actually, hurricanes, tornadoes, cyclones and typhoons are all members of the cyclonic family. Here are some definitions of terms:

Cyclone   A cyclone is a system of winds that may be several hundred miles wide and circulates about a center of low barometric pressure. It travels at 20 miles an hour or more, and usually from west to east in the United States.

Tornado   Commonly, a tornado—the most destructive and violent of all local storms—consists of winds rotating at 200 miles an hour or more. It may last from a few minutes to hours, cut a path of destruction from a few feet to a mile wide and move forward anywhere up to about 300 miles at a speed of up to 68 miles an hour.

Hurricane   The hurricane, a severe cyclone that originates in tropical waters, is a huge wind system as much as 500 miles in diameter. It is slower than a local twister, moving at 10 to 15 miles an hour. In the western Pacific, it is called a typhoon.

Blizzard   The severity of rain and snowstorms is measured by the number of inches of precipitation over a given period. By custom, the public has come to accept any snowstorm of prolonged intensity as a blizzard; actually, the Weather Bureau defines a blizzard as fine, dry snow driven by a wind of 35 miles an hour or more, reducing visibility to less than 50 feet, during a period of low temperature.

General Weather News

There are many ways of telling weather news and the journalist uses all of them, whether the weather is good or bad. Even if there is no story in the newspaper, the United States Weather Bureau forecast is nearly always published somewhere on Page 1. Either the government forecast or the paper's own prediction, obtained from private forecasters, is printed in a prominent position inside the paper. As for the electronic media, weather is one of their most prominent features and many stations have their own specialists.

Forecasts   Most daily newspapers also run the government weather table from various major cities, the regional weather forecast, the long-range weather forecast and the weather map with appropriate explanations. Radio and television run radar maps and give appropriate explanations. At airports and Coast Guard stations, meteorologists also are called upon frequently for interviews by all the news media.

The enormous amount of statistical weather data given to the public means that reporters should make it their business to be reasonably familiar with the principles of weather forecasting. No journalist can for very long escape writing or talking about the weather. When a weekend or a holiday is near, when there is a big sports event or an outdoor convention of consequence, the weather is an important part of the story. It cannot be ignored.

The basic facts that must be used in any weather summation include the latest forecast, mean and hourly temperatures when pertinent, humidity, barometric pressure, wind strength and direction and a comparison with the record highs and lows for that particular date and season. In hot weather, Americans torture themselves with a measurement called the temperature-humidity index (THI), which tries to estimate human discomfort (as if that were possible). To determine THI, wet and dry bulb temperature readings are added, then multiplied by 0.4, and 15 is added to the product. In theory, when the THI passes 75, half the people will be uncomfortable; when it reaches 80 or more, everybody feels awful.

Highs and Lows   It is an amiable and harmless journalistic custom to salute a "record" high or low for a particular date, which is slightly synthetic, since most government and other weather records are less than 100 years old. When all highs and lows for a single date, such as May 12 or December 13, are compared in the record, it is obviously possible to have a "record" day occasionally.

The ancient journalistic weakness for "firsts" can also be satisfied by checking on the weather for the first day of the season, the first storm of the winter, the first heat wave of the summer, and the hottest and coldest days of the month, season or year. To those who play the game of highs and lows, a reminder should be given that the "record" is not always established on the hour but may come between hourly readings.

Like everything else, the reporter must ask the Weather Bureau for the record because the information is not always volunteered; nor is it a good policy to depend on such supplementary services as the weather information supplied in some cities by telephone companies.

There is one other precaution that is recommended to everyone who writes about the weather — whether the story deals with disaster or is just a routine short. A glance out the window, just before writing, will sometimes save everybody trouble. Weather forecasting is far from perfect, and even the most efficient meteorologists have been known to change their predictions within an hour or less.

In resort cities and localities weather news sometimes is used for its promotional value. Thus, Florida media are likely to play the news of cold weather in northern states, from which so many tourists come, or rain in a rival tourist paradise such as California. Local weather, too, is more likely to be newsworthy in such areas.

Heat Waves, Cold Waves and Storms   When the hot spells of summer and the cold spells of winter set in, they are news. The classic patterns of weather reporting then are spread over several days, with hourly temperatures featured and enlarged upon by appropriate comparisons with previous days or years.

It is comparatively simple to document a heat wave or a cold wave with statistics from the usual sources. They are plentiful and available for the asking.

The accompanying events also are familiar and generally easy to cover. Crowds take to the parks, lakes, mountains and seashore in the summer heat, with a certain amount of official and business activity being curtailed at extreme periods.

During the winter a subzero cold spell can seriously disrupt both business and transportation but much of this material can be obtained from official sources, chambers of commerce and transportation information. Gathering such weather data takes time.

Handling a Weather Story

The most difficult thing for a newcomer to journalism to understand is that a heat wave, cold wave or storm, which is known to have occurred in the area, must be announced in the media and explained from beginning to end.

There is nothing unusual about this. A hundred thousand people may have seen the Super Bowl football game and millions of others may have watched it on television, but the newspapers and subsequent regular broadcasts still record the fact that there was a game, which side won, what the score was and the pertinent details. The evidence is impressive that the public is often particularly interested in getting more detail, background information and color on news of which it has some advance knowledge.

Since the weather is a universal topic of discussion, the first rule in any weather report is to begin at the beginning by telling what is right or wrong with the day, what the results are and why, and whether improvement can be expected.

Undated Weather Leads When storms engulf vast sections of the country, the wire services and leading newspapers write undated leads to give a panoramic picture of the calamity. Often, with some local changes, these are read on radio and television newscasts because they are tightly written, vividly told and present the reader and viewer with an information pattern that is easily understood.

Here is an undated lead on the brutally cold winter of 1982, the worst in the records of the National Weather Service in many places:

By David L. Langford
Associated Press Writer

An invasion of Arctic weather that has killed at least 65 people pushed southward Monday, sending temperatures to record lows across Dixie. In the north, a new blizzard walloped Buffalo, N.Y., with 25 inches of snow.

Many people, mostly elderly, froze to death in their homes.

Schools and factories were closed in many cities from Chicago, where Sunday's temperature of minus 26 degrees was an all-time record, to Atlanta, where Monday's minus five degrees was the coldest since 1899.

> Travelers were stranded across parts of Indiana, Ohio and Pennsylvania as the eastern two-thirds of the nation remained caught in one of the most severe cold waves of this century.
>
> Many highways across the Midwest were impassable with up to six-foot drifts. Scattered power outages were reported in several states as generating facilities became overloaded and lines snapped in the cold and wind.
>
> Augusta, Ga., set an all-time record at minus two. It was two below in Birmingham, Ala., eight above at Pensacola and 15 at Houston, coldest in 30 years.

General Disaster Coverage

The reporting and writing procedures described here also apply to the coverage of fires, as well as air, sea, train and auto accidents in general. In each area, however, there are specifics that have to be noted.

Fires   These are the basics for any fire story:

- Address of the burning structure.
- Casualty lists, assembled from fire and police officials at the scene, hospital authorities and relatives.
- Description of the structure — residence, office, loft or factory building; number of stories; type of construction — frame, brick, concrete, fabricated steel; number of occupants involved, and the building's owner.
- Whether the building was substandard, a tenement or still under construction.
- Time of discovery of the blaze, number of alarms, number of firefighters and vehicles responding, time the flames were under control or extinguished, effect on nearby buildings and traffic.
- Cause of deaths and injuries.
- Stories of survivors and heroic rescues.
- Unofficial damage estimate if available.
- Cause of fire, if announced by fire marshal's office. If there is a suspicion of arson, there should be an official statement to that effect.

Sea Disasters   The news of tanker oil spills, ship collisions, fires at sea and other nautical disasters usually breaks first by radio and is reported on by the United States Coast Guard. Because it takes a long time to determine responsibility for ship collisions, charges that one ship or another was at fault should be handled with the greatest reserve.

The first thing a reporter must try to do is to get a list of the passengers who are reported by the ship's agents or company to be aboard. Being out of touch with the actual scene of the disaster, the reporter must depend on Coast Guard and other radio reports for information until the survivors are brought in. Often, the news media hire aircraft to go to the scene of such a disaster, if it is at all possible. RCA Communications is another source.

The information required roughly parallels that of much other disaster coverage:

- Name of the ship or ships involved, descriptions of gross tonnage, year built, date last inspected. Location and time of accident.
- Passenger lists; but remember that some people on the list may not have been aboard.
- Radio information monitored from the scene for messages from the captain or captains involved on casualties and other details.
- Calls to the homes of listed passengers to check whether they were actually aboard. Some passengers may have sent messages.
- Insurance coverage of company agents and officials.

In the case of a tanker oil spill, radio messages are the prime source, but the Coast Guard and residents living near imperiled beaches are also important.

Train Accidents   News of a train accident often comes first from someone living near the scene. Because nobody has a passenger list, identification of the dead and the injured is always difficult. Officials at the scene seldom know any more than the reporters until it is possible to arrive at a tentative body count. These are the essentials:

- Train or trains involved (by time and place of departure and of destination), name of line, number of cars, type of engine, time and location of accident, approximate number of passengers involved.
- Estimates of casualties, based on an official source. There may be several estimates, often conflicting at first.
- Eyewitness accounts of survivors and people at or near scene.
- Cause of crash, if the statement is attributable to a responsible official.
- Description of the scene.
- Description of investigations that are under way.
- Information obtained from nearby hospitals, residences of those involved in the crash, funeral establishments, railroad waiting rooms and other sources.

Aircraft Accidents   There are two general types of coverage for air crashes.

When commercial planes are involved, the routine for covering sea and rail disasters is followed, with the help of federal, state and local authorities and company officials. The local airport is always a valuable source of news. Plane passenger lists are generally unreliable because there are often numerous no-shows.

If reporters can reach the scene, they can tell much of the story and survivors then fill in the details. But often the wreckage is inaccessible and the state police must be relied on for first reports.

When an Air Force, Navy, Army or Coast Guard aircraft is involved in an accident, the rules change sharply. The Defense Department's procedures for issuing information on aircraft accidents often curb independent reporting. The news media, in such cases, must depend on the military for initial reports of casualties. The restrictions become even tighter when a military aircraft carrying a nuclear weapon is involved. The laws concerning disclosure of atomic information provide stiff penalties for the unauthorized issuance of information in such cases.

Auto Crashes   This is by far the largest category of accidents, and the one that takes the highest annual toll of lives. Over holidays and summer weekends, the National Safety Council generally issues death forecasts that are widely reported by the news media. However, few individual auto, bus or truck accidents are covered in much detail because there are so many of them.

The only accidents of this type that receive special attention are those in which there are multiple deaths, such as school bus accidents in which a number of children die.

Earthquakes   Four out of five earthquakes occur around the borders of the Pacific Ocean. They also may be experienced with some degree of frequency from the West Indies across the Atlantic and Mediterranean and on to the Himalayas and East Indies. All in all, 1,200 seismograph stations detect about a half million temblors a year. But of these only about 1,000 cause specific damage, although up to 100,000 or more may be felt in some slight degree.

The measurement of earthquakes is done on the Richter scale, designed by the geologist C. F. Richter. Under it, the magnitude of the quake is made proportional to the logarithm of maximum recorded amplitude. These are typical Richter scale figures of earthquake magnitude:

2 — smallest shocks to be reported.
4.5 — smallest shocks causing slight damage.
6 — shocks that cause moderate destruction.
8.5 — largest known earth shocks.

While there is a considerable body of material about earthquake forecasting, such predictions should be handled with great caution. Headlines announcing a future quake, or broadcasts suggesting it is time to take to the hills, are not notably popular either in Japan or along the San Andreas Fault on the American Pacific coast. Such forecasts do not have irrefutable scientific acceptance to date.

The locality in which a small earth shock occurs also has something to do with the amount of interest it creates. A mild tremor means very little in most parts of Japan, where there are thousands of earth movements every year. But anything that even sends pictures swinging on the walls in the New York City area, where earth shocks are rare, stirs up the public and stimulates a kind of controlled alarm in the news media. A major China quake (8.5 on the Richter scale) was a brief sensation in the United States, then was treated almost routinely.

Nuclear Accidents

Aroused by frequent public demonstrations against the existing nuclear plants in the United States, many of them sponsored by small but dedicated environmentalist groups, the news media have given massive coverage to nuclear accidents.

The Story of Three Mile Island The most famous was the break-down of a nuclear reactor in 1979 at the General Public Utilities plant at Three Mile Island, Pennsylvania, which was regarded as a threat to the lives of people for many miles around its general area.

The *Philadelphia Inquirer* put 28 reporters to work over a 10-day period to find out how and why such an accident could have occurred. Its exclusive report, spread over eight pages, won it a Pulitzer Prize. Steve Lovelady's lead to that series presents, in brief space, the style, tone and content of that extraordinary journalistic effort:

> 4:07 a.m., March 28, 1979.
>
> Two pumps fail. Nine seconds later, 69 boron rods smash down into the hot core of unit two, a nuclear reactor on Three Mile Island. The rods work. Fission in the reactor stops.
>
> But it is already too late.
>
> What will become America's worst commercial nuclear disaster has begun.
>
> Unit two at Three Mile Island is out of control. And no one knows. No one will know, for hours.
>
> During the next six days, America — and the world — will watch in terror and dismay as the best minds available try to prevent apocalypse. They will see scientists grappling with events they have never anticipated; federal officials frozen by indecision for days; a small, previously obscure utility company haplessly repeating like a broken record that everything is all right; and a state government struggling fruitlessly to find out what is going on and what is to be done.
>
> What they will not see are the details behind these reactions — details more harrowing even than the general impression:
>
> Nuclear workers playing Frisbee outside a plant gate because they were locked out but not warned of the radiation beaming from the plant's walls.
>
> Federal officials meeting 55 hours after the accident to be briefed, and learning to their dismay that the experts could not describe what was going on.
>
> Company officials meeting behind closed doors eight days after the accident to discuss, not how to get the facts out, but how to keep the facts hidden.
>
> Broken valves fastened together with sealing compound.
>
> A state official trying for two days to get briefed by federal officials and, when he finally heard from them, being so shocked that he buried his head in his hands and cried, "Oh, my God. . . ."

This was the beginning of the inquiry, not the end. Two and one-half years later, in a major story on Page 1, the *Wall Street Journal* reported as follows:

By Arlen J. Large

THREE MILE ISLAND, Pa.—Two and one-half years after The Accident, the lights are still on in the control room of this dead nuclear power plant. A crew is always on duty, watching for flashing lights that would warn of a renewed and unwelcome chain reaction.

On March 28, 1979, the crew in this room misread those lights, assuming that cooling water was flooding into the hot core when it was actually draining out. As is often repeated, nobody got killed when the reactor overheated and broke down. But the accident has been a financial disaster for General Public Utilities Corp., the plant's owner. GPU's earnings have nose-dived, the price of its stock has collapsed from nearly $19 a share before the breakdown to $5 today, the shareholders get no dividends and the company's bond ratings are rotten.

Most embarrassing of all, the $1 billion estimated cost of cleaning up the radioactive mess has turned GPU into a national charity case. . . .

The Story of Diablo Canyon   When the great California atomic plant at Diablo Canyon was scheduled to open, in the early 1980s, hundreds of antinuclear demonstrators protested that it was unsafe. Within a few weeks, the government's Nuclear Regulatory Commission took drastic action. This was the story:

WASHINGTON (AP) — The Nuclear Regulatory Commission on Thursday suspended the operating license of the Diablo Canyon atomic power plant, saying it would require verification of earthquake protection equipment at the troubled California facility.

The NRC decision came at a closed meeting hours after a Congressional subcommittee hearing at which new questions were raised about the safety of nuclear power.

NRC Chairman Nunzio J. Palladino said the vote was 4–1 to suspend the license to test the first nuclear reactor at the yet-to-be-opened $2.3 billion plant. . . .

Even with the completion of an independent audit as proposed by the plant's owner, the Pacific Gas & Electric Co., and the lifting of the suspension, both Three Mile Island and the Diablo Canyon affair cast a deep shadow over the American nuclear industry. Only 72 plants were in operation at the time and proposals to have 200 in action by the turn of the century had to be scrapped. Nuclear power was a story the news media would cover for years to come.

• Short Takes

When you write about disasters, natural or manmade, watch these things:

- Base the lead on the human element—the casualties, the rescues, the homeless. The material damage comes second.
- If you don't have a solid casualty figure with firm attribution, it's better to generalize. Nobody can convict you if you can't estimate the number of dead and injured 10 minutes after a tornado, a fire or other disaster.
- In anything having to do with the weather, give the United States Weather Bureau forecast high up. And look out the window before you write the story.
- Remember that human experiences and good quotes distinguish a good story from a mere collection of statistics.
- Any story based on the weather should include reports of school closings;

power outages if any; traffic tieups; suspension of air, train and bus service, and the like.

- In compiling casualty lists, be sure that a death is actually related to a disaster. Too often, particularly in pieces about cold and heat waves, almost anybody who dies for any cause turns up as a weather victim. It should not be handled that way.
- Be careful about terminology. Not every snowstorm is a blizzard. Not every windstorm is a tornado. Make sure that you know the difference.
- In handling stories about fires or other building fatalities, the kind of structure should be given (wooden or brick or concrete), the height in the number of floors, the type of building (tenement, house, skyscraper), the time the blaze was reported, the number of families involved, the owner of the building. The cause of the fire should be attributed to a responsible official, particularly if arson is alleged. So should the damage estimate.
- In handling transportation accidents, writers should be careful not to assign blame. A collision does not imply that one party or the other was at fault. If charges are made, the response should be given by the accused party, if it is at all possible.
- Every effort should be made, in reporting commercial aircraft accidents, to determine the number of people and crew involved. In advance of a determination of casualties, that figure alone can carry a lead when the news first breaks.
- Military aircraft coverage is subject to military regulations. The writer may well get more over the phone from military authorities than the reporter can at the scene.
- Nuclear accidents can be overstressed and overplayed if the writer does not have a basic knowledge of the facts of nuclear power. Scare stories and hopped up leads are never justified in so serious a situation. All such stories must be handled with reserve.

CHAPTER 11

Sharpening the Lead

In writing a lead, the first instinct of the news technician is to play it safe, to "hang it on somebody," as the journalistic saying goes. The first instinct of the artist is to tell a story. And that is the difference between writing a bad lead and a good one.

Patterns for Leads

Suppose a crowd has collected about a wrecked automobile at a street corner outside a park. A passerby stops and taps a truckdriver on the arm.

"Hey, Mac. What happened?"

"Two kids got killed. Car jumped the curb and ran them down."

That's the story.

In effect, the truckdriver has performed the same function as a writer summarizing a news event. He has answered the essential question posed for anyone dealing with hard news:

"What happened?"

The news writer *could* tell it just as plainly and simply. An artist *would*.

An Overstuffed Lead   But just put a story like this before a writer who is mired in routine. More often than not, it will be messed up.

For under the ancient news formula so dear to all news technicians, the lead must contain both the facts and the source of the news, whether or not it is necessary to give the source the same prominence as the facts. Under this procedure, assuming the facts in the street incident just referred to came from a police chief, the traditional news writer would produce something like this:

> Police Chief J. W. Carmichael announced today that two children were killed outside Prospect Park, at Jackson Avenue and 16th Street N.W., when a "recklessly driven" automobile jumped the curb near where they were playing at 2 p.m. and ran them down.

This 40-word horror contains all the bad habits of the routine news writer. A tragedy such as this need not have its lead embellished with the name of a police chief. Nor is it necessary to have a partial quotation from his words of wisdom to make the story sound official, formal and important.

These things are stuffed into the lead mainly because the reporter, writer or editor — as the case may be — feels the news must be "hung on" some official to make it safe to use, particularly when there is an allegation of reckless driving. They forget that if the facts are wrong, no partial quote "hung on" a police chief will avert a libel suit.

The news technicians in broadcasting studios usually follow an identical routine. Sticking to the same procedure, they continue the error of "oversourcing" the story. That is, they go with the usual broadcasting procedure of giving the title of the source and the official's name before proceeding to the news. This is what makes so much daytime radio news an exercise in monotony.

Writing for the news media needn't be that bad.

The Crime of Monotony   There are two arguments against this kind of writing, whether it is done for newspapers or the broadcast media.

First, it is dull. It makes a monotonous official singsong out of a tragedy that should arouse a community. Even more important, a question of accuracy is involved even if libel is somehow sidestepped.

Either the facts are accurately reported or they are not. If they are accurate, the reporter does not need the police chief's name in the lead to guarantee them but can refer to him as the source in a succeeding paragraph. If the story is inaccurate, whatever the police chief says will not excuse the publication of the account.

The name of the police chief, therefore, should be used in a context that gives it more meaning. The event, not the source, should be stressed. The source in a story of this kind is a secondary consideration.

The Blueprint Lead   Even if the lead is not overstuffed and oversourced, it can still adhere to routine. Anybody who has ever done night rewrite knows the familiar blueprint that is used for such stories, and here it is:

> Two children were killed and 12 others injured today when an automobile hit them outside Prospect Park.

This is the way it's been done, alas, since the invention of the automobile:

2 KILLED, 12 HURT IN AUTO CRASH

For the benefit of lazy or inexpert news writers, the lead could be kept standing, with blanks for the figures for the dead and injured, the place, and the type of vehicle. For that matter, so could the body of the story. It makes every auto accident seem the same. And when the hasty reader glances over the page and spots the familiar headline, it evokes not even a glimmer of interest, much less of sympathy or indignation.

Answering the Question   The blueprint lead does not attempt to answer the fundamental question: "What happened?"

It grinds out statistics and records in prosaic language. Yet, in an event of this kind, a writer with a sense of artistry should take readers to the scene — to let them see it, hear it, smell the fumes of the wrecked automobile. That is possible if the event is described as it happened:

> A speeding yellow sports car jumped a curb outside Prospect Park today and crashed into a group of children at play, killing two of them. Twelve others were injured.
>
> Police Chief J. W. Carmichael, who hurried to the scene, attributed the accident to reckless driving.
>
> The dead children were. . . .

Thus, in two sentences totaling 29 words, the facts are packed into the beginning of the story in such a way that the public has a vivid image of what happened and how it happened. Facts — action — color — these are the ingredients of a fast-moving lead for a spot news story such as this.

What Makes the Lead Different?   In place of the humdrum "2 killed, 12 hurt" approach, readers are shown how this automobile accident differs from others. The lead is specific rather than general. It uses vigorous verbs in the active voice. It eliminates needless attribution and location, since they will be written into the story at appropriate points. The awkward phrases and unnecessary quotes of the official type of writing in the first lead are dropped.

In essence, these are the differences between sharp leads and dull ones. Dull leads are the product of habit, lazy writing and carelessness. They become weighted down with needless attribution, unnecessary partial quotes, hackneyed phrases.

There is no magic that creates sharp leads. They require a good news sense, a decent command of the English language and a show of effort by the writer. Above all, there must be an honest attempt to answer the question: "What happened?"

Effective Hard News Leads

Making Figures Mean Something   When the United States debt passed one trillion dollars, writers grappled with the problem of making that colossal figure mean something to the average citizen. The Associated Press came up with this illustrative lead:

> WASHINGTON (AP) — To neither cheers nor tears, the national debt now is at $1,000,000,000,000 — and rising.

That's a trillion dollars, 1,000 billion, about $4,700 for every man, woman and child in America. Counting it out, one dollar at a time for every second, would take 31,668 years.

The 13-figure milestone was reached Thursday and was greeted with little more than passing interest at the Treasury Department....

Proposals—Proposals—Proposals One of the worst features of legislative correspondence is the continual announcement of proposals by governors, mayors and lawmakers. The public is well aware that much of this is non-news, the submission of suggestions that never will be adopted. A correspondent for the *Milwaukee Journal* tried to put a little life into this usually dull story:

STEVENS POINT, Wis.—Gov. Dreyfus Thursday delivered a laundry list of proposals designed to help beleaguered municipal officials solve their budget problems.

Unfortunately, a number of officials attending the League of Wisconsin Municipalities said his suggestions just won't wash....

Holiday for Parkers The average story about traffic tickets has little appeal for most readers because the message is so often predictable: Pay up or else. But Ken McLaughlin, City Hall reporter for the *Watsonville* (California) *Register-Pajaronian*, came across a different kind of parking-violation story, and this is how he wrote it:

Nearly 400 Watsonville motorists have been given a rare opportunity. They're being allowed to tear up their traffic tickets.

The City Council last night voted unanimously to have the city attorney dismiss the 385-odd tickets issued to overnight parkers on the Ides of March....

What the council had done, McLaughlin reported, was to demand that the police enforce an anti-overnight parking law on nights when the streets were being swept, only to find that such selective law enforcement was unconstitutional.

Making Storm Damage Readable Where there are no casualties, storm-damage stories are batted out routinely on most newspapers. But not on the *Island Packet*, published twice weekly at Hilton Head, South Carolina. A reporter, Betsy Wakefield, wrote this lead on a story about high-tide damage and made it vivid for her paper's readers:

Two measures to prevent beach erosion took a beating under high tides and heavy winds last week.

Waves breached the seawall along North Forest Beach, and on Heron Street carried 12 feet of beach away beyond the wall.

In Palmetto Dunes, heavy surf cut a noticeable scarp in the dune, recently renourished with 800,000 cubic yards of sand from the Shelter Cove Marina. In some places south of the Hyatt, ten to 12 inches of the new sand were pulled offshore....

An Assortment of Good Leads

Whether the lead is a sentence, several sentences, a paragraph or several paragraphs, it should delineate the action and the locale of the story if it deals with spot news.

If it is about a person, it should sketch in the broad outlines of the subject's character. Background and interpretive leads must of necessity be explanatory. And feature leads may start almost anywhere as long as they are interesting and get the reader into the story.

Except for the stencils and blueprints in which routine writers deal, it isn't really possible to devise leads for all occasions. But the following assortment, assembled from familiar news situations and from a number of newspapers across the land, illustrates how varied good leads can be:

A Summary Lead   When a reporter is handling a running story for publication, or telephoning the facts to a rewrite person for the edition, the principal objective is to tell the news as it happens and tell it clearly. It isn't often, in such situations, that a brilliant lead, or even a clever lead, can be devised. Nor is it advisable to attempt to play tricks with words when the news in itself is tricky. The following is a summary lead that blends several important angles into a relatively brief space — a useful variant of the multiple-incident lead:

> CENTRAL CITY — An estimated 600 of the 1,263 inmates at the state penitentiary here ended a 48-hour takeover of two cell blocks last night by releasing 22 hostages after an agreement with state officials.
>
> Governor Harold Anderson announced that Warden Nicholas Golubovic, eight guards and 13 visitors, all taken captive on Sunday, had been set free unharmed.
>
> The governor said the agreement with the inmates, negotiated by Bert Engelhart, a columnist for the Central City News, included the establishment of grievance machinery to assess the prisoners' complaints about overcrowding and poor food. . . .

The paragraph linking the lead to the body of the story could briefly describe the manner in which the hostage takeover began. In the body of the story, each point in the lead would be covered in turn — the facts of the release, the negotiations, the agreement and a summary of less essential material.

The Tabular Lead   This type of lead, also a variant of the multiple-incident lead, is often used to report major announcements by governmental leaders, complicated documents like budgets and tax legislation, and wide-ranging news conferences. Its principal purpose is to convey information, not to sling words. Here is an example:

> The Central City Police Department is riddled with lax discipline, old-fashioned administration and inefficient procedures.
>
> While the city's police force is as large and as well paid as those in other municipalities of comparable size, standards for performance, promotions and job applications are sagging.
>
> These are the salient conclusions of a year-long survey of the Police Department, which was conducted by a panel of experts and made public at City Hall today.
>
> Mayor Harold V. Dawkins, who pledged that such a study would be made during his successful re-election campaign, stressed these major aspects of the report:

- The Police Department's record-keeping is inaccurate and open to serious question on other counts.
- Fewer than 20 percent of the force is assigned to patrol work on weekends, when crime usually reaches a peak.
- Patrol post boundaries are outmoded and police are assigned arbitrarily to three shifts in equal numbers, although high-crime hours are at night.
- Many police frequent bars while on duty and some late at night are found "cooping," a term for sleeping in patrol cars.

"This survey," the mayor said, "indicates that a thorough reform is needed in our Police Department and I'm going to see that a beginning is made, regardless of who is hurt. . . ."

Of course, each of the tabular points must be documented with quotes from the survey, so that the reader will be left in no doubt about the authenticity of the story. It is the editor's responsibility to see that the documentation is not cut on the copy desk or in makeup, thus leaving the reader in dazed ignorance of why these charges were made and on what material they were based.

Dual-Purpose Leads

Leads in this category are often done on the rewrite bank because writing specialists are familiar with them and generally handle them without much fuss. They tell the news, of course, but they also try to advance or anticipate it by one step. This dual purpose can be confusing to newcomers, but there really isn't any difficulty attached to the writing. Mainly, it is a technique.

Second-Day Leads   The simplest way to explain this is that a second-day lead shifts the focus of the story. For example, if the first-day lead is based on two killed in a fire, the second-day lead would be about the opening of an investigation. Yes, it is perfectly true that the investigation would be carried in the first-day story, but for the second day this would be the probable basis for further activity.

To take another familiar example: a prominent citizen's death is carried in the morning papers. For the afternoon papers and the PM cycle of wire services, the lead would shift to funeral arrangements. Or let us say the morning papers carry a major speech by the governor in his re-election campaign. For the afternoons, the focus would shift to the next step in the governor's schedule, plus reactions to his speech, both for and against.

In a few words, the news is constantly developing and the second-day lead keeps pace with it. The practice is called "updating."

But since there is nothing that is deader than rewriting an old clip at half the length, writers who have to update a story usually pick up a telephone, make a few phone calls and try to develop a little fresh news, to keep from repeating stories already published or heard over the air.

The verbs that are dear to the hearts of writers searching for second-day angles in old stories include such workhorses as *emerged, confronted, faced, awaited, expected, held, seemed, appeared* and others in the general area denoting continuing action. For instance:

First-day lead	George J. Dockweller appeared last night to have defeated his Republican rival for mayor, Ernest Quentin, by about 20,000 votes.
Second-day lead	George J. Dockweller emerged today as the victor in a hard-fought election for mayor. He defeated his Republican rival, Ernest Quentin, by 22,468 votes.

First-day lead	Three teenage robbery suspects were captured by police last night after a South Side grocery was held up.
Second-day lead	Three teenage robbery suspects were held for arraignment today in the theft of $15.22 from a South Side grocery.

First-day lead	At least 10 persons were killed and many others were injured last night in a collision between two Southeast Railway trains outside Union Station.
Second-day lead	Three investigations were under way today into the Southeast Railway wreck in which 12 persons were killed.

Second-day angles also apply to news in morning papers that broke for the papers of the previous afternoon. Wire services and the broadcast media often do not wait for a change in cycle but go with second-day stories while the original account is still being cleaned up.

Overnight Leads   The second-day principle applies, to some extent, to the handling of what are called overnight stories. These are reports of such continuing events as court cases, political campaigns and conventions in which there is sufficient public interest to have an early continuing story in the papers or on the air.

The difference is that reporters, in the main, are responsible for overnighters, as they are called. The simplest example would be the work of a reporter who is covering the state Legislature on the adoption of a new tax program. In writing for an afternoon paper, the reporter would file a piece giving the details of the program as they were announced by the governor's office. His overnighter would be based on interviews with key legislators on the chances for passage of the legislation, and it would be used in his first edition.

Another example of an overnighter, familiar to most readers and viewers, is the work of a crime reporter who must follow up a long and fruitless day of police maneuvering in a murder investigation. What can he do for his overnighter? In all probability, it will be an interview with the chief of detectives, analyzing the possible motives for the crime and the personality of the killer as developed from the available evidence.

The point is that there can be nothing artificial about an overnighter, except when it anticipates the news. ("Mayor Jones summoned the City Council into emergency session today for anticipated action on his budget for the next fiscal year.")

The reporters who are on beats, or who are working on continuing stories, always must have something fresh to report overnight, however slight it may be.

The burden is not so great on morning papers, because the first edition of AMs has the entire day's news from which to draw. So features, in the main, are the basis for most AM overnighters. And that is also true for the broadcast media.

Kelly Scott in the *St. Petersburg Times* did it differently when he covered the Rolling Stones' appearance before 60,000 people in Orlando's Tangerine Bowl:

By Kelly Scott

ORLANDO—Graying temples mingled with spiky punk hair, Lacoste shirts with tie-dyed halter tops, parents with children, heavy metal noise with clean, rhythm-and-blues flavored rock.

But the wild opposites drawn to the Rolling Stones' concert Saturday shared the same feeling for music, so the gathering of 60,000 in the hot, dirty playing field of Orlando's Tangerine Bowl was a smooth and affectionate affair.

It's been that way all over the country this fall as the Rolling Stones, one of rock's most mature yet continually popular bands, reconvened its faithful after a three-year absence from live performances. . . .

Then there's a personal lead that made history — the one that John Roderick of the AP filed from Peking (now Beijing) when he became the first American journalist to return to his former base since the Communist takeover in 1949:

PEKING—This is my first dispatch from China in 22 years. The news I have to report would have seemed incredible only a few weeks ago—Americans are welcome in the People's Republic of China.

So welcome were they that Roderick within a few years became the chief of a newly opened AP bureau in the Chinese capital.

Freak Leads The leads that pose a question, begin with a quote or ask "you," the reader, to be a part of the news were far from favorites of old-line editors. But all are cropping up in the news with greater frequency today. Here is a "you" lead for Halloween partygoers:

Want to rent a Halloween costume? If you live in the Washington area it will cost you $1 to $150, give or take a feather boa. You may be content to dress as a pirate or a rock star, but you can also go as a bunch of grapes or a six-foot rabbit. . . .

This is a more serious "you" lead, but the principle of getting the reader into the act is the same:

If you have worked long enough for a private company to earn a pension, don't worry that your money will ever be taken away from you. Congress has just passed a law protecting 30 million Americans covered by such plans, promising that nothing will interfere with your pension when you retire, even if the company fires you or goes bankrupt.

Writers can get personal and use a question lead on a routine story that otherwise would be dull — to wit:

> Give Ohio back to the Indians? Absolutely, the Indians say. They told a House subcommittee today that Ohio's remaining Indian tribes have filed claims for 117 million acres. That's roughly four times larger than the whole state.

And here's a quote lead on a feature story about a notorious character in the news whom most Americans have probably forgotten:

> HUNTINGTON BEACH, Calif. (UPI) — "I'm really a good soldier, a fighter," said Nguyen Cao Ky, former premier of South Vietnam who fled to safety while urging his troops to fight to the end.
>
> Interviewed at his home six years after his country fell to the Communists, Ky, who has just sold his liquor store here, expressed hope that he could battle his way back to his homeland some day.

The Contrast Lead　One of the standbys for well nigh 100 years is the contrast lead. In its most familiar form, it reports the election of a company president who began as a $4 a week office boy. This stencil, however, has become faded. Sometimes, a writer with an original turn of mind can adapt the same theme to a new subject. When Van Cliburn, the pianist, returned to this country from a musical triumph in Moscow, one reporter wrote:

> Harvey Lavan (Van) Cliburn Jr., of Kilgore, Tex., came home from the Soviet Union yesterday with 17 pieces of luggage. They bespoke his triumph as a pianist in Moscow. He had three when he went over.

The Delayed Lead　The *Wall Street Journal* frequently uses a delayed lead, known to the trade as "backing into a story," in its big Page 1 specials. There's an art to doing it, but the *Journal*'s writers are given more scope than many others to practice the fine art of writing. Here is a lead on a Page 1 *Journal* story about the Robot Age.

By JoAnn S. Lublin

LOUSIVILLE, Ky.—Two men in T shirts and work pants chat as they casually aim paint sprayers at clothes-dryer doors moving along an assembly line. Across the hall, in another glassed-in booth at General Electric Co.'s Appliance Park here, a robot silently sprays enamel on washing machine lids at a consistent, careful pace.

The robot, essentially a large, computer-controlled mechanical arm, "doesn't talk back and it doesn't take breaks," observes Clarence Engle, a fabrication manager at the giant manufacturing complex. It doesn't draw a pay-

check, either. By year-end, the two men's $8.14-an-hour
jobs "will be taken by robots," Mr. Engle says, and the
employees will be transferred to other work here.
   Industrial robots are rapidly moving into the U.S. labor
force. . . . Nearly 5,000 robots are currently toiling away in
the U.S.

The Anecdotal Lead   Magazines used to begin many articles with anecdotal leads, provided the anecdotes were bright and applicable and not too wasteful
of space. The practice seems to have dwindled in recent years in favor of a more
direct news approach. However, newspapers have been so eager to pick up pointers
from magazines to interest mass audiences that the anecdotal lead has had a rebirth
in the news columns. Here is one that began a series on divorce in the *Louisville*
Sunday *Courier-Journal and Times:*

> David and Kay Craig's two-year-old marriage is a second one for both and their
> story is one that is being repeated with increasing frequency across the country.
>   Each was married for the first time at 18. David's marriage lasted through five
> years and two children. Kay's first marriage ended in divorce after a year and eight
> months.
>   The Craigs (not their real name) are among the 13 million Americans who,
> according to the Census Bureau, at one time or another have been through a divorce.
> More than four million Americans currently list their marital status as divorced. The
> rate of divorces in this country has been and still is steadily increasing.

When the anecdote is short and pointed, as this one is, it can be used to bring
the reader quickly into a news situation that might not attract his attention if it
were routinely written. The trouble with anecdotal leads, as some magazine editors
concede, is that they do not really attract as many readers as unusual statements—
the basis of good straight news leads.

Besides, few anecdotes are good enough to occupy the amount of Page 1 space
that could otherwise be used for a news lead.

Gag Leads   There is no sadder face in a newsroom that that of the writer
who has just been ordered to write a funny story. When a situation is funny, the
practiced news writer lets it tell itself and modestly disclaims credit for a humorous
effect. Journalistic humor requires the skilled and practiced hand of an Art
Buchwald.

Knowing the limitations, the experienced journalist seldom trifles with
humor. As E. B. White of *The New Yorker* once wrote, "Humor can be dissected as
a frog can. But the thing dies in the process and the innards are discouraging to any
but the pure scientific mind." Nevertheless, the inventive mind of the journalist
sometimes is able to produce a delightful change of pace in the dull routine of an
average day's news.

Here was what Hal Cooper wrote for the AP when a woman broke her leg
trying to climb out of a locked London public toilet:

> LONDON—What's a lady to do when trapped in a loo?

But more often than not, the journalist who is asked to be funny on deadline feels like emulating Dorothy Parker; when asked to define humor, she once said, "Every time I tried, I had to go and lie down with a cold wet cloth on my head."

Some Classic News Leads

The sharp news lead crops up in every conceivable situation. It may be produced by a great name of journalism or by a relative unknown. It may set the stage for the telling of a momentous news story. Or it may describe the weather.

These are some of the classics that are recalled whenever American journalists discuss the fine art of sharpening a lead:

> (By Lindesay Parrott in the New York Evening Post on a St. Patrick's Day parade)
> Fifty thousand Irishmen — by birth, by adoption and by profession — marched up Fifth Avenue today.

> (By H. Allen Smith in the New York World-Telegram on a one-sentence routine weather forecast)
> Snow, followed by small boys on sleds.

> (By Harry Ferguson, UPI executive editor, on the execution of Bruno Richard Hauptmann)
> The State of New Jersey, which spent $1,200,000 to capture and convict Bruno Richard Hauptmann, executed him tonight with a penny's worth of electricity.

> (By Hugh Mulligan, AP special correspondent, on a dull day during the Vietnam War)
> SAIGON — Rama Dama Rau, Premier Ky's personal astrologer who predicted five years ago that the war would be over in six months, was drafted today.

> (By Shirley Povich in the Washington Post on Don Larsen's perfect World Series game)
> The million-to-one shot came in. Hell froze over. A month of Sundays hit the calendar. Don Larsen today pitched a no-hit, no-run, no-man-reach-first game in a World Series.

> (By Howard Benedict, AP, on the launch of the new space shuttle Columbia's second flight)
> CAPE CANAVERAL — One last time, nine minutes before liftoff, launch director George Page held the countdown clock. "Let's take our time and do it right," he told his crew. They did, and the space shuttle Columbia's blastoff was brilliant.

> (By Mary McGrory in the Washington Star on the Watergate conspiracy trial of H. R. Haldeman, once President Nixon's top aide)
> On the 30th day of his trial, H. R. Haldeman's eyes are like two burnt holes in a blanket.

> (By Robert J. Casey in the Chicago Daily News describing what happened after a Texas explosion wiped out a public school)
> They're burying a generation today.

(By Charley Williamson in the Yonkers *(New York)* Herald Statesman *on events in nearby Elmsford)*

Tranquility ran rampant in Elmsford last night. No accidents, no fires, no traffic violations, no wife-beatings and no dog bites.

• Short Takes

There is an art to sharpening a lead. It takes practice and experience to write good ones. Here are some things for writers to remember about leads:

- A spot news lead should answer the question, "What happened?"
- Where the facts do not point to a definite conclusion, it sometimes helps to try to visualize the story in headline terms.
- Be careful not to bury the lead under nonessentials. It is equally important not to overwrite and overstress leads.
- When it is necessary to use attribution in a lead, always go with the source closest to the news.
- If a lead cannot be directly attributed, use at least two independent checks on the information before writing the story.
- When an official source clutters the lead, and there is no doubt about the authenticity of the news, drop the source to the next paragraph.
- Avoid using negative leads or leads of an indefinite nature as much as possible.
- Always explain large figures or unfamiliar places if they are used in leads. Make them mean something to the reader.
- Where several angles of a story must be worked into a brief space, use a summary lead. A tabular lead, separating each angle into a brief one-sentence paragraph, sometimes clarifies such a summary.

Following a news break, second-day leads are based on the next important step as the story develops. It can be done on rewrite, but it should be based on new information if at all possible.

Overnight leads are developed by the reporter on the job for the first edition of the paper next day to maintain interest in a continuing story.

CHAPTER 12

Writing Under Pressure

Writing for a deadline is one of the severest tests in journalism. Not everyone can stand the pressure. Nor is there any psychological test that can determine who's good at deadline writing and who isn't. Furthermore, you can't pick 'em by looks, like TV anchors or fashion models, because some may resemble Walter Mitty on a dreamy summer's afternoon.

Traits of Deadline Writers

Sometimes young and relatively inexperienced journalists, after messing up a few leads, turn out to be very good at this mind-boggling art. But there also are veterans in the business, some with outstanding reputations, who groan when they are asked to whip out a 15-minute lead on anything ranging from a fire or an earthquake to the abduction of an archbishop's niece.

What it comes down to is personal preference, mind over matter and superior technical ability as a writer. A lot of practice also helps.

Rating Yourself Along   What does it take to handle a deadline-writing assignment?

First of all, you must know your own capabilities. Nobody expects you to blaze away at the VDT at 100 words a minute. But if you can do 60 or 70 words a minute on a story that you know well, and not have to stop to straighten out an awkward sentence or a sour phrase, the chances are that deadline writing won't bother you.

However, for writers who are naturally slow, it's a different story. If you are one of these, you must be careful. When you have only 15 minutes to a deadline and you're doing the lead on a Page 1 story, you are going to need all of that time to produce a two-take story of about 500 words or so.

The trick is to rate yourself along and not attempt to do more than you can naturally handle. That is the first and most important rule.

Next, try to produce a short lead that contains the essence of the story. The emphasis is on *short*. Then, at once, go into the documentation for a paragraph or two and make sure to pick out a good high quote, if there is one, immediately afterward.

By that time, you'll be ready for the second main point in the story with its documentation. The rest of the lead will consist of writing down into the existing story until you reach a suitable paragraph where you can pick up the remainder.

If your story is an original, without a pickup (a story already in the paper), just end it. Nobody ever objects to a period. In fact, the more periods you use, the better.

Why Build a Breaking Story?　When writing and editing can be done so quickly on a VDT and phototypesetters can spew out a story at phenomenal rates of speed, many newcomers to journalism question the need for worrying about new leads, inserts, adds and all the other techniques used in building a story.

This is the answer from Louis D. Boccardi, executive editor of the AP:

> Most newspapers do use VDTs for writing and rewriting stories. The VDT does make it much easier to assemble a story and plug in new information. But the machines in no way detract from the need to know how to write a lead, when one is needed, and where and when to plug in an insert or sub.
> The arts of building a story and rewriting continue to be mainstays of newspapers and wire services.
> It's true that with the highspeed wires, we [at the AP] can repackage a story quickly and make it unnecessary for the wire desk to do so at a newspaper. But the chore remains for local copy. Writers should know how to build a breaking story.

Don't Crowd the Deadline　One of the principal rules for deadline writing has always been not to crowd the deadline, except possibly with the lead story. When a story has to be put together in bits and pieces (new leads, inserts, etc.), it takes time to assemble them for the pasteup on the page. And not even a Pagination machine can shorten the process by much.

In short, despite the speed of the electronic process, the rule against crowding the deadline is still very much worth observing.

Consider the mechanics of putting a newspaper together: Its separate pages move into production on an orderly schedule for placement on the presses. Pages with large advertising layouts are nearly always plugged up early with type and sent in first to be photographed. The same is true of most departmental pages, copy for which is prepared well in advance. That leaves a cluster of fairly open pages plus

Page 1 for developing news, but these also must be moved along on schedule if the edition is to go out on time.

In consequence, copy from the newsroom must be sent into production in an even and well-regulated flow or everything will come out at the last minute, a half-dozen pages will be bunched for photographing and plate-making, and the edition will be late.

This routine places the burden for deadline production mainly on the writers. Now, few writers have the temperament that enables them to wait until five or 10 minutes before a copy deadline to begin a lead. Nor can every story be held until the last minute for one last fact, one last quote. That way lies madness. For when copy piles up on the editors' VDT, everything goes wrong.

It is essential, therefore, to start writing as soon as possible and finish the story well before the deadline. Just about the only story that can be held until the last minute is the lead story, and doing that isn't very good practice, either.

Organize! From these observations, it follows that the literary style of a deadline story is by no means as important as its organization. If a developing story is not done in such a way as to permit easy expansion and contraction, quick handling on a deadline becomes impossible. This is not as difficult to do as it seems. With just a little thought, a reasonable scheme for building almost any developing story can be worked out and maintained under pressure.

This is the writer's business. Sometimes, editors are helpful in making suggestions; generally, however, they leave writers to their own devices for fear that they will freeze on deadline and produce nothing. There is good reason for such editorial concern, for many a story on a rapidly changing event is made up of a succession of new leads, inserts and adds, a constant challenge to the talent and ingenuity of writers.

The wonder is not that such assembly-line writing jobs read as well as they do, but that they are even put together. The process is intricate. It requires experience, patience, coolness, great skill at organizing detail and a maximum of staff cooperation.

Of all these, the most important word is, "Organize!"

Deadline Writing Subjects

Thomas F. Chester of the *Knoxville Journal* came across a good story at the nearby village of Sevierville, Tennessee. United States Customs agents had seized a small airplane from South America that was loaded with cocaine, but its pilot and passenger fled from the airport.

A Cocaine Bust After checking on the exact amount of cocaine and its going price, Chester returned to his office in time to write this story under deadline pressure:

By Thomas F. Chester

SEVIERVILLE, Tenn.—Authorities have issued at least one warrant in connection with the seizure of 614 pounds of pure cocaine from a twin-engine airplane at Sevierville-Gatlinburg Airport.

The cocaine, with a wholesale value of $70–$80 million and a street value of $217 million, was the largest seizure ever taken from an airplane and the second largest haul of illicit drugs in U.S. history, the Drug Enforcement Agency said.

U.S. Customs agents tailed the red and white Beechcraft Queen Air 80 Friday from San Antonio, Texas, to South America, where the cocaine was loaded by two men. The place was flown back Monday night to this East Tennessee town 30 miles southeast of Knoxville.

Agents said the two men fled after the plane touched down about 11 p.m.

Thomas F. Chester of the *Knoxville* (Tennessee) *Journal* compiling a Page 1 story. (Photograph: Gary Hamilton. Copyright by the *Knoxville Journal*. Used by permission.)

The Tennessee Bureau of Investigation obtained a warrant Tuesday from the Trial Justice Court of Sevier County charging one of the suspects with possession of a Schedule II drug [cocaine] with intent to resale, Judge Charles R. Edwards said.

Steve Watson, special agent in charge of the criminal unit, would not comment on reports that at least two Gatlinburg men were being sought in connection with the bust. Authorities, however, staked out a house on Upper Alpine Drive in Gatlinburg after the men eluded agents at the airport. . . .

Encounter with Auto Thieves Sam Martino of the *Milwaukee Journal,* tracking down the facts on a high-speed chase between the police and two alleged auto thieves, came across a mother in nearby Waukesha who had snatched her four-year-old son from one of the thieves. It made a Page 1 story:

By Sam Martino

WAUKESHA—Sandra Poeschl, 34, of Monches, clutched her son, Keith, four, as they sat in a waiting room at the Waukesha Sheriff's Department Wednesday. She said she was thankful the two of them were safe.

Mrs. Poeschl had feared that her son might be kidnapped after two men in a stolen car had crashed into her car while the suspects were fleeing from police in a high-speed auto chase on I-94.

Instead, Mrs. Poeschl told authorities, the men stole her maroon Grand Prix after she had grabbed her son from one of them.

Mrs. Poeschl and her son became a part of a series of events Wednesday that began in Milwaukee when a man stole a car at gunpoint from another woman, who had driven into a parking lot near 2929 State St.

Later, that suspect and another man in the stolen car crashed into the rear of the Poeschl car on the ramp connecting Highway F and I-94. Mrs. Poeschl shouted that her son was hurt and crying, after which both men left the stolen car. One said,

"Let me check to see if he is OK."

"He had his arms on my boy and I grabbed my boy out of his arms," the mother said.

The two men then got in her car and sped off with it, she said. . . .

300 Nurses Strike a Hospital The strike against Cape Cod Hospital, the main facility in the heavily settled Massachusetts resort area, was a major story for the weekly *Register,* which has been published since 1836 in Yarmouth Port. It became even more important when the walkout of 300 nurses and 635 support personnel was settled within hours of the copy deadline for the weekly newspaper. David Damkoehler, who had been covering the story for almost three weeks, wrote a 2,000-word piece under deadline pressure that began:

> Department by department, beginning with critical care units, Cape Cod Hospital was being reopened this week after the settlement by contract compromise of a 17-day strike by registered nurses.
> The breakthrough in the strike occurred at about 2 a.m. Tuesday. At that time, Eaman Hogan, from the Massachusetts Nurses' Association, and Jerome Weinstein, bargainer for the hospital administration, had a tentative agreement which would put 300 nurses and 635 support personnel back to work, reopening the cape's central health care facility.
> First to vote on the tentative pact some eight hours after it was agreed upon were 229 registered nurses. Gathering for two hours of voting in strike headquarters at the Outrigger Inn Motel, 210 of the strikers endorsed the pact and put the ball in the court of the hospital trustees. A little more than three hours later, trustees did their part. A two-year labor pact was sealed and the strike was over. . . .

Parts of the Story

Developing stories can be no better than their parts because the parts are often written separately and out of sequence. To add to the confusion, there is no standard nomenclature for the separate parts, although the widespread use of computers eventually will bring that about. For the present, only the wire services have agreed on standard terminology to tie their material in with the computers of members or clients. In the following summary, the terms and symbols that are more widely used will be described in order to make sense out of the deadline-writing operation. Where terminology differs, the operation itself will be recognizable.

New Lead   The term *new lead* is used by many newspapers to denote a new start on a story that is in type or in the computer. It is often referred to as a *new top*, particularly by the broadcast media. Symbols vary widely and include *NL*, *Nulead*, *1st lead* and *1st LD*, the last being the most prevalent for computer use.

Wire services for many years have been accustomed to top their stories with a *1st LD*, then a *2nd LD* and so forth, which has caused some newspapers to follow the practice. However, the term *new lead* still lingers on and will be used here for illustrative purposes. The difference in terminology arose because newspapers, having specified editions, did not need as many fresh tops as the wire services and broadcast media.

Expanding the New Lead.   There are two basic numbering systems in wide use in print journalism. (Broadcast scripts, being differently organized, are discussed in Chapter 15.) Many newspapers number the separate takes of a news story consecutively, while others follow the first take with *1st Add* and the slug, *2nd Add* and the slug, up to *4th and Final Add* and the slug, or however long the story is. This same thing happens when a story is topped.

In topping an existing newspaper story slugged *storm*, for example, a writer would begin with the slug *New Lead Storm* on the first take of copy. This would be followed, under one system, by *New Lead Storm—2*, *New Lead Storm—3*, etc., until the final take, which would be marked at the end: *End New Lead Storm*, *Pick Up Type*, or *Pick Up Earlier*. Under the more cumbersome system of writing adds, which is used by wire services and many large newspapers, *New Lead Storm* would be followed by *1st Add*, *New Lead Storm*, *2nd Add*, *New Lead Storm*, etc., until the final take, when the same kind of concluding instructions would be written.

Fixing the Old Story If the old story is still in the computer memory system and not in the paper, it can be joined to the new lead very simply on a VDT with appropriate editing or corrections. What then results, in effect, is a fresh story.

But if the old story is in the paper and the fresh top is for a new edition, then a *markup* will show where the new and old stories fit. At the paragraph where the new lead is to be joined to the old story, the instruction would be written: *Pick Up after New Lead Storm* usually shortened to *PU NL Storm*. Computer language varies, so there are varying symbols for the latter.

However, many editors now see little point to this complicated procedure and instruct writers to put together an entirely new story on the VDT unless the account is abnormally long.

How the System Works For those who still need it, here is an example of how a new lead is written down into an existing story so that the two join smoothly at a designated paragraph. The technique is known as "making a clean pickup."

THE OLD STORY
Slug: Storm

The first snowstorm of the winter swirled over Centerville today, but the Weather Bureau said it would not last long.

With the first flurry of white flakes at 10 a.m., Forecaster F. L. Maynes announced that the snow was expected to melt rapidly. The 10 a.m. temperature was 31 degrees and Maynes said, "It's likely to go up above the freezing point."

But, he went on, "There is just a chance that the temperature will stay just where it is, and if that happens we'll be in for a real storm."

The street superintendent, A. R. Ward, took no chances. He put his entire force on a standby basis, tested his snowplows and arranged to hire snow removal trucks if they were needed.

xxx

THE NEW LEAD
Slug: New Lead Storm

An all-day snowstorm tied up Centerville today and threatened to reach a depth of 15 inches before tomorrow.

At least five persons died in auto accidents that were attributed to the storm. In the first four hours, up to 2 p.m., the snow reached a depth of four inches.

It snarled traffic, played havoc with bus schedules and made walking dangerous.

The snow crossed up the Weather Bureau. It predicted at first that the snow would change to rain. A later forecast warned of an all-night snowfall that would pile at least 15 inches on the city.

End New Lead Storm
Pick Up Type

In the markup that indicates where the new lead would join the old story, it is clear that the pickup point in the storm piece is the second paragraph of the old story. The new lead has been written with this in mind. The details of the storm would be added to the part of the story that remains in the paper.

Lead All   A *lead all*, as its name implies, tops a new lead. It is seldom used, for it is seldom needed. On newspapers, when a *lead all* is ordered, it is kept very short and generally is written so that it reads into the old story at the second paragraph. In wire service terminology, a *lead all* is simply a *2nd LD*.

Just about the only time that the *lead all* has any meaning is after a *new lead* has cleared production and a fresh break in the story occurs before the edition deadline. In such cases, the editor has the choice of using a *bulletin*, which sits atop the old story separated by a dash, or a brief new top that is joined to the old story. Generally, it is just as easy to do a *lead all* with the fresh break in a terse paragraph that turns the new material smoothly into the previous story. This is an example:

> *Lead All Storm*
>   Mayor Wallis closed nearly all city offices today as an all-day snowstorm tied up traffic and threatened to reach a 15-inch depth before tomorrow.
>
> End Lead All Storm
Pick Up Type

The markup would indicate the second paragraph of the previous new lead as the pickup point. If there were time, the mayor's statement would also be inserted into the story at an appropriate point in order to document the *lead all*.

Insert   An *insert* should be written in such a way that it will fit smoothly into an old story or a new lead. A lazy way of doing this is to begin an insert with the words, "meanwhile," "earlier," or "at the same time." These threadbare devices do not make for a smoothly joined story and should not be used, except on a deadline.

If an insert corrects material previously sent, it merely replaces the old paragraphs. If it adds to or elaborates on detail already in the story, it may be necessary to condense some of the type that is in the paper to make room for the new material. If that is done, it should all be a part of the same insert.

As is the case with a *new lead* or *lead all*, an insert must be accompanied by pickup directions unless the story can be fixed on a VDT. This applies to wire service and special copy sent by wire, too. To illustrate what happens to an insert, the mayor's statement, if put into the storm lead above, could easily be substituted for the third paragraph in this manner:

> *Insert A Storm*
>   The mayor took this emergency step as the snow snarled traffic, played havoc with bus schedules and made walking dangerous.
>   "I am asking all city department heads to close their offices by 2:30 p.m., he said, "with the exception of those that are directly concerned with clearing the streets. This is an emergency."
>
> End Insert A Storm

It is a good practice to name succeeding inserts with letters of the alphabet. In this way the sequence of inserts can be maintained, and there is also an automatic check on how many have been written. That is standard newspaper procedure but is not usually followed by wire services.

Add   Here is a case of confusion twice compounded. On newspapers that use the *add* system of numbering takes, the addition to a story presents no problem and is merely numbered in sequence to show where it should go. On papers that number the takes of a story consecutively, an *add* also goes at the end. It doesn't help much that some editors drop off the additional "d." But as long as everybody understands the system of the particular paper, it doesn't matter.

In the storm story, for example, the five persons whose deaths were attributed to the storm could be listed by name, age, address and occupation in an *Add Storm.* If greater prominence was desired, the names could be inserted higher in the story.

Bulletin   In the days when newsboys hawked newspaper extras and there were devices for inserting news on Page 1 without stopping the presses, the *bulletin* was a big deal in the newsroom. It is less useful now except when it is part of a wire service report or gives an important sports result. For the ordinary run of news in a newspaper, of what utility are a few words in boldface, topped by headlines in boxcar type, against the continuing narrative that any reader can hear by flipping on the radio or television set? And with pictures, too?

The newspaper bulletin, when used, consists of about 20 or 30 words and is placed on top of the story to which it refers, separated by a dash, if a *new lead* or *lead all* cannot be written. This would be a bulletin for the storm story:

Bulletin Precede Storm
　　Two autos collided on snowswept Route 82 north of Centerville at 2:40 p.m. today, killing at least six persons.

3 em dash

End Bulletin Precede Storm

For a fresh news break of overwhelming importance that refers to nothing already in the paper, no rational editor would go with just a few words. For example, if word was received of the death of the president of the United States while an edition was on the press, sufficient detail would be incorporated in a fresh Page 1, technically known as a replate, to make publication something more than a gesture.

Flash   A *flash* is reserved for the biggest kind of news, outside the sports pages. It is an attention-calling device to warn of a major news development. Typically, it consists of a dateline, three or four words, the name of the sender and the time. It cannot be used to print because it is so curtailed; it must always be followed by either a bulletin or some type of lead. This is a flash:

WASHINGTON—PRESIDENT IS DEAD

Kill   Another journalistic word that must be used with great care is *kill.* It means that material to which it refers should be destroyed.

On routine corrections it is advisable to use a different term, *eliminate*. For example, in doing a note on the previous storm insert, the correction would be: *"Eliminate Third Pgh New Lead Storm."*

The word kill should be saved for extraordinary situations. The mandatory instructions *Must Kill* can never be used on a newspaper without the permission of the editor in charge unless the reporter is filing from a distant point.

Sub   As its name indicates, a *sub* substitutes for a previous news account. *Sub Weather*, when it is written, would automatically dispose of the weather story that is in the paper. It is a newspaper term and is seldom used in wire service practice.

Of course, a sub is usually impractical except when it is short and eliminates a short previous account. In the weather story that has been built up over several hours, it would be foolish to do the news a second time for some purely esthetic reason.

The Effect of Terminals   All these technicalities used to be of great importance, but terminals and fast printing by photographic means have made it less necessary to transmit the news in dramatic bits and pieces. An entire new story can be sent and put into type now in the time it used to take to handle a short lead, except when a story is too long to be reset.

Piecing the Story Together

When the lead to a long news story is expected shortly before the deadline, much of the story must be written in anticipation of the lead. It must also be done in such a way that, regardless of what happens to shape the lead, the earlier part of the story will fit it.

This technique of writing a story backward is known in newspaper work as doing *B copy* or *B matter*. Some newspapers call it *A copy* or *A matter*. Still others slug it *running* or *lead to come*. For purposes of discussion, *B copy* will be used here as the term for the earlier part of the story that is written in anticipation of a lead to be done a few minutes before the deadline.

Running stories of this type often have to be written in several pieces, one stacked atop the other. The way they are assembled, in the order in which they appear in the paper, is *lead* (not *new lead*), *A copy* and *B copy*. Often the *A copy* is eliminated as a needless and complicating step so that the two pieces that remain are merely *lead* and *B copy*.

B Copy   This is a process that wastes space. It should be used only on major stories, or on sports events calling for detail that is written before the lead is begun.

It is wasteful because, by its very nature, *B copy* includes material that could easily be chopped from the end of a story. Except when it is done in chronological order, *B copy* contributes little to the art of good news writing.

Its sole justification is that no paper can do with just a paragraph or two on the outcome of an election, convention, trial, contest, sports event or similar account.

Thus, when a writer anticipates the passage of a new law, or a verdict, or an election of a mayor or governor or the end of a football game, *B copy* is used.

The trick is to write it in such a way that it will easily join to any lead that is written, regardless of how the lead may begin or end. In effect, the documentation for the lead is bound to be in the *B copy* somewhere.

Therefore, the way the *B copy* begins is important. In doing an election story, the *B copy* could start:

> *B Copy Vote*
>> The polls closed at 7 p.m.
>> During the day there was a heavy turnout of voters because of the interest in the election and the sunny fall weather. Much of the vote was in by 2 p.m., but lines still curled away from many a polling place at the closing hour.
>> The issues . . .

Similarly, in a news account of a trial, the *B copy* could begin with the hour at which the judge delivered the charge and gave the case to the jury. An account of a convention fight, leading up to the nomination of a particular candidate, could open with a summary of the remarks of the first speaker and continue chronologically. A baseball game or other sports account could fit snugly into the *B copy* pattern by beginning with the action and describing it tersely as it develops, inning by inning or quarter by quarter.

Necessarily, the writer must have a fair idea of which names or titles are to appear in the lead of the story. To avoid repeating full names and titles, these would be left out of the *B copy* and only the last names of the principal actors would be used. Such considerations would help to make the *B copy* and lead fit smoothly together.

Writing Backward

To illustrate the process of writing a story backward, here is a curtailed version of a murder trial verdict as done for a newspaper:

> *B Copy Getty*
>> The verdict climaxed a long, tense day of courtroom drama. Judge Davis gave the case to the jurors at 11:03 a.m. He charged them to acquit Miss Getty if they believed her to have been insane at the time of the slaying of her invalid father.
>> "But," said Judge Davis sternly, "if you find Miss Getty knew the nature and quality of her act, and knew in fact that it was wrong, then you must find her guilty of murder in the first degree."
>> Miss Getty was pale but calm as the judge gave his charge. Her mother, a large woman in a crumpled black dress, sobbed audibly.
>> For much of the afternoon, the courtroom was deserted except for a few clerks and newspaper reporters. Then, toward 4 p.m., word sped about the quiet marble corridors of the court house that the jury was coming in.
>> Thus, the stage was set for the last act of the drama that has fascinated much of the nation for the past two weeks.
>> The state had tried to prove that Miss Getty committed a "mercy murder"

when she shot and killed her father with his revolver. District Attorney Lindsey hammered away at the theme that no one has a right to take a human life.

Defense attorney Streator insisted, throughout, that Miss Getty was insane at the moment she pulled the trigger. He did not contend, however, that she was insane before or afterward.

Miss Getty was her own best witness. Testifying in her own defense, a tall, plain-looking girl with short brown hair, she kept a small Bible clutched in her hands. She told jurors quite simply that she could remember nothing of the events on the night her father was fatally shot, from the moment she entered his room until she came to in her own room.

The state was never able to shake her story.

End B Copy Getty
A Copy Upcoming

A Copy Getty

Miss Getty, summoned from the hotel where she had been staying, entered the low-ceilinged, oak-paneled courtroom at 4:16 p.m. to hear the verdict. Her mother and her attorney, Arthur P. Streator, were with her. District Attorney Mead Lindsey followed them.

Miss Getty still wore the simple black dress, with a small gold pin at the throat, in which she had appeared throughout the trial. A small black hat was pulled down over her straight hair. Her shoes were low, black, and flat-heeled.

Her mother was weeping as Judge Davis entered, short, red-faced, but grave. A few moments later the jury filed in to take its place and the courtroom waited tensely for the words that determined Miss Getty's fate.

End A Copy Getty
Pick Up B Copy

FLASH MARILOU GETTY ACQUITTED GRIMMEL 4:32 PM*

Lead Getty

Marilou Getty was acquitted today of the "mercy murder" of her father.

A jury of four men and eight women, most of them in tears, set the tall, 19-year-old choir singer free at 4:31 p.m. They had deliberated five hours and 28 minutes.

Miss Getty embraced her weeping mother, Mrs. Catherine Getty, and said:

"I was sure they would not find me guilty."

Supreme Court Judge Myron J. Davis dismissed the jurors but did not thank them for their services. To Miss Getty he said gruffly,

"You are free to go home with your mother. Try to take care of her."

By its verdict the jury showed that it had believed Miss Getty's story that she was temporarily insane when she fatally shot her father, Morgan R. Getty, a builder who doctors had said would die in a month of cancer. The slaying occurred last October at the Getty home, 365 Baldur Place.

End Lead Getty
Pick Up A Copy Getty, Then B Copy

Dummy Leads In the story of the Getty verdict, alternate paragraph leads would have been prepared to cover several possibilities if the paper had been

*Local papers use undated flashes on court trials, sports events, etc. Nationally, a flash is used only on news of major importance to the whole country.

closer to its deadline and unable to wait for a "live" lead from the courtroom. On receipt of the flash the correct *dummy lead* would have been placed atop the A Copy and sent to production with previously prepared headlines to match. Here is how some of the dummy leads would have looked:

> *Lead Getty—Acquit—Hold for Release*
> A Supreme Court jury today acquitted Marilou Getty, 19, of the "mercy murder" of her cancer-stricken father, Morgan R. Getty, last October 24.
> *End Lead Getty—Acquit—Hold for Release*

> *Lead Getty—1st Degree Murder—Hold for Release*
> Marilou Getty, 19, was found guilty of first-degree murder in Supreme Court today for the "mercy murder" of her cancer-stricken father, Morgan R. Getty, last October 24.
> *End Lead Getty—1st Degree Murder—Hold for Release*

Of course, other dummy leads would be prepared to follow the various additional contingencies. The practice, however, is not as widespread as it once was because it gives the public nothing it hasn't already received from the broadcast media, and very little of that.

● Short Takes

Here are the main things you should remember about writing under pressure:

- Rate yourself along. If you're a speed merchant, you can turn out a good 500-word piece on deadline. But if you work slowly, you must never attempt more than you can handle.
- Never miss a deadline.
- Don't crowd deadlines.
- Learn to organize your stories so you can always top them without having to rewrite the whole business.
- You have to be familiar with every type of story in the news because you never know when you'll be tossed into one of them. Read newspapers!
- If you're doing a new lead, write down into the old story to a point where the two join smoothly at a paragraph.
- If you're doing an insert, make sure it fits and reads as if it were part of the original story.
- Keep your bulletins short. A 20-word bulletin is par for the course.
- Never send a flash if you can send a bulletin instead. A flash can be used on the broadcast media, but not in print.
- Watch out for words like "kill" and "flash." They're rarities in the business and are reserved for major occasions.
- If you're writing B copy, leave out the first names and complete identifications of anybody who'll be in the lead. Make sure that your B copy starts in a way that will pick up smoothly no matter how the lead ends.
- Relax!

CHAPTER 13

Handling the Story on Rewrite

One of the best things that can happen to newcomers to journalism is to be assigned to the rewrite bank. There they spend the entire working day with professionals whose main interest is writing. In a highly practical way, they learn some of the essentials of the art by trial and error. And very often, in a tough spot, a few gruff words of advice from an older colleague will have a greater effect on a beginner than a dozen hours at a writing seminar.

The Fine Art of Rewrite

It is many years since rewrite people were confined to redoing dumb stories and turning out byline copy for energetic but illiterate legmen. Today's rewrite men and women are specialists—editors and reporters by turn—and are valued for their dependability and news judgment.

Introduction to Rewrite　The beginner who is put on rewrite usually fears the experience as a form of journalistic hazing. It isn't. Newcomers are not expected to produce a miracle on deadline. The emphasis, instead, is on the development of good writing habits—accuracy, clarity, orderliness and coherence.

New staff members are seldom tossed into the pressure cooker. They are given the more leisurely tricks—day rewrite for a morning paper (something like 11 a.m. to 7 p.m.) or night rewrite for the first edition of an afternoon paper (for example, midnight to 8 a.m.). It gives them a chance to work at a slower pace, to observe how others handle writing assignments and, above all, to read newspapers—their own and the opposition, local or suburban.

One of the first lessons for newcomers on rewrite is that the telephone becomes a virtual extension of their personalities. They take notes from reporters by phone; check press releases, obits and other vital statistics by phone; obtain interviews on the breaking news by phone; clarify obscure points in speeches and reports by phone, and conduct research by phone. Very often, in a working day, they will be on the phone, listening and asking questions, more than they will be writing at the VDT.

It always seems to surprise newcomers on rewrite that seasoned reporters seldom dictate their stories by telephone, except possibly on deadline, but turn in notes in an informal, conversational style. One youngster, in his first day on rewrite for a wire service, was so awe-stricken that he faithfully recorded every word telephoned by a reporter covering picket-line violence and copied the reporter's notes without change. The young writer was informed rather abruptly, when the story came up on an editor's VDT, that he was to write the story from the notes, not reproduce the notes verbatim.

Sometimes the same thing happens when a beginner is told to do a story from a press release. The beginner dutifully checks with the source to make certain the handout is genuine, asks a few desultory questions and then—impressed by the great corporation or government office that is the issuing agency—virtually copies the handout. Once again, the instructions from the desk are to base the story on the news, if any, and omit the self-serving statements in the press release. The music may be the same, but the lyrics have to be different.

How the Rewrite Bank Works   After a few such experiences, any intelligent beginner should discard the notion—prevalent in some journalism schools—that the rewrite bank is a refuge for tired old hacks. One experience such as this will put rewrite in better perspective:

There's been a major newsbreak close to an edition deadline. Several reporters are out on the story, covering various angles at widely separated points. Two editors are giving them directions as they phone in. The telegraph desk is watching the AP file as it develops out-of-town angles. The managing editor is holding Page 1, and the circulation director is in the newsroom to see what the fuss is all about.

At such a time, the burden of the operation rests on the rewrite bank. The person assigned to do the lead story is geared to such moments with notes and wire copy printouts piled around the rim of the desk in seeming disarray. Everybody watches that desk.

But the writer, with a glance at the clock, begins work nervelessly on the VDT—a paragraph or two at a time—so the editors can begin reading and processing, producing layout and headlines. Take after take flows from the machine into production until the story is complete. Without argument. Without fuss.

No hacks could be trusted to do this kind of work, day after day, week after week. Some may have tried it, but they haven't lasted very long. They don't have the know-how. And the beginner instinctively realizes it and begins to appreciate the importance of rewrite.

Duties on Rewrite   When a president is elected or a war begins, when a pope dies or a hurricane strikes a great city, the story must be written quickly. The lead must be available within a matter of seconds if the account is for a wire service, a newspaper deadline or immediate broadcast.

Nor do great events alone receive such spectacular treatment. In the ordinary run of local news it may be necessary to give quick handling to a fire, a robbery, a baseball or football game, the death of a prominent citizen or even an interview with a million-dollar sweepstakes winner.

In such situations, skilled writing specialists are called on. It is no time to spin theories or philosophize over the news. This is the spot that was made for the rewrite man or woman.

The Necessary Ingredients   The first quality of those who work at rewrite is the ability to turn out clear, accurate and interesting copy without hesitation under all conceivable circumstances. Facility and adaptability are other qualities that are mandatory on rewrite. Such writers may handle in the same working day a dramatic straight news story, a light feature, a thoughtful interpretive piece, or even a street tragedy tinged with human interest. The least desirable quality is temperament.

Anybody who wants to stay on the rewrite bank for very long must demonstrate sharp and accurate news judgment. Editors cannot forever be telling their writers what the lead should be. They must know, based on their background, their current reading and specialized knowledge. However, if it happens that an editor wants a lead other than the one that has been written, the slant should be changed without fuss.

What Writers Can Do

Competent writers can illuminate the bare details of reporters' work with considerable newsworthy material. Being detached from the event itself and under no compulsion to leap to the telephone with every new detail or file on a portable terminal, writers can afford to take a broader view and try to make their stories amount to more than a surface account. Frequently, they succeed.

For one thing, writers who are handling a continuing story will usually have a good idea of the background, the principal characters and the scene. For another, reporters who are out on such a story cannot consult the newspaper library, or morgue, for the fill-in information that is often so necessary to make a piece authentic as well as interesting. The two are not necessarily synonymous.

Nor can reporters divide what is happening at other points that may have an important bearing on the development of the story. In a sense, therefore, writers in the office actually are in a better position to tell what is going on than are the reporters in the field.

Finally, writers have direct and immediate contact with editors and can discuss operations with them. Where reporters would be hopelessly snarled up by space estimates or the lack of important background, writers handle such things in stride. Yet, for all their advantages, not even the cleverest member of the rewrite bank can make a story seem as real as that of a reporter who knows how to describe the sights, sounds and smells associated with the news. The best writers, in fact, are those who are too wise to try to counterfeit reality by imagining a news scene in too great detail. That way lies error and a resultant failure of credibility. Reporters will always be the legs, eyes and ears of a newspaper; no terminal, computer or camera can substitute for them.

Rewrite Procedures

There are no blueprints for working on a rewrite desk. No accepted body of procedure has ever been drawn up for this difficult and demanding job. Yet there are certain things that good writers do to reduce the hazards of processing the news. These are some of them.

Listening to Reporters   The old movies on the late-late show have made a burlesque out of the relationship between reporters and writers. Anybody who has ever seen the various movie and stage productions of the Hecht-MacArthur classic *The Front Page* will remember the line used by one of the reporters in the Chicago Criminal Court press room, "Hello, baby — get me rewrite." That's the way it was in 1927, but the legend persists that the reporter is a comic and the writer is some kind of creep.

The writer, invariably male, is usually depicted as a character, sometimes with a hat on, who keeps snapping "Yah — yah — yah" into the telephone out of the corner of his mouth, presumably to let the reporter know somebody is on the line. Or he may make nasty remarks about the reporter's professional and personal life.

If this were done on a major story, it would hopelessly jam the delicate machinery of news gathering and news transmission. The rewrite and reporting processes must be handled smoothly, and with a minimum of friction, or they break down. It is not unheard of for a reporter to hang up on an inconsiderate writer, which always requires a lot of explaining and causes unnecessary anguish.

Reporters are trained to tell their stories by beginning with a brief summary, then giving the pertinent details and incidentally spelling out difficult or unusual names and repeating figures. When they finish, they generally ask, "Any questions?" Considerate writers then conclude the communication process by filling in the blanks without coarseness, wisecracks or "Yah — yah — yahs."

The wiser and more experienced members of the rewrite bank always remember to ask reporters, if there is time, whether they have suggestions for a lead. But no writer with a professional newspaper background will ever try to tell reporters their business or suggest improved methods for covering a story. These are mainly the business of the editors.

Updating

When it becomes necessary to rewrite a clip from another paper or combine such old news with fresh material developed by a reporter or wire service, that is the job of the rewrite battery.

The first effort should be to try to get something fresh on the story by making a telephone call. There is nothing deader than rewriting an old clip that was originally based on an older handout. If writers can get nothing new, they should at least update the news by featuring a different slant and using a lot less of the whole story. The writer who merely repeats a previously published or broadcast story, or picks up words and phrases at random, does not last very long.

Devices to do away with the rehash include the use of chronological stories to reconstruct some major news event, the engagement of experts to criticize a cultural event or explain a new development in economics, the increasing trend toward lavishly illustrated stories, and even the publication of reporters' diaries when they are on a long and significant story.

Writing from PR Sources

The rewrite bank generally inherits the task of turning routine public relations copy into short news accounts where it is warranted. Whoever handles the story is well aware, of course, that a public relations release serves the interests of the issuing agency and that these interests do not necessarily coincide with those of the newspaper.

Tricks of the Trade For example, as most journalists know, it is a threadbare device to put a propaganda message in quotes, attributed to a prominent person, in the body of a press release. Some of the less imaginative publicity officials also persist in needlessly attributing an announcement to two or three persons or agencies they want to publicize.

It should not be assumed that a public relations announcement must always be discounted. Quite the contrary is true if it is issued from a responsible source and contains news of importance to the community. However, newspaper writers should take stock of whatever facts they have from public relations sources, before writing, and ask the simplest of all news questions: "What happened?" The lead and its documentation then may be separated from all the embroidery. The result may not precisely please the issuing agency, but that cannot be helped. The newspaper's first responsibility is to the public.

Here are two examples of how a sharp-shooting public relations office and a newspaper would handle the same set of facts:

1. *A Shift in Executive Personnel*

   J. Cadwalader Winnefall, president of the J. C. Winnefall Manufacturing Company, announced today that Evans B. Arctander, its general manager, had been designated head of the company's London office.

   In accepting the new post, Mr. Arctander wrote in a letter to Mr. Winnefall, "I am most grateful to you and to our executive board for having made the London office my next important post with our company and can assure you that I will do my utmost to serve the company there just as I have in the home office. I have looked forward for some years to a lightening of the heavy load I have been carrying."

The new general manager will be J. Cadwalader Winnefall Jr., who has been promoted from assistant general manager. Mr. Winnefall was graduated from Princeton four years ago. . . .

*   *   *

The J. C. Winnefall Mfg. Co. today named J. Cadwalader Winnefall Jr. as its new general manager. He replaces Evans B. Arctander, who has been shifted to the London office.

2. A Fund-Raising Report

Follet Hargreaves, chairman of the trustees of Graditton College, appealed today to its 30,000 living alumni to support its $3 million drive for a new athletic field house.

"Graditton deserves your loyalty and your support," he said at a report luncheon in the Graditton Faculty Club, which was attended by the chairmen of alumni committees. "I am sure that all alumni cherish Graditton traditions and want to see us flourish. To this end, the new athletic field house is a most necessary addition to our plant."

The chairman reported funds in hand and pledges of $62,000, an increase of $24,000 over last month. This brings the total contributions to date to $184,456 for the Graditton Athletic Field House Fund. Checks should be made payable to the fund. All contributions are tax-deductible.

*   *   *

Graditton College announced today that $62,000 had been contributed to a fund for a new athletic field house, bringing the total to $184,456. The goal of the campaign, which began last year, is $3 million.

A Rewrite Testimonial

Robert B. McFadden, who has served both as a general-assignment reporter and rewrite man at the *New York Times*, gave this assessment of the responsibilities on rewrite in an article for the *Bulletin of the American Society of Newspaper Editors:*

The rewrite man, at his best, must be a nearly ideal newspaperman—a thorough, fast, tenacious and objective reporter with an encyclopedic memory, voluminous contacts, the news sense of a great editor and the ability to write with speed, clarity, grace and an unshakable calm against deadline.

He must be willing to find human dramas buried in the seemingly impenetrable bedrock of welfare statistics and ponderous government reports. He must be able to convey the hoopla of parades and politics, the tragedies of plane crashes and urban riots, the intricacies of nuclear power and municipal budgets. He must find personalities behind the masks of politicians and celebrities, and articulate the frustrations of people snared in the webs of bureaucracy. And to tell it straight, he must somehow see—if it is only in his mind's eye—the weary faces of soot-streaked firemen, of sobbing tornado victims and of the children of poverty.

The late Paul Scott Mowrer, a Pulitzer Prize-winning reporter who edited the

Paris Post many years ago, said it best one frustrating day when he called the editor of the rival Paris Herald Tribune and made him an offer:

"I'll trade you three of my geniuses for one good rewrite man."

● Short Takes

Here are the main things to remember about handling a story on rewrite:

- *Don't interrupt reporters.* Listen to them until they finish with their notes and ask, "Any questions?" Then ask them to plug up the holes in the story.
- *Don't wait for the deadline to creep up on you.* When you have enough facts for a story, start writing. You can always top it, insert or add to it.
- *Cultivate a sharp news judgment.* You can't be running to editors all the time to ask what the lead should be. You do it. They'll tell you quickly enough if it's not what they want.
- *Don't expect to be praised much.* You're paid to do good work. If you do bad work, you'll know about it in a hurry.
- Remember that when you're rewriting a clip or a press release, you do have to try for a new angle by phone and check the available facts. Then, be careful about picking up somebody else's phraseology. The music may be the same but the lyrics must be different.
- *Watch those phony second-day angles.* It's better, when updating a story, to use a new fact you obtain yourself or a feature angle instead of using, "Joe Glutz was dead today . . ." So was Julius Caesar.
- Don't let press agents get away with a story they want to plant. *If there's no news in it, don't write it.* If there is news, do it straight and take the propaganda content out of it.
- *Remember that you always go with your own reporter,* in case of disagreement with the opposition in print or broadcast, unless and until he or she proves to be unreliable.
- This is the spot to repeat: *Go with what you've got.* The edition is not going to be held for your works of art.
- And, for emphasis, *when in doubt, leave out.* They can't sue you for what you don't write.

CHAPTER 14

Writing for Wire Services

Wire services meet deadlines every minute for the news media in America and the world. They supply news from all sources—local, state, national and foreign. They also provide pictures, features, analysis, criticism, cartoons and all the other byproducts of the news.

Inevitably, because of the nature of their work, wire service people are known as speedy reporters but seldom receive credit for their skill as writers. And yet some of the best deadline writing in American journalism has been done for the Associated Press and United Press International.

Quality and Style

In wire services as they are conducted today, there are many more opportunities for well-reported, thoroughly researched stories than there were 15 or 20 years ago. There is more emphasis on better writing. And there are greater incentives for originality and enterprise. Not every story must be ground out like so much sausage. Even on big news, when speed is essential, well-trained writers can produce readable, exciting stories.

These are the goals for young writers on wire services. They are worth the effort.

Wire Service Style The bigger the story, the simpler the language must be if it is to be quickly told and understood by a mass audience. This is an inviolate rule in writing for wire services (also called news agencies and press associations). Sentences should be brief. Dependent clauses should be turned into separate sentences where possible. The one- and two-syllable words—the familiar Anglo-Saxon words—should be the basis for this kind of reportage. Speed is useless if the writing is not clear and accurate.

Handling the Big Story

When walkways over the lobby of the Hyatt Regency Hotel in Kansas City collapsed, flinging dancing couples to their deaths, there was no time to debate the niceties of journalism. It was difficult enough to find out what had happened and get out the news, as the Associated Press's coverage shows.*

The first report came at 9:15 p.m. and could not indicate the scope of the tragedy:

> A273
> AM Walkway Collapse
> URGENT
>   KANSAS CITY, Mo. (AP)—One or more walkways over the lobby at the Hyatt Regency Hotel collapsed Friday night, leaving an unknown number of people killed and others injured or trapped, the Kansas City Fire Department said.
>   The accident apparently happened during a weekly dance contest. A hotel staff member estimated that at least 1,500 people were in the area at the time of the collapse.
> AP NY 07 17 2115 EDT

Moving the First Lead It was 24 minutes before a 1st lead moved, but two service messages meanwhile informed editors that there were at least six dead in the accident. The beginning of the 1st lead, a "writethru," or complete new story, follows:

> A 278
> AM Walkway Collapse, 1st LD—Writethru A273.
> URGENT
>   KANSAS CITY, Mo. (AP)—At least six people were killed Friday night when three sky bridges inside an enclosed courtyard at the Hyatt Regency Hotel collapsed onto a ballroom floor full of dancers, police said.
>   Police said an undetermined number of people were injured and they expected to find more dead.
>   As the first bodies were pulled from a tangle of twisted girders and broken glass, officials designated one room of the lavish downtown hotel as a temporary morgue.

---

*A bulletin has highest priority on the AP's "A" wire, the main trunk wire. An "urgent" comes next. Each "take," or segment of copy, is numbered and each bears a brief "slug" or name to identify the story from others on the wire. A flash, of course, takes precedence over everything. Times are in Eastern Daylight (EDT).

The accident apparently occurred during a weekly dance contest. A hotel staff member estimated that at least 1,500 people were in the area at the time of the collapse. . . .
AP NY 07 17 2139 EDT

Five minutes later, the story escalated with the discovery of more bodies and an estimate of fatalities by the Kansas City police chief. The AP signaled a major story as follows:

A280
AM Walkway Collapse 2nd LD A:278
BULLETIN
     KANSAS CITY, Mo. (AP)—At least 27 people died Friday night when three sky bridges inside an enclosed courtyard at the Hyatt Regency Hotel collapsed onto a ballroom full of dancers, police said.
     Police Chief Norman Caron said at least 100 people were injured.
MORE
AP NY 07 17 2144 EDT

Like the first story, this one was also a fresh account. But the extent of the tragedy mounted by the minute as rescue efforts intensified and the lists of dead and injured grew longer.

There was a 3d lead 28 minutes after the second. A 4th lead, with 39 dead, followed in 15 minutes. At 11:27 p.m., two hours and 12 minutes after the first notice, the AP filed this definitive account , given here in substantial part:

A 290
AM Walkway Collapse 5th LD A 278
URGENT
     KANSAS CITY, Mo. (AP)—Three "sky bridges" in an enclosed courtyard at the Hyatt Regency Hotel in Kansas City collapsed onto a lobby floor full of dancers Friday night, killing at least 43 people and injuring about 100, police said.
     Bodies were pulled from a tangle of twisted girders and broken glass where the concrete walkways fell to the floor. One room of the lavish midtown hotel was designated as a morgue.
     After talking with officials on the scene, Mayor Richard Berkley said there would be "more, many more deaths."
     One police officer said he could see "arms and legs sticking out all over" from under the debris as rescuers brought bodies out.
     "You couldn't believe it, it just started crashing, caving in," said Dorothy Johnson, a nurse who was having dinner at the restaurant overlooking the lobby. "We just sat there and watched it cave in."
     "There was a rumbling sound, exactly like a rolling clap of thunder outside and everything got real quiet for a moment. Then there was mass confusion," said Randy Dunford, whose wife was just about to walk onto a crosswalk when it fell.
     Police Chief Norman Caron said the injured who could walk were being placed on a city bus for transportation to a hospital. Others were being treated where they lay in the rubble.
     The ballroom beneath the walkways was crowded with people dancing to big-band

music at a "Tea Dance," which has become a Friday-night fixture at the latest luxury hotel to open in Kansas City.

A hotel staff member said at least 1,500 people were in the area when the collapse occurred. . . .

AP NY 07 17 2327 EDT

The bulletins, urgents, leads and writethrus kept piling up for the remainder of the AM cycle (the report for morning papers) and continued through the PM cycle (the report for first and subsequent editions of afternoon papers). When the rescuers finally finished work, there were 111 dead and hundreds of others injured. It was one of the worst tragedies in the nation's history.

The broadcast reporters at the scene had the advantage of ad-libbing their reports and getting to officials and survivors quickly with microphones and cameras. But the wire services, which file to both newspaper and broadcast members and clients, had to be just as fast and even more accurate, so the AP was more conservative in its early casualty figures.

There was no way, under the circumstances, in which either wire services or newspapers could have reported the story other than by going to inverted pyramid style for the principal account. It is worth noting that the AP filed no color story, using the news feature approach, during the first two hours after the collapse.

Despite the pressure for short, pithy leads, the AP's opening sentences in all accounts given here were longer than normal because the unique nature of the accident had to be described. That was, however, a departure from normal wire service style. Generally, this kind of writing has to be sharper and more compact than newspaper material.

A President Is Shot

Reporters can be no better than their sources. And that goes for White House reporters as well as all others. For they, no more than anybody else outside a small hospital room in Washington, did not know for 45 minutes on March 30, 1981 that President Ronald Reagan had been shot and seriously wounded outside a hotel in Washington, D.C. The White House press office had said at first that he had not been hit. Indeed, Reagan himself said later that he did not realize at first that he had been shot.

How Reporters Operate   The wire service and broadcast reporters and the TV camera crews were in place outside the Washington Hilton Hotel that day as President Reagan emerged after defending his economic program before a labor group.

Michael Putzel, an AP White House correspondent, wanted to ask a question and shouted, "Mr. President, Mr. President." Putzel related, "The President turned slightly toward us, a smile on his face. I thought he was going to stop to take a question.

"'Pop! Pop! . . . Pop! Pop! Pop! Pop!' I saw Reagan's smile freeze.

"Gunshots. Had to be. But the sound was ricocheting off the stone wall next to us. . . ."

Walter Rodgers, a White House reporter for AP radio, was near the hotel door after a brief shoving match with a young stranger who had elbowed his way into the press area.

An Eyewitness Account   "The President walked toward his waiting limousine," Rodgers said. "An instant later there were six light flashes accompanied by loud bangs. . . . I was standing next to the gunman and was knocked to the sidewalk in the melee. Four feet in front of me lay White House Press Secretary James Brady.

"I ran into an office and commandeered a phone. Broadcasting through the phone line, I told what I had seen. . . ."

The TV cameras were still transmitting the wild scene outside as the president was crammed into his limousine and driven away. Putzel, by that time, had sent an AP bulletin over the A wire, the wire service's main trunk line.

Dean Reynolds of UPI, also a White House correspondent, ducked as he heard the shots. He said,

"I dropped into a crouch but kept my eyes on the president. He appeared frightened, almost bewildered, just after the shots were fired. The Secret Service agents spun him around, shoved him head first into his limousine.

"All the while, agents kept shouting, 'Get back, get back.'

"The limousine pulled away.

"A nearby scuffle then caught my attention. A young blond man was being wrestled to the ground by several agents and police. The tops of two legs, clad in dark trousers, were visible from the pileup. . . ."

It was the young man Rodgers had pushed, John W. Hinckley Jr., who was borne off and charged with the attempted assassination.

Telling the Story   Both the wire service bulletins and the cameras told the same story: A young man had fired at the president, but the White House press office said he had not been hit.

The UPI file graphically illustrates the difficulty of covering so confusing an event.*

BC REAGAN   3–30
BULLETIN PRECEDE
    WASHINGTON (UPI)—SHOTS WERE FIRED AS PRESIDENT REAGAN LEFT A WASHINGTON HOTEL LOBBY TODAY. THE PRESIDENT DID NOT APPEAR TO BE HURT.
    UPI 03–30–81   02:31 PES

BC REAGAN   1ST ADD   3–30
    X X X HURT
    THE SHOTS SOUNDED LIKE FIRECRACKERS AS THEY EXPLODED FROM THE GUN AT 10 FEET RANGE.

*UPI material is sent in caps, AP usually in lower case. BC means "both cycles," AM and PM. PES means P.M., Eastern Standard Time. The pickup line includes the last word of the preceding paragraph. The details of slugging are left out for clarity's sake (see page 192).

REAGAN WAS PIVOTED BY SECRET SERVICE AGENTS AND SHOVED
INTO A CAR.
   UPI 03–30–81 2:39 PES

BC REAGAN 3–30
BULLETIN PRECEDE
   WASHINGTON (UPI)—PRESIDENT REAGAN WAS NOT HIT BY GUNFIRE
MONDAY, THE WHITE HOUSE SAID.
   UPI 03–30–81 02:40 PES

BC REAGAN RUNNING 2ND ADD 3–30
   X X X CAR
   THE FIRST LADY WAS NOT WITH THE PRESIDENT. HE WAS
ACCOMPANIED BY PRESS SECRETARY JIM BRADY, DEPUTY STAFF CHIEF
MICHAEL DEAVER AND OTHER ASSISTANTS.
   UPI 03–30–81 02:45 PES

Nobody celebrated any beats on this one. The confusion that occurred and the contradictory information that was issued, mainly because the White House press spokesman was shot and unable to function, complicated the reporting for everybody. At one point, some of the TV reporters mistakenly announced that Brady was dead.

Wire Service Operations

Wire services are the wholesalers of news. Leaving aside the networks and the larger newspapers that have their own Washington bureaus and foreign services, the agencies account for 90 percent of the foreign news and more than 50 percent of the national news in American newspapers and broadcast news outlets.

The Global Services There are four global services in the Western world and Japan. Of these, the Associated Press is the largest and most important. It is a nonprofit, cooperative agency that serves nearly 1,400 newspaper members and 3,600 broadcasters in the United States and more than 7,000 subscribers abroad. On a budget of $120 million annually, it employs 1,500 full-time reporters, editors and photographers in 120 bureaus and smaller posts in this country and 63 abroad.

The other American agency, United Press International, sells its service to almost 1,200 newspaper and several thousand broadcast subscribers in the United States and about 7,000 abroad. It operates on a budget of $80 million, has 145 bureaus in the United States and 78 abroad. In 1982, UPI was sold by its owner, the E. W. Scripps Company, to the Media News Corporation, organized by a group of newspaper and cable operators.

Reuters, the British agency, is a foreign service with a $25 million budget, many clients in the British commonwealth and elsewhere but only about 65 or 70 in the U.S. The fourth global agency, Agence France-Presse, is smaller than the three English-language giants.

Communist Agencies   In the Communist world, there are two dominant wire services: Tass, for the Soviet Union, and Xinhua, for the People's Republic of China. They are official agencies, run by their respective governments, and express their governments' point of view. Both have extensive exchange agreements with the Western agencies.

The National Agencies   On the national level, the global wire services function under agreements with agencies operating privately in various other countries or representing their respective governments. For example, the Associated Press and Canadian Press work together. So do United Press International and such national agencies as British United Press. Reuters exchanges news with the Press Trust of India among others. The Communist agencies work mainly with those of their client states and usually offer their services for little or nothing to anybody else who will use them.

The News Syndicates   Rounding out this system for distributing news at wholesale are the various news syndicates based on the national and foreign services of the larger and more important newspapers. Prominent examples in the United States are the New York Times and Washington Post–Los Angeles Times Syndicates; in Britain, there are smaller syndicates that also sell abroad.

A Flexible Network   The unique part of this flexible communications network is the ease with which it can relay the most urgent and dramatic news to the entire country and to the rest of the world as well. As an Indian editor once said, "Whatever happens in the United States, good or bad, the whole world will know about it in a matter of minutes."

The wire services maintain several hundred thousand miles of leased wires in the United States as well as leased cable and radio circuits overseas. Communications satellites help speed news and pictures to overseas clients.

Using Computers and VDTs   Terminals are used for editing and writing wire service copy, with transmission between the computers of the respective agencies and their clients. Most of the services move at 1,200 words a minute, so that important news can flash on the screens of client VDTs in a matter of seconds. With the exception of smaller papers and stations that have not converted to the electronic age and still receive copy by teleprinter at 66 words a minute, the high-speed electronic transmission of wire service news is standard in the United States and in larger centers abroad. News budgets and advisory messages issued by the wire services keep editors posted; to handle the news and edit the daily file, it is only necessary for an editor to call up a story on a VDT in a desirable order. The whole thing works silently, without clatter or fuss.

Wire Service Channels   Each wire service has its own routine, based on the needs of its members or clients, that differs from others in detail. But in the main, all resemble the AP, and that agency's operations are therefore described here as an example of the routine.

The AP delivers its service over a network of news, sports and financial wires. The transcontinental trunk wire that carries the main budget or report of news is called the A wire. It is filed 24 hours a day from New York in two cycles—one for afternoon papers (PMs), starting at 1 a.m., Eastern time, and another for morning papers (AMs), starting at 1 p.m.

The AP uses a species of VDT called a cathode ray tube (CRT).

In addition to the main transmission centers in New York and Washington, the AP directs its service through a series of "hub" centers, such as Chicago and Atlanta, each of which has its own regional computer system.

The Hub System It should not be assumed that all AM copy is shut off when the PM cycle begins, or vice versa. There is a necessary overlap in which copy is transmitted for both cycles. In addition to breaking news, the PM file consists of copy for an overnight schedule for the first editions of afternoon papers and the regular day-wire schedule for this and later editions. The same cycle carries day leads that often run past 1 p.m., when the night wire opens; similarly, the night wire runs leads past 1 a.m. on continuing stories.

To reduce the piecing together process, AP has a 1,200 wpm DataRecaps service in which up-to-the-minute writethroughs of breaking stories are offered to subscribers in completely assembled form. Mainly, this services copy on the "A" wire.

Paralleling the "A" wire is the "B" wire, carrying the most important regional news coast to coast and from Boston to Florida as well as all-points copy that cannot be accommodated on the "A" wire. Next in importance are numerous regional and state wires, many of which are in effect smaller trunk wires. As the system of hub and satellite bureaus indicates, still further subdivisions exist within specific areas. Very often, too, on subordinate circuits, a system of "splits" is used through which the wire carries general news for part of an hour and state or regional copy for the remainder.

While the "hub" bureaus may take over the "A" wire when they have major news to transmit, most of their copy for the "A" and "B" wires goes first to the general desk in New York City on collection wires that are driven by regional computers. It is in New York, therefore, that supervisors, copy editors and wire filers decide on news priorities and handle the copy for movement on the trunk wires in what is called a *quality control* operation. Washington alone is not "hubbed" and continues to file its copy direct.

Wire Service Procedure

The techniques of wire service handling of developing news differ from newspaper and broadcasting procedure in several respects.

Schedules Preceding the opening of each cycle, a schedule is sent to all editors on a given circuit to let them know what material is available for transmission to them. This schedule, or budget message, tells editors each story that they will get by slug, description and often by word count. It does not, of course, tell the precise time that each specific piece will go on the wire because that is bound to vary. The breaking news, which is handled as it happens, can knock out the most carefully prepared news budget.

There are slight differences in agency procedure but in the main they follow the same principles because they are always working on some paper's deadline. The various takes of their stories are moved in order, but not necessarily consecutively. They may be put between bulletins of other material that is given precedence.

Wire Service Slugging   For all these reasons it is not practical for a wire service story to be written in newspaper fashion, with the page slugs numbered 1–2–3–4. Instead, wire copy consists of a first take and a series of adds for most stories. Each add is easily identifiable because it bears the slug and dateline of the original and a time sequence of transmission.

Slugs in wire service work also are devised as a code to indicate urgency of transmission. Those generally used by the American wire services are *Flash*, *Bulletin* and *Urgent* in descending order of importance.

These are included in the "header" material, made necessary by the computer, that precedes each story. Under arrangements devised by the American Newspaper Publishers Association, both wire services include in their "header" lines such data as the story number, service level designator, pre-header select code, priority and category. All this sounds formidable, but actually it is quite simple to work with and it is necessary for editorial use. In this book, for purposes of uniformity and ease of reading, the "header" material will be limited to story numbers, slugs, time designations, signatures and pickup lines.

Transmission of a Wire Story   Here is a typical transmission of a wire story, selected at random from the AP file on an ordinary news day. It includes a bulletin, three succeeding takes and a correction. Note that there is no pickup line between the 1st and 2nd adds because they follow each other on the day's file:

> a158
> *Bulletin*
> PM Rover
> WASHINGTON (AP)—The White House asked Congress today for money to begin the development of a nuclear-powered rocket engine, the "Rover."
> 0228 1122 AES

> a159
> PM Rover 1st add a 158 02 28
> WASHINGTON: "Rover"
> For this and other scientific projects, Congress was asked for a total of $149.8 million for use in the fiscal year beginning July 1.
> In addition to the nuclear-powered rocket engine, the White House was asked for funds for a physics laboratory for basic physical and biochemical research and a specialized facility for further exploration into controlled thermonuclear fission as a potential source of electricity.

a160

"The projects will advance America's ability to harness atomic energy for the peaceful exploration of space," a spokesman said. "They will also help us chart new courses in nuclear science."

He said development of a nuclear-powered rocket engine will take time.

0228 1126 AES

---

a165

URGENT

PM Rover 3rd Add A 158 02 28

WASHINGTON: TIME.

A number of flight and ground tests will precede full use of the engine in space programs, the White House announcement added.

A total of $91 million is sought in the next fiscal year for the rocket development and the remaining $58.8 million to develop the new research facilities.

Both new research facilities will be built by the Atomic Energy Commission at its Los Alamos, N.M., scientific laboratory.

0228 1156 AES

---

a179

PM *Rover Correction*

WASHINGTON: Rover A158 Third Graf make read XXX thermonuclear fusion etc. (sted fission)

0228 1247 AES

Analysis of the Story   The AP decided the story should go on the wire at once and therefore marked the first paragraph as a bulletin. The AP used an "urgent" designation on A165 to make certain it was given the next order of priority. Note the method of identifying the location of corrections because the same procedure is used for placing inserts in moving stories.

If a "write-through" is ordered, something newspapers generally call a sub story, wire services often merely use the next numbered lead in the progression and at the end carry the notation "eliminates previous" or "no pickup."

There is another peculiarity in wire service procedure that is not generally in accord with newspaper practice. Because of the confusion in morning papers which carry undated leads with the notation that something happened yesterday, and dated leads of yesterday that something happened today, the wire services use the day of the week and drop all dates for morning papers. However, for afternoon papers, today — and not Monday or Tuesday — is usually used for leads, dated or undated.

Wire services, whenever possible, carry the total wordage and the number of takes in their "header" material and also include necessary labels and instructions, such as advance stories for a given date or the reason for a particular lead or insert.

But when big news is breaking — news of national and worldwide importance — the wires move the story first and the technicalities take second place.

Wire Service Standards   A wire service must meet the standards of thousands of editors of all shades of political and religious beliefs, all nationalities and sympathies. What may be of interest to one news organization may be of no consequence to a wire service, except if an editor requests special coverage, but what may seem interesting to a wire service does not always please its members or clients. Editors being what they are, it is difficult enough to satisfy one of them, let alone hundreds or thousands at a time.

The wire service, therefore, ordinarily takes great care to present all sides of a story that is controversial. It may not be the best way to handle a wire service report, but it is usually the fairest way.

Wire service people are not paid to take sides. They are the impartial sources of information for all sides.

• Short Takes

Here's what writers should remember in handling wire service copy:

- Use short sentences, 16 or 17 words or less, few adjectives and adverbs.
- Be sure that everything is attributed to an identifiable source. For unsourced stories, be sure that there are two independent checks before the material is transmitted.
- The bigger the story, the simpler the language must be if it is to be quickly told for a mass audience.
- Get it first, but be sure to get it right.
- Keep it short.
- Play it safe in stories that may be libelous. Use *acquitted* or *innocent* rather than *not guilty* in court stories because of the danger that the negative may be dropped in transmission.
- If you want to apply the standard for truth as a defense against libel, make sure it is provable truth.

CHAPTER 15

Writing for TV and Radio

Those who write for television must combine the skills and insights of the playwright, the motion picture scriptwriter and the practicing journalist. It is not enough to say that television writers must consider both the eye and the ear. In a real sense, they must unify in word and mood a jumble of sights and sounds and give them meaning.

This represents creativity at a high level. Good TV reportage, like good drama, is most effective when it appeals to reason rather than to emotion, when it strives to make its point through artistry instead of crude histrionics, when it uses restraint and understatement and lets humankind see at first hand the stuff of which it is made. To do this with an economy of words and a few carefully selected scenes each day in the span of a TV news network program is no mean feat.

A TV News Report

When U.S. Navy F-14 fighters shot down two Libyan jet aircraft in the Gulf of Sirte as an unexpected part of Mediterranean war games, Doug Tunnell and two camera crews were assigned to the story. The *CBS Morning News* wanted a dramatic segment on the Naples arrival of the U.S.S. Nimitz, the carrier from which the Navy jets took off.

Planning the Story   Tunnell, young in years but a veteran at covering combat operations, planned the story with care and took into account the problems of writing a script under pressure. This is how he described his operation:

> Our job that morning was clear. Both of our competitors (NBC and ABC) were planning heavy coverage of the Nimitz's arrival at Naples. There was no doubt that a story would be aired. But for our morning deadline (working six hours ahead of New York) we knew we would not have the pilots of the aircraft telling us what happened, or even a statement from the ship's commander. It was a question of providing Americans with their first closeup look at the ship and its men after the incident off the Libyan coast.
>
> At 0600 local time we employed a fast boat and a slow airplane to ferry our crews (two of them this time) out to get the pictures. I went with the boat.
>
> The script was written on the run, under extreme deadline and competitive pressure. There was little time to do anything fancy. The concept here was to provide as many "looks" at the Nimitz and its crew as possible and to give its return to port some context for viewers.

Handling the Script   In Tunnell's script, "Nimitz Arrives Naples," the writing is sharp and crisp, staccato in style, picturesque in narration. Like most TV scripts, it is put together on a split page, the narration (AUDIO) on the right side and the visual effects (VIDEO) on the other with appropriate directions. The timing of each shot is left out here because it isn't necessary to an understanding of the segment as a whole. The lead-in was narrated by the anchorman on the *CBS Morning News* for August 24, 1981, and the segment follows:

VIDEO	AUDIO
Ship sailing into port with sun backlight	The aircraft carrier Nimitz sailed into the Bay of Naples at dawn; fresh from forty-eight hours of war games in the Gulf of Sirte . . . and one minute of combat with the Libyan air force.
Closeups of aircraft	Lashed to the deck, some of the F-14's of the Navy's 41st Fighter Squadron. They are called the "black aces," whose pilots shot down the two Libyan jets.
Men on board Men gesturing "two"	It was the first known combat with a foreign force since the rescue of the Mayagüez six years ago. There could be little doubt that all of the Nimitz's 6,287 men knew the score.
Flag-raising ceremony aft	At 91,000 tons, one of the largest nuclear-powered ships in the world raised the American flag in the home port of the Sixth Fleet. (Open here for sound on tape of "The Star-Spangled Banner.")

General shots of ship and crew	There was no formal welcome for the Nimitz and its men. The ship is a frequent visitor to Naples during that six months of duty each year it spends away from home.
Aerials of Naples port	Naples is a NATO port, and Italy an American ally. But there is perhaps no other country in Western Europe that enjoys such cordial relations with Libya. Even though Muammar Khaddafi admits that his planes fired first, reaction to the incident here has been mixed.
On-camera bridge	Italy's defense minister, Leilio Legorio, commended the United States Navy for defending the freedom of the high seas. But in a recent interview, Legorio likened the war games in the Gulf of Sirte to lighting a cigarette in a dynamite deposit. "You have the right to smoke," Legorio said, "but not to start an explosion."
Aerials of ship	The Nimitz planes intercepted Libyan jets 47 times during the maneuvers, according to Pentagon officials. The Navy will not disclose how long the Nimitz will stay in Naples or where it goes from here. But officials have said there are no plans for it to return to the "shores of Tripoli" in the near future.

Doug Tunnell, CBS News, Naples

Analyzing the Script   After the segment was shown to American audiences and produced an immensely favorable reaction—it had been a long time since the nation had savored even a small victory—Tunnell analyzed his script and his problems in writing it as follows:

You'll notice the script's second line is one of those broadcast sentences without a verb. I employ the technique sparingly to explain an important picture that the viewer might not otherwise notice, but at the same time I provide the verbal staccato that lends itself to editing in a second quick shot.

Once the story shows viewers the main attraction, it moves rapidly into why we are showing them this ship, these men and aircraft. There is no one else to tell them. The press conference did not start until that afternoon.

I knew that out of the three network boats bobbing around the carrier that morning, only ours had been in position to shoot the flag-raising ceremony by two Marines on the aft deck. I wanted to make the most of that. It was an emotional sequence. So we opened the narration for the sound of "The Star-Spangled Banner" and gave our story something the others did not have.

But then I aimed to temper all the patriotism such scenes inspire with the fact that there was no great welcome for the Nimitz, and so I went on into the political context in which the incident occurred.

I considered it essential that the controversy that surrounded the incident should be mentioned. Again, there was no one else to mention it except me.

Italy's minister of defense had used a lovely analogy that I thought summed up the feelings of many in Europe. We did not have him saying it on camera. So I stepped to the bow of our boat and said it for him.

I did so in what we call an *on-camera bridge,* from one thought or sequence of pictures to another. I used the bridge instead of the close [closing remark] because at that early point in our coverage I simply did not know how our story would shape up. A bridge is an insert. It is easy to move around in the body of the story. A close is not. If you want to sum up in an on-camera close, the story must have come to some sort of conclusion. Otherwise, anything said may well be overtaken by events.

As it happened, there was no late-breaking development on this story. I went out on the most obvious of facts, which was all we knew about what the Nimitz would do next.

Techniques of TV News

Tunnell's understanding of the techniques of TV news is what made his Nimitz script work on the *CBS Morning News.* Unless writers do know the techniques and how to apply them, the result will be of little use to an electronic news organization.

That means they must be familiar with videotape, the minicam (miniature cameras) — the methods used in electronic news gathering (ENG) from the scene of a news story and with the operation of complicated studio equipment. This is not to say that working journalists must be able to operate a camera or handle a microwave transmission with the aplomb of an engineer. There are qualified staff people for those jobs. What the journalist does have to know is how to deal with the problems involved in these techniques. Otherwise, the best-conceived news assignment can end in disaster.

Videotape Videotape, that most flexible and remarkable process for handling sight and sound, has made possible many of the seeming miracles of television news. It is magnetic and can be played back immediately. It can be reused. It can be stored indefinitely without damage, catalogued, categorized and taken out for a rerun whenever necessary.

With the help of CBS engineers, KMOX-TV in St. Louis, the CBS affiliate there, began experimenting with portable cameras and videotape in 1973 and in the following year abandoned the use of film for news coverage. All kinds of adjustments and improvements had to be made. Different kinds of cameras had to be developed. Cameramen were given backpacks with necessary additional equipment. Soon the miniature camera — the now-omnipresent minicam — was a fact of life.

The Minicam A single operator can handle a 12-pound minicam, with a 20-pound backpack of battery-operated recorders. In essence, therefore, the minicam eliminates the need for the old three-member film camera crews with their mountain of equipment — what Professor Fred W. Friendly used to call television's "thousand-pound pencil." Sometimes, two-member tape crews are used on network assignments. With tape now dominant, the minicams have created more changes in television than anything since the industrywide adoption of color in 1965.

How Minicams Work Reporters and minicam operators work as a team and closely coordinate with their producers and news directors. It can't be otherwise. They travel in a mobile unit if they are assigned to transmit pictures and narration directly to the newsroom by microwave. In the case of a conference, convention, show or interview, a small electronic relay outside the studio is aimed at the mobil unit, which transmits a live microwave "feed" back to the studio. Whatever the reporter and minicam operator are doing is thus under the eyes of their news director all the time if he wants to watch them in action.

For outside scenes, minicams are even more effective. However, they aren't restricted to ground level. Some stations have helicopters equipped with minicams and microwave transmission for the coverage of forest fires, other natural disasters and traffic accidents. The small cameras are so sensitive that they can be used at night with relatively low light levels; they are at their best, of course, by day at brightly colored scenes.

TV Controls For many assignments, centralized control of news coverage has come to television with the minicam-videotape microwave system. Television's control, in fact, is even more sweeping than that of any newspaper editor. For a television news director can see and hear exactly how an interview is going with live coverage and can interrupt with instructions for the crew. Similarly, orders can be given to direct the work of mobile units or large staffs on a convention floor. Everything that comes in may be recorded, as desired, on the TV monitors beside the news director's desk. And both the director and the producer, as a result, have a much better idea of the development of the story.

How Writers Operate When television staffers are working toward a regularly scheduled news program, the pictures and narration accumulated on assignment give editors more time for their work. Cuts can be planned without undue haste, except as the deadline approaches. And there is also more time for writers to work on their scripts, to fit the narration precisely to the pictorial content. It also becomes possible to make more news on deadline and even during the program as it is being shown, always a risky business.

Regardless of how much is written about these important and complicated procedures, they are actually best learned by doing. Like the intricate problem of putting news and advertising together in a newspaper or magazine and producing a professional product on time, no amount of description or exhortation can be quite as enlightening as meeting the problem head-on. And this is where experience, background and a thorough knowledge of new procedures as well as standard ones count for a great deal.

Problems of Local TV Coverage

When disaster strikes, a story that might take 30 to 45 seconds on network TV becomes a major assignment for local TV news staffs in the affected area. They are the ones who have to go after the news under conditions that are often difficult and sometimes dangerous as well.

This is what KXAS-TV, Fort Worth, Texas, was up against when major floods hit north-central Texas, wrecked businesses and homes and left many families without shelter. Leah Keith, a member of the KXAS news staff, recalled:

> During the severe flooding that hit north Texas, we were hard-pressed to cover the story. The victims were literally spread out in dozens of places. What we couldn't wade to, we covered by helicopter. And, of course, the chopper was the best way to ferry over miles of flooded territory.
>
> Disasters like floods push our staff and our equipment to the limit. But on the whole, we were pleased with our coverage, especially after many flood victims called to tell us it was a help to them.

This is a segment of Leah Keith's flood coverage at Eagle Mountain Lake, north of Fort Worth:

VIDEO	AUDIO
Flood scene in north-central Texas. Shots of water at porch level. Shots of ducks floating near houses. Scenes of houses partly under water.	KEITH: Trout? Pike? Black bass? Anything you want is close to home. This ideal fishing spot is at the back-porch level. The fishing dock is under water. Fish and ducks have all but moved in the houses that are nearly submerged. At the lake the level is holding at four and one-half feet above flood stage. And residents are hopeful that their bad luck will take a turn for the better.
Two women surveying flood damage	WOMAN: Hope we don't get any more rain. If we do we're going to have a real big problem.
Keith (OC, walking along flooded lake edge) Scenes of flood damage at Eagle Mountain Lake	KEITH: More rain would be disastrous because the ground is soaked. Officials say that the ground is so wet it can't hold any more water, which means any rainfall will be 100 percent runoff. The residents now living at Eagle Mountain Lake have seen enough runoff to last them a lifetime. There are predictions of more rain. A heavy rain in the next day or two is expected.

```
              Eagle Mountain Lake has been dropping
              but heavy rains could bring it right
              back up.

              Leah Keith, Channel 5 Action News

              (From KXAS-TV, NBC affiliate in Fort Worth,
                  Texas, owned and operated by the Lin
                           Broadcasting Corporation)
```

The Completed Program

When a completed, regularly scheduled news program is shown on a national television network, it is generally put together so smoothly that the viewing public can't guess at the effort that has gone into it.

Making the Scene The cameras move, seemingly in the most natural and agreeable manner, from the anchorperson in the studio to live, videotaped segments of other portions of the program. On occasion, there is a pleasant variation of medium and close-up shots of the anchorperson. Usually, this key individual is portrayed as calm, decisive, authoritative and — as far as the men are concerned — solemn to the bursting point.

Behind the reader, which is what anchor men and women really are, the device of rear-screen projection may be used to show still pictures, maps, charts, sketches, even headlines on occasion through the use of flipcards on an easel. Or this may be varied by slide devices taking up the whole screen, known as *balops* or *telops*. Almost everything is done to maintain the viewers' interest, from cutting down all unillustrated remarks to working in feature videotape or library film when there aren't enough good new news pictures to give the program a lift.

When the program is over, the public necessarily must judge it by the substance it has just heard and seen. The techniques are applied in such slick fashion that they are seldom detected by the inexperienced eye. Were it not for such technical mastery, editors, writers, reporters and technicians could not even put a program together, for there seems to be no end to television's development as a news medium and to the devices that make it more efficient.

The Ratings One of the features of television news is its continued dependence on ratings. The weekly polls of the A. C. Nielsen Company, based on recognized sampling techniques, have been accepted with such finality that they have become the basis for a lot of editorial decision making.

The Nielsen firm is the largest in marketing research in the country. What it has been doing in radio since 1942 and TV since 1950 is to record the listening and viewing habits of a small sampling of American homes and project them on a regional or national basis each week. For TV, the sample has consisted of 1,170 homes out of a total of more than 80 million TV-equipped households. The identity of each sample home is carefully guarded and, by means of a device called an audimeter, is connected by special telephone lines to Nielsen computers. These machines sort out the channel selection information and provide the weekly totals on which news and entertainment programs stand or fall.

When it is considered that Nielsen's ratings affect billions of dollars in TV network commercials alone, there is reason to appreciate the influence they exercise over programming. A drop of one percentage point in a network news program rating, for example, is said by some TV executives to be equivalent to a cut of $1.5 million in advertising revenues. Nielsen is no longer in radio.

The success of TV news is based on its ability to attract millions of viewers—something on the order of 60 million of them for the three network news programs. Statistically, social scientists generally agree that the ratings are sound enough. Some argue that participants in the sampling are by nature viewers in larger volume than the national average and that out-of-home viewing audiences are seldom included. But few have challenged Nielsen's claim to accuracy, within 1.3 percentage points, of a typical finding that a program has attracted 20 percent of the viewing audience.

A TV Prison Inquiry

Here is a segment from the "NBC Nightly News," based on an investigation into the causes of rioting in the prisons of Michigan and other states. The anchorman introduces the subject and Roger O'Neil, the reporter who conducted the inquiry:

VIDEO	AUDIO
A released convict, Mark Murphy, signs prison release form. Murphy shakes hands with prison officials. Inmates roam prison yard (seen through bars). Armed guards patrol area. Injured inmate (patch over eye) seen. Shot of prison dormitory. Tents seen in Texas prison yard. Exteriors of Minnesota prisons.	O'NEIL: Mark Murphy, convicted of armed-robbery parole violation, was released from prison this morning. He's the first of almost a thousand convicts in Michigan who are getting early parole to ease the state's badly crowded prison system. The inmate riots in Michigan this past week speeded up an emergency plan to reduce by three months the sentences of almost all of Michigan's 13,000 prisoners. Michigan is not the only state, though, with too many prisoners. Twenty-nine states have court mandates to do something about prison overcrowding. In Texas, convicts sleep in tents. Wisconsin wants some of its convicts to go to Minnesota, where there is more room. And a judge in Maryland is fining the

Michigan inmates clear riot debris.	state for failing to end overcrowding.
Aerials of southern Michigan prison	Prison systems all over the country are caught in a catch-22. The public is demanding stiffer prison sentences for criminals. But that same public is unwilling to increase its taxes to pay for more prisons. Prison officials and inmates of Michigan say the riots were completely unexpected. The prison system has 1,400 more prisoners than it was designed to hold.
Warden Foltz interviewed	WARDEN DALE FOLTZ: I've been surprised that we've been this long before someone finally, you know, they just had enough.
McEntyre interviewed	ROY MCENTYRE (inmate): You can't manipulate, you can't move around, without constantly bumping into someone, step on somebody's feet, you know.
Wright interviewed	ERNEST WRIGHT (parolee): It's like being inside a sardine can.
	O'NEIL: Michigan is trying to free up bed space in its big prisons. But law enforcement officials charge early parole makes a sham out of the criminal justice system.
Armstrong interviewed	DAVID ARMSTRONG (prosecutor): Parole boards have become innkeepers of the criminal justice system and they release violent criminals to make room for more violent criminals.
Close with aerial of Michigan prison	O'NEIL: The response from state officials is: What else can they do?
	Roger O'Neil, NBC News, Jackson, Michigan

Radio News Operations

Outside the United States and other advanced nations, radio is the prime reliance of most of the world's peoples for their daily news. Where there are no newspapers, or where newspapers are few and under government control, radio is the only source of news for millions in Asia, Africa and Latin America.

Although radio does not have the clout of television in the United States it remains a formidable organization for disseminating news quickly. Despite the drawbacks of the all-news radio stations, with their repetitious programming and often bored news listeners, they are making a contribution to public knowledge. When major news breaks, they are always ready to go with it.

The Radio Wire   Local radio news reporters are often supported by detail from the AP and UPI radio wires and network feeds if the event is of sufficient importance. In major bureaus such as New York City, the agencies' radio services generally work on a three-cycle basis. These are the "early," from 11 p.m. to 7 a.m., corresponding to the "A" wire overnight file; the "day," from 7 a.m. to 3 p.m.; and the "night" from 3 to 11 p.m., both equivalent to the "A" wire day and night cycles. In smaller bureaus and overseas, the early and day files are combined into a single PM cycle and the night file is expanded into a longer AM cycle. But regardless of the system, the agencies' radio wires keep turning out the spot news summaries of headlines, roundups of news and such added broadcast material as sports, financial and weather summaries.

There is a news budget for each cycle of the radio wire, just as there is for the "A" wire. New tops, the radio equivalent of the new lead, are frequently filed to update pending material. Where there is an important new development, the radio wire carries bulletins for immediate use. In general, material is prepared and slugged in much the same basic manner as copy for any other agency wire.

In addition, there are voice recordings made by wire service correspondents who are on the scene at breaking news events.

Brevity Is the Rule   Radio writing must be brief. Developing news is usually written in the present tense. The work must be clear and to the point to cut down the risk of misunderstanding, always a radio bugaboo. Consequently, the short sentence and the one- and two-syllable words are features of the radio wire.

The following spot summary of five items illustrates the manner in which a radio wire headline roundup is prepared:

Here is the latest news from the Associated Press:

NEW YORK — A Liberian freighter has signaled it is taking on water and is in danger of sinking 470 miles east-southeast of New York.

NEW YORK — A British freighter has taken aboard three women and two men from the stricken yawl Petrel — also at the mercy of the Atlantic storm.

WASHINGTON — The Food and Drug Administration has asked a New York importer to recall all retail stocks of foreign dolls which have been found to be highly inflammable.

BURLINGTON, IOWA — A mysterious but apparently minor illness has affected workers at the Army ammunition plant near here and the federal government is investigating it.

CHICAGO — A new snowstorm is moving south across the central Rockies.

Expanding the Summary This is expanded into the kind of news summary that is more in evidence on the radio wire than anything else:

A Liberian freighter has signaled it is taking on water and is in danger of sinking in an Atlantic gale. The New York Coast Guard says the ship S. S. Georgia gave her position as about 470 miles east-southeast of New York. A spokesman said the cutter Vigilante out of Provincetown, Massachusetts, has been diverted to help the Georgia. The cutter had been en route to the 70-foot yawl Petrel — also being pounded by the storm.

A British freighter is standing by the stricken Petrel after taking aboard five of its ten passengers 360 miles southeast of New York. Three women and two men were transferred to the freighter Cotswold. The five other passengers — all men — have elected to remain aboard the Petrel until a Coast Guard cutter arrives to take it in tow.

The Food and Drug Administration has asked a New York City importer to recall all retail stocks of some imported dolls which have been found to be highly inflammable. The dolls, ranging in size from seven to sixteen inches, have been distributed nationally. Thus far, the administration adds, it has received no reports of any injuries involving the dolls.

A U.S. government report is expected within the next ten days on a mysterious, but apparently minor, illness that has afflicted workers on a project at the Army ammunition plant near Burlington, Iowa. Some 50 to 100 employees have been hit by the ailment in the past six months.

A snowstorm in the southern Rockies and the intermountain region has prompted heavy snow or hazardous-driving warnings for northern Arizona and western New Mexico. Several inches of snow fell on Kingman, Arizona, and one to three inches covered the ground today in southern Wyoming, Utah and Nevada.

A New Top With a change in the status of an item in the summary, the new top is sent without fuss, and directions are included for the information of station news directors. One way of doing it is as follows:

News Dirs: Following is new top for Ships section above:
(Ships)
The Coast Guard says 29 Greek crewmen aboard a Liberian freighter 470 miles southeast of New York report they may have to abandon ship. A Coast Guard spokesman says a rescue plane is flying over the stricken vessel — S. S. Georgia — and a rescue ship is only about 20 minutes away. The freighter's position is about 120 miles east of the disabled pleasure yacht Petrel, which appears to be holding its own. A British freighter has taken aboard five of the Petrel's ten passengers and is standing by the 70-foot yawl.
— Dash —
The Food and Drug etc. x x x picking up third graf original item.

The technique of attracting the attention of the listeners before actually telling them what is happening can be extremely helpful in news of a surprising nature. It comes under the old formula usually stated as follows: "Tell 'em what you're going to tell 'em, then tell 'em what you have to tell 'em, and finally tell 'em that you've told 'em." For example, when the King of Denmark died and was succeeded by his daughter, the NBC teaser at the beginning of the nightly news roundup said that there would be a story telling how "a young woman in Copenhagen, whose father died last night, became Queen of Denmark."

The Roundup   While a great deal of radio and television news is told in the present tense, it is by no means an inviolate rule. The roundups, which summarize the day's events, are usually handled very much like summaries in newspapers; moreover, there are newscasters who insist on the use of the word *today* in every past-tense item just to be sure that the listener understands when the event took place.

At its best, this radio-news-writing technique approximates superior newspaper or news-magazine journalism. But when it is misapplied, the effect is similar to that of reading yesterday's newspaper aloud. Mainly, much depends on who is doing the reading and what sense can be made out of the news.

Timing   The dominant mechanical factor in the preparation of any radio or television news program is time. Most newscasters read from 170 to 180 words a minute and calculate a 16- to 17-line page of typing (with one-inch margins) as requiring about a minute to read. For the average station, only the last few items are timed, with the elapsed time of the script marked in big numerals in the upper right hand side of the page so that the newscaster knows when to conclude. However, the more important the station, the more rigid are the time controls applied to the radio news programs. And on the networks, there is usually very little room for maneuvering. A five-minute newscast actually includes only three and one-half minutes of news, allowing for commercial and sign-off, and a 15-minute newscast runs somewhere between 12½ and 13½ minutes, depending on commercials. Radio news is still a necessity in the United States, particularly in rural areas where so much depends on accurate weather information, and for millions of motorists.

Cable TV and the News

About one-third of American homes are now hooked up to cable TV. By the end of the century, the figure is likely to go as high as 70 percent — perhaps more. With the coming of satellite transmission and the relaxation of restrictions on cable by the Federal Communications Commission (FCC), the future for the new electronic giant seems bright. Ted Turner's Cable News Network (CNN) was the first news service to take advantage of the new technology, but it won't be the last. For the era of telecommunications and electronic publishing has barely begun and a lot of surprises are in store.

This is a brief rundown on what is already in the works:

Teletext   Most of the larger new organizations, both print and broadcast, are experimenting with ways of sending information into the home. Some use cable; others use over-the-air broadcast channels. But the objective of the various tests is the same: to discover what kind of news the public wants and how much the public is willing to pay for this kind of service.

There are many teletext information systems, most of them activated by a keypad (a switching device you hold in your hand, much like a TV channel selector). CEEFAX and Oracle, from Britain, were the earliest. The British Post Office thinks it has a winner in PRESTEL, but it is very far from making money. Warner Communications in this country runs QUBE, a system in which viewers have a very limited capacity to send back a verdict on programs. Knight-Ridder and the American Telephone and Telegraph Company (AT&T) have tested a device called Viewtron in Coral Gables, Florida.

One problem with all of these is high cost. A second drawback, almost as important, is that the small screen can handle only about 150 words at a time, and the business of picking one's way through a schedule to hit on the right numbers or codes to punch for the desired 150-word page can get pretty complicated.

Of course, teletext is in its infancy. Some believe it will develop eventually into a form of home-delivered electronic newspaper.

Home Computers   This is another method of trying to sell and deliver information to people at home. The trouble is some computers are far more expensive than TV sets. However, some authorities estimate that there are now more than a million home computers that are actually installed and working, and retailers like Radio Shack are trying to sell even more. How do they work? An operation called CompuServe, a subsidiary of the income tax preparers H & R Block, can sell you a complete news report for your computer provided by a number of newspapers from Columbus, Ohio, to New York. But it's a lot more expensive than the 15 to 30 cents you pay for the home-delivered newspaper.

Satellites   This is a booming field. Instead of using land phone lines, large communications companies are bouncing their signals off satellites in space. The American wire services, AP and UPI, both have reduced their line costs through nationwide installation of earth receivers (dish antennas) on the roofs of their clients. The plans for the Gannett national newspaper, *U.S. Today*, were based on satellite transmission. The *Wall Street Journal* and the *New York Times* were among the first to put out satellite editions and proved that they work.

AT&T   The big newspaper and broadcast systems, however, are far less concerned about teletext and TV competition than they are about the telephone company's plans to enter the data distribution field. Under the terms of an FCC order, which soon came under congressional attack, AT&T agreed to give up its regional phone companies and concentrate on long lines and research. In return, the company was granted the right to get into the data business, which gave publishers the nightmarish concept of an AT&T news service distributed by phone lines. The telephone company denied it wanted to get into the news business, but that didn't allay suspicions. Some said the press ought to work with AT&T to develop a joint teletext market. It was a symptom of changing times.

Broadcast News and the Law

The broadcast industry, meanwhile, continued to pile up profits and develop its news services despite its innate nervousness over government licensing procedures. Government regulation and licensing, of course, go back to the very beginnings of radio. These rest on the principle that privately owned radio and TV stations use a public facility, the airwaves or ether. And that goes for teletext, which uses broadcast channels.

Moreover, the laws governing the broadcast media have included an "equal-time provision" and a "fairness doctrine." The former required broadcasters to give equal air time to candidates for public office. The latter broadened that rule by obliging broadcasters to give equal time to opposing points of view generally.

Another major provision of the law limited the number of stations owned by a single corporation or individual to seven, no more than five of which could be in the very high frequency (VHF) range normally used for most news and entertainment programs in this country.

All these regulations were based on the "theory of scarcity"—the notion that there were relatively few channels available for broadcast use in the nation and these should not be monopolized. However, there are more TV and radio stations now than there are newspapers, and the advent of cable TV means that many more channels are being made available. So the old rules to safeguard First Amendment rights on the air, broadcasters argue, no longer apply. They now seek equal status with newspapers under the law.

The FCC, in asking Congress to repeal both the "equal-time provision" and the "fairness doctrine," took the first step in what promises to be a long and complicated legal battle. More than any other area involved, broadcast journalism has a major stake in the outcome.

• Short Takes

- Writing for the broadcast media must be sharp and crisp and precisely timed. Particularly for radio, sentences must be short, and one- and two-syllable words should be used as much as possible.
- Except for the roundup news programs, most broadcast news is written in present tense or present-perfect tense. The reporting should be personal in style.
- For television, the narration must be fitted to the pictorial content.
- Because so much broadcast news must be written under deadline pressure, flexibility is a prime requirement for writers. They also must have unflappable personalities.
- Attribution for broadcast news comes at the start of a sentence or paragraph, not at the end as it does in much news that is written for print. Figures and

names are simplified as much as possible, figures being rounded off and middle initials and names being dropped in most instances.

- Pronunciation must be precise. When in doubt, consult a dictionary or the source directly involved. For example, one of the most mispronounced names is Pulitzer—pronounced *Pull*-it-zur, with the accent on the first syllable, and not Pew-lits-*ser*.
- Writers for TV should have a thorough basic knowledge of the workings of the minicam, videotape and ENG (electronic news gathering). Writers for radio should know how to handle changes such as new tops (new leads) and inserts with a minimum of fuss.
- There is an art to ad-libbing on the air, and not everybody can do it well. It is something that news people should practice by themselves before they attempt it in a real-life situation.

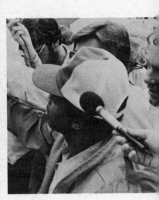

3
Principles
of Reporting

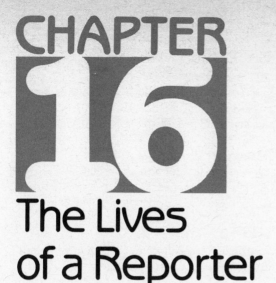

CHAPTER 16

The Lives
of a Reporter

It is a beautiful theory that reporters gather news so easily that they have time to stop for a drink and plot the undoing of any dastardly villain who dares to withhold information from them. In real life, though, most reporters are devout believers in Murphy's Law: If anything is likely to go wrong on an assignment, it will. And they govern themselves accordingly.

The Way It Really Is

Ned McCormack, a police reporter for the *Journal-News* in the pleasant Hudson Valley community of Nyack, New York, proceeds on the fixed notion that Murphy was an optimist. On a rainy Friday afternoon in October, he was halfway through a turkey sandwich when his city editor told him to drive to the New York City borough of Queens, on Long Island. New York police, in a followup to a $1.6 million armored car holdup in Nyack, had just arrested one suspect and killed another in a shootout.

Maps and Credentials Are Necessary McCormack learned by phone that the captured man was being questioned at the Forest Hills Police Station, but he didn't have the faintest idea of how to get to Forest Hills. A postage-stamp-size map of Queens didn't help much, but he started on his long drive, along partly flooded parkways. Inevitably, once he crossed the Whitestone Bridge over Long Island Sound and reached Queens, he got lost. But eventually he reached the Forest Hills Police Station only to be challenged by a policeman. Security was tight, and for good reason. The holdup gang had had drawings of the station in one of the houses that had been searched.

McCormack's police card helped him get through the police cordon to the fourth floor of the station house, but it was his bad luck that the New York City police commissioner had just finished a news conference. However, a public information officer, Deputy Police Commissioner Alice McGullion, had stayed behind to talk with a small group of reporters.

Hanging in There   McCormack had pieced together fragmentary details of the story on his car radio on the way to Forest Hills, but now he was getting the details backward. He heard McGullion give the account of the chase that preceded the shootout, but he didn't know how the suspects' car had been spotted. Just then, a TV reporter whisked McGullion away for a live report. McCormack was frustrated but he hung in there, followed the TV crew and eventually grabbed the exhausted information officer.

The *Journal-News* is an evening paper, but it has a Saturday-morning edition so McCormack had a little more time. He explained,

> Throughout the afternoon and evening, I called the city desk to fill them in on new developments. It's good to call as soon as possible just to let them know you're on the job. And talking to rewrite has advantages. If you're not sure of your facts, they'll ask questions and you can go back and get it right. I've never felt there was any disgrace in asking questions two and three times if the facts are in doubt.

Getting a Break   McCormack's persistence finally paid off. He put together a complete report of the chase and the gunfight, identified the dead man by his real name instead of his alias, and handled the arraignment of the captured suspect. He stayed close to the action throughout. And then, in the end, he got a break.

"After the captured suspect was led away," he said, "I talked with a cop who had been with McGullion on and off for most of the day. It turned out that this officer was the chief of detectives of Queens."

That helped a lot to give McCormack a complete story. He wound up his assignment, drove back to Nyack, called the desk and rewrite before he checked his notes and turned in for the night. "It pays to be lucky," he said.

Handling the Story   McCormack collaborated with Nancy Quirk Keefe, who had been in the office on rewrite, and produced a detailed story in Saturday's paper. It took a lot of writing as well as doing because it ranged across Rockland County, in which Nyack is located, and through neighboring Westchester County, just above the New York City line, as well as in the always-confusing borough of Queens on Long Island. This was how the story was handled in large part:

A license plate spotted on a car outside a Westchester apartment, and linked to the $1.6 million Brink's holdup and shootout in Nyack, triggered a high-speed chase across Queens Friday. It left one man dead and another in custody.

The arrested man, identified by New York City police as Nat Burns, is a Black Panther with several different aliases who had been on the run for 13 years.

The dead man was identified from his fingerprints as Samuel Smith, also known as Mtajori Sandiata, who had no known link to any terrorist group.

Both men were wearing bullet-proof vests. Their car had a large cache of ammunition, a loaded revolver and spare parts for a rifle. Burns was carrying $2,446 in cash.

Police declined to say that the two men were actually a part of the robbery Tuesday at Nanuet Mall in Nyack in which one Brink's guard was killed and two guards were injured, or a part of the shootout shortly after at the entrance to the New York State Thruway in which two Nyack police officers were killed.

As the story was told by Deputy Police Commissioner Alice McGullion, the chase began about 12:30 p.m. Friday. Three members of the Queens Task Force riding in an unmarked police car saw New Jersey license plate 573 LDO on a 1978 gray Chrysler Le Baron. The plate number had been broadcast earlier after it had been seen on a maroon Ford parked in front of a Mount Vernon apartment belonging to a woman known as Carol Durant.

Her real name, police said, is Marilyn Buck, an escaped prisoner who is said to be the only white member of the Black Liberation Army.

Lt. Daniel Kelly, a Queens detective, spotted the license plate number on the Chrysler as it drove on Foch Blvd., in Queens, not far from Kennedy Airport. The police car began the chase.

The Chrysler jumped a cement barrier and headed west. The detectives' car had hung back and blocked an intersection. The Chrysler rammed it.

The passenger opened the window and fired several shots, the police said. The car jumped the divider again and sped east. The two men jumped from the moving car and fled on foot. The car crashed into a factory building.

Both ran a short distance and separated. One police officer jumped from his car and chased the men. Detective Irwin Jacobson saw one of them coming over a fence and fired twice from his car. The man went down. Jacobson got out of his car, used the hood for a cover and fired twice more. The second shot was fatal to the man later identified as Samuel Smith.

The other man ran into a construction company courtyard,

turned and took a combat stance, feet spread apart, both hands on his weapon. The gun jammed.

He hollered, "I give up. Take the gun."

Police approached to handcuff him and, they said, the man tried to bite, kick and punch them. Three officers subdued the man, later identified as Burns. . . .

Putting It All Together   It all sounds so easy when it is told in orderly, readable form under big black headlines. But here was a case in which a reporter got lost, had to battle his way inside a police station, missed an important news conference, but kept trying and finally wound up with a detailed, fast-moving story. It took him the better part of eight hours to do the job.

The Routine Takes Guts

The knowing newcomer will nod and wink and say with assurance, "Oh, sure. But then you're talking about a small paper and a reporter who didn't know the territory. Now on a big paper, the reporter's got it made."

True, the *Nyack Journal-New*'s circulation is just under 50,000, which is relatively small for the New York metropolitan area. But sometimes reporters for the greatest papers in the land have even more trouble than Ned McCormack on fast-breaking stories. The ones that are spread over a long period of time can turn out to be the most difficult of all.

A Reporter Against the Mob   Gene Miller is one of the best in American journalism, but he was punched in the mouth on a story because he was doing his job. Throughout northwest Florida, he had become a marked man. Public officials accused him publicly of lying about them in his paper, the *Miami Herald*, one of the most powerful in the country.

Miller was harassed at every turn, spied upon, frustrated in every attempt he made to prove he was right—except for the last time. Then, after eight and a half years, he finally made the gates of Florida State Prison swing open for two indigent black men who had twice been wrongfully convicted of first-degree murder and twice sentenced to death. Miller did it because he had faith in the innocence of the two, Freddie Pitts and Wilbert Lee; because he was able to locate the real culprit and extract a confession, and because the *Miami Herald* backed everything he did.

Once the Governor of Florida freed Pitts and Lee on the evidence Miller had developed, the reporter's work was done. He said of the case: "It wouldn't go away and it wouldn't go away and it wouldn't go away. There was nothing to do about it but keep working and writing."

Miller won his second Pulitzer Prize for local reporting on that case, his first having come for freeing a man and woman in two separate cases after they had been convicted of murders they had not committed.

You Keep on Digging Such feats are rare in the annals of American journalism. Yet neither Miller nor his editors have ever credited his success to anything more than making accurate basic judgments and following a hard and often unrewarding routine until the work paid off. Much the same thing happened in the Watergate exposé conducted by Bob Woodward and Carl Bernstein for the *Washington Post*, except that the paper itself came under as heavy fire as the reporters. Challenges, including some by President Nixon's friends, were filed with the Federal Communications Commission against the *Post*'s ownership of two television stations, causing a drop of almost 50 percent in *Post* stock on the American Stock Exchange. But the paper never ceased to back its reporters—and the reporters kept on digging.

In all truth, much excellent reporting is based on routine—dull, persistent work such as the checking of records, the location of persons with specialized information, efforts to corroborate material already in hand, long vigils for informants who sometimes never show up. This can go on for months—even years, as in the case of Miller and the Woodward-Bernstein inquiries.

Reporters on the Job

It is easy to tell good reporters from poor ones. The good ones know that much of their working time will be spent on routine and are prepared to do it well. The poor ones brush off such mundane details as reading newspapers, checking names and addresses, asking questions about seemingly unimportant details and taking careful notes when they can.

Another important difference between the two is that the good ones are well aware that they will have to cover all kinds of stories, and most of them will be small, particularly for newspapers, while the poor ones keep hoping for a big news break that may never come their way. Even in the bad old days, reporting was sober, serious business; the glamor of *The Front Page*, if there was any, could be found primarily in the corner saloon.

Beginners usually have to learn such things the hard way. Once a neophyte wire service reporter was sent to a courtroom to pick up an appeals court decision and telephone the results to his desk. When he was given the papers, he flipped to the last page for the decision and got on the phone with it. Not until he returned to the office did he realize that he had reported a dissenting opinion; the majority's decision was somewhere in the middle of the report, but he hadn't bothered to look for it.

Going on Assignment Newspaper or wire service reporters, on a spot news assignment, waste no time in going directly to the source of the story. It is even more important for the broadcast media to get to the scene, for good pictures can't be taken by remote control and eyewitnesses don't hang around forever to give interviews about accidents, fires, holdups or natural disasters. The saddest reporter in town is always the one who shows up late and has to get a fill-in from a grudging colleague.

Making Your Own Breaks   Reporters can make their own breaks by doing their routine work well. Often, by checking both sides of a story, they will find an aggrieved person who will provide good leads for further inquiry. Through firmness and persistence they sometimes can persuade an aloof news source to talk. This was the routine adopted by Jack Anderson, the syndicated columnist, who has broken so many major stories, from the disclosure of the background of American opposition to India during the Indo-Pakistan War to the lobbying methods in this country and abroad of the International Telephone and Telegraph Company. Like Anderson, many another reporter has found that patience and dogged work have been rewarded with unexpected disclosures, but few have been favored with so many leaks from government sources.

Wherever it is possible, a thorough inquiry should be made into the backgrounds of the principal actors in the news. In a murder trial, during which the defense contended that death was due to an accident, a reporter discovered that the judge some years before had shot and killed a hunting companion by accident. During the investigation of a large corporation which was in financial difficulty, it developed that one of its principal officers had been a notorious ex-convict who had changed his name.

Ask—Ask—Ask!   How does a reporter accomplish such feats? Usually this is done by asking questions, often politely but always persistently — not just any questions, but one that is so phrased as to produce a newsworthy answer.

The reporter who breezes into the county clerk's office and asks gaily, "What's new?" is likely to be told, "Nothing." But if the reporter goes through court records in a systematic way, the results may be quite different. Donald L. Barlett and James B. Steele went through Philadelphia court records for months on end in an analysis of the administration of justice for the *Philadelphia Inquirer* and came up with a series that showed that innocent persons had been sent to jail, judges were inconsistent in sentencing and most of them did less work than others in cities of comparable size.

Aggressiveness   All editors want aggressive reporters, but that doesn't mean just a loud voice and tough talk. Loud and brassy reporters are their own worst enemies. The shouted question, the accusing finger, the dramatic manner are not calculated to endear any reporter either to a news source or to professional associates. Mostly, such persons are an embarrassment to their colleagues.

Nor does it ever help reporters to quarrel with their sources, or threaten or anger them. Such histrionics may jar loose one story, but they are likely to cost the reporter the confidence of a good source thereafter. To those who can be persistent, but still maintain an even temper and moderate manner, go most of the rewards of the professional news gatherer.

Sometimes it is the news source who is arrogant, overbearing and even threatening. The most even-tempered reporter may be angered under such pressures. However, as most reporters know, anger is not particularly helpful in gathering news, although it is on occasion becoming to an editorial writer. Experienced reporters, regardless of provocation, maintain their poise by staying off the defensive and asking questions.

Young reporters, going on their first assignments, invariably ask themselves before approaching their first awesome news source, "Why should he talk to me?" It is true that few reporters today command a personal following. Young reporters, however, need not feel abashed by lack of experience. They will be received not because of who they are but because of what they represent. From such beginnings they will learn quickly enough to make their own way by asking the right questions of the right persons at the right time.

Taking Notes   Some good newspaper reporters take a few notes now and then, scribbled on the back of an old envelope or a shred of copy paper. Others have taken notes about the weather even while crossing Times Square on a beautiful spring day. These are the established professionals whose methods vary in accordance with their temperament, their habits and their needs.

Today's reporters, especially the younger ones, are likely to find that considerable note-taking will be more useful to them than the casual attitude of veteran reporters. The reason is that modern reporting must be more careful, more thorough and, if possible, more accurate than the news gathering of 35 or 40 years ago.

Using Tape Recorders   One of the principal results of the increasing use of tape recorders is that more news has been put on the record at every level, from the village council to the committees of Congress, from the routine interview with a town police chief to the audience granted by a king. Some old-time reporters, long accustomed to writing politics by referring to mysterious unnamed sources, have found to their dismay that the politicians they once protected so zealously now rush into television talk programs with the most indiscreet remarks. And young reporters with tape recorders think nothing of asking the most exalted figures in the land to say for the record what they once would confide to only the most trusted veteran reporters. But tape recorders have their disadvantages, too. It takes a long time to transcribe an interview and to find a key quote unless a careful time record is kept.

This does not mean that the practice of so-called background reporting is in a decline. It does mean that journalists in general are putting up more of a fight to bring the sources of the news out into the open. The print media, in this respect, owe a debt of gratitude to the electronic journalists who have taken a giant step toward greater honesty in handling the news.

Checking Copy   Inexperienced reporters sometimes are placed on the defensive when officials, in public or private industry, demand the right to examine notes or tapes or approve copy before it is submitted to the home office. It is a fixed rule on all news organizations that their editors—alone—have the right to determine what reporters should do with their facts and how a story should be written. Overly aggressive news sources should, of course, be told this in a polite manner. Whenever there is insistence on the right to see a story before it is used, reporters can only refer their sources to their superiors and await the outcome. Reporters should never yield copy for examination, except under conditions of acknowledged censorship, or for military clearance when necessary. (See Chapter 19.)

Reporters and Their Offices

The relationship between reporters and their offices is changing in all parts of the news media. Where reporters once were regarded as freewheeling characters, particularly on fixed newspaper beats like City Hall and police headquarters, the rule today is close supervision of all reportorial activity.

There are three main reasons for the change in attitude. The first and foremost is that editors could afford to squander the time of $35-a-week reporters in the great Depression or let them go off on their own without worrying too much about the ultimate cost. But when weekly wage minimums for reporters on major news organizations today are in the $400 range, and up, and they can go to more than $700 a week, they are treated quite differently. Their time is important. And if they go into overtime at contractual time-and-one-half rates, they pose something of an issue. Any editor will ask, "Is this story worth such an expenditure?" And in television, where the cost of technicians and equipment has to be added in, the calculation of news values is anything but philosophical.

As has already been shown, the widespread use of terminals by newspapers and wire services and the swing to electronic coverage by television have in effect linked reporters more closely than ever before to their home offices. Journalists now would have to go to the polar ice caps, remote villages in India or China or the central Sahara before they could properly claim that they were out of touch. In any event, when editors have the opportunity to supervise, that is what they do, and reporters shouldn't be surprised by it. Thus, the concept of "teamwork" is greatly favored in most newsrooms; it gives a news organization added power and prestige to have special reportorial units available for investigations or other specialized work. Such units, naturally, are the most closely supervised of all.

Finally, the intricate character of much of the news in the latter part of the century has obliged editors and reporters to work in closer collaboration. When a city trembles on the verge of bankruptcy or a neighborhood is in revolt over the condition of its schools, when small and distant nations can choke off American oil and gasoline supplies and poor crops can send food prices soaring, news organizations have to coordinate all their resources if they are to serve the public properly. The era of the happy-go-lucky reporter is over.

Pool Reporting   Some of the reporting practices of earlier days still survive in this modern era of togetherness, the most important of which is the "pool," with one or two reporters representing a group.

The pool device is resorted to whenever there are large numbers of reporters and camera operators, both still and television, in a relatively limited space. Moreover, at major congressional hearings when public interest is high, as is the case at major political conventions, networks will use pool cameras to provide daily coverage. Regardless of the complaints of purists, such measures do not deprive the public of any essential information, and they are both useful and economical.

Disadvantages of the Pool   Nobody contends that the pool is the best way to cover a story. Far from it. For under the informal rules of pool coverage, those in the pool are bound by the agreement of their representatives on material that is to be used for background or put off the record entirely. (See Chapter 23 for gradations of attribution.) But those outside the pool, not being bound by the rules, can and do use such material if they hear about it—and that frequently happens.

An even more serious disadvantage occurs when hundreds of reporters are assigned to cover a trial in which there is great public interest but only a small courtroom is available. Sometimes the judge turns the whole matter over to the reporters themselves, which generally means that smaller papers and radio stations have to organize a pool or be shut out entirely; even if the judge tries to act as arbiter, not everybody receives complete satisfaction.

Almost all pool reporters inevitably face criticism by those who depend on them for not being more observant, for failing to report what the pool subject had for breakfast, or what the subject's demeanor was under certain circumstances. All of which adds to the unpleasantness of pool reporting for everybody concerned.

Call Backs   One of the most frustrating experiences for reporters is to call in with a major story and talk with somebody who knows nothing about the assignment. The delays involved in explaining who gave the assignment and why and what has happened since are likely to curdle the spirit of the most enthusiastic reporter. Yet this kind of faulty liaison is all too common in every news organization.

It is recommended professional practice for call backs by reporters to be handled by the person who originally assigned them or by someone on a later shift who has been briefed on what reporters are doing. Even a casual glance at the assignment list on the VDT often helps. Poor liaison between reporters and editors can quickly lead to demoralization.

Enterprise Reporting

This is the generic term given to almost anything off the beaten track of the day's news. It may be nothing more important than overhearing a city official's remark that his wife is house-hunting elsewhere, which turns out on inquiry to be the clue that he is about to leave his local office and has accepted a job in Washington, D.C. Or it may be a month-long inquiry by a reportorial team into the county's real estate records, which shows that a city councilman has been involved in questionable dealings. Whatever reporters turn up on their own is credited to their enterprise.

Much of this type of reporting is investigative in character, as might be expected, and is dealt with in detail in Chapter 28. The pertinent matter here is the extent to which enterprise reporting, as a team effort, has subordinated the work of individual reporters. On larger newspapers and in the few broadcast media that go in extensively for original reporting, the juiciest enterprise assignments go to teams primarily because there is a better chance that a team will produce a good series. The odds against an individual reporter in a complicated investigation are naturally much greater than they are against a team.

However, news organizations will have to continue to depend on the enterprise of individuals as well as teams to produce news outside the routine. The imperatives of team reporting do not, by any means, conflict with the individual enterprise of a reporter who follows up a hunch, a tip or even some other news organization's lead. No editor can afford to throttle or ignore this kind of effort, for the individual reporter remains the basis for independent journalism as it is practiced in the United States.

Good Taste and Bad Taste

Fifty years ago, newspapers adhered to strict Victorian standards of morality. Good taste was ordained in the main by what pleased a parson's wife. Bad taste was anything that "nice people" found to be vulgar or otherwise objectionable.

Changing Standards   That era is long behind us.

Two world wars, a major depression and years of civil and racial strife in our cities have created great social changes and swept away many of the taboos that encumbered the coverage of the news.

The *New York Times*, hardly an avant-garde newspaper, is an indicator of the extent of the change that has come to the press. In its Sunday magazine, a writer blithely led with a quote from a workman who described the Dallas airport, the subject of the article, as a "sumbitchin'" airport. And the *Times*'s book review, on its first page, graphically detailed Elvis Presley's sexual failings by quoting from a biography of him, the subject of a review.

Still, even on so important a matter as President Nixon's obscenities as recorded on the Watergate tapes, the press was divided on usage. And that wasn't entirely due to political leanings. Some editors honestly thought they were offending their readers by letting them know what kind of language the president of the United States used in the Oval Room in conducting the business of state. As a matter of journalistic candor, however, most papers of consequence did use the record in full as it pertained to presidential taste in self-expression.

Guidelines for Offensive Language   While it is difficult to generalize in such matters, most newspapers today apparently consider it necessary to print obscenities, profanity and vulgarity if there is a compelling and newsworthy reason for doing it. The Associated Press, often a guide in such matters, states the position negatively as follows in its stylebook:

"Obscenities, profanities, vulgarities. Do not use them in stories unless they are a part of direct quotations and there is a compelling reason for them."

The AP offers this example to its writers:

"In reporting profanity that normally would use the words *damn* or *god*, lower-case *god* and use the following forms: *damn, damn it* and *goddamn it*."

As far as television is concerned, "heck" is still considered to be just about the ultimate in four-letter words for a national audience.

Even in the advertising columns of newspapers, always a pillar of conservatism, there is a bit more explicit language. Some years ago, in advertisements for a revival of the Elizabethan play *'T'is Pity She's a Whore*, the last word of the title was represented by five racy dashes. Emancipation of a sort came with the long-running Broadway musical *The Best Little Whorehouse in Texas*, when the unofficial censors — at least in New York — gave up the struggle.

The line for respectable publications is vaguely drawn just about where the U.S. Supreme Court left it in *Miller v. California* in 1973 (see Chapter 19) by specifying that "community standards" would determine what was obscene. In any event, there have been no newspaper prosecutions of consequence under the obscenity statutes. And even among the "skins," the sexist magazines, there have been relatively few, and these were mainly for pictures, not words.

In effect, then, in today's society the use of four-letter words is no big deal if they are printed in a newsworthy context.

Pictorial Problems   When a young soprano enthusiastically removed her clothes in a performance of *Salome* during the traditional dance of the seven veils, it startled operagoers in Phoenix. A newspaper photographer snapped the picture, which was duly published, with some editing, and didn't seem to create much of an uproar in the Southwest.

But that doesn't happen very often, in or out of opera.

When Elizabeth Ray attained a degree of notoriety after revealing that she had been on a congressman's payroll as a stenographer — even though she couldn't type — the AP circulated a partly nude picture of her. Not many papers used it; most of them, however, arted out the interesting parts of Miss Ray's anatomy.

The fact is that nude art isn't a problem for the great majority of newspapers. They don't go for it and are therefore no competition for *Playboy* and the rest of the skins. In that respect, nothing much has changed in journalistic morality.

The real problem is in the use of horror pictures. The worst shocker of the Vietnam War, taken by an AP reporter, showed an aged bonze (priest) burning himself to death in a public square of Saigon in protest against the conflict. The reporter confessed himself to have been horrified as he saw the bonze, suddenly doused in gasoline, touching a match to himself in the presence of his fellow priests. Should the reporter have taken the picture? "I had to," he said. "It was news. I've never had any doubt of that."

The photo was so horrifying that American editors were deeply divided over using it. Some who did buried it in the paper. But a hardy few put it on Page 1.

That was the beginning of a spate of wartime horror pictures, and not only from Saigon. One photograph captured a Saigon general, pistol pointed at the head of a Vietcong prisoner, a moment before he pulled the trigger. The photo won a Pulitzer Prize. Another shocker, published during the Indo-Pakistan War, showed prisoners being beaten with rifle butts; it too was the subject of major concern in the United States.

Television, so circumspect in its choice of language, did not shrink from putting ugly and explicit film and videotape of live combat before the home audience, even though it created problems. It was a part of the return of a realistic age.

A newcomer to journalism, however, should not assume that there is a noncontroversial way to handle any sensitive subject, either in words or in pictures. Each case has to be decided on its own merits. And each news organization, large or small, print or broadcast, has its own mores, depending on the nature of its audience and the conviction of its editors. What is all right for an editor in New York or Chicago may be all wrong in Dayton, Ohio, or Puyallup, Washington.

Progress, if that is the right word, comes slowly in journalism. It took longer for the American press to get over the Victorian ideal of morality than it did for the British.

● Short Takes

These are some of the basic practices of reporting that you should remember:

- Persistence is the hallmark of a good reporter. You always have to hang in there, no matter how difficult the assignment is.
- Never forget to have proper identification and reporters' credentials (a police card, if you have nothing else) in your possession. You may be sent to places where you aren't known and aren't welcome. It always helps to have a good map of territory that's unfamiliar.
- Always keep in touch with your desk. On a breaking story, you ought to be sure to call in every 20 or 30 minutes.
- Don't ever resent questions from the desk or rewrite. They are trying to be helpful, not critical. You may have to ask the same question three or four times of different sources before you get an answer that checks out.
- When you give in a story, begin with a brief summation. (Fire on 23d and Fulton, four dead.) If you have names, once you give the summation, let rewrite have them next with ages, occupation and addresses. Spell the names phonetically (Alyce is the first name: A-Albert; L-Louie; Y-Young; C-Charlie; E-Eddie) so there will be no mistake. In giving figures over the phone, be careful about 9s and 5s—they can be mixed up.
- Always stick close to the main source of the news, a police official, a fire chief, a DA, depending on the type of story.
- Don't be afraid to ask all the questions if you're still unsure of the facts and other reporters seem ready to fold up.
- Don't be upset if you're not popular with the cops. Few reporters are. You're not in a popularity contest. It's your job to gather the news.
- Don't try to get information out of records in a hurry. Double check every entry. You can make mistakes by copying too hastily.
- If you're going to adopt a disguise or pretend to be someone other than a reporter, you'd better check first with your desk to be sure that you have approval. Some desks won't let reporters be play-actors for any reason. Others, particularly on investigative stories, welcome it. It's all a matter of policy.
- Remember to get all sides of a story. Frequently there are more than two sides. News can be very complex.
- Don't play District Attorney and go around accusing people without reason. You can't shock your sources into giving you news. Be aggressive, but show some sense in doing so. Shoving seldom helps.
- Take notes systematically. Leave a good space on the left side of your note-

book for a key word or two to show the subject matter of the notes as you take them. It is easier then to go back over them and digest the main points for an oral or written report.

- Tape recorders are always helpful. But remember that they take a long time to transcribe and you can't always find the key quote you want quickly. That's why penciled notes of highlights are needed.
- Unless you are a science writer or have authorization from your office for some specialized story, never permit anybody to check your copy before or after you turn it in to your desk. You are responsible to your editors, not to your sources.
- To meet standards of good taste, be sure to review office policy if you have a quote with obscene or profane language that you believe is necessary to the story. Generally, the rule is that offensive language in quotes can be used if there is a newsworthy reason for it, but some papers—and nearly all broadcast media—are still timid about four-letter words.
- Keep moving. Keep trying. And ask—ask—ask.

CHAPTER 17

Interviews, Speeches and News Conferences

Talkers are always in the news. Reporters come across them daily in any assignment involving interviews, speeches, news conferences, panel discussions or public statements. The principal problems in dealing with this outpouring of words are to check them for accuracy and to determine what will interest a mass public.

It isn't easy. A certain amount of art and news judgment, combined, is required to select quotes that mean something and turn them into a well-written news story.

Conducting an Interview

Jeannie Williams, a columnist for the *Rochester* (New York) *Times-Union*, has developed these eminently practical rules for reporters who are assigned to do an interview:

- Before you meet your subject, do a thorough job of research. Find out all you can about the person, using all available resources.
- Conduct the interview in a useful, comfortable place — a home, for example. Try to avoid a neutral environment.
- Open gently. Let the subject get warmed up. Unless you're on deadline, save your tough questions.

- Be a good listener. Forget yourself. Don't try to impress your subject with how smart you are.
- If the subject stops talking, don't interrupt. Just be quiet and often the person will continue in a more revealing fashion.
- Spend as much time as possible with the subject unless you're on deadline. The more time you have, the more details you'll get for your story.
- Get anecdotes. Assemble all the descriptive material you can handle.
- Use your perceptions and your intuition. Some ideas you get may be nonverbal: looks, the tone of the voice, a certain way the subject sits, stands or gestures. Maybe the person is trying to tell you something. Follow up gently with a remark, a question, to encourage comment.
- Play to the ego of your subject without being too obvious about it. It's not only famous people who like to be stroked. It helps maintain a good relationship.

Setting a Mood   Some experienced interviewers prefer to depend on circumstances, inspiration and lucky breaks for the opening of an interview, but they have a general plan well in mind for all else. Others, just as experienced but less confident, quite deliberately plan their opening remarks or questions. In any event, the main idea in beginning an interview is to set a friendly, easygoing mood for the proceedings.

Many an interview has been ruined at the outset by a crude or pointless observation, a bad joke or a question that betrayed antagonism. In such cases, subjects experienced in the ways of the news media simply limit their answers, say as little as possible and then excuse themselves.

It is a good idea, therefore, to begin by playing directly to the subject's own interest in granting the interview. If the subject is in politics, the natural approach is to remark on some recent accomplishment; in show business, the new play, film or musical is an obvious beginning; and in sports there is usually such a community of interest that there is seldom a problem once the interview can be arranged. It rarely pays to begin with some side issue such as the weather, the rudeness of the taxi driver on the way over or the decor of the subject's apartment. That kind of beginning only delays the reporter in getting to the point.

For Difficult Subjects   Interviewing people unfamiliar with the news media, particularly children, presents entirely different problems. Here, much depends on reportorial instinct. But the basic principle is still the same: to make the subject feel as comfortable and relaxed as possible and to encourage a free exchange of conversation and ideas. With children, it takes a lot of patience and, whenever possible, the cooperation of a parent or sympathetic family friend.

But in no case should arrangements for an interview be left to chance.

Timing   The one thing you do not do at the outset of an interview is to ask the subject how much time has been allowed unless, of course, the whole thing is to go on live television. By every possible device, the reporter should try to beguile and interest the subject in continuing the discussion and prolong the 15 or 20 minutes most busy people allot for an interview. The longer the session lasts, the better chance there is for a well-written, fully detailed piece.

A Story About "Old" Children

Cynthia Stevens, a young Associated Press correspondent in Johannesburg, South Africa, interviewed one of the most unusual children any reporter could meet during a visit to the nearby town of Orkney. The tiny boy, eight-year-old Fransie Geringer, was a victim of progeria, a rare and incurable illness that causes the body to age 10 times faster than normal.

When the reporter recovered from the initial shock of seeing a little boy in an old man's body, she began talking to him about his dreams and desires. He told her, with childish forthrightness, that he wanted to meet Pinocchio, the storybook character he idolized, at Disneyland in California.

Stevens wrote the story just that way. Within 10 days, the *Johannesburg Citizen* reported, more than enough money had been raised to enable the child, his parents and his 10-year-old brother, Paul, to fly to Disneyland. The reporter recalled:

> Meeting Fransie Geringer, an eight-year-old South African boy trapped in an old man's body by a rare "rapid-aging" disease, was enough of a shock. That combination of youth and age just didn't seem possible.
>
> So I was doubly surprised when a second progeria case, Mickey Hays, nine, emerged in Hallsville, Texas, following publication of Fransie's story. The boys' doctors had believed their patients were the only living victims.

Friendly Texans sent the second boy to Disneyland to meet Fransie. Stevens, who meanwhile was expelled by the South African government for unspecified reasons, joined the boys there and wrote:

ANAHEIM, Calif. (AP)—Shy, eight-year-old Fransie Geringer, a little old man who like Pinocchio longs to be a normal boy, met his fairy-tale idol at Disneyland Wednesday after a trip halfway around the world.

It was a wish-upon-a-star dream come true for the wizened, bald child from Orkney, South Africa, who suffers from a rare aging disease called progeria.

While Fransie smiled and giggled at Pinocchio's gestures—but said nothing—a new-found friend from Texas, a victim of the same disease, tweaked Mickey Mouse's ears and nose.

Fransie once thought he was alone in suffering from progeria, which ages its victims 10 times faster than normal, stunts growth and often results in death by the teen years.

The naughty wooden marionette, Pinocchio, has had special significance for Fransie since a Pinocchio doll was put in his crib in infancy. The 19th-century storybook character won a struggle to become a normal boy.

Then, Sunday, Fransie met 9-year-old Mickey Hays of Hallsville, Texas, and together the little boys went to Disneyland to meet their favorite characters. They toured the park after strolling around and riding a train with Mickey Mouse and Pinocchio.

Mickey headed straight for Mickey Mouse, the character he most admires, because "that's my name."

> "You're not a real mouse. You're a dressed-up girl," the cocky Texan told his new friend. "I knew that all the time."
>
> Fransie, a timid child, giggled throughout the private hour-long meeting as Pinocchio, a traditionally silent character, communicated by gestures. He didn't speak to his idol but soon followed Mickey's example and pulled the mouse's ears and nose.
>
> Pinocchio gave Fransie a Pinocchio watch and signed his autograph book with: "Fransie, be a good boy like me. Love, Pinocchio. . . ."

Fransie later saw the even more fantastic Disneyworld in Florida before returning home.

The Adversary Interview

It is true, of course, that the always-desirable friendly relationship between subject and interviewer cannot be maintained in interviews growing out of investigations. Thus, in cases where it is necessary to get an accused person's side of the story, the one-on-one interview is difficult to arrange and often has to be conducted by telephone.

But in those relatively few cases where a reporter does succeed in arranging a sit-down interview with someone involved in a difficult situation (usually it's done through a lawyer), the best thing that can be done is to maintain a formal but courteous attitude. The hard questions should be asked quietly but firmly, and without unnecessary finger-pointing or pencil-tapping. For this is no TV scenario but something real reporters have to do in real-life situations.

Interviewing a Victim

Most people who have been mugged on the street, or robbed in their home, store or office, are too uptight to discuss their experiences for the newspapers. Strangely enough, few object to being brought before TV cameras and questioned for the edification of millions of Americans at their evening meal. But when they see a pad and pencil, they often freeze. It's one reason why few reporters take notes in such an interview, but depend on their memories until they have a chance to make a sufficient entry in their notebooks.

This was the problem of Peter Perl, a reporter for the *Washington Post*, when he was assigned to interview a jeweler who had been robbed. Here, in essential part, is how he solved his problem:

> The call was ordinary enough. The man wanted to set up an appointment to look at some rings in the Wedding Ring jewelry store at 1909 I St. NW, co-owner Chris Booth recalled yesterday. Would Tuesday be all right? Yes. Could he have the phone number of the caller? Yes.

But by 3:30 Tuesday, it was clear that what had really been made was an appointment for robbery. Police led away one 18-year-old suspect; two undercover policemen and another 18-year-old suspect lay wounded, casualties in what had become the city's 22nd attempted jewelry store robbery of the year.

Robbery—indeed, gunfire—is nothing new to Booth. Three years ago in the same store, he said, a would-be holdup man shot him through the neck, and the bullet, which exited through his mouth, nearly killed him.

"The doctors said it was a miracle," Booth said. "It was a miracle nobody got killed here yesterday."

Booth describes himself as "paranoid" since his shooting and his cautious nature served him well Tuesday.

When the caller showed up for his noon appointment, Booth sensed "he looked like trouble." Booth quickly sized him up as being too poorly dressed to buy a custom ring and too persistent when Booth refused to open the electronically controlled front door he had installed since the last robbery.

More ominous, Booth said, was what he thought was a gun butt beneath the young man's jacket.

Right then Booth and his co-owner, Barry Michaelson, decided to call D.C. police. Within minutes, five plainclothes officers were positioned outside and inside the 12- by 15-foot jewelry showroom. While one of the undercover policemen was posing as a showroom employee, Booth and his partner hid behind a bulletproof enclosure with two other officers, Booth said.

When the young man returned, he was admitted by the bogus store employee, Booth went on. Then this happened:

"I heard muffled sounds and then the talking got louder and then the gunfire started. We hit the floor. . . . It sounded like machine gun fire," said Booth, speaking from the small store where the walls and blue carpet are now spattered with blood.

Police said one of the suspects opened fire without warning after the officers identified themselves. Yesterday the two suspects were charged with assault with intent to kill while armed. . . .

The whole story is told through the interview, mainly because that's the way the writer decided to organize it. Had it not been for Booth's quotes, it might have been just another report of a robbery and shootout in the nation's capital.

Interviewing and Writing

It can be deceptively easy to write a story about an interview. Just slap out a lead based on something the subject said, give the backup quote to show exactly how it was said, list the time and place of the interview, insert a couple of phrases ("flabby-looking, poorly dressed man"; "gawky, angular woman in a dress that looked like a gunnysack") and then quote, quote, quote and you're through.

This is a certain recipe for failure.

An interview of depth, in which the interviewer makes an honest effort to learn something about the subject, can't be written as a brush-off job, and it's always a mistake to try. For openers, writers should have a decent respect for their own ability. They should have a good ear — a sense of what's right and what's wrong about their use of langauge. They should be able to work easily with a strong character who comes through with such force that the image is formed in the mind before the writing begins. And they should have patience, kindness and a certain amount of sympathy for the subjects who have trouble when they try to express themselves — the most difficult kind of interview to write about.

Above all, they should be able to come up with a central idea for the interview — what John Galsworthy called "a spire of meaning." For this, next to the art of writing itself, is probably the most important characteristic of a successful story about an interview.

Telephone Interviews

The trouble with telephone interviews is that the other party can always hang up. It becomes necessary, at the outset, for the journalist — reporter or rewrite person — to establish some degree of credibility. This has led police reporters to begin with something like this: "I'm Bob Jones, calling from Police Headquarters. . . ." Or, "I'm Bob Jones, at Police Headquarters, and I want you to tell me. . . ."

The inference, of course, is that Bob Jones is a cop, not a reporter. It works on frightened people and there is no guarantee that the information they give over the phone is anywhere near correct. Almost anybody else will demand better identification of Bob Jones, and he may well wind up with a click in his receiver.

By coming right to the point, and asking the important questions, the reporter has the advantage of noting reactions. It isn't necessary to confront mobsters on their own turf and ask them right off if they killed a rival racketeer. Nor is it particularly healthy, if the reporter is alone. But reporters in such situations have never hesitated to discuss a murder with those who might be, at the least, material witnesses. Sometimes, reporters have received important information from such sources that was worth checking.

The best advice to any telephone reporter is to identify himself or herself at the outset by name and organization and immediately ask a question that is likely to produce an answer. It may not be much of an answer but it is, at least, a beginning. No reporter should tie up a subject on the telephone in a long theoretical discussion in the hope of trapping the person into some sensational disclosure. It's a waste of effort.

The only method that really works is to be fair, honest and businesslike, ask the questions that have to be asked, note down the answers and then, after the interview is complete, run a check on whatever information has been gathered.

Veracity

Dr. Alfred C. Kinsey, who interviewed thousands of men and women in connection with his sex studies, once was asked how he could tell if his subjects were lying.

"Very simple," he said with calm scientific assurance. "I look them right in the eye. I lean forward. I ask questions rapidly, one right after the other. I keep staring them in the eye. Naturally, if they falter, I can tell they are lying."

The reporter who was interviewing Dr. Kinsey nodded sympathetically over this expression of the master's views. A few minutes later, the distinguished scientist was somewhat startled to find the interviewer leaning forward, staring him in the eye, and asking questions rapidly.

The expert protested, "Now look here, that isn't fair. I just don't like what you're doing."

Most experienced reporters have learned that it does not pay to stare their subjects out of countenance. They become just as annoyed as Dr. Kinsey did when his own methods were turned on him.

The point is that there is no easy way of testing a subject's veracity. If reporters think they are being lied to, their only recourse is to check the statements that have been made in the interview. Subjects who are willing to lie in an interview are usually pretty accomplished, and cannot be upset by stares, grimaces or even outright challenges.

Handling Speeches

Most set speeches, particularly at conventions, can run anywhere from 10 to 30 minutes. At political conventions, there is no way of predicting an average length because politicians, as a group, are long-winded and seldom appear to know when to stop.

In any event, the typical set speech may contain a dozen or more points of fact or opinion. But if the reporter knows in advance that the story must be held to 400 or 500 words—about the limit for the average speech story inside the paper—it is obvious that no more than two or three points at best can be selected for inclusion in the news account.

Except in rare instances when the editor in charge decides what the lead shall be, the selection of material to be used in the story is the responsibility of the writer. Now and then, if there is a question of what to do, editor and writer may confer briefly before the story is turned out. But, usually, writers are on their own.

The more complicated the story, the simpler the sentence structure should be. And in writing about ideas, one idea to a sentence is a solid rule throughout.

The rule holds good, as well, for the selection of quotes. If the speaker's syntax is too involved but a quote is essential, then the only recourse is to use a partial quote even though it isn't a practice that can be generally recommended.

Selecting Material from a Speech   Here is the way a speech with several angles was handled:

Lead incident	The new director of the city's Museum of Modern Art promised today that he would broaden its benefits to the community.
Documentation for the lead	Dr. Frederick V. R. Langsam, the director, who succeeded the late Albert Arnold Bunker, made public his plans in a "White Paper on Art."
	The "White Paper" was summarized in a speech by Dr. Langsam before his Board of Trustees at the Museum's auditorium.
	"We are going to send some of our best pictures, including some Picassos, into the deprived parts of this community," he said.
	At the Museum itself, he added, such modern devices as indoctrination films and pocket-size tape-recorded guides would be used to explain the collection to the public.
Second incident	Dr. Langsam also said he might find some surprises in the Museum's treasure-trove of art, now stored in various warehouses.
Documentation for second incident	"As a good museum man," he explained, "I know that fashions in art change and some works of modern artists that have been stored now will find an appreciative public. This city is likely to have some surprises."
Third incident	The Museum's director conceded frankly that the Musuem's public image needed improvement.
Documentation for third incident	"People have thought of us as a stuffy old barn run by a lot of fuddy-duddies," he said, "and maybe they have been right. We're going to open up from now on, I can tell you."
Added detail	Among the measures Dr. Langsam proposed in his "White Paper" were improved relations between the Museum and the city's public schools. "Let's bring art to the children instead of leading the children into the Museum by the hand," he urged. He also wants to close the gap between the Museum and the State University to strengthen the Museum's reputation among art scholars.
	Dr. Langsam was a professor of art history at the State University before he assumed his present post. During his academic career, he won a reputation for springing surprises, known as "Langsam's Happenings," to attract the public to academic surroundings. He said there would be no "Happenings" at the Museum.

Some Precautions The most frequent question asked by young journalists, in their first jobs, is, "What happens if the speaker's remarks are untrue? How can we tell? And what can we do if we have to get the story in on deadline?"

This was precisely the situation that was exploited by the late Senator Joseph R. McCarthy Jr., of Wisconsin, when he created a climate of terror, after World War II, in his campaign against people he accused of being Communists, especially those in government. With few exceptions, newspapers gave banner headlines to his charges, even though he never was able to document them. It was not until after the televised hearings of McCarthy's groundless accusations against the U.S. Army that his hoax was exposed.

Nowadays, reporters are required to ask for proof of controversial statements, to seek comment at once from those who may be accused of wrongdoing and to report the facts along with the misstatements. Such corrections are often included in the same account as the one in which the misstatements are reported, together with comments by all parties to the incident.

Another necessary precaution, especially when speeches are written from an advance text, is to make certain the remarks are actually delivered without change. The newspaper is covered, until delivery is completed, through the use of a phrase high up such as "In a speech prepared for delivery," or "In an advance text, he said. . . ." When Betty Ford was First Lady, she arose to speak at a dinner in her honor at a New York hotel when the previous speaker, a distinguished American rabbi, collapsed and died on the platform. Mrs. Ford, with great presence of mind, asked the other guests to join her in prayer.

News Conferences

Ever since President Franklin D. Roosevelt popularized the news conference by holding two a week, it has spread throughout government at all levels and is also used by everybody from beauty queens to striking garbagemen. It has developed its own rules, its own set of standards, its own peculiar mannerisms. But as an entirely practical matter, most experienced journalists know that if a news conference develops no news in the first 20 minutes, it is likely to be a washout.

Running a News Conference   In the higher reaches of government, reporters expect to meet with the press spokesman or spokeswoman in particular offices at least once a day. That is especially true at the White House, where the presidential press secretary is always in demand. But when the press secretary is away making a speech, there isn't as much interest in him unless he spreads the word that he will have something newsworthy to say. And that sometimes leads to a misunderstanding at best, an argument at worst.

During David Gergen's tenure as White House press secretary, he once addressed an annual conference of the American Association of Advertising Agencies at a Washington hotel. He spoke with more candor than he usually did in his daily news conference and at one point, before taking on a tough question, asked:

"This is all off the record, isn't it?"

From the back of the room, someone shouted, "No!"

Gergen demanded, "Who are you?"

"The Associated Press."

"Well, can we put this on background [not for attribution]?"

"Nope."

The affair ended with the AP reporter, Mike Feinsilber, walking off with an exclusive story. At a news conference, he would have shared the story with anywhere from 20 to 50 colleagues, depending on the hour of the day.

The incident points up the weaknesses of the news conference as a mechanism for transmitting news. First of all, nothing can be exclusive; everything must be shared and shared alike by all in attendance and anybody who has a friend covering for him or her. Second, the person conducting the news conference may be able to dominate the proceedings very easily by answering simple questions, turning aside the tough ones and stalling on anything that might possibly be embarrassing. Experienced public officials and politicians are going to say exactly what they intend to say and nothing more, no matter how much fuss the reporters kick up. Finally, in the hands of an official like Henry Kissinger, a news conference can be used to manipulate the news media into circulating plausible explanations of unfortunate incidents.

A Local News Conference   News conferences are held every day at every level of government for every conceivable purpose. Chicago Mayor Jane Byrne used the news conference to reassure jittery citizens that she was fighting rising crime. Here is the way one of the Byrne news conferences was handled by Robert David and William Juneau of the *Chicago Tribune:*

> Mayor Byrne made an unannounced tour of the crime-ridden Cabrini Green housing project Thursday and promised its residents, "You are going to live in security and safety."
>
> In a news conference in City Hall shortly after the one-hour visit to the Near North Side project, the major said a comprehensive plan for the project's protection was being developed by Police Supt. Richard Brzeczek and Charles Swibel, Chicago Housing Authority director, with whom she toured the project.
>
> Asked if the residents she had met appeared frightened by the large number of shootings in the area in the last several months, Mrs. Byrne said, "No, but I'm sure they are."
>
> She said she had told them she was going to get the matter cleared up, adding, "They feel they need more police protection and they are going to get it...."

A News Conference for Spacemen   On a more glorified level, an informal news conference becomes a part of the ceremonial of welcoming home American spacemen after a successful mission and produces an integral part of the story. The way the two merge is demonstrated in this account of the flight of the Columbia space shuttle:

Lead: the landing	EDWARDS AIR FORCE BASE, Calif. (AP)—Spaceship Columbia crowned a busy, bittersweet mission Saturday, bursting like a silver wraith through mottled California skies to its second flawless desert landing.
Documenting the lead: color	With Joe Engle in command and Richard Truly beside him, the winged shuttle hit Earth right on time, right on target: the oil-black center line on wide-open Rogers Dry Lake in California's Mojave Desert.
	"Touchdown. Welcome home," said Mission Control.
	For Engle and Truly it was a perfect ending for a troubled mission, halted three days early only because an electric generator broke down. Crowds, estimated at 220,000 peo-

ple, cheered "Go" as Columbia passed overhead on its final approach to Runway 23.

Return to Houston   The astronauts headed quickly for home in Houston while technicians swarmed over the first ship to go into space twice. "The bird is real solid," said Engle as the 106-ton ship emerged from a 17-minute blackout and sped across the Pacific at five times the speed of sound.

News conference in Houston   A chilly but cheering audience of about 300 people greeted the astronauts when they arrived at Ellington Air Force Base near Houston.

"You can be proud of the talent that's right here in Houston and made this whole thing possible," Engle told the crowd, referring to the staff of the Johnson Space Center. Said Truly, "We really had a lot of fun."

"It's a great day for the U.S. and the space program," said James Beggs, head of the National Aeronautics and Space Administration, in introducing the astronauts following their quick physical exam.

"Sorry we got down here a couple of days early," Engle said of the short flight. He called the cut in flight time "kind of heartbreaking," but added, "We were awful glad that we were able to accomplish the things that we set out to do and got the main objectives of the flight done."

Truly said, "The real hero of the day is sitting out there on the lakebed. That is some kind of flying machine. . . . I think it's going to lead us to things we don't even dream of yet. . . ."

Getting Exact Quotes   Nearly all news conferences of importance are televised. Some, like the astronauts' conference at Houston, go on live and millions of people watch and listen. It follows that when writers repeat what the astronauts already have said to a national audience, the quotes have to be scrupulously accurate.

Since relatively few American reporters know shorthand (even British reporters with only a high school education usually are good at it), the main dependence for accuracy has to be on transcripts and tape recorders. It is possible to record accurately the few quotes of the astronauts with pad and pencil, but anything more intricate takes a lot more time. Nobody has yet devised a speedy method for taking key quotes off tape recorders after an extended news conference.

Fixing up Quotes   Before the electronic era, when pad and pencil journalists had to cover an extemporaneous speech and weren't sure they had the main quotes quite right, they would get together and agree on a version. Sometimes, they would consult the speaker, but generally he was unavailable. In any case, off would go the "fixed up" quotes to the nation, and there were few objections afterward.

That isn't possible now, of course. What most news organizations permit their writers to do is to smooth out garbled syntax now and then. Of course, this doesn't mean that a mobster being questioned about a murder can be made to speak the Queen's English. But where nothing very earthshaking is involved and it is possible to spare embarrassment for hard-working officials at news conferences and interviews, such corrections may be made.

It all depends on the news organization. Bitterly partisan correspondents and/or their newspapers tried to make President Eisenhower look silly by quoting with painful accuracy what he said at his news conferences. It never worried him particularly. It seemed only to increase his popularity. The same is true of people at the local level whom reporters have attempted to embarrass.

Football players are penalized for unnecessary roughness. The same isn't always true in journalism, but it happens sometimes. At the very least, it can cost reporters a few sources.

Responding to Questions   When a speaker responds to questions from the audience, and thereby makes news, a reporter should note the source for the record. Sometimes, that becomes important. President Eisenhower, who could be absentminded, once dropped the last paragraph of a speech through sheer forgetfulness, and it happened to contain the main news point of the address. A quick-witted reporter called to him, as he left the podium, "How about letting me use the last paragraph of the speech as an interview, Mr. President?" After an aide explained what had happened, Ike said rather guiltily, "Good idea, go ahead. And tell everybody else."

News Conference Rules   Whether the news conference is good or bad, or a mixture of both, it is conducted according to a few simple rules that should be well understood by all participants.

On the part of the news source, or a public relations representative, there is a tacit understanding that there is news to impart and explain that will be worth the time of the reporters who are assigned. On the part of the reporters, they agree to listen and report accurately but they make no guarantees of use in any form.

It is the responsibility of the news source to pick a time and place convenient to all, and provide a tape recorder or stenotype record. If TV and still photographers also are expected, the source must make appropriate arrangements. Where the news conference is one of a regular series — as at city hall or a state capitol — it is understood that everything is on the record and may be quoted. For other conferences, the source's public relations representative announces the ground rules and type of attribution, subject to acceptance by the reporters.

At most news conferences reporters understand that no one is to leave until the last question has been answered and that the door to the conference room will be closed. If there is to be any variation from this practice, it is generally announced before the beginning of the news conference, again subject to agreement.

For the average news conference, reporters expect that about 20 or 30 minutes will be sufficient. If it lasts much more than that, the senior reporter will end the affair abruptly by saying, "Thank you, Governor or Mayor So-and-So." Without further ado, everybody will leave the room. To avoid such an embarrassing situation, even the most eminent news sources have learned to compress their remarks. If they have a great deal to say, they hand out a prepared statement in advance and invite questions on it.

No news source in the world, except for the president of the United States, is supposed to be able to answer without hesitation every question thrust at him. Therefore, at most news conferences, the principal source will have subordinates answer some of the questions. Only at the White House does a president face the news media of the world and the nation with only a hasty warmup to guide him.

Conventions and Crowds

Young reporters often find themselves assigned to cover conventions. In every city and town, prominent and not-so-prominent citizens belong to at least one organization, and many are members of several. Committee meetings, luncheons, dinners, discussion groups and fund-raising efforts are part of the way of life in America.

   Procedure   Any assignment to cover a convention or another meeting of a fairly large group usually begins with a visit to the official, agency or public relations firm handling the arrangements. The reporter picks up all available mimeographed material, including the program, schedules, advance copies of speeches, biographies and historical notes. That is the basis for homework on any such session — political, social, academic or scientific. If such advances aren't available, the reporter is in for a dreary time of routine interviewing to get as much background as possible before the meeting opens.

   For some meetings, the story is usually an advance. What reporters try to do is to interview a prominent person involved in the session, perhaps an official or a speaker, to get away from doing a routine story. Sometimes, as in the case of a convention that attracts persons from all over the country, it is possible to do a roundup of national conditions in that particular industry, business or grouping.

   Most reporters like to work from advance texts of speeches; or, in the case of a gathering of physicians, scientists or academics, from abstracts of speeches or papers that are to be delivered. If the public relations people in charge of the meeting are efficient, they round up such material in advance. If not, the reporter has to do it — and it is a long, tiresome and often painful job.

   Crowds and Crowd Figures   At conventions, parades, political meetings and sports events, attendance figures are a part of the story. Reporters used to take a figure from some police official or public relations representative, who made a fast guess. That is no longer good enough.

   Much of the haziness about crowd reporting has long been dispelled. For instance, it has been found that, at best, Times Square in New York City can hold about 250,000 people. About the same number can line lower Broadway for a ticker-tape parade. As for the millions who supposedly jam the great squares and plazas of foreign cities, that myth also has been shattered.

   It is mandatory for a reporter to know the capacity of an auditorium, theater or other public place in order to make an accurate estimate of attendance. For a parade, the calculation is somewhat more complicated. The number of blocks along the line of march is known, and the average block length can be calculated. By taking samplings of the number of people per 100 feet along the line of march, an average density figure may be obtained. Simple multiplication will then produce a reasonably accurate crowd figure. Similarly, the dimensions of any large and well-known area in a city may be obtained (Trafalgar Square in London, Red Square in Moscow) and the crowd density may be observed, thus providing the main figures for a simple calculation. In important cases, a tabulating machine may be used. There is no reason for guesswork in arriving at crowd totals in an age in which so many electronic tabulating devices are available.

Researchers have shown that usual crowd densities may vary from 6.5 to 8.5 square feet per person, with 7 square feet as a reasonable average. Thus, knowing the outer dimensions of a crowd or making a fair approximation of it, anybody can put together very quickly a realistic estimate of the size of measurable gatherings. But if a crowd spreads out for many miles, thin here and dense there, it is foolhardy to put down a supposedly accurate figure and — in these days of omnipresent TV — any viewer knows it.

• Short Takes

Here are the things to remember in reporting on interviews and news conferences:

- Before you go to an interview that may be the basis for a story, check the background of your subject in your news library and biographical reference material. For relative unknowns, check school and employment records and call neighbors and others. The point is never to go unprepared, except in emergencies.
- Plan the interview. Ask your first questions in line with the interests of your subject. Once the subject starts talking, listen. And keep listening. It's the hardest thing to train reporters to do.
- List the key questions, put them in your purse or pocket after memorizing them and use them as the interview develops.
- Be careful about note-taking. If you can't use a tape recorder, which is the best way to handle the q. and a., then be sure that your note-taking doesn't choke up your subject. If it does, put pad and pencil away and make notes directly after the interview.
- Unless you are in an adversary-type interview, make the subject feel comfortable and relaxed. Don't stare at the subject or take signs of nervousness for unwillingness to talk. Be encouraging.
- For adversary-type interviews, play it straight. Ask your questions in a calm, reasonable and courteous manner and do not let yourself be provoked under any circumstances. Lead up to your toughest question but don't be afraid to ask it. Generally, it is best to have another reporter along as witness if you can't record.
- Be very patient in interviewing children. Ask for the help of parents and friends. And take the time to make the child feel some trust in you.

These are the principal points to remember about writing stories involving news conferences, speeches, interviews, panel discussions and public statements:

- Leads should be based on a newsworthy statement. It is never acceptable to write merely that someone held a meeting or someone made a speech. Tell what was said.
- Scatter the details, one idea to a sentence. The time naturally goes in the lead, but the place, the type of audience and the background of the speaker can go in subsequent paragraphs where they fit.
- In any story based on talk, other than a short, there should be a strong quote high in the story to document a paraphrased lead. In all stories, good quotes should be used instead of paraphrases with the possible exception of the lead.
- Anything that is said, quoted or in paraphrase must be directly attributed to the speaker. Avoid elegant variation in attribution. When in doubt about a verb, use "said."
- To avoid distortion, if something that is said is used out of context, the main thrust of the speaker's remarks should be given and linked to the material taken out of context.
- Reporters are required to ask a speaker or interviewee for proof of controversial statements and to gather replies from persons who may be accused of wrongdoing by a speaker.
- When material is written from an advance text, a clause high in the story should record that fact. Use "In a speech prepared for delivery," "In the advance text of a speech" or some variation of these. Remove it if the speech is delivered without change.

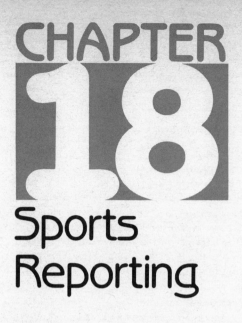

CHAPTER 18

Sports Reporting

This is the era of big-time college football, created in large part by the willingness of the broadcasting networks to spend millions of dollars on nationally televised games. It is also the era of the million-dollar-a-year professional athlete, enormous stadiums, fanatical fans and gamblers who will do almost anything to avoid losing a bet.

Such a combination is bound to add up to trouble, sooner or later, but it isn't often that either the sports pages or the sportscasters reflect so damaging a reality. In the mythology of the sports world, sports reporters are supposed to confine themselves to the stories of who won and who lost, or game called on account of the weather. When they don't, it's news.

Uncovering a Scandal

At a meeting of the American Society of Newspaper Editors, Charles Bailey, editor of the *Minneapolis Tribune*, put the case this way:

> I have a feeling of unease when I think about sports, both college and
> professional, in terms of the fact that we are not really doing a job of reporting on the
> true conditions. I am talking about college football in particular, but also most college

241

sports, the money involved and the practices involved. One has a hard time getting sports writers interested in digging into that story.

Brent Musburger of *CBS Sports* responded with the not-so-original observation that most communities believe sports writers "should not touch this grand entertainment" and went on:

> It is very unfortunate we are so hypocritical at the college level. Take a look at the money that is being generated by college athletics in terms of television contracts and tickets that are sold for those arenas. You wonder why athletes aren't paid in some way. . . . Even if the *Minneapolis Tribune* does a story or CBS goes in with 20 minutes in one, two or three different schools around the country, we are not going to change a thing. They are going to be back out there giving cars away, giving jobs to parents, because there is so much money at stake. It is an economic issue. They just ought to be honest with it and deal with it in some way.

A Hometown Story   Musburger's reference to hometown pride in local sports heroes was at the base of an outpouring of resentment in Tucson, Arizona, when the local *Arizona Daily Star* began digging into rumors about the alleged mishandling of the financial affairs of the University of Arizona's football program. Some large businesses canceled their advertising in an effort to stop the inquiry, editors of the paper said, and others started a boycott.

Despite these efforts to stop the inquiry, the two city-side reporters who were conducting the investigation, Bobe Lowe and Clark Hallas, broke a series of stories after working for three months, bringing about the resignation and indictment of the university's football coach on charges of financial irregularities in the football recruiting program. However, when the coach was brought to trial he was acquitted. Even though the reporters were awarded the 1981 Pulitzer Prize for investigative reporting, it did not endear them to the loyal supporters of the Arizona Wildcats. The coach's acquittal, coming as it did after the award of the prize, demonstrated once again that it is one thing for a newspaper to publish charges and quite another to persuade a jury to believe them.

Another Coach's Story   The outcome of the Arizona case, however, did not quiet the concern about irregularities, and worse, in intercollegiate sports. It was no city-side reporter or sports writer but a basketball coach, Richard (Digger) Phelps of Notre Dame, who made news in the 1980s by charging that some colleges were paying $10,000 a year to obtain the services of star basketball players. He accused two institutions, which he did not name, of making such payments from funds supplied by local sports booster groups, and the National Collegiate Athletic Association investigated.

At the time Phelps made his charges, 17 colleges and universities were on probation under NCAA rules for various violations, but for different reasons than those Phelps publicized. While some coaches accused the Notre Dame mentor of making charges after a losing basketball season, others supported him but conceded that such payments were difficult to prove.

Ralph Miller, basketball coach at Oregon State, called Phelps's $10,000 figure low and was quoted by the Associated Press as follows: "That figure was what they were talking about 10, 15 years ago . . . If they build big arenas, they have to fill them. It's all money in college sports nowadays, no doubt about that."

A number of other coaches agreed that there was a problem, not only in basketball but in football as well. However, they argued that the violations were not as widespread as Phelps had said. For the most part, on leading sports pages, columnists discussed the problem and gathered quotes from coaches and NCAA officials. But relatively few efforts were made immediately to conduct an independent check of his charges.

Changes in Sports Reporting   Sports editors and reporters are well aware of the criticism that has come their way. In Boston, there was no effort to play down or cover up a criminal investigation into a point-shaving scandal that rocked the Boston College basketball team. As a result, a youthful Boston College basketball player was convicted and sent to jail for ten years. Nor have sports editors always been complaisant about the rumors of wrong-doing in collegiate and professional sports. Years ago, Max Kase, sports editor of the *New York Journal-American*, won a Pulitzer Prize Special Award for turning over information to the district attorney of New York County about a looming basketball scandal. As a result, several local college players were convicted and sent to prison.

But then, New York and Boston aren't as likely to develop hometown pride in local athletes as are smaller communities. And in the big cities, there is less opportunity for booster organizations to bring pressure on the local news media not to interfere in the affairs of local colleges or universities.

Without much doubt, the emergence of television as a dominant influence in the presentation of sports to a mass public has made a difference in the public's perception of right and wrong. As George Solomon of the *Washington Post* has said, "TV buys events. TV puts on the event. And to make TV look good and sell all the commercials, the sport must look good."

Brent Musburger of CBS believes the charges to be overstressed. He says, "To a large extent we are in the entertainment business, which leads me directly into what we do as networks. Yes, we have to buy events. Then we have to make a profit out of them. So we have to attract an audience. And, yes, there is a certain amount of hype that goes into it."

Still, Musburger argues, newspapers also try to present the news in as appealing a way as possible because they, too, have to maintain circulation to attract advertisers and they, too, have to make a profit to stay in business. True enough, but the difference is that the newspapers don't pay large sums of money to put on national sports broadcasts. In consequence, to quote Solomon, "A lot of editors are demanding the same standards from sports reporters and sports journalists as they do from everyone else — that is, aggressive reporting, looking behind the scenes, digging, being a true reporter."

The Cult of Privacy   In professional sports, where outstanding athletes can earn enormous sums of money in a relatively short time, sports writers are under even greater handicaps. Because there is a tendency to criticize those players who collect millions and give substandard performances, the cult of privacy has taken firm hold among many teams. Once it was taken for granted that sports reporters and TV cameras would be welcome in team locker rooms or at practice sessions. But not today. Access to athletes in locker rooms is severely restricted by most professional sports teams. Dave Anderson of the *New York Times* says:

> When I was covering the [New York] Jets 10, 12 years ago, you could virtually walk into their locker room during the week at any time. You could go into a locker room before a game up until an hour before. You could walk on the practice field and stand behind the huddle in the middle of the field. Today, virtually all of that is gone. There is no way you can walk out on a practice field of any team. You can stay on the sideline.... During the week, many teams have situations whereby you are only allowed in the locker room, let's say, an hour or a half hour. You have to make appointments with players.... The coaches seem to think the more secrecy they have, the better. To me, the more secrecy they have, the worse it is.

In major league baseball, star players of the caliber of Steve Carlton and Dave Kingman have refused for years to speak to sports reporters and have gone their own way. And some younger players have had a powerful urge to imitate them.

The problem, therefore, is to obtain access to the millionaire athletes and their colleagues, and not every sports reporter is successful. The athletes appear to divide reporters into "good guys" — that is, cheer leaders — and "bad guys" — those who try to do an honest day's work.

There are some coaches, athletes and club owners who still resent women sports writers and try, by various means, to make it difficult for them to obtain access to athletes. But few women are fainthearted enough to be put off by such phony excuses as male modesty in locker rooms. Nor have women sports writers turned out to be the problem that some of their male colleagues predicted they would be. There still aren't very many of them.

Making a Beginning

It is a long way from such major concerns among the top figures in the sports reporting field to the beginner who wants to break into sports reporting for a newspaper or broadcast organization. Yet sports is almost a common denominator among working journalists today. Many of them had their first task of journalism covering sports as stringers at the high school level. And few have forgotten their experience.

Getting a Sports Job In a lot of American cities, high school sports have a wide following and, particularly in communities without college or professional teams, are a dominant community activity. On any autumn Saturday afternoon, from Riverhead, New York, to Wenatchee, Washington, and from Key West, Florida, to Monterey, California, thousands of people turn out to watch high school football. In many places, too, basketball is a magnet that draws townspeople to high school gymnasiums. Such sports as baseball and track traditionally have lighter attendance, but all are reported on in the local papers and local broadcast media.

Beginners generally inherit stringing jobs in high school from graduating classmates. Or, if they are particularly enterprising, they may find a nearby publication or station that gives no coverage to a high school within the general circulation area, and win the assignment. At any rate, the first time they report on a game, they may be told that the paper or station wants only the final score and how the victory was achieved. Then someone in the office writes a roundup including this information.

As the newcomer proves trustworthy, the assignments improve. In addition to the final score, other details are requested—the number of people attending the game, an interview with the winning coach or the player who scored the deciding points, plus a summary of the scoring by both sides. Once again, that story may be written by somebody else in the office.

It sounds so easy to do these things. But actually, as all beginning sports reporters learn, it is almost as difficult to pin down sources at the high school level as it is to gain access to the big-time professionals. The reasons are apparent. Coaches, for the most part, don't trust the judgment of youngsters to report what they say and— if they comment at all—it will usually be in pleasantries with little news value. The same is true of officials at the games and those teachers who have a special responsibility for athletics. Players, too, are often cautioned to say as little as possible on the air or for publication, to avoid making some statement that can be seized upon by a future opponent.

Working at the High School Level From these experiences, the beginner will learn persistence if nothing else. And that will be all to the good. But there will come a day when an assistant sports editor tells the beginner to write the story and bring it to the office or, better still, to come to the office and do the piece under supervision. That is always something to be remembered, even if the copy is heavily edited and bears little resemblance to the original.

Most young and inexperienced sports writers make the same mistakes. They deal in clichés instead of writing simple, straightforward English sentences. They load their copy with expertise, or what they believe to be expert comment, all of which is usually eliminated. And, worst of all, they betray a partisanship for the home team that makes their credibility suspect to anybody who merely wants a fair account of what happened.

The process of learning to write a sports story, therefore, takes time. Except in rare instances, beginners can't learn to do it well overnight. It helps to read the work of outstanding professionals. Above all, the job is learned best by continual practice.

Daily Sports Coverage Every year, depending on the size of the paper and the rate of turnover, a certain number of stringers are offered regular sports jobs. It is far more difficult to make a beginning as a sports broadcaster, because these jobs are even more limited. The progression is usually through the sports pages of newspapers in medium-size cities. Such papers, though, rarely hire more than one youngster a year. Very small dailies do not have enough staff turnover to warrant expectation of jobs for beginners, and the big metropolitan papers prefer to take on people with experience.

For the lucky ones who come up through the system and land regular jobs, the routine of daily sports coverage can develop into a pleasant life. Newcomers generally are assigned to writing the same high school sports they covered as stringers—an easy way of breaking in. The next step in the progression is to handle college sports if there is a nearby institution of higher learning. It takes awhile to graduate to professional sports coverage, particularly if professional teams are outside the paper's circulation area. But when the newcomer does get a professional assignment, it generally is to do either a color story on a major contest or to handle the play-by-play.

Regular beats—following a particular baseball or football team through the season—aren't practical for a small sports staff. Reporters may handle several different sports in a single week and have to adapt themselves to local conditions.

Interviewing Sports Figures

Bob Matthews, sports columnist for the *Rochester* (New York) *Times-Union*, has these suggestions for interviewing sports personalities:

- Make sure your first question is a good one so the subject will know you have something on the ball.
- Always be on a first-name basis with every player on a pro team. Sooner or later, one of them will goof up and it's a sports writer's job to ask him about it. Nothing turns off an athlete faster than a reporter who hasn't said hello to him all season but is quick to arrive after a costly error.
- Try for specifics. Don't settle for generalities. Ask why the center fielder dropped the ball in the last half of the ninth, enabling the opposition to score the winning run.
- I have one pet question I often ask athletes: "What do you think of sports writers?" They usually have definite opinions and branch off into how they've been misquoted, misrepresented, etc. It's a good way to build rapport and can lead to some good exchanges.
- Before I interview a national sports figure, I often phone a sports writer in his particular town for background and tips on how to approach the subject.
- Invariably there's a question I forget to ask or a point that needs clarification. So I always ask where the subject can be reached later in the day, just in case he's needed.

Patterns of Sports

Because most of the sports public knows the final score of the game from radio or TV before the paper comes out, sports writing in the TV age is different in many respects from what it used to be. Dave Anderson of the *New York Times* says:

A lot of my colleagues really seem to resent television. I may be different, but I enjoy television for this reason: I think television creates sports readers. Any time people see an event on television, they invariably want to read about it next day. To me, the beauty of television is that as soon as the game ends, they go off. . . . As soon as they go off, that's when we go to work. That to me is the great value of television in the sports business.

Other newspaper, magazine and syndicated sports writers have been pleasantly surprised by the self-evident truth that Anderson expressed. And they have adapted to the new dispensation by using many of the techniques of the feature writer—the bright anecdote, the sharp quote, the interview with all concerned in a disputed play or a disputed decision, the description of a part of the contest that television downplayed. Relatively few editors now want the fast summary lead on the final score; instead, they ask for the way it happened and the answers to all the questions the fans will be raising that night and the next day.

Damon Runyon, Bob Considine and Jimmy Cannon—three of the old-time greats in the sports writing business—would have been very much at home in today's sports pages. As the saying goes, they always played the angles and wrote the story for all it was worth.

Telling the Sports Story   Anybody who undertakes to write about sports must have an intimate knowledge of the assignment. The three greatest necessities are accuracy, restraint and a decent respect for the English language.

Sports followers invariably pride themselves on being experts. They like to hear and read about "inside" strategy, just as the literati gossip endlessly about the famous people on whom characters in a sensational new novel are supposedly patterned. However, some games are more easy to describe than others—and that depends on the patterns of the sport.

An essentially simple game like baseball is easily reported. The game's play-by-play, the result and the reasons for it can be quickly summarized, then documented with a description of the key plays. A few other details, and the account is complete enough for a postgame electronic roundup. But the written sports story must be different and it must have more detail.

Boxing and horse racing, too, have essentially simple patterns and need not be told in too complicated a fashion. What matters, particularly in television, is the detail that makes the tiny images on the small screen come alive—the blow-by-blow in a fight and the "call" in a horse race. By comparison, accounts of competitions in crew, swimming, tennis, polo and golf are handled with relative ease.

In football, however, the pattern of the game becomes increasingly complicated and difficult to follow. The effort of a play-by-play commentator here must be to simplify, wherever possible, and to explain to the viewer what happened and why it happened instead of prattling excitedly about the confusing technicalities. In a summary, oral as well as written, it becomes necessary to analyze the result, to select the principal plays and to give the public a sense of participation in the reporting. The writer, especially, must emphasize anecdote and detail.

The many events in track and field, each with special complications, also require a good deal of guidance from professionals who are intimately acquainted with the sport. This is particularly true during the spectacle of the Olympic Games every four years; in inexpert hands, such reportage may be the worst, rather than the best, of the year because some American commentators and reporters know only the United States' competitors as a rule and tend to give the results of each race as a triumph of American righteousness or a blow to the Stars and Stripes. Actually, in any track meet, the reporting can be done very nicely—and interestingly—if the expert-for-the-day studies the teams in advance, looks up the necessary background and records and comes to the field an hour before the meet starts to do a final checkup. To wait until the first event begins is to bog down completely in detail. But if it is known in advance that the pole vault, the mile run and the hurdles are likely to develop the most interesting contests, then the meet becomes a relatively easy matter to cover. What can never be anticipated is the unexpected event, such as the murders of Israeli athletes by Arab guerrillas that made so tragic a spectacle out of the 1972 Olympic Games in Munich, the wholesale withdrawal of black African nations from the 1976 Games in Montreal and the 1980 American boycott of the Moscow Games.

As for basketball, with its seven-footers and its statistical labyrinths, this is less a job for a sports reporter than for a certified public accountant. It is hard to follow on television and even worse to describe in print, but it has such a large and devoted following that it receives major coverage.

It is clear, therefore, that the patterns of sport have much to do with the pattern of sports journalism. The big-money sports such as horse racing, boxing, baseball and football are the ones with the most public appeal; in general, professional sports have the widest following. But college sports also attract millions of followers, and the TV contracts are much sought after.

New Interests   Two developments have broadened the audiences for both the sports page and sports events on the tube. One is the rise in participation for women's sports and the broader attention and funding that universities have given to them. In some parts of the nation, the excitement over women's sports, even at the high school level, has become a matter of consequence.

The second break in the traditional sports pages has been the interest in such audience-participation events as stock car racing, motor boating and sailing, hunting and fishing, skating and skiing and the like. Such events are not easy for TV to cover, and therefore offer something to newspapers that can interest their readers. The boom in soccer, so long considered a "foreign" sport, benefits all the news media.

Writing Techniques   The incomparable Red Smith, viewing an Army–Navy football game at Philadelphia, began his account as follows:

> As some churlish historian of America's great undergraduate pastime wrote years ago, "It was an ideal day for football — too cold for the spectators and too cold for the players." For 100,000 citizens of assorted nations, including Russia and Monaco, whose chattering teeth rattled like castanets upon the necks of bottles in Municipal Stadium yesterday, that just about sums up the match of Army and Navy.

Eventually, Smith got around to mentioning the size of the Army's victory, 22–6, which wasn't particularly important to him because everybody who read him knew it anyway. What was more important to his readers was his point of view:

> The entertainment seemed flat by comparison with Army–Navy contests of the past. It was just too perishing cold. Reluctant to quit a slugging match which they had traveled many miles to watch, the customers nevertheless started making their numbed way toward the exits when the first half ended, longing for a warm hotel room with the guy across the courtyard beating his wife . . .

Unlike Red Smith, most sports writers and commentators immmerse themselves in technicalities to such an extent that they often forget entirely about the game itself and the people who contest it and who watch it. The electronic reporters become slaves to their equipment. The newspaper reporters worry about writing three separate accounts of a single event in order to cover all editions of a newspaper — a time-consuming and expensive procedure that provides no advantage in these times of instant communication.

Advances and Summaries   Because the technique of doing multiple stories of one sports event is still practiced in a large section of the daily press, the essentials are recorded here without assurance that they will survive many more years:

1. *The Advance Story*   The advance begins with a situation lead, relating that two teams are facing each other or that a field of seven horses is ready for the big race of the day. The remainder of the story merely discusses the background of the event, gives whatever detail there is on the participants and the crowd, and winds up in such a way that the running account of the early part of the game can be added on. If the contest is under way before the edition closes, a brief high insert can give the early scoring. Necessarily, even in an early edition, the advance is bound to look foolish. It assumes that the public is entirely dependent on the newspaper to find out what happened and will buy a later edition to get the full details. This used to happen, but it hasn't for many years.

2. *The Running Story*   Depending on the style of the paper, the chronological story of the game is told as B copy (or B matter) or merely slugged "Running" or "Play-by-Play." As an edition approaches, a two-paragraph lead is written by the reporter at the scene or by an editor in the office and put on top of the opening of the chronological account. Once the event is over, a final wrap-up lead is written and the details of the end of the game are put at the bottom of the piece.

3. If the running story is well done within reasonable space, it should stand. But frequently, sports writers have the urge to do the whole exercise over again on the dubious theory that they will produce magnificent prose the second time around. Unfortunately, it rarely turns out that way.

These are trying circumstances for any journalist. If the objective is to keep pace with radio and television, it is impossible to attain. If it is to "save space" for the final story, the theory is lacking in practicality. Such "saved space" is always wasted space. The newsmagazines manage to do pretty well with their weekly summaries of sports and do not arouse great feeling among the sports-minded public that it is being cheated. Sooner or later, the newspapers will come around to the obvious — that the best way to do a sports story is to wait until the event is over and then give it the well-considered treatment it deserves. Few sports events are big enough to call for edition-by-edition coverage against electronic competition.

Statistics   The sports fans of the nation love statistics, and most sports pages provide them in abundance with columns of box scores, averages, racing detail, league standings and the like. Every reporter must learn at the outset how to keep an individual set of statistics and make sure they are accurate. But the wisest reporters know when to stop loading a story with "stats" and depend, instead, on the beauty and utility of the English language. Too many statistics can kill a story. Too few will make it unusable. The trick is to find a practical in-between point.

● Short Takes

Here are some of the basics that should be remembered about sports reporting:

- Sports reporters are measured by the same standards as all other reporters. They have to do more than just report the score; it is their business to be aggressive, to dig for the hidden story, to make sports pages mean something more than a repository for columns of agate results.
- One of the foremost problems today is access to athletes and locker rooms, at both the professional and the amateur levels. Reporters have to make it their business to ask the tough questions—which means that they can't let themselves be turned aside by a stern locker room janitor.
- Most beginners in sports get their first job stringing for a neighborhood paper and reporting high school scores. The high school sports beat is a testing ground for the next generation of sports writers. Usually, the best of the stringers gets first crack at an opening for a high school sports reporter and the progression starts there.
- The three necessities for a sports writer are accuracy, restraint and a decent knowledge of and respect for the English language. Phony expertise and cliché-ridden writing are the principal faults of newcomers.
- In a contest featured on TV, the newspaper sports writer has to emphasize something other than the score, even though the score does have to be repeated high up. This can be an anecdote, a sharp quote, an interview or an explanation of some occurrence that was fuzzed up by the TV reporters.
- In the thousands of contests that sports writers cover with little or no broadcast competition, the emphasis is still on writing the story straight and featuring the manner in which the game was won or lost. But even here, the feature approach always helps and—except for the brief summary story—good quotes are mandatory.
- Keeping statistics is an important part of a sports reporter's work, and he or she should devise a system that can be quickly scanned and summarized at the end of the game. Too many stats will spoil a story; too few will make it unusable. The point is to find the happy medium.
- Everybody in the business emphasizes sports writing styles. But mostly, this refers to the elite—the columnists and commentators who speak and write pretty much as they please. The young sports staffer is bound to the same rules that cover all reporters, however, and should not deviate from them without permission.

CHAPTER 19

The Press and the Law

Carol Burnett was angry. She had just read an item in the *National Enquirer*, a checkout-counter weekly, that implied she had been tipsy and disorderly in a fashionable restaurant.

The *Enquirer* had been printing that kind of gossip about Hollywood personalities for some time without being sued, and most professional entertainers, fearful of bad publicity, had refused even to protest. But this one was different.

First, Burnett forced a published retraction from the *Enquirer*. Then she sued for libel and won an $800,000 judgment. The *Enquirer* appealed, but at once was threatened with libel suits from others in Hollywood.

Like every other news organization, it had discovered to its cost that it was not immune from libel suits.

What Is Libel?

There is nothing very mysterious about libel. Generally, if you injure someone in print without sound legal grounds, you and your news organization have committed a libel and will have to take the consequences. If you do so on the air, it is slander — oral defamation; but if there is a written script for the broadcast, the infraction is libel.

In a very broad sense, there are two absolute defenses against libel. The stronger is *provable* truth. The second is *privilege*, or right, which means that the reporting is based upon a fair and true account of such public proceedings as court, legislative and other governmental records. But it is important, in both cases, to establish that no malice is involved.

Some writers mistakenly cite the right of fair comment on actions of public figures — politicians, entertainers and the like — as an absolute defense. But editorialists and commentators proceed at their peril when their criticisms or observations stray beyond purely professional concerns into peoples' personal affairs and exhibit *provable* malice.

Qualifications such as the use of terms like "alleged," "accused" or "suspected" are no defense against a libelous statement. Nor can reporters contend that they merely repeated something that turned out to be untrue and not covered by privilege. Even retractions are no defense against libel judgments. These, and a few other actions, are useful only as partial defenses and efforts to mitigate damages.

Libel by Legal Definition   Libel laws vary from state to state, as do legal precedents. As a result, there is no one catch-all legal definition. Nor have United States Supreme Court decisions always clarified a particular issue. Sometimes even the high court can be obscure and difficult.

For practical purposes, however, the New York State definition of libel (Section 1340 of the New York Penal Code) is a useful guide:

> A malicious publication by writing, printing, picture, effigy, sign or otherwise than by mere speech, which exposes any living person, or the memory of any person deceased, to hatred, contempt, ridicule or obloquy, or which causes or tends to cause any person to be shunned or avoided, or which has a tendency to injure any person, corporation or association of persons, in his or their business or occupation, is a libel.

Punishments for Libel   Civil libel, the category for most law suits, is an infraction against an individual. Criminal libel, which is comparatively rare, constitutes a crime against the state.

In civil libel, if proved, general or compensatory damages may be ordered. Plaintiffs do not have to prove monetary loss in such cases. Where monetary loss can be established, special damages may also be awarded. However, it is so difficult to prove financial damage through libel that such verdicts are uncommon.

But where malice in a civil libel case can be established, the roof can fall in. It isn't necessary for the plaintiff always to show hateful intent. Very often, gross negligence or ill will or a finding of reckless disregard of the truth are construed as malicious under the law. Then the penalties can be enormous, as the Burnett case demonstrated.

As for criminal libel, the state is the prosecutor and punishment may include both fines and prison terms in the case of individuals.

How to Stay out of Trouble

The first rule for staying out of trouble with the libel law is to check for accuracy *everything* you write or broadcast. An irascible and impatient journalist will snarl: "Oh, come on! Haven't you ever heard of deadlines?"

But it isn't the deadline story, or the big feature or the long-term investigation, that usually touches off a libel suit. Generally, it is the routine item — the ho-hum brief or bright squib that brings grief to a newsroom.

"Oops! I Didn't Mean It!"   Careless mistakes are often the most damaging to journalists. There was the case of a war veteran who captured a purse snatcher in a street chase, but was rightly annoyed when the local paper identified him as the thief and his quarry as a war hero. He collected $10,000 for that one through an out-of-court settlement.

Another instance of sheer carelessness caused a businessman to sue a newspaper that described his tactics as those of a "robber baron" — and name-calling is a no-no in libel textbooks. The newspaper settled by giving $25,000 to the businessman's favorite charity.

Then there was the case of a newspaper that published an interview in which a singer's manager, by implication, was accused of having mishandled her affairs. However, the newspaper omitted the facts on which the opinion was based, even though they had been given to the reporter. The manager accepted an out-of-court settlement.

It isn't enough to say of a stupid error, "Oops! I didn't mean it!" Checking copy is one way of avoiding mistakes. Another is the old safety-net rule: "When in doubt, leave out."

Fairness Is the Best Policy   It's all very well to insist on "telling it like it is," in the vernacular of Howard Cosell. But it's more important to be fair in the handling of news and comment. The best policy, by all odds, is to be scrupulously impartial, particularly in using sensitive material. There is no better defense against the charge of malice.

Once a story is slanted, once bias creeps in, then both journalists and their news organizations may be in deep trouble. And there is no easy way out once a libel suit has been filed. Litigation can go on for years, placing a very heavy financial burden on defending news organizations.

Preventive Medicine for Libel   The heat is on when libel papers are served, and everybody involved usually scrambles for cover. But quite sensibly, journalists are now being advised to take preventive medicine at the time a touchy story is being developed.

Louis D. Boccardi, as executive editor of the Associated Press, said:

> Part of the preparation for [possibly libelous] stories should include our answering, as journalists and not as lawyers, a series of "what ifs?" —
> What if we are sued, can I count on that confidential source?
> What if I have to rely on other support, do I have the proof I'll need?
> What if my notes are subpoenaed, and what steps can we take now to protect our interests?
> What if we are accused of recklessness, can I demonstrate the care we took?
> Preparing for the suit at the time you do the story is an awful lot easier than starting from square one when you are served with the papers 11 months later.

The Importance of Notes   The prospect that reporters' notes may be demanded by a judge, or that a jail sentence for contempt of court may be imposed if a reporter refuses to give them up, has led to a lot of panicky reactions. Some journalists, including a few respected veterans, advise their colleagues to destroy their notes in touchy situations. The same advice is being given to broadcasters with respect to their "outtakes," videotapes or film that are part of a record but never were used.

It would be better, in important cases, to arrange to put such material in the company safe and have the management handle the problem. Notes in a pad or on a wad of copy paper, like tape recordings, documents, still pictures, film and "outtakes," are important parts of the journalistic record of events that have been covered and should be carefully and systematically preserved. More often than not, notes help bolster the credibility of journalists as witnesses in court. They can scarcely be looked upon in all cases as instruments of potential difficulty.

"Who Goes to Jail?"   Journalists, often given to black humor, have been known to ask as participants in a libel case, "Who goes to jail?" Actually, in a civil case, nobody goes—unless an individual becomes involved in a contempt-of-court citation. Fines and heavy costs for legal services are the result if guilt is proved.

Who pays? In theory, everybody associated with a libelous story could be held accountable. But in practice, the management of the news organization bears the principal responsibility. When journalists of prominence are parties to the suit, they are also likely targets.

In one celebrated case, when a newspaper columnist made scathing attacks on a writer, the writer won a $75,000 libel suit against both the columnist and his news organization. But the papers that had published the offending column didn't have to pay. That is an exceptional case, however. In most libel suits, the news organization is considered the prime offender and the main defendant.

Danger! Use at Your Own Risk!

Journalists have learned from experience that libel suits in the following categories are the most difficult to defend:

1. Attacks on a person's character.
   - Calling someone insane who has never been confined to an institution.
   - Reporting that a person of good character is an alcoholic or a habitual drug user.
   - Imputing a loathesome disease to a person.
   - Stating or implying a lack of chastity and/or loose moral conduct to a person of good reputation.
   - Declaring someone is divorced or separated from a spouse when in fact a harmonious marriage exists.
2. Criminal charges.
   - Alleging that someone confessed to a crime when only a statement was given to the police. The term "confession" should be used sparingly if at all.

- Confusing a person of the same name with a criminal.
- Mistaking an indictment for wrongdoing by assuming it is a conviction of a crime.
- Reporting that someone was arrested when that person was only one of a number who were questioned about a crime.
- Using summonses, affidavits and police blotter entries in the mistaken notion that they are privileged. They seldom are, unless they become part of a formal court record.
3. Financial errors.
   - Calling a person a bankrupt when it is not true.
   - Injuring a person in his or her profession, calling or trade and causing financial loss.
   - Attacking a person's ability to earn a living.
   - Disparaging a person in such a way as to impair or destroy his or her credit, often through ridicule.
4. Mistakes in procedure.
   - Announcing a court action before papers are filed, particularly in divorce cases, and then learning there has been a settlement.
   - Repeating a libel when there is no defense of privilege.
   - Misquoting a court record.
   - Accusing a person who has never been convicted of having a criminal record, usually on the basis of charges that were dismissed.
   - Using an obit about a person who is still alive. In a famous case, Annie Oakley of circus fame collected from newspapers that erroneously reported her death.

Words That Can Hurt   Call a physician a "quack" in print or on the air without sound legal grounds and you'll almost certainly be in the middle of a libel suit. The same thing goes for "blasphemer" if it is applied to a minister, priest or rabbi, or "ignoramus" to a teacher. These and other terms of abuse, used without justification, can trigger court actions, as many of the following already have done:

liar	informer	fool
rascal	perjurer	idiot
nut	whore	jail bait
villain	bandit	oaf
swindler	cradle-snatcher	dunce
loan shark	B girl	chowderhead
phony	seducer	rogue

When such terms are used, it is nearly always because they are part of a public record that is privileged. But let a public official repeat the same term outside a courtroom or a legislative hearing in which a record is kept, and both print and broadcast journalists who make the exercise in name-calling public are asking for a libel suit.

Taking Chances   There is a widespread belief among journalists that certain classes of people are "libel-proof"—that almost anything can be said or written about them without danger of reprisal. Chiefly, these are gangsters with long criminal records; women with a record of convictions for prostitution; fugitives from justice, and inmates of mental hospitals or prisons and other correctional institutions. It is true that such people rarely sue, but that does not exempt the journalist from relaxing vigilance.

Moreover, despite their inclusion in libel laws, both dead people and corporations are not rated highly in newsrooms as libel risks. Neither are politicians who sue for millions close to election day.

These notions are debatable. Even if "dead people can't sue," in the conventional wisdom of newsrooms, their estates can. When Norman Mailer, the author, put fictional dialogue in the mouth of Marilyn Monroe in his book about the actress, her estate sued for invasion of privacy. Although the suit was dismissed, it took time and money to defend.

As for corporations, they *do* sue. Some, held by courts to be "public figures," must show malice to collect in libel suits. Others, termed "private figures," need only demonstrate "fault" — that is, error. Even political suits, brought in an obvious attempt to intimidate the news media, must be taken seriously.

How to Defend Against Libel

Libel suits filed against the news media are growing in alarming proportions. For journalists, therefore, it is more important than ever to know how to defend themselves and take effective counteraction. The following summation deals with both complete and partial libel defenses.

The Defense of Truth   When truth is invoked as a defense against libel, convincing proof must be offered in court for the veracity of the publication. It is not sufficient to show that a quotation from some other source, which turned out to be false, was accurately reported. Nor are juries impressed with affidavits and sworn statements by reporters that what they wrote was true. Legal authorities insist on *provable* truth if it is to be offered as a libel defense.

Even where state laws additionally require proof that malice was not involved in a publication, there is no serious challenge to provable truth as a complete libel defense. This right, won by John Peter Zenger in his New York libel trial in 1735, eventually became a major landmark in the struggle for press freedom. Today, the defense of truth against a charge of libel remains one of the pillars supporting the First Amendment.

The best proof of truth is documentary evidence, supported by the testimony of witnesses who can show that the defamatory story is true. Tape recordings, videotape and even reporters' notes sometimes become valuable exhibits.

When it isn't possible to present such an airtight defense, the plaintiff's background and reputation are examined in an effort to show that the plaintiff is of such poor repute that he or she cannot be libeled. But that is at best only a partial defense.

In any case, it is the *substance* of the charge that must be proved, not the manner in which it was made. It isn't sufficient to show that a police chief publicly accused a suspect of being a murderer while standing at the scene of the crime. Nor can a tape recording be introduced to prove that a politician, speaking in front of his own home, called one of his critics a bribe-taker. Since neither statement would be privileged, the news organization itself would have to prove the truth of the charges, not merely that they were made.

The Extension of Privilege   This defense is based on public policy. It underscores the right of the public to receive fair and true reports of the acts of its courts, legislatures and other official bodies and most but not all public officials.

One of the standard definitions of privilege is a part of Section 337 of the Civil Practice Act of New York:

> A civil action cannot be maintained against any person, firm or corporation for the publication of a fair and true report of any judicial proceeding, or for any heading of the report which is a fair and true headnote of the statement published.
>
> This section does not apply to a libel contained in any other matter added by any person concerned in the publication; or in the report of anything said or done at the time and place of such a proceeding which was not a part thereof.

What Is a Public Record?   That raises the question of what constitutes a public record. State laws vary. Some go beyond New York in permitting the quotation of remarks by certain officials outside the actual record. Other states are more restrictive.

A legislative reporter found to his dismay some years ago that a record had not been made of an important committee hearing, after which libelous charges had been published. Other reporters have learned that inferior courts in some states are not considered courts of record. Moreover, not every state declares police records to be privileged under the law.

Eternal vigilance, therefore, is the prerequisite for journalists. On a case-by-case basis, they must determine for themselves and their news organizations what is privileged and what is not. Secret police proceedings and secret meetings of public bodies, where no records are kept, must be considered dubious supports for the defense of privilege. So are legal papers before they are served and recorded.

The defense of privilege, therefore, is by no means as sweeping as that of truth, although it is just as complete when it can be invoked.

The Right of Fair Comment   Editorials, columns, critical articles and broadcast commentators' work are generally covered by the right of fair comment unless there is proof of malicious intent. It is a libel defense based on public policy — the right to express an opinion about those who seek public attention. The opinions or criticism may seem silly or illogical, but they are defensible in court as long as they are free of malice.

As a matter of prudent procedure, such writings or broadcasts ought to be based on fact and the facts supporting the opinion ought to be cited. Serious writers and critics have long recognized that opinions based on mere whimsy can be challenged. Thoughtful journalists do not, in consequence, take offense without good reason, and they document their opinions. Mere name-calling is never advisable.

The law specifies that the right of fair comment must be confined to matters of public interest or concern. These include government affairs; acts of such institutions as universities, hospitals and charitable foundations; public entertainment, and publicly offered printed and broadcast works.

Among those who invite criticism and comment are holders and seekers of public office, writers, public performers, athletes and others whose careers are based on public attention. But all are protected by law against intrusion into their private lives, unless their acts affect their public careers. A drunken public official cannot prevent inquiry into his or her weakness. Neither can police officers whose sex life opens them to criminal blackmail.

The Wavering *New York Times* Rule

The law of libel is subject to change. That is its most durable feature. And change can come about quickly, as the *New York Times* Rule illustrates.

The Law on "Public Officials"   A 1964 decision of the Supreme Court under Chief Justice Earl Warren gave the press a strong defense against libeling a public official. The case involved an appeal by the *New York Times* against a $500,000 libel verdict by an Alabama jury in favor of L. B. Sullivan, public safety commissioner in Montgomery.

Sullivan contended that he had been injured when the *Times* published an advertisement, paid for by a civil rights group, that circulated "unretracted falsehoods" about his work. The high court ruled for the *Times* with this judgment:

> The constitutional guarantees require, we think, a federal rule that prohibits a public official from recovering damages for a defamatory falsehood relating to his official conduct unless he proves that the statement was made with "actual malice"— that is, with knowledge that it was false or with reckless disregard of whether it was false or not.

The Law on "Public Figures"   In 1971, the Supreme Court broadened this landmark case to include a larger group it called "public figures."

In that case, *Rosenbloom v. Metromedia*, the Metromedia station WIP appealed a $750,000 libel verdict won by a nudist magazine distributor and obtained a reversal. The plaintiff — the magazine distributor — was held to be a "public figure," in the words of the majority decision — "a private individual [involved] in an event of public or general concern."

Therefore, the Court declared that the plaintiff had to show malice — a reckless disregard of the truth — and he hadn't done so. In consequence, the decision said, "A constitutional rule that deters the press from covering the ideas or activities of the private individual thus conceives the individual's interest too narrowly."

That was high tide for liberalism in the Court.

Squeezing the *Times* Rule   With Warren E. Burger as Chief Justice and conservatives on the Court, reaction set in. In *Gertz v. Robert Welch Inc.*, a libel judgment was upheld in 1974 for a private individual without proof of malice. The high court decreed that a private individual involved in public affairs had only to show some degree of "fault," possibly negligence by the defendant news organization. So Elmer Gertz, a lawyer, bore off a $50,000 award against a John Birch Society publication, put out by the Welch firm.

Two years later, the Supreme Court showed that it would be very restrictive about whom it chose to label a "public figure." That was in the case of *Time Inc. v. Mary Alice Firestone. Time* had reported that the socially prominent Mrs. Firestone had been divorced on the grounds of "extreme cruelty and adultery," which wasn't true. She had not been accused of adultery, and a Florida court awarded her $100,000 damages, ruling that she was a "private individual" who did not have to prove malice but only "fault." The Supreme Court upheld that decision despite *Time*'s protest that Mrs. Firestone was widely known, had held press conferences and was thought of as a "public figure."

Alan U. Schwartz, a distinguished legal authority, warned that the *Firestone* decision "severely limits" the legal definition of who is a "public figure" and told journalists that they were on shaky ground if they depended on it. After all, it is a lot easier to prove "fault" in a private person's suit than to show "malice" against a public figure.

Schwartz's caution was underlined in the Supreme Court's 1979 decision upholding a libel verdict in favor of Ilya Wolston, who had sued the Reader's Digest Company for publishing a book in which it was erroneously stated that he had been indicted for espionage. The high court held that Wolston had never before been a "public figure" because he had not "voluntarily thrust" himself into an investigation of Soviet espionage but had been "dragged unwilling" into it by the government. Thus, all he had to do was prove "fault," not malice.

The wavering *New York Times* Rule had become a weak shield for the press.

Other Defenses   Less frequently used libel defenses include:

- Publication resulting from the consent of the person libeled.
- Use of defamatory material in self-defense or as a reply.
- Privilege claimed as a participant in an official hearing.
- The statute of limitations (usually two years in most states).

But it is difficult to depend on any of these in front of a jury.

The Libel Data Center   More than 20 news organizations and libel insurance companies formed the Libel Defense Resource Center soon after a jury threw the profession into near-panic with a $9.2 million libel judgment against a small paper, the *Alton* (Illinois) *Telegraph*, which subsequently was reduced.

Research services and information on virtually all pending libel cases were made available at the center — located in Suite 3420, 30 Rockefeller Center in New York City — through James S. Kraus, the staff coordinator, and Henry Kaufman, the general counsel. At the beginning, there was no charge for services except for basic costs of handling requests for information.

Kaufman noted sadly that a majority of all libel suits are won ultimately by defendants.

Partial Defenses Against Libel

Where there is no complete defense against a libel suit, the best that can be done is to publish a retraction or an apology and hope for the best. Such hopes seldom are realized. Next comes a resort to partial defenses to try to cut down the size of the verdict.

Ten Alternatives   Here are 10 of the more important partial defenses that are used in an effort to show that the defendant tried to issue a fair and true report without malicious intent:

1. The conduct of the plaintiff gave "probable cause" for believing the charges to be true.
2. Rumors like the defamatory report had long been circulated and never denied by the plaintiff.
3. The libel came from a wire service report or another respected source.
4. The plaintiff's general character is bad.
5. The libel was used in heat and passion provoked by the plaintiff.
6. The libel had been told to the plaintiff before use and had not been denied.
7. The libel was committed in the heat of a political campaign.
8. A retraction or apology was issued.
9. The libel did not actually refer to the plaintiff, but to another person of similar name about whom the charge was true.
10. The libel was qualified as to source ("according to police") and merely repeated allegations ("the alleged crime," "the suspect," etc.).

The Public's Stake   Safeguarding a news organization against a libel suit is of obvious importance to journalists, but it is not the most compelling reason for emphasizing the care that must be taken in circulating news, views and opinion. The ultimate stake is public confidence in the news media, without which no privately owned news organization can long exist in an open society such as ours.

Reporters and Privacy

Suits for invasion of privacy are another serious risk for the news media. Floyd Abrams, a New York lawyer, calls them "the single most ominous threat to the First Amendment's guarantee of press freedom." The effect of privacy litigation is being felt increasingly by reporters, editors and all types of news organizations, large and small.

What Is Privacy?   The courts have generally taken a dim view of reporters who burst unasked into people's homes or private offices. Similarly, reporters who pose as somebody they are not or adopt disguises to get the news may find themselves on shaky ground in a privacy action.

In one widely publicized case, a United States appeals court upheld a $1,000 verdict for an "herb doctor" against *Life* magazine because two of its reporters had caused injury to his "feelings and peace of mind." What they had done was to enter his office, one posing as a patient and the other carrying a hidden camera, in an effort to show that he was practicing medicine without a license. Even though he later pleaded no contest to that charge, he still won his privacy suit.

Thus, in one broad classification of privacy actions, a reporter cannot injure the "feelings and peace of mind" of individuals by intruding into their homes or offices. To quote the court decision: "The First Amendment has never been construed to accord newsmen immunity from torts [civil wrongs] or crimes committed during the course of newsgathering."

It also means that news organizations had better be sure that there is a sound basis in public policy for the work of reporters if they are to assume disguises to get at the news.

Malice in Privacy Cases When a privacy situation is deemed "newsworthy" in a legal sense, the courts have held that a finding of malice is required before a judgment can be returned against a reporter or a news organization. This is a second large grouping of cases under the privacy law.

The issue first came up in the 1952 case of *Time Inc. v. Hill*, in which the Supreme Court reversed a verdict of $30,000 against *Life* magazine for invasion of privacy. The Hill family had charged that *Life* had identified them as a fictional family held captive by escaped convicts in the play *The Desperate Hours*. The Hills had indeed been held captive by convicts for 19 hours, but they had not been harmed. However, the fictional family had been tortured. The high court ruled against the Hills because they had not proved malice — that is, that the magazine had knowledge that what it printed was false or that it had done so with reckless disregard of whether the story was false or not.

Quite the opposite occurred in 1974 when the Supreme Court upheld a $60,000 verdict against the *Cleveland Plain Dealer* for invasion of privacy brought by Margaret Mae Cantrell, widow of a man who had died in a bridge collapse. Mrs. Cantrell complained that a reporter had visited her home in her absence and then written an article in which he gave the impression that he had interviewed her and found her and her children living in poverty.

The high court found the case "newsworthy" and also held that the defendant's act was malicious. Mrs. Cantrell, the Court declared, had been portrayed "in a false light through knowing or reckless untruth."

Thus, in privacy cases, portraying people "in a false light through knowing or reckless untruth" is as dangerous as "injuring feelings and peace of mind" through invasion of private homes or offices.

Truth in Privacy Cases The Supreme Court agreed in 1975 that the press had a right in privacy cases to use "true information . . . in court documents open to public inspection." But it added that at some future time it would decide "the broader question whether truthful publications may ever be subjected to criminal liability."

The case was that of a 17-year-old Georgia girl who had been fatally injured in a rape and later identified by a Cox Broadcasting Corporation TV station. Invoking a Georgia law that makes identification of rape victims a misdemeanor, the girl's father won a privacy suit against Cox, but the Supreme Court reversed the judgment by holding the Georgia law unconstitutional.

In effect, therefore, the high court showed that privileged documents could be used as a defense against privacy litigation as long as they contained "true information." As for the right to use the names of rape victims, it is a rare news organization that does so.

"The Right to Be Let Alone" Louis D. Brandeis, later to become an Associate Justice of the United States Supreme Court, once defined privacy as "the right to be let alone." He and Samuel D. Warren of Boston first laid down the principles of the privacy law in the *Harvard Law Review* in 1890. That law has since become a powerful instrument.

But there is nothing in the privacy statute that prevents reporters from covering any public event or public personage as long as they conform to standard journalistic practice — giving a fair and true account of the proceedings. Moreover, even Brandeis and Warren, fierce advocates of privacy, agreed long ago that individuals lose their right to privacy if they consent to publication or take part in the process. Today that goes for broadcast journalism too.

Reporters and Fair Trials

If you are a young journalist assigned to cover a court hearing, there is a chance that you may not be allowed in. Certain types of court hearings are now closed to the news media on the theory that even the most fair and honest reportage will somehow prejudice the right of fair trial. It is the proper concern of journalists, however, to oppose unnecessary secrecy by the courts and guard against the possibility of miscarriages of justice.

The framers of the Constitution intended the First Amendment's guarantee of a free press and the Sixth Amendment's equally strong assurance of a fair trial to coexist, not to be set against each other. But there is no accounting for judges, any more than there is for journalists, so open court reporting cannot be taken for granted.

Gagging the Press The issue of free press versus fair trial was raised by the Supreme Court in 1966 when it reversed a murder conviction against Dr. Samuel Sheppard of Cleveland. The high court ruled that "virulent publicity" and a "carnival atmosphere" had made a fair trial impossible. When Dr. Sheppard was tried again later that year, after having served nearly 10 years following his conviction in 1954, he was acquitted. A few years later he died.

The aftereffects of the Sheppard case, however, long survived him. Within 10 years after the Sheppard reversal, at least 50 judicial orders were issued imposing gags on the news media in court proceedings. But the worst was yet to come.

Closing the Courts   Journalists were lulled into a false sense of security when the Supreme Court in 1976 ruled that judicial gag orders were unconstitutional except in rare cases. The decision reversed a Nebraska judge who had forbidden the news media to conduct pretrial coverage of an accused mass murderer. But, instead of gagging the press, judges promptly began gagging news sources, and the effect was almost identical.

Even worse, in 1978 the Supreme Court decided in the *Stanford Daily* case that the police had a right to search a newsroom or other premises for criminal evidence merely by obtaining a search warrant.* They did so elsewhere, as well, with abandon. In the following year, in *Herbert v. Lando*, the high court ruled that journalists, like others, would have to submit to an exploration of their thought processes by plaintiffs in libel suits.

That set the judicial stage for what amounted to a confrontation between the bench and the news media. The issue was posed by the Supreme Court in 1979, in *Gannett v. DePasquale*, when it upheld a New York judge who had closed his courtroom to reporters for the Gannett Newspapers at a pretrial hearing in a murder case. For the majority, Justice Potter Stewart wrote:

> The Constitution nowhere mentions any right of access to a criminal trial on the part of the public; its guarantee, like the others enumerated [in the Sixth Amendment], is personal to the accused.

So, while ostensibly barring the press from pretrial hearings, where most criminal cases are actually decided, the *Gannett* decision in reality gave judges a signal to close courts at random, pretrial or not. And they did so. This, many journalists declared, amounted to a return to Star Chamber proceedings, the secret English courts of the 16th and 17th centuries.

The Consequences   The protests against the *Gannett* verdict amounted to a firestorm of public opinion. Some lawyers, notably Alan U. Schwartz, joined the attack with a warning that this was "a time of dark caution for the press and therefore for the country."

Courtrooms were closed to the news media in literally dozens of cases for a variety of reasons. Nor were closures confined by any means to pretrial hearings. Despite the Sixth Amendment's guarantee to the accused of "a speedy and public trial," open sessions of murder cases were closed to the press by judges who feared what they called prejudicial publicity. It was a sickness that spread through the land with unmatched virulence.

Finally, in 1980 the Supreme Court found in *Richmond Newspapers v. Virginia* that press and public *did* have the right to attend criminal trials in open court. Justice John Paul Stevens, in commenting on the decision, wrote that the high court "never before [had] held that the acquisition of newsworthy matter is entitled to any constitutional protection whatsoever."

---

*Such searches are barred under the Privacy Protection Act, which took effect in 1980 at the federal level and in 1981 at the state level. The FBI, however, is urging Congress to grant it immunity from the act.

It was premature, however, to call this a "reversal" of the *Gannett* decision. For as the Reporters Committee for Freedom of the Press learned in tabulating the number of court closings *after* the *Richmond* case, judges were still slamming the door on press coverage.

Between July 1979 and May 1981, the committee counted more than 400 closure motions in preindictment, pretrial, trial and postconviction proceedings. Of these, 241, or 60 percent, succeeded, with 217 being enforced or upheld on appeal and 24 more constituting direct prior restraint. Almost two-thirds of the closures were made to avoid jury prejudice from pretrial publicity. Other causes ranged from the protection of trial figures to the refusal of reporters to follow voluntary Press–Bar Guidelines of conduct (see page 267).

When Reporters Go to Jail

There used to be a popular misconception in newsrooms that journalists, like physicians and priests, enjoyed the privilege of confidentiality and could keep their sources secret. Sadly, it is not so. A number of reporters who tested the issue have gone to jail for contempt of court. And more are likely to follow them.

"You Can't Do That!"   The key decision came from the Supreme Court in 1972 in *Branzburg v. Hayes*. The high court held that journalists had no right under the First Amendment to refuse to tell grand juries the names of confidential sources and the information received from them.

In effect, Paul Branzburg of the *Louisville Courier-Journal*, Earl Caldwell of the *New York Times* and Paul Pappas of Station WTEV were punished with contempt citations for having refused, in separate cases, to disclose their confidential sources. Thereafter, the sorry parade began of reporters who went to jail because they had defied the courts' warning: "You can't do that!"

Four years later, the Supreme Court showed that it still meant what it had said in the *Branzburg* case. It refused to intervene in the case of four journalists for the *Fresno* (California) *Bee* who served 15 days in jail for refusing to disclose the source of secret grand jury testimony in a bribery case. And William T. Farr, then of the *Los Angeles Herald Examiner*, did time when he refused to reveal his source for an article about a murder trial. The high court took no action on his appeal.

The Stiffest Punishment   The worst sentence of all was imposed on Myron A. Farber, a reporter for the *New York Times*, and his newspaper when they were found in contempt of court in New Jersey for refusing to give a judge confidential files in a murder trial. Farber served 40 days of a six-month jail term in 1978, and the *Times* was fined $285,000.

The case was that of Dr. Mario Jascalevich, who had been brought to trial following the publication of a series of articles in the *Times* under Farber's byline. The indictment charged the physician with multiple murders in a hospital involving the drug curare, and the defense then demanded the confidential files kept by Farber and his newspaper. They refused, pleading that New Jersey's shield law gave them the privilege of doing so. Nor would they yield the files to the judge at the trial for a determination of whether the material was pertinent.

Farber's conviction followed. It was upheld by the state's highest court, and the Supreme Court rejected a review of the case. Eventually Dr. Jascalevich was freed without examination of the files, which led to Farber's release. But the damage had been done. And the shield law in New Jersey, as in other states, was found to afford little or no protection against a contempt citation.

The case did not end there, however. On his last day in office Governor Brendan Byrne of New Jersey pardoned both Farber and the *New York Times*.

The Courts Reconsider

The obdurate refusal of reporters and their news organizations to betray their sources has yielded some results, although the Supreme Court still refuses to protect journalists' confidentiality. However, eight of the 10 United States appeals courts have agreed that journalists do have the right, even though it may be qualified, to refuse to testify in criminal or civil cases.

Extending the Ground Rules In a 1980 case involving a libel suit against a Boston newspaper, the appeals court in Boston ruled that the newspaper would not have to disclose its confidential sources to a boat manufacturer until alternate methods of finding the desired information had been exhausted.

The appeals court in the District of Columbia went beyond that in 1981 when it turned down a request by two defendants in a racketeering case for the notes of a *Detroit News* reporter. When a journalist is called as a witness in a civil case, the court held, "the civil litigant's interest in disclosure should yield to the journalist's privilege. . . . Indeed, if the privilege does not prevail in all but the most exceptional cases, its value will be substantially diminished."

Why Reporters Must Fight The rationale behind the journalists' refusal to betray their sources was given eloquently by Daniel Schorr of the Columbia Broadcasting System when he risked contempt of Congress for refusing to tell where he had obtained a secret United States intelligence report. He did admit giving a copy of the report to the *Village Voice*, a New York weekly, which published it.

Invoking the First Amendment in testimony before a congressional committee in 1976, Schorr said:

> To betray a confidential source would mean to dry up many future sources for many reporters. The reporters and the news organizations would be the immediate losers. The ultimate losers would be the American people and their free institutions. In some 40 years of practicing journalism, I have never yielded to a demand for the disclosing of a source that I had promised to protect. But beyond that, to betray a source would be to betray myself, my career and my life. I cannot do it. To say I refuse to do it is not saying it right. I cannot do it.

The House committee did not cite Schorr for contempt. He later resigned from CBS and joined Cable News Network.

The Press Counterattacks The judicial offensive did result in a press counterattack. Many state legislatures passed "shield" laws that were intended to protect reporters' confidential sources and keep them out of jail. As in the Myron Farber case, the "shield" laws didn't help much because many judges ignored them. A few judges did recognize their validity — a small but significant gain.

A more effective device came from the Gannett Newspapers, which had been in the forefront of the battle to retain press freedom. The group distributed a 3½-x-5-inch card to all its reporters; when folded in half, the card displayed the text of the First Amendment on one outer cover and the following notice on the other:

> Journalists are America's guardians of the people's First Amendment rights to a free, unfettered press. Today more than ever, journalists must be prepared to move quickly and effectively to defend the public's right to know. To this end, Gannett offers its news staffers the enclosed statement, which may be read into the court record when a reporter is confronted with attempts to close the courtroom doors on the public and the press.

Inside the cover, Gannett's lawyers had prepared the following brief notice which gave the position of the press against arbitrary court closures:

> Your honor, I am _____ , a reporter for _____ , and I would like to object on behalf of my employer and the public to this proposed closing. Our attorney is prepared to make a number of arguments against closings such as this one, and we respectfully ask the Court for a hearing on those issues. I believe our attorney can be here relatively quickly for the Court's convenience and he will be able to demonstrate that closure in this case will violate the First Amendment, and possibly state statutory and constitutional provisions as well. I cannot make the arguments myself, but our attorney can point out several issues for your consideration. If it pleases the Court, we request the opportunity to be heard through Counsel.

To almost everybody's surprise, the device worked well. It was, after all, a challenge backed by the power and wealth of the largest group of newspapers in the land. Confronted with the possibility that an arbitrary or capricious court closing would be appealed and probably reversed, many judges consented to hear arguments. And after thinking over the decision, some maintained open courtrooms. No judge likes to be reversed, and Gannett's action guaranteed that a determined fight would be waged to knock out unnecessary court closings.

The press counteroffensive also produced a number of state "Sunshine laws" that were intended to keep official meetings and public records open to the press. They varied in effectiveness. Reporters soon discovered that they had better luck appealing directly to executive and legislative officials rather than to the courts.

In a turnabout, however, the press invoked the courts' help in cases brought under the federal Freedom of Information Act. Although the news media were slow to use it after its passage in 1967, the law soon became such a potent source of news that the CIA, the FBI, the Secret Service and other government offices pressured Congress to restrict its scope. In fact, as a Library of Congress survey showed, in a single relatively brief period more than 250 news stories originated through the use of the FoI as it became known.

Very often, the courts have been useful in directing recalcitrant government offices to yield information that was clearly in the public interest. But in cases bearing on national security and other exceptions noted in FoI, the results have not been as encouraging.

Press–Bar Guidelines　The struggle for primacy between advocates of press freedom and fair trial also produced limited cooperation between the news media and bench and bar. Press–Bar Guidelines were adopted in most states with a recommendation for voluntary use. Public-spirited lawyers and editors, in the main, did the drafting.

In the Washington State agreement, which was widely regarded as a model, the press was warned against using opinions before a trial as to a defendant's guilt or innocence, character, admissions, alibis or confessions and other information that could be prejudicial. However, it was agreed that, subject to the usual standards of accuracy and good judgment, there were no restraints on using the identity of the defendant, biographical material, the name of the investigating agency and the circumstances of the arrest.

Like the state "shield" laws, the Press–Bar Guidelines were well intentioned but they were just about as ineffective in resolving the dominant issues in the clash of free press versus fair trial. Most reporters found them of little help.

The Outlook　It is evident that the conflict between the news media and the courts will not soon be resolved and journalists should not expect that their problems will be eased. Out of the best of motives, the courts will have more differences with the news media on the degree of coverage of sensitive cases. But the news media will also insist on the right to publish and broadcast whatever they believe to be in the public interest.

These tensions are worrisome. But they also show the public that there are strong forces in our society that will continue to guard against violations of the basic rights of free press and fair trial. It is a lot less dangerous, on the whole, than the "everything-goes" atmosphere of the 1920s, when justice was administered too often in the manner of a three-ring circus.

Reporters and National Security

An outraged Air Force general once complained to the columnist Bob Considine that a young reporter was "lousing up security" at a large air base nearby. With righteous anger, the general demanded, "What should I do about this guy?" Considine retorted sharply, his voice tipped with irony, "General, why don't you shoot him?"

Like most experienced journalists, Considine believed that the government too often raises the cry of national security as a coverup rather than as a genuine objection. This, certainly, was true of President Nixon's denunciation of the Watergate inquiry as a betrayal of the national interest. A similarly groundless charge was invoked against the columnist Jack Anderson when he broke the secret State Department cables showing that the United States was "tilting" toward Pakistan in the India-Pakistan War of 1971.

The Pentagon Papers The most important test of the public interest versus national security occurred when in 1971 the *New York Times* published the top-secret Pentagon Papers. This was a record compiled by the Defense Department to show how the United States had been maneuvered into the Vietnam War.

The Department of Justice charged that national security was imperiled and obtained a court order halting publication. When the *Washington Post* then ran articles based on the same subject, it was also restrained. But after both papers had been under government censorship for 15 days, the Supreme Court on June 30 denied the government's right to impose any prior restraint on publication.

"Any system of prior restraints of expression comes to this court bearing a heavy presumption against its constitutionality," the majority decision said. It added that the government "thus carries a heavy burden of showing justification" for suppressing the articles but it "had not met that burden."

To no one's surprise, the *Times* concluded 10 years later that it had been right in making public the Pentagon Papers. Nobody of any importance disagreed.

The Problem for Reporters This is not to say that reporters have any right to play games with national security or that news organizations can betray national secrets. Professional journalists are well aware of their responsibilities.

The *New York Times* severely edited a story warning of the CIA-sponsored Bay of Pigs invasion of Cuba in 1961, following a request by President Kennedy; the President himself admitted after the fiasco that it would have been better if the *Times* had used the original account. As James Reston of the *Times* commented:

> No doubt the press does have to learn greater restraint than in the days when the United States was an isolated country but the government has to do the same. For the truth that makes men free is very often the truth they do not like to hear and also the truth that the government does not like to see published, either.

In this era of enormous Defense Department budgets, reporters assigned to look into local activities of the armed forces should not be scared off when some official screams, "National security!" These inquiries are legitimate matters of public interest, so the reporter's job, as always, is to get the facts. If national security is truly involved, it becomes a problem for the editor and publisher, the news director, the producer and the station owner.

Sex Cases and Obscenity

The basic decision in obscenity cases is the ruling of the Supreme Court in *Miller v. California* on June 21, 1973. The decision set "community standards" as the guide for deciding whether a publication, picture or broadcast was obscene. "Community standards" were defined as the opinions of a reasonable person, living in a community, about a newspaper, magazine or book, a photograph or film, a radio or television program.

In the same decision, the Supreme Court reaffirmed its refusal to apply the protection of the First Amendment to obscene materials. It defined a work as obscene if, taken as a whole, it (1) appealed to prurient interest, (2) exceeded the standards of candor in depicting sexual matters and (3) was "utterly without redeeming social value or literary merit."

Attitudes Toward Sex Cases   Most newspapers and newsmagazines have a relatively liberal attitude toward sex cases today, but they are still quite reserved about the use of obscenity except in such major public documents as the Watergate tapes. Editors can scarcely forget that their publications go into the home and that the government has the right, particularly under the "community standards" ruling, to clamp down on borderline material sent through the mails.

The so-called skin magazines — *Playboy*, *Penthouse*, *Hustler*, *Screw* and the rest of that gamey lot — are more likely targets for the law. *Hustler*, in particular, has been a continual object of government prosecutions. The argument made in behalf of the magazines is that censorship of the skins could lead to suppression of other publications, but it has never carried much weight.

A more important point is the contention by many lawyers of consequence — and not only those who defend the skin magazines for large fees — that the "community standards" ruling means that the standards of, say, Pocatello, Idaho, or Emporia, Kansas, may be imposed on New York City, Chicago and Los Angeles. Nobody so far has argued that the standards of the big cities may be imposed on small towns, however. That seems quite unlikely.

Over-the-air TV, never very daring as an innovative medium, has taken no chances so far with the "community standards" law and veers away precipitously from anything that borders on obscenity. "Heck" is still considered about the limit of permissible exclamations. Now and then, when an agitated guest bursts forth with something more dramatic on live TV and the beeper can't catch it, there are pained looks all around. But there have been hard- and soft-core "porn shows" on cable in various parts of the country that became obscenity issues locally. That could become a national nuisance.

Guidelines for Reporters   The congressional sex scandals and the "Abscam" investigations resulted in a fairly broad agreement that public officeholders couldn't let their private life interfere with their effectiveness as public servants. Disclosures of drunken conduct by one congressman and of the use of public payrolls to support the mistress of another may not have been prize-winning journalism, but they were widely published and broadcast. As for the "Abscam" scandals, in which an FBI agent posed as the representative of wealthy Arabs and bribed several congressmen and one senator, they solidified the feeling that public officeholders had to be answerable for their conduct at all times. That was confirmed when the Senate forced the resignation of Harrison Williams, Democrat of New Jersey, after his Abscam conviction.

Ben Bradlee, executive editor of the *Washington Post*, laid down this simple guideline for his staff about reporting on officeholders: "If it does not impinge on their public duties, what they do is their own business."

Alan L. Otten of the *Wall Street Journal* added:

> Many a reporter who feels he can't make a flat-out charge may still strongly suggest what he considers to be the case.

He won't call the Senator a drunkard but simply tell how the Senator slurs his words or stumbles around the Senate floor. He may not say a prominent political figure has a mistress, but simply report how often the two are seen dining together at posh restaurants.

Yet the general press rule remains that even politicians are entitled to have their private misdeeds ignored so long as their official activities aren't suffering.

Louis D. Boccardi, executive editor of the Associated Press, laid down these guidelines in sex cases for all staffers as criteria for using a story or passing it up:

1. Satisfy ourselves that the activity impairs or conflicts with a public official's public responsibility.
2. Satisfy ourselves that there is some documentation beyond an anonymous charge or even a named source of doubtful reliability.
3. Give the item, if we carry it, no more than the prominence it merits. . . .
4. Tell a member [of the AP] who asks for a story we've decided to pass — that we don't see any news in it. But if the member wants it, give it to him on a one-point basis by whatever means is feasible.
5. Always give the accused a chance for comment on the charge before we move the story.
6. When in doubt about the merits, consult the General Desk [in New York] before moving anything.

• Short Takes

These are your rights as journalists under the law:

- You may cover anything that is broadly shown to be in the public interest, provided you are accurate and fair in your report.
- You may rely on provable truth and privileged records as absolute defenses against libel.
- You must beware of *malice*—using a story knowing that it is false or recklessly disregarding whether it is false or not.
- You enjoy the right of fair comment on the public acts of public officials and public figures as long as you make no showing of malice. The best defense is to cite the facts on which your opinion is based.
- You have no right to enter private homes or offices unbidden and thereby injure a person's "feelings and peace of mind."
- You cannot invade privacy by depicting an individual in a "false light through knowing or reckless untruth."
- You have no constitutional right to withhold the identity of your sources and the information they give you. Therefore, you should be careful about making promises of confidentiality.
- You do have the right to file a formal protest with judges who close their courtroom, provided your news organization agrees.
- You cannot safely violate the secrecy of grand jury records or defy a judge's order, the likely punishment in both instances being a jail term, a fine, or both for contempt of court.

- You can't depend on "shield" laws to keep you out of jail if you are cited for contempt. Before you take any step in that direction, you had better be sure of the support of your news organization.
- You should not be deterred from carrying out an assignment to look into governmental actions because an official protests that you are violating national security. That determination rests with your editors or broadcast news directors.
- You should always remember that the government has no constitutional right to censor what you do, say or write, which, in legal language, means the imposition of "prior restraint on publication." You and your news organization, however, are liable for any laws you may violate by so doing.
- You should be aware that the Supreme Court has repeatedly held that obscene material may not be subject to the protection of the First Amendment.
- You should remember that, under *Miller v. California,* a 1973 high court decision, "community standards" are the guiding determination of whether a work is obscene; also, that the decision held a work to be obscene if, taken as a whole, it (1) appealed to prurient interest, (2) exceeded the standards of candor in depicting sexual matters and (3) was "utterly without redeeming social value or literary merit."

CHAPTER

20

Police Reporting

An angry, frightened woman telephoned Edna Buchanan, a police reporter for the *Miami Herald*, late one March afternoon and told of witnessing the kidnapping of an engaged couple that had ended in a gang rape. The witness identified one of the five neighborhood hoodlums who had been preying on passing cars as well as residents.

"I'm fed up," the caller said. "What happened was outrageous."

Nothing could be done to help the young man, who had been beaten by the gang, or his fiancee, who had been sexually assaulted. But Buchanan made it her business to interview other neighborhood residents, and she didn't stop until she had identified all the suspects. They were arrested, charged with rape, robbery and the use of a gun in the commission of a felony. The police gave the reporter credit.

"Edna's sources," said Police Sergeant Mike Gonzalez, "knew who they were, what they did, where they were and who played what role."

Covering Police News

The story was part of the daily — and often nightly — routine for Buchanan, who has covered police news for the *Herald* for almost 15 years.

"Police reporting is exciting work," she says. "I get to see what people are really like—what makes some turn to crime, what makes some become cowards, and some become heroes. It's a great job."

The Toughest Beat The police beat in Miami is the toughest in the country. For some years now, the Florida metropolis has had the highest crime rate of any city in the country, in statistics reported annually by the FBI. And in addition to crime, the beat includes coverage of fires, explosions, accidents of all kinds and rescues as well as departmental policies and charges affecting individual police officers and the activities of cooperating federal, state and local law enforcement agencies.

Any newcomer who is assigned to a police beat—even a beat less tough than Miami's—is going to be tested for courage as well as ability. For historically, that is where city and metropolitan editors generally start their best young prospects. On the *Herald*, they have the advantage of working with seasoned professionals like Buchanan. But very often they are on their own.

The Daily Routine Here is a summary of the police beat assignment for the *Herald*'s police reporters:

- Continual radio monitoring of all police calls and messages.*
- Continual monitoring of fire calls and services.
- Hourly telephone checks of federal, state and other municipal departments.
- Close liaison with police public-information offices and installation of related tele-type, beeper and communications systems.
- Immediate communication with the office by car radio, beeper and walkie-talkie.
- The *Herald* uses wake-up calls for reporters plus helicopters, planes, ships and speedboats for reporters and photographers.
- Examination of logs, uniform crime reports and arrest forms daily at police offices in Miami, Miami Beach and the Metro complex.
- Daily examination of booking sheets at the central jail.
- Access to special categories in the *Herald* library on all forms of crime and crime statistics.

The *Herald*'s editors have arranged for service by lawyers to back up reporters' requests for the release of information by the police. The lawyers also try to handle subpoenas issued by the courts, at the request of prosecuters or defense lawyers, to gain access to reporters' files and notes.

The newspaper has a policy of following up tips or complaints from citizens, such as the one given to Buchanan, on everything from illicit drug trafficking to police brutality, failures of the justice system or outrages in the streets. The paper also keeps files in the newsroom for identification of people involved in crimes, as

---

*Most journalists know that it is illegal, under Section 605 of the Communications Act of 1934, to divulge intercepted radio messages without the prior consent of the parties involved. But despite warnings by the Federal Communications Commission, the practice is almost universal in this country among news organizations. A constitutional test of Section 605 has never developed and, since the act itself is being modified, the whole issue may be moot.

victims or assailants, including the latest city directories, tax rolls and other helpful data.

The FBI's Uniform Crime Reports

The FBI issues each year a thick book entitled *Crime in the United States*, which is crammed with disheartening statistics. While lists of cities with the highest crime rates are regularly compiled from the book's section called "Index of Crime, Standard Metropolitan Statistical Areas," the FBI itself does not issue such a tabulation and discourages it as misleading for a number of reasons. However, the lists can easily be put together by checking the figures for the crime index total rate per 100,000 population.

While the list varies from year to year, three of the cities that have figured prominently among the "first 10" for some years are also the ones that attract millions of tourists annually — Miami; Atlantic City, New Jersey, and Las Vegas, Nevada. With the rate of crime in the average metropolitan area at the beginning of the 1980s set at 6,757.6 per year per 100,000 population, this was the rating of the three tourist centers: Miami, 11,581.8; Atlantic City, 11,481.3, and Las Vegas, 10,292.3.

The Rise in National Crime The FBI report for the decade 1971–1980 showed a 54.8-percent increase in the number of serious crimes committed nationally since 1971 and an almost 10-percent increase from 1979 to 1980. In fact, the report showed that violent crimes over the decade surged by 60 percent and property crimes escalated by 54 percent. Here is the FBI's tabulation:

National Crime, Rate, and Percent Change

Offense	Estimated crime 1980		Percent change over 1979		Percent change over 1971	
	Number	Rate per 100,000 inhabitants	Number	Rate per 100,000 inhabitants	Number	Rate per 100,000 inhabitants
Crime Index total[1] Modified Crime Index total	13,295,400	5,899.9	+ 9.4	+ 6.9	+54.8	+41.7
Violent	1,308,900	580.8	+11.1	+ 8.5	+60.3	+46.7
Property	11,986,500	5,319.1	+ 9.2	+ 6.7	+54.2	+41.1
Murder	23,040	10.2	+ 7.4	+ 5.2	+29.6	+18.6
Forcible rape	82,090	36.4	+ 8.0	+ 5.5	+94.2	+77.6
Robbery	548,810	243.5	+17.5	+14.8	+41.6	+29.5
Aggravated assault	654,960	290.6	+ 6.6	+ 4.1	+77.6	+62.5
Burglary	3,759,200	1,668.2	+13.9	+11.3	+56.7	+43.4
Larceny–theft	7,112,700	3,156.3	+ 8.1	+ 5.6	+60.8	+47.1
Motor vehicle theft	1,114,700	494.6	+ 1.6	− .8	+17.6	+ 7.6
Arson						

[1]Because of rounding, offenses may not add to totals.

The Crimes Defined   The Uniform Crime Reports (UCR) uses these definitions of the eight crimes included in the index:

murder and nonnegligent manslaughter   The willful (nonnegligent) killing of one human being by another. A total of 50 percent was attributed to handguns.

forcible rape   The carnal knowledge of a female forcibly and against her will. Assaults or attempts to commit rape are included, but not statutory rape (without force).

robbery   The taking or attempting to take anything of value from the care, custody or control of a person or persons by force or threat of force or violence and/or by putting the victim in fear. Street and highway crime was put at 51 percent.

aggravated assault   An unlawful attack by one person upon another for the purpose of inflicting severe or aggravated bodily injury. Attempts are included.

burglary   The unlawful entry of a structure to commit felony or theft. The use of force to gain entry is not required to classify an offense as a burglary. There are three subclassifications: forcible entry, unlawful entry where no force is used and attempted forcible entry. A total of 67 percent of the reported burglaries occurred in residential property.

larceny-theft   The unlawful taking, carrying, leading or riding away of property from the possession or constructive possession of another. It includes crimes such as shoplifting, pocketpicking and purse-snatching; thefts from motor vehicles; of motor vehicle parts and accessories and of bicycles in which no use of force, violence or fraud occurs. The volume of larceny–theft was 53 percent of the crime index total and 59 percent of the property crime total, with thefts from motor vehicles and the taking of motor vehicle accessories as the largest single crime, 36 percent.

motor vehicle theft   The theft or attempted theft of a motor vehicle. The average estimated total national loss in this category was $3.2 billion, with 75 percent of the thefts being automobiles, 13 percent trucks or buses and 12 percent other types.

arson   Any willful or malicious burning or attempt to burn, with or without intent to defraud, a dwelling house, public building, motor vehicle or aircraft, personal property of another, etc. The monetary value of property damage due to reported arson was $891 million; the most frequent target being structures, which comprised 54 percent of the total.

The FBI reported that 10.4 million arrests were made in 1980 for all criminal infractions except traffic violations, with persons under 25 comprising 70 percent of those arrested for Crime Index offenses. However, only 19 percent of the reported index crimes were cleared during the year, the FBI said, the rate for violent crimes being 44 percent and for crimes against property 16 percent.

The Police Reporters' Task   This statistical pattern vividly illustrates the magnitude of the task crime poses for the news media in general and police reporters in particular. For in any self-respecting community, unfavorable publicity affecting the business community always produces dismay. And this is particularly

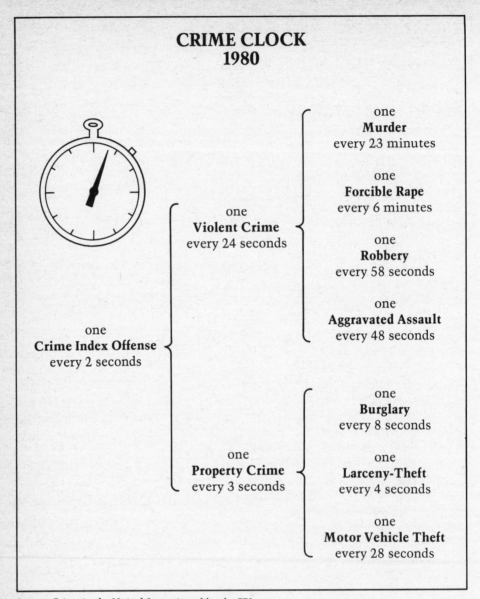

CRIME CLOCK
1980

one
Murder
every 23 minutes

one
Forcible Rape
every 6 minutes

one
Violent Crime
every 24 seconds

one
Robbery
every 58 seconds

one
Aggravated Assault
every 48 seconds

one
Crime Index Offense
every 2 seconds

one
Burglary
every 8 seconds

one
Property Crime
every 3 seconds

one
Larceny-Theft
every 4 seconds

one
Motor Vehicle Theft
every 28 seconds

Source: *Crime in the United States,* issued by the FBI.

true in places like Atlantic City and Las Vegas, which are dependent on attracting millions of visitors to try their luck at the gambling tables, and Miami, as well as some other Florida cities, in a state that annually draws 35 to 40 million tourists annually.

But not many newspapers in such areas try to bury the news or omit it entirely. As one editor put it, "This is not something we can keep a secret. We have to face it, report on it and trust that our citizens will be sufficiently angry and determined that they will insist on federal and state action to help reduce the threat of crime." That, in fact, is a substantial part of the anticrime movement throughout the country today.

Stories on the Police Beat

With violence rising in many American cities, large and small, a part of the police beat assignment necessarily has to do with delving into the causes of crime.

In states along the Atlantic Seaboard and the Mexican border, the FBI points out that much crime is drug-related. The drug traffic in itself is so huge as to be almost uncontrollable. In addition, there is continual warfare between narcotics smugglers and loosely organized gangs that vie for local control of illicit drug sales. No large city is immune from this type of mob violence, whether it is New York, Chicago, Los Angeles or Miami.

Then, too, there are major problems related to the massive influx of Cuban and Haitian refugees and millions of illegal immigrants from Mexico. It is no accident that the New York police have found that hardened criminals let out of Cuban jails, who joined the mass movement of more reputable Cuban immigrants, were settling in the least accessible areas of the Bronx and preying on their countrymen and others. But in the 1980s, the move to the north had ebbed and most Cuban emigres were settling elsewhere.

Still, the police story can't be told entirely in terms of major drug busts, Mafia-type gangland murders, large-scale robberies and other big-time crimes.

Edna Buchanan's bylines, for example, appear on all kinds of stories for the *Miami Herald* — fires, police shootouts, features and investigations. Within about one month, the following two accounts were among the interesting and detailed stories, most of them on Page 1, her assignments produced:

A Fire Story Buchanan received a call from one of her sources at 4 a.m. that several people, all members of the same family, had died in a fire that destroyed their home. It was a stormy night, but she phoned a photographer to meet her and got rolling in her car in the middle of a thunder-and-lightning storm.

"The fire was more than 40 miles away," she recalled, "and I got lost in south Dade County farmland in the rainy dark before dawn. I was driving with my gas indicator on empty."

Finally she reached a gas station and was able to get to the firefighters, who had been on the job and had returned to the firehouse, before the shift changed in Leisure City. Then she drove to the charred ruins of the home and talked with investigators, cops, neighbors, friends and relatives of the bereaved family.

"I set out at 9:30 a.m. to return to the office and write for the early edition," she went on. "Back at the office, I interviewed the medical examiner by phone and talked the cops into giving us a rough drawing of the layout of the house and the body positions. In the meantime — in case of argument or disagreement — I got the floor plans of the house from the courthouse. After polishing and writing through for later editions, I left the *Herald* at 9:30 p.m."

An incident report by the Public Safety Department, Dade County, Miami, Florida. Assumed names are used for defendants.

Edna Buchanan, police reporter for the *Miami* (Florida) *Herald*.

The fire story began on Page 1 and, with pictures, ran for a full page inside with sidebars. This was Buchanan's beginning on the main story:

A smoldering fire from a worn air conditioner wire ignited a sofa, raced across wall paneling and gutted a Leisure City home in an inferno that killed five children and their small dog Wednesday.

The parents, Redland Construction Co. superintendent John Paul Dixon, 54, and his wife, Barbara, 38, and their two other children, Delbert, 3, and Tracy, 19, were cut and burned but survived.

"A $10 smoke detector would have saved five lives," said Metro firefighter Anthony Spadaro. He carried two dead girls, five and six years old, from the house.

He found them in their bed, "beautiful little blonde girls in long nightgowns. One was resting her head in her hands like she was sleeping." Two baby dolls lay nearby.

A neighbor tried to rescue the children but was driven back by two snarling and snapping family dogs, a boxer and a bird dog, who tried in panic to protect the burning house.

Flames shot from every window, the doors were ablaze and a huge column of smoke rose skyward when the firefighters arrived at 2:54 a.m. The frantic parents and screaming neighbors shouted that five children were inside.

There was no sign of life within the modest 10-year-old, four bedroom home. Rescuers were forced back by flames and heat so intense that it melted the aluminum trim on the house.

A huge pumper equipped with 3,000 gallons of water arrived at 3:03 a.m. The flames were knocked down and firefighters were able to enter the house in five minutes.

It was too late for those inside.

Damage to the house, at 29445 SW 115th Ct., is estimated at $45,000, damage to the contents at $10,000.

Joseph Dixon, 13, died as he tried to escape.

A window screen lay atop his body in a back bedroom. His hands were cut. His pet dog, a miniature dachshund, lay dead at his feet.

Wanda Dixon, 6, and John Dixon's granddaughter, Misty Hogan, 5, died in their beds. Two more little girls, sisters Paula and Reba Dixon, three years old, died crouched, wedged in corners, trying to escape the flames. . . .

It is reportorial detail that makes this story. It takes the reader to the scene, makes the plight of the shattered family devastatingly real, adds poignant evidence to the firefighter's observation that a smoke detector could have saved them all. The story went on in this manner for more than a column.

A Cop's Last Night on the Job   This was a different story, about a cop's violent final night on the job. It also came alive through Buchanan's drive for detail, detail and more detail. Here is the start of that story:

After a rough and tumble ten-year career as a Metro cop, Officer James Melvin shot a man Sunday, his last night on patrol.

Melvin, who is moving away from Dade County to South Carolina, wounded one of three burglars he caught in the act, police said.

"He was upset. He wanted to get through a quiet evening his last night on the road," said Metro Police spokesman Pete Cuccaro.

But Melvin, who has won honors for bravery and heroic rescues in the past, was too conscientious a cop to ignore a suspicious truck during his final hours on the job, superiors said.

The truck was a pickup, parked at the rear of the Service Merchandise Mart and the vacated former Treasury Store, at SW 160th St. and US 1.

The truck was loaded with thousands of dollars' worth of stolen equipment, stereo and electronic, police said.

As officers searched the darkened building, they spied two men, identified as Richard Young and Ernest Holcomb, both 22, hiding in the ceiling work, police said. They added that both refused commands to surrender.

> Cornered, Young shouted an obscenity and rolled to one side, reaching into his waistband, police said. Thinking he was reaching for a gun, Melvin fired a shot, striking Young in the leg. Young is listed in good condition at Jackson Memorial Hospital. . . .

Following up a Story

Police reporting elsewhere in the United States differs only in degree from the intensive work that is demanded of the men and women on the police beat in Miami and other metropolitan centers. The same watchfulness, the same effort, the same dedication and the same professional knowledge and skill are called for from the people who handle police news in every city and town, regardless of size.

The routine may differ, depending on circumstances, but the stories are seldom if ever handed to reporters with a flourish and a bow from the participating police officers. If there is one lesson that beginners learn very early on the police beat, it is that they have to struggle — and sometimes even fight — for every fact they get. There is a limit to what even the best police sources can do for the news media, and reporters know it.

A Double Slaying in Kansas Even if there isn't anywhere near as much crime in Kansas as there is in New York, Illinois, Florida or California, people in Kansas are just as concerned about the rise of violence on the Great Plains as other Americans are in more dangerous areas. Reporters, too, know from experience that police news has to be carefully scrutinized.

Anita Miller of the *Topeka Daily Capital*, only a year out of the William Allen White School of Journalism at the University of Kansas, may not have had either the reputation or the experience of Edna Buchanan of the *Miami Herald*, but she worked with the same care and efficiency in developing the facts behind a double slaying. It was a sensitive story, to begin with, and Miller explained why:

> My story was a second-day story. The first story was sketchy because police hesitated to say anything, since one of their own officers was involved.
>
> It was a double slaying. A girl had been fatally shot by her former boyfriend, and the boyfriend then was fatally shot by a police officer in the parking lot of a major shopping center in Topeka.
>
> I didn't write the first-day story but I felt a follow-up was necessary because there wasn't much of a hint as to how the woman and man were associated. She was only 17 and he was 19.
>
> I happened to know one of the victims and I knew where the two had gone to school, so I began calling people at the school, including teachers, students and counselors. My main goal was to find some friends who might have been with the couple prior to the shooting, or knew what the girl was doing at the shopping center and how the man knew she was there.
>
> Digging for facts on a story like this was really frustrating. For every ten calls I made, only one would come up with good, current information. I was careful about

taking down what each acquaintance said until I had a clear picture in my mind of what the girl was really like and the chain of events that led to the shooting.

I didn't use information unless I felt comfortable with the people and had a good idea that they were telling me the truth.

Results of the Follow-Up   When Miller finally wrote her story for the *Capital*, she had checked all the facts she used and was confident that she had a story that would stand up. She didn't do a sob story—it isn't in her nature. The piece is straight throughout, with no flourishes and no attempt to do anything more than set out the facts behind a tragedy. Here is the substance of the story she wrote:

A 17-year-old Topeka girl who was fatally shot Thursday night at the White Lakes Shopping Center parking lot had recently stopped dating the man who shot her, acquaintances said Friday.

They asserted Linda M. Schneider, 324 Woodbury Lane, had dated Mark J. Thompson, 19, 919 S.E. Consuelo, about a year until they broke up two months ago.

"When they broke up she went to St. Louis [and stayed with relatives] to get away," Stacey Moore, 4012 W. 28th, said. "Then she moved back here with her parents about four weeks ago."

Thursday night Miss Schneider was at White Lakes Mall attending her first session at the Barbizon School of Modeling since her return to Topeka from St. Louis. One friend said Miss Schneider had wanted to be an airline stewardess.

Topeka police said Miss Schneider was fatally shot in the head by Thompson at 8:59 p.m. as she ran toward two police officers just south of the Sears Automotive Center outside the White Lakes Shopping Center complex.

Police said after the girl fell, Reserve Patrolman Gaylon Thompson, no relation to Mark Thompson, saw Mark Thompson point what was later determined to be a .38 caliber handgun and fire one shot at Officer Thompson.

The bullet ricocheted off the trunk lid of the patrol car. Officer Thompson fired three shots from his .357 magnum at the man, striking him in the head and right shoulder.

Mark Thompson and Miss Schneider were rushed to Stormont-Vail Regional Medical Center by ambulance. According to reports, Miss Schneider died at 9:41 p.m., Thompson at 9:46 p.m.

The police firearms review board ruled Friday that Thompson, 27, a two-year member of the reserve force, had fired in self-defense.

Acquaintances of Miss Schneider said she had been invited to attend a party at a friend's house in central Topeka after her class Thursday, but Thompson was not allowed inside when he went to the house. However, he learned that

she was at White Lakes and drove there, acquaintances
said. The slayings followed.

Are Police Reporters Insensitive?   People unfamiliar with newspaper work in general, and police reporting in particular, often assume that journalists are insensitive to all the tragedies about them on many occasions. A few may
be, but most reporters could be deeply affected if they weren't able to seal off their
personal feelings by casting a protective shell about their emotions. This, perhaps,
may give the appearance of insensitivity to human suffering, but appearances are
often deceiving. Miller summed up her own position this way:

> Talking to close friends and the family of a dead person really bothers some
> reporters, but it has never upset me much. Before I start an interview, I ask the
> people involved if they want to talk to me. I think it's important to give them a
> choice. If they refuse, then I don't pressure them. It's always necessary for me to
> remember that I'm approaching them at a sensitive time and I try to be
> understanding. If they won't talk, there's usually someone else who will be able to
> give me the information.

The columnist Jim Bishop, once a police reporter on the New York tabloid the
Daily Mirror, which went to the journalistic boneyard in the 1960s, put the case
this way: "I was a crime reporter. . . . A callus grows on your brain. The heart
becomes a cool stone. There is a shade of cynicism on the retina." And then, he
added, there comes a time when the reporter reads something about the piteous
victim of a crime and this happens: "Your throat slams shut and you throw the book
on the floor. . . ."

The Miranda Rule

Under the Miranda Rule, the police are obliged, with certain exceptions, to notify
defendants of their right to remain silent and to obtain counsel. The notification
must take place upon arrest. It became law when the Supreme Court in 1966
reversed the conviction of Ernesto A. Miranda, a 25-year-old mentally retarded Arizona truck driver, because he had not been warned of his right to counsel or that
his statements might be used against him before he confessed to raping an 18-year-
old girl. Miranda had been serving concurrent sentences of 20 to 30 years.

Chief Justice Earl Warren held for the 5–4 majority that police must inform
criminal suspects, when arrested, of their right to remain silent and to obtain counsel. While the Miranda ruling remains on the books, it has been weakened by subsequent high court decisions. In 1971, statements made by an accused person before
being informed of his rights were admitted under cross-examination. Four years
later, statements made by an accused person after being informed of his rights were
admitted as rebuttal testimony. And in 1976, the Miranda rule was held inapplicable
to grand jury testimony.

Copies of the "Miranda card," used by police to inform defendants of their rights upon arrest, were found on Miranda's body after he was stabbed to death in 1976 during a barroom brawl.

Working with Police Records

It isn't always easy for reporters to look at police records. As an entirely practical matter, police who have something to hide may make it difficult for an aggressive journalist to examine their work. Laws and practices vary from state to state. Where there are "Sunshine laws" that open records to the public and provide for open meetings of governmental bodies, easy access is provided to certain police files but by no means all of them. Elsewhere, contrary practices exist and the courts are not always cooperative.

The federal government's own "Sunshine law," approved in the fall of 1976 and signed by President Ford, lends congressional support to the concept of open meetings and open records with certain exceptions. For while the law obliges about 50 federal boards and agencies to conduct much of their business in public, confidentiality is maintained over matters including defense and foreign policy, internal personnel data, private commercial material, criminal and other law enforcement information and data that might invade an individual's privacy.

Dealing with the Police   The first things any reporter must know about the police department are its organization, its regulations, its relationship to other city departments and its point of contact with allied peacekeeping organizations in the state and federal government.

Whether the department is large or small, one official is usually designated to handle the news media. Sometimes it is the chief or commissioner, but more often it is a former journalist who is known as a secretary, an executive assistant or some other title covering a public relations role. Such officials can be helpful, if they are permitted to be, but they also are likely by the nature of their office to withhold more news than they issue.

It is necessary for reporters to protect themselves by maintaining good relationships with other officials who will, for a variety of motives, give them information or check facts. The more reporters know about police organizations, the easier it will be for them to acquire such sources.

Mere procedural knowledge of police routine is never enough. Reporters must also know the substance of criminal law, which varies by terminology and statute in most states, so that they can properly describe police activity. For example, a felony, which is a serious offense, may cover certain types of crime in one state, but the same crimes may be called misdemeanors, relatively minor offenses, in another.

Most professional police and court reporters have an excellent practical knowledge of the law, and some even have law degrees. It is virtually impossible to cover police and court news intelligently without acquiring a basic legal background.

Arrest Procedures   Here, in brief outline, is what happens when an arrest is made:

- The suspect may be brought in on a complaint or a warrant or he may be seized at the scene of a crime. But until formally charged and booked, he cannot be said to be under arrest.
- The booking consists of recording the suspect's identity, address and vital statistics in a large record together with the alleged crime, time and place of the arrest and the name of the arresting officer.
- The suspect is searched, his property is enumerated, sealed and given to the property clerk for safekeeping.
- The Miranda card, notifying the suspect of his constitutional rights, is read to him. He is informed that he may remain silent, that he may consult a lawyer or, if he doesn't have one, a lawyer will be provided. Before he can be questioned by police, he must sign a paper waiving these rights.
- If he signs, the police question him and put together a formal arrest report. In any case, he is photographed, fingerprinted, told he can make a telephone call and then he is put in a detention cell.

In some cities, notably New York, there is an arraignment either in a day court or in Night Court, as soon as possible after a formal complaint is drafted by a member of the prosecutor's office. The suspect then is given a chance to enter a plea. If the plea is not guilty, the presiding magistrate or judge sets bail.

Some defendants — depending on the charge and on their record, and on the amount of security that can be put up on their behalf — may be able to raise bail through a surety company after the hearing and thereby obtain release. If they can't raise bail, they are held in jail.

The prosecutor's office must now determine whether the evidence against the suspect is strong enough to warrant holding the suspect on a felony charge, in which event a case must be presented to a grand jury and an indictment must be returned, or whether to proceed to trial in a lower court on a misdemeanor, a lesser charge.

It is at this point that the courts take over. If it is decided to proceed with the misdemeanor charge, generally the trial is scheduled in a lower court without a jury. But if the felony charge holds good, and an indictment is returned, the suspect must await trial before a judge and a jury. Or, through their lawyer, suspects may plea-bargain with the prosecutor's office and consent to a guilty plea on a lesser charge.

In any event, once an arrest has been made, the police and court procedures are intricate and time-consuming. Generally, if the case warrants it, the reporter who was in on the arrest follows through to at least the preliminary hearings in the lower courts. Once an indictment has been returned, particularly in larger cities where there are regular court reporters on daily assignment, they take over the story.

News Values and Crime

The looting of small homes, the snatching of women's pocketbooks, the rumbles between gangs of juvenile delinquents and the small-time offenses of prostitution and gambling and the petty racketeering that flows from them are the commonplaces of crime in American life. Taken individually, they merit but a few lines, if anything at all, in the average paper and no mention at all in the broadcast media. It is the usual run of crime material — routine — uninteresting by old-fashioned editorial standards.

Yet these seemingly small events touch the lives of more people than headline crimes. In many communities, home robberies have outstripped the ability of the police to cope with them and have caused a steep rise in insurance rates. In the nation's largest cities the purse-snatcher and sneak thief are so common that most women and old people fear to walk alone. The rumble that is ignored by today's news media as the outburst of ill-trained and irresponsible street children becomes tomorrow's gang war. As for the streetwalker and the policy-slip salesman, the narcotics addict and the juvenile killer, they make little news by themselves, but in the mass they constitute a major social problem for the nation.

Toward Improved Reporting   Except for broad public service campaigns that are methodically conducted by many daily newspapers and the more public spirited broadcast journalists, the issues of inner-city decay, better protection for the home, juvenile delinquency and all the broad problems of crime prevention receive less attention than the stories of commission, detection and punishment of crime. There is not as much alertness over civil rights issues in the bulk of the American news media as there should be; nor, for that matter, is enough encouragement given to such sensitive areas as prison reform. Except when a spectacular crime occurs, a prison is convulsed by rioting or an inner city goes up in flames, crime prevention is treated as a rather dull but necessary aspect of the news. There is no doubt that it is more difficult to gather such news and that it takes more ingenuity and imagination to develop such stories. But it is not the usual pattern of the crime story as we know it. Hamlet never consulted a psychiatrist. Sherlock Holmes was not a probation officer.

Crime reporting is likely to be broadened considerably in its scope and influence as the public accepts some of the more fundamental developments in modern urban life as a challenge for reform, and not as the kind of existence that must be tolerated indefinitely.

Guide to Crime Reporting

Crime reporters often have to go behind the news. The following safeguards are worth following, therefore, in the coverage of the administration of justice:

Arrests   It is a serious matter to report that a person has been placed under arrest. When such a report is made, the exact charge against the arrested person should be given and it should be documented by either a record or attribution to a responsible official. If such documentation cannot be obtained, the reporter had better check the facts. The person in question may not have been under arrest at all. There are euphemisms in police work such as "holding someone for questioning," "asking witnesses to appear voluntarily to cooperate with an investigation" and similar statements which indicate the person is being detained but may or may not be subject to arrest. In many states an arrest is not formally accomplished until a prisoner is booked. The news, in any case, must be handled with care.

Accusations   It is commonly written that someone is being "sought for robbery," "suspected of arson" or "tried for murder." This is journalistic shorthand, which has gained acceptance through usage, but it is neither precise nor correct.

Persons are "sought in connection with a robbery," unless a charge has actually been made, in which case they are "charged with robbery." Persons under suspicion are not necessarily going to be charged with a crime, and it is generally not privileged matter to indicate that suspicion is attached to any individual by name. Where the police suspect someone, but lack proof, that person may be held as a material witness — which is far different from being accused of a crime. Therefore, cases of suspicion are not usually given too extensive and detailed news treatment if no privileged material is available for use. The practice of reporting that a defendant is being "tried for murder," while widely used, is obviously prejudicial and could be more accurately, if less dramatically, stated, as "being tried on a charge of murder," or "on a murder indictment."

Confessions   The use of the word "confession" to describe statements made by a person to the police or to prosecuting authorities is dangerous when it is not a matter of public record. The fact that a police chief or a prosecutor has claimed to have a confession, except in open court, may be used only at the risk of the news organization. Most press–bar voluntary agreements forbid the use of confessions until they are admitted in open court. The records are full of supposed confessions that backfired later for a variety of reasons and of persons who admitted crimes they could not possibly have committed. Unless and until it is established in fact that a person has confessed, approved procedure for reporters is to use such terms as "statement," "admission," "description" or "explanation." They convey the shade of meaning that is warranted by circumstances and do not subject the news organization to unnecessary risk.

The reporter must always remember that under the law individuals are presumed to be innocent until they have been found guilty.

Investigations   Certain stages of police investigations require secrecy in the public interest. This also pertains to some of the aspects of prosecutions and trials. The secrecy of the grand jury room and of a trial jury's deliberations are soundly based on public policy. Except under the most extraordinary circumstances, no reporter and no news organization have any right to interfere and few have ever attempted to do so.

Often, during the course of investigations, reporters are confined to listing the identities of witnesses who have entered or left a police station or grand jury room, if the names can be obtained. They have every right to try to interview such witnesses, if the circumstances are favorable, before and after appearances of this kind. But it is the business of the prosecution, defense lawyers and the witnesses themselves to decide whether or not they should talk.

For this reason investigations, in their earliest stages, are likely to produce a crop of speculative reports without much basis in fact unless editors insist on sounder reporting. Clever, publicity-conscious investigators can often hopelessly prejudice the position of hostile witnesses and others who oppose them if the news media do not hold rigidly to their code of presenting both sides of the story. That is why no claim by any investigators, regardless of their position and personal prestige, should be accepted and published at face value without some effort by a reporter to determine the soundness of the statements that have been issued.

Cases of Violent Death   Nowhere is there a greater tendency to jump to conclusions in the field of crime reporting than in the initial reporting of a violent death. The amateur reporter is invariably in a hurry to characterize the event as a suicide or a murder when it may be an accidental death. It is advisable, therefore, to report only what is known and avoid speculation in the absence of an official verdict by a coroner, medical examiner or some other competent authority.

An apparent suicide is one of the most difficult crime stories to handle. If the police report that a man was found shot to death with a bullet in his right temple and a revolver in or near his right hand, the story should be written in exactly that way. In the case of a police finding that someone "jumped or fell" to his death, the reporter should not go beyond the facts but use that phrase. If a woman is found dead in bed with an empty bottle labeled sleeping tablets beside her, no conclusions should be drawn.

In all such cases, it is proper to note any other circumstances that have a bearing on the story, particularly as to whether notes were left. It may not always be proper to publish such notes, even if the text is made available by the police, unless the material is privileged. Moreover, unless there is a formal announcement of suicide by a responsible authority, the news account can do no more than to note that an investigation is being made to determine whether the death was a suicide.

When violent deaths occur without any indication as to whether they may be accidents, suicides, murders or combinations of all three, the story should report the identities of the victims and the manner of their deaths. It is usually fruitless to try to unravel such a mystery in a newsroom. That is the job of the police and the prosecuting authorities. In the absence of any word from them, a factual account of the event must suffice.

A murder investigation often tempts reporters to venture into realms for which their profession has not really equipped them. Because a few reporters have achieved fame through phenomenal exploits, all reporters are scarcely justified in trying to play detective when a newsworthy personage has been "done in." Not many even attempt to do so because there is simply not enough time for the routines of both journalism and police work on a fast-breaking story.

Precautions   There are a few fundamental precautions of which reporters must take account.

The first is that police and prosecutors rarely will give them information on a silver platter. That means a tremendous amount of interviewing and research must be done in a very short time so that a coherent story may be written.

The second is that there can be no guarantee of police accuracy; in fact, an impressive body of evidence can be amassed to the contrary. That means police versions of names, addresses and other facts must be checked.

The third is that police and journalistic terminology are not necessarily identical. The legal term for a slaying is a homicide, but many news organizations loosely and incorrectly refer to such crimes automatically as murder. In a grand jury indictment the homicide eventually may be defined as first- or second-degree murder, depending on whether there was premeditation; or first- or second-degree manslaughter, depending on whether there was provocation or negligence. Since manslaughter is not murder, care must be used in defining a homicide. Indictments charging murder have been found to be deficient in the past, so writers should be precise in their statements whenever they refer to the legal basis of any charge.

Assessment of Blame Whenever there is a fist fight, shooting or collision involving police action, it is only human to wonder what happened and who was at fault. Often only a trial can determine this; therefore, most reporters use as many versions of the incident as there are witnesses if such extensive treatment is warranted.

Such accounts begin with a statement that two men had a fist fight in a night club, or that there was a shooting match, or that two automobiles collided. The body of the story then documents the noncommittal lead, giving such versions of the event as are necessary. The attribution of documentation of this type always presents a problem for writers who want to avoid using "he said," or "she said," or "the police said" in every sentence.

There are several ways of doing this. One is to quote the various versions, if they are brief enough. Another is to write, "The police version of the incident follows," and then report it without further attribution. In any case, unless there is some official assessment of blame, it is usually not necessary for the reporter to try to act in such matters.

Identification The identification of persons in crime stories sometimes leads to trouble, no matter how carefully it is checked. Confusion of persons with identical last names, mistakes in middle initials, mix-ups in addresses, misspellings of names and police errors all conspire against the reporter. There is no real safety in the familiar formula "The suspect gave his name as. . ." or, "The prisoner was identified as. . . ." If the identification is incorrect, the reporter and the news organization are in trouble.

It is usually a good rule, in stories that warrant it, to include material showing how the identification was made — by papers in the person's possession, by friends or relatives, or by other means. If there is any doubt, the reporter will find it does no harm to add a clause or even a sentence indicating that the identification was partial and remained to be checked. No news organization need regard itself as an oracle whose word is final, when the public knows that many things are possible between the commission of a crime and the conviction of a defendant.

Civil Disorder

The coverage of civil disorder imposes major responsibilities on journalists. On the one hand, they must exercise the greatest care not to spread rumors. On the other, they must expose themselves to danger if necessary to determine the magnitude of any street incident. But whatever they do, they must always be conscious that careless reporting or the provocative appearance of still or television cameras can cause untold harm in a tense situation, particularly in the crowded inner cores of many American cities.

Restraint in Conduct   The conduct of the journalist at the scene of action must be circumspect. A hard-hatted, swaggering white reporter in the center of an angry black community can provoke trouble. A television cameraman, training his instrument on a floodlighted crowd, is likely to get more action than he bargains for when fighting has broken out all around him. Nor is there any great sense in sending an armored truck bearing the name of a news organization into a trouble area. These are the things that cause the news media to be blamed for spreading disorder. Complete coverage is desirable at all times, but no one is thereby justified to put on a circuslike performance.

Restraint, such as was maintained in the face of wholesale disorders by street gangs in Detroit, is a necessity in reporting policy.

Defining a Riot   In both written and oral reports of any incident, every effort should be made to arrive at accurate evaluations. An isolated act of vandalism, or a street fight between two teenagers in the midst of a crowd, must not be called a race riot. And if shooting is heard in a crowded neighborhood at night, it is not automatically "sniper fire" until an investigation determines that snipers are at work. Nor are all fires the work of arsonists. Looting, too, should be carefully defined. Great damage can be done if radio, television and published wire service and newspaper reports exaggerate a few small incidents. Consequently, in the early stages of any civil disorder, the basic rule is to work and report with the greatest restraint.

Necessarily, once a news organization's editors have evidence to show that they are dealing with a riot of major proportions, there is no justification for not making a complete report available to the community at large. When reporters see arsonists setting fire and looters carrying merchandise from wrecked stores, these things must be communicated. Yet, the need for restraint and patient inquiry cannot be abandoned even in such circumstances. For when shooting breaks out, the reporter is never justified to leap to conclusions that all the damage is being done by demonstrators or that race is aligned against race. Jittery police and National Guardsmen have been known to fire away at almost anything that moves, sometimes with unfortunate results.

Reporters have to be more patient and more circumspect.

• Short Takes

These are the basics of covering the police beat:

- Police reporters check police and fire department radios, arrest records (where available), departmental liaison officers and associated sources. When they spot a story worth going out on, they call their city desk and make suitable arrangements.

- Police reporters do a lot of interviewing at the scene of a crime, a fire, an accident or other incident on a police beat. The heart of their work depends on a good deal of accurate detail and good quotes.
- Police reporters can't afford to be a part of the big blue machine. They must maintain their independence and investigate at once any story that indicates police negligence.
- There is no such thing as going with first police reports without checking the facts. Police reports themselves may not be accurate.
- Some stories, in which important angles are left hanging, must be cleaned up with second-day and sometimes third-day reports. A once-over-lightly isn't sufficient.
- Sometimes it pays to go deeper into a story that indicates a profound human conflict. Such stories may be told at first in three or four paragraphs. But if the police reporter suspects a much better story lies behind the initial report, he or she should try to sell the idea to the city desk and get help.
- There are restraints on the coverage of crime news. All suspects must be read their Miranda rights—their right to remain silent and to be represented by a lawyer. In some states, under voluntary Press–Bar Guidelines, there are agreements that reporters will not use a defendant's prior police record and other damaging detail in the arrest report. What can and cannot be used should be checked with the city desk.
- Police reporters must be familiar with the department they cover, its regulations and procedures, and must have a good working acquaintance with criminal law.
- The greatest care must be taken in reporting arrests. Sometimes people are detained for questioning, asked to give help to the police or held as material witnesses. But these actions are not arrests and it is libel per se to report that such people are under arrest. The test for an arrest is twofold: (1) The subject must be booked and formal charges must be lodged, and (2) both the booking and the charge must be attributed to a responsible police official.
- Similarly, in the event of a civil disturbance, no reporter should call the exchange of a few blows a riot. And particular care should be exercised never to term a disturbance a race riot, which is a major civil calamity.
- Reporters should beware of announcing confessions. Generally, what is done is to report that a suspect has made a statement, made admissions or given an account of the crime to the authorities, and the source of that intelligence should be named and identified by department and rank.

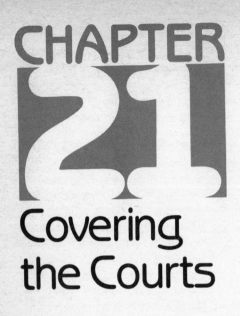

CHAPTER 21

Covering the Courts

Reporters who regularly cover the courts often establish good relationships with judges, prosecutors, defense lawyers in criminal proceedings and lawyers specializing in civil actions, court clerks and other court personnel. Those who stay on the job acquire such a wide knowledge of the law and legal precedents that they are sometimes consulted by lawyers. In rare cases, even a judge has been known to read the articles written by veteran court reporters with respect and grudging admiration. An outstanding reporter such as Anthony Lewis of the *New York Times*, who won a Pulitzer Prize for his court reporting, lectures regularly at Harvard Law School.

Without a continuity of court coverage, however, such individuals are bound to be rarities except when they happen to have law degrees. For the beginner, the first recourse is to learn the system and know how to operate within it.

The American Court System

In the United States, our legal heritage is unique. The court system is split into federal and state jurisdictions, each administratively separate, each independent of the executive and legislative branches of government. In some areas of the law, they each have exclusive jurisdiction; in others, they overlap.

The Federal System The federal courts were set up under Article III of the Constitution: "The judicial power of the United States shall be vested in one Supreme Court and in such inferior courts as the Congress may from time to time ordain and establish."

Of the two systems, the federal is the less complicated. It consists of about 500 judges and 12,000 other court officers and employees but is constantly under pressure to expand. There are three main levels of the federal judiciary: the district courts, the courts of appeals and the Supreme Court. Most federal judges are appointed for life by the president of the United States.

The district courts, having original jurisdiction in most issues involving federal law, handle cases in which citizens of two or more states are involved and in which there are alleged violations of the Constitution or other federal laws and suits affecting the federal government, the various states, foreign governments or foreign citizens. At least one district court exists in each of the 50 states and in the District of Columbia; the larger states have several each.

The next highest courts in the federal system, the courts of appeals, handle appeals from the district courts and cases involving the federal regulatory agencies. There is a court of appeals in each of 10 circuits set up in the 50 states and in the District of Columbia, with up to nine judges on each circuit.

At the apex of the system, the Supreme Court — the Chief Justice of the United States and eight associate justices — has the final decision on any case it decides to accept. The highest court also hears appeals from state courts if a constitutional issue of another federal law is involved.

Here are examples of stories that come out of the various federal court jurisdictions:

A Judgment in Equity The Associated Press carried the following lead on the long struggle for control of the Marathon Oil Company after Mobil Oil, the unsuccessful bidder, had gone all the way to the Supreme Court to try to stop a takeover by U.S. Steel:

> NEW YORK (AP) — After a seven-week struggle with a giant oil company, U.S. Steel Corp. on Thursday bought a controlling interest in Marathon Oil Co. and took the first step toward creating the nation's 12th-largest industrial concern.
>
> The long and costly fight over Ohio-based Marathon climaxed Wednesday with Mobil Corp.'s 11th-hour plea to Chief Justice Warren Burger for a temporary halt in U.S. Steel's bid.
>
> Just hours before the steel company's deadline to start buying Marathon shares, Burger rejected Mobil's request. . . .

A Damage Suit This is the announcement of a federal suit for damages, filed in Little Rock but carried in a version rewritten from wire services by *Today*, of Cocoa Beach, Florida:

> LITTLE ROCK — An Air Force sergeant who was injured in a Titan 2 missile silo explosion is suing the missile system's manufacturer, Martin-Marietta Corp., for $7.5 million.

Jeffrey Kennedy's lawsuit is the largest of four law suits resulting from a blast that killed one person and injured 21 others. Attorney William N. Carter of Little Rock filed the suit in U.S. District Court for Kennedy, 26, and his wife, Margaret, who live in Raymond, Me.

A Civil Rights Action   A civil rights law suit against Wisconsin state prison officials, heard in federal court, made history in a modest way, as the *Milwaukee Journal* reported. This was the lead:

One prisoner represented another in Federal Court Wednesday and, in so doing, made Wisconsin legal history.

Larry G. Solles, 31, serving a 60-year sentence for murder, left a maximum security cell at Waupun Correctional Institution to challenge the justice system from the other side.

Solles represented a fellow prisoner, Kenneth Jaworski, 33, in a $5.1 million civil rights suit against state prison officials. The jury trial began Wednesday before Federal Judge Robert W. Warren.

Jaworski, serving a three-year term for burglary, is suing prison officials over an alleged assault by guards at Central State Hospital in Madison. . . .

The State System   A major feature of the judiciary in the 50 states is that no two exactly resemble each other. State judicial systems are enormously diverse, consisting of more than 1,000 courts of different types and jurisdictions. In New York City alone, for example, there are more than 300 judges and specially appointed official referees who assist them and about 3,500 clerks, attendants and other staff workers. As for lawyers, they are more numerous in the largest city in the land than anywhere else except perhaps in Washington, D.C.

Basically, the states each provide in their respective constitutions for a group of general and special courts that hear civil and criminal cases, depending on the type of case, plus a roster of appeals courts.

Most of the so-called inferior courts, the lowest level, handle minor civil and criminal cases or, in the latter category, bind over suspects in serious cases for action by a grand jury. In a county subdivision, a justice of the peace may preside over such a lower court; in cities, they may be called police courts, magistrates' courts or specialized jurisdictions such as traffic court, family court, domestic relations court or juvenile or adolescents' courts. Inferior civil courts, sometimes known as "poor men's courts" because they are supposedly less expensive for litigation, are called city or municipal courts and handle cases with judgments limited to a fixed sum, anywhere from $3,000 to $6,000 in many cities and states.

It is not always certain that such inferior courts are legally courts of record and that their proceedings are privileged as to publication. The careful reporter will always ask the presiding jurist wherever there is even a shadow of doubt.

The workhorse courts—the courts of original jurisdiction for serious cases, both civil and criminal—are organized in most states on a county-by-county basis. They also handle appeals from inferior courts. These courts are known by different names—superior, common pleas, circuit, district and various specialized names adapted from the areas in which they are situated. (New York's workhorse courts are called Supreme Court, which is confusing.) In large cities, each such court may have several parts. In New York City, for example, there are 28 parts in a single workhorse court in Foley Square, Manhattan.

Where there is a heavy overload of criminal cases, there may be special and separate criminal courts known by such names as general sessions, oyer and terminer, or simply county courts. Still other courts may handle legal actions for divorce or marital separations, and surrogates' courts or probate courts handle wills. All are courts of record, and cases brought before them are privileged as to publication.

Above the workhorse courts in the various state systems are the appeals courts. Once again, the names do not always denote the importance of the functions of the various courts, which may be called anything from superior to supreme, or appellate to appeal—thus duplicating some of the names of workhorse courts in adjacent states. In the larger states, to relieve the load on the highest courts, an intermediate system is set up. Thus, in New York State, the decisions of the workhorse courts of original jurisdiction go to the appellate courts and then to the court of appeals.

Problems for the Courts   In addition to the technicalities of the judicial system, newcomers to court coverage will find some perplexing problems.

Year after year, the case loads of our courts grow heavier and the delays in reaching verdicts become more pronounced. For some time now the national average for court delays in bringing a case to trial has been about 30 months. Moreover, with new cases coming to trial at the rate of more than 8,000 a year in a populous area like New York County, there is little hope that the heavy burden on the courts will soon be eased. With two-thirds of all civil cases classified as liability actions, mainly involving automobiles, and with the crime rate shooting up all over the country, the cause of the judicial tieup is clear enough. It can take many years in some jurisdictions to obtain justice.

The greatest problem for the press, however, is the degree to which coverage of the courts is now inhibited. With the sanction of the Supreme Court, any judge can close a pretrial hearing to the news media—and a majority of cases are decided in such procedures. Furthermore, reporters investigating certain types of cases are always liable to be faced with a demand for their sources by a judge who has the power to jail them for contempt. (Gag rules and libel are discussed in detail in Chapter 19.)

Sources in Court Coverage

In the coverage of courts, as in every other aspect of journalism, reporters are only as good as their sources and their knowledge of how to gain access quickly to records. The reporters who are assigned to courts by the story, rather than as a regular beat, quickly discover this to be true. No matter how clever they are and how hard they work, the veterans on the beat are bound to have many more resources.

Most sensible editors know this to be true and generally send an experienced reporter with a newly assigned man or woman to open doors, make introductions and pay particular attention to such important sources as the clerk of the court and others. But where a beginner is shoved off to a court and told to struggle along, a friendly court clerk can help break the ice.

The Court Clerk   Regardless of the court's jurisdiction — federal, state or local — the clerk of the court is the key official for nearly all reporters. In that office will be found all the pertinent records and documents or there will be files and file numbers to trace whatever papers are needed.

Under the authority of a judge, clerks prepare trial calendars with the dates of various proceedings. They handle *dockets* (records with names of defendants, dates of arrest and a number that refers to the relevant papers in the case). The clerks also have records of all proceedings, judicial orders and transcripts (the latter available for a fee). They receive applications, motions and fines and transact other necessary court business. In major court trials, it is the clerks, generally, who make the arrangements with the news media for coverage; when space is limited, they decide who will be in the courtroom and who will be shut out and forced to listen on a public address system somewhere else in the courthouse.

It is the clerk who decides when a document in a law suit is a part of the court record and therefore privileged as to publication. A complaint, for example, cannot be considered as privileged until the clerk formally receives it, stamps it and records it. Summonses, for the most part, are seldom privileged. When in doubt, the reporter must always ask the clerk for a decision; in very important cases, it is worth reaching a judge to make such a determination.

The point is that legal papers are not graven in stone. They may be merely handed to the clerk but not filed by agreement pending negotiations of one kind or another; if the negotiations are satisfactory, the papers could be withdrawn and never filed. Should the reporter jump the gun and use such papers, carrying charges that amount to libel per se, the news organization involved could have what amounts to an erroneous story at best and a libel suit at worst.

Federal Sources   In federal courts, the first thing reporters must learn to do is to get the exact name of the court and its jurisdiction. There is a vast difference between a United States District Court for the Western District of Kentucky, for example, and a United States Court of Appeals for an area that includes Kentucky's Western District. It helps always to have the exact address of the building in which the court is located.

In the federal system, arraignments in the first instance are before United States commissioners, and cases against defendants are presented by members of the staff of the United States attorney for the particular district. These offices are major sources, therefore, along with that of the court clerk. In noncriminal actions brought in federal courts, the lawyers involved are also primary sources for news. For criminal cases, of course, defense counsel must ordinarily be consulted if an interview with a defendant is to be arranged.

The Position of Judges   The relationships of judges to the news media vary widely. As Chief Justice of the United States, Warren Burger was notably aloof to the news media and on frequent occasions expressed an unflattering view of reporters. Yet other judges at the federal and state levels can be more accommodating, although, for understandable reasons, few permit interviews on pending legal business.

Still, most reporters believe in introducing themselves to judges with whom they are bound to work on a day-by-day basis. There does come a time, particularly if a verdict is about to be reached in an important case, when reporters try to persuade jurists — usually through their law clerks or assistants — not to close the doors of the courtroom. A decent and mutually respectful relationship between judge and reporter can help smooth over such difficulties.

News from Prosecutors   So much news flows from the offices of prosecutors and their investigators that reporters must be constantly on guard against even an unconscious slant in their copy in the state's favor. Most reporters also make a point of knowing as many minor officials as possible — bailiffs, court stenographers, special police and the like. They learn to check court calendars daily, study the docket for new cases and maintain contact with developing cases. It is their job to keep their editors advised of pending schedules for the organization's "future book."

As for grand jury proceedings, these are secret until an indictment is voted, but reporters often develop a fairly accurate notion of what is going on by talking with witnesses and the prosecuting official who submits the evidence.

It should be remembered that an indictment is an accusation, drafted on the basis of one-sided evidence, and each separate charge or count must be proved in court. Everything in a grand jury action, therefore, must be heavily qualified. If the penalty for the alleged crime is given, reporters should point out that it will apply only upon conviction.

Defense Counsel in Crime Cases   To try to avoid prejudicial publicity, judges in a number of criminal cases seal up the opposing lawyers at the outset of a trial. In a way, this works a hardship on reporters who try, as best they can, to present a balanced account of the proceedings. Before the trial actually begins and all proceedings are out in the open, the prosecution has the advantage of being able to file its charges; moreover, the police generally will have given their reasons for making an arrest, but the defense may be ordered not to say much out of court.

Nevertheless, an able reporter will always maintain regular contacts with both defense and prosecution in criminal cases. This can be done during recesses in the courtroom, as well as before and after sessions. At the very least, the routine should be preserved, the requests for witnesses should be made and comments on the course of the trial should be solicited, whether or not they are given. In some instances, there will be chances for background briefings.

Reporters, however, should always be aware that when judges seal up sources at the outset of a trial, the utmost care should be taken not to appear responsible for violations of such orders. Citations for contempt of court are never easy to handle.

Opposing Counsel in Civil Cases   The issues in civil cases are sometimes of such a complicated nature that they require some explanation in advance of the trial. When such suits become newsworthy, it is well worth the effort to interview opposing counsel — and to let each know that the other is being consulted. This, too, is the route that generally has to be taken to interview the principals in such actions as, for example, matrimonial cases or child custody suits.

Civil Proceedings

Matrimonial cases, damage suits, petitions for injunctions and actions in bankruptcy or requests for receiverships are of primary interest to the news media in civil proceedings. And yet the vast bulk of civil suits involve automobile damage cases that seldom receive any attention in the press.

It is strange that this should be so. But unless a suit involving an automobile accident carries with it a huge settlement, there is seldom much public interest in the story. Suits for damages in such cases are so numerous that they are generally ignored.

Divisions of the Law Civil law, as distinguished from criminal law, has two main divisions: actions at law and suits in equity.

Actions at law deal primarily with property and personal matters such as damage suits and the enforcement of contracts.

Suits in equity are brought to compel or bar action. Injunctions and restraining orders, through which individuals and corporate bodies seek relief of various kinds, are also a part of this division of the law, as are foreclosures and receiverships.

However, the distinctions between the two branches of civil law are fading. Many states have abolished the differences between them and others are considering similar action. It is complications such as these, in addition to the vast extent of the field of civil law, that make it difficult to chart a general plan of procedure for reporters.

Even lawyers of experience, venturing into areas of civil law with which they are not familiar, cheerfully confess that they have to look up a considerable amount of material. It is therefore mandatory for a reporter not only to have a law dictionary handy but also to obtain sufficient technical background whenever a newsworthy civil suit crops up on the beat.

Cautions in Coverage Sometimes reporters know of civil actions before they are filed through tips from friendly lawyers or court attaches. In any case, by looking over the clerk's docket they can find any complaint or petition that has been filed in a civil action. They need only its serial number and a helpful official to look up the original petition and get the story from it.

Civil suits begin with the filing of the complaint, but in some states the mere act of filing does not constitute privilege. Once the petition is brought before a judge, however, it becomes a part of a judicial proceeding and is thereby privileged. The issue cannot come to trial, though, until defendants file their answer and legal skirmishing in the form of pleadings is concluded. As has been pointed out, all this may take many months. The lapse of time and the legal technicalities thereby conspire to limit the news value of many civil actions. They may, in due course, be settled out of court and noted in the record. In major law suits lawyers announce such settlements, but the run-of-the-mill civil actions come and go with few except those directly concerned being the wiser.

It follows that reporters should be wary of any civil action in which there is evidence of private negotiations to effect an out-of-court settlement. What this involves is a continual contact with lawyers for both sides because the court usually is not a party to such proceedings.

Handling News of Civil Suits

The following is an account of a verdict in a damage suit brought against an airline. It is unusual because neither of the plaintiffs was physically hurt, and yet they collected a record sum for their effort.

> CHICAGO (AP)—A retired judge and his wife complained that Delta wasn't ready when they were, and a jury awarded them $208,000 for being bumped from a flight. It is believed to be the largest award ever made to airline passengers denied their seats.
>
> Delta said it would appeal.
>
> A Circuit Court jury on Monday agreed with former Illinois Supreme Court Justice Thomas Kluczynski and his wife, Melanie, that they suffered "humiliation, indignity and outrage" when they were told all seats were filled because of overbooking on their Delta Airlines flight to Florida....
>
> The award against the airline, whose advertising slogan is "Delta is ready when you are," was more than twice the amount requested by in the lawsuit....

Civil Trial Steps   The Seventh Amendment to the Constitution specifies: "In suits at common law, where the value in controversy shall exceed $20, the right of trial by jury shall be preserved, and no fact tried by a jury shall be otherwise reexamined in any court of the United States, than according to the rules of common law."

By contrast with this constitutional principle for the conduct of actions at law in civil cases, suits at equity historically have been decided by judges without a jury. This is a heritage from the ancient English courts of chancery (headed by a chancellor and established as separate courts of equity to provide legal relief for injustices and establish certain claims and rights).

However, with the merger of law and equity in many civil courts, a number of tests have been devised in various states to determine whether a jury should indeed be impaneled where there is any doubt about legal procedure. Most states, in consequence, do require juries for a variety of civil cases except for those seeking injunctions or other forms of relief under the principles of equity.

These, therefore, are the principal steps for reporters to follow in covering civil cases in general.

A complaint and other relevant papers are filed with the court clerk for presentation to the court itself. This is the spot at which reporters begin their coverage.

In response to the plaintiff's complaint, the defendant files a reply with the court clerk. This, too, may be examined.

A trial date is set. The clerk records it if it is not announced in open court.

If the case is to be tried by a judge and jury, a venire (panel or group of people) is called and the jury selection begins. The first juror chosen is the foreman or forewoman.

If no jury is to be selected, the trial proceeds at once.

The plaintiff's case is presented first. This consists of an opening statement by the principal lawyer, in which the purpose of the action is defined and specific damages, proposals for relief or other requests are made. The defense may open here, or defer a statement until after the prosecution's case ends.

The plaintiff's witnesses then are called for direct examination, with the defense having the privilege of cross-examining each one. When the plaintiff's case is complete, the defense generally asks for dismissal of the action and states the grounds for the request.

At this point the judge has the right, with or without a jury, to decide to continue the case or dismiss it. In most instances, the defense's request is denied.

The defense's case is then presented, the opening statement first to show what is asked of the court and the general lines of the response to the plaintiff's case.

The defense's witnesses then are called on direct examination, with the plaintiff's lawyers having the privilege of cross-examination.

In both the plaintiff's and defense's cases, each side has the additional privilege of conducting re-direct and re-cross-examination of witnesses at the time they take the stand. Or they may be recalled for testimony at a later stage.

Once the rival cases are complete, the summing-up begins.

The plaintiff goes first, showing what has been testified to, making claims for adjudication by the court and attempting to knock down the position taken by the defense.

The defense's summation follows in kind.

If there is a jury, the judge then instructs the jury as to the points of law that are involved and lays out the possible verdicts that may be brought in. The jury then retires and, when its deliberations end, re-enters the court and hands up its verdict to the judge.

The judge may let it stand; if, however, the court believes it to be excessive, as in the case of a damage suit or an action for libel or slander, a reduction may be ordered.

If there is no jury, a judge usually concludes the case by taking it under advisement and announces a decision in due course, usually a week or so. This may be done in open court, it may be published in a law journal or merely handed to the clerk of the court for transmission to the parties to the dispute.

In any event, the verdict may be appealed and, generally, it is. In most civil cases where considerable amounts of money are at stake, both the initial case and the various appeals may take years.

Where the federal government or the state is a party to a civil action, as for example an antitrust case in the federal courts or an effort by a state to obtain relief against excessive utility rate increases, the procedure is essentially the same.

Matrimonials Newspapers that use a lot of matrimonial cases must be wary of libel suits. A lawyer may prepare a sizzling complaint for a wife in a divorce suit without knowing that she is, at that moment, about to be reconciled with her husband. Suits for divorce, annulment, separation and alienation of affections are, like crime news, popular with the commercial press. However, they are not particularly popular with reporters who cover them because of the very real difficulty in obtaining material that is privileged and fair to both sides. When the law permits still further complications, such as the sealing of papers in a divorce action, then the use of news of such suits becomes impossible until the trial begins.

It is, therefore, a matter of considerable risk to use an item about a divorce suit or separation involving prominent persons; only in Reno or other jurisdictions that cater to matrimonials can a reporter consider that such work is ever as simple as it seems.

Criminal Arrests and Trial Steps

In newsworthy cases, reporters follow the action from the time an investigation begins. Once an arrest is made, the defendant is arraigned, generally in an inferior court, and makes a plea, guilty or not guilty, after being provided with counsel.

If the inferior court has jurisdiction, as in the case of a misdemeanor, the case may be disposed of with an immediate hearing or with a hearing within a few days.

If a felony is involved, there is a preliminary hearing in the inferior court to determine whether the state, in the form of an assistant prosecutor, has sufficient evidence to have the defendant bound over for grand jury action. Once the defendant pleads and sufficient evidence is presented, the judge orders the defendant held for grand jury action and sets bail.

The Grand Jury A grand jury in most states consists of 23 members, although it may have as few as 12 members. Its mission is to hear the state's case against a defendant in a criminal proceeding, with the prosecutor presenting witnesses to show there is sufficient evidence to take the case to trial. In a 23-member jury, if 12 or more members believe there is sufficient evidence to prosecute the accused, an indictment is handed up. The accused is then rearraigned and pleads to the indictment.

A grand jury also may act on its own initiative, or on the allegations of private citizens who come before it with complaints. In such instances, what the grand jury votes is a presentment and, like an indictment, it is presented to a court.

Grand jury proceedings are secret, but reporters have the right—and frequently exercise it—of questioning people who are to testify before a grand jury or of meeting them after they testify. Knowing this, prosecutors and judges go to great lengths to protect witnesses from what they believe might amount to harassment. Sometimes courts issue orders forbidding any person connected with a particular case from discussing it with anybody outside the court itself.

Reporters and Criminal Trials So many moves are open to opposing counsel in a criminal trial and courts can proceed in so many different ways that directions for journalistic procedure are bound to be riddled with exceptions.

Reporters just have to cover the story, discussing questions and procedures with both sides and the court as well wherever there is any doubt. In some instances, it helps to talk with impartial legal sources—lawyers or even judges not connected with the case at hand. Such interviews generally occur on a background basis and are mainly for the reporter's benefit.

The Rights of Defendants   The Sixth Amendment to the Constitution is the basis for criminal trial procedures:

> In all criminal prosecutions, the accused shall enjoy the right to a speedy and public trial, by an impartial jury of the state and district wherein the crime shall have been committed, which district shall have been previously ascertained by law, and to be informed of the nature and cause of the accusation; to be confronted with the witnesses against him; to have compulsory process for obtaining witnesses in his favor, and to have the assistance of counsel for his defense.

For trial verdicts, the Eighth Amendment applies:

> Excessive bail shall not be required, nor excessive fines imposed, nor cruel and unusual punishments inflicted.

In addition, the United States Supreme Court held in 1967 that the "due process" clause of the 14th Amendment guarantees the right of a jury trial to accused persons in criminal proceedings by the states. The section reads:

> No state shall make or enforce any law which shall abridge the privileges or immunities of citizens of the United States, nor shall any state deprive any person of life, liberty or property without due process of law, nor to deny to any person within its jurisdiction the equal protection of the law.

Criminal Trial Procedures   The procedures in civil trials with juries generally apply to most criminal trials.

All the relevant papers—the indictment and applicable material—will be found in the possession of the court clerk. The docket number will show where the papers may be located in the files.

When the court meets on the trial date, jury selection begins with the examination of the venire panel. Each side has a certain number of challenges, peremptory and for cause, to get rid of people it doesn't want.

Then the opening address of the prosecutor follows, in which he or she details the crime and relates how the state intends to prove the defendant guilty. The defense may follow with its opening statement or delay until the end of the prosecution's case, except in such states as New York, where the defense must follow the prosecution.

The state puts on its witnesses next, with the prosecutor conducting direct examination and the defense cross-examining. Re-direct and re-cross-examination are permitted, if requested.

When the state's case concludes, the defense always asks for a direct verdict of acquittal on the ground that the charges have not been proved. The court usually denies such requests.

The defense's case follows. Its witnesses go through direct and cross-examination, as have those of the state.

Both sides then may put on rebuttal witnesses.

The summing-up follows—invariably a field day for lawyers in a criminal trial. The prosecution generally speaks first, and the defense closes, each seeking to convince the jury with arguments, pleas and rhetoric. Both sides rest their case after that.

The judge then charges the jury, sums up the law in the case, tells the jury its possible verdicts and explains the meaning of each verdict. The jurist also emphasizes that the state must have proved its case beyond a reasonable doubt.

When the jury returns to the courtroom, the foreman or forewoman announces the verdict. If it is a finding of guilt, the judge then may remand the prisoner and set a date for sentencing, or may pronounce sentence immediately, depending on the law in the state.

In some jurisdictions, juries may decide on the sentence or recommend a verdict to the judge. In others, the judge decides on the basis of the law, precedents, relevant information in the case and from probation officers what the penalty is to be.

Handling a Verdict   Here are two examples of how leads are handled upon the conclusion of a criminal trial. In the following, a reporter carefully used the term "innocent," which does not exist in law, instead of taking a chance on having the "not" drop out of a "not guilty" verdict.

> FALL RIVER, Mass. (AP)—Anne Capute, a nurse who said she only wanted to help a cancer victim endure agonizing pain, was found innocent Friday of murdering the patient with massive doses of morphine.
>
> A Superior Court jury of seven men and five women also found Capute, 44, innocent of illegally dispensing the drug to the patient, Norma Leanues.
>
> The jury, which listened to five weeks of testimony, took 13 hours to reach a verdict.
>
> "I'm just grateful, that's all. I thanked them for my life," Capute said after she hugged her family and attorney and thanked the jurors. "That's what I had to do. . . ."

Here is how a sentencing procedure was handled when it occurred at a separate hearing after the verdict in a murder case was handed up:

> SALT LAKE CITY—Joseph Paul Franklin, convicted of killing two black joggers, was sentenced to life in prison Wednesday by a jury that deliberated 2½ hours.
>
> Franklin, an avowed racist, could have been sentenced to death by a firing squad. Third District Court Judge Jay E. Banks set formal sentencing for 10 a.m. Monday.
>
> Franklin, 31, was convicted Saturday of first-degree murder in the shooting deaths of Ted Fields, 20, and David Martin, 18. The two were shot while jogging with two white girls. . . .

Plea Bargaining

Because of the tremendous overload of criminal cases, plea bargaining has become an established procedure in all but the smallest and least troubled jurisdictions. In large cities such as New York, Miami, Chicago, Los Angeles and others, prosecutors make no secret of their desire to dispose of certain cases—especially those in which their evidence is weak, by offering a deal to defendants to plead guilty to lesser charges and accept a sentence substantially more merciful than if they were to be convicted on the original charge. Defendants' lawyers are often quite active in this kind of negotiation, attempting to get the best deal possible for their clients.

When Plea Bargaining Begins   Reporters should be alert to any evidence of plea bargaining from the time of an arrest. The symptoms include repeated postponements of trial dates, conferences between prosecution and defense, continual consultations with defendants either in detention cells or while they are out on bail.

When is a plea bargain announced? Almost any time. It could come before the trial begins with a request for rearraignment of a defendant (there is an arraignment for pleading after an indictment), who then changes the record plea to guilty of a lesser crime. The judge generally requires a statement from the prosecution to show why the deal is being made. The defense, of course, has little to say in such circumstances.

The most dramatic instances of plea bargaining come in the middle of a trial. What usually happens is that a defendant, having been offered a deal, decides to accept it, so informs the defense lawyer and the prosecutor, then pleads guilty to a lesser charge.

Criticisms of Plea Bargaining   Prosecutors in large cities argue that they allow plea bargaining in lesser cases in order to concentrate on prosecuting hard-core criminals. However, the evidence does not seem to substantiate that kind of justification in many cases. It is true that plea bargains were arranged in some notable cases, including a selected few Watergate defendants, but critics point out that some hardened criminals also receive unexpected benefits from plea bargaining and spend relatively little time in prison.

The rise in the crime rate, however, is the best indication that plea bargaining is a fact of life in our courts and is likely to continue indefinitely.

Writing About Plea Bargaining   Here is how the *Chicago Tribune* reported the outcome of a plea-bargaining case:

> A 17-year-old woman who provided testimony leading to the conviction of an arsonist pleaded guilty to an arson charge Monday and was sentenced to 10 years in prison as part of a plea-bargaining agreement.
> Faith Byas testified at the trial of Jimmie Terrell, 27, of 6530 S. Halsted St., who was convicted of setting a fire that killed six persons in an uptown apartment building. She admitted earlier that she had been with Terrell at the time. She was charged with murder and aggravated arson; in exchange for her testimony, however, prosecutors dropped the murder charges. . . .

Covering a Criminal Trial

Every courthouse reporter hopes one day to cover a sensational criminal trial like that of Jean Harris, the head of a fashionable girls' school, who was convicted of the murder of Dr. Herman Tarnower, the Scarsdale diet expert, or that of Wayne Williams, who was convicted of two of the mass murders of young black children and youths in Atlanta. However, there simply isn't time enough for the average court reporter to do day-by-day coverage of the usual grist of criminal trials.

The Reporting Routine   If every reporter on a courthouse beat were to sit all day in a single trial, there would be precious little news about other courts and the prosecutor's office in the paper. Except for the most important and sensational trials, beat reporters have to make do by reading the relevant papers, sitting in on the opening of the trial, getting a fill-in on testimony from the court stenographer and from transcripts where available before covering the verdict.

In between, the reporter does have to check on other courts, grand jury actions, the court clerk's office and the prosecutor's office. It's all in a day's work.

Full Coverage of a Trial   When reporters are assigned to stick with a trial from beginning to end, preparation is the key to the best work. It pays to have fully prepared notes in advance, detailing the relevant dates and occurrences in the case; the names, addresses and phone numbers of opposing counsel; major figures and potential witnesses, and additions from time to time about the judge, the jury foreman and trial developments.

Sometimes, major testimony comes from persons whose names mean nothing to the public. In such instances, reporters generally say that a state or a defense witness testified to a particular point in the trial, then make the necessary identification in the third or fourth paragraph. An alternative is to describe the charge that was made at the trial, then identify the witness later in the story. Throughout, efficient reporters usually know what to expect next and they make their arrangements with their offices accordingly.

As the time approaches for the judge's charge to the jury, a brief history of the trial should be prepared if it has developed into a major news story. Once the jury retires, the history should be filed for newspaper use as B copy. Further material preceding the verdict, such as a jury's return to the courtroom for instructions, could then be sent as A copy to precede B copy. The jury verdict would, of course, constitute the lead.

Covering the Verdict   There isn't much difference in the way trial verdicts are presented by the news media. The broadcast reporters, having the first break, do their reporting in the present tense, the wire services and newspapers in the past tense. But the basic information and the presentation of the story are grounded on historic journalistic practice regardless of the time difference between newspapers and their faster rivals. Here is a verdict in a trial, giving the essential portions of the lead:

By Dudley Clendinen
New York Times News Service

NEWPORT, R.I.—As Claus von Bulow sat flushed, still and expressionless, a jury Tuesday pronounced him guilty as charged, of twice trying to kill his wealthy wife, Martha von Bulow, by injecting her with insulin.

Twenty-four times, as the seven men and five women rose one by one to be polled by the court clerk, von Bulow heard the word "guilty" roll out. He showed not a flicker of emotion at the verdict. The 55-year-old Danish businessman faces a maximum sentence of 40 years in prison.

"By God, we've done it," Stephen Famiglietti, the prosecutor, whispered to his boss, Susan McGuirl, the deputy attorney general of Rhode Island. He squeezed her hand as they heard the verdict.

The Rhode Island attorney general's office said that a previous state supreme court ruling had established that, should Mrs. von Bulow die, her husband could not be charged with murder since that would constitute double jeopardy.

The appeals will now begin, but Tuesday, after nine weeks of trial, 56 witnesses and 36 hours of deliberation, a jury has agreed with the suspicions first raised by a grieving family and Mrs. von Bulow's personal maid.

The 50-year-old Mrs. von Bulow, once called "Sunny" by her friends for her beauty and the sweetness of her temper, lies in a coma in Columbia-Presbyterian Hospital in New York, with no cerebral function left above her brain stem. For weeks, the defense suggested that she was the victim of her own weakness, of a self-destructive indulgence in alcohol, sweets and drugs. The jury has decided otherwise.

Von Bulow's lead counsel, Harold Price Fahringer of New York, made the defense statement for hundreds of reporters representing outlets around the world.

"I don't know if we will ever know how large a part his love affair with another woman took in this case, or his aristocratic background and Danish citizenship," Fahringer said.

"He took it like a man," said Fahringer, standing with his co-counsel, John F. Sheehan of Providence. "We intend to appeal."

When Sentence Is Pronounced In many states, a judge may pronounce the sentence on a convicted person immediately after the jury returns a guilty verdict. Sometimes, the court acts on a jury's recommendation; if there is no recommendation, the court may defer sentencing to hear arguments from opposing counsel. That is what happened in the von Bulow case. Here is the essential part of a news account:

NEWPORT, R.I. (UPI)—Claus von Bulow was sentenced to 30 years in prison Friday for twice trying to murder his heiress wife with insulin injections that turned her into a "sleeping beauty."

Von Bulow, 55, showed no emotion as Judge Thomas H. Needham sentenced him to 10 years on one count of attempted murder and 20 years—the maximum—on a second count involving the insulin shot that plunged his wife Martha (Sunny) von Bulow into a coma.

The court acted after hearing opposing counsel. The sentences are to be served consecutively and von Bulow would have to serve 10 years before becoming eligible for parole.

Needham continued von Bulow's $500,000 bail until next Friday when it will be increased to $1 million. He was convicted seven weeks ago after a sensational two and one-half month trial. The verdict is being appealed . . .

TV Cameras in the Courtroom

A majority of the 50 states now allow television coverage in some form in their civil, criminal or appellate courts. However, relatively few trials are covered by TV. Those that are, demonstrably interest a large and ever-curious public. But even in such newsworthy trials, what actually happens is that the cameras record the opening of the trial, a few highlights and the verdict.

What the Supreme Court Decided   It wasn't always so. As late as 1965, Billie Sol Estes, a Texas financier, won a reversal of his swindling conviction in the Supreme Court because his trial in a Texas state court had been televised over his objection and because of other circumstances. Estes's term in a federal prison based on a federal mail fraud conviction was not affected and has since been completed.

Just 16 years later, in 1981, the Supreme Court decided unanimously that the televising of trials, despite a defendant's objection, is within the sanction of the Constitution.

Legal authorities have since pointed out that this decision did not endorse or outlaw television in the courtroom. But it did give the states the right to experiment with TV if they decided to do so.

The ruling did not affect federal courts, including the high court itself, because they make their own rules. And while Chief Justice Burger remains on the bench, it is safe to say the red eye of the TV camera will not cause him to blink; his opposition to televised courts is widely known and frequently noted.

The Basis of the Decision   The case that led to the Supreme Court's ruling was that of two Miami Beach policemen, Noel Chandler and Robert Granger, who had been accused of committing a burglary. Just one camera was in the court and WPLG broadcast less than three minutes of the trial, but the accused men argued that their rights had been violated. Chief Justice Burger, in writing for the Court, decided against them. While his opinion pointed out that "dangers lurk in this, as in most experiments," that in itself did not warrant a complete prohibition on TV cameras in the courtroom.

It was a victory for Florida and 17 other states that had joined in carrying the fight to the high court. The issue thus has been passed to the states with varying results.

Juvenile Delinquency

The rising concern over juvenile crime is weakening the protection that has been given to children under 18 who are involved with the law. Their names are withheld in many states in the Union. However, instances of 13- and 14-year-old killers preying in gangs on defenseless elderly persons in large cities have outraged lawmaking bodies in some larger cities. In consequence, there have been moves to lower the age limit for juvenile crime to 13 or 14. This, combined with the U.S. Supreme Court's restoration of the death penalty for certain types of crimes specifically designated by individual states, raises at least the possibility that children who commit murder may be hanged or put to death in the gas chamber or electric chair.

It may not come to that. And yet the intensity of the debate about the responsibility of juvenile criminals, habitual or not, indicates that the body of law affecting juvenile delinquents is changing, and not for the better.

Covering Juvenile Courts   With rare exceptions, reporters are not permitted to enter a juvenile court or adolescents' court and cover the proceedings. It is sometimes difficult even to find out what is going on in this rather sensitive domain of the law.

What reporters must do, therefore, is to maintain contact with both court clerks and judges in such jurisdictions, even though they may say very little for the record. Actually, the tips on news stories in children's courts usually come from the offices of the prosecutor or the defense lawyers, sometimes both.

A court reporter who moves around and knows a lot of lawyers seldom has much trouble determining when a newsworthy case is about to be heard in a juvenile court. It then becomes the duty of the editor in charge to decide whether the story should be run and, if so, whether the child should be identified and photographed. Such decisions are never very easy to make. Nor do reporters, as a rule, generally show much enthusiasm for publicizing cases of child criminals.

But it is a part of the routine of court coverage and it can't very well be evaded. Justice for children is just as much a part of the press's responsibility as it is for the courts.

Terms Used in Court Reporting

Judges and lawyers have a language all their own, much of which goes into legal documents and decisions. Some of the words and phrases most frequently used are reproduced here for the information of reporters who are newly assigned to the courthouse beat.

Reporters cannot, of course, use all such terms and others even more complicated in a news story. They would hopelessly confuse the public. Professional practice requires each term to be briefly explained if it is used. For instance: "The defendant pleaded *nolo contendere* (no contest)." Better still, instead of using a term such as *nolle prosequi*, it may be stated as follows: "The prosecution announced it would drop the case." Except in a law journal, there is no reason to clutter up a news story with a lot of legal terminology unless the news cannot be told any other way. This procedure applies particularly to wire service correspondents and specials who cover important legal proceedings in other states for their newspaper. Pleas and other terminology that are familiar to the public in one state are not necessarily known, or even used, in adjacent states.

accessory   Person who assists in the commission of a crime, either before or after the fact.

acquit   To declare a person not guilty; to exonerate.

action at law   Proceedings instituted to enforce a legal right.

adjournment   Request for more time to find witnesses or important evidence, or other reasons.

administrator   Appointee of a court to administer the estate of a person who has died intestate (without a will).

affirm   Used by appellate courts to uphold a lower court decision. Failure to affirm is called a reversal.

allegation   An assertion, made in pleading, which its maker says will be supported with evidence.

arraignment   Process through which defendants hear the charges against them and plead guilty or not guilty, or no contest.

arrest   To take into custody by legal authority.

attachment   Authorization by the court in written form to take and hold a person or property.

attorney   Prosecutors and defense attorneys are lawyers and officers of the court, along with judges, court clerks and bailiffs.

autopsy   Examination by a coroner to discover cause of death; often, this includes dissection of a body.

bail bond   Security, usually furnished by a professional bondsman, to guarantee the appearance of an accused person in court. When individuals are ordered held without bail, the seriousness of the charge is such that the court refuses to turn them loose. When a bond of $5,000 is posted, if that is the amount of bail set by the court, the usual phrasing is that the prisoner was liberated in lieu of $5,000 bail, or simply, freed on $5,000 bail.

bailiff   A court officer who guards jurors, keeps order in courtroom.

bench warrant   Order issued by a judge for arrest of a person charged with a crime.

beneficiary   A person who receives an inheritance in a will, insurance policy, trust, etc.

bill of particulars   A statement setting forth the specifications in an indictment, information or complaint.

change of venue   Changing the place of trial.

codicil   Addition to a will.

commutation   Reduction of sentence.

concurrent sentence   Court decision that convicted defendants serve only the longest of several terms imposed. Consecutive sentence means they serve the sum of all terms.

contempt of court An offense against the court, punishable by a fine, jail term, or both.

consent decree Court order to which the defendant has consented.

corpus delecti Essence of the crime.

decree nisi Final judgment to take effect some time in the future.

defendant Party against whom an action has begun.

demurrer Defense plea that the charge does not constitute a crime, or cause of action.

deposition Taking of testimony from a witness before trial.

directed verdict Instruction by the court to the jury to bring in a particular verdict.

double jeopardy Plea that the defendant has already been tried for the same offense.

eminent domain Right of the government to take private property for public use, paying just compensation for it.

exculpatory To free a person from blame.

executor Person named in a will to administer an estate.

extradict Process of returning a prisoner from one state to another.

felony A serious crime, a misdemeanor being a minor crime.

grand jury Jury of 12 to 23 citizens that hears evidence against an accused person and votes an indictment if there is sufficient cause.

habeas corpus Writ requiring production of a detained person in court to inquire into the legality of the proceedings.

indeterminate sentence Sentence of "not more than" a certain term, and "not less than" another term of years.

indictment Document brought by the grand jury on evidence submitted to it by the prosecutor. A bill of indictment is also known as a true bill.

information Document filed by the prosecutor under oath instead of by the grand jury.

injunction Court order requiring those named to act or to forbear in certain actions.

interlocutory decree Preliminary mandate of the court.

John Doe inquiry Inquiry by a prosecutor to obtain evidence in connection with an alleged crime.

letters rogatory Document under which a witness in a foreign jurisdiction is examined.

letters testamentary Authority issued to executors of wills after they have qualified to permit them to perform their functions.

mandamus Court direction requiring someone to perform an act.

mandate A judicial direction.

misdemeanor Minor crime, as distinguished from a felony, which is a serious crime, such as a homicide.

mistrial End of a trial because of an irregularity.

motion to dismiss Motion attacking the basis of the action.

nolle prosequi Also, simply *nolle pros;* determination not to proceed with a case.

nolo contendere, or *no contest*   Plea indicating that defendant will not contest the charge.

obiter dictum   A judge's incidental or collateral opinion.

pardon   Action by executive relieving criminal from sentence.

parole   Release on pledge of reappearance at regular intervals, or on call.

plaintiff   Party who initiates litigation.

pleading   Document in which the plaintiff's claim or defendant's defense is set forth.

presentment   Document brought by a grand jury on its own initiative or upon allegations of private citizens.

quash   Motion contending an indictment is defective in form.

quo warranto   Writ by which government seeks to recover an office from a public official or a franchise from a corporation.

referee   Appointee of court.

replevin   Writ requiring production of property.

reprieve   Delay in execution of a sentence.

respondent   Party against whom an appeal has been taken.

sealed verdict   It is rendered in the absence of a judge, but opened by the jurist when court reconvenes.

subpoena   Court order requiring witness to appear and testify.

subpoena duces tecum   Court order requiring witnesses to produce certain documents bearing on the case for which they must appear.

suits in equity   A proceeding originally brought before a chancellor to compel defendants to refrain from doing something or to compel them to do something.

summons   Process of the court instituting an action.

veniremen   Members of a panel (venire) of potential jurors, called to be examined for jury duty.

voir dire   Examination of potential jurors.

writ of certiorari   Writ from superior to inferior court requiring the record to be sent to the former for review.

writ of supersedas   Writ by which proceedings are stayed.

• Short Takes

Here are some of the principal points to remember about court reporting:

- Always check the docket in the court clerk's office for the filing of new cases.
- Always check the office of the prosecutor for criminal complaints and cases that are going before the grand jury.
- You are dependent mainly on lawyers for other information.
- While judges have the right to close pretrial hearings on their own responsibility, they have no right to bar reporters from open court in any criminal case. Reporters should have authorization from their news organizations to protest such closings.
- In writing about court actions, be sure that the material you use is privileged if it contains material that is libelous per se. If there is any doubt, ask the judge.

- Keep in touch with the prosecutor's office whenever there is a probability of plea bargaining in a newsworthy case.
- Whenever you write about a jury verdict, be sure that you also specify the maximum and minimum punishment possible under the law. When punishment has been announced by the court, that must be combined with the verdict in the lead to the story.
- Make sure that everything you write about the courts is phrased in terms that the general public can understand. Avoid legalisms at all costs.

CHAPTER 22

The Ethics
of Journalists

A small boy toting what appeared to be a pistol robbed a New York City bank of $118 one wintry afternoon. When a nine-year-old boy surrendered to the FBI in the case two days later, and his lawyer called a news conference, reporters for newspapers and television staged a publicity carnival. The ethics of both lawyers and journalists were widely questioned, particularly after each blamed the other for creating a circuslike atmosphere about a child's misfortune.

The Boy Bank Robber Story

A teller at the branch of the New York Bank for Savings at Avenue of the Americas near 47th Street was stunned on the morning of February 25, 1981, when he saw a small boy pointing what seemed to be a pistol at him. After the teller gave the child $118, the robber ran from the bank and vanished. Two days later, someone tipped off a *New York Post* reporter that a suspect was about to surrender to the FBI, requested that other reporters be informed and directed the press to a lawyer, Mel A. Sachs.

The Reporters Move In The boy, identified as Robert M., was 4 feet 5, weighed 90 pounds and was dressed in blue jeans, a tan shirt and a tie. When he appeared at FBI headquarters, he had $20 on him and Sachs, his lawyer, said the rest had been spent on hamburgers, French fries, a movie and a $29.95 wristwatch that plays a tune. Dan Collins, a UPI reporter, set the scene:

"Have you ever seen 30 reporters and photographers bent over to the waist trying to interview a 4-foot-5-inch boy and waiting for one word to drop?"

Collins remarked, "U.P.I. was there because A.P. was there," and added that he had felt "caught in a competitive situation." That was to be the general excuse among reporters for the way they handled the story — competition.

E. R. Shipp, a court reporter for the *New York Times*, said she believed that "most of the reporters here were offended" by what she termed "a Mel Sachs production." Nevertheless, she conceded that she had been told by her editors "to get as much as we could," and she did her job.

The First Splurge   Television was in on the story, of course, and went with it, pictures and all. The *New York Times* ran the story on the first page, second section, with a picture. Under normal conditions, the metropolitan editor, Peter Millones, said, the *Times* would not have used the picture but, since it already had been on TV and everybody else had it, he thought omitting it would be pointless.

The *New York Daily News* and the *New York Post* both used the boy's picture on Page 1 and gave generous coverage to the story inside. The *News* had the name and address of the boy but didn't use them; however, so many details *were* used, including the name of the business of the boy's grandmother, that anybody who knew the boy could have identified him without the picture.

There was some soul-searching. Stephen J. Cohen, news director of WCBS-TV, argued that he would not normally have displayed pictures of a juvenile suspect but added, "Once it was on the front pages of the newspapers it was difficult for us to take the high road."

Justice for a Nine-Year-Old   Hearings in juvenile cases in New York City are nearly always private, but Robert M. was spared nothing. At his lawyer's request, Judge Edith L. Miller of Family Court held an open hearing a few days later and an even larger corps of reporters and photographers attended. Courtroom sketch artists also were at work during the boy's arraignment.

The lawyer entered a "not guilty" plea for the defendant and contended that he had only been "playing" in the bank. The lawyer blamed unspecified TV programs for the boy's actions. A trial date was set and the child was released in the custody of his family. Eventually, when the uproar about the case died down some months later, a Family Court judge ordered Robert M. to attend school regularly, undergo therapy and "commit no action which would be a crime if he were an adult." Pending regular reports on his progress "for a year or two," the court then suspended judgment. However, before long Robert M. was hauled into court again on another charge and this time there was no publicity circus.

The Moral Problem   Jonathan Friendly, who reports on the news media for the *New York Times*, commented on the ethical issue as follows in one of his stories about the first arrest:

. . . Reporters covering the story and editors who have displayed the stories and pictures of "Robert" in their newspapers and on the most-watched television news programs agree the story is a fine one. And if the coverage has overstepped an ethical line that no one draws in quite the same way, they say, that is the fault of the boy's lawyer and the reality of news competition.

In principle, the press has largely agreed with juvenile-justice authorities who say that children are too immature to judge the consequences of their own acts and should not be subjected to public scrutiny that could permanently mar their future.

However, there are no legal bars to identifying such children, either as suspects or if they are convicted, and the press reserves to itself the right to make a case-by-case judgment about whether to disclose a name or print a picture. There seems to be no disagreement on the newsworthiness of the robbery itself. . . .

The Limits of Press Morality

Since there is nothing to stop the news media from thrusting a child into the midst of a publicity hippodrome in the largest city in the land, it may well be asked whether there is a line, generally accepted by professional journalists, beyond which no reporter, correspondent, editor, news director or photographer should go.

What Is Permissible?   That question raises a number of others of a rather crucial nature. For example:

- What is there to stop a reporter from betraying a source he or she has promised to protect?
- Or violating a confidence on the theory that the story is too good to pass up?
- Or making up stories and manufacturing phony personalities on the theory that nobody will ever know the difference?
- Or inventing a quote on the theory that a speaker should have said it even if he didn't?
- Or invading private homes and offices and grabbing papers and pictures that might have a bearing on an investigation?
- Or having a love affair with a news source on a story in which both reporter and the source are involved?
- Or trading information between sources, such as obtaining a list of defense witnesses in confidence and then trading them to the prosecution in return for an exclusive story?
- Or assuming false identities in cases where such actions amount to nothing other than crass deception for no purpose based on public policy?
- Or accepting gifts and other largesse from news sources, advertisers or both?

In 56 years as a practitioner and teacher in the news profession and business, I have known of journalists who did such things—and some of them got away with it. Fortunately, they were few in number and not typical. But the very fact that evil practices are possible in journalism underlines the weakness of accepting mere newsworthiness as a standard of judgment for morality, in whole or in part.

In reality, newsworthiness is the very worst standard for deciding whether an act is ethical or not. The questions about what is permissible all dealt with situations that were, at the time, a part of major news developments. In each case, the reportorial acts were committed on the theory that "getting the story" is the only rule that matters.

However, the time for that kind of irresponsible journalism has long since passed. Even if some ill-advised reporter were to steal pictures or lie or cheat to get a big story, the consequences of such actions — once they were revealed — would lead to ultimate disgrace for the person and the news organization involved. Both the courts and the public are holding the news media to much stricter standards of conduct today.

What Price First Amendment?   There is nothing to stop journalists from doing anything that could be an affront to common decency, short of violating the law. The First Amendment makes it impossible for Congress or any other legislative or regulatory body in the land to pass a law licensing journalists, binding them to an acceptable code of conduct and devising suitable punishments — such as loss of a license — for infractions large or small.

Unlike physicians, lawyers or even plumbers, journalists cannot be regulated by any outside body, and the codes of conduct that professional societies adopt cannot be enforced. If journalists cannot act responsibly themselves, or if their news organizations cannot force them to do so under pain of dismissal, nobody else can do anything about it, unless they commit a crime or become involved in a civil court action in connection with their work.

It follows that self-control, responsibility and a decent sense of restraint ought to be stressed as important elements in the practice of journalism and, quite generally, they are. Most journalists of character and experience *do* profess to practice a certain amount of responsibility in dealing with the news. Here is one such instance.

"I Don't Ambush People"

William Owney, a 23-year-old reporter for the *Gainesville* (Florida) *Sun*, was just one year out of journalism school at the University of Florida when the city editor asked him to take a telephone call.

At first, it seemed like much ado about very little. An irate father complained that his little girl had been hit on her nose with a stick by another little girl while an older boy held the hands of the victim. The reporter sympathized but wondered aloud what the paper could do about it. The father announced that although the assailant was only six years old, he was having her arrested and brought to trial.

Bill Owney began taking notes furiously. Then he told the city editor he wanted to go out on the story and soon was on his way. He talked with the father who had telephoned in the complaint and learned that the lawyer for the six-year-old defendant was demanding a jury trial which, under Florida law, would have to be held in an adult court.

A Different Approach   Owney was appalled. He did something that is very different from the go-go-go image the public has of a reporter hell-bent on getting the story no matter who was hurt. The reporter said to the father: "Look, going public with a story like this will put you and your wife and your little girl in the center of a lot of public attention. It may be very unpleasant. Do you really want to do it?"

The father insisted.

Owney then went to see the family of the six-year-old defendant. To let him tell his own story of what happened:

> They were throwing great quotes around about not being afraid to put their little girl before a jury but I just had to stop them. I asked them, too, if they knew the consequences for the children in the case and for themselves. I don't ambush people. I want them to know what they're getting themselves into. But the defendant's parents, like the father of the other little girl, wanted to go through with it, no matter what happened.

The Settlement   On March 25, 1982, the *Gainesville Sun* carried Bill Owney's piece on Page 1 under the headline "1st Grade Girl To Go On Trial." It became a nationwide sensation for a few days until the local prosecutor, with good sense, insisted on an out-of-court settlement and refused to let a little girl face the jury. Instead, the case was put back in the Juvenile Court where it should have been settled in the first place. And eventually, the injured girl's parents received half the cost of their medical expenses, or $20, from the parents of the little girl who had wielded the stick.

It suited Bill Owney and it pleased his paper. Had he succeeded in convincing both sets of parents not to go to court, he would have had no story. And that, he said, would have been all right, too.

What the Polls Show

The attitudes of journalists toward the news, and the manner in which they deal with it, inevitably have an effect on the public's assessment of the news media. In the 1980s, a Gallup Poll of 760 persons showed that journalists maintain a respectable credibility rating among professionals, with the clergy standing first among the respondents with 71 percent, followed by physicians, 58 percent; police, 52 percent; journalists, 38 percent; businesspeople, 31 percent; members of Congress, 16 percent, and advertising executives, 12 percent.

Credibility of the News Media   However, in the same Gallup Poll, 61 percent of respondents said they believed "very little or only some" of the news, 33 percent agreed that most news reports are valid and only 5 percent believed everything they read or heard in the news media.

Another Gallup Poll, taken a few months earlier, showed that of 1,524 respondents 37 percent believed that the current curbs on the press in the United States are not strict enough, 32 percent believed the restrictions were "about right" and only 17 percent said they were too strict, the rest having no opinion. The restrictions included libel laws, findings of contempt of court and regulations having to do with police news and court coverage.

On accuracy in the news media, the same number of respondents were polled and 34 percent concluded that facts were inaccurately reported, 47 percent believed facts were accurately presented and 19 percent gave no answer.

It may be seen, therefore, that there is a dichotomy in the public attitude toward the news media as a whole and a sharp split between belief and nonbelief, credibility and lack of credibility. The First Amendment protection of the press, moreover, does depend on public support and, if that support should vanish, the press will be in deep trouble.

The Public and the First Amendment   It is not at all reassuring, in consequence, that the Gallup Poll of 1,524 respondents showed that only 24 percent were able to name correctly what the First Amendment is or what it deals with; among the college-educated, only 42 percent were able to do so.

The ethics of journalists and their moral position, therefore, are not mere theoretical matters. They are very important in helping to form public judgments of the profession and maintaining public confidence in the news media themselves. If either should ever disappear, then the First Amendment will go down with it.

"Jimmy's World" and the Journalists' World

On September 28, 1980, the *Washington Post* published a story under the byline of Janet Cooke with this headline:

Jimmy's World:
8-Year-Old Heroin Addict Lives For a Fix

This is how the story began:

> Jimmy is 8 years old and a third-generation heroin addict, a precocious little boy with sandy hair, velvety brown eyes and needle marks freckling the baby-smooth skin of his thin brown arms.
>
> He nestles in a large, beige reclining chair in the living room of his comfortably furnished home in southeast Washington. There is an almost cherubic expression on his small, round face as he talks about life—clothes, money, the Baltimore Orioles and heroin. He has been an addict since the age of 5.
>
> His hands are clasped behind his head, fancy running shoes adorn his feet and a striped Izod T-shirt hangs over his thin frame. "Bad, ain't it," he boasts to a reporter visiting recently. "I got me six of these."
>
> Jimmy's world is a world of hard drugs, fast money and the good life he believes both can bring. Every day, junkies casually buy heroin from Ron, his mother's live-in lover, in the dining room of Jimmy's home. They "cook" it in the kitchen

> and "fire up" in the bedrooms. And every day, Ron or some-
> body else fires up Jimmy, plunging a needle into his bony
> arm, sending the fourth grader into a hypnotic nod. . . .

The story continued in this manner for more than two columns. It was accompanied by a blood-curdling pen-and-ink sketch of a tiny black boy wincing in pain
as a big hand grasps one thin arm and another hand plunges a hypodermic needle
into a vein.

What Price Pulitzer Prize?   The story won a Pulitzer Prize, but the
celebration was short-lived at the *Washington Post*. Due to discrepancies in her published biography, Janet Cooke underwent night-long questioning by her editors and
finally confessed that there was no Jimmy and that the story had been invented.

"Jimmy's World" shook up the world of the journalist as no other story has
since the *New York Sun*'s "moon hoax" in the early 19th century. It raised serious
questions about journalistic ethics and journalistic morality that no one has
answered to the satisfaction of the profession. It also demonstrated to what lengths
young people can be driven by striving for a major journalism award.

The *Washington Post*'s Reaction   The reaction of the *Washington*
Post was to publish an 18,000-word analysis of what happened and why it happened
by William Green, the paper's ombudsman, who since has returned to his academic
post. Green began his account:

> "Jimmy" never existed, but his story convulsed the city and humiliated the
> Washington Post — proud house of Watergate investigation.
>
> The story was a lie and, after all its celebrated achievements, the Post owes its
> readers an accounting of its spectacular failure.
>
> How did it all happen? Why?
>
> This account was prepared from 47 interviews, primarily with members of the
> Post's staff. It was written by the Post's ombudsman, who is the fifth person to occupy
> the position of reader representative since it was created by the newspaper in 1970.
>
> This is essentially a story of the failure of a system that, in another industry,
> might be called "quality control." On newspapers, it is called editing.
>
> The fabrication of Janet Cooke's story eluded all of the Post's filters that are set
> up to challenge every detail in every news story the paper publishes. From the time
> she applied for a job, questions were not asked. Editors abandoned their professional
> skepticism.
>
> This narrative reconstruction suggests that "Jimmy" moved through the cycle
> of news reporting and editing like an alien creature, unimpeded by ordinary security
> devices. This account has available the marvelous tool called hindsight.
>
> It is also the story of a young and talented reporter, flaming with ambition,
> who showed irresistible promise of achievement. The Post accelerated her success,
> and may thereby have hastened her failure. . . . For Cooke, it was a personal tragedy.
> For the Post, it was inexcusable. . . .

How the Story Got By   It is worth summarizing, from the Green
account, how the Cooke story got by and actually won a prize, with the deflation of
all concerned when it blew up. These are the signposts along the way:

- Nobody at the *Post* asked Janet Cooke to identify "Jimmy" and his family for the confidential information of the editors and nobody even asked for "Jimmy's" address while she was on assignment.
- Nobody questioned the story when it was written or suggested the boy should be given help. Bob Woodward of Watergate fame, the top editor for metropolitan affairs, called it a "great piece." Ben Bradlee, the executive editor, said it was a "helluva job."
- Cooke was told, before the story ran, that it would be controversial, that she might be called before a judge to give her source and identify the boy and that she could back out and kill the story. She agreed it should be run.
- After the story was published, the mayor and police chief of Washington, D.C., launched a mammoth investigation to locate "Jimmy." They didn't find him and denied his existence.
- The *Post* sent a staff member, Courtland Milloy, with Janet Cooke to the neighborhood where "Jimmy" supposedly lived and they drove around for seven hours without result. Milloy came back, openly skeptical. But the *Post*'s publisher, Don Graham, wrote Janet Cooke a note of congratulations.
- Others at the *Post* began voicing doubts, among them her immediate editor, Milton Coleman. But the *Post* decided to submit the story for the Pulitzer Prize.
- In the Pulitzer proceedings, the story didn't win the jury verdict in the news-reporting category in which it was entered. But when the Pulitzer Prize Board met, the board itself shifted the story from the news category to the feature category and then voted it the feature-writing prize. One or two board members, reportedly, voiced doubts about the story, but the majority did not.
- When the prizes were announced, the AP correspondent in Toledo, Michael Holmes, was notified by the *Toledo Blade* that the AP's biographical information on Cooke did not check with the *Blade*'s. The AP had simply picked up the *Washington Post*'s biography, forwarded with her entry, and made public at Columbia University by the Pulitzer Board. Cooke had prepared it. It showed she had a master's degree from the University of Toledo. A check showed she had, indeed, graduated from the university but had no master's degree. When Holmes reported that to his New York office, the AP checked Cooke's claim to a degree from Vassar and study at the Sorbonne in Paris. Result: She had no degree from Vassar. As for her claim to have studied at the Sorbonne, she couldn't even speak decent French.

The *Post* finally decided to question Cooke. First she admitted she had made up part of her background. Then, after an all-night session, she signed this statement:

"Jimmy's World" was in essence a fabrication. I never encountered or interviewed an 8-year-old heroin addict. The Sept. 28, 1980 article in the Washington Post was a serious misrepresentation which I deeply regret. I apologize to my newspaper, my profession, the Pulitzer Board and all seekers of the truth. Today, in facing up to the truth, I have submitted my resignation. *Janet Cooke.*

Rocking the Journalists' World Many a newspaper throughout the land and all TV news programs featured the Cooke story when it broke with the *Post*'s announcement that "Jimmy's World" was a fake. For more than a year, every meeting of journalists argued over the case, philosophized over it and deplored it. More candid critics of the press had some sarcastic observations about journalistic ethics.

As a result of the Cooke hoax, today's journalists taken as a whole have the deepest concern about their own reputations and their own integrity. It is perhaps the paramount reason for the most general criticism of the profession: its defensiveness and its resentment of outside inquiries into journalistic conduct and journalistic morals. There is no doubt that such criticism persists. A recent *Washington Post* poll concluded that the public is "sharply critical" of the national press, mainly because of just such considerations.

Ethics, in short, is not just a sometime thing. There may be no enforceable rules of professional conduct for journalists, but every ethical violation that comes to public attention receives a stiff share of public censure. If enough of that piles up, Congress one day will take action and it will not be pleasant.

The Aftermath of "Jimmy's World" It would be heartening to point out that the overkill coverage of the nine-year-old bank robber in New York and the exposé of the mythical eight-year-old heroin addict in Washington had immediately beneficial results, but it would not be true.

Only a few weeks after the disclosure that "Jimmy" didn't exist, the *New York Daily News* sadly announced the forced resignation of one of its columnists after a British newspaper accused him of faking a story about a shootout between British troops and a youth gang in Belfast.

Within a month, under pressure of a large libel suit, the *Toronto Sun* announced one of its reporters had been fired and another was forced to resign after they admitted having no documentation for charges that a high government official had made stock profits by using inside government information.

The *New York Times*'s Hoax On February 22, 1982, the *New York Times* admitted in a Page 1 story that a 24-year-old American freelance writer had confessed that he had made up an article published in the paper's Sunday magazine about a trip he took to live with the Khmer Rouge guerrillas in Cambodia. Moreover, the writer confessed that he had concocted the article without ever leaving Spain, where he was living at the time. In an editorial headed "A Lie in the *Times*," Executive Editor A. M. Rosenthal said, "We do not feel that the fact that the writer was a liar and a hoaxer removes our responsibility. It is our job to uncover any falsehood or errors. . . . I regret this whole sad episode and the lapse in our procedures that made it possible."

It may be true, as many in journalism contend, that these were isolated incidents. But when the whole tab was added up, it amounted to a substantial amount of doubt that too many sharp practices still exist in journalism and something had better be done about it beyond passing resolutions of regret.

These are some of the results:

- Editors are more vigilant now about unsourced stories and are quicker to demand proof from reporters, including names, date and places where interviews took place, plus better documentation of charges.
- More newspapers are checking statements made in their newspapers. John R. Har-

rison, president of the New York Times Group, a chain of small newspapers, says each member newspaper checks the quotes in at least two stories every week and publishes the results on office bulletin boards. It may arouse a certain amount of resentment among reporters whose accuracy is questioned, but Harrison believes the check is necessary. It is no more than leading magazines have been doing for a long time.

- More efforts are being made to develop a set of ethical standards in the profession that will be broadly acceptable, beyond those published by the American Society of Newspaper Editors and other organizations. But many editors still believe codes are useless.
- The existing ombudsmen on about a score of American newspapers are receiving more attention from editors, but there is little indication that such a post ever will be universally adopted or even that it will increase in popularity.
- The National News Council, as an independent and privately funded body looking into the conduct of the news media, has received more attention but its support in the profession remains spotty.
- The Pulitzer Prize Board decided to abandon its practice of awarding a dozen newspaper prizes and seven nonnewspaper prizes in a one-day meeting, to avoid the appearance of undue haste. Instead, the 15-member board voted to hold two-day sessions to go over the jury reports in all categories. In addition, the board agreed to consult the respective juries before moving an exhibit from one category to another if a prize was likely to result from the exchange. It was also the sense of the board that there would be greater consultation with the juries on other matters, in particular on reversing jury verdicts.
- The National News Council got into the Pulitzer act by criticizing an award to Teresa Carpenter, a freelance writer for the *Village Voice*, a New York weekly, who was given the prize the *Washington Post* returned. However, the Pulitzer Board let the Carpenter award stand, holding that the council's criticism applied to an article about a murder that had not been the principal award-winning work.

Despite these attempts to make sure that nothing like the Cooke case ever happened again, there was a distinct air of unease during the 1980s among American journalists in general and among students and other newcomers to the profession. As one student put it in an ethics class at the University of Florida, "How do we know how much faking is actually going on and how can it be stopped?" It was a disturbing question and there were no easy answers.

One thing was certain: Editors aren't likely for some time to accept any story on faith, and they are even less likely to yield their authority over the run of the news to an impetuous and demanding reporter.

Ethics: An Overview

J. Montgomery Curtis, the former director of the American Press Institute, believes that ethical considerations in journalism have greatly expanded in recent years. This is his overview of the current position:

Invasions of Privacy. Is it ethical for news reporters to invade private homes, the private grounds, and indeed the private presences of innocent people caught in highly emotional situations? I think not. We continue to alienate a considerable part of the public by picturing innocent people in prose and photographs at moments when they should be allowed to grieve in private.

TV Incursions into Privacy. If anything, television is much worse than the print press in invading privacy. But what the TV people do with their microphones and cameras inevitably rubs off on the print press.

Objectionable Advertising. Is it ethical to print advertising for pornographic, X-rated movies? For nude theaters? For massage parlors that are used for prostitution? I don't believe it is. I think the press has a responsibility to refuse such advertising.

Unbalanced Reporting. Occasionally, young reporters with little sense and editors with even less sense print articles that depict certain unethical, immoral and certainly illegal practices in a highly favorable light. Two examples: Not long ago, a famous Sunday newspaper magazine came out with a cover showing two attractive youngsters, a boy and a girl, sniffing cocaine through straws. The article inside the magazine quoted several people by position, not by name, [a Congressman, a banker, a manufacturer, an educator], to the general effect that cocaine had benefited them through daily usage. To me, such an article is totally unethical. The same paper a few years ago used an article about a Miami Beach call girl who was supposed to have made between $35,000 and $40,000 a year. It was not the type of thing to recommend to the impressionable young girls who might be reading the paper. This also ranks as totally unethical, in my view.

No Gifts, No Freebees   Curtis has always advocated a strict policy for newspapers against the acceptance of gifts and other freebies by staff members. He recalls how Bill Terry, while managing the New York Giants years ago, informed the New York baseball writers who were traveling with the team that they had no right to criticize the players because the Giants paid travel expenses for nearly all of them. The exceptions were the *New York Times* and the *New York Daily News.* Curtis went on:

> When I started work on the *Buffalo Evening News*, I was surprised that the paper accepted no free tickets for movies, theaters, sporting events or anything else. We paid our own way. The one newspaper that accepted no freebies of any kind, ours, is still in business today and quite healthy. Two rivals merged and two others went out of business.
>
> The truth is that if a newspaper engages in unethical practices, the word soon gets around. People quickly know whether editors and reporters are on the take or not. This includes such things as excessive Christmas gifts from news sources, free meals for restaurant reporters, free trips to distant tourist centers and hotels and so on. And when word gets around, people lose respect for the paper.

The Obligations of Journalists

There is general agreement within the profession on the basic obligations of journalists. Briefly stated, they are as follows:

- To cover the news fairly, thoroughly and accurately
- To present the news truthfully
- To explain what the news means
- To protect sources wherever necessary
- To respect confidences if they are freely offered and willingly accepted
- To act at all times in the public interest and to be influenced by no other consideration
- To respect the law and the rights of privacy of people in the news and to deal with them with forthrightness and honesty
- To acknowledge error when it occurs and to make suitable corrections as quickly as possible.

Like all procedures, these can be abused or neglected by complacent reporters or sources given to perverting the truth or entirely withholding it. This does not make the measures any less necessary. Beginning reporters soon learn that they are judged by their colleagues, their editors and their sources on how well they observe these ground rules, how effectively they use them and how faithfully they observe them. There is, in journalism as in life itself, something more important than getting the big story and zinging the opposition. That is the preservation of a decent respect for the good of the profession in general and for one's own self in particular.

It is so easy to state these high moral principles but sometimes, when reporters are on the job, it is difficult to decide where the line should be drawn between what is permissible in news-gathering and what is entirely unethical. And there aren't any philosophical calipers to measure the difference.

When Reporters Are in Danger A reporter for a major metropolitan newspaper, assigned to investigate the Mafia, once asked his editors with a trace of sarcasm: "Do you really expect me to identify myself as a reporter for this newspaper wherever I go and explain what I am doing and why I am doing it?"

The editors, who had been properly concerned about widespread reports in the city of the infiltration of the Mafia into legitimate business, also wanted to safeguard the integrity of the newspaper and didn't like the idea of having the reporter masquerade as a hoodlum. What finally happened was that the reporter went on the assignment with permission simply not to identify himself unless he blundered into a confrontation and was asked who he was, what he was doing and why he was doing it.

That was one Mafia investigation that didn't get very far. There aren't many Sunday School characters in the underworld, and reporters, like informers, can run into rough treatment.

Several reporters for the *Detroit Free Press* had an even more difficult and dangerous problem. While they were investigating Michigan's mental hygiene system, they came across information suggesting that a number of mental patients — including four killers — were at large and there was no indication that police were searching for them.

This was a ticklish matter. Was it really the business of reporters to do police work? And yet if they didn't find the apparently missing persons, how could they prove the truth of their story?

After a lot of soul-searching, a top-level editorial decision was reached to try to locate 10 of the patients involved. The reporters, of necessity, had to adopt various guises to get information. But they determined in advance not to use quotes obtained from innocent persons while posing as someone other than a reporter. And they worried over possible invasion of privacy in the cases of social workers they interviewed and the ethics of obtaining confidential records in such circumstances.

In the end, all worked out well. Seven of the 10 persons on the *Free Press* list were located by the reporters, including the four killers. The deficiencies of the state's mental hygiene system were exposed. And widespread reforms were instituted.

When Is Deceit Justified? The *Free Press* has exposed abortion clinics, a surgery mill, discrimination against blacks by real estate agents and quack medicines by permitting reporters to assume disguises. While Neil Shine was the paper's managing editor, he defended the practice, saying,

> Our responsibility is to get information and if we can do it legally, we'll do it. I wouldn't let a reporter say he's a policeman. That's illegal. But I don't draw many lines. When our young medical writer heard about a guy selling phony arthritis medicine, she didn't go up to him and say, "Hi, I'm the medical writer from the *Detroit Free Press*. Are you a charlatan?"

The reporter pretended to have arthritis, bought $200 worth of medicine from the quack, then exposed him.

But Gary C. Schuster, Washington bureau chief for the *Detroit News*, got into trouble when he posed as a Michigan congressman so he could expose lax security at the signing of the Israeli-Egyptian peace treaty on the White House lawn. After he wrote his story next day under the flaring *News* headline, "Crashing a Moment in History," the Standing Committee of Correspondents in Congress rebuked him.

The *Wall Street Journal* isn't exactly a gung-ho paper bent on sensation, but it did publish a story about company–union conflicts by Beth Nissen, a young reporter, after she had worked for three weeks on the assembly line at the Texas Instruments plant in Austin. Laurence O'Donnell, managing editor of the *Journal* at the time, explained, "There was no other way of getting the story . . . and the information was worth getting."

This, too, was the justification for two other investigations by major papers, the *Los Angeles Times* and the *Chicago Sun-Times*. The Los Angeles paper ran a piece about psychiatric care at Metropolitan State Hospital, based on the two weeks a woman reporter worked there posing as a graduate student in psychology. The *Chicago Sun-Times*'s exposé was the celebrated Mirage Bar operation, which was run by reporters and served to disclose widescale bribery among Chicago officialdom.

"We couldn't have gotten the information any other way," said James Hoge, then the editor-in-chief. He conceded such campaigns should be conducted "with extreme caution and selectivity and only when certain standards are applied."

The *New York Times* is one of the relatively few major newspapers that refuse to let their reporters adopt disguises. Instead of being praised, a *Times* reporter was censured for putting on mechanics' overalls to try to interview the wife of a Russian defector while she was being detained in an airplane.

"Reporters should not masquerade," said the executive editor, A. M. Rosenthal. And yet when the *Times* believed it to be in the public interest, it printed top-secret government papers that had been stolen and delivered to a *Times* reporter.

What is ethical for some, quite clearly, depends on how big the story is, how strongly the editors feel about it, how effective the reporters are and the urgency of the public issue that is involved. The problem of whether reporters should disguise themselves seldom arises on a small city daily or weekly because somebody in town would almost certainly recognize the reporter and ask, "Hey, Joe, what're you doing working in a garage? I thought you wuz a reporter."

To quote an old-time editor, Casey Jones:

"Newspapermen sitting around talking about ethics are like women discussing their virginity. If you've got it, you've got it. And if you've lost it, that's your fault and you ain't gonna get it back."

Phonies, Freebees and Payoffs

There are three areas, however, in which an ethical line can be clearly drawn between what is right and what is wrong. These are, not necessarily in the order of importance, the phony story and the phony quote or "composite person"; the acceptance of free tickets, free trips, free vacations and free clothes, and an agreement, sometimes unspoken, that if a certain story is done in a certain way the reporter will never have cause to regret it.

Whatever It's Called, It's Still Phony   There have been reporters who made up quotes and even faked whole interviews and didn't seem to think anything was wrong about it. One woman, a reporter at a famous court trial, was sent to interview the defendant when the lights went out in the cell block where he had been held overnight. She returned with a complete interview in about 15 minutes, fast work in any league. The editor meanwhile had learned from a wire service that the defendant had slept through the entire ruckus.

"How come you got an interview when the AP says the guy slept through it all?" the editor asked.

The reporter shrugged. "That's what he would have said if he'd been awake."

Sometimes this same rationale is clothed in high-sounding phrases and noble rhetoric. For example, Ray Mungo, a figure in the antiwar movement of the 1960s, argues that facts are less important than truth and illustrates his point with an article in a Boston publication, *Avatar*, called "Report from Vietnam, by Alexander Sorenson." This purports to be an eyewitness account of torture in a Vietnamese village during the Vietnam War. However, Mungo says the report is fiction and Sorenson doesn't exist, but he contends:

> . . . Because it has happened in man's history, and because we know we are responsible for its happening, and because the story is unvarnished and plain and human, we know it's true, truer than any facts you pick up from the *New Republic*.

Based on that premise, the argument could also be made that Janet Cooke's story about "Jimmy's World" was the truth because somewhere, somehow, children are introduced to illicit drugs; only, she wasn't able to find such a child, Jimmy or anybody else. At one point, during her interrogation at the *Washington Post*, she called "Jimmy" a "composite."

These "composite" figures, a favorite device sometimes when writers can't find quite the type of person they want to illustrate a particular story, can cause more trouble than they are worth. Gail Sheehy's "Redpants," a prostitute about whom she wrote in *New York* magazine, was a "composite," only her editor eliminated that fundamental point from her article. Thus "Redpants" was made to appear to be a real person when, actually, she didn't exist.

The main point cannot be mistaken: Either an interview is real and honest and true or it is not. Either people in the news are real or they are not. You can't make things up to prove a point unless you are writing something clearly labeled fiction.

The Role of Freebees Automobile, film and flour companies and travel organizations have sponsored media events for many years to attract large numbers of journalists. Countries like South Africa have offered editors and reporters all-expenses-paid trips, hoping for favorable notice in their publications. Assorted companies with something to sell offer everything from cocktail parties to moonlight cruises, to cause the assembled journalists to think well of them.

In New York City, it would be possible for a reporter to live entirely on such largesse if his news organization would let him do it. But most responsible news organizations these days try to keep freebees for their staffs to a minimum, and some bar them entirely. The basic premise is that you don't get something for nothing in the news business or anywhere else. The acceptance of a favor implies that something of value will be given in return. And in the current state of journalism in the United States, that is more than most editors can tolerate.

Some reporters argue that it's necessary for them to have a drink with a news source once in a while, or to go to dinner with an influential person. That may well be true. But the cocktail-and-dinner circuit can be overworked and usually is, which is why it isn't very popular in the higher reaches of journalism. The more affluent papers have a policy of buying everything from theater tickets for their critics to trips for their travel writers; the smaller and less affluent ones have a choice of appearing to be bought or keeping their reporters at home.

For the beginning reporter, or the reporter who is new to a news organization, the only recourse is to ask what the policy on freebees is and then take care to observe it. This is one of the touchiest subjects in journalism, and for good reason. No news organization can afford to have staff members living high at someone else's expense. The rule is to avoid even the appearance of impropriety.

Relations with News Sources Experienced reporters know that they must keep a decent distance between themselves and even the best of their news sources. If it becomes known that a certain reporter is too chummy with influential Republicans, for example, opposing Democrats quite rightly may have grounds for suspicion. If a business reporter is seen too often with a powerful company president or board chairman, and then writes favorably about the firm's newly issued stock, others in the business community are bound to draw unfavorable inferences. If a film reviewer pays more than occasional visits to the home of a film star, and enthusiastically plugs the star's pictures, that also becomes the subject of comment and gossip.

Some years ago, a first-rate woman reporter for a good newspaper in a large Eastern city was assigned to the local political beat and became friendly with an influential political leader. She accepted lunch and dinner dates with him, traveled with him on assignment sometimes and even accepted a fur coat from him. Eventually, they had an affair that ended when the reporter left the paper and accepted a post with another paper in another city. She appeared to be doing well in her new job until the influential politician who had been her lover was indicted on fraud charges and the prosecution was determined to call her as a witness in the case. Her former paper, alerted that the story was about to break in the opposition paper in town, ran the whole story in depth, with the result that the woman lost her job on the out-of-town paper.

Feminists argued that a male reporter would never have been punished in a similar situation, had he become involved with a female news source. But it was pretty difficult to establish a case of discrimination in this instance.

The Standards Are Strict After the arrest of Kathy Boudin, caught while fleeing from the scene of a botched Brinks armored car robbery in which two policemen and a guard were killed, it was learned that she had been living in a New York City apartment under the name of Lynn Adams with a reporter for the *Stamford* (Connecticut) *Advocate* as her roommate. Boudin, a fugitive from justice for more than 10 years, told her roommate that she was working as a waitress to support her year-old son.

The reporter in turn informed her employers at the *Advocate*, a Times-Mirror group newspaper, that she had not known of Lynn Adams's real identity, but she also was too distraught, she said, to write anything about her erstwhile roommate. After a month-long investigation by the *Advocate*, which found nothing to corroborate or refute the reporter's story, she was discharged.

Kenneth H. Brief, executive editor of Connecticut Newspapers, controlling the *Advocate*, contended that there is "an inherent clash between an individual's constitutional rights and a reporter's responsibilities." He went on:

> By the nature of the job, a reporter is a reporter all the time. . . . If a reporter has a relationship with somebody who has done something unethical or illegal, what is the reporter's responsibility? The more the issue is addressed, the healthier it will be for the profession.

He contended the information the paper had published about the reporter and Boudin had not been "totally accurate" but did not specify what fault, if any, had been committed by the reporter. It was a harsh judgment, but not many editors said they would have acted differently under the circumstances.

Is Sports Reporting a Special Case? Younger sports writers who are fortunate enough to be assigned to travel with a professional team have been known to contend that they must have a closer relationship with sports figures than cityside reporters and their sources. This, sports reporters argue, is vitally necessary because they so often must develop feature pieces for newspapers and magazines after television has covered a game in its entirety.

Most editors are willing to grant that there is something to the argument, but not many sympathize with it. Professional athletes, by reason of their earning power, have become very large figures in the news and it is unlikely that any of them will single out particular reporters and bestow all their favors on them. Sports, like all other kinds of coverage, calls for something more than a few quick quotes, a smile and a pat on the back for a young reporter. And reporters cannot feel very comfortable if they have close ties to a few favored athletes on one team. The field is far too large for that kind of intimacy.

This is, fundamentally, the disadvantage of having the professional clubs pay for the salaries and upkeep of the TV sports broadcasters who cover the team's home games. No matter how broadcast journalists may protest that they are still independent figures and can call 'em as they see 'em, not many fans are likely to believe them. Too many cameras have been shunted away from too many embarrassing situations on the field, where that kind of reporting relationship exists, for broadcasters to establish a forthright claim of journalistic independence.

When to Omit News Detail

A country editor in Tennessee likes to tell the story of a woman, apparently some six or seven months pregnant, who came into his office one day and asked him not to publish news of her marriage, which had taken place the day before. It didn't take long for the editor to make up his mind. He agreed not to publish the news of the marriage. In a small town, where people would know the story anyway, he reasoned that it would serve no good purpose to publicize the marriage and thereby add to the woman's pain and embarrassment.

Withholding Names in the News Most news organizations don't use the names of rape victims or the addresses of people who have received threats or are otherwise endangered.

Now and then, a case develops that tests editors' judgments in a different way. One was the plight of a retarded teenager whose parents wanted to sterilize her because she could not understand the consequences of sexual relations and, the parents said, she could not have cared for a child if she had had one.

The news broke when the parents asked for a private hearing and a New Jersey court granted their request. Because the judge's decision was made in open court, UPI carried the names of the parents and their retarded daughter. H. L. Stevenson, the editor-in-chief, pointed out that, even if the name had been withheld, there would have been requests from other clients to disclose it. UPI's senior news editors, in fact, were about evenly split on whether to use the name or withhold it.

A Code of Conduct for Journalists

American journalists have always been wary of codes of conduct. While they may generally agree with the principles of such codes, they have invariably raised the possibility that government in some fashion will try to enforce them. That, of course, would lead directly to the licensing of journalists and the end of the free press.

Thus, in the following code that bears on the standards of journalists, it should be borne in mind that no enforcement is possible.

The ASNE Statement

The following Statement of Principles was adopted in 1975 by the American Society of Newspaper Editors to replace its 52-year-old Code of Ethics or Canons of Journalism:

PREAMBLE

The First Amendment, protecting freedom of expression from abridgment by any law, guarantees to the people through their press a constitutional right, and thereby places on newspaper people a particular responsibility.

Thus journalism demands of its practitioners not only industry and knowledge but also the pursuit of a standard of integrity proportionate to the journalist's singular obligation.

To this end the American Society of Newspaper Editors sets forth this Statement of Principles as a standard encouraging the highest ethical and professional performance.

ARTICLE I. Responsibility

The primary purpose of gathering and distributing news and opinion is to serve the general welfare by informing the people and enabling them to make judgments on the issues of the time. Newspapermen and women who abuse the power of their professional role for selfish motives or unworthy purposes are faithless to that public trust.

The American press was made free not just to inform or just to serve as a forum for debate but also to bring an independent scrutiny to bear on the forces of power in the society, including the conduct of official power at all levels of government.

ARTICLE II. Freedom of the Press

Freedom of the press belongs to the people. It must be defended against encroachment or assault from any quarter, public or private.

Journalists must be constantly alert to see that the public's business is conducted in public. They must be vigilant against all who would exploit the press for selfish purposes.

ARTICLE III. Independence

Journalists must avoid impropriety and the appearance of impropriety as well as any conflict of interest or the appearance of conflict. They should neither accept anything nor pursue any activity that might compromise or seem to compromise their integrity.

ARTICLE IV. Truth and Accuracy

Good faith with the reader is the foundation of good journalism. Every effort must be made to assure that the news content is accurate, free from bias and in context and that all sides are presented fairly. Editorials, analytical articles and commentary should be held to the same standards of accuracy with respect to facts as news reports.

Significant errors of fact, as well as errors of omission, should be corrected promptly and prominently.

ARTICLE V. Impartiality

To be impartial does not require the press to be unquestioning or to refrain from editorial expression. Sound practice, however, demands a clear distinction for the reader between news reports and opinion. Articles that contain opinion or personal interpretation should be clearly identified.

ARTICLE VI. Fair Play

Journalists should respect the rights of people involved in the news, observe the common standards of decency and stand accountable to the public for the fairness and accuracy of their news reports.

Persons publicly accused should be given the earliest opportunity to respond.

Pledges of confidentiality to news sources must be honored at all costs, and therefore should not be given lightly. Unless there is clear and pressing need to maintain confidences, sources of information should be identified.

These principles are intended to preserve, protect and strengthen the bond of trust and respect between American journalists and the American people, a bond that is essential to sustain the grant of freedom entrusted to both by the nation's founders.

• Short Takes

These are the principal ethical considerations that a newcomer to journalism should remember on initial reporting assignments:

- Play it straight. Don't try any tricks. Ask all the necessary questions and write a factual story about a sensitive issue straight down the middle.
- Protect your sources wherever necessary and respect confidences that are freely offered.
- Respect the law and the rights of privacy of people in the news.
- The instructions given to you by your editor or news director and your own loyalty to the public interest should be the only considerations that will influence you on assignment.
- When in doubt, always ask the editor who gave you the assignment to clarify any problem that arises.
- Do not represent yourself to be anything other than a reporter unless you have specific instructions from your news organization.
- Beware of accepting free trips, free tickets, free dinners or other freebees in connection with an assignment; even when you are not on duty, you should never accept any gift that will have the appearance of impropriety.
- Remember that a "composite figure" in a story is a made-up figure with mythical characteristics. The "composite figure"—if used in a news story—is

bound to create misunderstanding, and reporters should avoid creating this type of journalistic monster.

- All reporters should keep a decent distance between themselves and even the best of news sources. It does not pay to be too chummy with people who are in a position to influence the shaping of the news.
- If there is a strong reason to withhold a name or an address in connection with a news break, such as a kidnapping or a terrorist who is holding hostages, clear the position you want to take with the editor in charge and make sure that you both have the same understanding about what should be done.
- When it becomes necessary to work with law enforcement authorities, you should ask for guidelines from your news organization on how much cooperation is to be expected of you. Remember that newspeople should not be under the control of any source outside their own news organization.
- Always try to avoid becoming a part of the news. It is not your job to create news. Your assignment is to cover it, write or photograph it and explain it.
- Always try to go in the front door and don't look for short cuts.
- The same ethical considerations apply to all journalists.

4

Interpretive Journalism

CHAPTER 23

Attributing and Interpreting the News

There are circumstances under which reporters keep their own counsel about what is disclosed to them. If they didn't, there would be no investigative reporting worthy of the name and the whole structure of journalistic practice would be weakened.

Yet few beginning reporters and even fewer news sources have a precise understanding of the ground rules for giving and receiving information. This is because definitions vary from one person to another and from one circumstance to another. It shouldn't be that way, but it is.

Uses and Misuses of Attribution

Experienced reporters know that a certain number of sources who talk freely about a sensitive story are likely to cry "Foul!" when the story is published or used on the air. In most cases, the reaction is purely defensive. The sources, for one reason or another, feel compelled to deny the information they gave to the reporter in whole or in part, and sometimes particularly embarrassed sources deny they even talked with the reporter.

Therefore, on almost any controversial story, reporters actually anticipate that denials will be made once the news breaks and conduct themselves accordingly.

They know they must have the most convincing proof that they met their sources, talked with them and accurately recorded what was said.

Reporters' Defenses The best defense, naturally, is a tape-recorded playback of the entire conversation. Photographs of the source talking with the reporter help, too. Sometimes, not having access either to a camera or a tape recorder, a reporter will ask a source to sign and date a notebook beside the record of the conversation. In interviews that conceivably could wind up as part of a court record, reporters try by one device or another to work in pairs so that there will be a witness to what was said.

But nobody in journalism should be so naive as to expect that news sources, who are themselves open to criticism, will stand up for a reporter if they find themselves in a controversial position once the story is made known. When sources turn on reporters, there is always an implication that the news was obtained through journalistic trickery. Often the charge is made directly. And when that happens, the best reporters are the ones who have proof ready at hand to show that the accusation is completely untrue.

The Almost Perfect Defense When William Greider of the *Washington Post* began discussing the federal budget with David Stockman, the director of the Office of Management and Budget at the time, a tape recorder was used by agreement. Thus, when Greider wrote an article about his conversations for the *Atlantic* magazine and used quotations that were particularly embarrassing, Stockman couldn't challenge them. They were recorded on tape. The best Stockman could do was to argue that he hadn't expected to be identified as the source, to which once again reference was made to the tape recorder.

It was an almost perfect defense.

When Sources Stand Up Sometimes sources do come to a reporter's defense, although it doesn't happen often. One of the most spectacular defenses came from Alexander M. Haig Jr. during his tumultuous career as Secretary of State. Jack Anderson had published an item in his column to the general effect that Haig believed a "guerrilla" in the White House was out to get him.

Naturally, the White House promptly denied it. But Haig announced that Anderson's story was correct and even had a State Department spokesman summon the press to receive the information.

The Basics of Attribution

To understand the basics of attribution, it is well worth analyzing the main gradations as they are generally understood by experienced journalists, regardless of where they work and for whom. The following discussion is based on more than 50 years' experience in American journalism and is offered as the view of most professional journalists who are working today.

On the Record   Most American reporters operate on the basic premise that there are certain broad limitations to what is "on the record"—that is, material which can be used by the news media in exactly the form in which it is made available, quotes and all.

One limitation is any specific agreement or understanding made by reporters and their sources to withhold some or all of the news for a valid reason. If there is a matter of principle at stake here, rather than some technical reason, any such limitation should have the approval of the reporter's superiors.

Another limitation, even more important, is the body of law affecting the news media. This includes the law of libel, the law against invasion of privacy and certain broad statutes forbidding the use of certain kinds of news such as atomic secrets and other matters affecting national defense and, in numerous states, the names of juvenile defendants and relief clients.

For Attribution, but Not for Direct Quotation   The initial variant in the rule of putting as much news as possible on the record is to specify that there may be paraphrase, but no direct quotation. Reporters dislike this kind of limitation because direct quotations give authenticity to the news. Yet there are times when they must accept it.

Since American reporters as a whole do not take shorthand, nobody with an important statement of policy is willing to take chances. If an official does not have time to issue the statement in advance, and if no tape recorder is available, then the rule against direct quotation is usually invoked.

For Attribution to a Spokesman   After World War II, spokesmen blossomed in the federal, state and local governments. They cropped up in stories from Congress and the legislatures. When it became evident that the editorial bars were down, and the news media were so eager for news that they would accept even anonymous sources, spokesmen appeared as authorities for news about city halls, boards of education, police headquarters and even street cleaning departments. There were spokesmen for movie stars and gospel singers and football players. And the women's liberation movement had spokespersons.

Reporters could knock a lot of the nonsense out of the use of anonymous spokesmen by refusing to countenance the practice except where there is good reason for it.

Background   Anonymous attribution is the most difficult and confusing practice in American journalism, but at the same time it is one of the most important, for it is the key to the use of a lot of news for which nobody will be the authority. The reporter and the news media must take risks, for the only attribution of so-called background news is "well-informed sources," "official sources," "diplomatic sources," "officials" or no source at all but the reporter's name and the name of his or her organization.

The word "background" is in itself a semantic puzzle. In one sense, when it is used in connection with the writing of a story, background means the historical detail that helps explain some current event. In a reporting sense background means the use of material in a story without any attribution to the source by name or to any nation, state or organization the source may represent. The origin of the term in connection with reporting doubtless may be traced to the introduction of such material by a news source:

"Now, I can't be named as the authority for what I'm about to tell you but I'll give it to you on background."

A variation on this is for a source to remark to a reporter, "This is just background material for your personal use."

It is important for reporters to remember that they need not use background material if they see no real reason to do so. Not all background material, after all, is newsworthy. A lot of it is of trial-balloon character, to be withdrawn if it arouses opposition. Some of it is issued by sources who do not really know what they are talking about. And occasionally somebody tries to put over background material as out-and-out publicity for some cause, idea or person. It is a human peculiarity that editors who will not print a story when it is put on the record will sometimes fall for the same material when it is put out mysteriously for background by a conniving official (and, in a rare case, maybe a conniving reporter).

Background, as a journalistic practice, is as old as print. European foreign offices have used it as long as there have been favored correspondents and favored newspapers. It was adapted for American use during World War II by Washington reporters who generally credit Ernest K. Lindley, of *Newsweek* magazine, with being the first to employ it. Finding that high officials could not talk to him on the record, and being unwilling to talk to them off the record, Lindley persuaded them to give him needed explanations of current and coming events under a pledge that he would not identify them as his sources. Thus, background came to be a half-way house between on the record and off the record.

Officials and Background The background reporting device has spread from Washington into every state in the Union. Few news organizations in the United States today are able to identify all sources of all news because of the growing number of restrictions on use. Therefore, the "informed source" and the "official circle" have moved in as not particularly welcome guests in journalism at all levels.

Reporters and Background Writing in the *New York Times*, James Reston had this to say about background reporting:

> This is a remarkable rule, for it imposes upon the writer what can only be described as a compulsory form of plagiarism. That is to say, the official explains what he has been doing or is about to do or is thinking about doing, on the specific understanding that the writers may publish what he says on their own authority without any attribution to him or his department, or even to "an official source."
>
> The reporters are permitted under these ground rules to say that the government is planning to do these things or thinking about doing them, or if they are inordinately cautious, they can dream up such phrases as "there is one view in the government." But they cannot give any authority for what they are told.

Human nature and human conduct being what they are, it is inevitable that the source of a background story of importance eventually will be disclosed if there is controversy about it.

Reporters do try to protect such sources. The difficulty is that those reporters who are left out of a cozy Washington background dinner, which is given by an official to a favored few, invariably disclose what happened because they are under no pledge of confidence. On the contrary, having been beaten, they are entitled to some slight revenge, and disclosure is one of the best ways they can fight back.

It is the State Department primarily that has developed the backgrounder into a way of journalistic life, although regular backgrounding sessions are part of the routine at the Pentagon, on the Hill during congressional inquiries, at the White House and elsewhere in government.

During the Eisenhower administration, John Foster Dulles fancied himself as a molder of public opinion who could use the press as a weapon against his enemies. Often, he got away with devious tricks. But once, at Newport, Rhode Island, he gave warning anonymously on background that the United States wouldn't stand for an invasion of Taiwan by the Peking government, then went on the record as Secretary of State and was considerably milder for direct quotation. The trouble was that *Time* magazine blew his cover, with embarrassment to all concerned.

To get around this kind of disclosure, Secretary of State Dean Rusk in the succeeding Kennedy administration took to talking quietly to a few selected correspondents on what both referred to as "deep background." This meant that the material was primarily for "guidance," a word that can be variously translated, and that the correspondents pledged they would never—well, hardly ever—disclose that the meeting had taken place. In any event, "deep background" soon became a code word in journalism, like the British "D Notice."*

When Background Backfires It remained for Secretary of State Henry A. Kissinger, in the Nixon and Ford administrations, to make a travesty of background reporting. He posed so often as a "senior official" in briefing reporters on his plane, while on his many foreign ventures, that both sides took it as a joke.

The Dangers Involved This does not mean that reputable journalists can get away wtih dropping all attribution if it is inconvenient, or failing to give a source if they have one and can use it. That way lies trouble, as the following incident shows.

During a fatal uprising at Attica Prison in New York State after a final assault by the State Police, an official of the State Department of Corrections announced that hostages held by the prisoners had been found with their throats cut. Almost every reporter on the job was so convinced of the truth of this statement that it was generally used on radio and television and in the press without attribution and without checking. It would have been bad enough to publicize the views of a panicky state

*The British have a tough Official Secrets Act and, under it, a D (for Defense) Notice, sent to the media, warns that articles on certain subjects may violate the secrets law. Usually, the British press complies and suppresses information. The law carries punitive action.

official; however, it was compounding a palpable error to drop out all attribution and make most of the nation's news organizations the authorities for the hasty assumption.

It was not until two reporters for the *Rochester* (New York) *Times-Union* obtained autopsy reports next day from a reluctant Monroe County medical examiner that the truth was discovered. The reporters, Richard Cooper and John Machacek, disclosed that the autopsies had shown that the slain hostages died after being shot by police bullets (the rioting convicts had no guns). Thus, the whole focus of the story shifted and the investigation proceeded in a more evenhanded manner. For their work that day, Cooper and Machacek received a Pulitzer Prize for Local Reporting.

Off the Record   The trouble with putting something off the record is that, almost always, it will leak if more than two persons know about it.

That, however, is not the way responsible reporters look at off the record material in their day-to-day work. To them, off the record means that the information or quotations or documents cannot be used. It is, in effect, a pledge that a confidence will not be violated. This may sound unbelievably holy and high-minded but it is true. The leaks generally come from an opponent of the source.

Young reporters and others unfamiliar with the ways of journalism invariably ask why anybody would want to tell the media a secret that should not be revealed. As a matter of public policy, such actions are frequently taken. At the highest level of government, presidential movements — and sometimes those of other high officials — are not disclosed to the public even though the media receive broad advance notice of travel plans for purposes of coverage.

The Battle Against Secrecy   The attribution of news is a complicated and sometimes confusing business. The public neither cares about it nor understands it. All the fussing over unnamed sources merely makes well-intentioned people wonder.

And yet, reporters are caught in this trap which they have helped to devise. Accordingly, they learn from experience not to make agreements they cannot keep and clear with their offices if they are involved in a difficult ethical situation. The battle against secrecy is never-ending.

Interpreting the News

Basically, the interpretation of the news adds the factor of judgment to what is called straight news — the unvarnished recital of fact and poll-taking which may or may not represent the truth.

For example, a distinguished speaker may make news with a startling statement, but that does not necessarily mean his statement is correct. Accuracy, as all journalists know, represents something more than putting down quotes in order and getting middle initials straight. The interpretive writer is given the additional responsibility of considering the news in this perspective.

Not everybody on a newspaper or broadcasting station has this privilege. For the beginner, it is something that is generally put out of bounds except when special instructions are given by the editor in charge on a particular story. But on most stories about public affairs, in particular, interpretation is a necessity.

The difference between interpretation and editorialization, broadly, is this:

The interpretive writer explains the news, using suitable attribution to show why the explanation is valid, but stops short of making proposals or urging action on his or her own responsibility.

The editorial writer tells the reader or listener or viewer what should or should not be done about the situation, making it clear that the opinion expressed is that of the news organization.

The following are some of the ways in which interpretation may be legitimately used by the news media:

1. In the print media, interpretation may be written into the main news story or it may be made the subject of an analysis as a separate article. In the electronic media, an interpretive statement may be made during the course of a newscast; or, a separate commentary may follow by an analyst of established reputation.

2. For all media, the invariable rule is to give the news first and then, at an appropriate point, tell what it means. If there are several possible meanings, with no real indication of which may be correct, the fairest procedure is to give the report in precisely that way. In any event, the public must be given the facts on which an interpretation is based so that each individual may determine the soundness of the analysis in the light of the evidence.

3. If an interpretive lead is used on a story to give it meaning, the interpretation must be documented immediately. If the explanation is not complete and convincing, a straight news lead is better with a qualified interpretation interjected later.

4. The interpretive nature of a sidebar should be clearly indicated to the reader at the outset by some such approach as this: "Here is the meaning of the proposed two-cent increase in the state's gasoline tax," or, "This is how the new electric rate will affect your bills." The news, as such, should not be repeated in the sidebar on the assumption that the main story will make the basic facts clear.

5. The writer's byline goes on an interpretive story and serves as the best guarantee that an impartial explanation of events is being given. While it may be necessary at times to use such phrases as "Authorities said," or "Observers believed" or "Informed sources said," the reporter must in all cases have discussed the story with these unnamed authorities, observers, or informed sources. The opposition often can discover, quickly enough, when a reporter's informed sources are imaginary—sometimes with embarrassing consequences.

6. When a story explains itself, it should be told without recourse to interpretive techniques. If a story needs perspective in the form of background dates, or a paragraph about a previous action or decision, it should be given, but this usually does not constitute interpretation.

7. While much of the above may be adapted for use by writers for the electronic media, the main problem of presenting interpretation on radio and television is that relatively few journalists are permitted to do it.

8. In writing for news magazines or Sunday newspaper roundups, the tendency of the journalist often is to overanalyze and overinterpret. Even if readers know the basic facts of a given situation, usually a frail assumption, it is a mistake to ply them with too much opinion when they simply are not interested in it. This is the basic weakness of many an editorial page as well.

Examples of Interpretation

These are some of the ways in which interpretation is used to give meaning to the news:

The Interpretive Lead   In the following, the routine news lead would have been based on a White House briefing for labor leaders. Instead, the reasonably obvious conclusion was drawn:

> WASHINGTON — A proposal to merge the Labor and Commerce Departments into one super-Cabinet post appeared doomed today.
>
> Leaders of the AFL-CIO emerged from a White House briefing on the Administration's pet project without enthusiasm. Without labor's support, an Administration source conceded, the plan could not get through Congress.
>
> While the labor leaders reserved comment for the time being, it was learned that they would fight the program if it ever reached the House and Senate. One leader said, "If agriculture is entitled to a separate department, labor is, too." . . .

The Interpretive Paragraph   Particularly in reports of legal actions, it is not enough to say that a witness testified or was cross-examined. The purpose of the testimony or the cross-examination must be indicated as quickly as possible. One way in which it can be done follows:

> The state hammered away today at a key defense witness in the murder trial of Theron J. Wildener, who is accused of slaying a bank guard during a $100,000 robbery last year.
>
> In an hour-long attack on the testimony of Wildener's girlfriend, Emmaline Lindenhurst, District Attorney Millard Carew sought to shake her story that she and the defendant were riding in a car 40 miles from town at the time the robbery occurred.
>
> Repeatedly, he had Miss Lindenhurst tell her story and tried to trap her into inconsistencies. But the witness, a dark-haired, bespectacled, 29-year-old secretary, calmly answered his questions without a trace of nervousness. . . .

An Analyst's Conclusions   Often, in reporting an election, it is necessary to give conclusions rather than a cumulative total of elected representatives. Thus, the analyst goes beyond the figures at hand in the following lead:

> In a stunning upset, the Republicans appeared today to have wrested control of the Legislature from the Democrats for the first time in 20 years.
>
> While the Democrats still held a nominal advantage in the Senate as of 1 a.m., having elected 36 candidates while the Republicans had 33 seats, they were trailing in

all nine remaining contests. Thus, it appeared probable that the new Senate would consist of 42 Republicans and 36 Democrats.

In the House, the Republican margin was even greater, with 61 sure seats to 48 for the Democrats, and an even split likely on the remaining ten undecided contests. . . .

A Tabular Summary In stories about taxes, budgets, social security, and other matters that vitally affect millions of individuals, a tabular summary is often the simplest and the most effective way of explaining a complicated matter. This is one good method:

WASHINGTON — You'll pay more under the new Social Security Law that goes into effect next month but your retirement benefits will be greater.

The changes were voted at the last session of Congress and signed into law by the President. They affect almost every family in the United States.

Here is a summary, calculated by wage brackets, of what you and your employer will pay under the new law and the net increase: . . .

Fact-Sheet Method When a new program of wide public interest is undertaken, one of the easiest ways to present the factual material in a meaningful way is to draw up what amounts to a fact sheet. Thus, if a state undertakes a legalized lottery for the first time, the data could be presented as follows:

Here is how the state's new lottery will operate when it goes into effect:

Tickets will be priced at $1 each and will be available at state and city offices. There will be three drawings for prizes during the year, but separate tickets must be purchased for each.

The winning ticket in each drawing will be worth $100,000, with $75,000 for second place, $50,000 for third place, $20,000 for fourth place and $5,000 each for the holders of the next 11 tickets.

The lottery will be operated by the State Tax Commission for the benefit of the State Department of Education. . . .

Interpretive Sidebar Many newspapers, and nearly all radio and television stations, go out of their way to label separate interpretive pieces as "News Analysis" because they necessarily involve considerable personal judgment by the writer or commentator. The piece is generally all comment because the news is told separately and in detail.

As interpreting the news has become more popular in the news media, this kind of thinking and writing has become one of the imperatives of modern journalism. Certainly, the story of the complications of domestic and international affairs cannot be made comprehensible without recourse to analysis and interpretation. And not all this work can be left by default to syndicated columnists.

Precautions When interpretive writers describe the conclusions of a general body of opinion, such as "critics of the administration," or "independent-minded political leaders," they had better be sure of their ground and check with administrative critics or other representative figures even if such persons sometimes can't be quoted directly. The more conscientious analysts will call 15 or 20 persons and discuss a particular background issue before doing a piece about it. Those inside journalism soon find out who works and who does not.

It is also apparent that the public is becoming increasingly suspicious of those who hack away at a particular candidate, program or objective under the guise of quoting anonymous "observers" or "critics." The reporting of anonymous opinion does have a place in interpretive journalism, sometimes a very important one, but writers should do everything they can to discourage the impression that they are writing about their own prejudices or enthusiasms.

The dividing line between editorialization and interpretation, in this respect, is very clear. Analysts can and should give a balanced presentation of responsible opinion on important questions, but must not overstep the bounds and become an advocate, openly or covertly. Hortatory journalism is the province of the editorialist. During an election year the focus of public and press interest in government is the political contest. Most actions taken by elected executives, councils or legislatures are reported in the light of their effect on the campaign. But in between, the normal business of government goes on without interruption.

News Before It Happens

So much news is issued and processed before it actually happens that reporters are under a great disadvantage to give life to their copy. It is, after all, impossible to report the colorful details of a political speech or a rocket launching or a parade before they actually occur. Yet innumerable advance stories have to be written so that the course of events may be followed as they unfold. Nobody likes to do this, particularly for the electronic media, where coverage can be immediate as events develop, but there is no choice. The practice of circulating speeches before delivery, and making known other events before they actually occur, gives reporters the responsibility of using or withholding the material.

The Advance   For these reasons the advance has become a basic part of American journalism. It used to be done solely for the benefit of the press, but radio and television have long since dealt themselves in. Now the advance is a general technical problem for all concerned.

In essence, the handling of an advance is based on cooperation between the source and the news media, with reporters acting as go-betweens. If the source specifies that the material should be released at a particular time, the news media either comply with the request or do not accept the advance. The practice of holding a story for release is called an *embargo*.

The handling of an important speech or report illustrates this principle in its simplest form. It is common practice for the embargo to end at 6 p.m. so that the material can appear in all editions of morning newspapers as well as radio and TV newscasts. The embargo directions are always clearly given on the first sheet of the text of advance material.

If the first edition of a morning newspaper hits the street at 7 p.m., it is clear that the text of a speech to be delivered two hours later, or at least a news story about it, will appear under a prominent display. It will also be used by the broadcast media. The manner in which this is justified, both by the source and the editors, is as follows:

The lead will be based on whatever news there is in the speech and it will be written without qualification. But no lower than the second paragraph, it will be noted that the story is based on the release of an advance text with a phrase attributing the news to "a speech prepared for delivery." This qualification usually does not go in the first sentence because the lead then becomes too cumbersome. Here is an example of such an advance lead:

> Governor Williston charged last night that his Republican rival, J. Horton Denfield, intended to increase income taxes in the state if elected.
> In a speech prepared for delivery before the Tonawanda Democratic Club's annual dinner at the Hotel Biltmore, the Democratic Governor warned:
> "My opponent says our state must match income with outgo. He has pledged a balanced budget, but he refuses to specify what economies he will make to achieve it. I submit there is only one way in which he can accomplish his aim, and that is to raise the state income tax."

There would, of course, be a lot more of this based on the advance text. The same material would be used in the radio and TV newscasts so that it would be thoroughly familiar to any reader or listener by the time the speech actually was delivered. It would be the duty of the reporter, after writing the advance or giving in the essential facts to rewrite, to check the actual delivery against the advance text. If no substantial changes were made, the reporter would merely call in or dictate an insert to replace the second paragraph and eliminate all reference to the advance text.

To show that the speech was actually delivered, the sub second paragraph might read:

> The Democratic Governor was interrupted eight times by applause as he spoke at 10 p.m. before the Tonawanda Democratic Club's annual dinner at the Hotel Biltmore. He said:

The third paragraph and all the rest of the material culled from the advance then would be picked up and used as is. There would be no need for change. Occasionally, if there are interpolations in a speech that make some difference in the text, an additional insert will be used. It takes a major shift in emphasis to top an advance that has been used. Changes have to be kept to a minimum.

The growth of television campaigning in presidential and major gubernatorial and local elections has greatly reduced the value of advance speech texts for newspapers. There is little point in using an advance text when it differs materially from what actually is said on the air, as has been the case in recent political campaigns. This and the growth of what is known as the "basic speech," which candidates use over and over again in "whistle-stop" campaigning, have led many newspapers to drop advance texts altogether. Some candidates have been known to order their staffs to prepare any number of advance texts, merely to gain newspaper space, with no actual intention of ever delivering them.

However, there is still considerable value to advances on important government reports that are too complicated to be written on the run, to disclosures of major developments in science and medicine and space technology by both government and private sources. Such an advance gives reporters breathing time to study a story, to consult authorities in the field and to write a decent, well-considered account instead of a slapdash, and probably inaccurate, summary.

The Embargo

There are numerous types of embargoes. The most familiar one, and the easiest to work with, is the automatic release which specifies that material may be used in all editions that appear on the street after a specified time, and all newscasts as well.

Often, however, an embargo may specify that a release is "expected at about" a particular hour for all media. In such cases, the story cannot be scheduled definitely but must be held until it is certain that the speech is about to begin. Customarily, such material is used as soon as notification has been received that the delivery of the speech has begun. This kind of embargo applies to major advances such as the president's State of the Union message, the various governors' messages to their state legislatures and mayors' budget statements to their city councils.

Use of Embargoes   On complicated data, such as federal, state or local budgets or legislative or private programs to which extraordinary news significance is attached, several days may be given to the preparation of the story. On budgets, it is not unusual for public officials to hold a "budget school" for reporters to give them special instruction in detail and permit them to question experts. All material, whether it is printed or given out in the form of interviews or replies to questions, is then embargoed for a particular hour and issued for use by all media.

When an Embargo Is Broken   The universal rule on the breaking of an embargo, either by design or inadvertently, is: "A release that is broken for one is broken for all." The cases of deliberate violations of embargoes on major stories are so rare that each one becomes a *cause celebre.*

At the local and state levels powerful news sources, confronted with violations, have succeeded in holding the mass media to an agreed embargo time, but it is somewhat more difficult to contain the aggressively independent Washington press corps. It seems to be a sound rule, however, to notify a news source that an embargo has been broken and that, in consequence, rival reporters no longer feel themselves bound.

Changes in Advances

Sometimes, even when an embargo is observed in good faith, circumstances beyond anyone's control create such changes in the text that the advance lead is a false statement. There have been instances when speakers dropped dead between the time of the issuance of an advance and the delivery of the text. In other cases, mercurial speakers have discarded an advance text and talked at random. There have also been instances in which public officials have said one thing in their advance and quite another in their actual remarks.

Precautions   When there are significant changes between the advance and the live statement or speech, reporters should note them in their stories and try to obtain an explanation from the source. If the main point of the story has been nullified, then obviously it may be necessary to shift to some other angle, but it is mandatory to report as well what wasn't said and why it wasn't said. It is also accepted practice to let a source change an advance before release time, if there is sufficient reason to do so. But these changes, too, should be reported.

"Sealing Up" Reporters

The principal assets of reporters as a group are their ability, their integrity and their freedom from commitments other than those to their news organizations and their immediate families. Very early in their careers, nearly all find out that if one of these qualities is compromised, all are compromised. And that their integrity, basically, is the most precious of all.

For reporters who attain some degree of stature in their profession, it is almost foreordained that attempts will be made to sway their judgment, to persuade them to bend the news just a little in one direction or another. Few are ever affected by such blandishments. Those who are seldom last very long in active, day-to-day journalism.

In rare cases, where reporters are obliged to favor one side or another because of the policies of certain news organizations, they usually find that the very people to whom they are allied begin leaking tips and news to the opposition. Thus, the unfortunates are "sealed up" while the opposition reaps the benefits of being free of any ties. This is the price that extreme partisanship costs a news organization; worse still, where partisan policies continue for any length of time, the organization suffers a complete loss of public respect through lack of confidence in the impartiality of its news presentation.

It was this consideration that caused the American news media to protest disclosures that the Central Intelligence Agency had been using journalists as part-time operatives and demand full identification of those who were so employed. The rule is without exception: Journalists should stay away from situations in which they may find themselves compromised. The "sealed up" reporter is no reporter at all.

Sourcing Under PR Conditions

A reporter working with a responsible and experienced public relations agency or person is guided by a commonly accepted set of standards, principles and methods that have been developed over the years. Since this informal code is not recorded, and only exists because of its usefulness to the participants, it changes from time to time. Therefore, it is always prudent to review the ground rules with the public relations personnel who are directly involved before embarking on any major assignment.

Equal Treatment   Reporters have a right to expect equal treatment from public relations sources. This means that no great newspaper or network or newsmagazine will be given special breaks on a story, always a temptation when a public relations agency has a major news break that will make its client look good. However, other reporters have to demonstrate at least a show of interest to merit consideration — something editors may forget when they are making assignments.

It is generally assumed that a public relations agency or person is obligated to keep the confidence of reporters who check with them on exclusive angles of certain stories. Any attempt to leak the exclusive angle will not gain the gratitude of the press corps for the public relations unit involved; on the contrary, as soon as a violation of confidence is discovered, the unit or person who did the leaking will forfeit the trust of everybody on the story. The pledge of confidence that binds the publicist is no different than the one that seals up the reporter who accepts off-the-record information.

Attitudes Toward PR   Whenever reporters deal with public relations representatives, and it is almost impossible to avoid them except in small towns and modest organizations, their problem is to determine whether the news has been tampered with. Whenever they find distortions, half-truths or no truth at all, it is their job to get the story right before passing it on to the public.

Checking a Handout

There is no law that requires public relations people, in or out of government, to tell the whole truth and nothing but the truth. James Risser, a lawyer turned reporter for the *Des Moines Register*, was well aware of that and, unlike many of his colleagues, he was a diligent reader of press releases.

One day, in his regular routine, he came across a Department of Agriculture handout reporting that indictments had been returned in Houston against five ship inspectors for falsely certifying unacceptable vessels for the loading of grain. These inspectors, although federally licensed, were actually employed by a firm called the Houston Merchants Exchange, which aroused Risser's suspicions. He put the handout in his pocket and went to the headquarters of the USDA grain division in Maryland, where he learned that other grain inspectors had been indicted in New Orleans.

The news media had ignored the story. No other correspondent was bothering with it. But Risser, convinced he was onto something, decided it was worth investigating.

After studying court records in New Orleans and Houston, he began a series of interviews with government investigators, inspection firms and grain companies.

Then he invoked the federal Freedom of Information Act to gain access to USDA files, found evidence that grain shipping figures had been juggled and that foreign grain buyers had lodged more than 100 complaints against short weighting and the shipment of grain that was unfit for use.

Two months after beginning his inquiry, he broke a Page 1 story in the *Des Moines Register* about what he called "widespread corruption in the grading and shipping of U.S. export grains." In addition to his disclosure of the government's investigation, he wrote:

> The *Register's* own investigation indicates that the government's system of grading export grain and inspecting ships is full of conflicts of interest and the potential for a variety of abuses.
>
> As a result, foreign purchasers and countries that get humanitarian food aid from the United States may have received substandard grain and grain that was contaminated by being transported in dirty or insect-infested ships.

Now the Washington press corps came to life. And leading papers and the electronic media paid attention to the story. Before long, 57 individuals and companies were indicted on charges ranging from bribery to theft in the $12-billion-a-year export grain business. Eventually, more than 50 individuals and companies pleaded guilty to the charges. In the continuing inquiry, Congress approved remedial legislation and different methods of grain inspection were adopted.

And it all began because a reporter read a handout instead of throwing it in the wastebasket. Was he satisfied? Few good reporters ever are. Said Risser: "Many segments of the American press never did focus on the story, dismissing it as a dull farm issue."

Granted, few reporters have the freedom of movement and the luxury of weeks of time and a generous expense account, as was the case with Risser's inquiry. A few basic approaches can be taken, however, by any reporter who is willing to put in the effort.

The first and most important step is to seek access to the sources of the news — persons, places, records — within the bounds of law and sound journalistic practice. Such access is one sign of a guarantee of good faith; if it is denied, it may also be one possible sign of danger.

Translating this experience into terms of local news, reporters who are barred from the meetings of public bodies by closed doors generally learn to be suspicious of such "executive sessions." To be sure, some are necessary. But when a board of supervisors in town or county suddenly decides to hold a closed meeting in a motel at 8 a.m., it doesn't take much imagination to figure out that somebody is trying to conceal something.

The Publicity Specialists   This is not to say that anybody who has anything to do with public relations is to be mistrusted from the outset. Many are former journalists who have become government civil servants or corporate officers. Both in ability and reputation they differ widely, probably more so than journalists; moreover, few except at the higher levels appear to derive much satisfaction from the jobs they do. In moments of disillusionment, they apply to themselves every term from press agent to flack, and sometimes worse.

Yet, particularly in government, a well-trained specialist who deals with the news media can be helpful, and there are many whose reputations for candor and fairness are well deserved. It is not unknown for such specialists to serve the public interest against the policies of those who employ them, certainly a risky business. But then, "Deep Throat," the source who was the key to the earliest Watergate revelations, wasn't exactly a myth. Messrs. Woodward and Bernstein were lucky that he was on their side.

• Short Takes

Here is a brief summation of the way news is attributed and interpreted and the general practices involved.

- *On the record* means everything goes, quotes included.
- *For attribution, but not for direct quotation.* Everything goes, except for quotes. These must be paraphrased.
- *For attribution to a spokesman.* Use everything, including quotes, but put it on a spokesman for the such-and-such department, company or person, not using the spokesman's name unless he permits.
- *On background.* Everything may be used, including quotes, but attribution must be limited to "informed sources," "official circles," "a senior official" and so forth. The department or firm also cannot be identified unless permission is given.
- *For reporters' information only, not for immediate use.* Eventually the source may authorize some of the data to be used but never with attribution.
- *Off the record.* Nothing may be used. Reporters should not accept this kind of information except where it pertains to a moving story, such as a kidnapping, an official journey, a troop movement and similar material that eventually will be covered.
- Anybody who isn't a party to such agreements, and who picks up the information outside the meeting where it was imparted, may use it and sometimes, if there is good reason for it, identify the source, too.
- Leaks of information from responsible sources should always be examined as to motive and should be carefully checked before being used.
- It is common practice to put important speeches, reports and public documents such as budgets to be issued well in advance of publication under a time embargo. Once this material is accepted, the reporter is bound to observe the embargo and use the story only after the specified date and time.
- If an embargo is broken for one, it is broken for all. However, it is a good practice to notify the source before using.
- When there are major changes in an advance, those changes should be noted in the subsequent news account and reporters should find out why the changes were made.
- If it becomes necessary to use interpretation in the news, an inexperienced reporter or a reporter who is new to the organization should discuss the problem with the editor or news director in charge and obtain general guidelines.

Every newspaper and broadcasting organization handles this problem differently.

- The thing to remember about interpretation is that it *explains* the news and gives the facts to show that the explanation is valid. It does not attempt to evaluate or recommend what should be done about the particular event, for that is the province of the editorial writer.
- In a single story that includes interpretation, always tell the news first, then tell what it means. In a sidebar slugged "analysis," be sure not to duplicate the lead on the main story and go directly into what the event means.
- If anonymous sources are to be quoted to support the explanation, these sources must actually exist and the reporter must consult them. Good reporters, doing an analysis, may phone as many as 15 or 20 knowledgeable sources before writing such a story if they have the time.
- In dealing with public relations sources, reporters expect equal treatment. It is assumed that the public relations agency or person or department will keep the confidence of reporters who check for comment on an exclusive story before it is used. But ordinary prudence ought to be used in such queries.
- Always invoke "sunshine" laws or "open meeting" laws where they exist to challenge the right of any public body to hold closed meetings on public business.

CHAPTER

24

Public Opinion, Polling and Elections

Social science has made possible a thoroughgoing reform of outworn journalistic methods for measuring public opinion and keeping pace with major campaigns for public office. It has developed powerful statistical tools, most of which were made possible by the computer, to enable journalists to do a better job.

As Philip Meyer of the Knight-Ridder Newspapers has written in his book, *Precision Journalism*, "Social science has suddenly leaped beyond armchair philosophizing. It is doing what we journalists like to think of ourselves as best at: finding facts, inferring causes, pointing to ways to correct social problems and evaluating the efforts of such correction."

Journalism and Social Science

If all editors have not hailed this development with hosannahs, and if all journalists have not hurled themselves headlong into the breaking statistical waves, that is only characteristic of the innate skepticism of the profession. However, progress is being made.

There are, throughout the land, a modest number of reporters who have the qualifications to conduct a reliable scientific study of public opinion, who are adept at analyzing masses of statistical data and who are not afraid to work with computers and learn computer language. There are, as well, an increasing number of editors who are willing to employ them, news organizations that use their work regularly and sophisticated public officials and business and industrial leaders who know how to evaluate polling results.

Whom Do Polls Influence? Social science has shown us that, except in cases where public opinion is almost evenly divided, polls in and of themselves seldom can make perceptible changes in the mass mind. This is, of course, also true of much editorial opinion published in newspapers and newsmagazines and broadcast locally or by the networks. What polls can do, in the vast majority of cases, is to reinforce opinions that are strongly held.

Whom, then, do polls influence mainly? As nearly all responsible social scientists agree, the people who commission polling research are the ones who are most likely to change their opinions and their public positions to conform to the public opinion findings. This is more true, naturally, of the vendors of commercial products than of others. And yet many a political leader and nearly all recent American presidents have been powerfully influenced by the findings of their private poll-takers.

While the "bandwagon vote" conjured up by James A. Farley has little substance — even though the old master of the first two Franklin Roosevelt presidential campaigns fervently believed in it — many a politician still clings to the notion that last-minute voters will flock to his or her standard just to "ride with a winner." And they try by every conceivable device to create the impression that they are certain winners.

The main reason for this exercise in atmospherics is to keep wealthy corporations, individuals and labor unions in a mood to continue to make large financial contributions to particular compaigns. Senator Hubert Horatio Humphrey was convinced to the end of his days that a California Field Poll, which showed Jimmy Carter ahead by 25 percent before the California Democratic primary of 1976, prematurely dried up contributions and crippled a last-minute TV effort in the state by the Humphrey forces. Humphrey lost the primary by less than 5 percent.

Where the polls do have an enormous influence on voters is in the network projections of winners, based in part on the random sampling of voters' choices gathered immediately after they cast their ballots. In the 1980 presidential election, for example, the networks announced Ronald Reagan's victory and President Carter conceded defeat while the polls on the Pacific Coast were still open. The result, according to most reliable political estimates, was that a certain number of voters didn't even go to the polls in that area. Although this could not have changed the outcome of the presidential election, it could have had an effect on other close races in states in the Pacific time zone.

The Nature of Polling It is not in politics alone that poll-taking is of importance. The Nielsen ratings, to a very large extent, determine what we see on television. Nielsen and other commercial poll-takers are well into the critical surveys of whether old products should be changed or withdrawn and whether new products can be sold.

Polls also are taken on every conceivable subject. Within a few days in a recent year, poll-takers covered these issues:

- An Opinion Research Corporation Poll showed 75 percent of respondents mistrust big business.
- A Harris survey showed 62 percent of respondents mistrust big government.
- A United States Census Bureau study indicated that American women will continue to outnumber men for the rest of this century.
- A New York Daily News Poll determined that 77 percent of respondents had lost trust in public officials.
- And a Los Angeles Times survey disclosed that most jurors in a poll were against judicial press gags.

That was, by the way, only a small sampling of the American news media.

The Researchers   It merely proves, if proof were needed, that the public opinion survey and social statistical analyses have become the basis for a major industry.

Within a little more than a generation, the news media, the universities and the commercial polling organizations have established a formidable network for measuring the frequent and sometimes dizzying shifts in public sentiment. However, it is still true as it was a century ago when Lord Bryce wrote that "the obvious weakness of government by public opinion is the difficulty of ascertaining it." Wide differences of opinion may be caught very quickly, it is true, but when the margin of error approaches 3 percent on either side, most poll-takers agree, however reluctantly, that the acceptable margin of confidence usually has been reached.

No one, therefore, can quarrel with Winston Churchill's celebrated dictum: "Nothing is more dangerous than to live in the temperamental atmosphere of a Gallup Poll, always taking one's temperature. There is only one duty, only one safe course, and that is to try to be right and not fear to do or say what you believe to be right."

Two of the pioneering polling organizations still remain in the forefront of public opinion research — George Gallup and his American Institute of Public Opinion and Elmo Roper's organization. Among the others, Louis Harris and Daniel Yankelovich are both prominent and widely used. Of the young comers, few have been as publicized as Patrick H. Caddell, who worked for both the George McGovern and Jimmy Carter Democratic presidential campaigns while still in his twenties.

Of equal importance are the university research centers and the numerous social science researchers in academe, who are so often sought out to help with the various types of polls and other statistical studies. Among the oldest are the Michigan Survey Research Center and the National Opinion Research Center.

Finally, some of the stronger and wealthier news organizations are doing much of their own work, as witness the rapid adaptation of social science methods by the Knight-Ridder Newspapers. Others have joined forces and thereby shared costs as well as services, the CBS News–New York Times polls being one example. Then, there are the statewide polls, some going back for many years, including the Des Moines Register's Iowa Poll, the Minneapolis Tribune's Minnesota Poll, the New

York Daily New's New York State Poll and the Mervin Field organization's California Poll.

Measuring Public Opinion

Everybody recognizes the importance of public opinion in an open society but few agree on what it is or how it operates. Nor is it easy to define, even by social scientists.

What Is Public Opinion   In a far smaller and less complicated United States nearly a century and a half ago, Alexis de Tocqueville called it the "predominant authority" that acted by "elections and decrees." In a moment of disillusion with the vagaries of the British public, Sir Robert Peel was less admiring; to him, it was "that great compound of folly, weakness, prejudice, wrong feeling, right feeling, obstinacy and newspaper paragraphs which is called public opinion." In the early 1920s, Walter Lippmann argued that it was "primarily a moralized and codified version of the facts," and that "the pattern of stereotypes at the center of our codes largely determines what group of facts we shall see and in what light we shall see them." In our own time, a social scientist, W. Phillips Davison, has concluded that public opinion should be treated as a "consensus that influences the behavior of individuals who contribute to the consensus . . . a form of organization [that] is able to coordinate the thought and action of a large number of people."

Of one thing there is no doubt. Whether it is the "predominant authority," a "great compound of folly," a "pattern of stereotypes," or a "consensus," the measurement of what is called public opinion has become of transcendent importance in modern mass communications. It forms the basis of much advertising and merchandising practice, determines what shall and shall not be seen on television, locates new enterprises as varied in character as food markets and newspapers, provides trends (or the illusion of trends) in political campaigns at all levels of government and dominates the coverage of national elections. Journalists have not been able to escape the implications of this expanding activity. It has placed them squarely in the middle of the computer age.

Since newspapers have taken up "precision journalism," polling assignments have become a part of the regular routine. The *Chicago Tribune*, for example, has found that nine of 10 persons surveyed in Chicago favored mandatory hand-gun registration. The *Dayton* (Ohio) *Journal Herald* forecast the outcome of a city tax referendum with less than 2 percent error. In a survey of "white flight" to the suburbs as a result of school integration, the *Milwaukee Journal* found that the trend was exaggerated. And the Associated Press, in one of a number of surveys, looked for a relationship between cancer death rates and the rate of spending for research.

The Rise of the Pollsters   The practice of poll-taking goes back to 1824 when a Harrisburg *Pennsylvanian* straw poll indicated Andrew Jackson was ahead in the presidential campaign. Over the course of the next century, such newspapers as the *Boston Globe* and *New York Herald* conducted street corner polls. And at the beginning of the 20th century, advertisers began experimenting with market surveys, the true forerunner of the modern public opinion poll. The first "social-scientific" poll of public opinion was conducted in 1907–1908 by the Pittsburgh Survey, with the support of the Russell Sage Foundation. Another first was the *Kansas City Star*'s quadrennial selection of "sample precincts," from which it would calculate the winner of the presidential election and banner the result soon after the closing of the election booths in the land.

But none of these was as spectacular a success — and failure — as the *Literary Digest* Poll which began in 1916. For most of the presidential elections through 1932, the *Digest* sent out postcards to millions of persons and predicted the outcome with reasonable success. By 1935, there was so much concern over polling that a bill was introduced in Congress to prohibit the use of the mails for polls and stop this "vicious practice." The bill failed. But in the same year, Elmo Roper began his poll in *Fortune* magazine and the first Gallup Poll was issued by George Gallup's newly founded American Institute of Public Opinion.

In the 1936 presidential campaign, the *Literary Digest* calculated, on the basis of more than 2 million postcards received mainly from telephone users and automobile owners, that President Roosevelt would lose to Alfred M. Landon, his Republican challenger, by 42.9 percent of the vote to 57.1 percent. The outcome gave Roosevelt 62.5 percent of the vote, which enabled him to carry 46 of the 48 states. The *Digest* Poll thereby racked up a polling error of 19.6 percent, the largest ever known for a presidential election, and the magazine went out of business. The Gallup Poll, based on a scientific sampling of a few thousand respondents, called the election correctly but itself registered an error of 6.8 percent, larger than any it has since made. Of course the difference between the two was that the *Digest* sampled only prosperous people in a time of depression, those who had phones and cars, while Gallup reached a better cross-section.

Despite a relatively good record set by Gallup, Roper and other pollsters, the polling industry had to struggle for years to overcome the *Digest* debacle. Just as it was regaining public confidence, however, it came a cropper in the 1948 presidential election, when President Truman upset the favored Thomas E. Dewey. The picture of a grinning Truman holding up the *Chicago Tribune*, with a banner headline proclaiming a Dewey victory, is a favorite in every journalistic album of the era — and one the pollsters will never forget.

In 1948, Gallup was in error by 5.3 percent, Crossley by 4.7 percent and Roper by 8.4 percent and all understated the Democratic vote by these respective amounts. The Social Science Research Council blamed errors of sampling, interviewing and forecasting. Gallup himself argued that he failed because he stopped polling "about 10 to 14 days" before Election Day and thereafter Democrats who had been "leaning" toward Dewey changed their minds. He changed his sampling methods and began polling up to two days before Election Day.

The pollsters had some rough times after the Truman disaster, and some bright moments as well. In the close presidential race between Senator John F. Kennedy and Richard M. Nixon in 1960, both relied heavily on private polling advice, Kennedy on Louis Harris and Nixon on Claude Robinson of the Opinion Research Corp. Kennedy always gave credit to Harris for the findings on which his successful campaign was based. In the 1968 election, last-minute Gallup and Harris surveys indicated that there was a trend toward Senator Hubert H. Humphrey, the Democratic candidate, that was reflected in Nixon's narrow victory.

Luck as a Factor All poll-takers are well aware that they ignore the usual 2.5 to 3 percent margin of error in any national survey at their own peril. And this was particularly apparent in the exceedingly close 1976 presidential election, when most major polling organizations came up with predictions of 1 percent or less in favor of Jimmy Carter. George Gallup, the dean of pollsters, picked Ford by the same figure. However, Gallup and others covered themselves—pointing to the margin of error—and said the election was "too close to call."

The only one daring enough to make an unqualified forecast was Burns Roper, for the Public Broadcasting System, whose final survey gave Carter 51 percent, Ford 47 percent and the minor candidates 2 percent. He came within 1 percent of complete accuracy, the final vote giving Carter 51 percent, Ford 48 percent and minor candidates 1 percent. Said Roper: "Polling is part science and a helluva lot of human judgments. Fortunately, we made the right ones." And Gallup commented drily, "The plain fact of the matter is that you have to be lucky. You have to repeal the laws of probability."

Yet, poll-taking and election forecasting have become so deeply imbedded in the American political system—and in American journalism as well—that they have continued to develop despite all setbacks. Their credibility has suffered from time to time, particularly when hired pollsters of some repute issued findings that tended to support the positions of those who paid them. Yet, on the whole, this has not seemed to affect their public acceptance.

As a result of their 1976 experience, most poll-takers were overly cautious in the 1980 election and called it a tossup, a close election, and some even refused to predict a winner because their samplings showed such an even division. The only major poll-taker to break out of this bind was Louis Harris, who went on national TV in the closing hours of the campaign and forecast a large Reagan victory. A few hours after the polls opened, the news leaked out of Washington that Patrick Caddell, President Carter's private poll-taker, had told him that he could not win.

The Reagan landslide was thus a surprise to almost everybody in the polling business except for Ronald Reagan himself and his closest advisers. They had had assurance from their private polls that the victory would be theirs and that it would be very large, indeed.

Reasons for Forecasts It may well be asked why the news media go in so heavily for surveys of public opinion in connection with the reporting of politics and government, and elections in particular. One very good reason is that such forecasts, and the basis for them, are a part of the legitimate business of political reporters and their news organizations. An even more compelling reason is that no news organization worthy of the name can act as a mere recording device that plays back speeches and rival claims but does not undertake to evaluate them. When the public asks, "Who's ahead?" the question is worthy of a serious reply by trained reporters and commentators.

Polling Techniques

The oldest, least sophisticated and least dependable type of public opinion poll is the reportorial survey in which an editor sends several staff members out to talk to almost anybody they think will give them a good quote. Before the rise of the feminist movement, it used to be called the "man-in-the-street" poll, and it is still used by editors here and there.

The notion is that any reporter, unschooled in the simplest statistical procedures, can talk to 20 or 30 persons and come up with a valid reflection of the view of the community. Such exercises, no matter how carefully reporters go about their work, come near the truth only by the sheerest accident. The sample has not been picked at random according to the rules of probability and therefore can't be truly representative of the views of all persons in the region under consideration, known in statistical terms as the "universe."

The Random Sample   Many journalists still believe that a random sample consists of picking anybody you want to talk to on the street. The folly of that approach is readily apparent in a place like New York City, for example, where people picked at random at the fashionable corner of 50th Street and Park Avenue, in front of the Waldorf Astoria Hotel, will be no more typical of New Yorkers as a whole than those selected at the corner of 125th Street and Lenox Avenue, the crossroads in Harlem.

The definition of a true random sample specifies that everybody living within a given "universe" that is to be surveyed must have an equal chance of being selected for interviewing. If the selection is properly done, the sample need not be large. As statisticians are fond of pointing out, if an experimenter draws 100 balls from two casks of black and white balls, one with 100,000 and the other with 1,000 and each divided into a ratio of three black balls to seven white balls, the likelihood is virtually the same that the drawing will yield 70 white balls and 30 black balls from each cask. Thus, Gallup's usual random sample is about 1,500 and his and other national polling samples during a political campaign run to no more than 3,000 persons.

In any event, reliable research and news organizations always go to considerable trouble and expense to develop a random sample that will represent the "universe," whether it is a village, a county, a state or the nation as a whole. In some instances, a "universe" may consist of groups of people taken by irregular areas depending on the type of survey and the desires of the person in charge.

The Probability Method   The most difficult, time-consuming and costly technique is the probability method. It is also the most widely accepted.

In this process, nothing is left to chance that the sample will be truly selected at random. Trained interviewers are given a list of carefully prepared and pretested questions, certain addresses in specified areas, a list of selected apartments in such buildings and a group of persons to be interviewed in order (the oldest male, the oldest woman and so on) at certain times of the day or evening.

They are given a choice if the address turns out to be an empty lot, or an apartment is vacant, or the type of person to be interviewed isn't available after repeated calls. Then the interviewers are given a list of alternatives, the whole following a statistical pattern developed well in advance.

Various refinements are applied to increase the representative nature of the sample, including stratification. This means simply that where the "universe" includes several identifiable groups of persons, samples will be drawn separately from each group to make certain they are properly represented. This helps maintain the accuracy of the sampling process, whereas clustering — interviewing several designated types of persons in one house or apartment — tends to reduce it.

The Quota Method   This is the older type of sampling. It is also the one Gallup and most other poll-takers used through 1948 with disastrous results, causing it to lose favor to the better-rounded probability method. However, quota sampling is still done here and there.

Under this technique, interviewers are given a list of the types of persons to be located and talked to but the choices are pretty much left to their own desires. The trouble here is that, consciously or unconsciously, the personal prejudices of interviewers enter into the selection process.

The principal advantage of the quota method over probability is that it is faster and cheaper; in the end, however, it may not be much more reliable than the "man-in-the-street" poll.

A Question of Confidence   Using statistical tables of probability, polling organizations invariably determine the size of their samples on the basis of what is called a "confidence level" — in other words, a test of accuracy. If a Gallup sample totals 600 persons, for example, he calculates that the chances are 95 in 100 that a poll which divides 60 percent in favor, 40 percent opposed (or the reverse) will be within four percentage points of the true figure. This means that the number in favor will be somewhere between 56 percent and 64 percent. By doubling the sample to 1,200, Gallup holds that the error factor (using the same 95 in 100 criterion) is reduced to 2.8 percent. Doubled again, there is a further decrease to 2 percent.

It isn't any great mathematical feat, using statistical tables and relatively basic mathematical procedures, to work out the confidence level for any sample size and confidence level. Most surveys make it their goal to operate within 4 percent error at the 95 in 100 confidence level, which means a sample of 600 persons is adequate. At 3 percent, a sample of 1,067 is needed; 2 percent, 2,401; 1 percent, 9,605. These figures assume, of course, that there is an absolutely true sample based on probability. As for the size of the "universe" involved, those figures don't make much difference until they get below the 10,000 level.

For many years, it seemed to many that it was sheer madness to try to determine national trends by polling a handful of citizens in a town, a few score in a state, and between 1,200 and 3,000 nationally. And yet, barring technical and human failures that now are usually kept to a minimum, the system works. The Bureau of the Census has been using the probability method of random sampling for years to determine population growth (the house-to-house enumeration process occurs only once a decade).

Sampling Techniques   The basis of most sampling techniques consists of maps and other data from the Bureau of the Census. If these are reinforced with city directories or comparable tabulations, the raw material for establishing a sample is in hand.

In the probability method, the primary sampling units may be drawn at random (using a table of random numbers) from a list of all the counties and metropolitan areas in the United States. These are then further reduced to urban blocks and rural segments, also selected by the random process as it is known in statistics. Next, within each selected block or segment, every dwelling unit is listed and a fixed number is selected at random. Finally, in the selected dwelling unit, all adults are enumerated; from each, one person is chosen, again at random.

The sample thus selected has a high probability of reflecting all the characteristics of the "universe" from which it is drawn. Factors of age, sex, economic status, ethnic and religious group and other relevant items are all represented in the sample. It is in this manner that interviewers are provided with their list of persons to be located and asked the precise list of questions drafted by the polling organization.

In telephone polls, which are faster and cheaper, the number of names in a telephone directory in a particular city is divided by the size of the sample (600, 1,067, 2,401 or whatever). The quotient shows the number of names to be skipped, from the beginning to the end of the directory, to produce a true random sample. Then, the designated telephone numbers are called by researchers. To cover unlisted numbers, some social scientists advocate adding one digit at the end of each telephone number on the list.

The Uses of Polling   It is a familiar argument among pollsters, particularly those with an academic background, that the poll is more sinned against than sinning and that news organizations misuse polls by attempting to extract more information from them than they are able to give. To a certain extent, this may be true. However, as long as polling organizations offer their wares for sale and as long as they announce certain results within a given range of probabilities, it is only logical to hold them responsible for their output.

No one can claim absolute accuracy for any public opinion study, whether it is done person-to-person, by telephone or questionnaire. The allowance of 3 percent error on either side is fairly standard in political poll-taking, but the public tends to overlook it in a close political fight when there is perhaps only a 1-percent difference between the chief rival candidates. Moreover, some polls are put to grotesque uses toward Election Day when one side or the other will claim victory on the basis of a lead of as little as one-half of 1 percent.

While political polling is a hurry-up job with a considerable element of risk, and while TV ratings are also under constant criticism for the same reason, the social issues type of poll can be much more leisurely and often just as useful. The *Detroit Free Press*, in a study of black attitudes after the Detroit riots, took three weeks. A University of California study of the Watts riots took two years to produce. The *Miami Herald* took a considerable period for its inquiry into the militancy of blacks in the Miami area. And academic studies always take a great deal longer.

Depth Interviews   There are some practical-minded social scientists and political experts who have faith in a few depth interviews—solicited from various types of persons at specific locations — as a means of judging the mood of a particular "universe," which may be a small voting unit or even the entire nation. Such depth interviews may be conducted for two or three hours and encompass a variety of subjects. It is hardly fair to say that this kind of work is a projection of the "man-in-the-street" interview, done at a highly sophisticated level. These depth interviews require a rare combination of journalistic skills and social science background, plus shrewd political judgments.

One of the most successful practioners of the art was the political analyst Samuel Lubell, who did most of his own interviewing and calculated his own results. Lubell might select for a depth interview a man who resides in a low-costing housing development and works in a factory, a housewife who lives in the center of an area torn by controversy over school busing or another emotional issue, a farmer in the center of the Midwestern grain belt, a small home owner and other such typical American citizens. Out of the mix of their opinions and his own judgment, he shaped his conclusions.

Is the United States Overpolled? Although a Gallup survey has indicated that six out of seven Americans over 18 have never been interviewed in a poll, polling organizations agree that there is rising public resistance to their surveys. The work now takes much more time, it is more costly and more people simply don't want to be bothered. The reason is evident: In addition to polls by the government, universities and the news media, more than 1,000 commercial organizations are now in the business — which means the public is being asked to do a lot of the pollsters' work for free. "Perhaps," one pollster suggested, "we are not treating the respondent with respect as a human being."

Checking Trends The use of selected national or state voting units is a favorite indicator of political trends. Every major polling organization has a well-guarded list of such precincts, picked because they have accurately reflected the outcome of elections over a period of years. Of course, in landslides such as 1964 and 1972, it is easy to pick a winner by using the results in the model precincts and projecting them. Sometimes it can even be done before the polls close by taking a random sample among voters as they emerge from casting their ballot. But in a close election, model precincts are a risky guide.

Among newspapers, it is a time-honored custom for political writers to publish their forecasts on the Sunday or Monday before election. Necessarily, this is nowhere near as informative as it used to be because the publication of weekly surveys before Election Day has taken the edge off what used to be "the last word." Once again, it is no big deal to call a one-sided election; as for the close ones, predictions continue to be a gamble regardless of when they are made.

Polling Standards Here is a checklist of the information that should accompany any poll:

1. The sponsor of the poll;
2. Exact wording of all questions;
3. Definition of the population sample;

4. Sample size and, where needed, the response rate;
5. Allowance for sampling error;
6. Proportion of "don't knows" and others in sample who may not vote;
7. Method of interviewing and, where done,
8. Time period for interviewing.

Predictions

Any election forecast should have suitable qualifications throughout, even though the result may seem to duplicate many years of similar preelection accounts. This is a sample of the usual type of forecast lead:

> Mayor Hammond Garvell appears likely to win re-election on Tuesday if the vote is as large as expected.
> A sampling of typical voter opinion, plus talks with professionals in both parties and the findings of private polls, indicated today that the mayor was expected to defeat his opponent, Hereford Cates.
> But even Mayor Garvell's closest aides emphasized that, as an independent running for re-election, he must count on a heavy turnout at the polls—always a sign in this city that the independent voter is making his influence felt. . . .

"Foregrounding" Politics   A considerable segment of political writing in newspapers and newsmagazines and analytical comment on television is based on the summation and interpretation of coming events. The holding of conventions, listing of known candidates and issues and analysis of rival claims are subjects for reports of this type. Another is the planning for a campaign during a given period and the conclusions that may be drawn from it in terms of objectives.

Best known of all is the pre–Election Day summation giving the time, places and candidates involved in the voting, the registration figures, probable vote totals, analysis of issues, weather and whatever conclusions the writer or analyst wishes to make. On television, this type of information can only be given in sketchy form. It generally takes two solid pages of newspaper type to give the voter all the material he needs to make a decision on numerous candidates, propositions and referenda. This, certainly, is the place where a good newspaper is priceless and the electronic media are at a complete disadvantage.

Covering Elections

The early part of the 20th century was the golden age for political reporters. They were regarded as seers in their own right, the traveling companions of the great and near-great, the oracles who—in their own time and at their own pleasure—gave the people the Word. Arthur Krock of the *New York Times*, Charles Michelson of the *New York World*, Edward Folliard of the *Washington Post* and their associates were national figures. However, the coming of television changed all that.

The Reporters' Job   Today, the exposure of TV and its astronomical costs limit political campaigning in all except the marathon races of presidential years. The wise candidates try to save their principal pronouncements for TV and get by the rest of the time with a stock speech. But they are constantly on the move.

Consequently, political reporters for major news organizations outside TV are up against an almost impossible job. Their work is so concentrated that they have little time to talk to the candidates or their managers, let alone the voters. In a national campaign, if they try to see anybody at an airport or train or motorcade whistlestop, they risk being left behind. Nowadays, candidates will cover several states at a time in a single day. And because most candidates rely on the basic speech, that isn't news after the first few times it is used. Except in the hands of experienced reporters who know how to dig for the unusual in a political campaign, coverage tends to become a humdrum affair. More and more, it is the analysis that counts with many a newspaper.

Team reporting, based on surveys of public opinion, is being used by newspapers that can afford it. And where research is needed, one or two reporters may be assigned to do a lengthy background report on a candidate or an issue. Much of the news, therefore, becomes a matter of reportorial initiative rather than the rewriting of political handouts or the stale coverage of last night's TV appearance. For newspapers and wire services, it is more of a challenge and, on the whole, it leads to better reporting over a period of time.

The Political Routine

The electronic revolution that is reshaping the news media has enabled political reporters and commentators to use new and far more effective instruments in their work. At the beginning of the century, the task of obtaining and analyzing registration figures for all but the smallest elections was so time-consuming that only a few great newspapers and the top echelons of wire services made much of an attempt to do it. Now the computer has made statistical analysis of registration figures almost a routine matter. This, plus social science's new knowledge of the habits of the nation's voters, has given public officials, journalists and office-seekers alike new insights into the operation of the machinery of self-government.

There is no excuse today for any political reporter who does not know the geographical, social and ethnic backgrounds of the various areas of the nation. Nor can the journalists who cover politics ignore the need for a broad academic preparation for their work. It all may seem very glamorous to the beginner, who sees television floor reporters running around national conventions and buttonholing the elect of the country for interviews in front of the ever-present minicams with their instant replay videotapes.

Actually, that is only a small part of the job. Regardless of electronic advances in journalism, a certain amount of routine remains for every political reporter, and it has to be done well. For coverage begins with registration and proceeds through the nominating process, the preconvention maneuvers, the conventions themselves or the primary elections that have replaced them in many states, and then the coverage of the campaigns for all major candidates. What is involved here is a lot of traveling, interviewing, research and writing at all hours of the day and night; the reporter doesn't exist who can cover politics on a regular basis within the neat framework of a seven- or eight-hour day.

Covering Political Conventions

The old tradition of the "smoke-filled room," from which candidates like Warren Gamaliel Harding emerged and were thrust upon an astonished electorate in presidential elections, has been shattered by the growth of television. While many a politician sighs and wishes for its return, the "smoke-filled room" is now a part of history. Undoubtedly there will be what are known as "brokered" conventions of the two major political parties in the future, as there have been in the past, but it will be next to impossible to keep the wheeling and dealing secret.

This is the main reason for the dramatic changes in the national political conventions at which presidential candidates are nominated. At the 1960 and 1964 conventions of both major parties, the presence of television cameras and TV reporters and commentators led to continual disorder as publicity-conscious candidates and delegates crowded each other for exposure.

That, however, was but a foretaste of what was to come at the disastrous 1968 Democratic National Convention in Chicago, when masses of antiwar activists, seeking to punish the Democratic leadership for the escalation of the Vietnam War, disrupted the proceedings with riots and other demonstrations before the television cameras. The Chicago police, surging to attack the demonstrators, helped produce what turned out to be a political disaster for the Democratic nominee, Senator Hubert H. Humphrey. He was defeated by former vice-president Richard M. Nixon, the Republican candidate, in the November election.

Both parties tried, without much success, to reduce the confusion on the convention floor in 1972 by attempting to restrain television coverage. In 1976, finally, despite the use of hand-held minicams and videotape, TV people were ordered from the floor of the Democratic National Convention several times in order to disperse the crowds around the cameras.

Calm, order, and dullness were the rule of the day at the 1980 conventions. At the Republican convention, Ronald Reagan, the frontrunner during the primaries, was nominated in what amounted to a coronation. At the Democratic convention, with the exception of a last-gasp effort from Senator Edward M. Kennedy, who made a brilliant speech, President Carter wrung an easy renomination from the reluctant Democratic leadership and went down to overwhelming defeat in the November election.

Election Day The proceedings on Election Day, once so boisterous in the average American city, are reasonably quiet today. In big cities, with few exceptions, there is almost a holiday air with banks and bars closed and often schools as well. It is seldom that there is news of such chicanery as stolen ballot boxes, the multiple voting of floaters and other tricks of the bad old days. If an election is being stolen, the few remaining political bosses try not to make a public announcement of it. Trickery at the polls, in consequence, is rather difficult to detect, except in Illinois, as the 1982 gubernatorial election showed.

This does not mean that news staffs have an easy time of it on Election Day, however. On the contrary, the arduous business of interviewing voters after they have cast their ballots now begins with the opening of the polls. And as the voting progresses, the news no longer is based on an hour-by-hour estimate of how many have voted but on projections at sample precincts of the standings of the various candidates. Of course, not every news organization is equipped to do this, because it takes a major outlay of funds and commitments of staff and electronic gear. But those that do can make an Election Day story much more exciting than it has been in recent years.

Election Night The important thing about Election Night work is the effort that goes into organizing it. In the press and in the electronic media, the news staff that generally does the best job is the one that prepares for it with the greatest care. Sometimes the preparations for an Election Night begin as much as six months in advance. During the final weeks, the compilation of background figures, campaign materials, data covering everything from biographies to party platforms and the outlining of actual assignments are almost as important as the day-to-day coverage of the news. No good news organization goes into Election Night without complete, pretested planning and batteries of the best calculators and computers available, with trained personnel to run them.

Election coverage is the kind of thing the American news media do best. Once the polls close and the first figures start flowing from the newsrooms, partisanship is nearly always forgotten by the working journalists and all effort is concentrated on reporting who won, how victory was achieved and what it means. The union of wire services and the three major television networks for Election Night coverage has reduced the public's uncertainty over the outcome in all but the closest elections.

Tabulating the Vote The public's attention is riveted on the television screens on Election Night and the announcements, as soon as possible, of the winning candidates. The electronic performance is risky, but it is in the journalistic tradition. Gradually, the major television news organizations have learned the bitter lesson that newspapers absorbed in the years before the electronic media took primacy in such spot-news reporting. They have become far more careful with the announcement of who won—and why—and have generally adopted a stance of responsibility that befits the journalist far better than a wild-eyed claim of exclusivity. Their cooperation on presidential elections is in the public interest.

Even though television is first with the results and often first with the announcement of the winners, it cannot—by its very nature—provide the detailed tabulations of the voting down to the smallest districts and the totals amassed by every candidate in the various races. That is something good newspapers have always done superbly and they still continue to do so. Without this kind of service, it would be difficult for a democratic system to operate as well as it does.

Handling the Figures

The basis of any voting announcement, whether it is given by the wire services, television or rival media, is the vote total itself, the number of districts it represents and the identities of these districts. No fragmentary vote is worth anything unless the source is identified, so that it can be compared at once with previous records. Thus, any voting result that is important enough to be made known should contain the number of voting districts, the area and — if possible — the time as follows:

> 442 out of 1,346 election districts in Great Bear County, on the state's northern border, gave these totals at 10:32 p.m.:
> Jones (D)   60,024
> Smith (R)   50,555
> 26 election districts in the 64th Ward, in the heart of Central City's south side, gave these totals at 9:30 p.m.:
> Brown (D)   2,022
> Green (R)   2,366

The names of election units change, of course, from one place to another, but whether they are wards or districts, the practice is the same. On the basis of a sufficient cross-section of the voting, and a knowledge of past performance in the same area, a projection of the figures can be computed and an indicated voting result can be given. Thus, on the basis of a 25-percent voting return, an experienced political analyst can calculate what will happen and make an announcement that reads something like this:

> On the basis of returns from one-quarter of the city's districts two hours after the polls closed, Smith led by 40,622 to 32,634 for Jones, his Democratic rival. This gave him an actual plurality of 8,028 over Jones and an indicated plurality of more than 30,000 if the same vote ratio continues.

Political analysts know if it is possible for the same ratio to continue. They have all the statistics of past performances and they have tabulating machines and computers, with operators, so that it takes little time to work out a proper projection in all but the closest contests.

Where cities are heavily Democratic and rural districts are overwhelmingly Republican, as is usually true in such states as Illinois, New Jersey and New York, the initial returns from cities, being tabulated faster, often show Democratic candidates far in the lead. But this is where the analysts take over. They point out that the early figures may be misleading. As the returns come in from rural areas, they make projections of the vote to see if the usual Republican majorities are being piled up; if they are, then it is a relatively simple matter to match this projection against those of the cities and arrive at a tentative winner if the swing between the candidates is wide enough. But where the difference between the candidates' vote percentages comes to 3 percent on either side, the familiar danger point for most statistical compilations, the wise analyst concludes that it is best to await virtually complete results.

It has happened, although rarely, that candidates have conceded defeat on the basis of projected returns and gone to bed, only to find upon arising in the morning that they have won because of a surge of late returns in their favor. And sometimes, when only a handful of votes separates winner and loser, a recount may reverse the result. So caution in close elections is an article of faith in every newsroom on Election Night.

The stories of the election results — written and verbal — are based on the tabulated figures, and the majorities and pluralities are calculated accordingly. (A majority is the difference between candidates where only two are running; a plurality between two candidates is the difference where more than two are in the race. A candidate may have a plurality over the second person in a three-way race and a majority over the combined total of the opposition.)

Anchor persons on TV need judgment, stamina and verbal skills to a high degree, but they don't have to worry too much about organizing their remarks. Newspaper work is different.

The key to the successful newspaper story on Election Night is the organization of the piece. It should be assembled in such a way that it need not be completely rewritten every time a voting total changes. Often figures are left out of the lead for this reason. The lead is merely based on the fact that one candidate is leading, the actual returns being given immediately afterward in tabular style so that they can be changed quickly by substituting an insert.

Qualifying the Story　Until a vote is decisive, it is well in reporting on Election Night to use such qualifications as, "On the basis of scattered returns," or, "Partial and unofficial returns showed Smith had a narrow lead 30 minutes after the polls closed." Until the election has been decided, a careful writer qualifies the lead in this manner:

> Robert J. Epperson apparently was elected mayor last night by an indicated plurality of 40,000 votes.
> Although no concession of defeat came from his rival, Arthur Ahlgren, Epperson claimed victory on the basis of returns from half the city's districts which gave him a commanding lead. . . .

Sometimes, in a close election, a candidate may be the victor on the basis of final and unofficial returns and the loser may charge fraud, demand a recount or both. Circumstances dictate how the story should be presented, but it is only logical to report that one candidate has scored a victory that is being contested. The charges of fraud should be used in a lead only when there appears to be some basis for them.

When elections are very close, news organizations sometimes have to wait until the entire vote is counted before declaring a winner. In rare cases, the decision has to await the filing of official returns a week to 10 days after the election. But generally, an election is considered final when the rival or rivals of the successful candidate concede defeat.

There have been instances in which a candidate conceded defeat only to learn, when complete returns were in, that he had won. But that doesn't happen often.

Styles vary in the reporting of election results in newspapers. Some carry the actual figures in a box preceding the story, where readers can see them before they look at anything else. Others like to use a lead saying who won, and then immediately summarize the salient figures, even though television has already done the job. Here is a general style in use on many newspapers and wire services, which is also familiar to television audiences who have heard it present-tensed and read by exhausted second-string announcers late at night after the first team has gone home:

> Arthur J. Wingate scored a surprise victory last night over his Democratic opponent, George Berling, who was seeking a third term as governor.
>
> The Republican triumph in the state, which ran counter to a nationwide Democratic trend, was the result primarily of deep inroads that Mr. Wingate made into normally Democratic pluralities in Central City, largest municipality in the state.
>
> Governor Berling conceded defeat at 11:15 last night. The concession followed a conference with Gunnar Dahlquist, chairman of the Democratic State Committee, and Mayor Franklin Quest of Central City.
>
> At 12:32 a.m., with nearly complete statewide returns in, 10,132 out of 11,110 districts gave:
>
> Wingate (R)   2,834,263
> Berling (D)   2,378,767
>
> Nearly complete returns from Central City at that hour indicated that Mr. Wingate, 54-year-old industrialist from Willow Grove, had cut the usual Democratic plurality there to less than 400,000 votes. Four years ago, Governor Berling was able to carry the city by almost 700,000 votes. . . .

The unofficial results, reported on Election Night by the news media, are seldom upset by challenges, charges or recounts, but the final result must await the official canvass. When there is an election upset, it is major news.

• Short Takes

Here are some of the main things to remember about reporting on public opinion, polls and elections:

- Polling is based on the scientific use of statistics and must always include an announced probability of error, based on the number of people involved in the sample and the method of interviewing. No poll is ever going to be perfect.
- The least effective, and least scientific, poll is the one in which a reporter asks any dozen or so people for an opinion. That kind of poll is useless scientifically.
- A proper poll is based on the selection of a true random sample, in which everybody in a given polling area or group has an equal chance of being interviewed. The usual national telephone sample is about 1,500, which has a 3-percent margin of error on either side, in 95 out of 100 instances.
- The two main methods are (a) probability, in which the interviewer is given specific instructions on exactly where to go and whom to interview, and (b) the quota method, in which the interviewer is told the types of people to interview (young, old, men, women, etc.) and the number of each and left to his or her own devices. The probability method is generally used.
- Polling reports should include the population sample, the size and response rate, the wording of questions, the poll sponsor, allowance for error, the time period for interviewing and when and where the interviewing was done.

- Any poll that shows a narrower percentage of support between two candidates than the margin of error for the poll itself is not really worth much. It shows an election too close to call.
- In writing about elections, any partial vote total must include the number of voting districts reporting, the area, the time, the partial totals and the part of the vote that is still missing as to area and, if possible, past voting performance.
- Until an election has been decided by the concession of one or another candidate or the completion of the vote, all reporting of returns must be qualified. Vote projections, as used by the networks and major newspapers, should be announced with the margin of error involved.
- In very close races, the official returns—which may take a week to 10 days—are often the decisive count. In the case of recounts, court actions may be involved, and the final decision could take months to determine. But as for the great majority of election results, they are determined on Election Night on the basis of projections of partial returns and should be so labeled.

CHAPTER 25

Budgets, Taxes and Local Government

It is a major duty of newspapers at the local level to maintain a continual scrutiny of the cost of running our cities and states. At the federal level, there are watchdogs aplenty.

But locally, newspapers alone — with very few exceptions — have the staff and the funds to cover local government in all its aspects on a day-to-day basis. Moreover, a complicated budget for a town, city or county, or a school or other political subdivision, cannot be analyzed for worried citizens in 30 to 45 seconds of TV time. It also takes a bit longer than that, and a lot more space and reportorial time, to explain the reasons for budget deficits and projected tax increases.

The Basics of Budget Reporting

The story of budgets and taxes is at the very root of the reporting of local government. The excuse that such accounts are likely to be dull doesn't wash any longer. What happened when New York City faced bankruptcy turned out to be a cliff-hanger that produced excitement in this country and abroad. For if the city had defaulted on its bonds and other obligations, financial institutions and individual bondholders would have lost billions of dollars and the credit of the entire state of New York could have gone down the drain as well.

Outline of the Assignment   Nothing is more important to the cause of democratic self-government than a public presentation of the costs of government and the tax proposals through which officials seek to raise the funds to meet those costs. What the public wants to know, and what reporters must establish right off when a new budget proposal is presented, is whether it will be necessary to increase taxes and, if so, what kind and how much.

Without this kind of information, the public is left in the dark and it is possible for unscrupulous or incompetent officeholders to play all kinds of tricks with public funds. To be sure, reporters with a good background in standard accounting practices and a knowledge of computer operations can dig into a government budget presentation at the local level and sometimes they can come up with some unpleasant truths that make headlines. But budget reporting, as a rule, isn't all that heroic. It involves a lot of painstaking, step-by-step journalistic routine and conferences with responsible municipal officials.

Every budget story must be told with regard for detail. In outline, this is the way the story generally develops:

- The total amount to be spent over the next fiscal year (usually from July 1 to June 30).
- The amount of increase or decrease over the preceding year.
- If there is an increase, the ways in which the city will raise the money:
1. New taxes, and if so, what kind and how much;
2. Increased taxes now on the books, particularly for property and business levies, and how much of each;
3. Increases in fees and license charges;
4. Economies such as staff reductions, and how many and how much is to be saved; elimination of services, exactly which ones and the costs involved, and revision of employee benefits and perquisites;
5. New bond issues, and if so, how much and what will the interest charges be.
- Pay increases or decreases for employees; new hiring, if any.
- The largest departmental expenditures in the budget, with each one listed, and the exact amount by which each is to be increased or decreased. Generally, this involves the police and fire departments and the sanitation services, transportation and street repair and, where the city makes a large contribution of its own, schools and welfare services.
- Statements about the budget by the mayor and/or city manager and budget director, and from the political opposition on the City Council or other legislative body.
- Explanation of the debt service item. This is always a large sum in most city budgets. In consists of the interest charges that the city must pay bankers and private individuals who buy city bonds, which are issued in order to raise money for specific projects or to meet various types of deficits. The debt service should be reported as an increase or decrease over the previous year and the story should give the latest charges of interest on the newest city obligations.

Making Tax Estimates   Sometimes, for understandable reasons, public officials are not willing to admit that their spending plans are going to cost the public more money in the form of higher taxes. It then becomes the responsibility of the reporter to determine how much of a tax increase is likely and what areas it will affect, usually property taxes and general business taxes.

Where there are private citizens' budget organizations, their executive directors always are a big help in such situations and generally they permit direct quotation. Failing that, tax estimates may often be obtained from the political opposition but they are likely to be suspect. If reporters try to make a forecast of their own, however, they are on shaky ground because too many variables are involved.

Types of Budgets The budget outlined here is called an operating or expense budget, which is financed mainly by property and business taxes, fines, licenses, permits and service charges, revenue sharing from state and federal governments and miscellaneous sources.

Some cities also have capital budgets, separate accounts for capital expenditures on new projects such as bridges, roads, buildings and so on that are financed by bonds or other forms of city indebtedness outside the general expense budget.

A more recent innovation is the performance budget, which accompanies the operating budget and explains, generally on a line-by-line basis, exactly how and why the money is being spent and what the duties of the departments or officials involved may be.

Local Government and Budgets

The two principal types of local government consist of the following:

Mayor-City Council This is the most familiar type of local governmental authority. The mayor is responsible for drafting the budget and submitting it to the Council, which then has the authority to make changes, but must finally adopt it before the beginning of the next fiscal year. Very often, the mayor has the services of a senior official who may be termed a city manager or a chief operating officer. In large cities, the office of the comptroller is of great importance in the budgetary process.

City Commission-City Manager In this type of government, a number of elected commissioners, say five or seven, choose one of their number to be the mayor and also elect a vice-mayor, but the entire commission has the overriding authority on any specific issue, such as the budget. The commission delegates the day-to-day operation of the city to a professional manager. In a variation of this system, the City Council is the elected body and hires the manager, and that official runs the city, prepares the budget and calculates the amount of taxes that will be needed.

Whatever the system, some single person—either a mayor or a city manager or a budget director—must take the responsibility for making up a budget and presenting it for adoption. This is not just an overnight job but requires literally months of consultation and negotiation between the budget-makers and departmental heads on the one hand and affected city groups, such as property-owners and business executives and unions, on the other.

Scheduling a Budget Process This, in general, is the way budget-making proceeds:

January 2–15. Submission of departmental estimates to the budget-makers.

January 15–February 15. Negotiations between department heads and budget-makers. Investigation for the reasons for some of the requests.

February 15–20. Tentative departmental allowances referred back to department heads by the budget-makers.

February 20–March 20. Conferences with department heads requesting review of their tentative appropriations and adjustments, where justified.

March 20–April 20. Drafting of the budget.

April 20–May 10. Submission to the top city official, either mayor or city manager, for a review of all appropriations and fundraising proposals. Adjustments and changes again negotiated.

May 15. Submission of the budget to the City Council or City Commission, as the case may be, with a message from the top city official, the mayor or city manager.

May 15–30. Debate and adjustments in the legislative body.

June 1–10. Public hearings on the proposed budget.

June 15. Final date for adoption of the budget.

July 1. Beginning of the new fiscal year and the beginning of operations under the new budget.

The dates set forth here are, of course, merely suggestions to show how the process works. But for most cities in the United States, this is believed to be a reasonable schedule.

Making up an Operating Budget

An operating budget, the most common and necessary type of financial document, consists of two parts: (1) proposed revenues and (2) proposed appropriations. Generally, income matches outgo, and that is called a balanced budget. Many city governments operate under laws requiring them to work only under balanced budgets.

Sources of Revenue The principal source of revenue for most city governments is the property tax. This is expressed in a unit called a mill levy, a mill being 1/10 of 1 cent. In theory, the property-tax rate is expressed as a certain number of mills for each dollar of the assessed valuation of a property; in reality, this is multiplied by 100 and it becomes a certain number of dollars for each $100 of the assessed valuation of a property.

Suppose a city's property is valued at $200 million, and $15 million is calculated to be the amount to be raised by property taxes. Dividing $15 million by $200 million makes the mill levy $.075 for each $1 of assessed valuation. Multiplying both by 100 makes the rate $7.50 for each $100 of assessed valuation. Thus, on a $50,000 house, the tax would be a whopping $3,750. That is a very high tax rate for residential property in a small to medium-size city.

Other sources of revenue include business taxes, fines, licenses, permits, charges for services, revenues from other governments such as a share in state sales taxes and revenue sharing from the federal government, and miscellaneous areas of income.

Appropriations   In most city governments, the largest sums are appropriated for the police and fire departments, sanitation and debt service. Recreation, engineering, administration and community development costs are in the second rank of departmental fund totals. Schools, a major item, usually are run on joint contributions from state and county governments as well as local revenues. Among other departmental costs are finance, law, public relations, parks, libraries, community services and various nondepartmental functions.

Welfare, one of the greatest costs in most governments, usually is carried in large part by the state and federal governments, with minimal contributions from cities. The great exception to that rule is New York City, where, for political reasons, the city has been saddled with the bulk of the cost of sustaining more than a million people on the public assistance rolls.

Writing About Budgets and Taxes

Budget stories range in total sums from about $600,000 for a small community like Martha's Vineyard (Dukes County), Massachusetts, to the billions of dollars that it takes to run New York City. These accounts are usually simply told and care is taken to explain any complications that may arise. This is the beginning of a budget story in the *Vineyard Gazette*, Edgartown, on Martha's Vineyard, as written by Andrew J. Shanley:

> The county advisory board took from the Dukes County news and information bureau and gave to Community Services and the county jail as the board met this week to set its preliminary county budget for the next fiscal year.
>
> This is the first year the board has had final say over the budget and the session Tuesday afternoon showed tension between the board and the county commissioners.
>
> The commissioners had proposed a $42,000 budget for the information bureau. The advisory board cut $10,000, eliminating a part-time position and money for printing and rent.
>
> The board gave Programs on Alcohol $5,000 and Visiting Nurses $1,000 more than had been allotted by the commissioners. They also increased the jail budget by $7,000 for a part-time jailer even after the commissioners had included money for one additional jailer.
>
> To balance the budget, the board took $3,000 from the airport budget. . . . The bottom line assessment figure to the Island towns is $606,557 in both the board's and commissioners' budget, which represents level funding for the year ahead.
>
> The board will hold a public hearing on the budget Jan. 21. . . .

Ken McLaughlin, City Hall reporter for the *Watsonville* (California) *Register-Pajaronian*, took a different tack in describing a final City Council budget session for that city:

> After six years on the City Hall beat, my philosophy is to keep budget stories as short as possible and to use as few numbers as possible. I always make an extra effort

with budget stories to add humor and describe the interaction of personalities. In addition, I always try to talk the city editor into running a graphic of a "pie" with budget stories. This is probably the best way to show the people how their money is being spent, which, after all, is really the only reason we report what goes on at these sessions.

A Typical City Budget Operation

The annual budget of Knoxville, Tennessee, which is reasonably typical of most cities of its size in this country, ran around $60 million in the early 1980s and was prepared by Lewis A. Gorham Jr., the director of the Office of Management and Budget, for Mayor Randy Tyree and the Knoxville City Council. Under local law, it had to be in balance.

The Situation of the City   At a time when recession had hit hard at the large industrial cities of the north, Knoxville regarded itself as being fortunate. As the home of the University of Tennessee and the Tennessee Valley Authority, its employment record was better than most and it was in a fairly stable position. Moreover, although it was a city of modest size, with 185,000 population, it sponsored a World's Fair in 1982 on a 70-acre site beside the winding Tennessee River and attracted millions of visitors. As an additional boost to its bid for tourism, it continued to be the gateway to the lofty wooded vastnesses of the Great Smokies National Park.

Analyzing the Budget   The operating budget drafted for the World's Fair year, fiscal 1982, ran to 601 pages and the performance budget, which explained the functions of the various parts of the city government and its beneficiaries, totaled 290 pages. Budget director Gorham gave this advice to reporters who received the two bulky volumes — advice that applies to the analysis of most budgets:

> The first things any reporter should do on receiving a proposed budget is to look at the summary, up front, of income and outgo, the anticipated revenue and the proposed appropriations, and then read the mayor's accompanying message. This is the big picture — the extent of the city's commitments, the measures that will have to be taken to bring the budget into balance and the basic decisions on whether taxes will or will not be raised and whether the work force will have to be reduced.
>
> Next, both the covering message and the summary will point to the improvements in services that are being proposed — the addition of more police, for example, and the provision of more city buses. I find that too many accounts of budget proposals are centered mainly on the questions of more taxes, if they are proposed, and new staff reductions while subordinating the very real efforts of most city governments to maintain and improve services to the public.
>
> The name of the game isn't always to damn the government. Sometimes, the government might be given a little credit, too, particularly if it performs well in adversity.

It is necessary, of course, for any reporter who handles a budget story to be thoroughly familiar with the way a city government is organized and how its powers

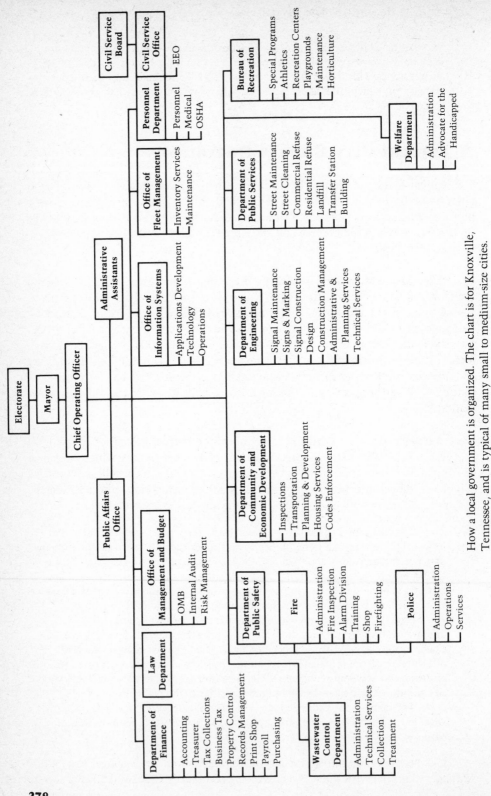

How a local government is organized. The chart is for Knoxville, Tennessee, and is typical of many small to medium-size cities.

are exercised. This is outlined in a chart that will be found in any printed budget document, listed with the summary; the chart, naturally, is not the whole story. The personalities involved, and their relationships, are more important, but it takes on-the-job experience in City Hall coverage to determine how the human side of government affects the way it actually operates.

The Final Budget   After prolonged City Council debate, more interdepartmental negotiations and talks with leaders of union and other employee groups, the final operating budget as adopted was increased to $58,405,684 but it still averted the imposition of new taxes or increases in existing property and business taxes. The total amounted to an increase of 4.8 percent over the previous year's $55.7 million.

This is the way the budget summary looked:

General Fund Budget Summary

Revenues		
Property taxes*	$31,387,381	53.7%
Business taxes	7,545,033	12.9%
Fines, licenses & permits	801,909	1.4%
Transfer from other governments	13,149,886	22.5%
Charges for services	2,788,626	4.8%
Miscellaneous	2,732,849	4.7%
	$58,405,684	100.0%
Appropriations		
Administration	$1,499,877	2.6%
Finance Department	908,297	1.6%
Law Department	319,515	.5%
Information systems (computers)	585,149	1.0%
Office of Management & Budget	229,883	.4%
Police	11,876,718	20.3%
Fire	11,778,978	20.1%
Civil Defense	102,361	.2%
Public Service (sanitation, transport, etc.)	9,081,947	15.6%
Engineering (street lights, roads, etc.)	1,577,673	2.7%
Welfare	78,672	.1%
Recreation (rec centers, pools, etc.)	3,223,515	5.5%
Parks and Zoo	400,000	.7%
Auditorium–Civic Center	976,648	1.7%
Libraries	802,100	1.4%
Community Action Committee	223,720	.4%
Metropolitan Planning Commission	284,500	.5%
Grants	274,810	.5%
Schools (only the city contribution)	1,984,333	3.4%
Community & Economic Development	2,091,552	3.6%
Debt Service (interest charge on bonds)	7,232,365	12.4%
Nondepartmental appropriations	2,544,893	4.4%
Grant awards	328,178	.5%
	$58,405,684	100.0%

*The estimated total assessed valuation for the fiscal year is $520,550,031. The tax levy (mill rate) therefore would be: Property taxes divided by total assessed valuation multiplied by 100. Allowing for a certain percentage budgeted for taxes that cannot be collected for one reason or another, this comes out to a rate of $6.10 for each $100 of assessed property valuation. It also is calculated that every 1 cent in the tax rate will generate an estimated $49,568.17 in revenue that can be collected.

A Story About the Final Budget   On the basis of these figures and the mayor's letter of transmittal to the City Council, a final story was written based on the Council's adoption of the budget:

The City Council adopted a $58.4 million balanced budget last night for the fiscal year beginning July 1 that provides for pay increases for city employees of up to 10%, eliminates 35 city jobs and calls for no new taxes or tax increases.

The budget is 4.8 percent higher than the current $55.7 million budget, but Mayor Tyree said, "Given a 10% inflation rate and fixed and mandated costs over which we have no control, I believe we have acted responsibly in adopting a budget that maintains essential service delivery and controls the growth of city government."

These were major provisions in the budget:

1. An across-the-board 10% cost of living raise for all non-uniform city employees with annual salaries below $10,000, 7.5% for all nonuniform employees with salaries above $10,000 and $75 a month more for all uniform employees.

2. Elimination of 100% coverage by the city in the deficit-ridden city employee health insurance fund. Employees now will pay 20% of the cost with a $100 front end deductible and the city will pay 80%.

3. The Recreation Department is hardest hit in the employee reductions, with some centers being closed. Total city employees now stand at 1,915, a decrease of more than 20% from the 2,407 work force when Mayor Tyree took office.

4. A new police class that may go as high as 50 employees and overtime funding for police work are provided for in connection with the World's Fair.

5. A $421,000 appropriation is provided to match a federal grant of $4.2 million for 30 new buses.

The mayor also announced that a $275,000 budget appropriation would go to 29 social service agencies because "recent disastrous cuts in federal aid make it necessary that we fund these agencies to the fullest extent possible."

Tyree pointed out that the economies provided for in the budget, plus revenues from the World's Fair, made it possible to avoid tax increases, leaving the property tax rate at $6.10 for each $100 of assessed valuation. . . .

Changes in Budgets During the Year   It should not be imagined that budgets, once adopted, are then frozen for the entire year. Unexpected costs, such as storm damage and snow removal, can make supplemental appropriations necessary. These and other factors, as well, can throw the most carefully administered budget out of balance and force hard-pressed city administrations to borrow money or to issue tax anticipation notes against income expected in the succeeding fiscal year.

General Fund

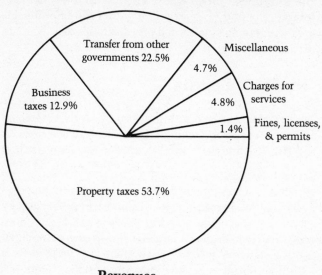

Revenues

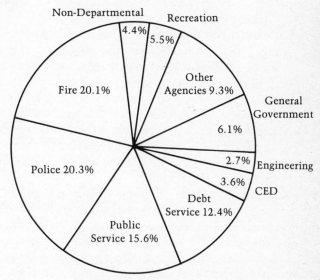

Appropriations

A "pie chart" showing income and outgo for the Knoxville operating budget.

City Hall reporters are well advised to be alert at all times for such changes and to follow up with direct departmental interviews to go to the source of the problem.

The budget routine outlined here for the city of Knoxville and the illustrative news story will differ in degree from the fiscal operations in other cities, but the basic requirement of matching income with outgo while maintaining essential services will be the same for all municipalities, large or small.

That, too, is the reporting principle applicable to budgets for school districts, counties and state and federal government subdivisions. But no budget story can ever be done in a fast shuffle. It takes a lot of time, a great deal of care and interminable checking, through interviews with public officials and private groups that maintain a close watch over public financing.

Definitions of Budget Terms

The following definitions of budget terms have been provided by Lewis A. Gorham Jr., director, Office of Management and Budget, City of Knoxville, based on research by Thomas Sherran, of the Public Administration Program of the University of Tennessee:

balanced budget This occurs when proposed revenues are equal to proposed expenditures. Many state and local governments require balanced budgets by law.

block grants Block grants are given primarily to general purpose governmental units in accordance with a statutory formula. Such grants can be used for a variety of activities within a broad functional area (for instance, Omnibus Crime Control and Safe Streets Act of 1968, Comprehensive Employment and Training Act of 1973).

bond anticipation notes This is to temporary borrowing for capital financing. These temporary notes are usually serviced from the proceeds of bond sales and enable the borrower to reduce the cost of interest during construction of large projects.

budget expense Outlay incurred for a specific time for goods and services and chargeable against revenues collected and held by public authorities.

capital budget A plan of proposed outlays that are associated with large expenditures for capital items, usually financed by borrowing. Capital items are dominant features of the physical environment—for instance, buildings, roadways, parks.

categorical grants This type of federal grant can be used only for a specific program and is usually limited to narrowly defined activities.

debt limit Total allowable government credit obligation.

debt service The amount of principal and interest due on outstanding obligations such as bonds, notes, lease purchases and so forth, in any one year.

formula grants This type of federal assistance allocates federal monies to states or their subdivisions in accordance with a distribution formula prescribed by law or administrative regulation.

general obligation bond Bonds whose payments may be financed by all taxpayers of the issuing governmental units. They are secured unconditionally by the full faith, credit and taxing powers of the issuing government.

general revenue sharing Advocates of the State and Local Fiscal Assistance Act, passed in 1972, sought to make federal monies available to lower levels of government without the traditional federal controls governing expenditure. It is based on the theory that those units of government closest to their respective interests can make better decisions because they better understand their needs.

line item budget   Consists of authorizing each expenditure line by line, item by item, thus producing a budget format commonly referred to as object of expenditure.

matching grants   A financial arrangement under which the grantor agrees to pay some fraction of the unit cost of the recipient.

mill levy   Refers to property taxation in mills, which is 1/10 of 1 cent per dollar of valuation, instituted by local government.

performance budget   Here, budget data are classified in terms of performance objectives. Criteria are established and monitored throughout the year, such as miles of streets cleaned, response time of emergency vehicles and so forth.

program budget   A budgetary format in which line item budget data are rearranged into a program structure so that, regardless of existing organizational location, complementary activities are grouped under common objectives. This helps decision-makers to resolve major policy questions.

project grants   This type of cooperative agreement provides federal funding for fixed time periods for specific projects or the delivery of specific products or services.

revenue anticipation notes or **tax anticipation notes**   Refers to short-term borrowing by local governments against a current year's property taxes or other revenues.

revenue bonds   Bonds issued to finance the acquisition, construction or improvement of revenue-producing facilities with their principal and interest requirements payable solely from the revenues generated by the facility. Ordinarily, these are secured only by the subsequent generation of revenues.

serial bonds   These bonds are primarily of two varieties: straight serial bonds and annuity serial bonds. Both ordinarily mature in regular, annual installments that are fixed at the time of issue of the bonds.

zero-based budget   A budget in which decision units are identified and established by program managers. These in turn require the preparation of several different packages for each of the decision units, which are ranked by priority.

Expanding the Reporting of Government

Most newspapers and the more responsible broadcast organizations see to it that the offices of the mayor and city manager, commissioners, Council members and other top local officials are thoroughly covered.

However, in larger cities, the growing dependence of such authorities on their public relations people tends to remove them from immediate access by local reporters. Now, instead of being tossed into the hurly-burly of news conferences, some media-wise officials save their news—and their availability—for much-desired personal appearances on local television.

Finding New Sources for News   The news media have changed, too. Instead of letting a reporter sit and await the pleasure of the mayor, whiling away the hours at penny ante in the press room at City Hall, most newspapers insist on enterprise coverage of city affairs. That means reporters get a chance to delve into promising but untouched areas of local government on their own for days at a time in order to produce a special story or series, and most of them welcome it. The growth of the team reporting concept in local affairs has helped open up a lot of different news resources as well.

Once the local reporter moves out of City Hall, the main problem is to find reliable and cooperative officials who will explain the details of their operations. Younger journalists usually depend on reporters already on these beats to break them in, but sometimes that presents difficulties. Journalism, after all, remains highly competitive at every level.

It is basic, therefore, to acquire primary background knowledge of the various forms of government beyond the local level. In counties, for example, the traditional method of government through old and well-established county boards of commissioners is giving way to a county executive–county legislature operation. On the state level, the governor and legislature remain the principal news sources, but the interplay of politics sometimes becomes a dominant factor in formulating state programs affecting local communities. And in metropolitan areas, forms of government such as the Tennessee Valley Authority and the New York–New Jersey Port Authority cut across state lines and continue to develop formidable powers all their own.

Reporters must be familiar with these systems and their adjuncts. They must also have a knowledge of the pertinent charters and constitutions, plus the source materials and daily records that are available for inspection, before they can hope to get a maximum of meaning out of public meetings and news conferences with officials.

It is an old reportorial habit to write stories in terms of persons rather than problems, colorful incidents rather than studied analyses of material in which the public should be interested. All journalists know that it is much easier to sell a story if the name of a controversial official is attached to the lead in some way, such as being for or against a particular proposal. The news media like the specific, abhor the abstract.

The State and Public Policy   At the state level, news breaks are infinite in their variety. The public's business often requires chief executives to speak out on a variety of issues. Here, for example, is the way the *New Hampshire Sunday News*, in Manchester, handled an unexpected warning by the governor of the state against fiscal irresponsibility:

> WATERVILLE VALLEY—It is time for New Hampshire to develop a comprehensive approach to its budget problems and stop trying to "cut a little, tax a little, gimmick a little," Gov. Hugh J. Gallen said Saturday.
>
> Speaking at the annual State Employees Association convention, the governor said the growth of state spending must be reduced. He noted that for nine of the last 14 years, New Hampshire's spending has outstripped its income.
>
> The governor said he would oppose proposals to make selective cuts (such as laying off state employees while leaving agency managers untouched) or passing a "hodge-podge assortment" of taxes to balance the state budget, which may be as much as $70 million in the red.

"While the old standby of cut a little, tax a little, gimmick a little may appear attractive, it has been a poor policy in the past and it is a poor policy today," Gallen said. . . .

State governors also have to be responsive to public needs and frequently will take the initiative in putting out proposals on everything from environmental issues to consumer affairs. In Utah, the *Ogden Standard-Examiner* sent its business editor, Cliff Thompson, to cover a meeting on power rates—usually a dull subject. But Utah's governor unexpectedly took a hand in the controversy, with this result:

By Cliff Thompson

Gov. Scott Matheson says the cost of meeting the state's growing electrical power demands should be fairly allocated to protect residential users from unreasonable rate hikes while encouraging continued industrial growth.

But he admits that won't be easy to accomplish.

Matheson's position was outlined in a letter read to the Ogden area Chamber of Commerce-sponsored meeting Monday between officials of the Utah Power & Light Co. and some of its biggest industrial users.

There was general agreement by both power company executives and industrial customers that UP & L faces a "tough, complex" question coming up with $300 million to $400 million a year to build new generating plants for the 1980s.

"I consider utility pricing issues to be one of the major policy items Utahns will face in the 1980s," Matheson wrote. . . .

At the legislative level of state coverage, reporters often have to go with incomplete stories because that is the nature of the legislative process. Where two houses are working on numerous proposed laws midway through a legislative session, almost anything can happen and reporters have to cover themselves. Here, for example, is such a partial story in the *Berkshire Eagle* of Pittsfield, Massachusetts, written by the paper's legislative correspondent, A. A. Michelson:

BOSTON—Even though there are more than 1,000 bills still bottled up in legislative committees, there is talk that the Senate will call it quits for this session at the end of the coming week.

"That's what the Senate leadership told us this week," Sen. Peter C. Webber, R–Great Barrington, said last night.

Rep. Dennis J. Duffin, D–Lenox, vice chairman of the House Ways and Means Committee, said he had heard of the plan "but I'll believe it when I see it. There's a tremendous amount of important legislation pending."

The idea, Webber explained, is for the Senate to go into recess for the winter holidays, not final adjournment. The legislators have only three weeks left in which to act on pending proposals. After that, all bills not acted on in the current session are dead. . . .

News at the County Level   Many counties in the United States have special authority beyond that of the cities within their jurisdiction and often make major decisions that deeply affect the quality of life in those municipalities.

This is how Barbara Johnson of the *Fort Myers* (Florida) *News-Press* began a story about beach erosion that could cost county taxpayers millions of dollars:

> To the sun-drunk sun-worshippers who week-end on Captiva Island, the furious two-year debate over enlarging South Seas Plantation's eroded beach might seem to be just so much environmental esoterica.
>
> But now a companion project by the Captiva Erosion Prevention District to rebuild the rest of the island's shore line is getting under way. The cost is estimated to be between $7 and $8 million.
>
> District officials are speaking of new island property taxes and county-wide tax revenue. The erosion prevention district has applied for state and federal permits to rebuild the island's remaining shore line.
>
> District Chairman Richard Butze said the erosion has become a menace to island property owners. On some parts of the island, he added, homeowners this year have watched four to ten feet of beach drop into the Gulf of Mexico. . . .

In the *Milwaukee Journal*, sewer funds made news. What was involved was a $1.53 billion antipollution program for the Milwaukee Metropolitan Sewerage District, and it took a certain amount of explaining, as the following story demonstrated:

> County officials, including nearly all 25 members of the County Board, packed a room in the Courthouse Friday to hear if a judge would find the county in contempt for defying an order to provide $55.7 million for the Milwaukee Metropolitan Sewerage District.
>
> Circuit Judge Daniel P. Anderson of Sheboygan County had been asked to force the county to come up with the money. Officials warned that the Milwaukee District's $1.53 billion anti-pollution program would come to a halt for lack of funds if the $55.7 million cannot be paid.
>
> Recently, Judge Anderson ruled that County Executive O'Donnell and the County Board must provide the $55.7 million, which they have failed to do. Lawyers for the county argued their client should not have to pay the money pending appeal. . . .

The Work of Reporting Teams   Through detailed investigation of land purchases, tax records and other available official documents, individual reporters and reporting teams have come up with a lot of news that could never have been obtained through the old routine of coverage by the beat.

One of the most brilliant investigations in recent years, which was conducted for six months by the investigative team of the *Indianapolis Star*, exposed widespread corruption in the Indianapolis Police Department and won the Pulitzer Prize for Special Local Reporting. It resulted in the dismissal of the director of public safety, the removal of the police chief and virtually all ranking police officers, and the defeat at the polls of a prosecuting attorney who was charged with a cover-up of the scandal. Here was the first of more than 400 stories that led to such spectacular results:

Widespread corruption in the Indianapolis Police Department—including graft and protection for prostitution, narcotics, bootlegging and gambling—has been uncovered in a six-month investigation by the *Indianapolis Star*.

Involvement in corruption by dozens of Indianapolis policemen is not limited to taking money, but has led some members of the department into criminal activities, the probe showed.

Allegations of bribery and wrongdoing over a period of five years are being investigated by the FBI and other federal agencies. Information obtained by the *Star* has been made available to federal investigators.

The *Star* investigation showed that vice operations in the city over the last decade add up to an estimated $40 million annual "pie" while the illegal narcotics trade is well over that figure.

The majority of illegal money filters up to high-ranking policemen and a few key political figures.

Aided by 28 policemen who—disgusted with what has been occurring—provided statements, tape recordings, records or other assistance, the investigation showed that corruption reaches into many areas of the department and includes high-ranking policemen.

Eight Marion County sheriff's detectives also provided information and other assistance, including statements from persons with direct knowledge of graft.

In all, reporters interviewed more than 400 persons, including a total of 60 policemen plus several former policemen. . . .

There followed 15 itemized charges supported by documented evidence, a careful and well-checked case that stood up for the most part under the most searching examination. Even though two of the reporters were indicted in retaliation on trumped-up charges of bribing police, nothing stopped the *Indianapolis Star*. The reporters were cleared, the police were not. The investigation was a model for planning, execution and results.

• Short Takes

These are the principal things to remember about reporting on budgets, taxes and local government:

- The first requirement is a basic knowledge of the functions of local government, the manner in which budgets are prepared and the manner in which the need for tax increases is determined.
- If a budget is increased over the previous year, the reporter must determine as quickly as possible where the additional money is coming from. It must be derived either from economies through decreases in staffs and services, increases in existing taxes or the levying of new ones, or the sale of bonds or tax anticipation notes.
- If taxes are to be increased, the first test is to determine how much the property tax will rise and what this will mean to the average homeowner.
- Pay increases or decreases for city employees should be noted, with exact amounts wherever possible.
- Where there is an increase in debt service—the amount a city pays in interest

on the bonds it issues—the reporter should know how much interest the city now pays on its bonds. (Municipal securities are tax-exempt under federal laws.)

- In writing budget stories, the lead should specify the total amount of the proposed or final operating budget and report on whether tax increases or new taxes are requested. A summary of the main points of the budget should follow, with the body of the story elaborating on the principal developments.
- The tax levy (called a mill rate) is determined by dividing the sum needed for property taxes by the total assessed valuation of all property involved, multiplied by 100. If the budget allows for a small percentage of property taxes that may not be collected, this should be subtracted from the property-tax total before the final calculation is made.
- Team reporting is often required at the local level if a detailed inquiry is being made into governmental affairs. Since governmental affairs at the state level are even more complicated, such devices as the in-depth report and the "take-out," a detailed account using a feature-style approach, are sometimes used to describe such developments.

CHAPTER 26

The Big Story: Washington and the World

In every global center of communication, the news media in effect provide a national and international platform for newsmakers, good and bad. Of these, Washington is by all odds the most important.

Regardless of where the news originates, it is magnified when it passes through Washington and other great world news centers. This process of amplification is the basis for the communication of the news of governments and their peoples both internally and externally in free societies. It is also, unfortunately, a powerful mechanism that may be seized upon by terrorists with a fancied grievance, who commit an outrage against public order and thereby have their puny voices amplified a thousandfold.

The Washington Correspondents

Among the 70,000 full-time journalists employed by American news organizations, a comparatively small number become Washington or foreign correspondents on a permanent basis. For those who have the knowledge, background, ability and good fortune to survive the rigorous tests of practical journalism, the privilege of covering the outstanding national and international developments of our time is among the finest rewards the profession has to offer.

Whether reporters are at work in the White House, the Congress or elsewhere in Washington; in the chanceries of foreign nations or on some desolate battlefield, their highest duty is to record and explain the decisions that affect hundreds of millions of people. Theirs is, in the main, the story of an age of political, social and economic upheaval — an era in which man has unleashed the terrifying power of the atom and walked on the moon, sent photographic robots to explore outer space and launched global satellites in orbit to insure better communications on earth.

What the Public Wants   However, if news organizations based their national and world coverage on what they think the public wants, there would be precious little of either in our daily news budgets except for major news breaks. It is one of the ironies of our time that when the United States remains the most powerful nation on earth and has vast global interests, the American people are so little interested in events outside their own immediate affairs at home.

At peak periods, such as the Vietnam War, the Watergate scandal, tensions in the Middle East and in Eastern Europe, there is of course a demand for other than local news. And most people have a demonstrable interest in the outcome of elections, even though only about half of those eligible bother to vote. But otherwise, from Broadway to Main Street, local news represents the main interest of the vast majority of our own people.

Dan Rather at the 1980 national conventions. CBS News Photo.

Why, then, do our principal news organizations devote so much time, effort and money to the coverage of national and international affairs? It is, quite simply put, a principal part of the journalist's duty to provide the public with the news it must have if it is to participate in the decision-making processes of a free society.

When National News Is Local

Editors who have spent their careers grappling with the intricacies of national news know all too well how little attention the home front pays to matters of high policy. They are always alert, therefore, to develop a local angle on major developments in Washington. These are some of the ways in which local reporters are assigned to trace the effect of national policy decisions on the average citizen:

Budget Cuts Any large reduction in the federal budget can have a devastating local effect. Offices of local members of Congress or of one of the two senators usually know in advance where to look for casualties. Anything from federal revenue sharing (money returned to the states and localities by the federal government) to school lunch programs can be deeply affected. Local budget officials are always ready to protest and are good sources.

Social Security This is one of the most sensitive areas of government. Anything that happens to such benefits, or to Medicare or Medicaid, usually winds up on Page 1 or the evening newscasts. Local Social Security officials are obvious sources, but the people on Social Security are the ones most immediately affected and the best sources.

Unemployment A change of a few 10ths of a point in the national unemployment figures can affect hundreds of thousands of families. It is up to the local reporter to find out, from the nearest state employment officials, what this means to each community. And it is very much worth doing. The human stories on the unemployment line make these figures take on new meaning.

Taxes Whether taxes are cut or increased, the first place to look for an effect on a community is among its businesspeople and its industrial plant. These employers, always sensitive to tax changes, know pretty well what the new figures will mean to the community at large. Local bankers and, in a college town, university professors can provide the necessary explanations of the policy changes.

Consumer Price Index (CPI) The CPI is the measurement of inflation nationally. It is issued monthly by the Bureau of Labor Statistics (BLS) of the Department of Commerce. When inflation goes to double-digit figures (more than 9 percent), it is no mere national statistic. Local news organizations, as soon as possible, translate that national figure into what it actually means at checkout counters and other mass businesses on which local living depends. We have learned to our cost that inflation can create as much turmoil in a local economy as unemployment.

The Washington Scene

The news corps in the nation's capital numbers about 2,000 permanent representatives from all countries, including our own, during peak periods for news. The number of stringers (part-time correspondents or brief visitors) varies by the day and no one can say how many are truly reliable.

Perhaps a score of great news organizations dominate the coverage of events in Washington. Of these, the most important for the bulk of newspapers and broadcast media are the wire services, Associated Press and United Press International. They provide anywhere from one-half to two-thirds of the coverage in the national engines of information, plus backup coverage for the networks, the great newspapers and their syndicates and the newsmagazines.

The Influentials Mass coverage, however, is not necessarily the most influential coverage. The Washington bureaus of our most important publications and broadcast news organizations usually have the greatest impact on the *leaders* of public opinion. Both in and out of government, a great deal of attention is paid to what is published in such major newspapers as the *Washington Post*, the *Wall Street Journal* and the *New York Times*, in *Time* and *Newsweek* and *U.S. News & World Report* and what is broadcast in the national network news reports. The flagship papers of the biggest chains — Knight-Ridder, Los Angeles Times-Newsday, Chicago Tribune and Gannett — also have a special influence.

It follows, then, that the major reporters for the leading news organizations as a rule also have an impact on the thinking of many of their journalistic colleagues. David Broder of the *Washington Post*, for example, has been regarded for a number of years as the single most influential journalist in the nation's capital. Others in comparable positions with news organizations of primary importance in Washington also have a kind of journalistic coterie of professional readers and listeners.

There is, as many Washington correspondents are the first to admit, a rather lamentable tendency among the Washington news corps to bid more for professional applause than public understanding. It is an all too human failing.

Probably the most important factor in the coverage of Washington is the extent of the adversary relationship between the news corps and the administration in power, whether it is Republican or Democratic.

Jack Nelson of the *Los Angeles Times*, a Pulitzer Prize-winner before he went to Washington, put the case this way:

> I don't think the problem is so much with the Washington press corps,
> although we have our problems, particularly in covering the White House. The
> problem is that there are a lot of people who have reached a pinnacle of power and
> who don't believe that the American people have a right to know what the
> government is doing. I have seen it in every administration. I don't exclude any of
> them. That is the real problem, and it is not particularly a problem of the
> Washington press corps.

Leaks in the Government Pipeline Every president without exception has had trouble controlling leaks in his administration. For better or worse, even the most capable and high-principled figures who have access to presidential planning and thinking will spill a story to a favored reporter for reasons of their own. Often, it is done to try to influence presidential policy against the subject that is being leaked to the news media. Sometimes, one Cabinet member will fall into a feud with an equally powerful colleague and each will leak derogatory information against the other. In the case of the Pentagon, where huge sums in the defense budget are at stake, the armed services on occasion will leak information in an attempt to prejudice congressional action against rival service programs.

Reporters, on their part, justify printing or broadcasting such data by arguing that, even if one noble soul refuses to become a conduit to the public, many another in the news business will be eager to publicize such exclusive information.

News Centers in Washington

Those who are assigned to work in Washington as members of established bureaus are lucky because their associates ease the breaking-in period and provide advice on such problems as housing, commuting, schools for children and so on. But for those who go to the capital for the first time on their own, it is a bewildering and sometimes traumatic experience. Newcomers are well advised to make themselves known to the chiefs of the wire services and syndicates to which their organization subscribes, their congressional delegation and key information personnel in such strategic spots as the White House, State Department, Pentagon and the House and Senate press galleries.

Before any such contacts are made, however, it is necessary to have proper credentials. These would include the usual personal-identification documents — auto licenses, credit cards and the like — and a letter from a qualified editor or news director in your news organization that indicates why you are in Washington, for how long and the general purpose of your reporting assignment. Such letters generally are duplicated and copies may be given wherever they are necessary.

Because of the publicity attached to the National Press Club, and the proximity of news teletype machines, loners in Washington sometimes try to work there on the basis of a temporary membership. However, as a rule, they are likely to be overwhelmed there by press agents of all kinds. It is a much sounder practice to work out of a place like the Senate press gallery, when Congress is in session, or to pick a particular story each day and follow it through, whatever the location. One inflexible rule for newcomers in Washington is to get to all assignments well ahead of time to meet the newsmakers and their staff personnel. Another is to insure that there is quick access to a telephone or wire for filing — sometimes far easier said than done in Washington on a major story.

In a book of this nature, which can include only a survey of overall Washington coverage rather than an in-depth study, all that can be attempted is a brief enumeration of the principal sources of news and a few suggestions on what to do and what not to do. These are as follows:

The White House The president of the United States, being the single most important news source in the country as well as the most influential, is given intensive daily coverage by every important news organization in the nation and others abroad. So are the members of his family, his friends and close associates.

Yet the press facilities at the White House are poorer than at many a state house or even a city hall. Only a small number of correspondents regularly assigned to the White House have one of the tiny cubicles plus telephone in the press room; the rest have to scamper for their communications on deadlines.

The president's press secretary is generally available once or twice a day for news conferences, announcements or background material. He and his assistants are the gatekeepers who can ease the newcomer's approach to members of the presidential staff and the various offices directly responsible to the president. The better-known correspondents, of course, make their own appointments and often conduct a substantial part of their business by telephone except on breaking stories. On days when the president is having a news conference, it is usual for 300 or more correspondents to attend if there is advance notice. If the conference is hastily called, only the regulars have time to attend.

The broadcast media are always on call and ready to work at the White House, but are no longer dependent on the unwieldy cameras on tripods that were set up in the reception room to catch important visitors as they left the president's office. With the minicam and videotape, TV people are mobile enough now to vie with other reporters in watching side entrances for visitors who seek to avoid publicity. TV crews can also get into the Rose Garden on short notice if a presidential news conference is called there on the spur of the moment.

A number of news conferences of officials, many for background, are held in a small conference room for reporters that was built over what was once a swimming pool. And when the president is about to travel, the 200 to 300 correspondents accompanying him must make their arrangements through the White House. There may be times on the White House beat when reporters sit around aimlessly and wait for something to happen, but such periods are infrequent. The president, the nation's No. 1 newsmaker, keeps the correspondents occupied with his activities.

Congress   If the president of the United States and the principal members of his Cabinet choose to be reticent about a policy or an issue, the Congress of the United States very quickly fills the news vacuum. Next to the White House, the "Hill" is the most important point for news in the capital. Reporters who regularly cover the Senate and the House have a good working relationship with the majority and minority leaders of both Houses, as well as with other legislative officials. They know the committee chairmen and develop efficient methods of keeping in touch with them. Whereas background conferences and other "I'll-tell-you-but-don't-quote-me" expedients are almost the rule in the executive branch of the government, the members of Congress generally put everything on the record. They want their views known. As elected officials, they seek to publicize their actions and their positions on the issues of the day; the voters all too easily forget a senator or a representative from whom nothing is heard for weeks at a time.

For the newcomer, the press galleries in both Houses are about the most convenient places to work in Washington. The superintendents and their small but able staffs in the press galleries know more than most reporters about schedules, speeches, committee hearings and the numerous other facets of the news that may be expected during the course of a congressional day. Advance copies of major (and a lot of minor) speeches are readily available, either in the press galleries or through the offices of the respective authors. The press gallery officials and other members of congressional staffs can be exceedingly helpful at times in reaching senators or representatives, either by telephone at their offices or by message on the floor of one of the two Houses. Reporters quickly learn that they cannot take the time to make the rounds in the Senate and House office buildings, except where the story makes such a procedure necessary. It is easier to use the telephone.

As the Congressional Directory shows, the sources of news in the Congress are manifold. And as the Congressional Record testifies each day, there are many speeches and other pronouncements that never attract public notice until they are published; moreover, a published speech may be considerably different from the original version because members of Congress have the right of correction and of extending their remarks. A final caution to the newcomer (and to many a veteran as well) is the warning to be familiar with the procedures in both Houses; without such knowledge, much of the intricate maneuvering that takes place during the legislative process cannot be translated into terms understandable to the public. It is a journalistic truism that there is so much news in Washington that it becomes a problem not of what to use, but of what to eliminate.

The State Department   In the massive gray State Department building on "Foggy Bottom," about 50 or 60 correspondents regularly cover diplomatic affairs and several hundred others come rushing in whenever there is a crisis. The inadequate press room, with its tiny cubicles for the reporters, is a chamber of echoes but is used for lack of something better. The wire service staffs, which have slightly larger quarters, do much of their work by dictating to their main offices in Washington.

Primary sources at State are the departmental news divisions, situated near the press room, and the office of the assistant secretary of state for public affairs on the sixth floor. In addition, the correspondent who is known and respected has access to most of the major officials of the department, up to and sometimes including the secretary of state. Nearly any correspondent can arrange through the small group of press officers to gain access to the desk officials in direct contact with embassies and ministries abroad. This kind of information usually is put out on a background basis. For more direct news reporting, the primary resort is the daily news conference by one of the senior officials in the Public Affairs office. The machinery at State is flexible enough to handle queries or requests for reactions at almost any time of the day, but once the "lid is on" in the evening it takes something akin to a war scare to produce news out of the department.

The secretary of state and his immediate aides schedule their own news conferences from time to time, but always in consultation with the White House. The printed matter available at State is mountainous in scope, but little of it is new except an occasional White Paper or other policy pronouncement that is issued as a document. Yet State can be a valuable research facility to those correspondents who know how to operate there and whose offices permit them to spend some time in preparing a story.

The Defense Department   Any bona fide correspondent with business in the Defense Department has very little trouble gaining access to the proper officials in the Pentagon. But getting news is something else again. In periods of crisis, restrictions abound.

Regardless of the difficulties of obtaining vital information, the machinery for developing and handling news at the Pentagon is probably the most elaborate ever devised for any department of government in this country. The Defense Department (DOD) has its own information setup under an assistant secretary of defense, which includes representatives of all military services, and a big press room on the second floor of the Pentagon where each service has a desk staffed by a number of officers. In addition, the Army, and Air Force have its own staff of information personnel (Army and Air Force each has a consolidated external and internal information programs). In all, nearly 1,000 officers in the Pentagon are assigned to some facet of public relations activities. In turn, they direct the information and public relations work of small staffs and individuals at each post and base throughout the world; thus, a small army of public relations officers is assigned specifically to work with press and public and within the armed forces themselves.

The Supreme Court   The nation's highest tribunal has almost quadrupled its case load in 30 years. In 1950, it handled 1,335 cases, in 1980, 5,144 cases. Of the approximately 200 cases on the court's weekly list, only four or five are actually heard and the rest are denied review. And yet, the load and the responsibility are enormous for the dozen or so reporters who regularly cover the Court and the extra 20 or 25 who come in for special cases of particular interest. During the year, which runs from the traditional "first Monday in October" to about July 4, the Court generally hands down 130 to 150 opinions — the laws by which the nation is governed.

It isn't an easy job to cover the high court. As Justice Oliver Wendell Holmes said, "The law embodies the story of a nation's development through many centuries, and it cannot be dealt with as if it contained only the axioms and corollaries of a book of mathematics."

Treasury   One of the most important innovations developed by the Treasury Department is the "Budget School" held for several days prior to the release of the federal budget. Correspondents, many with special training in economic affairs, have a chance to study this formidable document and talk with the nation's leading authorities on it before presenting their accounts to the public.

This kind of preparation is woefully lacking in many other areas of coverage in Washington, where it is needed. The Treasury has shown that it is possible to enter into a workable agreement with the news media on matters of importance to the public, such as government expenditures and the prospect of new taxes, to give correspondents time for study and reflection. In affairs of this nature, the few paragraphs scrambled together for a deadline 10 minutes away can sometimes be totally misleading. It is better to wait, in agreement with the source and with the competition, and give the whole story in proper perspective.

In periods of economic tension, the Treasury is also the source of news about monetary policies and the various temporary controls on prices and wages that accompany them from time to time.

Agriculture The correspondents who cover the Department of Agriculture, like those at State, Defense and the Treasury, are generally highly specialized in the field and work for news organizations with a particular interest in the subject. The daily routine of agricultural reports is ably carried by the wire services. But for detailed, in-depth reportage on matters of importance to both farmer and consumer, the news media must turn once more to the specialist.

Other Areas All except the largest and richest news organizations necessarily are unable to staff the many other important government departments daily. Consequently, the Justice Department, the Labor Department, the Departments of Commerce, the Interior and Health and Human Services, to name only a few, are covered by the wire services for the majority of the Washington news corps. Individual correspondents with a special interest in the affairs of Justice or Labor, for example, may spend much more time there than others. Or the whole group may strain the facilities of a single department, such as Labor, during a national strike emergency. The point is that even the large news corps in the nation's capital has to work on the firehouse principle for everything except the top newsmaking sources.

Among the regulatory agencies, the news media have a natural and abiding interest in almost anything that is done by the Federal Communications Commission. And, with the rising interest in consumerism, more attention is being paid to the Federal Trade Commission. Otherwise, the regulatory agencies and the Postal Service are probably the worst-covered newsmaking organizations in Washington on a day-to-day basis.

Freedom and Security

The government and the news media will always agree to the general proposition that no news should be made public in time of crisis that violates national security. However, no agreement appears to be possible on exactly what constitutes national security in any given set of circumstances. It follows that the responsibility of determining what information should be withheld is exercised primarily by the government. However, when and if the press learns that information is being wrongfully withheld for reasons other than national security, its responsibility is to make prompt disclosures of such material in the public interest. That is the substance of what is known as the adversary relationship with government.

This posture of basic conflict between a democratic government and the free press has been the subject of continuing discussion between journalists and responsible public officials for many years. The relationship is by no means typical only of the United States. As long ago as the Crimean War, in the middle of the 19th century, William Howard Russell's disclosures of tragic mismanagement of the British military brought great prestige to *The Times* of London and caused the downfall of the Aberdeen government. Such instances may be documented in every practicing democracy where there is an effective, competent and critical free press.

It is the prevailing theory that the public interest is best served by a continuing rivalry between the two forces. However, if the conflict is pushed to excess, and if all restraint is abandoned by both government and the news media, then the probable result could be anarchy.

In national and international affairs, where so much impinges on national security, correspondents and editors are well aware of all the eloquent philosophy on both sides of the question of whether to reveal or suppress. Despite all the pressures upon them, it will be their decision finally as to what material in their possession will be passed on to the public. This is the highest responsibility of journalists in an open society. To exercise it, they must stand or fall on their own judgment.

The Presidential News Conference

It is a peculiarly American custom to have the president of the United States regularly face the questions of newspaper, wire service, newsmagazine and radio-TV correspondents. Until the turn of the century, it had occurred to no president to do this, and the newspapers themselves were not particularly interested. Then, President Theodore Roosevelt took to talking with reporters and consigning them to the "Ananias Club" when they published stories he did not like. President Wilson initiated the occasional press conference.

The founding of the presidential news conference as we know it today was the work of President Franklin Delano Roosevelt. As a past master of the art of handling reporters and editors, and a talented politician who enjoyed jousting with the press, he saw to it that news conferences were held on the average of twice a week during his four terms. President Truman continued FDR's system. Although he did not hold as many news conferences as his predecessor, they were every bit as expert.

Under President Eisenhower the final shred of protection for a chief executive was ripped away. Historically, presidents had been given the privilege of having their answers to all questions published in indirect discourse. When presidents permitted direct quotation of a few words or perhaps a sentence, it was a major event. But, once Eisenhower permitted TV cameras to record the presidential news conference and go on the air with the film, following review, it was impossible to keep the press from using direct quotations. So, after a brief check, presidential news conferences in the Eisenhower regime were on the record.

Of all the presidents in the latter half of this century, President Kennedy was the best liked by the Washington news corps and Presidents Johnson and Nixon were the most disliked. President Ford, after a brave beginning, took to avoiding news conferences as much as he could and generally wasn't very happy with the reporters. Nor was President Carter any more at ease with the news corps, especially during his time of troubles with the Iranians who held 52 Americans hostage for 444 days.

It remained for President Reagan to cut down the number of formal news conferences to six in his first year and to restore some semblance of order to the process by persuading reporters to quit jumping up and shouting at him when they sought recognition. Although he transmitted information readily, he frequently detoured the bulk of the newspeople and used brief televised statements, which did not endear him to the Washington reporters.

The course of the news conference, in short, has been downhill both in prestige and as a newsmaking device for much of the 1970s and 1980s.

The United Nations Story

Since the United States has been pushed into a minority position, outvoted or checkmated by a majority of developing countries that have links with the Soviet bloc, the UN has become unpopular in America. Outbursts of anti-American oratory, crises affecting the Arab states or the black nationalists of Africa and the pretentious maneuvering of the Soviet bloc have little interest either for the American public or for many correspondents except when it touches a sensitive national nerve.

Yet for as long as there is a United Nations and for at as long as its headquarters remain in New York, it is a story that will be covered.

Problems of Coverage   The UN is not difficult to cover. The problem, like that of the State Department, is that there is too much talk, too little action. Most of the large national delegations have press officers, a few of whom are first rate. The UN itself has a small group of capable career press officials who work for the secretary-general. At the UN documents counter, relevant materials are easily available; in the UN library, there is a backlog of information on every pending issue and a lot of issues that have been forgotten.

The procedures of the UN, the rules of its main organizations and the interpretations of the Charter are complicated, but not more so than those of any government. Well-qualified correspondents have never had much difficulty in moving around the UN. The main problem of coverage is that there is so little of it that matters.

Methods and Sources   These are the four principal sources for the UN story:

1. The open meetings, speeches and resolutions of the various components of the organization. These are chiefly the General Assembly, the Security Council and Economic and Social Council with their subsidiary committees.
2. The foreign delegations that, however reticent they may be about their own business, generally may be relied on in a highly unofficial way to give background information on what is going on elsewhere.
3. The United States Mission to the UN. This is an extension of the State Department, but it has its own public affairs and information officers, plus an excellent library.
4. The United Nations' own information staff and the resources of the secretary-general. Over the years the UN has developed a system of chronological reporting of all major meetings, with takes of copy available for correspondents an hour or so after delivery. This small news staff clears through a city desk of its own on the second floor of the UN Secretariat building and may be consulted by correspondents.

Physically the center of UN press coverage is the third floor of the Secretariat building, where the press liaison, documents center, briefing room and some correspondents' offices are located. Wire, cable, telephone and other communications facilities are available here, too. Accreditation is handled easily, and with a minimum of red tape, the chief requirements being a letter from a managing editor of a newspaper, or other appropriate official, requesting privileges for a correspondent.

Foreign Correspondence

There is an almost universal feeling in American newsrooms, where such things matter, that the big story overseas is not often told in terms that can be communicated easily to average readers and viewers. The usual surveys, with their findings of minimum use of foreign news in a large section of the American press and even less in the broadcast media, are depressing to anybody who has worked in the field and knows how much talent and effort and money go into foreign news coverage. Admittedly, the crisis story, the war story and the personal stories about colorful characters get through in volume. But the straws in the wind, the stories that should put the American public on guard, are not widely used.

The Flow of Foreign News Foreign dateline news is available to the American news media in large quantities on a daily basis, but comparatively little of it is used outside the large centers of population.

The wire services each distribute around 200,000 words a week from foreign sources. The news syndicates — newspapers like the *New York Times*, the *Washington Post-Los Angeles Times* and the Knight-Ridder Newspapers — also distribute foreign dateline news from their own correspondents to subscribing news organizations. The three broadcasting chains and the newsmagazines are other originating sources of foreign news.

Finally, many of these news organizations have agreements with foreign wire services and news organizations for what amounts to an exchange of services. In short, when there is a major break in foreign news, the American people usually receive the details quickly, efficiently and in large volume.

Breaking a Story The public's impression of the foreign correspondent as a dashing figure, predominantly male, and swaggering around in a trenchcoat, has little basis in fact. The correspondents in the Vietnam War, because of the nature of the conflict, were often under fire. In the less deadly but more frequent wars in the Middle East and Central America, correspondents also risk their lives to find out what is happening. It is seldom that a story is handed to them on a silver platter. Like any local reporter going out on a tough assignment, they accept risk as a part of their work.

Frequently, foreign correspondents who are right at the scene of a big story can't be sure of what is happening within their line of vision. It was particularly true of the assassination of the Egyptian president Anwar Sadat in 1981. Every reporter who was present at the military spectacle in Cairo saw men dressed in soldiers' uniforms shooting at Sadat and others in the reviewing stand, but the first word on the wires was that the president had been unharmed. Soon afterward, there were reports that he had been hit.

Let Fred Rothenberg, the AP's television writer, tell the rest of the story:

The reporter had just dropped a bombshell on her editor: President Anwar Sadat was dead. Billy Newman and Lou Grant? No, it was real TV — Dan Rather, managing editor of CBS Evening News, and Scotti Williston, reporting from Cairo.

And it happened live, in full view of the American public.

Rather's reaction was the same as that of any other editor. He was visibly shocked.

The earlier information from Cairo and Washington suggested that Sadat was safe. How had Scotti Williston learned Sadat was dead? How reliable was her information? Could she believe her sources?

In a firm voice, she said the sources were reliable and that she believed them. With the nation watching, CBS gave first word that another world leader had been assassinated. . . .

When Foreign News Is Local

With the increasing involvement of the United States in world affairs, editors of even the smallest and most parochial of news organizations have learned that foreign news need not necessarily carry a foreign dateline. A lot of it turns out to be local, although it may be foreign in origin.

When the oil crunch came and the flow of Arab oil suddenly was halted, every news organization in America told the story in terms of long lines of indignant Americans waiting and swearing at the gas pumps.

When Japanese and German automobiles took away a share of the once-dominant American car market, the woeful tale was reflected in scare headlines about unemployment in the capital of the American motor industry, Detroit, and in every automobile showroom in the nation.

When the Carter administration slapped a partial boycott on the sale of grain to Russia as retaliation for the Soviet invasion of Afghanistan, the story evoked howls of rage from wheat farmers in the Midwest. They were placated when the Reagan administration — in its first year — canceled the boycott.

The lesson is clear enough. The scant bit of foreign dateline news in the average American paper on an average day is by no means the extent of the foreign story in this country. Almost every day, a local reporter is working on a story that originated abroad, as witness the following:

- In response to the Soviet arms buildup, the new American missile system and its defensive outposts are bound to affect the lives of millions of Americans in the less populated areas of our country. It is a major story of our time and it is being told in local terms.
- Our great multinational corporations have major enterprises abroad, which adds to employment there; in return, foreign multinational corporations are building plants here to turn out everything from automobiles to computers. But, lamentably, many more American jobs are lost abroad than are being created here by foreign companies. And that, too, is a local story.
- Fully one-quarter to one-third of American agricultural products are sold abroad and the acceptance of these products by foreign peoples is of enormous interest in

the areas where they are grown. There is nothing very foreign about the way this story is covered and written in the farm belt.

- Anything that tends to interfere with the flow of foreign oil to the United States is bound to have an effect on the way we transport our food, our clothing, our manufactured goods, our raw materials. And it also will have an inevitable effect on the amount of use we give the cars that we drive to work and back.

- There is an ethnicity characteristic of much of our foreign news, as witness the enormous interest in news about Poland and other parts of Eastern Europe in Chicago, Pittsburgh and other centers in which Slavic immigrants settled early in this century; news about Israel and the Arab states in New York, Boston, Miami, Los Angeles and other centers with large Jewish populations; news about the Irish time of troubles in Boston, New York and other centers settled by large numbers of Irish immigrants; news about Germany in Milwaukee and St. Louis; news about the Scandinavian countries in Minnesota, Wisconsin and western Washington; news about Central American fighting that galvanizes every Spanish-speaking community. The list could go on to cover many other nationalities as well.

The point cannot be overstressed. Foreign news must be told in terms that mean something to the people in a particular community. And very often those terms are translated into local interests.

The Foreign News Corps

The foreign correspondents on permanent assignment for American news organizations overseas vary from 350 to 400 in noncrisis periods to 700 or more when there is intense American public interest in a developing story. It takes at least double that number of editors, technicians and other supporting personnel to keep the reporters' dispatches and videotape moving.

In addition, a number of important regional newspapers of the caliber of the *Miami Herald* and the *St. Louis Post-Dispatch* send correspondents from the home office or their Washington bureaus directly to spot assignments overseas and pull them back when the story is over. And there are thousands of stringers — part-time correspondents — in every part of the world who service the American news media for varying periods on a piecework basis.

This is by no means an all-American show. The wire services in particular have found that "locals," the term for indigenous journalists, can do a better job at cheaper rates on some types of assignment than American correspondents sent from homebase and maintained at greater expense abroad. There are, in consequence, numerous bureaus in various parts of the world where "locals" are in control. This is also true, but to a lesser extent, of the corps of correspondents maintained by the great newspapers, the networks and the newsmagazines.

Who Are the Correspondents? The foreign correspondents who handle the bulk of the news on a day-by-day basis for America are usually mature journalists with a superior record of professional performance and a good education.

It is not unusual to find among them men and women with advanced degrees. Some are Nieman Fellows at Harvard and there are even a few Rhodes scholars.

They travel a great deal from established bases and usually are given new assignments every three years. In combat zones, the first thing they learn to do is to keep their heads down. A dead correspondent may be a hero, but news organizations naturally prefer to have their staffers hale of body and sound of wind. And as for rising to the heights and defying dictatorial governments, correspondents find out very soon that being expelled through provocation is not the high road to success.

How to Be One   The manner of becoming a foreign correspondent is still as great an uncertainty as ever, despite all the talk about modern personnel methods. Some are chosen for the job and trained rigorously for it with special courses in great universities and hours of practice in a foreign language. Many more happen to be at the right spot at the right time and fall into it. A few adventurers persuade editors to try them, with indifferent results as a rule (although sometimes there are pleasant surprises). The rest of the foreign correspondents work their way up slowly in the news agencies and on newspapers having foreign staffs, and quite often are picked off by the ever-watchful newsmagazines and electronic media for their own foreign staffs.

While most of the dependable older men and the few women who are established foreign correspondents can count on fairly decent pay, there are youngsters who are willing to work for less than they could earn on a police beat at home. It is only when the action is rough and the risks are very great that the younger people tend to get top preference, particularly in war zones. In television's first war, the Vietnam conflict, the youngsters often dominated the battle coverage.

That, too, was the experience in the trouble-wracked Mideast, especially in the long and brutal Lebanese civil war.

Foreign Language Studies   The foreign correspondent who gets by with a knowledge of English and some *table d'hôte* French is a dying breed. Most of today's younger correspondents are fluent in at least one foreign language, and some know two. If there is a choice between a tongue-lazy reporter who can't handle a foreign language and someone who is just as capable and has foreign language training, it is obvious that the trained correspondent will be selected. Moreover, it is difficult to get by in Latin America without knowing Spanish; in the Middle East without Arabic; in India without Hindi; in Japan without basic Japanese, and in China without at least a working knowledge of Chinese.

How They Work   Most foreign correspondents believe their first duty is to tell the story of the people of the nation to which they are assigned, not merely the official acts of the government and the various press ministry announcements. The job is difficult and demanding, requiring long and sometimes irregular hours of work at periods of the day and night that can break up family life. It is no accident that the divorce rate among foreign correspondents is comparatively high.

Where correspondents are assigned to cover an entire country, such as India, or several countries, such as the northern sector of the South American continent, it is apparent that they have to depend on the local mass communications facilities to keep themselves informed. However, they soon find that they have to do more than read papers, listen to the radio, watch TV, see what the wires are sending and be friendly with American embassy and host country information people. They have to develop their own sources, their own story ideas, their own methods of operation — and that takes time and a lot of money. Without counting transmission tolls, the average news organization excluding wire services can expect to pay more than $100,000 a year to keep a single American foreign correspondent in a post — and a good deal more in places like Moscow and Peking. No wonder more "locals" are now used!

Correspondents in authoritarian lands, such as the Soviet Union, China and many of the developing countries, can expect to be tied very largely to official sources. In the dwindling number of democratic lands, there is freedom of action if correspondents know what they want to do and how to go about it. It isn't often that editors want to lead correspondents by the hand, or even make the attempt, despite the availability of miracles of modern communication. Foreign correspondence is still a highly individual operation and it should remain so.

Combat Correspondence   The bitter experiences of American combat correspondents in Vietnam in the 1960s were repeated in the 1980s in both the Middle East and Central America. For those who went to report these wars, and particularly the TV camera crews, danger was all about them. It was inevitable that casualties would mount as contending factions tried to discourage Americans from covering any side except their own. Once again the death toll among newspeople mounted; but this time, Americans were not the only ones to suffer. In the war in El Salvador, four Dutch members of a TV crew were killed in what some called a "crossfire" and others "out-and-out murder."

Propaganda   It is a great popular delusion that the average American overseas is a ready victim for the wiles of foreign propaganda. The American politician who participates in a foreign conference is usually despaired of in advance. As for foreign correspondents, even their own editors sometimes refuse to believe them if their stories happen to coincide with claims that are being put out by a propaganda agency.

The fundamental difficulty here is to define propaganda and separate it from the journalistic commodity that is called news. Propaganda need not necessarily be based on false or misleading information; the "big lie," in fact, has certainly been less effective in the past than the truth — when the truth happened to serve, propaganda ends. Of course, few propagandists are foolish enough to label their more subtle ventures, but no propagandist is likely to deceive an experienced correspondent for very long.

Transmission of Information   Under current practice by news organizations with large volumes of news to transmit, circuits are contracted for on a time basis. A global wire service, for example, could keep 24-hour circuits going for two-way transmissions across the Atlantic. Under such circumstances, copy is transmitted in much the same way across or under oceans as it is over land lines or in the newsroom of a major organization. The old coded messages now have only interoffice service functions.

For a foreign service like that of the *New York Times*, transmission of certain kinds of data at 1,000 to 1,500 words a minute is not unusual. The wire services move as fast. Moreover, the system of telephone dictation into recording devices, which are quickly transcribed, is gaining favor at a number of overseas points as a rival to Telex. For both television and the print media, the satellite system has been a great advantage; with the increase in satellites and the growth of sophisticated cable channels, enormous improvements already are in sight. Transatlantic satellites eventually will provide some 42,000 simultaneous voice-data channels or 24 full-time color television channels. And the adaptation of laser technology and transmission by light along glass fibers is bound to broaden current facilities.

Press rates for foreign news are set by the International Telecommunications Union, mainly through the annual meetings of representatives of participating governments at Geneva and elsewhere. It is a general procedure that carriers must charge government-fixed rates and these can vary widely under transmissions paid for by the word rate, instead of a fixed time period.

Censorship

An even greater impediment to the flow of news across national borders than transmission costs is the rise of censorship in new and pernicious forms. In one guise or another, censorship exists over more than three-quarters of the earth's surface and it is gradually gaining even in the home of free expression, Western Europe.

In Communist Lands The crude total censorship of the early 20th century, in which dispatches were held up or mutilated in whole or in part, is no longer as widespread as it once was. Instead, particularly in the Communist world, the system has been changed to place correspondents in the position of censoring themselves for fear of being expelled.

Thus, the Soviet Union formally abolished censorship in 1961 and permitted Western correspondents to inaugurate two-way teletype communication with their home offices if they wished to do so. A certain amount of liberalization followed. Correspondents, cautiously testing the boiling point of the regime, learned they could transmit some criticism in low key and even speculate on the course of events behind the Iron Curtain. But they also found out that the Soviet Union was as quick as it ever had been to expel correspondents it deemed unfriendly and to bar from within its territory news organizations it held to be essentially hostile.

In China, too, correspondents experienced no formal censorship in the accepted sense of the term but they were held on a tight leash in both their movements and what sources they were permitted to contact. An exception was made for correspondents who went to China with American presidents or vice presidents.

The censor the correspondent never sees and the harsh voice that cuts off a telephone connection in a monitored call are the two figures in a censorship pattern that are the most difficult to bear. These are usually minor officials with set instructions, which they often interpret with unreasonable strictness. All correspondents can do is to file protests and carry their appeals to the authorities of their own embassy as well as those of the country to which they are accredited. They don't often win a battle of this kind, but they must always stand their ground for as long as possible.

In the Third World During the 1980s, the center of the struggle to keep information flowing freely across national borders shifted to UNESCO—the United Nations Educational, Scientific and Cultural Organization. There, a number of third world countries in Asia, Africa and Latin America began clamoring for a "New World Information Order." The Soviet Union seized on the issue, for it suited the Kremlin's purpose to stir up continued suspicion of American news media with their tradition of press freedom.

The new order, despite denials from UNESCO supporters, was calculated to bestow the blessings of the United Nations on any government that wished to prevent any foreign correspondent from sending dispatches or tapes from within its borders. This was clothed in fine diplomatic language, of course: The ultimate purpose was to disclose only "truth" about a given country, not "propaganda lies." Translated into realistic terms, this meant that the countries involved would tolerate no critical correspondence and would encourage only "positive"—that is, favorable—articles.

The complaints were aimed primarily at the Western news agencies, news syndicates, networks and newsmagazines—and especially those in the United States. Third world diplomats repeatedly called for the creation of an indigenous wire service—and the American news media continually offered to train personnel and provide the necessary hardware. But, of course, such agencies could not succeed because they were predicated on the circulation only of favorable reports—and news from the third world could never be all that favorable.

The "New World Information Order" had to be taken seriously, however, because it threatened widespread censorship of the news. In fact, a number of countries suffering from dictatorial rule didn't wait for the passage of requisite resolutions by UNESCO but installed their own set of guidelines for correspondents. Accordingly, the number of expulsions of foreign correspondents of American nationality became a regular—and extremely unpleasant—feature of world news coverage in the 1980s. And in some Latin American countries, licensing of foreign correspondents became a reality.

Leonard Marks, former director of the United States Information Agency, put the case this way:

> The kernel of the question is: Shall the state be powerful or shall the individual be powerful? And the press is just another manifestation of this problem. It won't go away because it's part of the tide that sweeps throughout the world when countries throw off their colonial yokes, when they try to enter the family of nations and become a vital part of the world. They have natural aspirations. How do you help them?
>
> I believe we've got to help them through developmental aid. We've got to show

them that having a variety of media is in their interest. When you talk to a journalist in a country where the government controls, you find within his bosom that he wants to be able to express his opinion. He doesn't feel that the guy who occupies the job of censor can do a better job than he. And some of the leaders have recognized that their national development will be aided by competitive forces. True, they don't like criticism but they recognize that there are advantages.

The intelligent ones, those who are sophisticated in world affairs, understand that if the free world media do not have access, if the media cannot report to the large developed countries the progress or the problems of the underdeveloped world, then bankers will not make loans, tourists will not be attracted, technical assistance will not be forthcoming.

• Short Takes

These are some of the basic points to remember about Washington and foreign correspondence:

- It is important to translate national and international news into local terms and, whenever possible, to demonstrate their effect on the lives of average Americans. A war threat in the Mideast, for example, could mean long lines at the gasoline pumps; or, for Midwestern farmers, a boycott on sales of grain to Russia might mean the difference between profit and loss for a year. A large budget cut in Washington inevitably will affect everything from local funds for local improvements to school lunches.
- The factor of adversary relationships between reporters and government is one of the realities of national and international coverage.
- In relation to the 70,000 full-time journalists employed by the American news media, the numbers of correspondents who work in Washington and abroad are relatively small, and newcomers sometimes wait for years to win such a post. However, any newcomer is likely to get a piece of the action locally at almost any time and should be familiar with national and international issues in the news. It is a part of the job.
- Stereotypes of national and foreign correspondents are misleading. Mainly, such reporters have greater responsibilities and, in combat areas, greater risks than others.

CHAPTER 27

The Specialists

Out near the San Andreas Fault in California, you don't wait for earthquakes to happen if you're in the news business. You prepare for them.

David Perlman, science editor of the *San Francisco Chronicle*, has covered earthquakes in California since 1952 and has a contingency plan for local emergencies. He knows how because he is a specialist and his paper and staff associates depend on him.

Useful as general assignment reporters usually are, they are the first to recognize when they are out of their depth. That is when the specialists are absolutely necessary in science, medicine, law and economics — to mention only four fields in which special knowledge is mandatory for practicing journalists.

In such newer fields as consumerism, the environment and atomic energy, a certain amount of special training, background knowledge and experience also are necessary, particularly for investigative reporters.

Leaders among the news media are applying greater resources, both in human and financial terms, to satisfy the public's increasing demands for more competent coverage of these and other specialized areas. And more young journalists are persuaded that it is worth their while to develop an interest in a specialty.

Science Writing

There is nothing theoretical about David Perlman's interest in earthquakes in California. And people who read the *San Francisco Chronicle* know it. For ever since

408

1906, when a great quake razed a large part of the city and set the shaking ruins afire, people in the area have been well aware that their only real defense against a recurrence is advanced knowledge. And Perlman has it, to the extent that anybody can in so unpredictable an area. He writes:

> I covered my first major earthquake at Tehachapi in California in 1952—flying down in a Red Cross plane to the tiny town where 14 people were killed in a temblor registering 7.7 on the Richter scale. We slept in the open for several nights on army cots which shivered and shook with every aftershock, and we filed stories via the railroad telegraph.
>
> Today our earthquake coverage involves continual contact with the seismologists at Caltech in Pasadena, at the University of California in Berkeley, and at the U.S. Geological Survey in Menlo Park. I usually write scientific "explainers" when a quake strikes, while we send as many reporters and photographers as needed to the sites of significant damage—be it San Fernando, the High Sierra, the Imperial Valley, or wherever.

Contingency Planning Like 120 million Japanese, who accept the reality of daily earth shocks as a part of their lives, people in towns and cities near the San Andreas Fault in California know that earthquake reporting is serious business. These are a part of the *San Francisco Chronicle*'s plans for any serious contingency. Perlman writes:

> We assume that phone lines and even power will be out, but that somehow cars will be able to roll. So we have preassigned photographers (whose cars are all

David Perlman of the *San Francisco Chronicle*.

equipped with radios) to drive as quickly as possible to the highest spots around San Francisco, where they would serve as local command posts and communications links to our central radio in the city room.

And if the city room is inoperative, our chief photographer's car would be parked in an open lot next to our building—there to serve as a focus for all city desk activities. (In 1906, the San Francisco papers all printed a joint edition in Oakland and we could probably find a newspaper plant somewhere in the Bay Area that would be similarly operable.)

It is noteworthy that the *Chronicle* apparently does not place major reliance on the Federal Emergency Management Administration, which didn't function as well as the news media in covering the Mount St. Helens eruption. But FEMA, for as long as it is able to continue in existence in the face of continual budgetary cutbacks, is bound to be a source in any disaster operation.

Covering a Quake The way a specialist covers an earthquake is somewhat different from and a lot more detailed than the way a general assignment reporter would go about the same job. This was how the *San Francisco Chronicle* led off its coverage of a "moderate" quake that took no lives (issue of January 25, 1980):

By David Perlman

Quake results   Rumbling aftershocks shook the Bay Area last night as damage assessment and repairs continued in the wake of a rolling earthquake that swept through much of Northern California yesterday morning.

Timing and damage   The initial quake, lasting nearly a minute, caused minor injuries and damage near its epicenter and forced 7,100 workers to leave the huge Livermore nuclear weapons laboratory.

Danger discounted   Last night, laboratory officials said a 30,000 gallon container of "very, very low level" radioactive tritium was leaking at the rate of four gallons an hour. The material, used in fusion research, was leaking into an asphalt container and was not considered by lab officials to be dangerous.

Magnitude of quake and aftershock   The "moderate" quake struck in a remote section of southeastern Contra Costa County at ten seconds past 11 a.m., with a Richter magnitude of 5.5. It was followed within the next three minutes by two aftershocks—one with a magnitude of 5.2 and the other measuring 4.8.

Two more aftershocks occurred yesterday evening—one of 4.6 magnitude at 9:12 p.m. and the second of 4.4 at 9:24 p.m.

Extent of quake   During the big morning quake, residents reported feeling the ground roll beneath them as far away as Reno, nearly 200 miles east of San Francisco; Monterey, 150 miles south, and Santa Rosa, 50 miles north.

Trains still run   The BART system halted all its trains for five minutes after the quake, but trains in the tunnel beneath San Francisco

Clay Ladd, reporter of the *San Francisco Chronicle* covering the Livermore, California, earthquake, January 1980. (Photograph: Susan Gilbert)

Road damage and repairs

Bay were allowed to go to the nearest station before the shutdown. No damage was reported on the lines.

Country roads and some larger highways near the epicenter buckled and cracked and an overpass along Interstate 580 at Greenville Road became impassable when earthworks and paving on the east side of the structure slumped three to eight inches.

> **General damage**
>
> The structure did not break but traffic had to be diverted off 580 and cars soon backed up several miles. Highway crews began clearing away chunks of tar and concrete. Resurfacing was completed and the bridge was reopened by late afternoon.
>
> Throughout the Bay Area, shattered windows, swaying high rises and groceries piled in the aisles of markets provided typical marks of the kind Northern California experiences. . . .

Most of the rest of the story was taken up with interviews with earth scientists in the area, both governmental and academic, to determine what caused the quake and whether a recurrence could be expected in the immediate future. This was, to the science writer, one of the most important aspects of the staff's coverage. He commented on his own experience:

> It was easy enough writing the first-edition story because the aftershocks obligingly subsided in plenty of time. But when more of them hit during the night, I had to rush back to the office and patch up the new information in a hurry. But that's the fun of the newspaper business!

Progress in Science Writing   Humankind's giant vault into space has done as much as anything to stimulate the trend toward specialization in journalism. When Neil Armstrong in 1969 stepped on the moon's surface and said, "This is one small step for a man, one giant leap for mankind," he also marked a major development in the reporting of science news.

Through all six moon journeys in which manned landings were made, and all the subsequent experiments that were climaxed by the trips of the space shuttle, the journalists told the story behind the marvelous TV pictures in terms that a mass public could understand. These, plus the space explorations of distant planets, have broadened the methods the news media use to communicate science news. Such experiences have given the trained newscasters and science reporters an advantage over their less skilled colleagues. As a young general assignment reporter observed ruefully, "You can't explain what you don't fully understand."

What Is Covered   Out of the enormous amount of material that is published in scientific and scholarly journals, it is obvious that only a small part can be translated into popular terms and used widely by the news media commanding a mass audience. Consequently, a considerable volume of science news of a technical nature appears in specialized publications first. Scientific conventions account for almost as much news of science, being prime sources of new developments and new ideas. Entirely on their own, science writers study almost anything bearing on the development of atomic energy and space exploration for the germ of a significant news account. Sometimes they learn of such developments from their own sources in government and industry; on other occasions, they may be able to deduce clues to future developments from their own background and knowledge.

The increasing emphasis on studies of air and water pollution has deepened public interest in such matters and broadened the scope of the writer of popularized science. This is also true of the emphasis on medical reportage and progress in improving conditions in hospitals. But whole areas of mathematics, physics and chemistry and other natural sciences are still relatively uncovered in the daily and periodical press because the developments are so far above the level of public understanding.

The Energy Crunch   Nowhere is there greater need for informed and dispassionate reporting than in the field of energy, on which the Untied States and other industrialized countries are so dependent. To put the case directly:

Today, electric power provides about 30 percent of the energy consumed in America. Of that total, a little less than half is generated by burning coal, 15 percent by burning gas, 13 percent by burning oil, 12 percent by hydroelectric power and only 11 percent from nuclear reactors. Thus, in the first half of the 1980s, only a small part of America's energy needs—if that much—comes from nuclear power, and there are no more than 72 operable nuclear power plants in the land.

Yet nuclear power has generated major demonstrations against the "nukes" from coast to coast and has resulted in wide public fear and misunderstanding. In consequence, no informed person believes we can now come anywhere near building and operating the 250 nuclear plants we were expected to have in the year 2000. Moreover, the cost of building such plants has virtually tripled.

The accident to the nuclear facility at Three Mile Island and its aftermath have done much to undermine public faith in nuclear power. But what happens now? This is the conclusion of a report by the National Academy of Sciences entitled "Energy in Transition: 1985–2010":

> A balanced combination of coal and nuclear electricity is preferable on environmental and economic grounds to the predominance of either. Coal and nuclear power are the only large-scale alternatives to oil and gas in the near term, before about 2000, as the use of fluid fuels begins to wane.

It is going to take a lot of informed reporting, based on hard scientific evidence, to change the public's mood, however. And today there are few industrial giants who are willing to take the risk of undertaking to build more nuclear plants than are currently scheduled for construction.

Consumerism

When Pete McKnight was editor of the *Charlotte* (North Carolina) *Observer*, he warned his colleagues in the American Society of Newspaper Editors, of which he was past president, "Consumer reporting is one of the big new fields that change has forced upon us. Consumer protection is a fact of life. It is not going to go away, even if it does set your advertising manager to trembling."

The Challenge   To a profession whose support is so dependent on advertising, that indeed is the challenge. It can scarcely be met by a few general assignment reporters, sent out at random, as consumer stories emerge, to cover each one separately. The more responsible news organizations have found it necessary to maintain a group of knowledgeable consumer specialists, who are reinforced from time to time with staff people; even among smaller newspapers with an interest in consumer news, there is usually at least one reporter whose regular assignment is the consumer beat.

More than in any other subject area of journalism, consumer news requires the strict separation of the editorial department from the advertising and business offices if the press is to maintain its credibility with the public. For consumer news cuts across all the traditional departmental lines, from life-style pages to financial, from real estate to sports, and more often than not it dominates Page 1.

Growth of Coverage A few pioneering consumer organizations, with pitifully small resources and skimpy publications, struggled for years to awaken the interest of the public in a crusade against shoddy products, overpricing, misleading advertising and the other signs of an overly commercial age. But for much of this century, few consciences were stirred except among the more progressive editors and managers of the news media. Along Madison Avenue, it was even hinted darkly that people who suspected the good faith of big advertisers were dupes of Communism at best and plotters against the security of the republic at worst.

The first to break through the barrier of indifference and neglect was a public-spirited lawyer. Ralph Nader, who managed to marshal the support of a group of talented young adherents in a whole series of campaigns to protect the interests of the consumer. Then, in a period of soaring inflation that sent the cost of living rocketing, the public itself began to face up to a distressing situation. The nation's campuses, ever sensitive to such movements, became staging areas for consumer groups that sought new recruits. And consumerism, at last, became a fact of life for the American press. Even the broadcast media had to take notice when the crusade against cigarettes reached such a pitch that cigarette commercials were eliminated from the air by law. Health news, on a day-to-day basis, became important to a large and demanding public.

Range and Methods Editors approach consumer reporting in various ways. The larger news organizations use specialists who do nothing else. Those who want consumer news but can't afford specialists expect their regular reporters to contribute pieces of interest to consumers. Business writers, for example, can do specialized pieces on how consumers can get satisfaction for their complaints. Sports writers can give much more advice than they do on such consumer details as where to park cars outside stadiums, the best methods of travel to various contests, costs, availability of meals and other details. All recipes in the family pages should carry approximate costs. And in travel and entertainment stories, costs should be included as a matter of course.

As the case was put in a report by Jack Foster, editor of the *Palm Beach* (Florida) *Times*, "Consumer reporting is all around us. It is no longer something out of the ordinary, if indeed it ever was."

Consumer Campaigns Consumerism has been effective in journalism in several different ways. Leading newspapers are originating their own inquiries in response to complaints, one of the byproducts of the various Action Line columns of recent years. And all newspapers, even the most sluggish, are being obliged to reexamine their policies on using material that formerly was considered a harmless bonus for an advertiser. In this respect, television, usually so timid wherever advertisers are concerned, lags behind the printed media.

Campaigns that once were considered taboo are now being undertaken with the helpful resources of a news organization. The *Des Moines Register*, for example, gave full support to Nick Kotz's examination of unsanitary practices in meat packing plants, the result being the passage of the Federal Wholesale Meat Act and a Pulitzer Prize for the reporter. Campaigns against unsanitary restaurants now are considered almost routine in some cities of the nation. And major papers like the *Wall Street Journal* do not hesitate to expose unscrupulous business practices wherever they are found. The 1982 Tylenol scare was a national sensation.

The automobile industry, despite its heavy advertising budgets, has been forced on the defensive in numerous instances to justify its safety standards and merchandising practices. The food sections of family pages, so long immune from critical inspection, have undergone an even more searching examination. And the phony plugs to advertisers and the acceptance of favors that have been so disgraceful a part of some financial, real estate and sports sections have come under fire from both within and outside the ranks of professional journalism.

Just how far consumer reporting will develop depends entirely on the skill and devotion of the journalists who undertake this specialty and the amount of support they receive from their news organizations. Several hundred of them are on the job today. But certainly, now that so many barriers have fallen, there can be no return to the comfortable situation where major advertisers felt that the average newspaper would always try to make up in departmental news for whatever injuries they may have received in the headlines on Page 1.

The Environment

No less than consumerism, the relationship of people to their environment and the increasing public concern over pollution have generated broadening interest in the news. The great industries that recklessly contaminated the atmosphere, despoiled the earth of its beauty and polluted the water supply are being called to account. Cities that casually dumped their sewage in rivers, lakes and inland seas are finding themselves threatened by their own filth. New York City, a special case, has learned to its cost that it must cease dumping sludge in the ocean because it contaminates beaches for miles around. And even well-meaning citizens have learned that, through their own foolish disposal measures, they are among the worst polluters of all.

A Measure of Progress   There has always been a certain amount of interest in the conservation of natural resources in the United States and the development of the resources of the earth for the benefit of all peoples. But for more than a century after the founding of the nation, the constructive measures undertaken by the press were limited to such innovations as those of the editor of the *Pennsylvania Gazette*, Benjamin Franklin, who introduced the yellow willow to America and devised a practical system of lightning rods.

The muckrakers of the early 20th century were the forerunners of the environmentalists of today. But their influence, in general, was limited to the period of Theodore Roosevelt's presidency, primarily because he had a deep interest in the protection of natural resources and was not afraid to attack "the malefactors of great wealth." However, it was no newspaper, but an indignant novelist, Upton Sinclair, who attacked the meat industry in *The Jungle*. And it was no national columnist, but a little-known chemistry professor and editor, Edwin Fremont Ladd of the *North Dakota Farmer* and *Sanitary Home* magazine, who was among the earliest agitators for pure food and drug legislation. The press, with few exceptions, was preoccupied with the political and economic scandals of the day.

Environmental developments were covered, of course, but there appeared to be no special concern over the state of the earth and the atmosphere even after World War II. Once again, it was a book, *Silent Spring*, by Rachel Carson, that called public attention to a development of consequence—the effect of the pesticide DDT on wildlife. Out of the national debate that ensued, a new consciousness was created of the precarious nature of humankind on earth. It was a time when the public also began paying attention to the historical warnings of overpopulation, diminishing resources for sustaining life and the rising threat of pollution on every side.

But when the Love Canal scandal broke in New York in the late 1970s and editors realized thousands of families were living over or near abandoned chemical dumps that threatened their health, local reporters did not have to do a great deal of investigating to find that similar situations existed in their own area. The upshot was the issuance of a national list of dangerous abandoned chemical sites that had to be cleaned up. It was a major step forward in the development of environmental reporting as a daily newspaper assignment in many parts of the country.

Economic News

When rocketing interest rates threatened both the automobile and housing industries in the early 1980s and helped spin the nation into recession, many a news organization asked, "Why?" The answers were not easy to come by because economic news, for the most part, had never been a staple of American journalism even in the Great Depression. More often than not, it was relegated to the business section of newspapers and given to reporters who couldn't or wouldn't get excited about covering fires and playing cops and robbers.

The seriousness of the American economic situation, however, prompted a turnabout in general economic reporting. Efforts were made to find reporters who knew the difference between a bond and a stock, an expense budget and a capital budget.

When the *Wall Street Journal* became the largest newspaper in the land with more than two million daily circulation, and TV programs like Louis Rukeyser's *Wall Street Week* pulled in four or five million viewers weekly, a lot of newspapers got the message. While economic reporting wasn't *in*, it at least became a necessary part of the daily coverage of events.

The long-deferred recognition of economic news was accompanied by equally important changes in the way it was written and told. There is no longer an excuse for making economics dull. In professional hands, such a story can be told in informal, popular and often uninhibited style. Whether the subject is business or labor, the stock market or foreign trade or the innumerable offshoots thereof, the innovators on the *Wall Street Journal* are often the first to show their irreverence for stuffy old forms of writing. This, without doubt, is one of the reasons for the phenomenal growth of the *Journal* into the largest daily newspaper in the land.

Nor is the *Journal* alone in profiting from changes in the presentation of economic news. All the leading business pages in rival newspapers have been affected by the movement toward improved content and livelier style. The McGraw-Hill magazines, headed by *Business Week*, and the Fairchild group, of which the daily *Women's Wear* is the most prominent, both have found prosperity in their sponsorship of the unorthodox.

Labor News

When the principal effort of the federal government was designated as an attack on inflation, the local headlines and local evening news programs very soon reflected worsening unemployment. Many reporters throughout the land found themselves assigned to interview government officials, plant managers, university professors and union leaders. But relatively few have much knowledge of the labor movement in this country, let alone the complicated economic issues that have resulted in scary unemployment figures.

The problem is not new in American journalism. During every economic turndown since World War II, there has been agitation at professional conferences for the improvement of reportorial training in the coverage of problems affecting the labor force. But once recovery begins, the urgency for better labor reportage appears to wane.

It is perfectly true that the nation's leading newspapers and newsmagazines have had labor reporters for years and have, on the whole, told the labor story fairly and impartially. It would be unthinkable today for a newspaper of stature in New York, Chicago, Pittsburgh, Detroit or Los Angeles, for example, to fail to maintain regular and detailed coverage of labor affairs. But elsewhere in the country, until very recently, the labor story has usually been told as a series of disconnected episodes. While many smaller newspapers and even a few local stations have tried within their resources to keep a fair balance between labor and management in the news, some have not.

In the columns of a good newspaper, news of labor affairs is by no means confined to unemployment, strikes and lockouts or violence on the picket lines. A more sophisticated approach to the reporting of conflicts between industry and labor has developed, so that a good newspaper takes care not to label itself a proindustry partisan in every dispute but tries to give both sides of the story.

Education News

With more than 60 million Americans going to school, the coverage of education today is a challenge to all the news media. There is greater room for progress in the reporting of education news than in many another specialty. But it will take well-trained journalists to do the job—men and women who understand the problems of the schools and know how to write about them.

The old journalistic weakness for emphasizing trouble rather than achievement is only a part of the difficulty in achieving a balanced presentation of the news of education. In many cities, the extreme sensitivity of school administrations to criticism handicaps even their defenders when they embark on a purely fact-finding mission. Such sensitivity often is exceeded only by that of the press itself when it is under heavy community criticism. In such situations, there is little possibility for a constructive dialogue and school and press drift into postures of mutual hostility. This is particularly true in some of the struggles over school integration and busing in Northern cities.

When the schools are in the forefront of the news, however, cool, careful, impartial reporting must become the order of the day.

This was the pattern to which both the *Boston Globe* and the *Louisville Courier-Journal* and *Times* adhered when integration crises gripped the schools of their respective cities. What they did provided guidance for both hard-pressed parents and teachers as well as much-needed support for the children who went to class daily under difficulty.

It would be well if the noncrisis news of education were covered in the same spirit, but often it is given only minimal attention. Some universities in America are covered by student stringers for major papers and wire services, but not at all by the broadcast media, except when there is a riot or some other disorder. Many an education writer has tried to devise some better method for the daily coverage of higher education, but not many have succeeded.

News of Religion

The news of religion for many years suffered an extremely low priority in the daily press except on weekends and religious holidays. The changed attitude that is so apparent today in a large section of the press, including television, scarcely means that the editors have suddenly "got" religion.

What has happened is that the extreme conservative wing of American religious leadership—the "Moral Majority"—has found a new outlet for its frustrations in political activity. It boasted that it helped elect Ronald Reagan as president and did much to defeat liberal Democratic senators. It also threatened to boycott television programs of which it disapproved, and the threat was enough to get a small amount of reform in blatantly violent programming.

Thus, while news of religion in general still was given minimal coverage, the activists of religion repeatedly made Page 1 and the network evening news programs. They were held up to critical examination on programs like *60 Minutes*, and created a mingled atmosphere of controversy, criticism and fierce partisanship. The "Moral Majority" movement, in short, attracted more attention than anything or anybody since the violent political sermons of the Reverend Charles E. Coughlin, the "radio priest" of the 1930s, whose parish was in Royal Oak, Michigan.

The conservative movement stirred up controversy in other areas as well. Its political supporters in Congress made renewed efforts to establish a prayer routine in the public schools despite constitutional bars against the mingling of religion and secular affairs. To get around that prohibition, President Reagan proposed a constitutional amendment. And book-banning in public libraries became news in some communities because conservative preachers made an issue of books they particularly disliked for various reasons.

Religious leaders became involved in politics in other ways.

Liberal church leaders and members, both Protestant and Catholic, supported the movement to protest the South African policy of *apartheid*, the separation of races. And the Polish pope, John Paul II, became the spiritual leader of worldwide protests against the Soviet-inspired military crackdown by the Polish government against the Polish labor union, Solidarity.

In this manner, the news of religion once more came to forcible attention of Americans. It was the strongest kind of evidence that the Monday-morning column of sermons (and a few others on Sundays in communities with large synagogues) was no longer adequate to tell the story of religion in the American press. Editors specializing in news of religion for the wire services and the larger newspapers dealt with many issues beyond the regular religious observances. Nor was it unusual for reporters on all news organizations in the land, large and small, to find themselves engrossed in an assignment dealing with issues arising out of deeply held religious beliefs. The struggle waged by the forces for and against abortion, for example, was probably the single most emotional issue in American life during the 1980s and it deeply involved communities in every part of the land. It was a symbol of changing times.

The Cultural Story

The audience for cultural affairs in the United States now is larger than the sports audience in most major metropolitan centers, but the news media have been slow to take advantage of it. Most of the reviewing and critical writing about the lively arts appears in the larger newspapers, the weekly magazines and the wire services. Smaller newspapers use syndicated copy, for the most part, but may run a few locally written reviews of books, touring theater and musical attractions and occasional art exhibits. Films are more widely reported on and reviewed than anything else on the cultural scene. And only the smallest papers neglect to run the daily and weekly television listings.

While television itself does very little reviewing and criticism of a serious nature, it is the one universal medium with the capacity to bring great theater and great music to nearly all American homes. That kind of TV programming doesn't occur very often. But when it does, it is nearly always a national event of importance.

Editorials

The editorial page is undergoing a much-needed revival in importance and the editorial voice of radio and television is a little stronger. Even some newsmagazines are coming around to the need for a separate section for editorial comment. The new stress on editorial opinion is due in large part to the expansion of public-service journalism; for, without the strongest kind of editorial support and the total mobilization of the resources of the entire news organization, many a crusade would wither and die in a few days.

There are many definitions of what editorial opinion should be, and how a properly conducted editorial page or editorial program should operate. Certainly, it must be something more than the voice of the proprietor, the vehicle for promoting his own interests and prejudices and those of his leading editors. Properly conducted, an editorial section should represent a community or region of the country; many, of course, contend that they speak for the nation but not very many could prove it if challenged. Moreover, such a section should be a marketplace of ideas, and not a grab-bag of columns and reprints intended to please all segments of the audience.

What Editors Believe   It is customary, in any discussion of the editorial function, to note that editorial pages rank comparatively low in any survey of readership of newspapers, and programs devoted to editorial opinion are close to the bottom in radio and television audience measurements. What these surveys do not show, however, is the quality of those who read the editorial page and listen to editorial programs. In most communities and regions, it is primarily the leaders who pay the closest attention to editorial content and who are the most likely to be influenced by it. Thus, despite low total diffusion, the editorial section can have an impact on the decision-making process and community leaders are well aware of it.

● Short Takes

These are some of the things to remember about specialists in journalism:

- Every young reporter should begin, as early as possible, to cultivate a specialty. In today's complicated world, journalists with specialized knowledge are very much in demand.
- Science writing is of importance in everything from the coverage of earthquakes to claims about instant cures for the common cold. It is of special interest in anything having to do with atomic power and other aspects of the energy crunch.
- Consumer reporting cuts across all departmental lines in a news organization. A consumer reporter has to have specialized and dependable sources and the strength and courage to stand by the reporting of unpleasant and controversial facts.
- Environmental reporting was given a big boost through the discovery that hidden sites for the dumping of chemical waste, much of it toxic, existed in most parts of the United States. The reporting of water shortages, the opening of

national lands for private exploitation and other aspects of environmental concern are regularly in the news.

- Any recession brings renewed interest in the reporting of economic news. It is no longer something that can be safely relegated to the financial page and it can't be done solely by the *Wall Street Journal*. Every news organization now is trying to find better ways to tell the economic story and it is going to take specialists to do it. The same is true of labor news, particularly in times of high unemployment.
- News stories about education, religion and cultural affairs all have their specialized aspects and are important on larger news organizations. In smaller organizations, the reporter with an interest in any one of these often does work on such stories without being specially assigned. Many give their own time to the job, even though it is not demanded of them.
- It is a rare beginner who makes the jump from school or a first job directly to the editorial page or a spot as a columnist. It has been done, but each case is extraordinary. It pays to know how an editorial page operates and what makes columnists run, but the one thing young reporters cannot do is to let the paper's editorial policy guide their reporting. No reporter can go out on a story with a fixed idea of what he or she is looking for and expect to do a fair and honest job.

CHAPTER 28

Investigative Reporting and Campaigning

Andy Knott, a hard-driving six-footer with the energy of a threshing machine, became an investigative reporter for the *Chicago Tribune* soon after his graduation from the University of Tennessee. For three months, he worked undercover as an Emergency Medical Technician for five private ambulance companies in Chicago. Then he wrote a six-part series for the *Tribune* entitled "Ambulances—Unsafe at Every Turn," which disclosed scandalously poor maintenance of many private ambulances and widespread abuse of patients. The result: major reforms, made mandatory by new state and city laws and regulations.

Public Service Journalism

Andy Knott's campaign, based on his own investigative reporting under the guidance of the *Tribune's* editors, is one example of the manner in which public service journalism works in the United States. Others of major importance have been a campaign by the *Charlotte* (North Carolina) *Observer* against "brown lung disease," created by the cotton dust that is responsible for the deaths of thousands of textile workers; the *Nashville Tennessean's* crusade against a resurgent Ku Klux Klan, based on undercover work by a reporter who became a Klan member, and the *Philadelphia Inquirer's* campaign against the reckless disposal of hazardous-waste chemical products.

There are many others of current interest in which newspapers, both large and small, have taken unpopular positions based on principle and carried out investigations against the angry objections of powerful adversaries. The record shows, as well, that the broadcast media also are going into the field with signal results, as the popularity of the CBS program *60 Minutes* demonstrates.

How Campaigns Begin Many campaigns are quite deliberately planned to meet a long-felt community need. Others develop naturally out of news breaks that point to the probability of dangerous abuses. Often, they come about by accident, as witness the following:

A woman wrote a letter of protest to the *Detroit News*, touching off its campaign to free four men who had been wrongfully convicted of murder in New Mexico. A congressional secretary confided her woes to a sympathetic stranger seated next to her on a bus, who happened to be a *Washington Post* reporter, and who proceeded to break the congressional sex scandals. A photographer in Buffalo happened to take a picture of a city truck unloading supplies at a private contracting job, thus revealing a major municipal scandal that rocked City Hall. A penciled notation on a card, found by a reporter for the *Seattle Times*, resulted in clearing a University of Washington professor of charges of Communist activity. A wrinkled newspaper clipping about an Air Force lieutenant who was losing his commission because some of his relatives were left-wing sympathizers led to a great television exposé by Edward R. Murrow.

A few campaigns, usually the most exciting of all, are brought about by the reporters themselves who delve into a suspicious situation long before their editors are aware of it and, in effect, commit the paper to a public service campaign. This was the story of the Watergate investigation of the *Washington Post*, brought about by Bob Woodward and Carl Bernstein. It was also the way Andy Knott's campaign began against ambulance dangers in Chicago, although in his case the editors grabbed up his idea quickly and supported it.

The Ambulance Story Knott had been pitching several investigative ideas at his boss, Bernard Judge, the Chicago editor of the *Tribune*, from the time he joined the staff. Finally, Knott came up with a proposal to look into the private ambulance operation, which had brought a Pulitzer Prize a decade previously to William Jones, then a *Tribune* investigative reporter and now the managing editor. The plan was to take another close look at a much-criticized service, and both Jones and Judge approved it.

The first thing Knott had to do was to qualify for certification as an emergency medical technician (EMT). Under Illinois law, this meant more than 100 hours of classroom work at a local junior college, three hours of field training and at least 10 hours of work in a hospital emergency room. The reporter completed the course successfully.

Support by the Paper The most important factor Knott had going for him was the full support of a powerful paper. It meant — win, lose or draw — that he would never be defenseless. If he was hurt, he would be cared for. If he got into

Andy Knott of the *Chicago Tribune* in his uniform as an emergency medical technician, assigned to ride private ambulances. His investigation resulted in major changes to make the system safer and more responsive to public needs. (Copyright, the *Chicago Tribune*. Used by permission.)

legal trouble, he would be defended. There was no advance guarantee that he'd find anything wrong — the ratio of successful investigations to failures is about one in five in the United States — but he knew that a washout wouldn't cripple his career. He was just beginning.

Was there personal danger? He didn't know. But he realized that it would be no fun riding a racing ambulance through heavy traffic beside a gung-ho driver. These were risks and they were a part of the job.

Under the guidance of William Recktenwald, a senior *Tribune* investigator who also had worked on the original story, Knott took these additional steps while he was studying to be an EMT:

- Examined ambulance company records in Springfield, the state capital, and learned that the private firms billed the state $2 million a year in the Chicago area.
- Checked into Dun & Bradstreet corporate records.
- Reviewed records of suits in United States Tax Court in Washington, federal court in Chicago and Cook County Circuit Court.

- Made himself familiar with all state and local laws bearing on private ambulances, emergency vehicles and good samaritan laws.
- Used his first name, Tom, to put together a background as Tom Knott of Georgia, plus references that weren't checked; obtained a "hard card," (chauffeur's license) plus the necessary certification from the Illinois Department of Public Health and the Chicago Board of Health.

Then Knott wrote of his employment:

> I got a job at the first place I applied and was working on an ambulance less than a week after I first walked in the door. I stayed there about a week and a half. The company was reputable and we used it as a benchmark to judge other companies.
>
> The second company, where I stayed three weeks, was located on and served the South Side of town. I alternated north, south and west to reduce the risk of running into people from other companies.
>
> Quitting one job and moving to the next was not always accomplished with the greatest of ease. It was easy to get a job, for sure, but it was hard to just up and quit. . . . The hours were exhausting. Most EMTs in Chicago work 60 hours a week, ten hours a day, six days a week. In all, I worked more than 400 hours. After each day, I would return home and write a long memo on the day's activities. These were painfully detailed memos and added up to more than 250 pages by the time I started writing my six-part series.

It was unusual, to say the least, for so young and relatively inexperienced a reporter to be put on a major assignment of this character. But, in the Woodward–Bernstein manner, it all worked. Knott recalled:

> Although I wanted to do this story very much, I was not quite prepared for the loneliness of the task. Because I was considered young and green, my editors were very concerned about my performance. When the investigation began, only five people knew of it. When I went undercover, I just disappeared from the office. My peers at the *Tribune* knew I was doing an investigation but they didn't know what it was about. I had very few people to talk over my problems and concerns with and, to make matters even tougher, I was under strict orders to limit my social life severely. The editors were afraid bar talk might get me into trouble.

Writing the Story   It all turned out well. Knott did all his six articles before the series went into print. With all his findings and his background of investigation, this is how he led off his first story:

> I'm exhausted after a long, tense day of high-speed ambulance riding through the streets of Chicago.
>
> This day began at 7 a.m. When we finally limp back to the garage 13 hours and two ambulances later, we have no beacon lights, no siren, no power steering, no shock absorbers. The brakes are in terrible shape.
>
> My partner, Bob, who is driving, isn't doing much better. He stopped twice to drink beer today and he says he's "popping" Valium to keep going.
>
> At one point, I thought I'd be killed. With a beer can in one hand and the other on the wheel, he almost lost control of

the ambulance as we wove at high speed down a South Side street.

We were "running hot" at the time—lights flashing and siren blaring—even though it was a non-emergency call. I don't know how fast we were going. The speedometer didn't work.

On this day, I also saw fraud and theft. And I can't forget how we terrified the lunchtime crowds as we zipped down busy Michigan Avenue on the wrong side of the street.

I'm expecting more of the same tomorrow and I'm not sure how much longer I can take it.

Today was by no means my worst day. What I've described happened again and again in the 500 hours I worked undercover as a certified emergency medical technician (EMT) for five of the city's private ambulance services.

Many of their ambulances are dangerous. In my three months on the job, our service to the sick and injured was rarely efficient or safe.

The poor condition of many ambulances was the most immediate major fault we discovered. The Chicago Board of Health is required to inspect them annually. That check is no more than a joke.

But so many elements of ambulance service are bad that it's hard to say what is the "worst." The problems, which will be examined in detail in subsequent articles, include the following:

Vehicle condition: Tires were bald. Brakes were mushy. Safety lights and signals didn't work. Some ambulances had structural damage or body corrosion. Rain leaked through the roof; road grime came through holes in the floor.

One ambulance I worked in caught fire from a short circuit in the wiring while we were carrying a patient. Another fish-tailed and nearly rolled over because its shock absorbers were shot. Another had 3 to 4 inches of play in the steering wheel, making accurate steering difficult.

Patient care: Patients in private ambulances were cursed, threatened and subjected to rough treatment. A mental patient was allowed to wander unattended. Another had bronchial trouble but was subjected to an EMT's cigarette smoke.

Worst of all was the time when we were transferring an ill man from a hospital to a nursing home and an EMT told me, "If his heart arrests, don't do anything. Let him die. If his heart stops in the ambulance, just don't tell me."

Equipment condition: Ambulances I worked in were usually short of bandages, sterile water to cleanse wounds, gauze, oxygen masks, splints and neck braces. One didn't have any first-rate linen.

Soiled linen was used repeatedly. Some ambulances did

not carry fire extinguishers or oxygen tanks, both required by the city, or spare tires.

It took an extra 30 minutes to get a woman with a ruptured stomach lining to a hospital because we didn't have a stair chair to get her down a narrow stairway.

Running Hot: Private ambulances consistently run hot, with lights and sirens going, when there is no emergency. On runs I made, it might have been necessary only one time of every five times we did it. At other times, lives were needlessly endangered.

The practice resulted in the death of a 19-year-old EMT in September after he'd been on the job only two weeks. The ambulance he was riding in and a car collided at a Park Ridge intersection and the ambulance rolled over. Police said the ambulance was running hot on a non-emergency call.

EMT attitudes: Most EMTs in Chicago are underpaid, ($3.50 an hour is typical) or they work on a piecework basis, which forces them into a frantic pace. The quality of care suffers as EMTs, brutalized by the system, transfer their frustrations to patients.

Though I saw some good EMTs at work, too many were inept. One didn't even know how to take blood pressure readings.

Nothing in my training fully prepared me for what I saw. . . .

Results   Once the *Tribune*'s series ended, changes were swiftly instituted. Governor James R. Thompson signed a bill into law in September 1981, making it mandatory for every ambulance in the state — public and private — to undergo inspection twice a year. The Chicago City Council at the same time moved to tighten local inspection and regulation laws affecting private and public ambulances. EMT training also was required of ambulance company dispatchers.

The campaign was a classic instance of cooperative effort between a young reporter, directed by knowledgeable editors, and public authorities who acted decisively as soon as the results of a newspaper investigation were brought to their attention.

An Investigation of Local Industry

It requires courage, clout and a lot of money to take on a dominant industry, on which the prosperity of a whole region of the country depends. This is what the *Charlotte Observer* did when it investigated the incidence of byssinosis, or brown lung, the disease caused by inhalation of cotton dust.

The *Observer* was well aware at the outset that the powerful textile industry, largest in the Carolinas, would fight its inquiry and its findings. But more than 391,500 Carolinians work in the textile industry, one-third of them in plants that process cotton. At the time the series was published, 18,000 Carolina workers had been disabled by cotton dust, but only some 320 had received compensation.

This was a typical reaction from one of the leaders of the $17 billion industry, W. B. Pitts, president of Hermitage, Inc., who wrote:

> How shameful it is for the Knight family and its organ, the *Observer*, to take the side of OSHA and the oppressive bureaucrats against the magnificent Southern textile industry. It is sickening to see the gutless minions of the news media siding with a few crybaby Americans who obviously are looking for a handout from the very hand that fed and clothed their families.

Taking the Public's Side   Nevertheless, the *Observer* continued its long inquiry, in which 15 members of its staff participated, and blasted open its campaign against brown lung disease. This is the lead on a summary of the 22 articles. It was written by a staffer, Bob Drogin, who then was 27 and had only been on the paper for three years.

Cotton dust is a killer in Carolina mills.

Already 18,000 Carolina workers are disabled by byssinosis, or brown lung, the lung disease cotton dust causes. Only about 320 have received compensation.

Now, six years after officials ordered mills to clean up, about 115,000 of the Carolinas' 391,500 textile workers remain exposed to dust in cotton mills. Health officials say at least 10,000 North Carolinians still work in dust levels that can kill.

It is a case of deadly neglect.

According to last week's Observer series on brown lung in the Carolinas:

- At least five textile companies didn't tell some workers they had been diagnosed with brown lung.
- Companies have contested 80% of the 936 North Carolina brown lung compensation claims and virtually all of about 200 South Carolina claims.
- Both industrial commissions have ignored state laws requiring companies to report on workers diagnosed with occupational diseases such as byssinosis. The North Carolina Commission has violated its own rules by approving company-written agreements in which workers forfeited all future claims.
- The commissions have approved compensation in only about 320 of 1,136 claims filed. Settlements often didn't cover lost wages and medical expenses. Some workers died waiting for compensation.
- Some doctors who advise the commissions on brown lung cases also see patients for textile companies; one former South Carolina medical panel member was a consultant for two textile firms. . . .

The End of a Campaign   Editor Richard A. Oppel recalled that within less than a year after the series ran, North Carolina textile workers had received $4 million in compensation for byssinosis, more than had been paid out in the previous nine years. And one mill worker in South Carolina, disabled by brown lung, was awarded $86,000 compensation.

Commission files in both states were opened to the public in reponse to the *Observer*'s editorial pressure. The North Carolina Labor Commission increased its inspection staff by 11 people and the state's Industrial Commission put on three additional deputies to speed up compensation decisions.

The campaign won for the *Observer* the Pulitzer Prize gold medal for meritorious public service. The jurors called it an example "of how a newspaper can effectively and dramatically use its editorial resources to expose and draw public attention to an important and previously ignored problem — in this case a disease that disables and kills thousands of workers."

Exposing the Ku Klux Klan

J. W. Thompson, a career Army man who took early disability retirement as a sergeant and earned his living as a cabinet-maker, was a member of the Ku Klux Klan for a year. When he quit, he resumed his true identity, Jerry Thompson, an investigative reporter, and wrote a series of articles on his experiences for his newspaper, the *Nashville Tennessean*.

It was a courageous thing to do. As John Seigenthaler, publisher of the *Tennessean*, wrote some months after the Thompson series was published, "Jerry Thompson always was in danger of discovery and lives today under police protection."

Inside the Klan   This was how Thompson wrote the lead for his Klan series:

The Ku Klux Klan today holds a strange, disturbing attraction for frustrated, fearful middle-income men and women — and a dangerous potential for violence and terror.

I know. For the last year, I have been a Klansman. I have worn the white robe and hood. I have twice taken the oath pledging my life to the Klan. I have twice been "naturalized" into separate Klan empires. I have paid my Klan initiation fees and my Klan dues.

I have fired Klan crosses, collected contributions at Klan roadblocks, marched in Klan street demonstrations and helped disrupt public order at a public meeting with shouts in a Klan chorus. I have attended KKK den meetings where men armed with pistols and automatic rifles mouthed their routine racist rhetoric: "The niggers and the Jews are ruining the country."

Clad in Klan garments, I have picketed the President of the United States, demonstrated against a TV station show-

When the *Nashville Tennessean* decided to expose the working of the Ku Klux Klan, it chose reporter Jerry Thompson to infiltrate the Klan as J. W. Thompson, a former Army sergeant. Here he wears the Klan's hood and robe. (Picture by staff photographer Jimmy Ellis. Copyright by the *Nashville Tennessean*. Used by permission.)

ing a documentary about the KKK, and been jeered by black citizens. And I have concealed the pistol of an ungarbed fellow Klansman beneath my flowing robes when he thrust it at me as a policeman approached.

Through it all I was acting out a role—working as an investigative reporter for the Tennessean, striving to discover just how dangerous the Klan is, endeavoring to penetrate the secrecy veil that has obscured much of the Klan's life since its founding in Pulaski, Tenn., more than a century ago. . . .

The Findings These were Thompson's conclusions, buttressed by an independent outside investigation by other *Tennessean* reporters and a photographer:

1. The Klan must be disarmed. Many Klansmen routinely carry guns on their public marches and demonstrations. State and federal laws need to be strengthened so that police can deal with this growing threat of violence.

2. The Invisible Empire of the Ku Klux Klan, headed by Bill Wilkinson, of Denham Springs, La., grows more dangerous each day, with a paramilitary training camp near Cullman. This militant faction of the Klan, of which I am a member, bears close scrutiny by the authorities. The Justice Department agrees and has asked federal agencies to cooperate in an effort to combat the danger of violence posed by Wilkinson's group.

3. The rival Klan faction, of which I am also a member, the Knights of the Ku Klux Klan, headed by Don Black of Birmingham, is less militant because it is losing members. Still, its wizard, Black, is vehemently anti-Semitic and equally hostile to blacks. A Texas branch of this Klan also operates a paramilitary training team. Obviously, Black's Knights cannot be ignored.

Unhappily, despite the exposé, very little has been done either to disarm the Klan, close its training camps or reduce the threat of violence. But the *Tennessean* and Seigenthaler, its publisher, have never regretted going into the investigation. Nor has Thompson been sorry that he gave a year of his life to the inquiry.

A TV Investigation

Because television is a visual medium and TV reporters work under severe limitations of time, the investigative job for TV has to be done differently. A two-part series on space weaponry by David Andelman, which was broadcast on successive nights on *The CBS Evening News with Dan Rather*, illustrates the essential points of difference.

Beginning an Investigation As was the case with Andy Knott's investigation of ambulances for the *Chicago Tribune*, David Andelman developed the idea for his CBS investigation. He wrote:

> This series grew out of some reading I'd been doing on this subject as much as a year before. At the time of the launch of the first space shuttle, I became further intrigued with the uses of military shuttles that were to follow, all of which were shrouded in the deepest secrecy. Looking into the uses of the military space shuttles led me to the much broader question of the nature and use of space weaponry.

CBS Evening News liked the idea and Alan Weisman was assigned as producer.

Investigating a Top-Secret Subject Andelman went on:

> We began by extensive phone work while a researcher dug up everything published on this subject over the past couple of years (much of which turned out to be somewhat unreliable). In the course of our phoning, we realized that the issue was extremely broad, but potentially far more serious than we had thought. Weapons decisions taken quietly today appeared likely to be nearly irreversible, committing the U.S. and by corollary the Soviet Union to MX-type missile programs perhaps 10 years down the pike.
>
> We decided, therefore, to outline a three-part series (this was ultimately

reduced to two parts), then sat down to figure out whom we should talk with on camera (of 25–30 people we had consulted by phone or in person). We settled on six key interviews. I took off across the country to do them (two were in Washington, three in California, one in Boston). Weisman began to work up a series of graphics that were, after all, the heart of the piece, and he rounded up obscure footage of some of these weapon prototypes in action.

I shipped back the interviews as they were done, Weisman transcribed them, looking for the best "sound-bites." By the time I had returned to New York, he had already sketched out an outline of the two parts (where the sound would go, the graphics, etc.) and we began work on the detailed script. We had been consulting by phone in the evenings after each interview.

The scripts must have gone through five or six drafts, each draft being pared down (with 22 minutes in the *CBS Evening News*, our early drafts would have eaten up a third of each show.) We then spent a day doing the very complex on-camera bridges (shot with two cameras in the main control room of the "Evening News"— we used it as a "set," the computer graphic animations we had prepared rolling on the main monitor behind me as I began talking.)

Both pieces were finally screened for the executives of the *CBS Evening News* and Dan Rather, too. Dan made some very useful suggestions on where both pieces could be trimmed, there were some negotiations back and forth, and finally both pieces ran on consecutive evenings.

Broadcasting the Investigation   The first of the two Andelman pieces on space weaponry was in effect a primer on space weapons, what they are, how they may be used. The "lightning bolt"—a laser beam of intense light—was one of the potential weapons included, but there were others just as exotic. The principle, however, was to introduce the millions of viewers of the *CBS Evening News* to a complex subject that was going to cost taxpayers a lot of money—much more than most of them realized.

Here is the audio part of the second piece, with the graphics and other illustrations in the video part of the script omitted:

RATHER: Speaking of missiles, the Defense Department has just
    sent Congress its so-called "definitive report" about
    research into directed-energy weapons, particularly laser
    weapons. The report is classified, but sources tell CBS News
    it recommends increased funding to determine just how
    effective lasers could be against a variety of targets. As
    David Andelman reports in Part Two of his investigation into
    the movement toward militarization of outer space, firing
    lightning bolts through the atmosphere is an idea whose time
    is coming--rapidly.
DAVID ANDELMAN: Since the early 1960s, the United States has been
    developing lasers for use by the military. Prototypes have
    destroyed revolving targets, and airborne targets, and have
    even been installed in planes for air-to-air combat. But using
    a laser to fire at a target in space presents some different

problems. A land-based laser firing at an orbiting satellite
would need huge power and clear skies to hit its target.
Without sufficient energy and the large mirrors needed for
aiming, the beam would disperse as it passes through the
clouds and end up too weak to effect the target. But a laser in
space with enough power and precise aiming could conceivably
hit a Soviet ICBM as the ascending missile broke through the
clouds.

ROBERT FOSSUM (Defense Research Project Agency): Specifically,
we would have in orbit a sequence of lower-altitude battle
stations, say on the order of 20, or that order of magnitude—
number of—of battle stations. At any one time, several of
these would be within visible range and laser-weapon range of
a mass attack. A target assignment would be given. One must
then acquire on the battle station that particular target,
then track the target because both the target and the battle
station are moving.

ANDELMAN: The laser would not fire at the missile's warhead. The
beam would lock on to the second stage, the booster, bathing
it with intense light, heating it during the ascent and before
the warhead has a chance to arm itself.

SENATOR MALCOLM WALLOP (R—Wyoming): I honestly believe, from
what I have seen with my own eyes, that we could put together
and orbit this prototype satellite within—within the next
four to five years.

ANDELMAN: But the skeptics abound. They say the idea is far more
costly than supporters think, that conventional weapons could
to the job just as well, and that the Russians could simply
harden their missiles or trick the lasers into firing at the
wrong targets.

WOLFGANG PANOFSKY (Stanford Research Laboratory): You can deploy
deceptive screens and alternate targets which fool the
sensors and/or aerosol sprays which hit the target. You can do
all sorts of things with very little weight.

ANDELMAN: Nevertheless, companies like TRW, Rocketdyne, Hughes
and United Technologies are hard at work perfecting the
mirror's tracking system and energy sources for the battle
stations. Funding for laser technology now runs about $200
million a year. But the Defense Department, in a top-secret
report to Congress, is now requesting an additional $250
million over the next five years.

   The Soviets too are spending a lot of time and a lot of
money developing directed-energy weapons. But there is no
hard evidence that they are any closer to an operational
system than the United States. And as research of all sorts
continues, so does the crucial question: is the dawn of space

```
         weaponry the end of the old arms race or merely the beginning
         of a new one?
FOSSUM:  We have avoided for various policy and national reasons
         the idea that we should go to space with weapons systems. It is
         almost inevitable in my mind that we will have to consider
         going to space with weapon systems at some time in the not-
         too-distant future.
WILLIAM PERRY (former Undersecretary of Defense):  I think it
         would be an extremely desirable objective for the United
         States to try to nip this space war in the bud, to stop it
         before it starts. It is still early enough to do that. Now,
         four or five years from now the opportunity to stop it may be
         gone. That is, the advances made by both nations by then may be
         so great that it is a clock whose hands cannot be turned back
         any longer.
ANDELMAN:  We're really at a crossroads right now.
PERRY:  I think we are, I think we are.
ANDELMAN:  In accepting the Albert Einstein Peace Prize recently,
         George Kennan, one-time U.S. ambassador to Moscow, remarked
         that the arms race "had reached such grotesque dimensions as
         to defy rational understanding." The Soviets and the United
         States, he added, "are like victims of some sort of hypnosis,
         men in a dream, like lemmings headed for the sea." And perhaps
         he might have added, out into space.

David Andelman, CBS News, New York.
```

Breaking New Ground   There are seldom any specific results that can be traced to this kind of in-depth investigative reporting about a controversial new family of projected space weapons. That it is necessary, no informed person can doubt. Andelman commented after the broadcast:

> In a newspaper series on a topic such as this, any reader could go back and find a Part One of a two-part series or, for that matter, skip over parts that are not intelligible or useful to him. Not so for television. At the same time, there's far less time to waste on fundamentals and on "recapping" what has gone before. But we do like to think that we broke lots of new ground on an important subject.

The Mirage Bar Story

The investigative art is by no means confined to men, although they are usually given the fattest assignments and the most prominent roles. The great exception is Pam Zekman, the *Chicago Sun-Times*'s crack investigative reporter, who has run a dozen major inquiries with dramatic results. She was the proprietor of the Mirage Bar, which was run by *Sun-Times* reporters to prove that thieves sell stolen goods with impunity. They accumulated the evidence and brought about major reforms.

in the city's penal system. Although it is taken for granted that reporters will adopt disguises for good reason to obtain necessary results, always with the consent of their paper, the Mirage Bar story didn't win a Pulitzer Prize because some of the board members thought it was "too deceptive."

This raises the issue in journalism of where righteousness ends, in adopting a disguise, and where unethical deception begins. It always has to be decided on a case-by-case basis by the news organization involved, and there are no set rules by which to judge such a moral issue. In the Mirage Bar case, however, Zekman certainly lost no prestige; in fact, she and her colleagues did win a number of prizes and industry-wide accolades.

Other women who have done first-rate work on investigations, and who have shared Pulitzer Prizes, include Ann deSantis of the *Boston Globe*, Lucinda Franks of UPI and Myrta J. Pulliam of the *Indianapolis Star*. The evidence is abundant, regardless of disguises, that women investigators do their jobs with as much skill and spirit as men.

The Bolles Case

The case of Don Bolles of the *Arizona Republic* should serve as a constant reminder to all journalists both of the dedication and the courage that are required of investigative reporters who venture into dangerous situations. The reaction to his murder in downtown Phoenix, while he was on the track of gangland connections with official Arizona, should also serve as an inspiration.

After Bolles was killed, 36 reporters and editors from different news organizations came to Arizona and many of them spent up to six months in the state, under the leadership of Bob Greene of *Newsday*, to try to finish the work that the Arizonan had begun. It was a unique cooperative effort, financed in part by most of the 20 news organizations that were represented, to show that no investigative reporter could be harassed or slain without inviting the most serious consequences.

The series of articles produced by the Investigative Reporters and Editors Inc., as the group called itself, was published and broadcast in whole or in part by a number of the participating organizations, but not in Bolles's own paper. The charges of links between business and politics and organized crime in Arizona, in a number of instances, bore out allegations that he had first made.

Campaign Objectives

It used to be said that the primary objective of most campaigns was to put wrongdoers in jail and get innocent persons out of jail. These, naturally, are the most spectacular results of campaigning. But there are many others, as this discussion has made abundantly clear. It sometimes happens that, without any declared intent, a major public service is performed because a news organization and its staff do their work of informing the public under extreme difficulties and in superlative fashion. This often occurs in the coverage of natural disasters or civil disorders. It results occasionally when a reporter, out of sheer conviction, risks life and limb to get a story that can be obtained in no other way.

The campaign that attempts to sound an alarm also has a long and honorable history. It goes back almost to the beginning of the republic, when editors were imprisoned for protesting the Alien and Sedition Acts, and includes many of the heroes of American journalism, from Isaiah Thomas to William Lloyd Garrison and Elijah Lovejoy. In modern times, these journalistic sentinels have included those who warned against the rise of Hitler, who foretold disaster for the United States in the earliest days of the Vietnam commitment, who fought against the destruction of the nation's natural resources. In substance, their deeds have ranged from the bravery of Mel Ruder, editor of the weekly *Hungry Horse News* in Montana, who risked his life to warn his community of rising flood waters, to the persuasive editorial warnings of Philip F. Kerby of the *Los Angeles Times* against judicial censorship of the press.

Numerous newspapers have tackled the problem of oil spillage. The situation has created an editorial mood that has spread across the country and involved even the smallest papers. Here, for example, is the way a California weekly, the *Pacifica Tribune*, presented the issue:

> Oil! Oil! Oil!
> Untold gallons of it fouled Pacifica's beaches yesterday, killing unknown numbers of marine birds, maiming others, and bringing an estimated 1,000 people swooping down on Pacifica to engage in the great oil battle.
> The oil seeped ashore Monday night, the early morning high tides leaving great gobs of the stuff high up on the beach, the surf covered with oil streaks, and two more huge oil slicks lingering off shore. . . .

In attacking a housing crisis brought on by the deliberate burning of slum buildings for whatever insurance could be collected, the *St. Louis Globe-Democrat* began its piece this way:

> Last April City Fire Marshal Arthur C. Newman called arson a grave threat to the future of the city. Since then, a fire captain and others have died in arson fires, and untold thousands of dollars worth of slum property has been deliberately destroyed.
> And the fires continue to burn, in many cases, fire officials say, so someone can make a buck. . . .

In some campaigns, the news stories are quite factual and restrained in tone but the alarm is sounded on the editorial page with thunderous emphasis. This was the case in the successful effort of the *Winston-Salem* (North Carolina) *Journal* and *Sentinel* to prevent strip miners from tearing apart the beautiful hill country of northwest North Carolina. One of the major editorials took this approach:

> The rolling hills and valleys in northwest North Carolina are among the most beautiful anywhere. But the land in Ashe, Alleghany, Wilkes and Surry counties won't be beautiful much longer if strip-mining gets a foothold in the area.
> Strip-mining might get that foothold if landowners and concerned citizens in the northwest aren't careful. The Gibbsite Corporation of America, which has

obtained options on thousands of acres in the northwest and in southwest Virginia, is conducting studies to see if gibbsite — a mineral found in the area — can be extracted easily and cheaply from the soil for use in producing aluminum. If the studies prove that strip mining would be profitable, Gibbsite apparently will exercise its options. . . .

One weapon against an unwelcome intruder is a public outcry. Such a protest helped Orange County keep Texas Gulf Sulphur from spoiling its beauty, and perhaps widespread resistance would make Gibbsite think twice.

If the people of the northwest should allow strip-mining to get a substantial foothold and if large parts of that scenic countryside become a virtual wasteland in a decade or so, they will have nobody to blame but themselves.

The point cannot be overemphasized. If a campaign is to mean anything, it must be undertaken with vigor and supported by the resources of the entire newspaper — from Page 1 to editorial, from pictures to cartoons.

This is something that few broadcasters have learned to date in their laudable efforts to emulate the crusading press; it is one thing to do an effective documentary, it is quite another to arouse the public without the editorial intervention of the management itself.

Does Campaigning Pay? There have been few campaigns of consequence that have added substantially to the circulation of a newspaper or the audience of a radio or TV station. Nor have very many reporters become as wealthy almost overnight as Woodward and Bernstein.

The record shows depressing instances in which campaigners for worthy causes in the press and broadcast media have lost circulation and advertising, become the targets for boycotts and even lost their jobs. The exposé is not the royal road to success, by any means.

The *Arkansas Gazette* paid for its championship of school integration in Little Rock with heavy monetary losses and the eventual resignation of its editor, Harry Ashmore. Several newspapers that ran campaigns against unscrupulous used car dealers lost automobile advertising. And in a classic case, the *Wall Street Journal* lost its General Motors advertising because it published information about new models before the auto giant was ready; however, GM soon came back into the paper.

One discouraged small-city editor, who tried and failed with a perfectly good campaign, even thought of giving up crusading altogether because it was so little appreciated. And J. Montgomery Curtis, while director of the American Press Institute, once came across an old Maine editor who refused point-blank to have anything to do with a campaign to improve his community, saying "Son, the durn town ain't worth it."

True, crusading isn't easy. Nor can anything of consequence in a community be accomplished quickly or cheaply merely by viewing with alarm. Most campaigns are won simply by hard, consistent work, backed by a determined editor and publisher. Such was the case in the *Louisville Courier-Journal*'s drive to tighten Kentucky's laws against strip-mining, which took four years before the Kentucky legislature finally passed what was then called "the toughest strip-mining legislature in America." More often than not, even a modest crusade takes a good deal longer than either editors or reporters anticipate at the outset.

The issue is not whether crusading journalism pays but whether it is necessary. The answer must be overwhelmingly yes.

Toward the Future

If anything at all is certain about the concluding years of the 20th century and the opening of the twenty-first, it is that American society will undergo drastic changes and journalism will have to reflect them. In no sense can it be said that social and economic pressures on this nation are likely to decrease; the outlook is quite the opposite. Even such necessary and long-delayed political reforms as government consolidation, an equitable taxing system and the elimination of towering injustices in the treatment of the sick and the needy, helpless children and the elderly may have a chance of success.

The nation will have need of a more efficient and broadened system for the dissemination of news, ideas and opinions. What we are seeing today in the adaptation of newspapers and wire services to the computer age and the development of the electronic media is only the beginning of the changes that are ahead for journalism. It is useless to speculate on whether there will be giant screens for TV across our living room walls, instant production of newspapers in the basement whenever we want them or production of voluminous statistics from distant data banks at the touch of a finger. The genius of science, interacting with the laws of supply and demand, will determine how much instant journalism we can have, what form it will take and how much we can actually absorb.

There are several things that are more important to the journalist than research and development, much as they are needed in a profession that has been backward for too long in such matters. The first and greatest of these is the continued protection of the freedoms guaranteed in the First Amendment, which are under increasing challenge in times of social change and worldwide political upheaval. For without a free press, the journalist becomes a mouthpiece for government, a lackey of the powerful, a robot who performs mindless duties in a graceless style.

While it is a temporary relief to have the United States Supreme Court strike down judicial gag orders and other prior restraints on publication, no journalist can feel secure if reporters sit in jail in violation of judicial orders to disclose their sources to the authorities and act, in fact, as servants of the government. It is a disturbing, even a threatening, trend.

Second only to the perpetuation of the rights of a free press is a reconsideration of the substance of journalism. And that bears upon the preparation and the beliefs of those who are intimately concerned with the identification, gathering, distribution and presentation of the news. Because, whatever definition may be offered, news actually tends to be what the journalist says it is. And the current definition of what the journalist treats as news is simply not good enough. Television and radio will have to be something more than glorified bulletin boards; newspapers, wire services and newsmagazines will be obliged to shape their reports to a greater extent toward areas that more deeply affect the public interest.

Finally, journalism must stand for something if it is to continue to be respected in a democratic society and given constitutional protection. It is not enough to be the harbinger of bad tidings; in primitive societies, such messengers were killed and journalists, in modern times, have frequently felt the sting of public animus merely because they did their duty. No less than the holding of public office, the difficult task of informing the public is a public trust. It is therefore inevitable that the concept of journalism as a public service is bound to increase in strength. Today, it is a trend. Tomorrow, it will be a necessity.

● Short Takes

Here are some of the basic points to remember about campaigning and investigative reporting:

- Campaigns must have the wholehearted support of the news organization— newspaper or magazine or broadcasting station—or reporters will find themselves helpless to continue. Even though one reporter may be the main investigator, the whole organization must give the inquiry its backing. And if legal trouble results, the reporter must have a proper defense, supported by the management.
- Campaigns based on the premise that the press is the watchdog over the public's business should show results. If there is a need for an inquiry, however, it should be undertaken whether there is any advance guarantee of results or not.
- It is manifestly true that not every campaign or investigation that is undertaken will pay off in a dramatic way. The ratio of success to failure is about one in five in the United States.
- Reporters undertaking investigations of crime or suspicious organizations are always in personal danger and they and their editors must realize it. Don Bolles of the *Arizona Republic* was murdered during his crime inquiry. Jerry Thompson of the *Nashville Tennessean* remained under police guard for a long time after he became a Klan member for a year and then wrote an exposé.
- TV investigations, because of the visual nature of the medium, usually take a lot longer to complete than newspaper inquiries. On network TV, with the exception of special programs like *60 Minutes,* the time allowed for national coverage is relatively modest. TV reporters usually have to do a much tighter job of writing than their colleagues in print.
- The substance of many an investigation is based on examinations of public documents such as land sales, tax records and court actions. The objective, in examining such data, is to determine first of all if there is a *pattern* of suspicious circumstances that might indicate wrongdoing. If the pattern exists, it should be followed up with a detailed inquiry.
- A campaign or an investigative report should be written in a calm, restrained manner. This is not the place for hype. The lead ought to indicate broadly the nature of the inquiry and the principal results, the reason the investigation was undertaken, the length of the inquiry and the participants. Generally, the first article emphasizes the main results and succeeding articles give details of each

main finding. The last article ought to contain recommendations and proposals for remedial action.

- Whether campaigns are undertaken in the public or private sector, they ought to be so fashioned and so directed as to serve the public interest. In most investigations, both news organizations and reporters will find it to their benefit to work with prosecuting authorities. Except when the prosecutor's office itself is involved in an investigation, it seldom helps to fight the people who will eventually have to decide whether sufficient evidence exists for criminal charges.

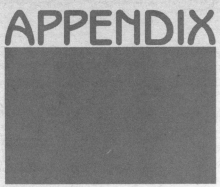

APPENDIX

A Glossary for Journalists

This glossary is divided into three parts. The first consists of terminology commonly used in newspapers and wire services. The second includes the principal terms used in computer technology for newspapers and wire services, and has some limited application to the electronic media where computers are used. The third applies solely to broadcast journalism.

1. For Newspapers and Wire Services

A copy   Also known as *A matter*. Part of a news story, based mainly on advance material, that is later completed by placing a lead on top of it. Used by newspapers mainly.

ad   An advertisement.

add   Additions of any kind to a news story.

advance   News story based on factual material about a forthcoming event, such as the advance text of a speech, parade line of march, etc.

agate   5½ point type; as a unit of advertising, 14 agate lines equal one column inch.

AMs   Morning newspapers.

angle   An approach to a story; also, various parts of a story.

441

ANPA   American Newspaper Publishers Association.

AP   Associated Press.

APME   Associated Press Managing Editors.

assignment   Duty given to a journalist.

bank   Also called a *deck;* the part of a headline that usually follows the top or the cross line, often both.

banner   A headline across Page 1, of four columns or more; sometimes known as a *streamer*. It is often confused with a *binder*, a headline across the top of an inside page.

B copy   Also known as *B matter*. Part of a news story, based mainly on advance material, which may be completed by topping it first with A copy and then with a lead. Many newspapers omit the A copy and top B copy with a lead directly.

beat   An exclusive story; also, a series of places regularly visited by a reporter to gather news.

Ben Day   Process named for Editor Ben Day of the *New York Sun*. It is a shading pattern of dots or lines used in photoengraving as background for photos, type or line drawings.

BF   Bold-face type. It is heavier and darker than regular type.

body   Part of a story that follows the lead. Also, the name of type in which regular newspaper reading matter is set.

box   Brief story enclosed by a border; many modern boxes have only top and bottom borders. Those put in the middle of a related story are called *drop-ins*.

bulldog   Early newspaper edition.

bulletin   Brief dispatch containing major news. Usually no more than 20–30 words.

byline   Signature on a story.

c & lc   Caps and lower case (small letters).

caps   Capital letters. Also called *upper case*.

caption   Descriptive material accompanying illustrations, cartoons, etc.

center spread   Also called a *double truck* on tabloids. The two pages in the center fold of a newspaper.

city editor   Boss of the local news staff in the United States. Now called metropolitan editor by some papers.

city room   Properly, the news room. Seat of the editorial operation of a newspaper.

clip   A newspaper clipping. Called a *cutting* by the British.

copy   Universally known as the name of material written by a journalist.

copy desk   Where copy is edited, cut and headlined.

copy editors   Also called *copyreaders*. They edit and headline the copy. Not to be confused with *proofreaders*, a function of the precomputer mechanical staff, whose duty was to catch errors in proof.

correspondent   When reporters go out of town, they sometimes call themselves correspondents. In broadcast media, a correspondent is a job classification of more importance than the basic reporter.

cover   To obtain news.

credit line   To credit a picture, cartoon, etc., to the source.

crop   Reducing the size of an illustration before it is put into printed form.

crusade   Also known as a *campaign*, a *series*, a *long reporting job*. It is an effort by all parts of an editorial staff to persuade the public to act, or to refuse to act, in some matter involving the public interest.

cub   An untrained newspaper person, usually a reporter. A term used more by the public than by newspaper people, who generally call a beginner a first-year reporter.

cut   An engraving, but also applied to all kinds of newspaper illustrations.

cutlines   The part of a caption that describes an illustration.

dateline   The place from which a news story is sent. Many newspapers now omit the date from the dateline.

deadline   Closing time for all copy for an edition. There are different deadlines for the city desk, news desk, copy desk, closing of pages in the composing room, etc.

deskman or woman   An editor in the newsroom.

dingbat   Decorations in type.

dope story   Also called a *think piece;* soft news, supposedly based on reliable opinion, which seeks to develop trends.

dummy   A drawing, usually freehand, outlining the position of news stories and cuts on a page by designating slugs and kinds of headlines.

ears   Boxes on either side of the nameplate on Page 1 of a newspaper — one usually encloses the weather, the other the name of the edition.

edition   Remake, or revision of some of the pages of a newspaper, including Page 1.

editorial   Comment on the news in the name of the news organization itself.

em   Through usage this term has become interchangeable with a pica, the name applied to a lineal measurement of 12 points (one-sixth of an inch) or to a square of 12-point type. Originally an em was the square of any size of type.

en   Half an em. Also called a *nut* to avoid phonetic confusion.

file   The act of dispatching copy to or from a news center, except when it is sent by a messenger.

filler   Small items used to fill out columns where needed.

flag   Newspaper nameplate on Page 1.

flash   In general news, a rarely used message of a few words describing a momentous event.

folio   Page number and name of paper.

folo   Also called *follow, follow-up, follow story*. Sequence of news events after a news break.

future book   Date book of future events.

handout   Generic term for written publicity.

head   Name for all headlines.

hold for release   Instruction placed on news that must not be used until receipt of a release, either automatic or by message. Used as *HFR*.

HTK   Abbreviation of *Head to Kum* (printers' spelling). Placed on copy when the headline is to be completed after the copy is cleared.

human interest   News or features with emotional appeal.

insert   Addition to a story written in such a way that it can be placed anywhere between the end of the first paragraph and the beginning of the last paragraph.

italics   Type face with characters slanted to the right, as contrasted with roman, or upright, characters.

jim-dash   A 3-em dash.

jump   Continuation of a story to another page.

jump line   A continuation line.

justify   To fill out a line of type, a column of type or a page of type.

kill   Elimination of news material at any stage in the processing.

layout   Arrangement of illustrations.

lead   Beginning of a story, which may be a sentence, a paragraph or several paragraphs, depending on the complications involved.

libel   Any defamatory statement expressed in writing, printing or other visible form.

ligature   Two or more united characters of type, such as æ, fi.

lobster   The working shift that usually begins with midnight and runs through to about 10 or 11 a.m.

logotype   Also called a *logo*. A single matrix containing two or more letters used together, such as AP or UPI. It is also another name for the flag, or nameplate.

lower case   Small letters.

makeover   Redoing a page.

makeup   Assembling the newspaper or magazine.

markup   A proof or clipping, pasted on paper and marked to show where changes are to be made and what new material is to be used.

masthead   Statement, usually on the editorial page, of the newspaper's ownership, place of publication and other offices. Sometimes confused with the flag or nameplate.

morgue   News library.

must   When this word is put on copy, it means the story must be used.

new lead   Also called a *New top, Nulead or NL*. It is a fresh beginning on a story already sent or in the paper and is so written that it joins with the old story smoothly at a paragraph that can be designated at the end of the new lead. A *lead all* is a short top that fits on a new lead.

obit   An obituary.

offset   A system of printing. Also known as *cold type*.

overnight   Also called *overnite* or *overniter*. It is a story for the first edition of an afternoon newspaper of the following day; also, for the overnight cycle of a wire service. In morning-newspaper terminology an overnight refers to an assignment to be covered the next day.

overset   Type left over from an edition. Usually wasted.

photocomposition   Typesetting by photography, replacing metal.

pica   12-point type, and also a lineal measurement of 12 points.

pick up   Also written *pikup* in printers' shorthand. This is the name for that portion of a story in type that should be placed at the end of a new lead, or other news material.

pickup line   Line at top of wire service copy that includes the word "add," the point of origin of the story and the last few words of the preceding page. It is used to assemble the whole story in order. Often shortened to PU.

play   The display given to a story or picture. Most editors talk of playing a story, rather than playing it up or down; these latter expressions are more frequently used by the public.

PMs   Afternoon newspapers.

point   Basic printing measurement, roughly equivalent to 1/72 of an inch.

pool   Selection of one journalist or a small group of them to cover for a large group.

precede   Brief dispatch, such as a bulletin or editorial note, that introduces a story but is separated from it by a dash.

printer   Also called a *Teletype* or *TWX*. It produces copy by electrical impulses actuated by a perforated tape, or some other means.

proof   Inked impressions of type for the purpose of making corrections.

rewrite   A writer for a newspaper or wire service, whose work consists in part of redoing stories and in part of writing original copy for the reporters who turn in notes by telephone or wire.

rim   Outer edge of copy desk. Extinct where terminals are used to read copy.

running story   Another name for the B copy — A copy — lead process. Usually it means a chronological story of an event topped by successive leads as the news changes.

runover   Another name for a *jump*.

scoop   An exclusive story.

shirttail   Additional material, related to a longer story and separated from it by a dash.

short   A brief story.

sidebar   A separate piece, related to a main story on the same subject.

situationer   An interpretive story describing a particular news situation.

slot   Seat of the head of an old-fashioned horseshoe copy desk.

slug   Each story has a name, which is called a slug.

split page   First page second section in a paper of two sections.

spread   Any story that takes a headline big enough to be used at the top of an inside page.

stereotype   Plate cast from a mold or image of a page of hot type.

stet   Copy editors' and printers' instruction, "Let it stand."

stick   About two inches of type.

stringer   Occasional correspondent paid by the amount of space per story. The length of the clippings is called the "string."

swing shift   A shift operated by workers who swing from one shift to another on different days.

take   A page of copy.

thirty   Telegraphers' Morse code symbol for "The End."

turn rule   Sometimes written as *T.R.* "T.R. for 2d ADD STORM" means a second addition to a story about a storm is expected.

UPI   United Press International.

wire service   A press association, a wholesaler of news.

wrapup   Also called a roundup. Summary of events in a broadly developed news situation.

2. For Computer Technology

alphanumeric   Use of both letters and numbers in print or otherwise.

autofunctions   Commands placed on copy to instruct computer in type sizes, column widths, etc.

bandwidth   Specifies range within a band of wavelengths, energies or frequencies.

baud   Transmission speed. In computer language, a typical rate would be 1,200 bits (or 150 characters) per second.

bit   In a computer tape or memory, this is the physical manifestation of a bit by electrical impulse, a magnetized spot or a hole.

bitstream   A network's complete flow of digitalized information.

byte   Unit of binary digits processed by a computer.

chip   A tiny piece of silicon on which minicomputer circuitry is printed.

code   Assignment of functions or routines.

coding form   Prepared programming instructions.

commands   Use of various symbols on a terminal to tell computer how a story is to be processed.

computer   Electronic machine for storing and processing news and other data.

core   Principal storage place of a computer, its main memory.

CPU   Central processing unit of a computer for input, output and storage.

CRT   Cathode ray tube. The AP calls its terminals CRTs. Most CRTs are Video Display Terminals.

cursor   Indicator for editing changes on a terminal which is the size of a single character and takes the form of a mobile block of light.

data   Information processed by a computer.

database   All the text stored in a computer system.

database manager   A computer that oversees all database operations, handling incoming stories for editing and sending outgoing to composing room.

diode   device that rectifies alternating current.

directories   Schedules that may be called up on terminals to see what stories are available.

DM   A control function of terminals, enabling key users to obtain a master directory of stories.

drum full   Signal from computer on terminal that storage drum has reached its capacity.

dump   Changing stored material from one computer unit to another.

edit   Programs for handling textual material.

edit mode   Position of terminal after a story has been called to the screen for handling.

font   Face and size of a type face.

hardware   The entire production system, as distinguished from software, the news and other data it processes.

head   This still means headlines in terminal-computer usage and they are written on terminals and handled by computers.

header   Basic information placed at head of story including writer's name, date, slug of story and department for which it is intended.

index   In some computer programs, it means directory or schedule showing the first three to five lines of a story.

insert   Placing additional material in a story already on a terminal or stored in a computer.

interface   An electrical command between parts of hardware — the machines "speaking" to each other.

invalid command   When one is made, the terminal screen reports it.

keyboarding   Keystrokes through which data is put into the system.

kill   One of the basic commands on a terminal.

modem   Device that uses an interface between two other parts of the hardware of a production system.

more   Instruction typed at end of a take of copy when it is to be continued.

multiplexor   Device through which computer handles material at the same time from several interconnected machines.

OCR   Optical character reader, also known as a scanner, which converts specialized typewritten material into electrical impulses which then are recorded either on punched tape or stored in a computer for later editing on a VDT.

on line   Units interfaced into the computer system, as contrasted with units that operate independently.

output   Data from a computer system, either in the form of tape or a printout.

paper tape reader   Device used to put OCR output in computer when OCR is not part of system.

purge   Elimination of data from system.

queue   Order of priority in various schedules, each schedule being known as a queue.

reperf   A tape perforator.

roll up, roll down   Commands moving text on a terminal screen.

slug   In a terminal, this may be the name of the story, registered in six to eight characters after the writer's name, or it may designate all the header material placed at the top of the story.

sort   Arranging material in desired sequence.

system   Combination of computer programs.

terminal   Generic name for electronic typewriterlike devices with TV-type screens on which news and other editorial material is written and processed.

UF, CF   Instructions for typesetting on certain types of terminals.

VDT   Video Display Terminals, the most widely used form of CRTs, sometimes called a "super-typewriter" because it has a typewriterlike extension from what looks like a small TV screen. Used to write, correct, change and edit stories, write headlines and process the material through the computer system to the composing room. Also stores material in memory banks.

wrap   Command used in editing on some types of VDTs.

3.   For the Broadcast Media

ABC   American Broadcasting Companies.

academy leader   Film marked off in seconds, spliced to newsfilm, as a lead-in.

anchor man or woman   Chief newscaster.

Arbitron   Audience measuring device used by American Research Bureau.

atmospherics   Electrical disturbances in atmosphere.

audio   Sound transmission, or reception.

audio frequency   Vibrations normally audible to human ear.

audiometer   Audience measuring device used by A. C. Nielsen Company.

back timing   Exact length of closing segment of newscast, timed in advance, to determine moment when segment should begin for program to end on schedule.

balop   Card, picture or similar object flashed electronically on a viewing screen. (The term is derived from Balopticon, an opaque projector trademarked by Bausch and Lomb, used for such work.)

BBC   British Broadcasting Corporation.

blooper   Embarrassing error.

blow up   Enlargement of portion of picture, chart or map.

bridge   Written segment joining film clips of a differing nature.

bring it up   Order for increase in volume.

cable television, or CATV   A system of wired television in which programs are received by a central source and redistributed to subscribers for a monthly fee plus original installation fee. Central reception is based on efficient high antenna that intercepts signals, which then are channeled by wire to subscribers.

call letters   Station's signature.

cathode ray tube   Tube that produces picture on its large fluorescent end surface by means of electron beam emanating from its cathode, or negative, electrode.

CATV   See cable television.

CBC   Canadian Broadcasting Company.

CBS   Columbia Broadcasting System.

coaxial cable   Long copper tubing containing large number of wire conductors held in place by insulating discs, making possible transmission of television signals, telephone and telegraph messages simultaneously.

communications satellite   Space vehicle placed in orbit about earth to facilitate global transmission of data by radio, TV and radio-telephone signals. Echo I, launched in 1960, was the first. Other early examples Telstar, Relay, Syncom.

compatibility   System in which color broadcasts may be received in black and white on sets not specially equipped to receive color.

CU   Close up.

cue   Signal in script or by hand or word to start or stop speech, movement, film, tape, sound effects, music or other parts of program.

cut   To eliminate, to halt.

cutaway   Subsidiary scenes that can be fitted by film editor into main action.

dead area   Also called "blind spot." It refers to areas where reception is difficult.

diode   Two-element electron tube or semiconductor that changes (rectifies) alternating current into pulsating direct current.

dish   Paraboloid microwave antenna, directional in nature.

double projection   A system in which two projectors are used, one for sound and the other for visual material, in producing a segment of integrated news-film and sound.

easel shot   Also called limbo; an object such as a still photo or a chart or map that can be picked up by a studio camera.

ECU   Extreme close up.

electron   Particle of matter, a constituent of the atom, that carries an elementary charge of negative electricity.

ENG   Electronic newsgathering, a combination of the use of the minicams *(which see)* and videotape which makes possible immediate transmission and replaces film. Also called *EJ* (electronic journalism) and *ECC* (electronic camera coverage).

ether   Upper region of space, or the rarified element that is supposed to fill it.

facsimile   Radiotransmission of printed matter and photos.

fading   Fluctuation of sound or image in broadcasting.

FCC   Federal Communications Commission.

feedback   Sharp noise or hum, such as may be caused by microphone placed too close to a speaker.

fidelity   Degree of accuracy with which sound or visual material is reproduced in radio or television.

flip card   Card containing material (charts, pictures, credits, etc.) that may be flipped before camera in studio.

fluff   An error in speaking or reading from a script.

FM   Frequency modulation, a virtually static-free system of broadcasting by radio. It adjusts the frequency of the transmitting wave in accordance with sound being sent, as contrasted with AM, or amplitude modulation, which adjusts the wave in accordance with its maximum departure from normal.

frame   One of a series of pictures on film; there may be 24 to 28 frames of film shown in a second.

from the top   Begin all over.

Geiger counter   Device for detecting radioactivity.

generator   A machine that converts mechanical into electrical power.

ground   Connection from broadcast receiver to the earth.

Heaviside Layer   Also called Kennelly-Heaviside Layer. It is the ionosphere region of electrically charged air that begins about 25 miles above the earth's surface and makes possible the transmission of radio waves over great distances.

high frequency   A frequency is the number of complete cycles of alternating current that occur in one second; high frequencies are between 6,000 and 30,000 kilocycles.

Iconoscope   A trademarked electron pickup or camera tube that uses an electron scanning beam to convert photo-emissions into television signals.

Image Orthicon Tube   A trademarked electron pickup or camera tube, a refinement of the Iconoscope.

interference   The effect of two electrical waves on each other.

interlock Separate projection of sound and film, locked together in synchronization. Expression describes a type of film, for example, as "16 mm color interlock."

intro Introduction of a filmed or tape portion of a program in script or spoken form.

jamming Interference from an undesired source, effectively blocking the reception of signals.

jump cut Undesirable element of television, in which there is an irregular or unnatural continuation of movement.

Kenotron An electron rectifying tube.

Keypad Pad with buttons, used to call up information on a TV screen.

kilowatt A unit of electric power. A watt is the work done by one ampere electric current under a pressure of one volt. A kilowatt is 1,000 watts.

Kinescope Trademarked picture receiving tube, either by direct view or projection. It also refers to the film, sometimes called a "kinnie," that is made from the monitor kinescope as the program is in progress.

laser Concentrated light beam. Acronym for "light amplification by stimulated emission of radiation."

level Volume of transmitted sound.

light wave technology Use of glass fibers 90 microns in diameter (a micron is one millionth of a meter) to carry light in the form of a laser beam which, when activated into electrical impulses, substitutes for copper coaxial cables for cable TV, computers, aircraft systems and telephones.

limbo Objects such as charts, pictures, etc., that can be picked up by studio cameras. Also called easel shots.

live On-the-spot broadcast or telecast.

live mike An open microphone.

long wave Radio waves with a length of 600 meters or more and frequencies under 500 kilocycles.

low frequency A frequency below radio frequencies, usually between 10 and 100 kilocycles, one that can be heard by the human ear; an audio frequency.

LS Long shot.

LTP Living telop (which see).

MCU Medium close up.

microwave Very short electromagnetic waves, usually between one and 100 centimeters in length; basis for microelectronic circuits in line of sight transmissions and in space technology.

minicam Hand-held miniature TV camera using videotape that can transmit pictures direct to studios for instant use, eliminating costly and time-consuming film processing.

monitor To view or hear a program.

monochrome image Black and white.

MS Medium shot

NAB National Association of Broadcasters.

NBC National Broadcasting Company.

newsfilm Film of current events designed for use on television, usually developed in the negative, after which a positive print is made for use on the air.

night effect Attenuation of transmitted or received signals, usually after sunset, often attributed to changes in the ionized upper atmosphere.

on camera Script notation of what is to be shown.

out cue Last few words of a strip of sound on film or sound on tape, indicating that next section of newscast must be started.

out takes Material that is filmed or videotaped but not used.

pan Moving the camera horizontally to include several objects or scenes in its sweep.

PBS Public Broadcasting System.

photoelectric cell Cell containing a substance sensitive to light that controls emissions of electrons, either from a cathode ray tube or similar source.

prop Various devices—so-called stage properties—used in a televised news program or documentary.

radiation Transmission of radio waves through space in every direction; in its widest sense, the term refers to all forms of ionized radiation, including electromagnetic, particle and acoustic.

radio channel The band or bands of frequencies within which a transmitter is permitted to operate by law.

radio frequency It is incapable of being heard by the human ear, as contrasted with audio frequency which refers to radio waves that can be heard.

radio wire The wire service teletypes that are hooked up specifically to a central source that provides news written for radio and television use at periodic intervals.

roll cue Three to four seconds' signal before newsfilm segment must be shown on a news program.

RP Rear screen projection, requiring the use of a positive transparency that projects a picture in back of the television newscaster on a full screen.

RPM Refers to revolutions per minute of a recording—commonly 33, 45 and 78 RPMs.

scan Causing a beam of electrons to sweep rapidly across a surface in a succession of narrow lines, varying in brightness, so that a transmitted image is faithfully reproduced. In the U.S., the standard is 525 lines every 1/30 of a second.

segue Overlapping of dialogue, sound effects or music, one fading in as the other fades out. Pronounced "seg-way."

signal Electric energy that conveys coherent messages.

SL Silent film.

slug Title for each piece of film considered for use in a news program; also used as a title for each piece of radio copy.

SOF Sound on film.

SOT Sound on tape.

split page Method by which television news script is written, with audio directions in one column on one side of the page, and video directions on the other side of the page in a second and separate column.

standby Written account of an event, held for use in case filmed version fails for any reason. Standby copy is then read.

static Disturbing electrical effects, caused by atmospheric electrical phenomena that disrupt sound in electronic receivers.

still   Single photograph used in television, usually an 8-x-10-inch glossy. Less satisfactory copy, of course, is also used at times.

straight up   When the second hand reaches 12, "straight up."

switch   Shifting from one locale to another, introducing the change in scene with a call in throw cue and signaling the switch back to headquarters with a return cue. A hot switch is a switch without warning.

switcher   One who does the actual switching of the program at an order from the news director.

TCU   Tight close up.

Telenews   Newsfilm syndicate, formally titled News of the Day.

teletext   System that distributes data through a radio or TV frequency.

telop   Like a balop, this is a card or picture flashed electronically on a viewing screen from an opaque projector. *TP* is abbreviation.

track up   Insert videotape or film track.

transistor   Arrangement of semiconductor materials, usually germanium and silicon, separated by a vacuum, that takes the place of a vacuum tube; used as a voltage and current amplifier and for other functions of a vacuum tube. The transistor, in effect, has replaced the vacuum tube.

transponder   Radio or radar set that emits a signal of its own when activated by coded impulses. Signals usually are returned in code.

UHF   Ultra high frequency band, consisting of Channels 14 through 83, as contrasted with VHF, very high frequency, the commercial broadcast band consisting of Channels 2 through 13.

UPI Newsfilm   Newsfilm, formerly Movietone News, distributed by United Press International.

VCU   Very extreme close up.

VHF   Very high frequency, Channels 2 through 13, the commercial broadcasting band.

video   Pertaining to or used in the reception or transmission of an image on television, as contrasted with audio, which refers to sound only.

videotape   A band of magnetic tape that records image and sound simultaneously and can be played back and rewound in seconds. It can be stored indefinitely, erased, used many times over a period of years.

videotex   Generic term for systems that display computer-based data unadapted TV sets. Two major parts of videotex are teletext (or broadcast videotex) and Viewdata (which is called up by telephone).

vidicon   Type of television camera often used for closed circuit, industrial and military work.

Vizmo   A 5-x-7-inch transparency used in rear screen projection.

Viznews   British Commonwealth newsfilm group, titled Brzina Viznews, to indicate the countries involved—Britain, Australia, New Zealand, India and some others.

Vizs   Plural of Vizmo.

VO   Voice over, meaning dialogue or live narration over silent film or studio action.

VOF   Voice on film or tape.

Voice of America   U.S. government broadcasting service overseas, a part of the U.S. Information Agency.

VTR   Videotape recording.

wave   Moving electronic disturbance in a medium, such as space, having a regularly recurring time period.

wavelength   Distance between any point in a wave and the corresponding point in the wave immediately preceding and following it.

wave trap   A circuit that can be tuned to cut out any undesired signal.

wired radio   Form of radio transmission in which current carrying the signals is sent over established wire systems, such as telephone or telegraph lines. The equivalent for television is the system known as CATV, which generally provides its own wire system hooked to telephone poles already in place.

wrapup   Rounded narration and/or filmed news program that summarizes a single major event or the day's news.

Acknowledgments

Grateful acknowledgment is made herewith of copyrighted and other material contributed to the fifth edition of *The Professional Journalist* that did not appear in previous editions.

Chapter 1
Brenda Webber, "11 of 15 Convicted in Drug Smuggling Trial," *Gainesville* (Florida) *Sun*, Sept. 13, 1981, p. 1. Copyright by *Gainesville Sun*. All rights reserved. Reprinted by permission.
Doug Tunnell, "Pope Arrives at Castel Gandolfo," *CBS Evening News with Dan Rather*, Aug. 16, 1981. Copyright, *CBS Evening News with Dan Rather*. All rights reserved. Reprinted by permission.
Anita Miller, "The Whippoorwill Tragedy," *Topeka* (Kansas) *Daily Capital*, June 19, 1978, p. 1. Copyright by the *Topeka Daily Capital*. All rights reserved. Reprinted by permission.
Susan Biskeborn and Paul Vitello, "Drama Inside a Water Tower," *Newsday*, Melville, N.Y., April 25, 1981. Copyright by *Newsday*. All rights reserved. Reprinted by permission.
Thomas F. Chester, "Ministries by Mail," *Knoxville* (Tennessee) *Journal*, Oct. 15, 1980, p. 1. Copyright by *Knoxville Journal*. All rights reserved. Reprinted by permission.

Chapter 2
Mike Tierney, quotation from article about Super Bowl Week in New Orleans in *St. Petersburg* (Florida) *Times*, Jan. 27, 1981, p. 1. Copyright by *St. Petersburg Times*. All rights reserved. Used by permission.
Sharon Fitzgerald, "Tommie Okoh Warner Found Guilty," in the *Oak Ridger*, Oak Ridge, Tennessee, Aug. 1, 1980, p. 1. Copyright by *Oak Ridger*. All rights reserved. Used by permission.
Longview (Washington) *Daily News*, articles on Mt. St. Helens eruption are from the *Longview* (Washington) *Daily News*, May 19, 1981. Copyright by *Longview Daily News*. All rights reserved. Used by permission.
Knoxville (Tennessee) *Journal* and *The New York Times*, assignment sheets used by permission.

Chapter 3
Chuck Johnson, explanation of VDTs, in letter from Chuck Johnson of the *Milwaukee Journal* used through the courtesy of Mr. Johnson and the *Milwaukee Journal*.
Barbara Abel, VDT copy and other directions for VDT use are from the *Milwaukee Journal* instruction book.
Joseph Ungaro, definitions and discussions of other machines are from material contributed by Joseph Ungaro, Executive Editor, Westchester-Rockland Newspapers. Used through the courtesy of Mr. Ungaro and Westchester-Rockland Newspapers.

Chapter 4
E. B. White, quotation from William Strunk, Jr. and E. B. White, *Elements of Style*, 3rd ed. (New York: Macmillan, 1979).
H. B. Hough, quotation from letter to author.
Madeleine Blais, "Who's Going to Love Judith Bucknell?" from the *Miami Herald* in a special reprint section, 1980. Copyright by the *Miami Herald*. All rights reserved. Used by permission.

Chapter 7
Gainesville (Florida) *Sun*, gun robbery short, Nov. 6, 1981, p. 10A. Copyright by *Gainesville Sun*. All rights reserved. Used by permission.
William M. Bulkeley, Fire alarm booth story, *Wall Street Journal*, Oct. 26, 1981, Sec. II, p. 1. Copyright by *Wall Street Journal*. All rights reserved. Used by permission.
David Andelman, report on failure of Russian couple's dash for freedom, from *CBS Evening News* with Dan Rather, Aug. 28, 1981. Copyright by *CBS News*. All rights reserved. Used by permission.
Edna Buchanan, story of rescue of trapped couple in *Miami Herald*, May 4, 1981, p. 1. Copyright by *Miami Herald*. All rights reserved. Used by permission.
Steve Fry, story of missing child in *Topeka Capital Journal*, Sept. 17, 1981, p. 1. Copyright by *Topeka Capital Journal*. All rights reserved. Used by permission.

Fred Barbash, Sandra D. O'Connor sworn in as first woman on United States Supreme Court, by Fred Barbash. *Washington Post*, Sept. 26, 1981. p. 2. Copyright by *Washington Post*. All rights reserved. Used by permission.

Chapter 8
Anita Miller, "The Funeral of Becky Jackson." *Topeka Capital-Journal*, Jan. 21, 1981, p. 1. Copyright by *Topeka Capital-Journal*. All rights reserved. Used by permission.
Dwight Perry, obit from the *Weekly Register* of Yarmouth Port, Mass., Aug. 27, 1981, p. 51. Copyright by the *Weekly Register*. All rights reserved. Used by permission.
Ethel Rollin-Brown, obit from the *Los Angeles Times*, Oct. 12, 1981, p. 2. Copyright by *Los Angeles Times*. All rights reserved. Used by permission.
Associated Press, Doc Livingston obit, day report, Oct. 1981. Copyright by AP. All rights reserved. Used by permission.

Chapter 9
Don Olesen, acid rain story, from *Milwaukee Journal*, "Insight" section, Sept. 13, 1981, p. 24. Copyright by *Milwaukee Journal*. All rights reserved. Used by permission.
John R. Camp, "The Man Who Stands in Two Places," *St. Paul Pioneer Press*, extracted from exhibit submitted for a Pulitzer Prize in 1979. Copyright by *St. Paul Pioneer Press*, All rights reserved. Used by permission.
Michelle Naspinski, "A Mother for the Retarded." *Orlando* (Florida) *Sentinel-Star*, Oct. 19, 1981, p. B–1. Copyright by *Orlando Sentinel-Star*. All rights reserved. Used by permission.
Lyn Bailey, "Marco the Magnificent." *Watsonville* (California) *Register-Pajaronian*, Feb. 1, 1979, p. 8. Copyright by *Watsonville Register-Pajaronian*. All rights reserved. Used by permission.
Sylvia Moreno, "Search for a Surrogate Mother." *Newsday*, May 31, 1981, p. 18. Copyright by *Newsday*. All rights reserved. Used by permission.
Gina Thomas, story about a surprise sentencing in *Today*, Cocoa, Florida, Oct. 23, 1981, p. 1. Copyright by *Today*. All rights reserved. Used by permission.
Associated Press, computer marriage story in day report from Sunnyvale, California, Oct. 25, 1981. Copyright by AP. All rights reserved. Used by permission.

Chapter 10
Peter Mancusi, New England blizzard story in *Boston Globe*, Dec. 7, 1981, p. 1. Copyright by *Boston Globe*. All rights reserved. Used by permission.
David L. Langford, undated Associated Press storm lead in night report, Nov. 21, 1981. Copyright by AP. All rights reserved. Used by permission.
Steve Lovelady, introduction to *Philadelphia Inquirer*'s series on Three Mile Island, April 8, 1979, p. 1. Copyright by *Philadelphia Inquirer*. All rights reserved. Used by permission.

Arlen J. Large, analysis of Three Mile Island nuclear breakdown two and one-half years later. *Wall Street Journal*, Oct. 21, 1981, p. 1. Copyright by *Wall Street Journal*. All rights reserved. Used by permission.
Associated Press, Diablo Canyon story, night report, Nov. 20, 1981. Copyright by AP. All rights reserved. Used by permission.

Chapter 11
Associated Press, "U.S. Debt Passes Trillion Dollars," night report, Oct. 23, 1981. Copyright by AP. All rights reserved. Used by permission.
Milwaukee Journal, "Dreyfus Laundry List Doesn't Wash," Oct. 24, 1981, p. 22. Copyright by *Milwaukee Journal*. All rights reserved. Used by permission.
Ken McLaughlin, parking ticket fiasco, *Watsonville* (California) *Register-Pajaronian*, May 12, 1980, p. 1. Copyright by *Watsonville Register-Pajaronian*. All rights reserved. Used by permission.
Betsy Wakefield, "High Waves Breach Seawall," *Island Packet*, Hilton Head, S.C., Oct. 20, 1981, p. 3. Copyright by *Island Packet*. All rights reserved. Used by permission.
Kelly Scott, Rolling Stones story, *St. Petersburg* (Florida) *Times*, Oct. 25, 1981, p. 25. Copyright by *St. Petersburg Times*. All rights reserved. Used by permission.
Leon Daniel, Nguyen Cao Ky lead in United Press international night report, June 22, 1981. Copyright by UPI. All rights reserved. Used by permission.
JoAnn S. Lublin, robot story lead in *Wall Street Journal*, Oct. 23, 1981, p. 1. Copyright by *Wall Street Journal*. All rights reserved. Used by permission.
Howard Benedict, lead for Associated Press on second flight of space shuttle Columbia in Associated Press day report, Nov. 12, 1981. Copyright by AP. All rights reserved. Used by permission.

Chapter 12
Louis D. Boccardi, remarks on VDTs, from letter to author.
Thomas F. Chester, cocaine raid story, *Knoxville* (Tennessee) *Journal*, March 25, 1981, p. 1. Copyright by *Knoxville Journal*. All rights reserved. Used by permission.
Sam Martino, "Mother Saves Son in Auto Chase," *Milwaukee Journal*, Oct. 22, 1981, p. 1. Copyright by the *Milwaukee Journal*. All rights reserved. Used by permission.
David Damkoehler, "Nurses Strike Settled," in the *Weekly Register* of Yarmouth Port, Mass., Aug. 27, 1981. Copyright by the *Weekly Register*. All rights reserved. Used by permission.

Chapter 13
Robert D. McFadden, letter to author about rewrite. Dec. 10, 1981.

Chapter 14
Associated Press, walkway collapse in Kansas City hotel from day and night reports, July 17–18, 1981.

Copyright by AP. All rights reserved. Used by permission.

Michael Putzel and Walter Rodgers, eyewitness accounts of Reagan shooting from Associated Press Log, April 6, 1981. Copyright by AP. All rights reserved. Used by permission.

Dean Reynolds, leads on Reagan shooting from United Press International day and night reports, March 30, 1981. Copyright by UPI. All rights reserved. Used by permission.

Chapter 15
Doug Tunnell, "Nimitz Arrives Naples." *CBS Morning News*, Aug. 24, 1981. Copyright by *CBS News*. All rights reserved. Used by permission.

Leah Keith, 1981 Texas floods from KXAS-TV, Fort Worth. Copyright by Lin Broadcasting Co. All rights reserved. Used by permission.

Roger O'Neil, Michigan prison investigation on *NBC Nightly News*, May 28, 1981. Copyright by *NBC News*. All rights reserved. Used by permission.

Chapter 16
Ned McCormack, story of shootout following armored car holdup, in *Nyack* (New York) *Journal-News*, Oct. 24, 1981, p. 1. Copyright by Westchester-Rockland Newspapers, Inc. All rights reserved. Used by permission.

Chapter 17
Jeannie Williams, advice on interviews. Published courtesy of Jeannie Williams and the *Rochester* (New York) *Times-Union*.

Cynthia Stevens, story from Associated Press Log Nov. 30, 1981. Copyright by AP. All rights reserved. Used by permission.

Associated Press, Fransie Geringer story datelined Anaheim, California, from Associated Press report Nov. 15, 1981. Copyright by AP. All rights reserved. Used by permission.

Peter Perl, interview with robbery victim in *Washington Post*, Nov. 19, 1981, p. B-1. Copyright by *Washington Post*. All rights reserved. Used by permission.

Associated Press, Mike Feinsilber-David Gergen exchange in Associated Press Log Nov. 2, 1981. Copyright by AP. All rights reserved. Used by permission.

Chicago Tribune, Mayor Byrne news conference, March 20, 1981, p. 1. Copyright by *Chicago Tribune*. All rights reserved. Used by permission.

Associated Press, landing of spaceship Columbia from day report Nov. 15, 1981. Copyright by AP. All rights reserved. Used by permission.

Chapter 18
Charles Bailey, Brent Musberger, George Solomon and Dave Anderson, quotations from the Proceedings of the American Society of Newspaper Editors, 1982, in panel discussion of sports reporting.

Arizona Daily Star, series, Tucson, Jan. 13, 1980–July 17, 1981, "Mason is acquitted." Reprinted by permission of the *Arizona Daily Star*.

Associated Press, March 26–27, 1982, details of charges by Richard Phelps and others, from New Orleans.

Bob Mathews, advice on sports interviewing from staff memorandum for the *Rochester* (New York) *Times-Union*. Used by permission of Mr. Mathews and the *Rochester Times-Union*.

Chapter 19
Colonel Henry Woodward Sackett, Harold L. Cross and E. Douglas Hamilton. "What You Should Know About Libel," booklet distributed by the Graduate School of Journalism, Columbia University.

Harold L. Cross, "The People's Right to Know" (New York, Columbia University Press, 1953).

The Constitution of the United States, Analysis and Interpretation, prepared by the Legislative Reference Service, Library of Congress. Edward S. Corwin, ed. (Washington, 1953).

S. D. Warren and L. D. Brandeis, "The Right to Privacy," 4 Harvard Law Review (1890).

Louis D. Boccardi, "Law of Libel: Where It Stands," AP Log," Feb. 4, 1981.

Alan U. Schwartz, "Danger: Pandulum Swinging—Using the Courts to Muzzle the Press," *Atlantic* (February, 1977), p. 29 et. seq.

Floyd Abrams, "The Press, Privacy and the Constitution," *New York Times Magazine*, Aug. 21, 1977, p. 11 et seq.

"Court Watch Summary," in *The News Media and the Law*, June–July, 1981, published by the Reporters Committee on Freedom of the Press, Washington, D.C., pp. 52–53.

Sheppard case reversal, *New York Times*, June 7, 1966.

Fresno case reported in UPI day report, Sept. 18, 1976. Farr case in *New York Times*, July 1, 1976, p. 17.

Farber case analyzed in *The News Media and the Law*, Vol. 2, No. 3, October, 1978, p. 2; decision reported in Matter of Farber, 78 N.J. 259, 394 Atlantic Reporter, 2nd series, 330.

"Federal Appeals Courts' Ruling Strongly Support Reporters' Right to Keep Sources Secret," *The News Media and the Law*, June–July, 1981 p. 13.

Daniel Schorr, testimony before Congressional Committee, Associated Press day report Sept. 15, 1976. House committee decision on Schorr in AP day report Sept. 22, 1976. His resignation, AP day report, Sept. 28, 1976.

Newsweek, material on Freedom of Information Act, February 2, 1976, p. 50; see also "The News Media and the Law," June–July, 1981, p. 3 et seq.

"Guidelines for the Reporting of Criminal Proceedings," issued by the Press-Bar Committee, State of Washington, Seattle.

Floyd Abrams, "The Pentagon Papers: A Decade Later," in *New York Times Magazine*, June 14, 1981, p. 22 et seq.; James Reston quotation in *New York Times*, May 10, 1961.

Citation of major decisions quoted:

Burnett v. National Enquirer Inc. (#C-157213 Cal. Super. Ct., Los Angeles Cty., March 26, 1981); Frosch

v. Grosset & Dunlap, (427 N.Y.S. 2d 829 App. Div., 1980) (Marilyn Monroe case); New Yort Times v. Sullivan (376 U.S. 254, 1964); Rosenbloom v. Metromedia (403 U.S. 29, 1971); Gertz v. Robert Welch Inc. (418 U.S. 323, 1974); Firestone v. Time Inc. (409 U.S. 875, 1976); Wolston v. Readers Digest Assn., Inc. (443 U.S. 157, 1979); Dietemann v. Time Inc. (449 F 2nd 245, 1971 before U.S. Court of Appeals, 9th Circuit); Time v. Hill (385 U.S. 374 No. 22, argued Apr. 27, 1966, reargued Oct. 18–19, 1955, decided Jan. 9, 1967); Cantrell v. Forest City Pub. Co. (419 U.S. 245, 1974); Cox Broadcasting Corp. v. Martin Cohn, (420 U.S. 469, 1975); Nebraska Press Assn. v. Stuart (427 U.S. 539, 1976); Zurcher v. Stanford Daily (436 U.S. 547, 1978); Herbert v. Lando (441 U.S. 153, 1979); Gannett v. DePasquale, (443 U.S. 368, 1979); Richmond Newspapers v. Virginia (448 U.S. 555, 1980); Marks v. Vehlow (#13901, Idaho Sup. Ct., 1980); Texas v. Yahyal Al-Omari et al., (#188280, Cty, Ct. of Law No. 3, Travis Cty., Texas, Sept. 2, 1980); Bruno & Stillman v. Globe Newspapers (633 F 2nd 583, 1st Cir., 1980); Zerelli v. Smith (#79-2466, 79-2480, D.C. Cir., April 13, 1981; Miller v. California (413 U.S. 15, 1973).

The author gratefully acknowledges assistance by Floyd Abrams in the preparation of this chapter.

Chapter 20
Miami Herald police beat assignment sheet. Used by courtesy of the *Miami Herald.*

FBI Uniform Crime Reports from "Crime in the United States, 1981." The author acknowledges the assistance of Roger S. Young, assistant director, Office of Congressional and Public Affairs, FBI. Crime definitions are extracted from this report.

Edna Buchanan, fire story from *Miami Herald,* Oct. 27, 1981, p. 1. Copyright by *Miami Herald.* All rights reserved. Used by permission.

Edna Buchanan, "A Cop's Last Night on the Job," *Miami Herald,* Sept. 21, 1981, p. 2-B. Copyright by *Miami Herald.* All rights reserved. Used by permission.

Anita Miller, "Double Slaying in Kansas." *Topeka Capital,* March 11, 1978, p. 1. Copyright by *Topeka Capital.* All rights reserved. Used by permission.

Chapter 21
Associated Press, Marathon Oil decision, day report Jan. 8, 1982. Copyright by AP. All rights reserved. Used by permission.

Today, "Army sergeant's suit" Cocoa, Florida, Oct. 18, 1981, p. 20A. Copyright by *Today.* All rights reserved. Used by permission.

"Prisoner Is Lawyer for Fellow-Convict," Oct. 21, 1981, p. 1.

Associated Press, "Couple Win Suit Against Delta," night report, Oct. 7, 1981. Copyright by the AP. All rights reserved. Used by permission.

Associated Press, "Nurse found innocent," day report, Oct. 24, 1981. Copyright by AP. All rights reserved. Used by permission.

Chicago Tribune, plea bargaining case, March 17, 1981, p. 1. Copyright by *Chicago Tribune.* All rights reserved. Used by permission.

Dudley Clendinen, story on the Von Bulow verdict from *The New York Times,* March 17, 1982, p. 1. Copyright © 1982 by The New York Times Company. All rights reserved. Used by permission.

United Press International, Von Bulow sentencing, day report May 8, 1982. Copyright by UPI. All rights reserved. Used by permission.

Chapter 22
The New York Times and *New York Daily News,* news accounts of nine-year-old bank robber, Feb. 26, 1981.

Jonathan Friendly, commentary from the *New York Times,* March 8, 1981, p. 20. Copyright © 1981 by the New York Times Company. All rights reserved. Used by permission.

William Owney, "First Grade Girl to Go on Trial" from *Gainesville* (Florida) *Sun,* March 25, 1982, p. 1. Copyright by *Gainesville Sun.* All rights reserved. Used by permission. The author's interview with William Owney was on April 10, 1982.

Janet Cooke, lead on the "Jimmy's World" story from the *Washington Post,* Sept. 28, 1980, p. 1. William Green's lead on his 18,000-word explanation of the Cooke hoax from the *Washington Post,* April 19, 1981. Both copyright by the *Washington Post.* All rights reserved. Used by permission. Other source: Janet Cooke's NBC *Today* show interview on Feb. 1–2, 1982.

J. Montgomery Curtis, remarks in a letter to author, Jan. 15, 1979.

David Shaw, ethics story in *Los Angeles Times,* Oct. 23, 1981, p. 1, and article in *The Quill,* December, 1981, p. 24.

Don Corrigan, "The Janet Cooke Tragedy," *Journalism Educator,* October, 1981, pp. 8–9; article on Gary Schuster by Donald P. Baker in *Washington Post,* May 20, 1979, p. C-1; comment by H. L. Stevenson, in *UPI Reporter,* April 12, 1979.

The New York Times, story on Cambodian hoax, Feb. 22, 1982, p. 1.

Chapter 23
James Risser, first grain embargo article in *Des Moines Register,* May 4, 1975; his observations in the *Bulletin of the American Society of Newspaper Editors,* September, 1976, p. 17.

Chapter 24
Definitions of public opinion from Alexis de Toqueville, *Democracy in America* (New York: Vintage Press, 1954); Walter Lippmann, *Public Opinion* (New York, 1922), p. 197; W. Phillips Davison, *International Political Communication* (New York, 1966), p. 66. See also Seymour Martin Lipset, "The Wavering Polls," *The Public Interest* (Spring, 1976), pp. 70–89, and George Gallup, "The Sophisticated Poll Watcher's Guide," (Princeton, N.J., 1972), p. 200–201.

Patrick Caddell, conclusion that Jimmy Carter could not win in 1976, Associated Press night report, November 4, 1976.

Polling standards based on material prepared by National Committee on Published Polls in Philip Meyer, *Precision Journalism* (Bloomington, Ind., 1973), pp. 185–186.

Chapter 25

The author is indebted to Lewis A. Gorham Jr., director of the Office of Management and Budget, Knoxville, Tennessee, for much of the technical detail and definitions in the discussion of budgets and taxes and to Mayor Randy Tyree and Mr. Gorham for the use of Knoxville's city operating and performance budgets.

Andrew J. Shanley, report on the Dukes County, Massachusetts budget in *Vineyard Gazette*, Edgartown, Martha's Vineyard, Dec. 25, 1981, p. 1. Copyright by *Vineyard Gazette*. All rights reserved. Used by permission.

Ken McLaughlin, report on the Watsonville, California budget in the *Watsonville Register-Pajaronian*, June 17, 1981, p. 9, elaborated in letter to author Nov. 11, 1981. Copyright by *Watsonville Register-Pajaronian*. All rights reserved. Used by permission.

The New Hampshire budget in the *New Hampshire Sunday News*, Manchester, Nov. 1, 1981, p. 1. Copyright by the *New Hampshire Sunday News*. All rights reserved. Used by permission.

Ogden (Utah) *Standard-Examiner*, story about the problem of power rates, Dec. 1, 1981, local-metro page. Copyright by the *Ogden Standard-Examiner*. All rights reserved. Used by permission.

A. A. Michelson, story about Massachusetts State Senate in *Berkshire Eagle*, Pittsfield, Dec. 12, 1981, p. 17. Copyright by *Berkshire Eagle*. All rights reserved. Used by permission.

Barbara Johnson, story about beach erosion in *Fort Myers* (Florida) *News-Press* Sept. 21, 1981, p. B-1. Copyright by *Fort Myers News-Press*. All rights reserved. Used by permission.

Milwaukee Journal, story on Wisconsin anti-pollution program, Oct. 23, 1981, p. 1. Copyright by *Milwaukee Journal*. All rights reserved. Used by permission.

Indianapolis Star, exposé, Feb. 24, 1972, p. 1.

Chapter 26

There is a very large literature on the New World Information Order, including the following:

"The UNESCO Fight: Williamsburg to Nairobi," *IAPA News*, Oct.–Nov., 1976; UNESCO's Assault on News, *Washington Post* editorial, July 10, 1976, p. A-22; Clayton Kirkpatrick, "The Lessons from Nairobi,"

in *ASNE Bulletin*, January, 1977; Don Bohning, "Demanding a New World Information Order," *Miami Herald*, Oct. 8, 1978, pp. 4–5 E; William Attwood, "To Rid the Garden of a Rattlesnake," *New York Times*, Dec. 9, 1978, p. 22; Robert U. Brown, Editor & Publisher, May 19, 1979, p. 52; *New York Times* editorial, "UNESCO as Censor," Oct. 24, 1980, p. A 32; "Reporter Licensing Weighted by UNESCO," *New York Times*, Feb. 15, 1981, p. 11; M. L. Stein, "UNESCO Debate Muted in Kenya," *The Quill*, January, 1982, p. 10; "New Information Order: Debating Pragmatics," by Alan Riding, *New York Times*, Jan. 24, 1982, p. 4-E; "UN Ambassador Blasts UNESCO's Role," *Editor & Publisher*, Sept. 19, 1981, p. 9. See also D. R. Mankekar, *Whose Freedom? Whose Order?* (Delhi: Clarion Books, 1981.)

For foreign correspondence, see H. L. Stevenson in *UPI Reporter*, "22 Journalists Murdered in 1981," Jan. 7, 1982, and "World Press Freedom Continues to Deteriorate," *Editor & Publisher*, Jan. 2, 1982, p. 7.

Chapter 27

David Perlman, story on California earthquake, *San Francisco Chronicle*, Jan. 25, 1980, p. 1. Copyright by *San Francisco Chronicle*. All rights reserved. Used by permission. Explanatory letter to author by David Perlman Dec. 2, 1981.

San Francisco contingency quake coverage plan used by permission.

Chapter 28

Andy Knott, ambulance investigation in *Chicago Tribune*, March 15–20, 1981. Copyright by *Chicago Tribune*. All rights reserved. Used by permission. Details in letter from Andy Knott to author Dec. 18, 1981.

Charlotte Observer, series on "brown lung" disease excerpted from Pulitzer Prize-winning exhibit, 1980, in Columbia University Library; Bob Drogin story in *Observer*, Feb. 10, 1980. Copyright by *Charlotte Observer*. All rights reserved. Used by permission.

Jerry Thompson, "Exposing the Ku Klux Klan," series in *Nashville Tennessean*, beginning Dec. 7, 1980. Copyright by *Nashville Tennessean*. All rights reserved. Used by permission.

David Andelman, series on space weaponry, *CBS Evening News* With Dan Rather June 10, 1981. Copyright by *CBS News*. All rights reserved. Used by permission. Details in Andelman letter to author.

Photo Credits: page 1, top, David Burnett; bottom, © Michal Heron 1981 page 24, middle, © Sepp Seitz 1980 page 25, bottom, © Michal Heron 1981 page 103, middle © Michal Heron 1981 page 210, middle, Wide World Photos.

Index

DUE DATE